United Nations University Series on Regionalism

Volume 33

This book series offers a platform for innovative work on (supra-national) regionalism from a global and inter-disciplinary perspective. It started with the World Reports on Regional Integration, published in collaboration with other UN agencies, and now publishes theoretical, methodological and empirical contributions related to various themes on interregionalism from academics and policy-makers worldwide. All book proposals are reviewed by an International Editorial Board and final approval on manuscripts also comes from the board.

The series editors are particularly interested in book proposals dealing with:

- comparative regionalism;
- comparative work on regional organizations;
- interregionalism
- the role of regions in a multi-level governance context;
- the interactions between the UN and the regions;
- the regional dimensions of the reform processes of multilateral institutions;
- the dynamics of cross-border micro-regions and their interactions with supra-national regions;
- methodological issues in regionalism studies.

Accepted book proposals can receive editorial support from UNU-CRIS for the preparation of manuscripts.

Please send book proposals to: pdelombaerde@cris.unu.edu and lvanlangenhove@cris.unu.edu

Dimitris Katsikas
Maria Antonieta Del Tedesco Lins
Andrea Ribeiro Hoffmann
Editors

Finance, Growth and Democracy: Connections and Challenges in Europe and Latin America in the Era of Permacrisis

Springer

Editors
Dimitris Katsikas
National and Kapodistrian University of Athens
Athens, Greece

Maria Antonieta Del Tedesco Lins
Institute of International Relations
Universidade de São Paulo
São Paulo, SP, Brazil

Andrea Ribeiro Hoffmann
Institute of International Relations
Pontifical Catholic University of Rio de Janeiro
Rio de Janeiro, RJ, Brazil

ISSN 2214-9848 ISSN 2214-9856 (electronic)
United Nations University Series on Regionalism
ISBN 978-3-031-68474-6 ISBN 978-3-031-68475-3 (eBook)
https://doi.org/10.1007/978-3-031-68475-3

This work was supported by [Faculdades Catolicas] ([33.555.921/0001-70]).

This Springer imprint is published by the registered company Springer Nature Switzerland AG
The registered company address is: Gewerbestrasse 11, 6330 Cham, Switzerland

Acknowledgments

This publication was realized with the support of the Erasmus + Programme of the European Union (620963-EPP-1-2020-1-BR-EPPJMO-NETWORK) and we also acknowledge funding by FAPERJ - Fundação Carlos Chagas Filho de Amparo à Pesquisa do Estado do Rio de Janeiro, Processes SEI-260003/011887/2023 - APQ2 (E-26/210.389/2023) e E-26/201.205/2022 – Scholarship.

"The European Commission support for the production of this publication does not constitute an endorsement of the contents which reflects the views only of the authors, and the Commission cannot be held responsible for any use which may be made of the information contained therein."

Contents

Chapter 1
Introduction: A New Era? Permacrisis and the Challenges to Financial Stability, Economic Growth, and Democracy

Dimitris Katsikas, Maria Antonieta Del Tedesco Lins, and Andrea Ribeiro Hoffmann

Contents

Introduction

We live in a world shuddered by multiple and profound crises. From the global financial crisis and the Eurocrisis that followed, to the pandemic, Russia's invasion in Ukraine, the consequent energy and inflation crises, the continuously evolving climate crisis, and the brewing tension among the world's major powers, the last few years have been marked by political and economic instability, leading many to talk about a new era in the world's history. New concepts have emerged to describe this era. 'Permacrisis' is one of these concepts. For Collins English Dictionary, permacrisis was the word of the year 2022. It refers to 'an extended period of instability and insecurity, especially one resulting from a series of catastrophic events'.

D. Katsikas (✉)
National and Kapodistrian University of Athens, Athens, Greece
e-mail: dkatsikas@pspa.uoa.gr

M. A. Del Tedesco Lins
Institute of International Relations, University of São Paulo, São Paulo, SP, Brazil

A. Ribeiro Hoffmann
Institute of International Relations, Pontifical Catholic University of Rio de Janeiro, Rio de Janeiro, RJ, Brazil

D. Katsikas et al. (eds.), *Finance, Growth and Democracy: Connections and Challenges in Europe and Latin America in the Era of Permacrisis*, United Nations University Series on Regionalism 33, https://doi.org/10.1007/978-3-031-68475-3_1

This is different from the traditional conception of crisis derived from the Greek word *κρίση* (judgement), which denotes 'a moment of opportunity' (Turnbull, 2022), i.e. when an event shakes the status quo forcing us to consider new options for action. The traditional notion of crisis then is characterized by temporality; on the contrary, permacrisis implies that 'crisis-as-context ceases to be a crisis … and becomes a fundamental feature of the system' (Henig & Knight, 2023:3). In other words, we are now living in a 'new normal', which is more volatile and unpredictable than the past (Zuleeg et al., 2021).

Tooze's (2022) definition of 'polycrisis' also implies a new context, in which 'the whole is even more overwhelming than the sum of the parts'. Implicit in these concepts is the idea that the world is now different; globalization and technological progress have created an interconnected and interdependent world, where separate, peripheral crises interact and reinforce each other. These interdependent shocks are likely to occur with higher frequency, because of recent structural changes which seem to represent a break with the recent past. In international economics and politics, we witness the rise of a multipolar world and, along with it, a multiplication and intensification in the conflicts of interest and tensions over international issues. One of these issues is the climate crisis, which has also been accelerating continuously crashing through new thresholds towards a tipping point with unpredictable implications. Technology's impact on our lives has also increased dramatically, particularly since the COVID-19 pandemic, creating new challenges for the economy and the labour market in particular.

While this new turbulent era is best conceptualized at the global level, its implications are manifested at the regional and local levels, and more often than not, they materialize in different ways, given the variation of socio-economic contexts and institutional legacies across the globe. In this context, in this volume we focus on how permacrisis has been experienced and dealt with in Europe and in Latin America. To do so we propose to employ the analytical lens of comparative regionalism, a perspective that examines and compares regional processes and organizations in all the regions of the world from an equal foot in terms of methods and theories, i.e. trying to avoid 'Eurocentrism' in the studies of regionalism and regional organizations (Katzenstein, 1996; Fawcett, 2004; Shaw et al., 2012; Acharya, 2012; Solingen, 2014; Börzel & Risse, 2016).

Permacrisis in Europe and Latin America

The examination of Europe and Latin America has theoretical interest because they represent two very different types of processes of regional integration and establishment of regional organizations. The most striking difference is the centrality of the European Union (EU) in Europe, against a plurality of regional organizations in Latin America, which has expanded even further particularly since the 1990s (Bianculli, 2016). A comparative analysis helps us identify the strengths but also the potential weaknesses of regionalism to deal with the challenges of the permacrisis era.

Europe, where talk of a polycrisis in public discourse first appeared (Junker, 2016), has perhaps suffered more than any other region from repeated shocks. In addition to global crises like the pandemic and the climate crisis, the EU has also had to deal with shocks of a distinctly regional nature (e.g. Brexit and the 2015–2016 Mediterranean refugee and migration crisis) or with shocks whose impact was felt much more intensely in Europe (e.g. the global financial crisis and the subsequent Eurocrisis or the Russian invasion in Ukraine and the ensuing energy and inflation crises). Academic literature has already started to investigate the implications of this new reality for EU's integration dynamics (Zeitlin et al., 2019; Jones et al., 2021; Ferrara & Kriesi, 2022; Anghel & Jones, 2023). Despite Jean Monnet's oft repeated dictum that European integration will progress through crises, the evidence shows that integration deepening is not inevitable after a crisis, and even when it occurs, it is often incomplete and ambiguous (Jones et al., 2016, 2021). On the contrary, it is widely acknowledged that the recent crises have posed a significant challenge for the EU, as they test the Union's institutional and policy limits and strengthen the politicization of the integration process, already on the rise after the Maastricht Treaty (Hooghe & Marks, 2009; Zeitlin et al., 2019). On the positive side, the experience from multiple crises may lead to institutional and policy learning, as demonstrated by the comparison of EU's different responses to the Eurocrisis and the pandemic (Wolff & Ladi, 2020). Having said that, different crises have different characteristics and raise different coordination and policy challenges. It is not surprising, therefore, that EU's successful reaction to the pandemic was not replicated in the case of the war in Ukraine and the ensuing energy crisis, demonstrating the need for more comparative analysis of crisis responses (Anghel & Jones, 2023).

The concept of 'permacrisis' applies perfectly to Latin America as well. For four decades, the continent has faced successive crises, most of them originating from macroeconomic imbalances. Although the effects of the global financial crisis were less severe than those of the crises in advanced economies, the region was not immune to the pandemic and the effects of the war in Europe. In Latin America the impact of the pandemic has been in fact particularly hard: despite having 8.4% of the world's population, it had 26.7% of deaths by COVID-19, and extreme poverty increased from 27.8% of the population in 2014 to 32.1% in 2022 (CEPAL, 2023). In some of the countries of the region, the decrease in the quality of life of the middle classes and the increase in inequalities opened space for extreme political proposals, putting democracy at risk. The persisting political polarization within and among countries has hindered the consolidation of a solid consensus on the revival of regionalism, despite the change of regime in Brazil from former President Bolsonaro to a third mandate of President Lula and the latter's intention to foster Latin America integration (Ribeiro Hoffmann, 2023).

Our focus is on finance and its connections to growth and democracy. This choice is deliberate and lies at the heart of the Jean Monnet Network 'Crisis-Equity-Democracy for Europe and Latin America', which funded the research conducted for the book. Scholars involved in this research network have argued that finance plays a crucial role for economic growth and stability but can also become a destabilizing factor, as the global financial crisis and subsequent episodes of financial turbulence have aptly demonstrated (De Souza Guilherme et al., 2021). The most recent episode occured in the USA, in March 2023, when three of the four largest banking failures in US history occurred, marked by the fastest run on deposits ever recorded; its resolution required a major intervention by the Federal Reserve and government authorities to prevent a financial meltdown (Beams, 2023). We have also argued that the political spillover from the global financial crisis and its handling catalysed a resurgence of populist and nationalist rhetoric and politics, which (reinforced by subsequent crises) has driven democratic deterioration across the globe to a tipping point (Freedom House, 2023).

Objectives and Structure of the Book

From a comparative regionalism perspective, this book has three main objectives: First, to critically analyse and evaluate the response of regional organizations and governments in the EU and Latin America to the crises that have shook these regions in recent years. This analysis takes place at two levels: one political and one economic. On the politics front, the *first part* of the book examines the challenges to democracy stemming from the recent crises, employing a regional perspective. More specifically, the chapters on Latin America, while acknowledging that democratic crises are not something new in the region, identify new challenges to democracy and examine their impact on regional and interregional relations. In this context, in the first chapter, Monica Herz and Andrea Ribeiro Hoffmann examine the rise of far-right regimes in the region focusing on Bolsonaro's government in Brazil. Their analysis shows that Bolsonaro's government contributed to the decay of democracy in Brazil, led to disengagement with the multilateral system, and undermined regionalism in Latin America while weakening relations between the EU and LAC.

José Briceño-Ruiz, in his chapter, stresses the fact that democratic crises have occurred with high frequency for several decades in Latin America. However, he, too, highlights the novel features of recent democratic crises in the region. He shows that democratic crises are now less likely to come from traditional military coups d'état than political strategies of democratically elected governments, such as polarization, undermining of the opposition, impeachments and more generally lawfare tactics, and non-traditional military interventions. The continued challenges to democracy and the ensuing political instability undermine the ability of Latin American countries to address the new challenges of permacrisis, like climate change, immigration, and shifts in the international economic and political order. The author focuses on the role of regional institutions and in particular that of the Organization of American States (OAS) in helping to address the democratic crises that Latin American countries have experienced since the 1990s. He argues that despite some initial successes, gradually the effectiveness of the organization in handling such crises has declined, making the coordinated response of the region to the challenges of permacrisis more difficult.

Finally, Tiziano Breda focuses on another recent trend, inspired by El Salvador's president Nayib Bukele, and his hard-line policies on criminality. The success of Bukele's approach in reducing crime exercises an increasing appeal for many other politicians in the region that seek to emulate it. The problem is that the policies adopted by Bukele, while successful, often violate human rights, depend on the concentration of power in the hands of the executive, and 'are nurturing a growing movement of punitive populism'. While Breda's analysis shows that this policy paradigm has remained mostly rhetorical until now in other countries, it could have a long-term impact on actual policies in the region, eroding the quality of democracy.

The chapters discussing Europe are somewhat more optimistic, despite the challenges facing the EU, not least the rise of populist, Eurosceptic, and far-right parties in recent years. Bettina Guilherme examines comparatively the handling of the Eurozone debt crisis and the pandemic, from a legitimacy point of view, focusing in particular on the role of the European Parliament (EP). In contrast to the Eurozone crisis, when intergovernmentalism dominated negotiations, during the pandemic, the EU reverted to its traditional 'community method' of legislation. The latter includes an active role for the European Parliament, which, during the pandemic, was able to contribute substantially to the design of the Recovery and Resilience Facility (RRF), EU's flagship fiscal initiative to combat the pandemic and its economic and social consequences. Moreover, the EP was able to promote transparency and the rule of law in the governance arrangements agreed. While far from perfect, the EU's response to the pandemic crisis endorsed solidarity as a guiding principle, improving thereby its legitimacy vis-a-vis the European citizens.

The next chapter by Dimitris Katsikas picks up where Guilherme's chapter left off by examining in more detail the popular legitimacy of the EU during the permacrisis era. The author seeks to assess the impact of permacrisis as 'an extended period of stress and insecurity, on European citizens' support towards European integration'. To do so, Katsikas employs Easton's (1975) concept of diffuse support and uses Eurobarometer data to examine the impact of consecutive crises on it over the last 15 years. Moreover, given that different crises have led to different rifts within the EU, he separates the data into three groups of countries: (a) southern Europe, (b) eastern Europe, and (c) northern/western Europe. The findings show that overall, public support for the EU has increased during this period, despite the significant decline observed during the Eurozone crisis, across all groups of countries. Therefore, the democratic legitimacy of the EU appears strengthened. However, the data also reveal potential problems; the share of people who do not trust the EU or are dissatisfied with the way democracy works in the EU has risen over time, while there is evident variation in the responses among the three geographical groups during different crisis episodes. Overall, therefore, despite the positive results, there are signs of heightened politicization of the EU and therefore support for the idea of an intensifying constraining dissensus, which could prove an obstacle to further integration initiatives.

On the economics front, the *second part*, focusing on the EU, examines fiscal and financial stability and resilience. These aspects are considered crucial, given the significant problems of the European banking system and the limitations of the Union's fiscal capacity, both significant factors for the deterioration from the global financial crisis to a full-blown Eurocrisis in the previous decade. More specifically, the chapter by George Andreou examines the EU's fiscal reply to the pandemic, the NextGenerationEU programme and its main component, the RRF, already mentioned above, and their uneasy co-existence with the more standard arsenal of the EU's fiscal tools and particularly the so-called cohesion policy. Andreou shows how the NextGenerationEU and the RRF are part of an EU tradition of resorting to the establishment of new ad hoc, off-EU budget tools in response to external shocks. While these tools proved crucial for economic and social resilience during the pandemic, their co-existence with EU's cohesion framework, with which they share, to a certain degree, similar objectives and priorities, poses numerous challenges in terms of fragmentation and duplication of proposed investments, implementation arrangements, funds, and levels of governance. Moreover, their shorter implementation period and lighter bureaucratic burden may even impact adversely the timeline of implementation of the 'normal' cohesion policy programmes.

Similar concerns over the effectiveness of policy interventions, this time in the area of finance, are expressed by Mikael Mäkipää, David Howarth, and Scott James. In their chapter they focus on the reforms that were promoted in the aftermath of the global financial crisis (GFC), to address the too-big-to-fail (TBTF) problem in the banking sector, which led to public bailouts, contributing thus to the deterioration of public finances and the Eurozone crisis that followed. The authors engage in a comparative examination of several European countries (the UK, France, Germany, the Netherlands), the EU level, and the USA, across a range of regulations including capital requirements, liquidity and resolution rules, and structural reforms. While acknowledging that many changes were made, the authors argue that with the exception of structural reforms (i.e. reforms relating to the organizational set-up of banks, particularly with respect to investment and non-investment activities and the ring-fencing of the latter) in the USA and the UK, the reforms promoted cannot effectively tackle the TBTF problem. Structural reform proposals in the EU were not implemented, while many of the other regulations outlined in the Basel III package were watered-down when transposed into EU law. The authors argue that this is due to national authorities' concerns over competitiveness and the lending ability of their domestic banking sectors. As a result, the systemic threat posed by the TBTF problem remains unresolved.

The final chapter in this part, by Dimitris Katsikas, examines in more detail one of the areas discussed by Mäkipää et al. In particular, the chapter focuses on one of the most important innovations of the Banking Union, EU's flagship reform, the adoption of the *bail-in* principle in the resolution of failing banks. The bail-in principle was introduced to eliminate publicly funded bailouts, break the link between banks and sovereigns, and instil discipline in financial market participants. Katsikas examines the implementation of the bail-in principle, in two major banking crises, in Cyprus and Italy. The analysis of the way the bail-in principle was implemented in these crises shows the significant political economy constraints at play. In both cases, bail-in requirements were not fully implemented, and even in cases where some burden sharing did take place, certain investor categories were compensated. Even in the case of Cyprus, where an extensive bail-in was implemented, this was limited to certain categories of investors and banks. In both cases, public bailouts were not averted. What is more, it is shown that these political economy constraints have been largely internalized in the new regulatory framework, which allows multiple resolution options, involves many actors, and allows local authorities substantial leeway.

In the *third part*, focusing on Latin America, given the region's past record and future development challenges, we examine the interaction between politics, finance, and economic growth. The chapter by Maria Antonieta Del Tedesco Lins serves as an introduction to the region's turbulent recent economic and political history. Del Tedesco Lins focuses on the experiences of the three largest economies in the region, Argentina, Brazil, and Mexico, during the past 15 years, demonstrating how they are trapped in a state of economic stagnation, from which they seem unable to escape. This situation is the result of structural deficiencies in the economy, but it also reproduces socioeconomic inequalities in a vicious cycle, which seems to get worse, given recurrent external shocks, such as the pandemic. The author argues that beyond economic fundamentals, we also need to look at political factors and, in particular, the interaction between political instability and the underlying economic dynamics. The joint discussion of economic and political developments shows that political turmoil impacts adversely the economy and obstructs the effective handling of external shocks. The latter remain unresolved, gradually feeding into economic and institutional structural weaknesses reproducing and sustaining a permanent state of stagnation.

Given the importance of trade for economic growth in Latin America, the chapter by Julieta Zelicovich focuses on the impact of permacrisis on the governance of trade relations with the EU. She shows how the challenges of permacrisis, like climate change and the need for sustainable development, have driven changes in unilateral, regional, and interregional trade rules. In this context, Zelicovich identifies three new key mechanisms that have been shaping interregional trade governance in recent years: the modernization of existing free trade agreements and conclusion of pending negotiations, the establishment of a new type of trade-related cooperation sectoral agreements, and unilateral reforms. These mechanisms do not show the same dynamics, and they carry different political economic implications. In particular, the weak regional coordination in Latin America and the vulnerable state of many economies in the region, Zelicovich argues, have allowed the push for extraterritorial application of unilateral reforms and the pursuit of bilateral over interregional or sub-regional agreements, by the EU, rendering the interregional trade relations increasingly asymmetrical.

The chapter by Giselle Datz focuses on another chronic problem of the Latin American region: sovereign debt crises. Datz shows that starting from the Brady plan, which was catalytic for the resolution of the debt crisis of the 1980s, the adoption of ad hoc, market-based solutions to the problem of sovereign defaults in Latin

America, and elsewhere, has failed to provide the necessary systemic institutional solution and has, indeed, created more coordination problems between public and private actors involved in the process of debt restructuring. Therefore, even when such crisis episodes have been successfully handled, the broader problem remains, and new episodes plagued by dysfunctional restructuring negotiations always emerge. In this sense, as the author concludes 'the past thus remains an insufficient prologue to a future where sovereign debt restructurings are a predictable part of permacrisis'.

The second objective of the book is to contribute to a better understanding of the promised benefits and risks of digital currencies and fintech, more generally, for economic growth, financial stability, and inclusion. The standard of information and transparency in these markets is very asymmetric across different levels (local, regional, global) and actors involved (individuals, companies, private financial institutions, central banks, and regulators), with both economic and political consequences. In this sense, digital currencies and fintech can be seen as a way to address some of the issues that have led to crises in the recent past but could also be a new source of crises themselves. In the *fourth part* of the book, several chapters engage with this cutting-edge problematique, from both theoretical and policy perspectives, with some of the chapters discussing regional aspects.

In the first chapter of this part, Christian Ghymers discusses the potential benefits of one of the most promising innovations in digital finance, the introduction of central bank digital currencies (CBDCs). For Ghymers, CBDCs offer significant benefits, such as 'significantly faster, safer, cheaper payments than cash or bank accounts, particularly for cross-border payments'. Moreover, they are expected to reduce bank profitability and make monetary policy more efficient. But the most important contribution of CBDCs for Ghymers is their potential as a 'game changer' of the international monetary system. Through their technological features, which can eliminate the difference between domestic and cross-border transactions, the creation of a safe, cheap, multilateral system of payments can become a reality. Ghymers does not stop there and proposes to go one step further. Taking full advantage of their technological potential, the adoption of CBDCs could lead to the creation of a global safe asset, an e-SDR, to be issued by the IMF, which would become the international lender of last resort. This would allow the management of global liquidity multilaterally, ensuring global stability and rectifying the asymmetric dollar-based and crisis-prone international monetary system.

In the next chapter, Stephan Schulmeister deals with the darkest aspects of digital finance, examining the rise and features of cryptocurrencies and, more specifically, the bitcoin. Schulmeister does not engage in a technical analysis of bitcoin but rather tries to examine its emergence as part of the great transformation of capitalism that has been taking place since the 1970s into financial capitalism. Bitcoin and other cryptocurrencies, which have no intrinsic value and are not connected to other currencies or valuable commodities (like stablecoins), thus lacking price limits dictated by fundamentals, rely on psychological and speculative drivers and as a result display very high volatility. After reviewing the literature, Schulmeister argues that most bitcoin transactions are related to trading and speculation, have little impact on the real economy, and are being used to fund illegal activities. As such bitcoin and other cryptocurrencies constitute for Schulmeister the ‘incarnation of finance capitalism’, taking the process of financialization to the extreme, deepening the separation of finance and the real economy, and through their pronounced volatility and speculative drive continuously sustaining financial instability as a constituent feature of permacrisis.

The next chapter by Maria Antonieta Del Tedesco Lins and Andrea Ribeiro Hoffmann returns to the CBDCs. Their aim is to examine the potential economic, social, political, and international repercussions of CBDCs, by focusing on the case of a particular country: Brazil. In recent years Brazil launched a highly successful instant payments system called Pix and plans to launch a central bank digital currency, Drex, in 2024. The authors argue that there are significant potential benefits domestically, in terms of costs and inclusiveness, provided however that a robust regulatory framework, which ensures transparency and privacy protection, is created. While Brazil seems to be moving fast domestically, it has been less active at the international level, particularly vis-a-vis other countries and organizations in the region. Given the significant opportunities and challenges that lay ahead for the international monetary system, as a result of both the increased geopolitical and geoeconomic rivalries among great powers, particularly between the USA and China, and the ongoing digitalization process, there is a need for more international cooperation on the future of digital monetary relations. For the authors, Brazil should exploit this opportunity by engaging more actively with other countries and international organizations in the region and also with the EU.

The next two chapters by Anastasia Kotovskaia and Panagiotis Barkas echo the argument of Del Tedesco Lins and Ribeiro Hoffmann about a balanced approach between market innovation and regulation, this time for fintech. Both chapters demonstrate how through the use of technological and financial innovation, and data science, fintech companies have emerged as a dynamic force in modern finance, delivering new products and services. Beyond the obvious benefits of increased consumer choice, which translates into cheaper and faster services, fintech holds the promise of financial inclusion for populations previously excluded from the traditional banking system, particularly in developing countries. Kotovskaia in particular argues that fintech can narrow the gender aspect of financial inclusion, as women often face higher barriers to accessing financial services. Moreover, discussing Latin American countries, Kotovskaia believes that the region has the potential to become one of the biggest fintech markets in the future, a development which could substantially improve financial inclusion in the region. All these benefits notwithstanding, the author calls for caution, as she analyses several risks associated with fintech, particularly those relating to vulnerabilities in data management and protection, cybersecurity, and operational resilience. Barkas engages with the same topic, but he focuses more on consumer protection and the risks that arise from market failures and psychological and cognitive factors that affect consumers’ financial decisions. To do so he relies on the use of concepts and tools from microeconomics and behavioural economics, which describe, and offer suggestions to address, the aforementioned challenges. Also, the author stresses the importance of synergies in promoting responsible and effective regulation, both within borders, through the collaboration of governments, companies, the academic community, and civil society but also internationally between national regulators and international regulatory organizations, as the enhanced financial interconnectedness and interdependency, which brings the world of fintech, entail more contagion and consumer-related risks of a transboundary nature.

The third objective of the book is to promote the mutual understanding about the challenges of permacrisis in Europe and Latin America and advocate for their cooperation at the multilateral and bi-regional levels. This objective is particularly important for our Jean Monnet Network and very topical, given the EU CELAC Summit 2023 that took place on the 17th and 18th of July, in the context of which our network participated in the fifth Academic Summit of the Permanent Academic Forum LAC-UE at the University of Alcalá, 6–8 July 2023. The past experience and future prospects of both multilateral and interregional EU-CELAC cooperation for tackling the permacrisis challenge are reviewed in the *fifth and final part* of the book.

More specifically, the first two chapters put forward innovative proposals for addressing, at the multilateral level, some of the key challenges of permacrisis. Christian Ghymers kicks off this part with an ambitious proposal for reforming the international financial and monetary system, which he deems necessary to secure the funding that is needed for de-carbonization. Ghymers describes the huge amounts required over the next several decades for de-carbonization investments and the related transition costs and shows how current financing levels are wholly inadequate to cover these expenses. It is not simply a matter of political will and political economy considerations; the author argues that the way the financial and international monetary systems operate imposes structural constraints on the international community's ability to mobilize and disperse geographically, as needed, the necessary funds. Accordingly, Ghymers proposes a financial international public intervention to complement current taxes on CO_2 emissions. This will provide positive incentives ('bonus') for new de-carbonization investments, thereby reducing their high ex ante uncertainty and making them viable. Ghymers also proposes a safe asset at the multilateral level and the corresponding upgrading of IMF into a global lender of last resort, an initiative which, if combined with the transition to new CBDCs, could lead to the creation of an e-SDR, as outlined also in a previous chapter by the author.

Stephan Schulmeister also puts forward a novel -but simple to implement- reform of the global financial system. Schulmeister argues, in line with the discussion of permacrisis in this introductory chapter, that the transformation of the global financial system during the last several decades has contributed to the constant sense of uncertainty and the recursive episodes of financial instability, which are constituent features of permacrisis. In contrast to the still dominant efficient market hypothesis, Schulmeister shows that the modern financial system follows a series of 'bull' and 'bear' swings, which increase volatility, dampen the real economy, and prevent the uninhibited funding necessary for the green transition. According to Schulmeister, this model of operation is due to the dominance of algorithmic trading and technical analysis, at the expense of the proper analysis of fundamentals. To remedy this problem, the author advocates replacing the current continuous trading model with electronic auctions that will take place at specific intervals during the day, e.g. every 3 h; this would slow down asset trading and reduce volatility, as it would eliminate short-term profit-seeking through the exploitation of high-frequency price data and would force traders and investors to consider more seriously market and asset fundamentals in their decisions.

The need for multilateral and interregional cooperation is the focus of the next chapter by Nicola Bilotta. Bilotta discusses the new emerging reality in the international monetary system which he argues is characterized by three developments: economic dislocations, geopolitical tensions, and digitalization. These developments could lead to international monetary fragmentation if different economic blocs establish parallel, non-complementary systems. According to the author, CBDCs offer an opportunity to overcome such challenges, if countries cooperate to establish interoperable institutional arrangements. While cooperation needs to be promoted multilaterally, Bilotta also argues in favour of increased cooperation between the EU and LAC in the framework of the EU-LAC Digital Alliance, as they share a common interest in shaping the new digital global financial and monetary architecture according to their own principles, while strengthening their autonomy vis-a-vis the USA and China. According to the author, this should be seen as a strategic move, which would enable the participating regions and countries not only to improve and facilitate interregional transactions but also to influence, through their combined market weight and the ability to withhold access to their network of CBDCs, the shaping of global rules and standards.

The final chapter of this volume, co-authored by Andrea C. Bianculli, Laia Brossa, and Jacint Jordana, reviews six decades of interregional relations between the EU and Latin America. More specifically, the authors examine the evolution of these relations since the 1960s, through the analysis of the policy instruments used to organize these relations. In doing so, they introduce a novel database which catalogues and categorizes the policy instruments used during this period. This database constitutes a distinct and valuable original contribution of the Jean Monnet Network 'Crisis-Equity-Democracy in Europe and Latin America'. In their analysis, Bianculli, Brossa, and Jordana show that agreements, particularly those relating to trade, have been the most frequently used policy instrument. It is worth noting that agreements tend to be bilateral, throughout the period under examination. On the other hand, interregional agreements, which have been sought by the EU since the 1990s, never really took off. The clearest example of the challenges they face, due to their deeper agendas and the involvement of numerous actors with different interests, is the agreement between the EU and Mercosur that has been negotiated for more than 20 years. The authors note that shocks such as the Eurozone crisis have affected the EU's ability and appetite for funding. Moreover, in the context of an increasingly intense global competition, the idea that certain Latin American countries should be 'graduated' and not benefit from developmental aid or preferential treatment arrangements has also shaped preferences in the EU. On the other hand, in today's increasingly multipolar world, characterized by great power rivalries and the decline of multilateralism, the EU aims to strengthen and rebuild relations with

Latin America, as demonstrated by the recent EU-CELAC Summit and the provision of €45 billion for investment through the Global Gateway platform, mostly on renewable energy and digital services. Clearly, developments in the international order open up new opportunities for cooperation between the two regions, as discussed by several chapters in the volume.

Finance, Growth, and Democracy in the Era of Permacrisis

The era of permacrisis poses tremendous challenges for all regions and countries in the world. Some of these challenges require immediate response, as was the case during the pandemic, while others demand a continuous effort to address problems and build resilience, as is the case with the climate crisis. In this book we invited several authors, with different backgrounds, to examine some of these challenges from an interdisciplinary and comparative perspective with a focus on Europe and Latin America. As outlined in the previous section, some of the chapters engaged with the way different shocks were handled by governments and regional organizations, while others emphasized the conditions which produce the shocks. All of them provide valuable insights into the challenges we face, and most of them offer suggestions on how to address them more effectively.

Without attempting to provide a full analysis of the findings and suggestions of the book's 20 chapters, we engage here in a brief discussion of the evidence provided, to draw some common interpretive threads. One such thread is the importance of highlighting the structural shifts and transformations that have led to the various shocks examined in the book. Finance, in line with our Jean Monnet Network's rationale, has emerged as an area which is crucial in this respect. The transformation of finance over the last few decades, through processes such as globalization, securitization, financialization, and, more recently, digitalization, has not only changed the nature of the global financial system but of capitalism itself. As was shown by different chapters in this book, this transformation has significant and broad repercussions in the context of permacrisis.

Thus, for example, the chapters by Schulmeister demonstrate how innovations like cryptocurrencies and algorithmic trading increase volatility and risk, rendering thus the system crisis prone. At the same time, other structural shifts impede the resolution of crises once they erupt. Datz, in her discussion of the market-based solutions, promoted to deal with sovereign debt crises, Mäkipää et al. in their analysis of the TBTF problem and Katsikas in his review of the implementation of the bail-in principle, highlight and analyse the political economy constraints, which are endogenous in the way financial capitalism has evolved and which inhibit both the conclusive resolution of crises but also more ambitious regulatory reforms to avert similar crises in the future. As a result, crises often remain unresolved or are partially resolved, without addressing their underlying structural causes, a practice which in effect sets the ground for the next crisis episode.

Another, equally important side effect, highlighted by Ghymers, is the fact that in the way the international financial system operates, it is impossible to find the resources necessary to fund the green transition and to combat the climate crisis timely. It seems, therefore, that the structural transformations that have shaped financial capitalism have created strong endogenous constraints to our ability to deal effectively with the challenges of permacrisis, which can only be removed with an ambitious paradigm-shifting reform of modern-day capitalism itself.

On the other hand, this does not mean that until such a systemic change is accomplished, governments or regional organizations are helpless in the face of crises. The chapters by Guilherme and Andreou show that the EU's reaction to the pandemic was much better than that of the Eurozone crisis. Fast reflexes in an array of policy areas gave EU member states the necessary leeway to deal with the challenges raised by COVID-19, and an ambitious fiscal intervention with the Recovery and Resilience Facility provided the necessary resources to deal with its economic and social consequences. As a result, as Katsikas demonstrates, popular support and therefore the democratic legitimacy of the EU are now higher compared to the pre-GFC period. Of course, this does not mean that all is well with the EU; in the same chapters, Guilherme mentions some of the old political economy rivalries between member states that emerged once again during the pandemic; Andreou warns about the governance and implementation consequences of overlapping ad hoc arrangements with permanent institutional mechanisms, while Katsikas notes the rising share of citizens who are dissatisfied with the way the EU operates and the latter's increased politicization, which is bound to make crisis handling even more challenging in the future, as dissatisfied citizens increasingly turn to populist, Eurosceptic, and even far-right parties.

In Latin America, things seem to be even more difficult, given the absence of both a significant governance centre at the regional level and the burden of a long legacy of democratic and economic crises. Indeed, the chapter by Briceño-Ruiz demonstrates this mutually reinforcing vulnerability, between unstable national democracies and weak regional organizations, which are unable to intervene effectively to resolve them. What is more, these crises are increasingly characterized by new features, as Briceño-Ruiz demonstrates in his categorization of undemocratic political strategies. Even more worrisome is the rise of far-right ideology in the region as documented by Herz and Ribeiro Hoffmann. Focusing on the case of Brazil, the authors show that illiberal regimes not only affect domestic democratic and human rights but also shape external relations as well, undermining both regional and interregional cooperation, which makes it even harder to address the common challenges of permacrisis. In this context, certain states' efforts to deal with a crisis on their own can actually lead to further deterioration of democratic standards, as Breda demonstrates with Bukele's policy paradigm. The failure to cooperate regionally has also negative economic consequences. As Zelicovich shows in her chapter on the governance of interregional trade between Latin America and the EU, the former's lack of effective regional cooperation has allowed the EU to effectively dictate the terms of trade governance.

The comparative analysis of the two regions clearly demonstrates the existence of a strong tradition of regional cooperation and existence of regional institutions in both cases. However, while in Europe, the EU has become the leading institution and provided states with the ability both to manage more effectively recurring crises (through a process of institutional learning) and to shape the rules of multilateral and interregional governance to their advantage, in Latin America, a plurality of organizations has been created, with different memberships and mandates as well as relevance for their member states' foreign policies. The current status of what is practically a paralysis of most organizations, mainly in South America, with the possible exception of CELAC, shows how regionalism in Latin America has become a hostage of political polarization and has failed to become a stable platform for engagement and deepening of cooperation, even during acute crises that impacted all countries, such as the pandemic. Democratic crises in leading countries in the region, such as Venezuela under the governments of Chavez and Maduro or Brazil under the government of Bolsonaro, have contributed to this paralysis and the weakening of regional organizations, including Mercosur.

When assessing the potential of the EU and Latin American regional organizations to handle specific issues addressed in the book, such as digital and fintech challenges, it is clear that they have limited experience and capacity to foster cooperation in the case of Latin America. Lins and Ribeiro Hoffmann show how even in cases where countries are very proactive, such as Brazil, initiatives have been mainly limited at the domestic level and have not fostered common regional approaches. In the EU, on the other hand, there are legislative and policy initiatives undertaken at the regional level, primary among them the preparation for the launching of a digital euro in the near future. Moreover, as Barkas and Kotovskaia discuss, there are regulatory arrangements designed to facilitate the expansion of fintech in the EU but also to buttress consumer protection, including the privacy of data. Still, there is a long way to go yet, as technological innovations and artificial intelligence, foremost among them, set new challenges to regulatory authorities daily.

Finally, several chapters have discussed the significance of multilateral cooperation for systemic changes at the global level, such as Ghymer's proposals for decarbonization investment incentives and the introduction of a digital SDR, Schulmeister's proposal for replacing algorithmic trading with electronic auctions, or Datz's proposal for a multilateral sovereign debt restructuring mechanism, and cooperation at the interregional level, as argued, among others, by Bilotta and by Bianculli et al. From the point of view of the Jean Monnet Network that funded and guided this research, we believe that promoting interregional cooperation between the EU and Latin America, mainly via interregional initiatives such as the EU-CELAC Partnership, but also bilaterally, with states such as Brazil—as long as such arrangements are not unduly asymmetrical in terms of their content—is key for promoting stability and growth in the context of permacrisis. Relations among the EU and Latin America have been based on common values regarding democracy and human rights, and these are preconditions for cooperation regarding inclusive growth and finance and the promotion of equity in the long term.

References

Acharya, A. (2012). Comparative regionalism: A field whose time has come? *The International Spectator, 47*(1), 3–15.

Anghel, V., & Jones, E. (2023). Is Europe really forged through crisis? Pandemic EU and the Russia – Ukraine war. *Journal of European Public Policy, 30*(4), 766–786.

Beams, N. (2023). *2023: A year of financial turbulence*. World Socialist Website, 29 Dec 2023. https://www.wsws.org/en/articles/2023/12/29/xato-d29.html

Bianculli, A. C. (2016). Latin America. In T. A. Börzel & T. Risse (Eds.), *The Oxford Handbook of Comparative Regionalism*, 154–177. Oxford University Press.

Börzel, T. A., & Risse, T. (Eds.). (2016). *The Oxford handbook of comparative regionalism*. Oxford University Press.

CEP.AL. (2023). *Panorama Social de América Latina y el Caribe 2022*. Publicación de las Naciones Unidas LC/PUB.2023/6. Impreso en Naciones Unidas. https://repositorio.cepal.org/handle/11362/48518.

De Souza Guilherme, B., Ghymers, C., Griffith-Jones, S., & Ribeiro Hoffmann, A. (Eds.). (2021). *Financial crisis management and democracy*. Springer Cham.

Fawcett, L. (2004). Exploring regional domains: A comparative history of regionalism. *International Affairs, 80*(3), 429–446.

Ferrara, F. M., & Kriesi, H. (2022). Crisis pressures and European integration. *Journal of European Public Policy, 29*(9), 1351–1373.

Freedom House. (2023). *Freedom in the World 2023: Marking 50 Years in the Struggle for Democracy*. Washington DC

Henig, D., & Knight, D. M. (2023, April). Polycrisis prompts for an emerging worldview. *Anthropology Today, 39*(2).

Hooghe, L., & Marks, G. (2009). A postfunctionalist theory of European integration: From permissive consensus to constraining dissensus. *British Journal of Political Science, 39*(1), 1–23.

Jones, E., Kelemen, R. D., & Meunier, S. (2016). Failing forward? The Euro crisis and the incomplete nature of European integration. *Comparative Political Studies, 49*(7), 1010–1034.

Jones, E., Kelemen, D., & Meunier, S. (2021). Failing forward? Crises and patterns of European integration. *Journal of European Public Policy, 28*(10), 1519–1536.

Junker, J.-C. (2016). *Speech at the annual general meeting of the Hellenic Federation of enterprises*. European Commission. https://ec.europa.eu/commission/presscorner/detail/en/SPEECH_16_2293

Katzenstein, P. J. (1996). Regionalism in comparative perspective. *Cooperation and Conflict, 31*(2), 123–159.

Ribeiro Hoffmann, A. (2023). In Anuario CEIPAZ 2022/2023. Policrisis y rupturas del orden global. https://ceipaz.org/anuario-2022-2023/

Shaw, T., Grant, A., & Cornelissen, S. (Eds.). (2012). The Ashgate research companion to regionalisms. Farnham, UK: Ashgate.

Solingen, E. (2014). *Comparative regionalism: Economics and security*. Routledge.

Turnbull, N. (2022, November 11). Permacrisis: What it means and why it's word of the year for 2022. *The Conversation*.

Tooze. A. (2022) *Welcome to the world of polycrisis*. Financial Times, October 28. Retrieved January 20 from Welcome to the world of the polycrisis

Wolff, S., & Ladi, S. (2020). Pandemic politics and European Union responses. *Journal of European Integration, 42*(8), 1025–1193.

Zeitlin, J., Nicoli, F., & Laffan, B. (2019). Introduction: The European Union beyond the polycrisis? Integration and politicization in an age of shifting cleavages. *Journal of European Public Policy, 26*(7), 963–976.

Zuleeg, F., Emmanouilidis, A. E., & Borges de Castro, R. (2021, March 11). *Europe in the age of permacrisis*. European Policy Centre (EPC). Commentary.

Part I
Democracy in Times of Crisis: Regional Perspectives

Chapter 2
Crisis of Democracy and Multilateralism: Effects of Bolsonaro's Far-Right Government on EU-LAC Relations

Monica Herz and Andrea Ribeiro Hoffmann

Contents

Introduction

The crises of democracy and of multilateralism are crucial phenomena to understand international relations, as well as relations between the Latin America and the Caribbean (LAC) and the European Union (EU) at this point of history. Diamond (2021) argues that while between 1974 and 2005 many states became democratic, since 2006, a democratization 'recession' erupted, with declining numbers of democratic transitions and multiple occurrences of democratic decay such as Brazil, Nicaragua, Venezuela, Hungary, Poland, Turkey, and Russia. Democratic decline has also reached the core of Western democracies with Donald Trump's election and the growing foothold of far-right parties and leaders in many European countries such as Italy and the Netherlands. Backsliding of democracy or de-democratization processes suggests that the mainstreaming and normalization of the far right are an international historical process as both contagion and mutual support take place (Mudde, 2019; Krzyżanowski et al., 2023).

De-democratizing agents have acquired some common features despite national and local specificities. The drive to destroy institutions that represent collective

M. Herz (✉) · A. Ribeiro Hoffmann
Institute of International Relations, Pontifical Catholic University of Rio de Janeiro, Rio de Janeiro, RJ, Brazil

D. Katsikas et al. (eds.), *Finance, Growth and Democracy: Connections and Challenges in Europe and Latin America in the Era of Permacrisis*, United Nations University Series on Regionalism 33, https://doi.org/10.1007/978-3-031-68475-3_2

debate, negotiations, and decision-making processes may start at the national level but has clear and dangerous international implications as it unfolds in the international arena. As far-right leaders progressively moved from the margins of political life to positions of power in several countries, it becomes crucial to fully understand their positions and actions in relation to the multilateral system, as well as their interconnected strategies. In their concrete actions on the diplomatic level, far-right leaders seem to have a convergence of action centred on three main axes, going beyond national particularities: unashamed advocacy for a conservative, authoritarian, and traditional worldview; denialism of science; and destructive posture towards multilateral institutions geared towards inclusion. They have been trying to influence and steer the international agenda, sometimes undermining norms and institutions, such as with the denial of climate change and the health crisis during the COVID pandemic, sometimes advancing a conservative agenda such as in the case of sexual and reproductive rights, evidenced with the creation of the Geneva Consensus in 2020 (Drumond & Rebelo, 2023). The Agenda 2030 is accused by some of these leaders of being an instrument to weaken sovereignty and establish a new world order for the benefit of collectivism and tyranny (Vox, 2022); the very concept of universal human rights collides with a political project that exalts a retrospective nationalistic utopia based on traditional values (Dip, 2023).

The rise of the far-right and authoritarian movements and leaders is a central process in the era of 'permacrisis' that we discuss in this edited volume. The Jean Monnet Network 'Crisis-Equity-Democracy' has explored the relations between economic and financial crises and democracy over the last 6 years from an interdisciplinary perspective. The literature on democratic crisis and the rise of the far-right have raised several possible drivers of these processes, such as the impact of neoliberalism and the 2008 financial crisis on material economic inequalities and on individual and collective subjectivities. Wendy Brown opens the door to an understanding of the despise for institutions, laws, and norms that are portraited as limiting the liberty of the individual. She has engaged in the debate on the topic connecting the discussions on authoritarian worldviews, neoliberalism, and traditionalism. Brown investigates the interaction between neoliberal formulations of freedom and resentment, and she argues that the association of nationalism with a version of liberalism focusing on the defence of sovereignty and on anti-statism allows us to refer to 'authoritarian freedom' (Brown, 2019). This neoliberal worldview, based on Friedrich Hayek's writings and widely implemented worldwide since the Reagan-Thatcher governments in the early 1980s, attempts to demolish the collective fabric of societies and bases the new social order on markets and morality. Neoliberalism defends the dystopia of an inegalitarian order in which individuals and families would be politically pacified by markets and morals and subtended by an autonomous and authoritarian but de-politized state (Brown, 2019, p. 17). Traditional values are thus presented as an essential supplement to free markets, and the capacity of tradition to produce social harmony, conformity, and integration is stressed. Inclusion, civil rights, constitutionalism, social justice, and resource distribution by state policies are under attack by potent social groups that have clung to a concept of liberty based on the expansion of market rationality to all spheres of life and that is striped of the political valences that attach it to popular sovereignty (Brown, 2019, p. 13).[1]

The global spread of the economic theories of Hayek and the so-called Austrian school of economics have been propagated internationally for decades through a dense and sophisticated network of research institutes and think tanks, the origins of which date back to the creation of the Mont Pelerin Society in 1947 (Mirowski & Plehwe, 2015) and of which today Atlas Network represents the most visible and influential face. In this context, political acts are seen as a threat to *liberty*. Liberty is seen to thrive not only when the logic of markets prevails but also within the private family sphere, where traditional values are preserved. The concept of liberty put forward here pertains to freedom to compete and treats the result of this competition, whether it be inequality or pain, as natural and functional to social order.

In the discourses of far-right leaders such as Donald Trump, Jair Bolsonaro, and Javier Milei, state-administrated social policy, planning, and social justice contrast with this world of liberty. Other leaders use the state and social policies to ensure popular support, such as Viktor Orban; the relation between authoritarian leaders and neoliberalism varies in different countries and regions. In Latin America, the Chilean military dictatorship of Gen. Pinochet (1973–1990) is a historical exemplar case of authoritarianism and neoliberalism, followed by Bolsonaro and Milei. The choice of the *red pill* (liberty) in the movie *Matrix* became an icon of the far-right's cultural online world. Liberty is sought against the 'cathedral', or the liberal intellectual elites, who share a common cosmopolitan, 'globalist' world vision opposed to the traditional values. In line with this logic, far-right and authoritarian actors resolve the permanent tension between order and justice in favour of *repression*. Law and order themes are expressions of this preference. Security is prioritized over other core values, and police forces and armed forces are treated as privileged social groups as they are supposed to guarantee order and use violence in a legitimate way.

This chapter discusses the crises of democracy and multilateralism and its effects on EU-LAC relations, focusing on the case of Brazil under the government of Bolsonaro. The next session contextualizes Bolsonaro's government and foreign policy in the Latin American far-right, and the third session analyses the effects of his foreign policy on EU-LAC relations. The final remarks briefly discuss the changes of Brazilian foreign policy after one year of Lula da Silva's third mandate and the possible effects on EU-LAC in the near future.

[1] For further discussion on Brown's work, see Herz and Summa, forthcoming.

The Rise of the Far Right in Latin America and Bolsonaro's Government

Sanahuja and Burian (2020) argue that the far-right in Latin America share some common characteristics, one of them being a particular interpretation of nationalism, since xenophobia is not a central issue for the far right in this region, as is the case in Europe. In Latin America the 'other' is associated with everything that challenges the national, which is in its turn understood as a homogenized concept, so issues such as the recognition of social diversity or plurinationality are perceived as a threat to the nation. 'Rather than the combination of xenophobia and nationalism, it seems more appropriate to think of a combination of nationalism and sovereignty, as a rejection of various foreign things' (p. 18, our translation). Despite the common characteristics, Latin America is also plural, including the relation between far right and populism, given the historical experience with left-wing populism in the region (Mudde & Kaltwasser, 2012; Kaltwasser & Van Hauwaert, 2020). The recent rise of the populist far right in Latin America is summarized by Zanotti et al. (2023, p. 3):

> Things started to change in 2017. In Chile, the former Independent Democratic Union (UDI) congressman José Antonio Kast left the party to run for president as an independent. With a discourse not unlike the PRR's [Radical Right Parties], he surprisingly obtained almost eight percent (8%) of the vote share in the presidential election. In 2021, Kast was the most-voted candidate in the first round, with nearly 28 percent of the vote, being defeated in the second round, but obtaining 44 percent of the vote. In Brazil in 2018, Jair Bolsonaro, a former army captain with a similar discourse, became the first PRR president in the region. Bolsonaro won the presidency by obtaining more than 46 percent of the vote in the first round and around 55 percent in the second round.

Even if part of a global trend, Bolsonaro's government must be understood in the context of domestic particularities derived from the Brazilian political system, political culture, and society, as well as his leadership. Bolsonaro was elected on an anti-rights platform, marked by hate speech against indigenous peoples, LGBTQIA+, blacks, and women; cleansing the nation from these alleged corrupting influences has been put forward as a mission. Bolsonaro adopted an ideological foreign policy that must be understood in the context of a transnational far-right trend that acquires unique features in Brazil (Herz, 2022). Bolsonaro's foreign policy has played an important role in his government, unlike other experiences in Brazilian history, where foreign policy was a marginal part of the domestic political debate. Almeida (2021) argues that Bolsonaro's foreign policy was the most formidable and bizarre rupture in diplomatic standards and foreign policy in the country's national history. He called the phenomenon 'bolsolavismo diplomacy' due to the influence of Olavo de Carvalho, a Brazilian right-wing thinker who lived in the United States and who assumed the role of Bolsonaro's 'guru'. Still according to Almeida, the rupture caused by the 'bolsolavismo diplomacy' included the abandonment of multilateralism, which is associated with 'globalism', a concept linked to Marxism, and the threat of global solidarity to sovereignty and national interests.

Adaptation to international norms and institutions that marked the foreign policy of the post-democratic period was put into question. South-South cooperation, a drive for regional integration in Latin America, and attempts to put forward proposals for environmental norms that are acceptable to the Global South were disregarded. Basic premises with which previous governments had worked were abandoned, and in Latin America the investment in regional coalitions and multilateral institutions that had characterized Brazilian foreign policy at least since 1994 was shelved (Herz, 2022). The slogan 'Brazil beyond anything', adopted by President Bolsonaro when still a candidate, in line with Trump's terminology, expresses a traditional concept of sovereignty in which the focus is on the relationship between the state and the nation, and global governance is put aside. Multilateral international and regional institutions were treated as either irrelevant or a threat. The UN system was treated as the expression of the decadence of Western civilization because of its practices, policies, and ideas on inclusion and norms on universal human rights (de Carvalho Hernandez, 2022).

Gomes Saraiva and Costa Silva (2019) differentiate what they call the 'ideological axis' of Bolsonaro's government, including former-Foreign Minister Ernesto Araújo and Eduardo Bolsonaro, who are directly influenced by Olavo de Carvalho, and, to a lesser extent, neo-Pentecostal churches that are sympathetic to their ideas and a 'pragmatic axis', in which they include the military, especially the former Vice President Hamilton Mourão, members of the Chamber of Deputies, and the agrobusiness interest groups. The increased influence of ideology in Brazilian foreign policy is not an isolated phenomenon; on the contrary, some of these traits can be observed in the foreign policy of other leaders from the far-right in the world, including former US President Trump and Hungarian President Orban. According to Sanahuja and Burian (2023), these leaders share a vision of a reactionary internationalism and anti-cosmopolitanism, which, according to them, is a new expression of the friend-enemy distinction in Carl Schmitt's sense. Key factors to understand the rise of the far-right in the world are the hegemonic transition at the global level and the crisis of globalization, evidenced in the 2008 financial and economic crisis, a process that led to a reaction of the 'losers' (real or perceived) in a Polanyian counter-movement, and the questioning of the liberal international order and the idea of cosmopolitanism, multiculturalism, and progress. They reject modernity and ideas associated with the (European) enlightenment.

Sanahuja and Burian (2020) argue that in Latin America 'globalism' and cultural Marxism are constructed as the main enemy of the 'people', differently from Europe, where the main 'other' are immigrants and Islam. Another element in Latin America is the perception of diversity as a threat to cultural homogeneity: 'In this region, not all right-wing parties of this type have strong xenophobic or Islamophobic components, without saying that there are no negative attitudes or securitarian discourses on immigration. However, in this type of discourse, the "other" is often associated with the "foreign"—which calls into question the national—or, on occasions, with plurinationality and the recognition of socio-cultural diversity, in contrast to a homogenizing conception of national identity, understood as something homogenous, hierarchical and ordered. Rather than a combination of xenophobia and nationalism, it seems more appropriate to think of a combination of nationalism and sovereignty, in terms of rejection of the foreign or diverse' (op.cit, p. 18). Neopatriots are nationalists and reject multiculturalism and any regional or global norm that restricts sovereignty; they also blame 'international elites' for propagating 'cultural Marxism', a concept that in Bolsonaro's case includes leaders from Hugo Chavez to Emmanuel Macron, foreign NGOs such as Greenpeace, and activists such as Greta Thunberg and even Pope Francis (op.cit., p. 30).

Zanotti et al. (2023) also highlight regional specificities of what they refer to as the 'populist radical right' and their traits of nativism and authoritarianism. They argue that while in Europe, ideological nativism is articulated through the preference for anti-immigration policies, in Latin America, the markers of difference to identify 'others' are not the immigrants but rather, religious, racial, and ethnic minorities, persons who identify as LGBTI+, and feminists. In the case of Bolsonaro, indigenous groups, quilombolas, and afro-decendants have been the major target of othering and exclusion. The concept of authoritarianism has regional variances too; radical right parties 'express their ideological authoritarianism not only as a preference for stricter measures in terms of law and order, but also as support for morally conservative policies' (op.cit., p.10). Bolsonaro has both characteristics: 'Bolsonaro embodies the growth of neoconservatism and its attempts to prevent access to equal rights, especially for women and members of the LGBTI+ community, though the defence of traditional family values. Concerning traditional moral values, Bolsonaro stressed two popular themes, the idea of "gender ideology" and non-partisan education, attracting allies in religious groups promoting censorship and mobilizing against, for example, the inclusion of sexual education in school curricula' (op.cit., p. 10). Still according to Zanotti et al. (2023), another specificity of Bolsonaro's far-right regime is the place of the military and military dictatorship: 'in Bolsonaro's discourse, the politicization of a nationalist sentiment goes hand in hand with authoritarianism and a reactionary nostalgia for the military dictatorship' (op.cit, p. 11). This can best be illustrated with his own words on the occasion of the vote for the impeachment of former president Dilma Rousseff, when he dedicated his vote to the 'Brazilian traditional family', to the memory of Colonel Carlos Alberto Brilhante Ustra, one of Dilma Rousseff's torturers during her detention during military rule, and to the Armed Forces (op.cit., p. 11).

The political ideology of top members of Bolsonaro's government, including himself, former Foreign Minister Ernesto Araújo, and the former Minister for Women, Family and Human Rights, Damares Regina Alves, is another key element to understand Bolsonaro's foreign policy; however, other elements are relevant too. During the last couple of decades, Brazilian foreign policy has been evolving from a top-down strategic policy decided by the Ministry of External Relations, based on consensual values, norms, and orientations, or by the president and his close advisors, as captured by the concept of 'presidential diplomacy', to more horizontal and complex processes. Milani and Pinheiro (2013) discuss the theoretical perspectives to study foreign policy, i.e. foreign policy analysis (FPA), and the literature of Brazilian foreign policy since the end of the Cold War and argue that in Brazil 'new' actors and factors had become more relevant to understand the debate, formulation, and implementation of foreign policies, such as the constitutional competences of the executive and legislature, the role of parliamentarians, of different executive agencies such as the General-Secretariat of the Presidency, ministries such as health, education, or culture, sub-national units such as states and cities, and the civil society. They argue that Brazilian foreign policy could be studied as a public policy, i.e. both the state organs and the government are involved in action at the international level, but they excluded social and economic actors such as business, NGOs, and social movements from this concept as it must include some level of direct connection with the state. They also discuss the relations between these processes of decentralization and loss of control of the foreign policy by traditional actors, such as the Ministry of External Relations (Itamaraty), with the process of democratization, arguing that pluralization does not necessarily imply a more democratic or a more effective foreign policy as it may lead to fragmentation, ambiguity, and inconsistencies.

Lopes (2020) shares this last point of view, arguing that from President Fernando Henrique Cardoso to Jair Bolsonaro, this combination of factors has prompted an epochal shift in Brazil's external relations, whose bottom line might be the demise of the Ministry of External Relations as the chief formulator of foreign policy, while other governmental bureaucracies, political parties, and individuals take over as the gravity centre in the process of policymaking, turning the contents of Brazil's foreign policy slightly more responsive to social inputs but less predictable and coherent over time. The concept of 'intermestic' is a useful concept to understand these changes. According to Long (2017), the concept was coined by Bayless Manning in 1977 and describes matters that are profound and inseparable both internationally and domestically. The idea of intermestic is related to a notion of linkage developed by James Rosenau, Robert Putnam's 'two-level-game' perspective, as well as Helen Milner's theory about how domestic politics influence international actions; it was used both as a process and as a type of issue. According to Manning, intermestic foreign policies are influenced primarily by interest groups and congress, in political processes that are also open to external influences. Manning saw these processes as resulting from increasing interdependence and argued that congress members seek to protect their constituents and interests 'regardless of foreign policy implications', i.e. foreign policy was more a residual output of domestic, shorter-term/electoral cycle concerns, instead of being led by long-term strategic objectives (Long, 2017).

The Effects of Bolsonaro's Foreign Policy on EU-LAC Relations

EU-LAC relations evolved in many levels: bilateral relations between the EU and individual LAC countries; interregional relations with sub-regional organizations, such as EU-Mercosur, and the comprehensive interregional relations with the whole region, channelled via the EU-CELAC Strategic Partnership since 2013. These relations are affected by several factors such as transnational relations among social and economic actors, global multilateral norms and practices, and EU's and LAC countries' foreign policies. Brazilian foreign policy is one among these factors, but given Brazil's size and leadership, it has historically significantly influenced EU-LAC relations. Bolsonaro's foreign policy had an impact on EU-LAC relations on two main levels: firstly, by prioritizing Brazilian bilateral relations with the United States and downplaying relations with LAC countries and regional integration. Brazil's withdrawal from CELAC in 2020 undermined the EU-CELAC Strategic Partnership as it had been a key country in the establishment of CELAC, along with Mexico (Ribeiro Hoffmann, 2021).[2] Secondly, by favouring ideological alliances with far-right governments, parties, and leaders such as Hungarian Prime Minister Viktor Orban, the Spanish Vox Party, and the Madrid Foro (Sanajuha & Burian, 2023) over institutionalized, multilateral, state-based relations, a characteristic of EU relations with third countries and ideologized foreign policy in several areas such as climate change and human rights, putting into question key values underlying the EU-Brazil Strategic Partnership and EU-Mercosur relations.

Mercosur is a particular case in the context of Bolsonaro's foreign policy and important to EU-LAC relations since this is considered one of the exemplar cases of interregionalism promoted by EU foreign policy especially in the 1990s, other examples being the Andean Community, the Central American Common Market, and the Caribbean Community, also in the LAC region, ASEAN in Asia, and SADC and ECOWAS in Africa. Mercosur, and regional integration, had been supported by all Brazilian governments until Bolsonaro, despite the variance in the priority accorded to free trade in the models of development (Briceno, 2013). In line with the overall dismissal of regional integration, Bolsonaro's first Minister of External Relations, Ernesto Araújo, and his Minister of Economics, Paulo Guedes, favoured the 'flexibilization' of Mercosur, allowing member states to negotiate international trade agreements individually and reduce tariffs unilaterally, what would have meant in practical terms the end of this project of regional integration and the aim of creating a common market in the Southern Cone, since Mercosur would have been rolled back into a free trade area. However, by the beginning of 2021, the opposition and resistance to Bolsonaro's government succeeded in pushing for

---

[2] Regional integration in LAC was a priority of Lula's foreign policy then. He convened the 1st Summit of Latin America and the Caribbean on Integration and Development, in 2008, in Salvador, and in collaboration especially with Mexican President Felipe Calderón, CELAC was formally created in December 2011, in the context of the 3rd Latin American and Caribbean Summit on Integration and Development, and the 22nd Rio Group Summit, in Caracas. Thereafter Venezuela became a third country leading CELAC's agenda and framing it ever more as an 'anti-imperialist', meaning anti-USA organization, competing with the Organization of American States (OAS). Despite this, the EU established a dialogue with CELAC in 2013, replacing the political dialogue between the EU and LAC countries that evolved from the dialogue with the Rio Group, itself established during the conflicts in Central America in the 1980s. In 2013 and 2015 Ministerial Summits took place and established Actions Plans, but until 2023 no Summit took place due to the polarization of regionalism in LAC (Ribeiro Hoffmann, 2021, pp. 132–133).

changes leading, among others, to the replacement of his Minister of External Relations (Saraiva & Alburquerque, 2022). While Minister Araújo had close links with Bolsonaro's son, Eduardo Bolsonaro, then President of the Commission of External Relations at the congress and was one of the main pillars of Bolsonaro's ideologized government and foreign policy project, Minister França had a low administrative profile, and the ministry lost power in the formulation of Brazilian foreign policy. Opposition to Bolsonaro's domestic and foreign policies in intermestic processes contributed to the preservation of Mercosur as a customs union, with a common external tariff and mandate to negotiate international agreements, among them the trade agreement with the EU.

The EU-Mercosur agreement has a long history. An 'Interregional Framework Cooperation Agreement between the European Community and its Member States, of the one part, and the Southern Common Market and its Party States, of the other part' was signed and entered into force in 1999 with three pillars: political dialogue, development cooperation, and trade negotiations. While the first two pillars have led to consensus and memoranda of understandings, trade negotiations were suspended and reopened on several occasions (Doctor, 2007; Meissner, 2016; Bianculli, 2020). The last relaunching of these negotiations took place in 2016, after the end of so-called 'left turn' and 'post-hegemonic' regionalism in Latin America, a concept of regional integration that prioritized the consolidation of regional infrastructure projects and social policies over trade liberalization (Riggirozzi & Tussie, 2012). In this period, presidents favouring trade liberalization took power in Brazil (Vice-President Temer replaced Dilma Rousseff after her controversial impeachment, in 2016) and Argentina (Mauricio Macri, in 2015). In Paraguay, neoliberal Horácio Cartes had been in power since 2013 and was succeeded by also neoliberal Mario Abdo Benitez, in 2018, and, in Uruguay, centre-left Tabaré Vazquez was replaced in 2020 by neoliberal conservative Luis Lacalle Pou. The suspension of Venezuela from Mercosur in 2016 on the grounds of failing to incorporate the normative acquis of the customs union into domestic law and in 2017 for having violated Mercosur's democracy clause, the Ushuaia Protocol, also favoured a relaunching of the EU-Mercosur negotiations (Ribeiro Hoffmann, 2023a).

Despite the change of Minister of External Relations of Bolsonaro's government and the survival of Mercosur and the EU-Mercosur agreement, another problem led to a new problem to EU-Mercosur negotiations. As Bolsonaro's government far-right profile became clear over time, this created a problem for EU-Brazil and EU-Mercosur relations since these relations have been historically driven not only by free trade interests but also by values such as democracy and human rights and, more recently, sustainable environment and climate change. While democracy and human rights conditionalities have been eroded in both regions as indicated in their lack of effectiveness to address the democratic backslide of countries such as Venezuela, Brazil, Hungary, and Poland, climate change activists were not silenced. The criticism of Bolsonaro's domestic and foreign policy on the environment and climate change generated powerful national and transnational collaboration including the 'Brazilian Front Against the Mercosur-EU and Mercosur-EFTA Agreements' (FASE et al., 2023) and the European Parliament and, ultimately, a successful movement to impede the ratification of the EU-Mercosur agreement (Fontes, 2023, Da Silva & Fearnside, 2022). The low expectations of gains from economic actors, as reported in consultancies by the EU (LSE, 2018) and by the Brazilian government (Maduro et al., 2020), also contributed to this result (Baltensperger & Dadush, 2019; Caetano, 2022; Mata Diz, 2022).

Final Remarks

We argued that Bolsonaro's far-right government in Brazil contributed to the decay of democracy, disengagement with the multilateral system, and weakening of regionalism in Latin America, as well as relations among the EU and LAC. The election of President Lula da Silva gave a new impetus to democracy and a change in Brazilian foreign policy: Brazil returned to CELAC and participated in CELACs 7th Presidential Summit in the first month of his mandate, in January 2023, and hosted the 11th South American States Presidential Summit in May 2023. The warm reception of Venezuelan President Maduro in this meeting was, however, divisive, showing that Venezuela is still an obstacle to the deepening of regional cooperation in Latin America. Maduro's recent declarations about his interest in annexing part of Guiana's territory of Essequibo further complicated the situation (Osborn, 2023). After almost one year in power, Lula's regional agenda has been, however, watered down to some infrastructure projects, such as the bioceanic routes connecting Brazil with the Pacific Ocean (Brazilian Ministry of Planning and Budget, 2023). At the political level, Brazil also hosted in Belém do Pará the Summit of Heads of States of the Amazon Cooperation Treaty Organization (OTCA), in August 2023, but the follow-up is yet to be seen.

As regards the relations with the EU, the EU-CELAC dialogue was resumed after seven years, and the 3rd EU-CELAC Summit of Heads of States and Governments took place in Brussels on 17–18th July 2023. The Summit was held under the theme 'Renewing the bi-regional partnership to strengthen peace and sustainable development', and its main formal Summit outcomes included the 'EU-CELAC 2023 Summit Declaration' and the 'Road Map 2023–2025'. Reception by experts was mixed (Nolte & Alvarez, 2023; Ribeiro Hoffmann, 2023b; Ghymers, 2023), but in the current context of 'permacrisis', small steps must be celebrated. The EU-Mercosur negotiations were also resumed under Lula's government, but there are still disagreements on the treatment of climate change, agriculture, and governmental procurement. The election of Javier Milei in Argentina in November 2023 has increased the level of uncertainties further. The effect of Milei's election on LAC and on the relations with the EU must be assessed beyond the EU-Mercosur agreement; his success shows that the far-right still has electoral power in Latin America, and his connections with Bolsonaro and 'bolsonarismo' as well as far-right leaders in the world, including Europe, are strong and likely to influence the political landscape in the region and EU-LAC relations in the near future.

References

Almeida, P. R. (2021). *O Itamaraty Sequestrado: a destruição da diplomacia pelo bolsolavismo, 2018-2021*. Diplomatizzando, ebook Kindle.

Baltensperger, M., & Dadush, U. (2019, September). *The European Union-Mercosur Free Trade Agreement: Prospects and risks*. Bruegel Policy Contribution Issue n° 11.

Bianculli, A. C. (2020). Politicization and regional integration in Latin America: Implications for EU–Mercosur negotiations? *Politics and Governance, 8*(1), 254–265.

Brazilian Ministry of Planning and Budget. (2023), Boletim IDSA, n° 1, Julho de 2023. https://www.gov.br/planejamento/pt-br/centrais-de-conteudo/publicacoes/boletim-idsa-1-julho-23-1.pdf. Accessed 3 Sept 2023.

Briceño Ruiz, J. (2013). Ejes y modelos en la etapa actual de la integración económica regional en América Latina. *Estudios Internacionales (Santiago), 45*(175), 9–39.

Brown, W. (2019). *In the ruins of neoliberalism: The rise of antidemocratic politics in the West*. Columbia University Press.

Caetano, G. (2022). *Analysis and foresight of the European Union-Mercosur Association Agreement*. Occasional paper FC/EU-LAC (4) EN. https://eulacfoundation.org/sites/default/files/2022-04/Especial_FC_EULAC_4_EN.pdf

Da Silva, M. D., & Fearnside, P. M. (2022). Brasil: meio ambiente sob ataque no governo Bolsonaro. *Amazônia Real*. https://amazoniareal.com.br/brasil-meio-ambiente-sob-ataque-no-governo-bolsonaro/. Accessed 25 Dec 2023.

de Carvalho Hernandez. (2022). A política externa em direitos humanos do governo Bolsonaro e a crise da ONU: o backlash é também verde e amarelo. In Barbosa, J.R., & Oscar, A.P.H. (orgs), *Extremismos políticos e direitas: Bolsonaro, Trump e a crise das "democracias"*. Editora Cultura Acadêmica

Diamond, L. (2021). Democratic regression in comparative perspective: Scope, methods, and causes. *Democratization, 28*(1), 22–42.

Dip, A. (2023). Extremists and hate groups meet at UN to 'reclaim' human rights declaration. *Open Democracy*. https://www.opendemocracy.net/en/5050/political-network-for-values-human-rights-meeting-un-extremists-hate-groups-abortion-gender-family/. Accessed 25 Dec 2023.

Doctor, M. (2007). Why bother with inter-regionalism? Negotiations for a European Union-Mercosur agreement. *Journal of Common Market Studies, 45*(2), 281–314.

Drumond, P., & Rebelo, T. (2023). Norm spoiling, gender washing and the pushback against women's rights in Brazilian foreign policy. *Globalizations*, 1–19.

FASE et al. (2023). Por que parar o Acordo Mercosul-União Europeia? https://fase.org.br/pt/acervo/documentos/por-que-parar-o-acordo-mercosul-uniao-europeia/. Accessed 25 Nov 2023.

Fontes, C. (2023). Acordo União Europeia-Mercosul depende de compromissos ambientais e texto mais rígido, diz eurodeputada. *Folha de São Paulo*, 27 de fevereiro de 2023.

Ghymers, C. (2023). *Una Cumbre birregional agridulce entre la UE y América Latina y el Caribe*. https://jeanmonnetcrisisequitydemocracy.com/policy-brief-1-una-cumbre-birregional-agridulce-entre-la-ue-y-america-latina-y-el-caribe-christian-ghymers/. Accessed 25 Nov 2023.

Gomes Saraiva, M., & Costa Silva, Á. V. (2019). Ideologia e pragmatismo na política externa de Jair Bolsonaro. *Relações Internacionais, 64*.

Herz, M. (2022). A conservative foreign policy for Brazil. *Latin American Policy, 13*(2), 376–388.

Hoffmann, R. (2021). La Celac: Integración regional y multilateralismo global. In G. Molano-Cruz & J. Briceño-Ruiz (Eds.), *El regionalismo en América Latina después de la post-hegemonía*. Universidad Nacional Autónoma de México.

Kaltwasser, C. R., & Van Hauwaert, S. M. (2020). The populist citizen: Empirical evidence from Europe and Latin America. *European Political Science Review, 12*(1), 1–18.

Krzyżanowski, M., Wodak, R., Bradby, H., Gardell, M., Kallis, A., Krzyżanowska, N., Mudde, C., & Rydgren, J. (2023). Discourses and practices of the 'New Normal' Towards an interdisciplinary research agenda on crisis and the normalization of anti-and post-democratic action. *Journal of Language and Politics*.

Long, T. (2017). Coloso fragmentado: la agenda "interméstica" y la política exterior latinoamericana. *Foro Internacional, 57*(1), 5–54.
Lopes, D. B. (2020). De-westernization, democratization, disconnection: the emergence of Brazil's post-diplomatic foreign policy. *Global Affairs, 6*(2), 167–184.
LSE. (2018). *Sustainability Impact Assessment in support of association agreement negotiations between the European Union and Mercosur.* Inception Report. London School of Economics and Political Science.
Maduro, L., Da Motta Veiga, P., & Rios, S. P. (2020). Acordo Mercosul-União Europeia. Impactos normativos/regulatórios no Mercosul. Nota Técnica Número IDB – TN – 1997. Banco Interamericano de Desenvolvimento, Instituto para a Integração da América Latina e Caribe (INTAL).
Manning, B. (1977). The Congress, the executive and intermestic affairs: Three proposals. *Foreign Affairs, 55*(2), 306–324.
Mata Diz, J. (2022). The Mercosur and European Union relationship: An analysis on the incorporation of the Association Agreement in Mercosur. *Europe and the World: A Law Review, 6*(1), 1–19.
Meissner, K. (2016). Interregionalism re-loaded: Assessing the EU-MERCOSUR negotiations. *St Antony's International Review, 11*(2), 95–120.
Milani, C. R., & Pinheiro, L. (2013). Política externa brasileira: os desafios de sua caracterização como política pública. *Contexto Internacional, 35*, 11–41.
Mirowski, P., & Plehwe, D. (Eds.). (2015). *The road from Mont Pèlerin: The making of the neoliberal thought collective, with a new preface*. Harvard University Press.
Mudde, C. (2019). *The far-right today*. Polity.
Mudde, C., & Rovira Kaltwasser, C. (2012). *Populism in Europe and the Americas: Threat or corrective for democracy?* Cambridge University Press.
Nolte, D., & Alvarez, M. V. (2023, Julio 26). La Cumbre CELAC-UE entre luces y sombras. *Latinoamérica, 21.* https://latinoamerica21.com/es/la-cumbre-celac-ue-entre-luces-y-sombras/. Accessed 25 Dec 2023.
Osborn, C (2023, June 2). South American presidents come to Lula's Party, but check his leadership. *Latin America Brief.* https://foreignpolicy.com/2023/06/02/south-america-summit-lula-maduro-brazil-venezuela/. Accessed 4 Dec 2023.
Ribeiro Hoffmann, A. (2023a). Mercosur at 30: Political ideologies and (de) legitimation strategies. *International Affairs, 99*(3), 1043–1061.
Ribeiro Hoffmann, A. (2023b). EU-LAC relations after the 2023 Summit: What now? *Regional Integration, 16,* 129–135. https://ejournals.epublishing.ekt.gr/index.php/periphery/issue/view/2027/915. Accessed 27 Dec 2023.
Riggirozzi, P., & Tussie, D. (Eds.). (2012). *The rise of post-hegemonic regionalism in Latin America*. Springer.
Sanahuja, J. A., & Burian, C. L. (2020). Internacionalismo reaccionario y nuevas derechas neopatriotas latinoamericanas frente al orden internacional liberal. *Conjuntura Austral, 11*(55), 22–34.
Sanahuja, J. A., & Burian, C. L. (2023). Las "nuevas derechas" y la ultraderecha neopatriota: conceptos, teoría y debates en el cruce de ideología y globalización. In J. A. Sanahuja & P. Stefanoni (Eds.), *Extremas derechas y democracia: perspectivas iberoamericanas*. Fundación Carolina.
Saraiva, M. G., & Albuquerque, F. L. (2022). Como mudar uma política externa? *CEBRI-Revista Brazilian Journal of International Affairs, 1*, 148–166.
Vox. (2022). *VOX define la Agenda 2030 como una herramienta de adoctrinamiento.* https://www.voxespana.es/noticias/vox-define-la-agenda-2030-como-una-herramienta-de-adoctrinamiento-20221219?provincia=jaen
Zanotti, L., Rama, J., & Tanscheit, T. (2023). Assessing the fourth wave of the populist radical right: Jair Bolsonaro's voters in comparative perspective. *Opinião Pública, 29*, 1–23.

Chapter 3
Democratic Crises in Latin America and the Responses of Regional Institutions: An Evaluation of the Case of the OAS

José Briceño-Ruiz

Contents

Introduction

Democracy has become a normality in Latin America. Most of the countries of this region are now ruled by governments elected in free elections, and peaceful political alternation has become a reality. This notwithstanding, democracy is also at risk in Latin America. It is valid to assert that permacrisis is one of the features of the democratic experience in the Latin American countries since the process of transition that began in the late 1970s and the early 1980s. In this context, the promotion and protection of democracy become even more important when the political polarization and social and economic crises are used as excuses to weaken the democratic practices in the region.

Regionalism has become an instrument to promote and protect democracy in the Americas. The early involvement of regional schemes took place in the 1990s in the Organization of Americas States (OAS) in a context of transition and early consolidation of democracy in the Southern Cone and the Andes. This paper analyzes the role of the OAS in addressing the democratic crises the Latin American countries

J. Briceño-Ruiz (✉)
National Autonomous University of Mexico – UNAM, Mexico City, Mexico

D. Katsikas et al. (eds.), *Finance, Growth and Democracy: Connections and Challenges in Europe and Latin America in the Era of Permacrisis*, United Nations University Series on Regionalism 33, https://doi.org/10.1007/978-3-031-68475-3_3

have experienced since the 1990s. It is argued that despite initial successes such as the OAS' response in the cases of Perú and Haiti in the 1990s or in the mediation in Venezuela in 2003, after 2009, the efficiency of the OAS was much lower.

This chapter is divided in three sections. The first section presents a conceptualization of the diverse forms of democratic crises that have occurred in Latin America. In the second section, the theoretical debate about the role of international institutions in the protection of democracy is presented. In the third section, we analyze the recent crises in Latin America and the responses of the OAS. In this section, the OAS intervention in these democratic crises is also evaluated.

Democratic Crises: Concepts and Varieties

Juan J. Linz describes democracy as "a government pro tempore, a government in which the electorate at regular intervals can make those governing accountable and impose a change" (Linz, 1985: 16). Adam Przerowski proposes a definition of democracy in which alternation is fundamental. For him, "democracy is a system in which parties lose elections. There are parties: division of interests, values, opinions. There is competition, organized rules. And there are periodic winner and losers" (Przerowski, 1991: 10).

In his classical book *Polyarchy*, Robert Dahl defines democracy as "a political system one of the characteristics of which is the quality of being completely or almost completely responsive to all its citizens" (Dahl, 1971: 1). According to Dahl, for a government to be responsive to the preferences of its citizens, these latter should have "unimpaired opportunities." For these conditions to be achieved, the institutions of the society must provide at least some guarantees: (1) freedom to form and join organizations; (2) freedom of expression; (3) right to vote; (4) eligibility for public office; (5) right of political leaders to compete for support; (6) right of political leaders to compete for votes; (7) alternative sources of information; (8) free and fair elections; and (9) institutions for making government policies depend on votes and other expressions of preference.

Levitsky and Way simplify Dahl's framework arguing that a "procedural minimum" definition of democracy includes four key attributes: (1) free, fair, and competitive elections; (2) full adult suffrage; (3) broad protection of civil liberties, including freedom of speech, press, and association; and (4) the absence of non-elected "tutelary" authorities (e.g., militaries, monarchies, or religious bodies) that limit elected officials' power to govern (Levitsky & Way, 2010: 5–6). However, these authors include an additional condition: "the existence of a reasonably level playing field between incumbents and opposition" (Levitsky & Way, 2010: 6).

In our view at least six factors have become the main causes of the democratic crises in Latin America in the last three decades: generalized upheavals and the increasing political polarization; the emergence of populist leaders democratically elected that decide to destroy democracy and led to what Levitsky and Way describe as "competitive authoritarian regimes"; and the proliferation of impeachment and lawfare and nontraditional forms of military intervention. As it is explained in a next section of this chapter, these diverse types of crises lead to an undermining and, in some cases, even the disappearance of some of the guarantees that characterize democracy. When that happens, a democratic crisis occurs.

Generalized upheavals refer to massive mobilizations of economic, political, and social actors against the policies (especially the economic policies) implemented by certain governments. When these upheavals are radicalized, they produce levels of political instability that cause an existential crisis of the political regime. As Panizza argues (2009), the ascendancy of the left in Latin America was accompanied by an empowerment of the popular sectors. However, this also produced an increasing polarization and political instability, expressed in political protest in the form of street demonstrations, disturbances, road blockages, or the occupation of public buildings and public spaces. This has produced a political turmoil that in some cases have led to the collapse of constitutionally elected governments (Panizza, 2009: 198). In other cases, those protests were used as an excuse to promote nontraditional military interventions.

Political polarization is one of the features of politics worldwide in the last few decades. Figures such as Hugo Chávez, Cristina Kirchner, Donald Trump, and Jair Bolsonaro, for example, have polarized their democracies.[1] When polarization appears, the logic "us vs. them" permeates the working of the whole political system replacing the traditional logic of democracy based on normal competitive politics. Jeniffer McCoy defines political polarization "as a process of simplifying politics, leading toward a division of society into two mutually antagonistic camps" (McCoy, 2023: 1). In another paper written with Tahmina Rahman and Murat Somer, McCoy defines polarization as "a process whereby the normal multiplicity of differences in a society increasingly align along a single dimension, cross-cutting differences become instead reinforcing, and people increasingly perceive and describe politics and society in terms of 'Us' versus 'Them'" (McCoy et al., 2018: 18). The process of polarization "simplifies the normal complexity of politics and social relations. Polarization does so by aligning otherwise unrelated divisions, emasculating cross-cutting cleavages, and dividing society and politics into two separate, opposing, and unyielding" (Somer and McCoy, 2018: 5).

Another variety of crisis emerged from populist leaders democratically elected that use democracy to destroy democracy. Fareed Zakaria describes those regimes as "illiberal democracies," the leaders of which are elected, reelected, or reaffirmed through referenda but that consistently ignore constitutional limits on their power and deprive their citizens of basic rights and freedoms (Zakaria, 1997: 22). Leonardo Morlino prefers the concept of hybrid regimes. For him, a hybrid regime is "a set of institutions that have been persistent, be they stable or unstable, for about a decade,

[1] Different studies have been published about these cases of polarization. For the case of Venezuela, see Corrales (2011) and García Guadilla and Mallen (2019). For the case of Argentina, see Schober (2017) and Torcal and Carty (2023). For the case of the United States, see Abramowitz and McCoy (2019). For the case of Brazil, see Goldstein (2019) and Iamamoto et al. (2023). See also Herz and Ribeiro Hoffmann chapter in this book.

have been preceded by an authoritarianism, a traditional regime (possibly with colonial characteristics), or even a minimal democracy and are characterized by the break-up of limited pluralism and forms of independent, autonomous participation, but the absence of at least one of the four aspects of a minimal democracy" (Morlino, 2009: 82).[2]

Levitsky and Way (2010) use the category "competitive authoritarianism," a hybrid regime type that shares characteristics both of democracy and authoritarianism. For Levitsky and Way:

> Competitive authoritarian regimes are civilian regimes in which formal democratic institutions exist and are widely viewed as the primary means of gaining power, but in which incumbents' abuse of the state places them at a significant advantage vis-a-vis their opponents. Such regimes are competitive in that opposition parties use democratic institutions to contest seriously for power, but they are not democratic because the playing field is heavily skewed in favor of incumbents. Competition is thus real but unfair. (Levitsky & Way, 2010: 5)

It is important to highlight that a competitive authoritarian regime is not the same as a fully authoritarian one. In the competitive authoritarian regimes, the opposition parties could compete in elections held regularly. This notwithstanding, in competitive authoritarian regimes the incumbent violates at least one of three defining attributes of democracy: (1) free elections, (2) broad protection of civil liberties, and (3) a reasonably level playing field (Levitsky & Way, 2010: 7).

Another risk to democracy, especially in Latin America, is the increasing judicialization of politics. Catalina Smulovitz (2022: 232) mentions aspects such as the replacement of the popular vote for the decision of a few, the politicization of justice, and the social effect of regression of certain judicial decisions as examples of this judicialization. Another aspect is the recent emergence of what in Latin America has been called lawfare. This is a concept originally developed in the United States and China in the 1990s, the central idea of which was the use of law as a tool of war. In Latin America, the concept of lawfare was transformed and began to describe a new political strategy in which the judicial power is the main actor. Camila Vollenweider and Silvina Romano describe lawfare as:

> The improper use of legal instruments for the purposes of political persecution, destruction of public image and disqualification of a political adversary. It combines ostensibly legal actions with extensive press coverage to put pressure on the defendant and his entourage (including close family members) in such a way that he or she is more vulnerable to accusations without evidence. The goal: to make it lose popular support so that it does not have the capacity to react. (Vollenweider & Romano, 2017: 19)

The former Brazilian Minister of Foreign Affairs, Celso Amorim, in a paper written with Carol Proner, describes lawfare as the "use of legal apparatuses as unconventional strategies to destabilize opponents and political opponents" (Amorim & Proner, 2022: 16).

---

[2] According to this Italian pundit, for a minimal definition of democracy, we need at the same time (a) universal suffrage, both male and female; (b) free, competitive, recurrent, and fair elections; (c) more than one party; and (d) different and alternative media sources (Morlino, 2009: 277).

Smulovitz argues that lawfare is not really a novelty in Latin American political reality. For her, there is some kind of partisan bias in the conceptualization of lawfare. There are reasons to agree that left-wing scholars tend to describe lawfare as a kind of activity that has as main target political leaders located in left of the political spectrum (see, e.g., Vegh-Weis, 2023), by forgetting that Nicolas Maduro in Venezuela and Daniel Ortega in Nicaragua have recurred to lawfare to attack political opponents. In consequence, it is valid to argue that, novelty or not, lawfare is a reality in current Latin American politics. As the Brazilian scholars Cristiano Zanin, Valeska Martins, and Rafael Valim assert: "lawfare is a serious issue and for this reason deserves significant and thorough attention. Simplifying it as a mere rhetorical instrument, even with the best of intentions, is as damaging as the skepticism or prejudice with which some view it" (Zanin et al., 2022: 83).

Impeachment has been another problem in Latin America. Pérez-Liñán (2018: 1) asks if impeachment is a functional equivalent of traditional military coups. In our view, there are reasons to think that the response to this question is affirmative. Pérez- Liñán and Polga-Hecimovich (2019: 3) assert that "most authors seem to implicitly accept that coups and presidential downfalls share some common causes." The fact is that between 1992 and 2016 eight presidents were impeached in Latin America. Certainly, impeachment is a legal mechanism established in most democratic constitutions. The problem is that in Latin America, impeachment has become a tool to expel some political leaders from the presidency, even if they have not clearly committed a crime that justified their destitution. This is the reason why Pérez-Liñán argues that the "impeachment procedure has been consistently 'stretched' for political reasons" (Pérez-Liñán, 2018: 2). The consequence is that there is a risk that "impeachment loses legitimacy as a tool of accountability when politics, rather than arresting illegal behaviour, become the sole motivation for removing the president" (Llanos & Marsteintredet, 2021: 2).

Finally, even if the military are not the central actors of democratic ruptures through coup d'états, it does not mean that they totally disappeared from the political scenario. As said previously, coup d'état directly executed by military is not the rule in Latin America, but some cases have occurred, for example, in Paraguay in 1996. Similarly, a new kind of military intervention has emerged that is called in this paper "nontraditional military intervention." In these cases, the military have participated in the destabilization of the democratic regime, and they have even demanded the resignation of the president, but, conversely to previous periods in the history of Latin America, afterward they have not taken control of the state and its institutions. This happened in Venezuela in 2002, Honduras in 2009, and Ecuador in 2010. In the case of Brazil, Ioris and Schneider observed "the return of the military to the centers of power" (2022, p. 19).

The International Promotion and Protection of Democracy

The literature on transition to democracy tends to consider it as basically associated to domestic political processes or specific national historical conjunctures that are not necessarily linked to external factors. However, this approach to the issue has been contested by a literature that highlights the international dimension of democratization. Thus, Laurence Whitehead edited in 2001 a book in which a group of pundits examined the extent to which international factors could influence the process of democratization (Whitehead, 1996). These external actors adopt narratives and encourage actions that make them promoters and protectors of democracy.

Democratic promotion is a concept that describes international actions aiming at contributing to the transition from authoritarian regimes to democracy. Inken von Borzyskowski and Mert Kartal (2023: 84) argue that when describing the actions of external actors to encourage democracy, "external" means to focus on the international community and not on the activities originating exclusively from inside the country. "Encourage" implies deliberate attempts to promote democracy rather than nondeliberate attempts to foster it, such as contagion. Another concept is democratic protection, described by Hawkins (2008: 375) as "activities that offer tangible or intangible rewards or penalties to the state as a whole for aggregate behavior with respect to democratic standards."

The role of external actors in the promotion and protection of democracy has been critical. Wolff and Wurm (2011) focus their analysis on states with consolidated democracies as external promoters, by arguing that they develop a democratic foreign policy that includes actions to encourage that kind of political regime. By contrast, Jon C. Pevehouse (2002) concentrates his analysis on the actions of states that he calls "young democracies." For him, these countries use regional international organizations in the processes of consolidating democracy. The fact is that both consolidated and young democracies use regional organizations (or more properly regionalism) as spaces to promote and protect democracy.

Thus, regional institutions have become important external actors in the promotion and protection of democracy through diverse mechanisms (Van der Vleuten & Ribeiro Hoffmann, 2010). The first of them is the approval of the so-called democratic charters or democratic clauses, regional legal instruments that condemn the rupture of the democratic order and establish sanctions to the perpetrators of such violations. These legal instruments condition the participation in a scheme of regional integration or cooperation to the respect of democratic rules. On the other hand, most of these clauses include actions and mechanisms to protect democracy when a political crisis emerges, especially in young democracies.

The Democratic Crisis in Latin America

Latin America democracies have had to deal with important challenges after their consolidation. Different crises have occurred in the framework of classification presented in the previous section of this paper. The coup against Jean Bertrand Aristide in Haiti in 1991 and Lino Oviedo's coup d'état attempt in 1996 in Paraguay were cases of traditional coups. Bolivia, Paraguay, Peru, and Venezuela have experienced diverse crises in the last 30 years. Ecuador, Guatemala, and Honduras have also undergone dramatic periods of democratic instability. Brazil is presented as an example of judicialization of politics lawfare and polemical impeachment.

Generalized upheavals, the best example of which was the so-called Caracazo, were critical in the crisis in Venezuela since 1989, a country that at that moment was considered a model of democracy in Latin America. Between 2003 and 2005 upheavals caused the resignation of Presidents Gonzalo Sánchez de Lozada and Carlos Meza in Bolivia. A similar situation occurred in Ecuador in 2005, where protests caused the resignation of President Lucio Gutiérrez.

Another problem of Latin American democracies is the increasing political polarization, to some extent promoted by the traditional elites that feared the loss of their privileges. This was the case in Venezuela on 11 April 2002, when a group of military officers rejected Hugo Chávez as president, but a military junta did not take control of the state, and the businessman Pedro Carmona was appointed president. In 2009, the military arrested and expelled from the Honduran territory the President Manuel Zelaya, but the president of the congress Roberto Micheletti became president. In 2010, members of the Ecuadorian Armed Forces and National Police fostered a revolt against Rafael Correa. The police and armed forces occupied the National Assembly building, and Air Force shut down Mariscal Sucre International Airport in Quito and José Joaquín de Olmedo International Airport in Guayaquil. The rejection of the Public Service Organic Law approved by the congress under the auspice of Correa's government led to a political crisis that was described by Correa as a coup d'état. In another case, Williams Kaliman, commander of the Bolivian Armed Forces, "suggested" to Evo Morales to resign in the context of a political turmoil due to accusations of electoral fraud in 2019, but the political opponent Jeanine Añez was the provisional president.

We also have observed cases of the emergence of competitive authoritarian regimes, hybrid democracies, where elections are held regularly but where political liberties have been undermined and political alternation has almost disappeared.

The first case was the so-called self-coup by the Peruvian president Alberto Fujimori in 1992. Fujimori decided to dissolve the congress and reorganize the judicial power. He also suspended various articles of the constitution, and by the Decree Law 25,418, Fujimori implement economic reforms and adopted severe anti-terrorist policies (Table 3.1).

Venezuela is a paradigmatic case of competitive authoritarianism. Hugo Chávez arrived in power in free elections in 1998, and his posterior reelections were legal in terms of transparency and political competition. However, from 2007 onwards,

Table 3.1 Main democratic crises in Latin America and OAS responses: 1991–2023

Type of crisis	Country/year	Event	Regional responses
Coup d'état	Haiti, 1991	Coup d'état against Jean Bertrand Aristide	Military intervention (non-OAS)
Competitive authoritarianism	Perú/1992	Alberto Fujimori self-coup	Declaration
Competitive authoritarianism	Guatemala/1993	Jorge Serrano's attempt of self-coup	Declaration
Impeachment	Venezuela/1993	Impeachment to Carlos Andrés Pérez	None
Coup d'état Impeachment/ upheavals	Paraguay/1996 Paraguay/2000	General Lino Oviedo's attempt of coup d'état Political Crisis during the presidency of Raúl Cubas	Declaration
Political polarization Nontraditional military intervention	Venezuela/2001–2003	Protest pro and contra Hugo Chávez Brief coup d'état in April 2002	Facilitation
Generalized upheavals	Bolivia 2003/2005	Protests against Sánchez de Lozada (2003) Protests against Carlos Meza (2005)	Facilitation
Generalized upheavals	Ecuador/2005	Protest against Lucio Gutiérrez (2005)	Facilitation
Political polarization	Bolivia/2008	Attempt of secession of some regions controlled by opponents to Evo Morales	Facilitation
Political polarization Nontraditional military intervention	Honduras/2010	Manuel Zelaya calling for a referendum Zelaya detention and expulsion	Suspension
Political polarization Nontraditional military intervention	Ecuador/2010	Political crisis and polarization Attempt of coup against Rafael Correa	Declaration
Lawfare Impeachment	Paraguay/2013	Contested impeachment to Fernando Lugo	Facilitation
Political polarization	Venezuela/2014	Massive protests against Nicolas Maduro's government Violation of human rights	Declaration
Lawfare Impeachment	Brazil/2016	Contested impeachment to Dilma Rousseff	None

(continued)

Table 3.1 (continued)

Type of crisis	Country/year	Event	Regional responses
Political polarization Competitive authoritarianism Lawfare	Venezuela 2017/2019	Protest against the attempt of the dissolution of the parliament Political persecution and violation of human rights Lawfare against political opponents Rejection to the convening of a National Constitutional Assembly Proclamation of Juan Guaidó as interim president	Mediation Attempt of suspension
Political polarization Nontraditional military intervention	Bolivia/2019	Protests pro and contra Evo Morales Accusations of fraud in general elections Military call to Evo Morales to resign	Facilitation
Political polarization Competitive authoritarianism Lawfare	Nicaragua/2019–2022	Protests and violence in the streets Increasing control of Daniel Ortega of the state institutions Lawfare against candidates of the opposition parties	Declaration
Political polarization Lawfare Attempt of self-coup	Perú/2021–2022	Congressional attacks to Pedro Castillo Judicial persecution to Pedro Castillo Pedro Castillo's attempt of self-coup Protests and violence in the streets	Declaration

Source: elaboration by author

Chávez began a process to control the judicial and electoral power using the parliament, which was under his control, due to the decision of the opposition parties not to participate in the parliamentary elections of December 2005. A decade later, Nicolas Maduro deepened the authoritarian nature of the political regime in Venezuela, especially after the elections of 2015 in which the opposition took control of the parliament. Maduro's government used the Supreme Court to neutralize the parliament and in 2017 convened a National Constitutional Assembly purportedly to draw up a new constitution. The elections held in 2019 were called by this constitutional assembly and not by the electoral power, while the executive controlled de facto the other powers. This took place in a political scenario of political polarization with violent protests in the streets against Maduro, to which the government responded with severe repression and violation of human rights. Similarly, the government implemented a lawfare strategy against political opponents.

The Nicaraguan regime also works in the logic of a competitive authoritarian regime, even if there are reasons to think that after the 2021 election it became just a traditional authoritarian government. Daniel Ortega was elected in free elections in 2006 and was reelected in 2011 and 2016. However, the political climate in Nicaragua was quite polarized with protests in the streets against Ortega and an increasing control of the parliament and judicial power by the executive. Significant protests occurred in 2018, and the response of the government was a violent repression and the arrest of political opponents. The paramount moment of the crisis was the 2021 elections when the authoritarian nature of the regime was revealed. Opposition parties were cancelled, and the most important political opponents were prevented from running in the elections by using lawfare. As a result, Ortega was easily reelected with 75% of the votes.

Lawfare and impeachment as political tools have also been part of the democratic crisis in the region. One of the first cases of impeachment happened in Venezuela, where Carlos Andrés Pérez was suspended as president due to accusations of political corruption. However, impeachment as political instrument became a real problem in Latin America after the questionable impeachment of Fernando Lugo in Paraguay in 2013 and Dilma Rousseff in Brazil in 2016. In both cases, impeachment responded more to political reasons than to a desire to condemn illegal behavior of presidents. In the case of Lugo, the impeachment was performed in just 48 h, which raises serious doubts about the respect of right of defense of the impeached president. In the case of Brazil, although the impeachment lasted several months, it was considered that the "*pedaladas fiscais*,"[3] the argument fostered by the political opponents, was not a constitutional cause of impeachment.

Lawfare has become a cause of political crisis in Brazil, Peru, Nicaragua, and Venezuela. The most famous case of lawfare was the judicial persecution performed by the attorney Sergio Moro in Brazil against Luiz Ignacio Lula da Silva. Lula was condemned to 12 years in prison and was impeded to participate in the general elections in 2018, when he was leading the polls. Moro was appointed as minister by Jair Bolsonaro once he became president. In 2021, the Brazilian Supreme Court annulled Lula's convictions. In Venezuela, Nicolás Maduro has used lawfare to impede opponents such as Leopoldo López, María Corina Machado, and Antonio Ledezma to participate in elections. In Nicaragua, Daniel Ortega-controlled courts have impeded leaders like Juan Sébastian Chamorro, Cristiana Chamorro, and Arturo Cruz, among others, to run in elections.

The case of President Pedro Castillo in Peru is more complex. On the one hand, since his arrival in power he experienced a sort of lawfare manifested in various judicial processes against him and different attempts of impeachment. This could be

[3] *Pedaladas Fiscais* (pedaling in English) was described as an action of the federal government that allowed the administration to fund a program for family farmers using money that was not reimbursed until several months later. By doing this, the administration was bypassing the congress.

Table 3.2 Guarantees violated in the Latin American democratic crises

Type of crisis	Guarantees violated
Political polarization	Freedom of expression Risk in the broad protection of civil liberties, including freedom of speech, press, and association
Competitive authoritarianism	Free and fair elections The existence of a reasonably level playing field between incumbents and opposition
Lawfare	Right of political leaders to compete for support Free and fair elections Eligibility for public office Right of political leaders to compete for votes
Impeachment	Right of political leaders to compete for support
Nontraditional military intervention	The absence of nonelected "tutelary" authorities (e.g., militaries, monarchies, or religious bodies)

Source: elaboration by author

described as a sort of "parliamentary harassment." However, his failed attempt of a self-coup in 2022 was an expression of a desire to adopt the logic of an authoritarian competitive regime.

All these modalities of political crisis in Latin America implied a violation of the guarantees proposed by Dahl and reformulated by Levitsky and Way, as shown in Table 3.2.

The Regional Responses of the OAS

Based on Heine and Weiffen (2014), it is argued in this chapter that three simple forms of responses could be given by regional institutions to the democratic crisis, as shown in Table 1. The first one is described as *declarations*, essentially manifested in agreements, decisions, or resolutions approved by the regional institutions in which they express their concern about particular political or social events that could imply a risk for democracy or in which they manifest their support to a democratic regime. The second one is *facilitation*, which happens when the regional institution decides to intervene in the political process of a country that is experiencing upheavals, political polarization, or events that imply a severe risk to democracy. This intervention is manifested with the promotion of mediation or electoral observation. The third response is the imposition of *sanctions*, which occurs when a break in the democratic order takes place and the regional institution decides to adopt measures to isolate the perpetrators of a democratic rupture.

The responses of the OAS have been diverse. In 1991 the hemispheric scheme approved the resolution 1080, in which the countries agreed to act in case of "sudden or irregular interruption of the democratic political institutional process or of the legitimate exercise of power by the democratically elected government in any of the Organization's members?" (OAS, 1991; Resolution 1080). As Feldmann (2015:

2) asserts, the Resolution 1080 was invoked in the crisis in Haiti in 1991, in Peru in 1992, in Venezuela in 1992, in Guatemala in 1993, in Paraguay in 1996, and Ecuador in 2000. However, in all those cases the OAS just made declarations expressing its concern about the risk to democracy and condemning any illegal rupture of the democratic order. This is not a surprise because the Resolution 1080 does not have mechanisms to sanction a violation of the democratic order, and the OAS can only "look into the events collectively and adopt any decisions deemed appropriate, in accordance with the Charter and international law" (OAS, 1991, Resolution, 1810, paragraph 2). Due to this, in 1992, the Washington Protocol was signed, in which sanctions were approved when a democratic break occurred.

The Interamerican Democratic Charter (IADC), approved in 2001, is a much more complex instrument in defense of democracy. Three situations are foreseen in the charter. The first occurs when "the government of a member state considers that its democratic political institutional process or its legitimate exercise of power is at risk." In this case, the state "may request assistance from the Secretary General or the Permanent Council for the strengthening and preservation of its democratic system" (IADC, 2001; art. 17).

The second one refers to situations that "arise in a member state that may affect the development of its democratic political institutional process or the legitimate exercise of power" (IADC, 2001, art. 18). In this case, the Secretary General or the Permanent Council may, with prior consent of the government concerned, arrange for visits or other actions to analyze the situation. The Secretary General will submit a report to the Permanent Council, which will undertake a collective assessment of the situation and, where necessary, may adopt decisions for the preservation of the democratic system and its strengthening (IADC, 2001, art. 18).

The final case occurs when "an unconstitutional interruption of the democratic order or an unconstitutional alteration of the constitutional regime that seriously impairs the democratic order in a member state" takes place (IADC, 2001, art. 19). If this situation persists, a country is impeded from participating in the OAS' institutions.

The Secretary General may request the immediate convocation of the Permanent Council to undertake a collective assessment of the situation and to take such decisions as it deems appropriate. The Permanent Council may undertake diplomatic initiatives, including good offices, to foster the restoration of democracy. If such diplomatic initiatives prove unsuccessful, or if the urgency of the situation so warrants, the Permanent Council shall immediately convene a special session of the General Assembly. The General Assembly will adopt the decisions it deems appropriate, including the undertaking of diplomatic initiatives, including good offices, to foster the restoration of democracy (IADC, 2001, art. 20).

If those diplomatic initiatives fail, a special session of the General Assembly shall take the decision to suspend said member state from the exercise of its right to participate in the OAS by an affirmative vote of two thirds of the member states in accordance with the Charter of the OAS (IADC, 2001, art. 21).

Thus, it could be argued that the IADC includes facilitation and sanctions as mechanisms to deal with democratic ruptures while at the same time allowing a government that is threatened by a risk of democratic break to ask for assistance.

Notwithstanding all these good intentions, the fact is that OAS' performance in defense of democracy through the IADC has been weak and in some political and academic circles in Latin America severely criticized. Even the action of Secretary Generals such as José Miguel Insulza and Luis Almagro have been condemned.

The illegal detention and expulsion of President Zelaya in 2009, the Paraguay impeachment in 2012, and the long Venezuelan crisis between 2013 and 2019 show the failures of the implementation of the Charter.

In the case of Honduras, the OAS decided to suspend the country. However, the new regime led by Micheletti remained in power, and Zelaya was never restored as president. As a result, the OAS modified its strategy and opted for the promotion of dialogue between the different Honduran political actors that ended in new elections with the observation of the OAS and the restoration of Zelaya's political rights. In fact, Insulza stated: "why the issue of Honduras continued in discussion. The reason is because economic sanctions do not work; they merely hurt the people that endure them directly" (Insulza, 2009, September 10). This was exactly the same strategy the OAS implemented in the case of the Paraguayan impeachment. In this case, the OAS' strategy was different to that adopted by Mercosur and UNASUR, which decided to suspend Paraguay from the respective regional blocs.

In the case of Venezuela, the situation was different. In the early period of political polarization (2001–2004), the OAS rejected the coup d'état to Chávez in April 2002, and the hemispheric scheme was actively involved in the promotion of a political dialogue to find a solution to the polarization in that country. Secretary General César Gaviria directly acted as a mediator, in collaboration with the Carter Center, which led to the recall referendum in 2004. However, when the crisis reemerged after the death of Chávez and the rise to power of Nicolas Maduro, the situation was quite different. As the IADC gives the states the opportunity to request assistance, Maduro's government opted to avoid the OAS involvement in the solution of the increasing political polarization and general upheavals in 2014. Instead, Maduro's regime opted for the mediation of UNASUR, even including actors such as the Vatican. When the violation of the democratic rule deepened in 2017 (attempt of dissolution of the parliament and convening of a National Constitutional Assembly), attempts were made in OAS to activate the IADC for Venezuela, approve sanctions, and suspend Venezuela, but they did not work because most of the CARICOM countries supported Venezuela and as "blocking minority" impeded the implementation of the Charter.

Another polemical OAS intervention occurred in Bolivia in the 2019 electoral process. The elections were part of a complex process due to the polarization that existed around the legality of Morales' reelection. The day of the elections the crisis emerged when the preliminary count was suspended with some 84% of polling stations counted and the results showed that a ballotage would be needed. When the count was resumed 24 h later, Morales led the election with a margin that made the ballotage unnecessary. The reaction of the anti-Morales part of population was protests and upheavals, while the Minister of Defense Kaliman "suggested" to Morales to resign. Under those pressures, Morales resigned, and a confused and not very constitutional process of political transition took place.

The OAS electoral mission presented on 21 October a press release in which it seemed to confirm the accusations about fraud in the election. The report stated a "deep concern and surprise at the drastic and hard-to-explain change in the trend of the preliminary results [from the quick count] revealed after the closing of the polls" (OAS, 2019a). Two days later, the electoral mission issued a report in which it reiterated the criticism to the electoral process. In the report it is argued that "the changes in the TREP [quick count] trend were hard to explain and did not match the other measurements available" (OAS, 2019b: 3). However, reports elaborated afterward by Long et al. (2019) and another report written by Idrobo et al. (2022) showed that there was no real evidence of fraud in the elections. The Bolivian election was a crossroad in the weaking of the OAS as promoter and protector of democracy.

In other crises, the OAS has not been able to stop the undermining of democracy in the region. In the polemical impeachment of Dilma Rousseff in 2016, the OAS made no declaration despite the evidence of the political bias of that process. In the case of Nicaragua, Ortega's antidemocratic actions continue despite the OAS' declarations. In the case of political instability in Peru, especially after the arrival in power of Pedro Castillo in 2021 and his failed self-coup in 2023, the OAS has not been an actor in the solution of the crisis.

Conclusions

Despite the democratic progress Latin America has experienced since the end of the 1970s and the early 1980s, the region also has undergone diverse political crises that have undermined the process of consolidation of the democratic regime. The crisis of democracy in Latin America certainly precedes what in this book is described as permacrisis. However, current Latin American democratic crises are more challenging as political regimes and regional institutions need to also tackle other crises such as migration, climate change, or hegemonic transition in the international system. Certainly, although there have been some attempts of traditional coup d'état (e.g., in Paraguay), the risk for democracy does not come mainly from the military but from new political strategies of destabilization. Increasing polarization, general upheavals, the emergence of competitive authoritarian regimes, lawfare, impeachment used as political tool, and nontraditional military interventions are the new mechanisms that trigger the democratic crises in Latin America.

Regional institutions such as the OAS have become actors in the promotion and protection of democracy in Latin America in the framework of those crises. Although the idea of democracy was part of several OAS declarations since the 1940s, the approval of the Resolution 1080 in 1991 and the signing of the Washington Protocol in 1992 implied the creation of regional mechanisms to protect democracy. These were further strengthened in 2001 with the signing of the IADC. Based on those hemispheric norms, the OAS has been involved in the handling of important democratic crises in Venezuela, Honduras, Paraguay, Bolivia, or Perú. However, the assessments of the effects of those mechanisms vary. As Feldmann asserts: "while certainly not negligible, it is also true that their impact has been rather modest and contrasts sharply with the loud rhetoric that accompanied the creation of the mechanisms" (Feldmann, 2015: 2). This view is shared by other experts such as Freitas Lacerda and Silva de Freitas (2018) who argued that the OAS was losing its credibility in the promotion and protection of democracy because it failed to find a rapid and satisfactory solution to the rupture of the democratic order in Honduras and Paraguay. Other experts, such as Thomas Legler, have a more nuanced approach to the issue. For him, defending democracy has become more problematic due to hemispheric and regional circumstances, especially by what he calls a "hemispheric order upheaval" "a particularly disorderly type of regional order transition in which interstate cooperation is seriously impeded by institutional balancing and the coexistence of power vacuum, crisis of authority, leadership deficit, and institutional dysfunctionality" (Legler, 2020: 137).

Several factors could explain the poor performance of OAS regional mechanisms for the defense of democracy, including the ideological cycles that the region has experienced in recent decades, the way that such mechanisms were conceived, the need for a clearer definition of what is meant by "democratic crisis," and the overlapping of South American and Hemispheric spaces to manage the crises. Due to space limitations, it is not possible to analyze these factors here. However, they have contributed to the undermining of the efficiency of regional mechanisms for the defense of democracy.

References

Abramowitz, A., & McCoy, J. (2019). United States: Racial resentment, negative partisanship, and polarization in Trump's America. *The ANNALS of the American Academy of Political and Social Science, 681*(1), 137–156.

Amorim, C., & Proner, C. (2022). Lawfare e geopolítica: América Latina em foco. *Sul Global, 3*(1), 16–33.

Corrales, J. (2011). Latin America: A Setback for Chávez. *Journal of Democracy, 22*(1), 122–136.

Dahl, R. A. (1971). *Polyarchy. Participation and opposition.* Yale University Press.

Feldmann, A. E. (2015). *Divisions at the heart of Latin America Regional Democratic Efforts.* Carnegie Endowment for International Peace.

Freitas Lacerda, J. M. D. A., & Silva de Freitas, J. (2018). A atuação da Organização dos Estados Americanos (OEA) e de sua burocracia internacional na defesa da democracia no continente americano. *Sociedade e Cultura, 21*(2), 176–194.

García-Guadilla, M. P., & Mallen, A. (2019). Polarization, participatory democracy, and democratic erosion in Venezuela's twenty-first century socialism. *The Annals of the American Academy of Political and Social Science, 681*(1), 62–77.

Goldstein, A. A. (2019). The new far-right in Brazil and the construction of a right-wing order. *Latin American Perspectives, 46*(4), 245–262.

Hawkins, D. (2008). Protecting democracy in Europe and the Americas. *International Organization, 62*(3), 373–403.

Heine, J., & Weiffen, B. (2014). *21st century democracy promotion in the Americas: Standing up for the polity*. Routledge.

Iamamoto, S. A. S., Mano, M. K., & Summa, R. (2023). Brazilian far-right neoliberal nationalism: Family, anti-communism and the myth of racial democracy. *Globalizations, 20*(5), 782–798. https://doi.org/10.1080/14747731.2021.1991745

Idrobo, N., Kronick, D., & Rodríguez, F. (2022). Do shifts in late-counted votes signal fraud? Evidence from Bolivia. *The Journal of Politics, 84*(4), 2202–2215.

Insulza, J. M. (2009). *Challenges for the consolidation of democracy in the region and the future of hemispheric integration.* 10 Sept 2010. https://www.oas.org/en/media_center/speech.asp?sCodigo=11-0075

Interamerican Demcocratic Charter (IADC) (2001). Available at: https://www.oas.org/en/democratic-charter/

Ioris, R., & Schneider, A. (2022). *Anti-corruption and democracy: Neo-liberal authoritarianism in Brazil*. University of Denver, Institute for Comparative and Regional Studies. Paper Series 2022/75.

Legler, T. (2020). A story within a story. *European Review of Latin American and Caribbean Studies/Revista Europea de Estudios Latinoamericanos y del Caribe, 109*, 135–156.

Levitsky, S., & Way, L. A. (2010). *Competitive authoritarianism: Hybrid regimes after the Cold War*. Cambridge University Press.

Linz, J. (1985). *Democracy: Presidential or parliamentary does it make a difference*. Paper prepared for the project, "The Role of Political Parties in the Return to Democracy in the Southern Cone," sponsored by the Latin American Program of the Woodrow Wilson International Center for Scholars, and the World Peace Foundation. https://pdf.usaid.gov/pdf_docs/PNABJ524.pdf

Llanos, M., & Marsteintredet, L. (2021). The political limits of presidential impeachment: Lessons from Latin America. *GIGA Focus Latin America, 4*, 1–11.

Long, G., Rosnick, D., Kharrazian, C., & Cashman, K. (2019). *What happened in Bolivia's 2019 vote count? The role of the OAS electoral observation mission*. Center for Economic and Policy Research.

McCoy, J. (2023, September 1). *Latin American democratic resilience and political polarization in comparative perspective*. Paper presented at the American Political Science Association.

McCoy, J., Rahman, T., & Somer, M. (2018). Polarization and the global crisis of democracy: Common patterns, dynamics, and pernicious consequences for democratic polities. *American Behavioral Scientist, 62*(1), 16–42.

Morlino, L. (2009). Are there hybrid regimes? Or are they just an optical illusion? *European Political Science Review, 1*(2), 273–296.

Organization of American States. (2019a). *Statement of the OAS Electoral Observation Mission in Bolivia*. https://www.oas.org/en/media_center/press_release.asp?sCodigo=E-085/19

Organization of American States. (2019b). *Preliminary report of the Electoral Observation Mission in Bolivia*. https://www.oas.org/documents/eng/press/Preliminary-Report-EOM-Bolivia-23-10-19.pdf

Organization of American States (OAS). (1991). AG/RES. 1080 (XXI-O/91), Representative Democracy (Resolution adopted at the fifth plenary session, held on June 5, 1991). https://www.oas.org/juridico/english/agres1080.htm

Panizza, F. (2009). *Contemporary Latin America: development and democracy beyond the Washington consensus*. Zed Books.

Pérez-Liñán, A. (2018). Impeachment or backsliding? Threats to democracy in the twenty-first century. *Revista Brasileira de Ciências Sociais, 33*(8), 1–15.

Pérez-Liñán, A., & Polga-Hecimovich, J. (2019). Explaining military coups and impeachments in Latin America. *Democratization*. https://doi.org/10.1080/13510347.2016.1251905

Pevehouse, J. C. (2002). With a little help from my friends? Regional organizations and the consolidation of democracy. *American Journal of Political Science, 46*(3), 611–626.

Przeworski, A. (1991). *Democracy and the market: Political and economic reforms in Eastern Europe and Latin America*. Cambridge University Press.

Schober, A. (2017). Widening La Grieta In Argentina: How Cristina And Nestor Kirchner Power-Consolidating Policies Leave Behind A Social Rift. *Tipping Points, The SAIS Europe Journal of Global Affairs*, (20), 63–74.

Smulovitz, C. (2022). Del "descubrimiento de la ley" al "lawfare" o cómo las uvas se volvieron amargas. *Revista SAAP, 16*(2), 231–259.

Somer, M., & McCoy, J. (2018). Déjà vu? Polarization and endangered democracies in the 21st century. *American Behavioral Scientist, 62*(1), 3–15.

Torcal, M., & Carty, E. (2023). Populismo, ideología y polarización afectiva en Argentina. *Revista Argentina de Ciencia Política, 1*(30), 128–157.

Van der Vleuten, A., & Hoffmann, A. R. (2010). Explaining the enforcement of democracy by regional organizations: Comparing EU, Mercosur and SADC. *JCMS: Journal of Common Market Studies, 48*(3), 737–758.

Vegh Weis, V. (2023). What does Lawfare mean in Latin America? A new framework for understanding the criminalization of progressive political leaders. *Punishment & Society, 25*(4), 909–933.

Vollenweider, C., & Romano, S. (2017). *Lawfare. La judicialización de la política en América Latina*. Centro estratégico latinoamericano de geopolítica. https://www.inep.org/images/2022/LawfareT.pdf

Von Borzyskowski, I., & Kartal, M. (2023). Democracy assistance by international organizations. In N. A. Seltzer & S. Lloyd Wilson (Eds.), *Handbook on democracy and security* (pp. 84–111). Elgar.

Whitehead, L. (Ed.). (1996). *The international dimensions of democratization: Europe and the Americas* (pp. 3–25). Oxford University Press.

Wolff, J., & Wurm, I. (2011). Towards a theory of external democracy promotion: A proposal for theoretical classification. *Security Dialogue, 42*(1), 77–96.

Zakaria, F. (1997). The rise of illiberal democracy. *Foreign Affairs, 76*(6), 22–43.

Zanin, C., Martins, V., & Valim, R. (2022). *Lawfare: Waging war through law*. Abingdon: Routledge.

Chapter 4
Fighting Crime and Preserving Democracy in Latin America

Tiziano Breda

Contents

Introduction

Latin America has been plagued by a series of crises over the past few years, in what this volume defines as "permacrisis", as discussed in the introduction, and meaning "an extended period of instability and insecurity, especially one resulting from a series of catastrophic events" (Collins English Dictionary 2022 mentioned in Katsikas et al., this volume). The economic stagnation of the second decade of the twenty-first century, which followed the boom of commodities prices in the 2000s, the exodus caused by political crises such as those of Nicaragua and above all Venezuela, the dreadful impact of the COVID-19 pandemic, the consequences of Russia's war on Ukraine, and the ever-growing global drug consumption have all contributed to shake the socio-economic grounds of the region. In particular, the setbacks in the economic and education sectors caused by the lockdowns imposed during the pandemic and the shifts in drug trafficking and peddling operations associated with border shutdowns have fed the recruitment pool of criminal organisations engaging in turf wars for the control of smuggling and extortion activities. This has in turn led to the deterioration of security in many Latin American

T. Breda (✉)
Istituto Affari Internazionali – IAI, Rome, Italy

D. Katsikas et al. (eds.), *Finance, Growth and Democracy: Connections and Challenges in Europe and Latin America in the Era of Permacrisis*, United Nations University Series on Regionalism 33, https://doi.org/10.1007/978-3-031-68475-3_4

countries, including those who were known as oases of peace, such as Costa Rica, Chile, Argentina, and Ecuador. Insecurity has become a top concern for most citizens across the Western Hemisphere, which has translated into mounting pressure for governments to come up with solutions to address violent crime.

Only one country has experienced a counter-trend in the fight against criminal gangs: El Salvador. The country's president, Nayib Bukele, has gained international acclaim for his unapologetic stance on cracking down on gangs and reducing violent crime. His administration's hard-line approach has led to a notable decline in gang-related violence, transforming El Salvador into a symbol of successful anti-gang policies in the region. Between 2022 and 2023, his government claims to have arrested more than 70,000 people tied with gangs, dismantling their operation and prompting extortion to subside and homicides to nosedive from a rate of 17.8 per 100,000 inhabitants in 2021 (already considerably down from 51 in 2018, just before Bukele took office in 2019) to just 2.4 in 2023. The results of his policies are appreciated by most Salvadorans, who widely believe the country's security situation has improved, translating into an approval rate of well over 80% that led to his re-election in 2024. The apparent efficacy and the wide popularity of Bukele's methods have appealed to a growing number of Latin American politicians who have started to use them as rhetoric tools to either criticise sitting governments' inefficacy or rally support for their presidential campaigns.

However, Bukele's practices are rooted in undemocratic premises of disrespect for certain human rights and the concentration of power in the hands of the executive and are nurturing a growing movement of punitive populism that risks eroding the democratic standards in other regional countries. National and international human rights groups have reported thousands of violations, including the use of excessive force, arbitrary detentions, and restrictions on freedom of expression and assembly, besides the denial of the right to legal defence and a fair trial. Moreover, the very premise of Bukele's approach is the absence of scrutiny from any other branch of the state, deriving from the amount of power he has managed to concentrate by controlling the legislature and the judiciary, to the detriment of the country's democratic checks and balances.

Luckily, there are a few practical reasons why El Salvador's draconian measures cannot be implemented elsewhere or at least cannot yield the same security results. Furthermore, electoral processes in 2023 show that promising to mimic Bukele's methods is not an electoral game changer, as other factors play into voters' decision to elect their representatives. Nonetheless, as long as El Salvador is able to maintain or deepen its security achievements, the popularity of these measures will keep growing, spreading the notion that only the suspension of democratic rights and the militarisation of societies can bring a solution to violent crime. This carries with it the risk of erosion of democracy in Latin America.

This article seeks to examine the risks posed by the spread of Bukele's anti-gang campaign in terms of democratic setbacks while also assessing its electoral impact on the wider Latin American region. It does by firstly presenting the growing challenge represented by the rise in criminal activities in various Latin American countries, displaying El Salvador's outstanding "exception" in a region where security has turned into citizens' main concern even in the once safest countries. It then describes the appeal of Bukele's measures and the emulation by a growing list of policymakers in several countries, from local administrators to presidential candidates and even sitting presidents, laying out the risks of eroding respect of human rights and democratic norms associated with these measures. Finally, it assesses the still limited impact of Bukele-style rhetoric in presidential elections undergone by Paraguay, Ecuador, Guatemala, and Argentina, displaying the other elements that play into voters' decisions to pick candidates that do not necessarily anchor their campaign plans on mimicking Bukele's methods. Nonetheless, it flags that the sway of Bukele's rhetoric is likely to grow further in the future and can have long-term impact on public policies throughout the region, unless it is met with an effective and sustainable alternative which is not based on rights suppression and executive control.

Crises and the Rise of Crime in Latin America

Latin America, a region characterised by high socio-economic disparities and varying degrees of development, has historically faced numerous challenges in dealing with violent crimes perpetrated by illegal armed groups with or without ideological motives. While the 2010s saw an overall reduction of violence levels across the Western Hemisphere, in recent years some countries—including traditionally less violent ones—experienced an uptick in criminal activities and homicides associated to them. The impact of the COVID-19 pandemic on the livelihood of millions of people, particularly on young students whose education was impacted by school closures, and the shifts in drug trafficking routes forced by border shutdowns fed the recruitment pool for criminal organisations throughout the continent (United Nations Office on Drugs and Crime, 2020). In turn, as both petty and organised crime thrived, ill-equipped and sometimes corrupt governments were unable to adequately mitigate the pandemic's impact on their countries' populations. As a result, insecurity has become a main concern for citizens in several countries, while trust in national institutions is wavering.

Latin America also suffered from high levels of income inequality, and the pandemic exacerbated this problem. The most marginalised communities suffered disproportionately as they lacked access to quality healthcare and faced increased job insecurity. The economic divide between the rich and the poor widened, leading to a negative impact on social cohesion and stability (Economic Commission for Latin America and the Caribbean, 2022). The pandemic hit the informal sector particularly hard, which employs a significant portion of Latin America's workforce, exposed to the lack of social protection and income instability. With lockdowns and restrictions, many informal workers lost their sources of income, leading to a surge in poverty rates (United Nations Development Programme, 2023). School closures and the shift to remote learning had detrimental effects on education in many countries, as millions of students lacked access to the necessary technology and Internet connectivity to participate in online classes. This digital divide disproportionately affected students from lower-income families, hindering their educational progress and exacerbating existing inequalities in access to quality education (United Nations International Children's Emergency Fund, 2020). Furthermore, the strain on healthcare systems in Latin America was immense, with many countries facing shortages of medical supplies, intensive care unit beds, and healthcare personnel. These shortages resulted in difficulties in providing adequate care to COVID-19 patients and led to increased mortality rates, contributing to fostering discontent among enraged citizens.

Against this backdrop, organised crime adapted quickly to the new reality. In Mexico and Central America, drug cartels and gangs even took advantage of the governments' inability to alleviate the humanitarian consequences of lockdowns. For example, they enforced their own restrictions but also suspended some extortion payments and even provided food handouts to locals, in order to win their hearts and minds, as well as consolidate their criminal governance (International Crisis Group, 2020). Border and air traffic shutdowns favoured the development of maritime drug trafficking and modified the dynamics in drug peddling, co-opting the food delivery sector (United Nations Office on Drugs and Crime, 2021). Meanwhile, cocaine and marihuana production in countries such as Colombia, Peru, and Bolivia continues to grow unchecked, while synthetic drug production literally skyrocketed, meeting an increasing demand also related to the mental distress caused by the prolonged lockdowns imposed by several governments to contain the pandemic (ibidem).

In addition, Latin America has experienced extraordinary migration flows in recent years, which have further attracted the interests of criminal organisations involved in human smuggling and trafficking, as well as those willing to recruit their members among migrants. Even before the pandemic, millions of Venezuelans had left their country to resettle mostly in South American countries such as Colombia, Peru, Ecuador, and Chile, while hundreds of thousands of Nicaraguans did the same to neighbouring Costa Rica. Both exoduses were prompted by those countries' political crises and the crackdown on dissent perpetrated by the authoritarian governments of Nicolás Maduro and Daniel Ortega. The socio-economic meltdown prompted by the COVID-19 pandemic fuelled these flows but also diverted them and prompted new ones, making north-bound migration towards Mexico and the USA to skyrocket and reach unprecedent levels (Solomon & Hesson, 2023). As a result, human smuggling is buoying, and criminal groups making a profit of it, such as the Gulf Clan in Colombia and the Venezuelan Tren de Aragua, are thriving.

The combined increase in drug production and demand, as well as the potential workforce for criminal groups involved in extortion and drug and human trafficking activities, turned out to be an explosive mix for the region. As soon as mobility restrictions were lifted, turf wars for the control of both international and local traffics broke out in a wide array of countries, and also petty crimes spread across the region, affecting even the once safest countries. As an illustration, Costa Rica—among the least violent and most developed countries of Central America—recorded a rate of 12.6 homicides per 100,000 inhabitants in 2022, the highest in the country's history, with violence concentrated in coastal locations such as Limón and

Puntarenas, crucial maritime drug trafficking hubs. This trend has further continued in 2023, with homicides increasing by another 40%, as of September (Voss, 2023). In Chile, murders surged by 43% in 2022 and kidnappings by 77% (Ramos Miranda, 2023). A survey by market research firm Ipsos published in May 2023 found that violence has become the primary topic worrying Chileans, despite the country's historically low levels of violence and criminality (IPSOS, 2023). Also in Uruguay, the government has struggled to tame a homicide rate that jumped by a quarter in 2022 and is now triple that of neighbouring Argentina, where security has nonetheless rivalled the hyperinflation-torn economy as citizens' main concern (Burns, 2023). The most striking case, however, is undoubtedly Ecuador. Over a decade ago, the Andean country, sandwiched between coca-producing countries such as Colombia and Peru, had managed to reduce levels of violence following a process of "legalisation" of the country's main gangs, including the notorious Latin Kings, promoted by former President Rafael Correa (2007–2017). The power vacuum left by their exit from the scene and that of FARC rebels after the 2016 peace deal in Colombia, however, appears to have been filled by a growing number of criminal groups with links to Mexican drug cartels and the Albanian mafia which have been vying for control of the territory and prisons for drug trafficking and distribution, sparking a wave of violence that has prompted a fivefold increase in annual homicides between 2016 and 2022 and is foreseen to further worsen in 2023, having already grown by 58% compared to the previous year (Pellegrini & Mosquera, 2023).

The Rise of Nayib Bukele and El Salvador's "Security Miracle"

Amid this surge of violent crime and mounting security concerns for millions of Latin American citizens, El Salvador has stood out as an unlikely exception. Under the leadership of President Nayib Bukele, the country, once known for being the world's murder capital, has experienced an extraordinary drop in levels of violence over the past few years, reporting a lower murder rate than Costa Rica in 2022, for the first time in its history.

When Nayib Bukele took office in 2019 as El Salvador's youngest president (37 years old), the country was the second most violent in Latin America, with a homicide rate of 51 murders per 100,000 inhabitants, even though it was already experiencing a decrease in violence since its peak in 2015, when nearly 1 in every 1,000 people was violently killed (Dalby & Carranza, 2019). Criminal gangs such as the Mara Salvatrucha, or MS-13, and the two factions of the 18th Street gang spearheaded the killings, amid an all-out war with state forces that broke out after a truce they negotiated with the Mauricio Funes government in 2012 had fallen apart in 2014 (International Crisis Group, 2017). In the first 2 years of the Bukele administration, levels of violence continued to decrease at a faster-than-ever pace, with 2021 reporting 17.6 homicides per 100,000 inhabitants (InSight Crime, 2022).

Several gang testimonies and investigative reports attributed the stark decrease to an informal deal of non-aggression his government brokered with gangs leaders (Martínez et al., 2020).

In March 2022, however, the picture changed completely. Gangs—the MS-13 in particular—went on a killing rampage that left 87 people dead in the span of 3 days, more than those reported in the whole previous month. The killing spree was allegedly triggered by a rupture in the negotiations with the Bukele government and dealt a huge symbolic blow to the president's image (Martínez, 2022). In response, Bukele took a U-turn in his approach to the gang issue, launching an unprecedented dragnet on criminal groups, anchored on a state of exception that restrains some citizen rights, including the right to a fair trial, renewed monthly by the legislature; mass arrests of suspected gang members and collaborators (over 73,000, as of October 2023); legal reforms that harshen sentences related to gang crimes, including membership, and lower the minimum age for being charged as an adult to 12; and the construction of a new mega jail, supposed to host up to 40,000 inmates (International Crisis Group, 2022). The government has also promised to double the army's size and has given it a prominent role in public security (Aguilar, 2023).

Albeit hard-line or "iron-fist" tactics are not new in El Salvador and have actually never worked to tame the expansion and penetration of gangs into the Salvadoran social fabric, the scale of the crackdown is certainly unprecedented and has yielded outstanding results. Gangs, who had learnt to use their ability to alter levels of violence to extract political concessions from successive governments, did not expect that the killing spree would be met with such a sweeping crackdown and so extended in space and time. In disarray, most of their medium-to-high ranking figures went into hiding or fled the country, while the government captured dozens of thousands of their lower-ranking members and collaborators, dismantling many of their operations throughout the country. As a result, gangs' presence in hundreds of neighbourhoods waned, extortion requests subsided, and gang-related homicides nosedived, with authorities reporting only 7.8 homicides per 100,000 inhabitants in 2022, a rate that further decreased in 2023 (InSight Crime, 2023). This has also contributed to maintain Bukele's sky-high popularity rate at around 90%, resulting from a perceived improvement in the security realm: 97.7% of interviewees of a June 2023 survey by IUDOP believed the security situation had improved (Instituto Universitario de Opinión Pública, 2023). The Bukele administration has also launched a communication campaign to portray the transformation of El Salvador into one of the safest countries in Latin America, by inviting dozens of youtubers and journalists to report the changed situation in neighbourhoods that were once gangs' strongholds, as well as the new mega prison, making sure the reportages would spread throughout the hemisphere (Paises & Olivares, 2023). Furthermore, several Salvadoran government officials and lawmakers have either received other countries' representatives or travelled to other countries in the region such as Peru, Argentina, Honduras, and even the USA, to showcase the country's security results and promote its replication elsewhere (Coca Pimentel, 2023).

The Appeal of Bukele's Methods in Latin America

The apparent efficacy and popularity of Bukele's methods have understandably grabbed the attention of a growing number of politicians in several Latin American countries, particularly those experiencing a deterioration of their security situations, nurturing the growing temptation of punitive populism (Freeman, 2023).

The call for the implementation of Bukele-like measures to tackle violent crime has been used in mainly three ways: by opposition representatives to discredit the inability of those in power to deal effectively with this issue or pressure them into taking more extreme measures; by presidential candidates who have in some cases dubbed themselves their respective countries' "Bukeles" in order to win votes; and by incumbents in order to rein in public criticism around insecurity. Lawmakers and/or local administrators in Colombia, Chile, Ecuador, and Peru have promoted these methods on several occasions: in August 2022, days after a bomb attack killed five in Guayaquil, Ecuador, the city's mayor asked, "Who fights insecurity in El Salvador, a mayor or the president? It's Bukele! … Copy it, as simple as that" (Breda, 2022). The implementation of Bukele-style security policies was also a proposal advanced by several presidential hopefuls in countries that went through electoral processes in 2023: Sandra Torres in Guatemala, Payo Cubas in Paraguay, Patricia Bullrich and Javier Milei in Argentina, and Jan Topic in Ecuador all promised to crack down on gangs and drug groups and referred to what is happening in El Salvador as a model to mirror, leading some observers to believe Bukele's tactics could influence elections and be mimicked elsewhere (Porter, 2023). However, for reasons explained below, this prediction has yet to materialise.

Lastly, a few governments have either considered or actually copied Bukele's measures and rhetoric. After Costa Rica's security minister, Jorge Torres, called for his government to implement such measures, President Rodrigo Chaves backed away, arguing the country does not have a military and respects citizens' rights (Mejía, 2023). In parallel, Honduras' President Xiomara Castro actually imposed a state of emergency and launched a "war on extortion", emulating Bukele's "war on gangs" (Breda, 2023a, b, c). In Peru, despite stressing that the differences between the two countries make it impossible to implement the same measures and expect the same results, President Dina Boluarte imposed a localised state of emergency in three districts of the capital Lima (Aquino et al., 2023). In only a couple of cases have progressive governments openly averted Bukele's policies: Gabriel Boric in Chile and Gustavo Petro in Colombia. The latter, in particular, has engaged in a public spat on Twitter/X with Bukele, arguing that in order to improve public security, it is better to build universities instead of prisons (Rojas, 2023), insisting also on his "Total Peace" plan, which is anchored on negotiations with illegal armed groups to end Colombia's prolonged internal conflict (Breda, 2023a, b, c). Both presidents, however, face in turn a crisis of public legitimacy at home, with approval rates hardly above 30%. Brazil's President Inácio Lula da Silva has also traditionally been against a heavy-handed approach to fight crime (Rodrigues & Caiuby Labate, 2016), favouring poverty eradication and violence prevention instead, but the recent rise in crime in the country has compelled him too to lean more substantially on the military to rein in criminal groups' activities (Paraguassu, 2023), even though keeping distance from Bukele's dragnet.

Risks for Democracy

There are a few practical reasons why El Salvador's draconian measures cannot be implemented elsewhere or at least cannot yield the same security results. However, the spread of the notion that only the suspension of democratic rights and the militarisation of societies can bring a solution to violent crime carries with it the risk of erosion of democracy in Latin America.

First of all, it is unlikely to replicate Bukele's methods elsewhere. Their success is deeply intertwined with the clearly defined criminal landscape in El Salvador, a tiny and densely populated country where criminal activities were mostly controlled by three almost hegemonic criminal gangs (MS-13 and the two factions of the Barrio 18), whose areas of influence had been clearly marked for years. It is also tied to the authorities' capacity and preparedness to imprison tens of thousands of gang members and maintain control in jails: El Salvador can count on over 45,000 police and military officers with public security duties, outnumbering by far the rate of security officer per inhabitants of most Latin American countries. These forces had also built a database of the around 120,000 active gang members, aspirants, and collaborators present in the country and had previously re-established their authority in jails, previously used as gangs' headquarters, by enforcing "extraordinary measures", which impose a strict isolation regime to inmates held in security jails, including the prohibition of family visits and reduced leisure time.

Most of all, however, the problem with Bukele's methods lie in its undemocratic practices. Salvadoran and international human rights groups have reported thousands of violations, including the use of excessive force, arbitrary detentions, and restrictions on freedom of expression and assembly (Human Rights Watch, 2022). In particular, the government itself has admitted to have released over 7000 of the more than 73,000 people detained until September 2023—implicitly acknowledging that one in every 10 arrests was unjust—but human rights group Socorro Jurídico Humanitario claims the number of unjust detentions can be around 20,000 (Deutsche Welle, 2023). A leaked police document actually recognises that around 57,000 people detained under the state of exception have clear links with the gangs, while 43,000 gang members, hopefuls, and collaborators are still at large (Valencia, 2023). Civil society organisations have also reported the death of at least 300 people in overcrowded cells, many of which with clear signs of torture, although the government has vehemently denied any allegation but only allowed visits of journalists or loyal human rights ombudsmen in controlled settings (Calvo, 2023). Furthermore, a legislative reform has authorised the judiciary to hold hearings of up to 900 defendants at the same time, virtually annihilating their rights to a legal defence and to a fair trial (Miranda, 2023). All things considered, Salvadorans have been living for almost 2 years with certain civil rights suspended.

The state of exception also poses significant risks to democracy. It gives the government sweeping powers, which can be used to suppress opposition and dissent, and is grounded in President Bukele's concentration of power in the hands of the executive, undermining the checks and balances that are essential for a functioning democracy. Since 2021, Bukele's party holds a supermajority in the Legislative Assembly, which approves without debate any initiative coming from the executive and has dismissed ten out of fifteen Supreme Court judges and the Attorney General, as well as one-third of ordinary judges and police officers and replaced them with loyalists. Therefore, neither ordinary nor constitutional judges dare to oppose the directives coming from the presidency. The very premise of the endless perpetuation of the state of exception in El Salvador is the absence of any independence from the executive by the other branches of the state.

2023 Elections: The Limits of Bukele's Influence

In 2023, several Latin American countries went through important electoral processes, testing the value of Bukele-style, anti-crime proposals as tools for electoral support. Luckily, the democratic tenure of the region has mostly resisted the temptation represented by punitive populism, hinting that the success and popularity of Bukele and his policies are not sufficient, alone, to win elections. In fact, promoters of Bukele's policies—some of whom defining themselves as their countries' "Bukeles"—did not win any presidential election. Paraguayo "Payo" Cubas and Patricia Bullrich came in third places in elections in Paraguay and Argentina, while Jan Topic ranked fourth in Ecuador. In Guatemala, Sandra Torres was defeated in the run-off by progressive Bernardo Arévalo de León, who promotes a more progressive agenda focused on addressing the root causes of violent crime while strengthening security forces' professionalisation and investigative capacity (Delcid, 2023).

A number of elements help explain why proposals to emulate Bukele are insufficient to win an election. First of all, the quality and credibility of candidates remain decisive features that play into citizens' electoral preferences. Amid a wave of anti-incumbent victories, the perception that a candidate would foster the status quo increases voters' aversion towards them, as it happened in the case of Torres in Guatemala (Breda, 2023a, b, c). Furthermore, although the imitation game of Bukele's promoters raises public visibility and attracts some consensus, it ends up annulling the novelty of policy proposals that can be perceived by the public as a lack of creativity. Also, even though crime is high in the priorities of citizens across Latin America, other pressing issues such as social and economic policies play into their voting orientations. The candidates who are perceived to have more solid proposals on how to energise the economy and improve the provision of services are more likely to gather popular support. Finally, the presence of strong civil societies, averse to extreme human rights suppression and keen on preserving democratic checks and balances, is also a factor that shall be taken into consideration: despite Milei's victory in the run-off of Argentina's elections, the unexpectedly strong performance of Sergio Massa and his party, *Unión por la Patria*, may hint at a substantial societal counterweight to any attempt to punitive populism.

However, it must be noted that, even though the promotion of Bukele-style methods does not ensure an electoral victory alone, it certainly contributes to improving electoral performances of populist candidates and can play into run-off political calculations. In Paraguay, Payo Cubas obtained 20% of votes in his first presidential campaign bid. The same applies to Jan Topic, who gathered over 14% of votes. In those countries where elections foresee a second round, run-off candidates look to gain those votes, and this might involve making alliance with those losing candidates or borrowing some of their proposals. As an illustration, the anti-crime rhetoric of Daniel Noboa harshened substantially between the first and second round, from promoting job creation to promising to build a prison ship where to lock dangerous criminals (Kueffner, 2023). He was eventually elected president of Ecuador. Similarly, in Argentina, Bullrich's anti-crime proposals were eventually absorbed into Milei's discourse in order to win the run-off with the moderate, Peronist candidate Sergio Massa.

All in all, even though the appeal of Bukele's methods is not yet a decisive game changer in elections and the region is mostly holding up vis-à-vis the temptation of punitive populism, its influence in regional politics should not be understated. In particular, the risk lies in the spreading notion that security can only be achieved through the suspension of citizen rights and the concentration of executive power, to the detriment of the rule of law and democratic checks and balances. Unless other regional leaders are able to address citizens' security concerns and come up with alternative policies that manage to curb violent crime while respecting the separation of powers and the hard-fought citizen rights, this notion is likely to keep on taking roots in a growing number of Latin American citizens, scared by the rise of criminal activities and angered at the ruling class's inability to solve their problems, with far-reaching consequences for the quality of democracy in an already troubled region.

Conclusion

As Latin America grapples with the spread of Nayib Bukele's popular anti-gang campaign, concerns regarding democratic stability and electoral outcomes come to the forefront. While Bukele's approach has successfully reduced gang-related violence in El Salvador, the risks it poses to democracy, as highlighted in this article, cannot be ignored. The suppression of rights and concentration of power his draconian measures imply represent serious setbacks in the quality of democracy in El Salvador, and the appeal of his methods risks making the list of politicians mimicking them grow, threatening the democratic tenure of other countries as well. This is all the truer at a time when various Latin American countries deal with a tide of violent crime, while growing popular disenchantment at the traditional political party system and the distortion in the information prompted by the rise of alternative communication channels further contribute to creating a breeding ground for punitive populism.

However, the electoral experiences of Guatemala, Paraguay, Ecuador, and Argentina in 2023 suggest that endorsing Bukele's tactics and discourse does not singlehandedly guarantee electoral success. On the contrary, other elements play into voters' decision to elect certain candidates, such as primary concerns in other areas than security, the quality and credibility of candidates, and the presence of strong civil society organisations and institutions. Nonetheless, the permacrisis afflicting several Latin American countries is likely to continue to affect the regional crime dynamics, leading to the security situation in many places and with it nurturing the demand for effective policies that provide immediate relief, along the likes of those offered by politicians proclaiming punitive populism manifestos.

For his part, Bukele remains a reference for a wave of punitive populism which is doomed to grow if violent crime keeps on penetrating the socio-economic fabric of Latin American countries' societies and governments across the region are unable to come up with an alternative, sustainable, and popular solution that is centred on strengthening authorities' investigative capacities, uprooting institutional corruption, and thus reducing impunity rates, in full respect of human rights.

References

Aguilar, J. (2023, September). Post-conflict remilitarization and militarism in El Salvador. In *Remilitarization in Central America: A comparative and regional analysis*. IBI Consultants. https://www.ibiconsultants.net/remilitarizationreport-elsalvador/english

Aquino, M., Pulice, C., & Berkrot, B. (2023, September 18). Peru declares state of emergency in parts of capital after crime spike. *Reuters*. https://www.reuters.com/world/americas/peru-declares-state-emergency-parts-capital-after-crime-spike-2023-09-18/

Breda, T. (2022, December 15). Latin America likes Bukele's 'war on gangs.' That's a problem. *World Politics Review*. https://www.worldpoliticsreview.com/el-salvador-gangs-bukele-human-rights/

Breda, T. (2023a, July 25). Bukele's 'war on gangs' model won't work for Honduras' Castro. *World Politics Review*. https://www.worldpoliticsreview.com/honduras-gangs-violence-xiomara-castro-bukele-el-salvador/

Breda, T. (2023b, September 14). *Can regional governance help safeguard Guatemala's democracy?* IAI Commentaries. https://www.iai.it/it/pubblicazioni/can-regional-governance-help-safeguard-guatemalas-democracy

Breda, T. (2023c, October 21). Petro's reality check: Colombia is not that easy to change. *Aspenia Online*. https://aspeniaonline.it/petros-reality-check-colombia-is-not-that-easy-to-change/

Burns, N. (2023, March 9). As Argentina's economy sputters, security concerns shape its campaign. *Americas Quarterly*. https://www.americasquarterly.org/article/as-argentinas-economy-sputters-security-concerns-shape-its-campaign/

Calvo, G. (2023, June 25). Más de 300 personas murieron en las cárceles de El Salvador durante el régimen de excepción: "La gran mayoría es inocente". *Infobae*. https://www.infobae.com/america/america-latina/2023/06/25/mas-de-300-personas-murieron-en-las-carceles-de-el-salvador-durante-el-regimen-de-excepcion-la-gran-mayoria-es-inocente/

Coca Pimentel, V. (2023, August 29). 'Plan Bukele' debe ser implementado en Perú lo más pronto posible, según alcalde de distrito en El Salvador. *Infobae*. https://www.infobae.com/peru/2023/08/29/plan-bukele-debe-ser-implementado-en-peru-lo-mas-pronto-posible-segun-alcalde-de-distrito-en-el-salvador/
Dalby, C., & Carranza, C. (2019, January 22). *InSight crime's 2018 homicide round-up*. InSight Crime. https://insightcrime.org/news/analysis/insight-crime-2018-homicide-roundup/
Delcid, M. (2023, August 21). ¿Quién es y qué propone Bernardo Arévalo, candidato ganador de las elecciones en Guatemala? *CNN*. https://cnnespanol.cnn.com/2023/08/21/quien-es-que-propone-bernardo-arevalo-candidato-guatemala-orix/
Deutsche Welle. (2023, July 20). *SJH: hay 20.000 personas inocentes detenidas en El Salvador*. https://www.dw.com/es/sjh-hay-20000-personas-inocentes-detenidas-en-el-salvador/a-66373375
Economic Commission for Latin America and the Caribbean. (2022, June 13). *The sociodemographic impacts of the COVID-19 pandemic in Latin America and the Caribbean*. https://repositorio.cepal.org/items/8dc36966-3e36-4a44-b2a3-1788e4f88451
Freeman, W. (2023, February 16). Nayib Bukele's growing list of Latin American admirers. *Americas Quarterly*. https://www.americasquarterly.org/article/nayib-bukeles-growing-list-of-latin-american-admirers/
Human Rights Watch. (2022, December 7). *El Salvador: Widespread abuses under state of emergency*. https://www.hrw.org/news/2022/12/07/el-salvador-widespread-abuses-under-state-emergency
InSight Crime. (2022, February 1). *InSight crime's 2021 homicide round-up*. https://insightcrime.org/news/insight-crimes-2021-homicide-round-up/
InSight Crime. (2023, 8 February). *InSight crime's 2022 homicide round-up*. https://insightcrime.org/news/insight-crime-2022-homicide-round-up/
Instituto Universitario de Opinión Pública (IUDOP). (2023, June 19). *Evaluación ciudadana del cuarto año de Gobierno del presidente Nayib Bukele*. Boletín de prensa Año XXXVII, No. 6. https://uca.edu.sv/iudop/wp-content/uploads/2023/06/Bol-Eva-Gob-4to-anio.pdf
International Crisis Group. (2017, December 19). *El Salvador's politics of perpetual violence*. Latin America Report n. 64. https://www.crisisgroup.org/latin-america-caribbean/central-america/el-salvador/64-el-salvadors-politics-perpetual-violence
International Crisis Group. (2020, November 13). *Virus-proof violence: Crime and COVID-19 in Mexico and the Northern Triangle*. Latin America Report n. 83. https://www.crisisgroup.org/latin-america-caribbean/83-virus-proof-violence-crime-and-covid-19-mexico-and-northern-triangle
International Crisis Group. (2022, October 5). *A remedy for El Salvador's prison fever*. Latin America Report n. 96. https://www.crisisgroup.org/latin-america-caribbean/central-america/el-salvador/96-remedy-el-salvadors-prison-fever
IPSOS. (2023, April). *What worries the world?* https://www.ipsos.com/sites/default/files/ct/news/documents/2023-05/Chile%20Report%20-%20What%20Worries%20the%20World%20Abril%2023_Espan%CC%83ol%20%281%29.pdf
Katsikas, D., Del Tedesco Lins, M. A., & Hoffmann, A. R. (this volume). Introduction: A new era? Challenges to financial stability, economic growth, and democracy. In *Finance, growth and democracy: connections and challenges in Europe and Latin America in the era of permacrisis*. Springer.
Kueffner, S. (2023, October 13). *Ecuador presidential hopeful wants violent prisoners put to sea*. Bloomberg. https://www.bloomberg.com/news/articles/2023-10-13/ecuador-presidential-hopeful-wants-violent-prisoners-put-to-sea
Martínez, C. (2022, 17 May). *Collapsed government talks with MS-13 sparked record homicides in El Salvador, Audios Reveal*. El Faro. https://elfaro.net/en/202205/el_salvador/26177/Collapsed-Government-Talks-with-MS-13-Sparked-Record-Homicides-in-El-Salvador-Audios-Reveal.htm
Martínez, C., Martínez, Ó., Arauz, S., & Lemus, E. (2020, September 6). *Bukele has been negotiating with MS-13 for a reduction in homicides and electoral support*. El Faro. https://elfaro.net/en/202009/el_salvador/24785/Bukele-Spent-A-Year-Negotiating-with-MS-13-for-a-Reduction-in-Homicides-and-Electoral-Support.htm

Mejía, J. C. (2023, January 27). *Presidente de Costa Rica rechaza imitar políticas de Bukele*. El Salvador. https://www.elsalvador.com/noticias/internacional/presidente-costa-rica-descarta-implementacion-regimen-excepcion-el-salvador/1035009/2023/
Miranda, W. (2023, July 28). *Mass trials in Bukele's El Salvador: Legal reform will allow hearings of up to 900 prisoners*. El País. https://english.elpais.com/international/2023-07-28/mass-trials-in-bukeles-el-salvador-legal-reform-will-allow-hearings-of-up-to-900-prisoners.html
Paises, M., & Olivares, G. (2023, May 19). Los evangelistas de Bukele. *Revista Factum*. https://www.revistafactum.com/los-evangelistas-de-bukele/
Paraguassu, L. (2023, 1 November). Lula militarizes Brazil's main ports, airports amid rising crime. *Reuters*. https://www.reuters.com/world/americas/brazils-lula-signs-decree-military-security-ports-airports-2023-11-01/
Pellegrini, S., & Mosquera, J. S. (2023, August 14). *The killing of Villavicencio: A symptom of rising political violence ahead of Ecuador's snap elections*. The Armed Conflict Location & Event Data Project (ACLED). https://acleddata.com/2023/08/14/the-killing-of-villavicencio-a-symptom-of-rising-political-violence-ahead-of-ecuadors-snap-elections/
Porter, E. (2023, July 25). El Salvador's iron fist on crime will crush Latin American democracy. *Washington Post*. https://www.washingtonpost.com/business/2023/07/25/el-salvador-s-iron-fist-on-crime-will-crush-democracy-in-latin-america/9d74f4b6-2adc-11ee-a948-a5b8a9b62d84_story.html
Ramos Miranda, N. A. (2023, January 23). Crime, inflation hammer support for Chile's Boric in tough first year. *Reuters*. https://www.reuters.com/world/americas/crime-inflation-hammer-support-chiles-boric-tough-first-year-2023-01-23/
Raziel, Z. (2023, August 20). 'Plan Bukele' debe ser implementado en Perú lo más pronto posible, según alcalde de distrito en El Salvador. *El País*. https://elpais.com/internacional/2023-08-20/el-autoritarismo-de-nayib-bukele-contagia-la-politica-latinoamericana.html
Rodrigues, T., & Caiuby Labate, B. (2016). Brazilian drug policy: Tension between repression and alternatives. In *Drug policies and the politics of drugs in the Americas* (pp. 187–208). Springer. https://scholar.google.com/citations?view_op=view_citation&hl=pt-BR&user=SKXEuvYAAAAJ&citation_for_view=SKXEuvYAAAAJ:-f6ydRqryjwC
Rojas, J. D. (2023, March 23). On security, Bukele and Petro have a problem in common. *Americas Quarterly*. https://www.americasquarterly.org/article/on-security-bukele-and-petro-have-a-problem-in-common/
Solomon, D. B., & Hesson, T. (2023, September 23). Migrant encounters at U.S.-Mexico border on pace to reach record highs in September. *Reuters*. https://www.reuters.com/world/americas/migrant-encounters-us-mexico-border-pace-reach-record-highs-september-2023-09-21/
United Nations Development Programme. (2023, June 2). *Mapping the socioeconomic consequences of COVID-19 in Latin America and the Caribbean and the adopted responses for recovery*. https://www.undp.org/latin-america/publications/mapping-socioeconomic-consequences-covid-19-latin-america-and-caribbean-and-adopted-responses-recovery#
United Nations International Children's Emergency Fund. (2020, July). *Impact of COVID-19 on children and families in Latin America and the Caribbean*. https://www.unicef.org/lac/media/14381/file/UNICEF_LACRO_COVID19_impact.pdf
United Nations Office on Drugs and Crime. (2020). *The impact of COVID-19 on drugs and crime*. https://www.unodc.org/unodc/en/data-and-analysis/coronavirus.html
United Nations Office on Drugs and Crime. (2021). *World drugs report 2021, COVID-19 and drugs: Impact outlook*. https://www.unodc.org/res/wdr2021/field/WDR21_Booklet_5.pdf
Valencia, R. (2023, September 22). *El Salvador police reports contradict Bukele's triumphalism*. InSight Crime. https://insightcrime.org/news/el-salvador-police-reports-contradict-bukeles-triumphalism/
Voss, G. (2023, September 26). *Costa Rica breaks homicide record amid security coordination*. InSight Crime. Struggles. https://insightcrime.org/news/costa-rica-breaks-homicide-record-amid-security-coordination-struggles/

Chapter 5
The European Union Will Be Built on Solidarity: Lessons Learned and the Financial Crisis Management of the COVID-19 Pandemic

Bettina De Souza Guilherme

Contents

I have always believed that Europe would be built through crises, and that it would be the sum of their solutions. (Jean Monnet, 1978, p. 417)

Europe will not be made all at once, or according to a single plan. It will be built through concrete achievements, which first create a de facto solidarity. (R. Schuman, 1950, p. 7)

B. De Souza Guilherme (✉)
Pontifical Catholic University of Rio de Janeiro – PUC-Rio, Rio de Janeiro, Brazil

European Parliament, Brussels, Belgium

European University Institute, Robert Schuman Center for Advanced Studies, Florence, Italy
e-mail: bettina.desouza@europarl.europa.eu

D. Katsikas et al. (eds.), *Finance, Growth and Democracy: Connections and Challenges in Europe and Latin America in the Era of Permacrisis*, United Nations University Series on Regionalism 33, https://doi.org/10.1007/978-3-031-68475-3_5

Introduction

Ever since the outbreak of the global financial crisis (GFC) in 2007/2008, the European Union (EU) seems to pass through a never-ending wave of crises such as the migration crisis, climate change, the COVID-19 pandemic, war in Ukraine with the energy and inflation crisis following and most recently the conflict in the Middle East. This new reality of poly- and permacrisis required the EU to constantly adjust and reform. Crises management responses, however, vary in their legitimacy, which affects the evolution of the EU in the long term, and its resilience. In a previous publication in the context of the research conducted by the Jean Monnet Network 'Crisis-Equity-Democracy for Europe and Latin America', I focused on EU's crisis management of the global financial crisis (GFC) and subsequent sovereign debt crisis (SDC) and showed that they were managed in an intergovernmental way, largely sidelining the European Parliament (EP) and national parliaments, creating a 'double democratic deficit' (De Souza Guilherme, 2020).

In this chapter, I analyse the financial crisis management of the COVID-19 pandemic and argue that the EU has overall learned from the lessons of the management of the GFC crisis and provided a more legitimate response. I draw on the concept of legitimacy by Vivien Schmidt (2013), who builds on Fritz Scharpf's (1999) concept of input and output legitimacy.[1] Schmidt adds a third dimension, which refers to what goes on in the 'black box' of governance between input and output, namely, what went on in the political system itself, and calls it 'throughput' legitimacy. Schmidt considers that regarding the EU, 'throughput legitimacy builds upon yet another term from systems theory, and is judged in terms of the efficacy, accountability and transparency of the EU's governance processes along with their inclusiveness and openness to consultation *with* the people' (Schmidt, 2013, p. 2).

The chapter is structured in three sections, the first section analyses the EU initial responses to the COVID-19 comparing it with the response to the GFC. The second section analyses and explains the changes introduced in the financial management of the COVID-19 crisis, in particular, the creation of the Recovery and Resilience Facility (RRF) in 2020, which represents a complete paradigm change for the EU and was even called a 'Hamiltonian moment' by the Olaf Scholz, Germany's finance minister at that time. The third section discusses the role of the EP in this process and how it contributed to the input and throughput legitimacy of the response. The concluding section argues that the management of the COVID-19 crisis strengthened EU's legitimacy and contributed to its resilience, reflecting Jean Monnet's and Robert Schuman's visions.

---

[1] According to Scharpf the exercise of governing authority is legitimized as a manifestation of collective self-determination and consists on input-oriented legitimacy (government by the people, implying that political choices are legitimate if and because they reflect the will of the people, that is, 'if they can be derived from the authentic preferences of the members of a community' (Scharpf, 1999, p. 6), and output-oriented legitimacy, i.e., political choices are legitimate 'if and because they effectively promote the common welfare of the constituency in question' (op. cit.).

EU Crisis Response to the COVID-19 Pandemic: First "Lockdown" in History and Initial "Déjà Vu" Reaction of Resorting to National and Intergovernmental Measures

When the COVID-19 pandemic broke out, the EU member states immediately resorted to purely national emergency measures, first in terms of health policies, with lockdowns, and then with financial and socio-economic measures. Confronted with a potentially 'lethal virus', member states took the historic decision to lock down their economies and confine their citizens to their homes and to give to the protection of human lives maximum priority over all other interests and rights. Some member states also closed the borders to other member states, most affected by the pandemic to prevent contagion. The initial crisis response was largely intergovernmental, marked by national measures, initially lacking solidarity and once again sidelining the EP.

This response gave a *déjà vu* impression of the global financial crisis response. One could wonder whether any lessons had been learnt from the previous crisis and if the EU had succeeded in establishing the appropriate rules, tools and mechanisms, which had been missing in the previous GFC, to become more resilient for future crises.

On the positive side, the European Commission (EC) and the European Central Bank (ECB) seemed to have learned the lessons from the past crisis and reacted very fast and efficiently to the pandemic. On March 19, 2020, the EC adopted the State aid Temporary Framework to enable member states to use the full flexibility foreseen under state aid rules. One day later followed the proposal to activate the General Escape Clause of the Stability and Growth Pact. Both allowed the member states to engage in emergency measures to support the economy in the context of the coronavirus outbreak. Additionally, on April 2, 2020, the Commission proposed a new instrument, 'Support to Mitigate Unemployment Risks in an Emergency (SURE)', which was adopted by the Council on May 19 (Council, 2020a) and became operational as of the 1st of June. SURE gave member states the possibility to request EU financial support for employment measures retroactively from the 1st of February and was a predecessor of a fiscal capacity scheme, financed by bonds and relying on national state guarantees. Also on the positive side, the ECB did not take 5 years to take over the role of a lender of last resort (Schmidt, 2020) and launched a policy package of asset purchases, a new wave of targeted longer-term refinancing operations (TLTRO III), the pandemic emergency purchase programme (PEPP) (ECB 2020), which acted as a powerful market-stabilizing force, and in 2022 the Transmission Protection Instrument (TPI). Additionally, measures foreseen in the initial phase included the EIB's €24.4 billion European Guarantee Fund (EGF) in response to COVID-19, which had the potential to leverage €200 billion, and the creation of a COVID-19 credit line designed to support ESM members.

In terms of input legitimacy at the EU level, none of the above-mentioned, early crisis, management measures involved the EP. The SURE regulation was based on the emergency Article 122 TFEU, which does not involve the EP in the adoption process. With the pandemic, there was a surge in the use of Article 122 TFEU, which allowed once again the sidelining of the EP. State aid falls under the sole competence of the EC, health under the sole competence of the member states, and the EP is not involved in the procedure of triggering the escape clause nor did it have a role in the adoption of SURE. However, the EP adopted its resolution on a recovery programme on April 17, 2020 (European Parliament, 2020a), ahead of the Franco-German proposal from May 18, (Elysee, 2020) and the ensuing Commission's proposal of May 28 on the Recovery and Resilience Facility (RRF) (European Commission, 2020) and finally the European Council's conclusions of July 21 (European Council, 2020).

Fasone (2022) pointed out that the EP indeed proposed a first outline of the main features of the RRF, which seems to be overlooked in most of the academic literature. The exchanges on and the adoption of the resolution took place during the critical phase of crisis management when the decisions on whether to pursue an intergovernmental approach or whether to make a breakthrough in the direction of EU bonds and common debts were being debated.

Agreement on the Recovery and Resilience Facility (RRF): A 'Hamiltonian Moment'?

When the pandemic struck, the EU found itself without any fiscal capacity and many of its member states with limited fiscal space. Instead, the euro country member states had established the intergovernmental European Stability Mechanism (ESM) providing loans with conditionality for its members. However, member states were reluctant to ask for ESM support due to its stigma associated with its previous interference into national policies through the adjustment programmes and because of their already very high debt levels as a legacy of the previous crisis. Consequently, they pushed for grants and community bonds guaranteed by the EU budget (MFF). It was necessary to counterbalance the great disparity in terms of fiscal space to engage in emergency policy measures concerning the health crisis and to stabilize the economy and employment, as well as to counteract distortions and the weakening of the internal market in an era in which global free trade was questioned and under threat.

Member states that had more leeway due to lower debt levels could better take advantage of the waiving of the state aid restrictions and were able to support their businesses. Furthermore, it was exactly the 'frugal states' (Austria, Estonia, Finland, the Netherlands), also known as 'frugal four', which, on the one hand, were the most reluctant to establish any kind of common fiscal capacity and, on the other hand, pushed most for further waiving of state aid regulations. This development threatened to create an uneven level playing field and distortions in the internal market. According to the Competition State aid brief (European Commission, 2022, p. 2), state aid measures approved by the Commission in 2020 and 2021 alone had amounted to '€3.1 trillion, representing 11.4% of EU27 annual GDP' and 'more than half of these budgets were approved in Germany, around 15% in Italy and France, 5% in Spain, and around 2% and below in other Member States'. These measures gave the impression of a lack of solidarity and generosity from these member states, while the EC appeared overly generous in broadly loosening the state aid measures. This seemed unfair since the Commission has the obligation to ensure the functioning of the internal market, and this asymmetry in state aid disproportionally benefitted some member states compared to others. Moreover, the Commission had been very rigid to the debtor countries in the euro crisis. Without any EU recovery package, these measures began to be increasingly put into question.

I argue that there are three main reasons why the crisis management of the pandemic took a different path than the one of the GFC and the euro crisis: first, lessons had been learnt from the previous crisis; second, because of the different nature and framing of the crisis; and third, because of the adoption of different tools and mechanisms. These factors are explored next.

Lessons Learnt?

Several lessons were learnt from the previous crisis, particularly when referring to the swift reaction and the generosity of the emergency measures of the EC and of the ECB. Another important lesson was to avoid withdrawing the measures too early as it turned out very costly in the previous crisis, as Buti and Papaconstantinou (2021, p. 6) pointed out: 'that EU countries were too quick to "declare victory" and embark in sharp fiscal retrenchment', reminded of 'Olivier Blanchard's analysis (see Blanchard & Leigh, 2014) on the "fiscal multipliers" which were much higher under large negative output gaps, especially if monetary policy approaches the effective lower bound', implying that budget consolidation in the early crisis in advanced economies deepened and protracted the crisis. Buti additionally highlighted the difficulty of coordinating national policies to achieve an appropriate euro area fiscal stance.

The experience of the euro crisis clearly exposes the limits or failure of intergovernmental fiscal coordination in crisis times and strengthens the call for a fiscal stabilization capacity at the EU or EMU level.

Different Crises or Rather Different Framing?

Both crises were global and of major impact and had been declared the worst since the Great Depression in the 1930s. However, contrary to the GFC, which was a systemic (Schulmeister, 2020, Ghymers, 2020) and endogenous crisis, originating from within the financial and economic system and architecture and caused by imbalances and fiscal shocks (Buti & Papaconstantinou, 2021), the pandemic was an exogenous crisis, which started with the spread of a lethal virus leading to supply and demand shocks.

A second factor that turned out crucial for the handling of the crisis was the question of 'responsibility' and the framing of the crisis. The COVID-19 pandemic originated as a health crisis and fell rather into the category of a natural catastrophe for which none of the EU member states could be held responsible. Waas and Rittberger (2023) emphasized the importance of the framing of crises for the choice of the policies to be applied and pointed out that a group of nine member states representing 60% of the EU GDP employed for the pandemic the 'European solidarity frame' by publishing an open letter to Council President Louis Michel, in which they highlighted that 'we are all facing a symmetric external shock, for which no country bears responsibility, but whose negative consequences are endured by all. And we are collectively accountable for an effective and united European response' (Governo Italiano, 2020, p. 3).

This frame stands in stark contrast to the 'national responsibility' frame which was applied to the GFC when Greece revealed in October 2009 that its deficit-to-GDP ratio was considerably higher than previously reported. As a consequence, the global financial crisis was re-framed from a systemic global financial crisis into a sovereign debt crisis (SDC), which was a consequence of bad national politics and did not deserve solidarity measures which would only lead to moral hazard. Greece was blamed for the immorality of wasteful spending and of deceiving the other EU partners, paving the way for punitive measures even going as far as to threaten expulsion, the so-called GREXIT. Financial assistance was only granted when the risk of contagion became a real threat to the existence of EMU, and it was provided in the form of loans combined with punitive austerity measures. The framing of sovereign debt crisis led to a situation that solidarity actions such as mutualized debt or EU bonds were completely out of the question, and the crisis management was done in a conflictual way by mutual accusations and public shaming. EU institutions (ECB and EC) were instrumentalized to execute the austerity measures in the debtor countries, and by way of excluding the community method, mediation between creditor and debtor countries was not really attempted, and decision taken was opaque and lacked transparency and democratic accountability. By re-framing a systemic crisis into a sovereign debt crisis, the cost of a systemic crisis could be rolled on debtor countries and solidarity measures excluded.

Additionally, in terms of output legitimacy, the crisis management of the GFC and SDC was marked by policy mistakes and was not a success story. The contractionary effects of the austerity measures were not smoothed by expansionary measures from the countries with more fiscal leeway. On the contrary, these countries further reinforced the economic contraction with their desire to lead the example of budget consolidation. The financial crisis ended up being much deeper and longer because of the measures adopted. Griffith-Jones (2014) pointed out the clear implication that countries would have grown more and would have seen their debt-to-GDP ratios fall more if they had engaged in less austerity. Apart from aggravating the crisis, these measures had additionally clear distributional consequences, which furthermore undermined the legitimacy of the SDC crisis management and trust in the EU.

With regard to input legitimacy, the GFC and SDC had been marked by the sidelining of the EP and by an increasing asymmetry and disparity in the involvement of and accountability to the national parliaments between creditor and debt countries resulting in a democratic regression (De Souza Guilherme, 2020). The democratic and political consequences were the loss of trust in the EMU, and the EU, but even more in traditional parties, with a consequent rise of new and more radical parties, polarization and euro-scepticism. In short, the price for the lack of democratic legitimacy of the previous crisis management was the transformation of the political landscape at the national and international levels rendering the political system more volatile, political alliances less reliable and as a consequence the EU governance and the multilateral system more crisis prone.

The pandemic on the other hand originated as a health crisis and as such was symmetric in its potential to affect all EU member states. However, the virus affected member states at different times and to different degrees. Additionally, there was a strong asymmetry in the fiscal space to adopt the health, economic and social measures needed to protect their citizens and economy. By coincidence, it was precisely some of the countries, which had been strongly affected by the financial crisis, where the pandemic raged strongest in the initial phase of the pandemic. There was a lack of masks and respiratory equipment as well as experience on how to address the virus overall. The budgetary consolidation measures from the previous crisis had included cuts in the health sector and administration, which had weakened the member states' capacity of crisis response in the pandemic, worsening the situation.

In spite of this, the 'frugal four', but initially also Germany, tried to use the same argumentation of 'national responsibility' as in the sovereign debt crisis. They argued that each member state was responsible for its own fiscal space and the lack of capacity for crisis management and resilience by not reducing debts in time and acquiring a fiscal buffer. Following these arguments, they rejected the request of a common debt instrument issued by the EU presented by the nine member states including France, Italy and Spain sent in an open letter to Council President Charles Michel on 25 March 2020. At the forefront of the 'frugal four', Dutch Finance Minister Wopke Hoekstra demanded that the EU should investigate why some states had insufficient fiscal capacities to effectively tackle the economic impact of the pandemic (Von der Buchard et al., 2020).

Different Tools and Mechanisms

The impact on public opinion of the dramatic scenes from the southern countries, struggling with the pandemic and burying thousands of their beloved ones, raised a call for solidarity particularly when confronted with a crisis, which threatens to affect all member states and can be blamed on no one. In this context, the 'frugal four's' stance provoked repulsion and public outrage in many member states.

Portugal's Prime Minister António Costa also called Hoekstra's demand 'repugnant' and accused him of 'undermining what the spirit of the European Union is' (ibid). The provocation of the Dutch finance minister Hoekstra was seen as another moral crisis and turning point for a catharsis in the European financial crisis management. With the public moral outrage these comments had provoked, the dynamic in favour of a recovery package based on community bonds gained momentum.

The same day, May 26, 2020, the president of the European Commission Von der Leyen described in a speech in front of the European Parliament the leadership and solidarity at EU level in the first weeks as partly painful:

> When Europe really needed to be there for each other, too many initially looked out for themselves. When Europe really needed an 'all for one' spirit, too many initially gave an 'only for me' response. And when Europe really needed to prove that this is not only a 'fair weather Union', too many initially refused to share their umbrella. (Von der Leyen, 2020, p. 2)

Germany's role and position were key to decide which direction the recovery programme would take. Indeed, Germany found itself in the delicate situation of having agreed in the national parliament to spend hundreds of billions of euros on state aid measures while at the same time sharing the unpopular position of the 'frugal four'. Thus, she found herself under strong pressure to abandon its resistance to common debt issuance to which it finally gave in. Waas and Rittberger (2023, p. 1) explain the motives for the German U-turn in the following way:

> First, to avoid a 'common bad' of a large-scale economic contraction, proposals for an EU-wide fiscal response became a political imperative. Second, the successful framing of the crisis as 'nobody's fault' rendered the call for European solidarity as the dominant standard of legitimacy to which all governments subscribed. Third, governments whose preferences were not aligned with this standard faced mounting normative pressure and isolation.

Finally, the Eurogroup meeting of April 8 already indicated the U-turn on the recovery plan but had still not found an agreement on the issue of common debt issuance or tying it to the MFF. It was precisely in this time that the EP adopted its resolution of April 17, 2020, on EU coordinated action to combat the COVID-19 pandemic and its consequences.

European Parliament and Recovery and Resilience Facility

This section analyses the role of the European Parliament in the response to the COVID-19 crisis and therefore to the strengthening of its legitimacy. The EP is the only institution whose representatives have been directly elected by the people to represent them at the EU level. Its role is deliberative and legislative, and it is responsible for holding accountable the executive. EP's positions represent compromises between the interests of citizens adhering to different ideological and social backgrounds, countries, regions and stakeholders. It is important to analyse the EP's role in regard to the choice of the EU crisis management by way of the community versus the intergovernmental method, the scope, content and financing of the recovery and resilience package, its implementation as well as its role in in terms of holding the executive accountable. Democratic legitimacy rests on the belief that citizens can elect representatives to parliaments to ensure that governing authorities are responsive to their preferences. Departing from the assumption that parliamentary accountability should occur at the same level where political decisions are taken, the RRF being decided by the community method falls into the category of pooled political authority requiring a two-pronged parliament accountability both at the domestic level (national parliaments) and the supranational level (the EP) (Rittberger, 2023).

In contrast to the GFC and SDC, the fact that the pandemic was a symmetric crisis affecting all EU member states and for which no member state could be made responsible led to the decision to create a recovery and resilience programme for all of the EU instead of limiting it to the euro area and to adopt the RRF within the legislative framework of the EU. In consequence of this decision, the EP could play a much more important role as co-legislator and the crisis management gained in legitimacy, transparency and accountability.

As described before, during the first months of the pandemic the EP found itself once again sidelined by a crisis response which sought recourse to intergovernmental and national measures and was based on a legal basis and competences which excluded the EP. However, as Fasone (2022, p. 5) argues, the EP was successfully fighting back and played an important role in promoting a 'grand bargain' during this first phase, which also influenced the decision to give preference to the communitarian way:

> Although this may have been overlooked, some MEPs were the first proponents of what later would become the RRF. Before the Commission initiative and the Franco-German proposal for an EU recovery fund, indeed, in early April, Luis Garicano and Guy Verhofstadt (RENEW) proposed a "European Reconstruction Fund" (Schelkle, 2021). In the EP Resolution of April 17, 2020, the contours of the future NGEU were already set.

The success of the proposal of the two leading figures in the liberal group Renew was due to the fact that, on the one hand, it was based on elements which had already found an agreement and had been adopted in previous EP resolutions, such as Eurobonds for future oriented investments and new own resources (European Parliament, 2011), a fiscal capacity, which would serve a stabilization function(European Parliament, 2017, 2018), and a budget of a sufficient size to provide fiscal capacity (European Parliament, 2011). On the other hand, it represented a compromise between those who were in favour of risk sharing and wanted common issuance of bonds and those who favoured risk avoidance and insisted in stringent conditions and the monitoring by targets, milestones and a combination of investment and reforms. They presented it as a grand bargain in which the EU would issue bonds and the interest would be covered by the EU budget, which would be increased through new own resources. Therefore, none of the costs would be paid by any of the member states for another member state. Yet it presented a step forward in the direction of a transfer union by directing grants to regions and sectors, which needed it most. However, the recovery fund was to be temporary and tied to the duration of the MFF. Furthermore, the funds were to be conditional on the achievements of milestones, such as investments and reforms in policy areas which are European priorities.

At the same time, the two politicians were well connected to the other institutions and important players and thus were able to exchange, develop and promote these ideas simultaneously in the different institutions at a critical moment when the discussions in the Council were in an intensive phase. Within the EP the resolution was negotiated and submitted by four of the big mainstream political groups (parties) and bore therefore a considerable political weight, the European Peoples Party (EPP), the Social Democrats (S&D), the Renew Liberals (Renew) and the Greens, and was adopted on April 17, 2020, before the presentation of the Franco-German proposal.

The EP used its resolutions of April 17, 2020, 'on EU coordinated action to combat the COVID-19 pandemic and its consequences', (European Parliament, 2020a) and the following one of May 15, 2020, 'on the new multiannual financial framework, own resources and the recovery plan' (European Parliament, 2020b) to increase the pressure for the recovery programmes to be established through the regular EU community legislative method, as part of the new MFF and not as an intergovernmental agreement. The EP explicitly expressed its disappointment about the recourse to national actions instead of common action and about the lack of solidarity at the early phase. Additionally, it warned about the risks of an uneven level playing field in the internal market without any community action and—last but not least—outlined its proposals which then became to a great extent the blueprint for the RRF.

In the negotiations with the Council the EP was successful in determining the overarching priorities for the RRF in the form of the six pillars of policy priorities which became Article 3 on the scope of the RRF.

> (1) green transition; (2) digital transformation; (3) smart, sustainable and inclusive growth, including economic cohesion, jobs, productivity, competitiveness, research, development and innovation, and a well-functioning internal market with strong SMEs; (4) social and territorial cohesion; (5) health, and economic, social and institutional resilience, with the aim of, inter alia, increasing crisis preparedness and crisis response capacity; and (6) policies for the next generation, children and the youth, such as education and skill.

Throughout the negotiation process with the Council the EP tried to promote democracy and legitimacy by strengthening ownership, transparency, inclusive decision-taking, accountability and the rule of law. Additionally, the EP promoted policies for the common good improving inclusion and resilience such as the green transition, the European pillar of social rights and sustainable social market economy and gender inclusion and mainstreaming. Part of the success in promoting its agenda can be explained by its tactic of issue linking as the RRF was negotiated in parallel with the own resource decision (ORD), the MFF and the rule of law regulation, and results were interlinked and formed an informal package (Montero et al., 2021). On December 16, 2020, an inter-institutional agreement (IIA) (European Parliament, 2020c) was concluded on the introduction of several new own resources, of which the plastic packaging was the first to be adopted, with a binding roadmap and a passage ensuring a role for the EP in all legislation based on Article 122, which might have an impact on the MFF.

In spite of the EP's success in influencing the blueprint and the scope of the RRF, it was considerably less successful in increasing its own role in the process of the RRF. There is no role foreseen for the EP regarding the drafting, evaluating and monitoring of the national RRF plans. The role of the EP in this important process of economic governance and coordination does not go beyond its very limited role in the European Semester. Yet the RRF procedure has been coupled to the European Semester and by doing so has given it more teeth. Before, the procedure of economic policy coordination of national economic and social policies was lacking ownership and compliance. The RRF, by contrast, can steer policies and promote EU objectives and has distributive and disciplinary effects through considerable EU funds. Considering the EP's role as co-legislator of the RRF, in defining the overarching objectives, and as Fasone (2022) pointed out, as a budgetary authority on an equal footing with the Council on the ground of Article 14, para. 1 TEU, the EP should have been granted more powers in order to fulfil its role. The EP had wanted to institutionalize a recovery and resilience dialogue between the Union institutions in which the representatives of the Council and its preparatory bodies, the Commission and the Eurogroup should be invited. Accountability to the EP in the RRF, as in the European Semester, is only foreseen for the EC.

In the context of the RRF, the dialogue found its way into the regulation in the form of a structured dialogue with the EC, which was organized every 2 months by the competent committees of the EP (the Committee on Economic and Monetary Affairs (ECON) and the Committee on Budgets (BUDG)). According to Article 26, of RRF, the Commission had to inform the EP about the following items: (a) the state of recovery, resilience and adjustment capacity in the Union; (b) the recovery and resilience plans of the member states (c) and their assessment; (d) the main findings of the review report; (e) the status of fulfilment of the milestones and targets of the recovery and resilience plans of the member states; and (f) payment, suspension and termination procedures. Moreover, in order to make it more like a dialogue, the regulation foresees that the 'Commission shall give due consideration to the views expressed by the EP', whatever that may mean. 'Democratic accountability' would imply that the process would lead to adjustments and improvements following the input from the EP, yet it seems rather that the main advantage of the scrutiny rights over the Commission lies in the increased transparency.

In terms of transparency the EP gained equal rights to access of information as the Council, simultaneously and on equal terms and without undue delay and also achieved introducing a recovery and resilience scoreboard on milestones and targets.

EU member states, on the other hand, succeeded to improve their role in the RRF governance process as compared to the European Semester. It is now up to the member states to submit the first draft of their national RRF. The EC then evaluates them according to the criteria of relevance, effectiveness, efficiency and coherence but may also suggest modifications in bilateral exchanges and submits the evaluation to the Council for a final approval and monitors the implementation. This change of procedure can be considered a game changer and considerably enhances ownership, the respect of citizens' priorities and thus legitimacy. While the EC's idea of ownership is mainly to improve compliance and by doing so to strengthen the output and throughput legitimacy of EU socioeconomic governance (Vanheuverzwijn & Crespy, 2018: 14), the EP is in favour of having the member states to decide the national measures in order to achieve the policy objectives which will strengthen responsiveness to citizens' choices expressed in national elections and at the same time emphasizes the need for democratic accountability to improve ownership and compliance both at the European and national levels (Rittberger, 2023)

An increased national ownership and inclusiveness, or horizontal legitimacy, and a strengthened accountability would increase democratic legitimacy of the national programmes and have long been among the priorities of the EP given the poor record of the implementation of the national plans within the European Semester process. Concerning strengthening horizontal legitimacy, the EP succeeded to anchor the reporting requirement on the consultation of local and regional authorities, social partners and civil society in Article 18, paragraph 4 (q).[2] Last but not least, the EP exercises additional powers of scrutiny and political pressure under EU budgetary and discharge procedures and resolutions such as on the European Semester or on the annual report on the RRF and by written or oral questions.

Conclusions

Olaf Scholz saw in the creation of the Recovery and Resilience Facility a 'Hamiltonian moment'. Even though it might not go that far, this chapter showed how, as summarized by Waas and Rittberger (2023), it provided 'concrete achievements which first create a de facto solidarity' and how it broke with a paradigm and paved the way in the direction of a fiscal union in the future. Moreover, it helped to avoid the 'common bad' of a large-scale economic contraction and of a social and economic crisis and to promote the European 'public good', or to put it in Scharpf's words (1999, p. 6), it 'effectively promotes the common welfare of the constituency in question', which considerably increased its (output) legitimacy.

When comparing the intergovernmental GFC and SDC management with the RRF based on the community method, we see that the latter clearly outperformed the former in terms of input, throughput and output legitimacy. While the GFC and SDC management brought about a double democratic deficit and erosion of democracy (De Souza, 2020), the EP had a stronger role in the creation of the RRF, contributing to its design, formulating the overarching policy pillars and therefore

[2] That reads: 'For the preparation and, where available, for the implementation of the recovery and resilience plan, a summary of the consultation process, conducted in accordance with the national legal framework, of local and regional authorities, social partners, civil society organisations, youth organisations and other relevant stakeholders, and how the input of the stakeholders is reflected in the recovery and resilience plan'.

contributing to its input and throughput legitimacy. The process is more transparent, particularly in terms of equal access to information; the social pillar and gender equality and the promotion of the involvement of regional and local authorities, social partners and civil society, pushed by the EP, rendered the RRF more inclusive and transparent at the national level.

That said, first evaluations already show that there is a lot of room to improve their involvement, which the EP already addressed with the designed scrutiny. Another important aspect, which is still missing, is the reporting on the involvement of national parliaments in their legislative, budgetary and scrutinizing competencies on the national RRF plans and the national implementation of the programmes. Increased accountability and responsiveness to citizen's priorities can only be achieved in an alliance between the European and national parliaments. The national parliaments are already partners and not competitors of the EP to ensure and promote democracy and accountability and improve legitimacy, for which the Conference of Parliamentary Committees for Union Affairs (COSAC), the European Parliamentary Week and the Interparliamentary Conferences on Stability, Economic Coordination and Governance (SECG) and Interparliamentary Committee meetings have been set up, but more can be done.

The EP also was not successful in its quest to introduce into the regulation the mandatory accountability of the member states, the Council and the president of the Eurogroup. It has not given up these efforts though and has re-inserted these requests in its position on the reform of the economic governance rules. Also important to RRF's legitimacy is that it has acquired great support in the population and seems, therefore, to well reflect the preferences of EU citizens and the 'will of the people':

> About half of respondents (51%) across the EU, answered that they were aware of a Recovery Plan for their country to support economic recovery from the COVID-19 pandemic. 74% expressed that they thought that it was a good approach for the EU and seven in ten replied that it is a good approach for their country that the EU Recovery Plan 'NextGenerationEU', is based on a principle of solidarity, as Member States agreed to provide financial support to each other to emerge stronger from the COVID-19 pandemic. (European Commission, 2023a, b, c, p. 3)

The RRF was created as temporary fiscal capacity, yet it has already brought about a paradigm change. Whether it has paved the way for a 'Hamiltonian development' will much depend on the proper use of the funds and its success. The RRF already made the EU more resilient for the COVID-19 pandemic as well as for the economic shock due the Russian war against Ukraine and the subsequent energy and inflation crises. Additionally, the fact that almost 40% of the total allocation of the plans should contribute to measures aimed at reducing net greenhouse gas emissions and almost 30% of the plans' allocation is dedicated to social expenditure will serve to improve the resilience of the European Union.

Confronted with increased instability in the era of poly- and permacrisis due to wars and conflicts, climate change and an increasingly multipolar world, with increasingly unstable alliances due to the rise of autocratic and populist governments within and outside of the EU, the need to finance or stimulate investment in European common goods and welfare and strengthen resilience will only increase.

The experience of the RRF will either result in a sequence of temporary stabilization functions or lead to a permanent fiscal capacity ideally by an increased EU budget which signifies a major leap forward towards a fiscal union. This chapter showed that crisis management within the legal framework of the EU and with solidarity has paid off for all member states and strengthened the European Union and its legitimacy, becoming more resilient and reflecting Jean Monnet's and Robert Schuman's visions.

Disclaimer

The opinions expressed in this chapter are the sole responsibility of the author and do not necessarily represent the official position of the European Parliament or of any other EU institution.

References

Blanchard, O., & Leigh, D. (2014). Learning about fiscal multipliers from growth forecast errors. *IMF Economic Review, 62*(2), 179–212.

Buti, M., & Papaconstantinou, G. (2021, April). *Does the EU ever learn? From the financial crisis to the Covid-19 crisis: Looking back to move forward.* EUI School of Transnational Governance (STG) Policy Papers, Issue 7.

Council (2020a), Regulation (EU) 2020/672 of 19 May 2020 on the establishment of a European instrument for temporary support to mitigate unemployment risks in an emergency (SURE) following the COVID-19 outbreak. July 21

De Souza Guilherme, B. (2020). The double democratic deficit. In *Financial crisis management and democracy: Lessons from Europe and Latin America*. Springer.

ECB. 2020. Decision ECB/2020/17 of 24 March 2020

Elysee. (2020). *French-German initiative for the European recovery from the coronavirus crisis.* https://www.elysee.fr/en/emmanuel-macron/2020/05/18/french-german-initiative-for-the-european-recovery-from-the-coronavirus-crisis. 18 May 2020.

European Commission. (2020). *Proposal for a Regulation of the European Parliament and of the Council establishing a Recovery and Resilience facility, COM (2020) 408 final.*

European Commission. (2022, October). Competition: State Aid brief, Issue 3.

European Commission. (2023a). Flash Eurobarometer 515, *EU Recovery Plan 'NextGenerationEU'*, Report 2023.

European Commission. (2023b). *Communication on Recovery and Resilience Facility: Two years on A unique instrument at the heart of the EU's green and digital transformation*, COM(2023) 99 final.

European Commission. (2023c). *Report on Public Finances in EMU 2022.* Institutional Paper 256 | October 2023.

European Council. (2020). European Council Conclusions of 17–21 July 2020.

European Parliament. (2011). *Resolution of 6 July 2011 on the financial, economic and social crisis: Recommendations concerning the measures and initiatives to be taken (2010/2242(INI)).*

https://www.europarl.europa.eu/sides/getDoc.do?reference=P7-TA-2011-0331&type=TA&language=EN&redirect. Accessed 1 Mar 2020.
European Parliament. (2017). *Resolution on the budgetary capacity for the euro area in 2017*. https://www.europarl.europa.eu/doceo/document/TA-8-2017-0050_EN.html. Accessed 1 Mar 2020.
European Parliament. (2018). *Draft report on the proposal for a regulation of the European Parliament and of the Council on the establishment of a European Investment Stabilisation Function* (COM(2018)0387 – C8-0241/2018 – 2018/0212(COD)), Committee on Budgets and Committee on Economic and Monetary Affairs, Rapporteurs: Reimer Böge, Pervenche Beres.
European Parliament. (2020a). European Parliament resolution of 17 April 2020 *on EU coordinated action to combat the COVID-19 pandemic and its consequences* (2020/2616(RSP)). https://www.europarl.europa.eu/doceo/document/TA-9-2020-0054_EN.html
European Parliament. (2020b). European Parliament resolution of 15 May 2020 *on the new multiannual financial framework, own resources and the recovery plan* (2020/2631(RSP)).
European Parliament. (2020c). European Parliament resolution of 17 December 2020 *on the Multiannual Financial Framework 2021–2027, the Interinstitutional Agreement, the EU Recovery Instrument and the Rule of Law Regulation* (2020/2923(RSP)).
Fasone, C. (2022). Fighting back? The role of the European Parliament in the adoption of next generation EU. *The Journal of Legislative Studies, 28*(3), 368–384.
Ghymers, C. (2020). The systemic nature of the global crisis and some principles for tackling it. In *Financial crisis management and democracy: Lessons from Europe and Latin America*. Springer.
Governo Italiano. (2020). Letter to Charles Michel, 25 March. http://www.governo.it/sites/new.governo.it/files/letter_michel_20200325_eng.pdf
Griffth-Jones, S. (2014). From austerity to growth in Europe: Some lessons from Latin America. In J. Stiglitz & D. Heymann (Eds.), *Life after debt: The origins and resolutions of debt crisis*. Springer.
Monnet, J. (1978). *Memoirs: The architect and master builder of the European Economic Community*. Doubleday.
Montero, C., et al. (2021). Pragmatism and the limits to the European Parliament's strategies for self-empowerment. *Politics and Governance, 9*(3), 163–174.
Rittberger, B. (2023), *Democratic control and legitimacy in the evolving EU economic governance framework* (pp. 733–742). European Parliament, PE.
Scharpf, F. (1999). *Governing in Europe: Effective and democratic?* Oxford University Press.
Schelkle, W. (2021). Fiscal integration in an experimental union: How path-breaking was the EU's response to the COVID-19 pandemic? *Journal of Common Market Studies, 51*(S1), 44–55. https://doi.org/10.1111/jcms.13246
Schmidt, V. (2013). Democracy and legitimacy in the European Union revisited: Input, output and 'throughput'. *Political Studies, 61, 2–22.*
Schmidt, V. (2020). *Europe's crisis of legitimacy: Governing by rules and ruling by numbers in the Eurozone, Oxford.*
Schulmeister, S. (2020). The road from prosperity into the crisis: The long cycle of post-war economic, social and political development. In *Financial crisis management and democracy: Lessons from Europe and Latin America*. Springer.
Schuman, R. (1950). *The Declaration of 9 May*. https://data.europa.eu/doi/10.2775/065
Van der Buchard, H., et al. (2020) *Dutch try to calm north-south economic storm over coronavirus*, Politico, March 27, 2020. Published online https://www.politico.eu/article/netherlands-try-to-calm-storm-over-repugnant-finance-ministers-comments/. Accessed 22 Dec 2023.
Vanheuverzwijn, P., & Crespy, A. (2018). Macro-economic coordination and elusive ownership in the European Union. *Public Administration, 96*(3), 578–593. https://doi.org/10.1111/padm.12413

Von der Leyen, U. (2020). Speech by President von der Leyen at the European Parliament Plenary on the European coordinated response to the COVID-19 outbreak on 26 March, 2020, Brussels online: file:///C:/localdata/bdesouza/Downloads/Speech_by_President_von_der_Leyen_at_the_EP__-_COVID_19.pdf%20(5).pdf. Accessed 10 Dec 2023.

Waas, L., & Rittberer, B. (2023). The Berlin puzzle: Why European solidarity prevailed in the adoption of the Corona recovery fund. *European Journal of Political Research*.

Chapter 6
Revisiting the Democratic Foundations of European Integration During the Permacrisis

Dimitris Katsikas

Contents

Introduction

In recent years, the European Union (EU) has been in a constant state of crisis. Although permacrisis has affected the whole world, compared to other regions, the EU has had to deal with additional idiosyncratic shocks, like the Eurocrisis, in the aftermath of the global financial crisis, the refugee crisis of 2015–2016 and Brexit. The implications of this situation for European integration were acknowledged in 2016 by Jean-Claude Juncker, president of the European Commission at the time. Having in mind the Eurocrisis, the refugee crisis and the Brexit referendum, Juncker coined the term 'polycrisis' to describe 'the confluence of multiple, mutually reinforcing challenges facing the EU'. Since then, more crises erupted: the pandemic, the Russian invasion of Ukraine and the ensuing energy crisis, the rise of inflation to its highest levels since the 1970s and more recently the new flare-up in the long-standing conflict in the Middle East.

On a global level, the number and intensity of the shocks and the multilevel challenges they entail, as well as the inability of global governance mechanisms to

D. Katsikas (✉)
National and Kapodistrian University of Athens, Athens, Greece
e-mail: dkatsikas@pspa.uoa.gr

D. Katsikas et al. (eds.), *Finance, Growth and Democracy: Connections and Challenges in Europe and Latin America in the Era of Permacrisis*, United Nations University Series on Regionalism 33, https://doi.org/10.1007/978-3-031-68475-3_1

respond satisfactorily, could further strengthen the dynamics of regional integration observed in recent decades. On the other hand, this new environment poses significant challenges for existing regional integration schemes, such as the EU, as they come under pressure to effectively handle the crises but also to redefine their priorities and redesign their strategies and policy tools, to enhance their resilience.

Given its member states' diverse interests, its incomplete institutional structure and limited policy capacity, the EU often lacks the ability to devise and implement policies in response to fast-evolving crises. The inability to deal effectively with an unfolding crisis in turn undermines the EU's basic legitimacy source: its ability to improve the material well-being of European citizens. This became evident during the Eurocrisis, when fiscal conservatism, domestic political calculations and moral hazard considerations shaped a 'go-it-alone' adjustment process for crisis-hit member states which produced extremely negative socio-economic results, undermining greatly the image and credibility of the EU in the eyes of European citizens, particularly in the South (Kriesi, 2018; Verney & Katsikas, 2020). On the other hand, most analysts tend to agree that the EU's reaction to the pandemic has been both prompt and comprehensive, compared to previous episodes (Boin & Rhinard, 2023; Brooks et al., 2023), restoring thus, to some extent, the image of an organization capable of delivering prosperity-improving results under conditions of crisis.

The impact of crises on European citizens' attitudes towards the EU is important because these attitudes underpin the European project's democratic legitimacy. This is a crucial aspect of the process of European integration, not only because the EU is a normative order (Bellamy & Weale, 2015), but also because legitimacy is a necessary corollary to further integration, which becomes increasingly necessary as consecutive crises call for institutional deepening in several policy areas. Accordingly, the objective of this chapter is to evaluate the impact of successive crises on EU's democratic legitimacy. To do so we examine public support towards the EU. We employ Easton's (1975) distinction between diffuse and specific support, focusing on the former, to gauge the impact of permacrisis, as an extended period of stress and insecurity, on European citizens' support towards European integration. We use Eurobarometer data on different aspects of public attitudes vis-à-vis the EU during the last 15 years, focusing on the potential impact of four major crises: the Eurocrisis, the refugee crisis, the pandemic and the Russian invasion of Ukraine. Due to space limitations, the analysis is mostly descriptive and is meant to discern and document major trends in popular support towards the EU during the permacrisis era.

The next section discusses the issue of EU's democratic legitimacy and the theoretical debates around it. The section after that describes and briefly discusses the four major crises that impacted the EU in the past 15 years, which are expected to have affected popular support for European integration. The following section presents and discusses the data from the Eurobarometer surveys. The last section discusses the findings and relates them to the literature.

The Foundations of EU's Democratic Legitimacy

Before the crisis, the EU's record in terms of democratic legitimacy was mixed. Historically, European integration proceeded without major political contestation in European societies, as it was always thought as an issue of low political salience in domestic politics, and European elections were typically treated as a 'second-order' election (Reif & Schmitt, 1980). The deepening and widening of the integration process that followed the Maastricht Treaty changed this. European integration became increasingly intertwined with issues pertaining to core aspects of national sovereignty and identity, making it more controversial and politicized and thus increasingly part of domestic party politics. As a result, the general public's 'permissive consensus', enjoyed by European elites in previous decades (Lindberg & Scheingold, 1970), was gradually replaced by an intensifying 'constraining dissensus' (Hooghe & Marks, 2009). This was manifested, for example, with the emergence of (typically marginal) Eurosceptic parties in many European countries, both on the left and the right side of the political spectrum.

The permacrisis era that begun with the global financial crisis increased further the politicization of the EU both at the national and European levels (Zeitlin et al., 2019). The Eurocrisis was accompanied by a rise in Euroscepticism manifested both in opinion surveys and the increased support for Eurosceptic parties in many countries (Hernández & Kriesi, 2016; Verney & Katsikas, 2020). While some consider politicization as a sign of further integration which brings unavoidable political transformations (e.g. Genschel & Jachtenfuchs, 2018), others see it as a problem, as it inhibits decision-making in the EU, creating a 'politics trap' (Laffan, 2021). The latter is more likely to occur during times of crisis, when intensified politicization is typically the result of diverse and often contrasting views, on the appropriate response, which reflect broader politico-economic interests and societal attitudes, leading to divisions, like the North-South rift that emerged during the Eurocrisis.

The rise of Euroscepticism undermines the democratic legitimacy of the European integration project, which has been contested from the beginning. Even before the global financial crisis, there was a heated academic debate about the 'EU's democratic deficit', which revolved around two main issues: the weak democratic institutional credentials of European governance and the limited affinity felt by European citizens towards the EU (Weiler et al., 1995; Follesdal & Hix, 2006; Hix, 2008). While some scholars rejected the institutional critique, arguing that the EU is a limited-purpose organization which should not be held to an ideal standard of democracy more appropriate for nation states (e.g. Majone, 1998; Moravcsik, 2002, 2008), the claim that the EU citizens do not understand or identify with the EU has been much harder to contest.

In this context, prior to the global financial crisis, there was substantial consensus that the EU derived its legitimacy mainly from its ability to deliver economic prosperity to European citizens. In other words, the EU enjoyed *output* legitimacy, that is, legitimacy based on the positive prosperity outcomes of the authority it exercised. On other hand, *input* legitimacy, that is, legitimacy based on the representation of the interests and values of the people in policymaking, by ensuring the accountability of policymakers, for example, through elections, was lacking (Scharpf, 1999; Schmidt, 2013).

Permacrisis: The EU Under Strain

The recurrent crises over the past 15 years, and the way these were handled, upset the previous balance. The first major shock was the global financial crisis and particularly its subsequent evolution into the Eurocrisis, which divided the EU into creditor and debtor member states and pitted them against each other. The management of the Eurocrisis weakened further input legitimacy, particularly in the countries of the Eurozone periphery, which suffered most from the crisis. The terms of the bailout agreements were dictated by the creditor countries, following ad hoc, intergovernmental and highly asymmetrical negotiations, which left no room for domestic politics. This was reflected in the explicitly expressed discord of societies with government policies in crisis-hit countries, which led to political upheaval and in some cases radical transformation of the political system, without, however, substantially affecting the content of the implemented policies, a situation described by Schmidt (2015) as 'politics without policies'. At the same time, questionable practices at the EU governance level and the constant invocation of a 'state of emergency' at the domestic level led to further weakening of institutional checks and balances (Katsikas, 2020). On the other hand, output legitimacy also suffered because of the economic deterioration experienced by the countries in crisis. The result was a rise of populism and Euroscepticism and not only in the South but also in the North (e.g. True Finns, AfD, etc.).

After the crisis, economic recovery improved the material conditions of European citizens—with the exception of Greece, which experienced a deep and long-lasting crisis. However, soon, the EU found itself faced with another shock. In 2015, in the space of a few months, more than a million people, coming for the most part from Syria, crossed the borders into the EU, mainly from the so-called eastern corridor, i.e., the Greek border with Turkey, and to a lesser degree from the 'central Mediterranean corridor', that is, the sea crossing from North Africa to South Italy (IOM, 2016). The refugee crisis that unfolded over the following months revealed a new rift, this time between member states in western and central and eastern Europe. The latter, led by the Visegrád group of countries, rejected the creation of a joint EU mandatory mechanism to distribute refugees to EU member states and resorted to unilateral—but often coordinated—measures, which ended up closing entirely the Balkan route towards northern Europe for refugees, leaving them stranded at the northern border of Greece (Kriesi et al., 2021). The influx of refugees eventually slowed down following a shift of policy towards re-bordering EU's external borders, including through an agreement with Turkey, to prevent more refugees from reaching the EU. The resolution of the crisis left a bitter taste, as the EU was unable to find a commonly agreed solution, and the behaviour of certain member states undermined the legitimacy of the EU both as a competent crisis manager and as a political entity that embodies a set of humanitarian values (Murray & Longo, 2018). The crisis further fuelled the rise of populist, Eurosceptic and far-right parties across Europe.

The period after the refugee crisis was characterized by relative stability and a strong recovery of the European economy from the Eurocrisis. Even Greece was able to finally recover and complete its third bailout programme in August of 2018. This period of calm did not last long; in early 2020 the COVID-19 pandemic, the worst global health crisis for a century, broke out. Beyond its devastating humanitarian toll, the pandemic has also had a profound impact on the economy. As with any epidemic, the isolation of infected people to contain dispersion of the virus unavoidably led to the disruption of economic activity, while the increased uncertainty impacted on both consumption and investment, further intensifying the recession (Gourinchas, 2020). Things got even worse as governments, in their effort to 'flatten' the epidemic curve, imposed lockdowns. Despite the 'symmetrical' character of the shock, the impact across member states was highly uneven; countries with less developed health systems and reduced fiscal capacity—the countries hit hard during the Eurocrisis displayed both weaknesses—would not have the means to effectively manage the crisis. The early reactions were not encouraging; once again, member states' first course of action was unilateral measures, including closure of borders, travel restrictions and exports bans (Brooks & Geyer, 2020), disrupting the functioning of both the Schengen area and the single market. The old rift between fiscally conservative member states and countries seeking more fiscal solidarity emerged again, as the former rejected the latter's proposal for the issuance of common debt to deal with the pandemic. Fortunately, under the increasing pressure of the crisis, cooperation among member states gradually improved, and the European institutions seized the momentum to push for a bolder and more active handling of the crisis. Policy activism from the European Central Bank (ECB) and the European Commission, the relaxation of fiscal constraints and the increased cooperation in health and crisis management were perceived as positive steps during an unprecedented crisis. Fiscal measures were also agreed, the culmination of which was the Next Generation EU initiative, which offered member states significant amounts of funds, much of it in the form of grants, to combat the pandemic and its economic consequences. These initiatives, in conjunction with the adoption of a joint procurement strategy for vaccines, contributed greatly to the handling of the pandemic.

The pandemic crisis was not over when the next major shock occurred. In February 2022 Russia invaded Ukraine, provoking the first war between two sovereign states in the European continent since WWII. The shock had an existential dimension for the EU, as it challenged the primary purpose of its own creation, which was to safeguard peace in Europe. The reaction of the EU towards this new crisis seemed to follow a pattern that was the reverse of that during the pandemic. In contrast to the pandemic's weak early response, there was a strong initial condemnation of the invasion and coordinated action to impose unprecedented sanctions to Russia. However, as time went by and the crucial aspect of the economic impact of these sanctions on European economies started being felt, coordination became looser, and disagreements on the way forward emerged, as European economies exhibited different degrees of dependency on Russian energy and had unequal access to alternative sources. At the same time, the inflation wave triggered by the war and the ensuing sanctions created domestic political pressure for incumbent governments. The result was more uncoordinated unilateral actions from various member states and a coordinated recess on certain aspects of EU policy towards the climate crisis, to accommodate pressures for access, at least in the medium term, to alternative fossil fuel sources. In this context, the EU's reaction in terms of its actorness, intra-European solidarity and ability to adapt to changing circumstances seemed lacking compared to its reaction to the pandemic (Anghel & Jones, 2023).

Public Support for the EU During the Permacrisis

The different responses of the EU during the permacrisis era have sparked a scholarly debate regarding the causes for this inconsistent performance and its results on European integration (Hooghe & Marks, 2019; Zeitlin et al., 2019; Wolff & Ladi, 2020; Jones et al., 2021; Genschel & Jachtenfuchs, 2018; Ferrera et al., 2022). A consensus that seems to emerge in the literature is that each crisis episode has distinct characteristics, and these should be considered when assessing their impact on European integration (Ferrara & Kriesi, 2022; Anghel & Jones, 2023). This is because different crises shape different interest constellations and therefore divisions about the appropriate response, leading to what Zeitlin et al. (2019) have called 'polycleavage'. While this may be true, the interaction between the different crises and their overall effect—given the EU's varying performance—on public support towards the EU remain unclear. While for some European citizens the EU may be seen as a breakwater against the tides of continued international turbulence, for others it may be seen as one of its causes. In this chapter we attempt to determine whether and how the extended period of crises and prolonged uncertainty have affected public support towards European integration.

To do so, and following previous work done in this area for the Jean Monnet Network 'Crisis-Equity-Democracy for Europe and Latin America' (Verney & Katsikas, 2020), we employ the well-known distinction made by Easton (1975), between *specific* and *diffuse* support in a political system. Diffuse support is defined as 'support that underlies the regime as a whole and the political community' (1975:445), whereas specific support refers to the satisfaction members of a political system 'feel they obtain from the perceived outputs and performance of the political authorities' (1975:437). It follows that diffuse support is more enduring and 'will not be easily dislodged because of current dissatisfaction with what the government does' (Easton, 1975:445). In contrast, 'specific support… varies with perceived benefits or satisfactions. When these decline or cease, support will do likewise' (Ibid: 439).

In this context, we would expect to see specific support to rise or fall in the aftermath of a crisis episode, depending on the European citizens' evaluation of the EU's reaction. On the other hand, we expect diffuse support to exhibit less variation during a particular crisis, but continuous dissatisfaction with the way the EU deals with consecutive crises could very well lead to a generalized dissatisfaction with the EU itself. Indeed, this is the challenge posed by permacrisis; the recurring occurrence of shocks not only tests the ability of officials in authoritative European institutions at a particular point in time to deal with a crisis but questions the ability of the EU institutions as such to rise to the task. Accordingly, in this chapter we focus on the impact of permacrisis on diffuse popular support for European integration.

To assess the impact of permacrisis on the attitudes of European citizens, we review data for an extended period of time. More specifically, we employ data from a survey in 2006—which is used as the pre-crisis basis against which data from subsequent surveys can be assessed—and data from ensuing surveys with a 2-year frequency, i.e. surveys from 2008, 2010, 2012, 2014, 2016, 2018, 2020 and 2022.[1] We strive to use data from the same (autumn) edition of the Eurobarometer surveys to ensure a higher degree of comparability of the responses, although in some cases this is not possible.[2] Moreover, given that different crises have led to different rifts within the EU, we have separated the data into three groups of countries: (a) the countries of southern Europe, (b) the countries of eastern Europe and (c) the countries of northern/ western Europe.[3] This categorization will provide a more fine-grained image of the attitudes of citizens in different European regions.

To test the effects on diffuse support, we employ three questions. First, a question on trust; according to Easton (1975: 447–450), trust is one of the two ways in which diffuse support is expressed (the other being legitimacy). Trust means that citizens 'feel that their own interests would be attended to even if the authorities were exposed to little supervision or scrutiny' (Ibid:447). It is a necessary corollary to the exercise of authority which otherwise would need to apply coercion for the implementation of its decisions. Trust is cultivated through socialization but also through extended experience with a regime—continued dissatisfaction with the latter's performance under different incumbents may lead to a loss of trust to the regime itself. To explore this aspect of diffuse support, we employ here a Eurobarometer question which asks whether people 'trust the EU'.

A second question which speaks directly to the issue of democratic (input) legitimacy at the EU level is a question which measures the public's satisfaction with the way democracy works in the EU. Given that EU is comprised of states with established democratic systems, and that European citizens' commitment to democracy is deeply embedded (Kriesi, 2020), the less European citizens are satisfied with the way democracy operates in the EU, the more likely they are to consider the EU illegitimate.

[1] This was not possible for all the Eurobarometer questions used. For the second question on democracy, data were not available for 2008, while for the third question on attachment to the EU, data were not available for 2008 and 2010.

[2] More specifically, for the 2006 survey, the questions of interest were included in the spring edition, while for 2020 and 2022, there was a change in the timeframe of the surveys and for both years we use the data of the summer edition.

[3] Ireland was excluded from the analysis as during the Eurocrisis years it should be included in the southern group of countries, but for the rest of the period it would fit better—given its socio-economic and politico-institutional characteristics—in the northern group of countries.

Finally, a third question addresses the more emotional aspect of diffuse support, as it gauges people's attachment to the EU.[4] Lindberg and Scheingold (1970) first made a distinction between *utilitarian* and *affective* support, with the former referring to a cost-benefit analysis of EU membership and the latter to a broad and often emotional acceptance of abstract values at the heart of the European integration project. This emotional link with the EU can be considered as part of or closely related to diffuse support (Boomgaarden et al., 2010:244).

Figure 6.1 presents the data for the first question, on trust. The findings show significant differentiation between the three groups of countries but also some common trends. The most evident common development in the attitudes of respondents in all three groups is the decline in trust towards the EU during the Eurocrisis. This is more pronounced and lasting for the countries of the South where citizens' trust deteriorates from 57% in 2006 to a low of just 28% in 2012 (with an astonishing 63% of respondents saying that they do not trust the EU), in the midst of the crisis. The levels of trust (distrust) remain low (high) until 2016 and start to gradually recover from 2018 onwards and particularly in 2022, when they exceed the 50% threshold again, remaining however lower compared to the pre-crisis period. The decline is also quite steep for the countries of eastern Europe, which see a drop in the levels of trust from a high of 59% in 2006 to a low of 45% in 2012. However, this does not last long, and in 2014 there is already a small recovery, which however is reversed in 2016, when the clash over the refugee crisis erupts in the EU. From

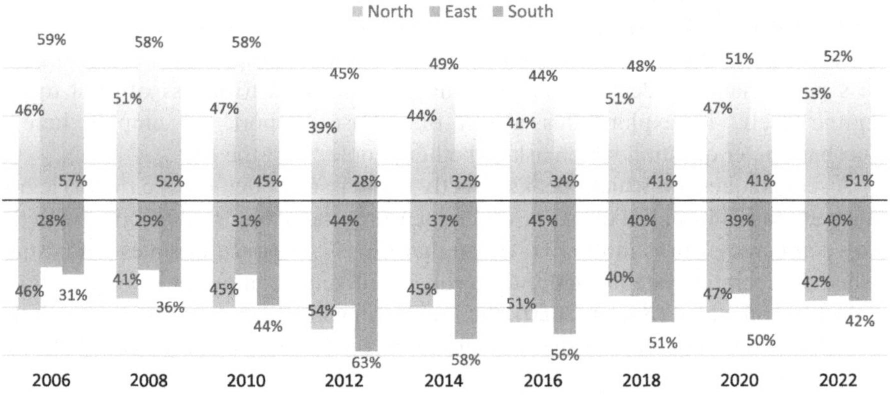

Source: Eurobarometer surveys (65.2, 70.1, 74.2, 78.1, 83.2, 86.2, 90.3, 93.1, 97.5)

Fig. 6.1 Trust in the EU

[4] More specifically, the questions were (a) Trust in EU: *I would like to ask you a question about how much trust you have in certain media and institutions. For each of the following media and institutions, please tell me if you tend to trust it or tend not to trust it: the European Union; (b)* Satisfaction with democracy*: On the whole, are you very satisfied, fairly satisfied, not very satisfied or not at all satisfied with the way democracy works in: the European Union; (c)*Attachment to the EU: *Please tell me how attached you feel to: the European Union.*

2018 onwards things gradually improve, and by 2022 52% of respondents say that they trust the EU. The variation in trust levels is most limited for the countries of the North. As with the other groups of countries, the most pronounced movement is related to the Eurocrisis, when following a slight improvement in 2008 there is a decline of 12 percentage points in the levels of trust by 2012. After that the trend is upward, although there are brief reversals both in 2016, during the refugee crisis, and in 2020, during the pandemic. In 2022 the level of trust for these countries stands at 53%, higher but very close to the levels of the other groups. It is noteworthy that this is the only group for which the citizens' level of trust is higher in 2022 compared to 2006.

Figure 6.2 presents the data for the second question, on democracy. For the group of southern countries, the pattern is similar to that for the trust question. There is a dramatic drop in satisfaction levels during the Eurocrisis, which reaches its nadir in 2014, at 30%, while dissatisfaction peaks in 2012 at 58% and remains very high also in 2014. From 2016 there is a substantial improvement which peaks in 2022 at 57%; this is 9 percentage points higher compared to 2020 and 5 percentage points higher compared to the pre-crisis period in 2006. For the group of eastern countries, the pattern is similar to that of the southern countries, although the movement is much less pronounced. There is a limited drop in satisfaction from a high of 55% in 2006 and 2008 to 49% in 2014. Afterwards, the satisfaction levels increase again, surpassing the pre-crisis levels in 2020, at 59%. The difference with the former group is that in 2022 there is a slight decrease to 57%. Finally, the northern countries display a somewhat different pattern, with dissatisfaction being expressed later in the Eurocrisis, in 2014, and increasing further during the refugee crisis in 2016—albeit in both cases the decline in satisfaction is small. Satisfaction levels increase substantially in 2018 and record a slight reversal in 2020, during the pandemic, before recording a substantial increase to 60% in 2022. It is worth noting that this is 10 percentage points higher compared to the pre-crisis period. Overall, in all groups of

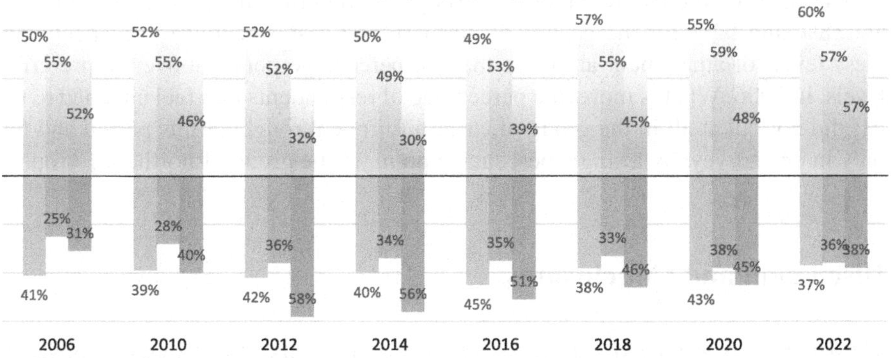

Source: Eurobarometer surveys (65.2, 70.1, 74.2, 78.1, 83.2, 86.2, 90.3, 93.1, 97.5)

Fig. 6.2 Satisfaction with democracy in the EU

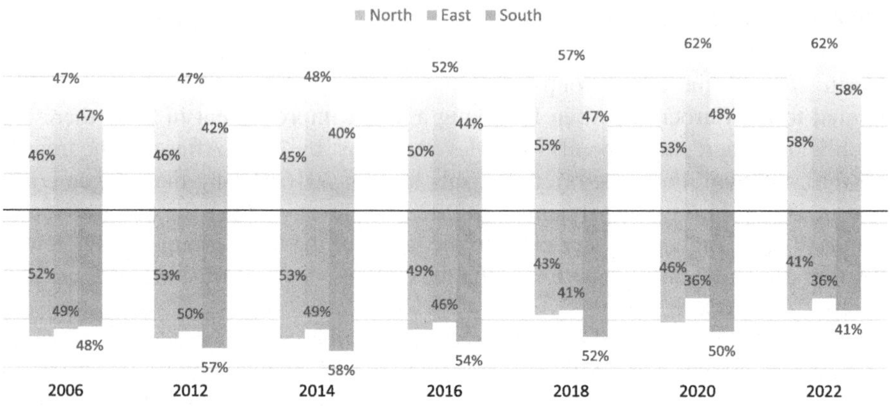

Source: Eurobarometer surveys (65.2, 77.3, 83.2, 86.2, 90.3, 93.1, 97.5)

Fig. 6.3 Attachment to the EU

countries, satisfaction with the way democracy works in the EU is higher—in some cases substantially so—compared to the pre-crisis period.

Figure 6.3 presents the data for the final question on citizens' attachment to the EU. The responses follow a different pattern compared to that observed for the two previous questions. Here, there is no major downward movement for any of the groups, with the partial exception of the group of southern countries, where the percentage of respondents who feel attached to the EU falls gradually from 47% in 2006 to 40% by 2014. However, this decline is relatively mild compared to the decline in trust and satisfaction with democracy in the EU. Moreover, the levels of positive responses start to gradually increase from 2016 onwards recording an increase of 10 percentage points between 2020 and 2022. As a result, by 2022 the percentage of respondents that feel attached to the EU is 58%, much higher compared to the pre-crisis period.

The same is true for the other two groups of countries; the percentages in 2022 are 58% and 62% for the groups of northern and eastern countries, respectively; these levels of attachment are more than 10 percentage points above the pre-crisis levels, in 2006. What is more, the percentage of respondents that feel attached to the EU did not fall at all in the group of eastern Europe throughout this period and fell only in one survey, by a single percentage point, in the group of northern Europe.

Discussion and Conclusions

The EU has experienced several shocks in recent years. As discussed above, its performance as crisis manager was not consistent during this period; in some cases, like the Eurocrisis and the refugee crisis, its handling cannot be considered successful, while in others, like the pandemic and, up to a point, the Russian invasion of

Ukraine, EU's performance was undoubtedly better. Given the EU's inconsistent performance across different crisis episodes, what has been the aggregate impact of permacrisis on citizens' diffuse support for European integration?

Examining Eurobarometer data over a period of more than 15 years, this chapter has sought to provide a first answer to this question. The findings presented in the previous section point to interesting and somewhat unexpected conclusions. First, there does not seem to be an overall loss of popular support for European integration. On the contrary, in two out of the three *indices* of diffuse support examined here, the level of support for European integration in 2022 is substantially higher compared to that of the pre-crisis period. What is more, in these two indices (democracy and attachment) the increase in positive replies is significant for all three groups of countries examined, although there is a clear differentiation in terms of the magnitude of the improvement. Respondents from the countries of northern Europe demonstrate the least volatility in their answers and the biggest overall increase in positive replies in both questions, followed by the respondents in eastern Europe and then by those from the countries of the South.

The issue of trust presents more difficulties for the EU. The protracted Eurocrisis and the ensuing failure to tackle effectively the refugee crisis submitted European citizens to a prolonged period of negative economic and political circumstances which impacted negatively their levels of trust. It is worth noting that during this period (2010–2016), the level of satisfaction with democracy in the EU was also on a strong downward trend but recovered in subsequent surveys. Once lost, trust is much more difficult to regain; the only exception were respondents from the countries of the North, who by 2022 seem to trust the EU more than they did back in 2006. Still, for all three groups, the majority of respondents in 2022 say that they trust the EU. Although a causal analysis of the trends we observe is beyond the scope of this chapter, a tentative explanation for this differentiation could be the fact that northern European societies display overall higher levels of interpersonal and institutional trust, compared to societies in the South and East of Europe.

Despite the overall strengthening of support, not all evidence is positive for European integration. For the first two questions, the percentage of respondents who state that they do not trust the EU or that they are dissatisfied with the way democracy works in the EU has risen over time and has remained at substantially elevated levels in 2022 compared to the pre-crisis period. The data therefore seem to suggest a bifurcation of citizens' attitudes, whereby neutral answers (I don't know) have declined, and both positive and negative answers have risen. This outcome is consistent with the idea that the EU has become more and more politicized during a period marked by successive crises. Interestingly, this is not true for the question on attachment where positive replies have increased and negative ones have decreased at the same time, indicating that more rational negative assessments related to the previous questions do not necessarily translate into negative emotions about the EU.

The variation in the responses throughout this period is also of interest. The deep socio-economic trauma experienced during the Eurocrisis, particularly in the countries of the South and to a lesser degree in the East, is clearly reflected in the respondents' replies during 2010–2014. A similar but less pronounced trend is documented for respondents from the North during the same period—albeit for different reasons—which demonstrates the depth of the rift in the EU during that time. On the other hand, there are reversals in the recovery trend of the replies in both the northern and eastern group of countries in 2016, which indicate the dissatisfaction with the handling of the refugee crisis and the new rift that emerged between these groups of countries during that crisis. Minor reversals are also observed for respondents from the North in 2020, during the early stages of the pandemic, and for respondents from the East in 2022, reflecting perhaps different degrees of sensitivity in different societies for particular issues (e.g. in the North for the restriction of individual freedoms during the pandemic and for some societies in the East, for the 'clash' between the EU and Russia).

Overall, the picture that emerges is hopeful for European integration; the turbulent era of permacrisis has not impacted negatively diffuse support for the EU. On the contrary, the EU seems to have benefited in terms of popular support, strengthening thereby its democratic legitimacy. On the other hand, the deterioration during the Eurocrisis years and the 2016 reversals indicate that this legitimacy hinges upon the EU's ability to deliver results. A protracted failure to cope effectively with successive shocks can lead to rapid delegitimization. Indeed, this is more likely to occur now compared to the pre-crisis period, as there are signs of heightened politicization and therefore support for the idea of an intensifying constraining dissensus, which could prove an obstacle to further integration initiatives. Finally, the findings provide support for the idea of differentiated shocks and their impact on European integration; there is clear variation in the replies of respondents coming from different groups of countries across different shocks.

References

Anghel, V., & Jones, E. (2023). Is Europe really forged through crisis? Pandemic EU and the Russia – Ukraine war. *Journal of European Public Policy, 30*(4), 766–786.

Bellamy, R., & Weale, A. (2015). Political legitimacy and European monetary union: Contracts, constitutionalism and the normative logic of two-level games. *Journal of European Public Policy, 22*(2), 257–274.

Boin, A., & Rhinard, M. (2023). Crisis management performance and the European Union: The case of COVID-19. *Journal of European Public Policy, 30*(4), 655–675.

Boomgaarden, H. G., Schuck, A. R. T., Elenbaas, M., & de Vreese, C. H. (2010). Mapping EU attitudes: Conceptual and empirical dimensions of Euroscepticism and EU support. *European Union Politics, 12*(2), 241–266.

Brooks, E., & Geyer, R. (2020). The development of EU health policy and the Covid-19 pandemic: Trends and implications. *Journal of European Integration, 42*(8), 1057–1076.

Brooks, E., de Ruijter, A., Greer, S. L., & Rozenblum, S. (2023). EU health policy in the aftermath of COVID-19: neofunctionalism and crisis-driven integration. *Journal of European Public Policy, 30*(4), 721–739.

Easton, D. (1975). A reassessment of the concept of political support. *British Journal of Political Science, 5*, 435–457.

Ferrara, F. M., & Kriesi, H. (2022). Crisis pressures and European integration. *Journal of European Public Policy, 29*(9), 1351–1373.

Follesdal, A., & Hix, S. (2006). Why there is a democratic deficit in the EU: A response to Majone and Moravcsik. *Journal of Common Market Studies, 44*, 533–562.
Genschel, P., & Jachtenfuchs, M. (2018). From market integration to core state powers: The Eurozone crisis, the refugee crisis and integration theory. *JCMS Journal of Common Market Studies, 56*(1), 178–196.
Gourinchas, P. O. (2020). Flattening the pandemic and recession curves. In R. Baldwin & B. Weder di Mauro (Eds.), *Mitigating the COVID economic crisis: Act fast and do whatever it takes.* a VoxEU.org eBook, CEPR Press.
Hernandez E., & Kriesi H. (2016). The electoral consequences of the financial and economic crisis in Europe. *European Journal of Political Research, 55*, 203–224.
Hix, S. (2008). What's Wrong with the European Union and How to Fix It, Cambridge: Polity.
Hooghe, L., & Marks, G. (2009). A post-functionalist theory of European integration: from permissive consensus to constraining dissensus. *British Journal of Political Science, 39*(1), 1–23.
Hooghe, L., & Marks, G. (2019). Grand theories of European integration in the twenty first century. *Journal of European Public Policy, 26*(8), 1113–1133.
IOM. (2016). Migration Flows to Europe: The Mediterranean Digest.
Jones, E., Kelemen, R. D., & Meunier, S. (2021). Failing forward? Crises and patterns of European integration. *Journal of European Public Policy, 28*(10), 1519–1536.
Juncker, J. C. (2016, June, 21). Speech at the annual general meeting of the Hellenic federation of enterprises, Athens. http://europa.eu/rapid/press-release_SPEECH-16-2293_en.htm
Katsikas, D. (2020). European Union's democratic legitimacy after the MoUs: The political legacy of an economic crisis. In B. De Souza Guilherme, C. Ghymers, S. Griffith-Jones, & A. Ribeiro Hoffmann (Eds.), *Financial crisis management and democracy*. Springer.
Kriesi, H. (2018). The implications of the euro crisis for democracy. *Journal of European Public Policy, 25*(1), 59–82.
Kriesi, H. (2020). Is there a crisis of democracy in Europe? *Polit Vierteljahresschr, 61*, 237–260.
Kriesi, H., Altiparmakis, A., Bojar, A., & Oana, I.-E. (2021). Debordering and re-bordering in the refugee crisis: a case of "defensive integration". *Journal of European Public Policy, 28*(3), 331–349.
Laffan, B. (2021). *Europe's Union in the 21st Century: From decision trap to politics trap* (RSC Working Paper 2021/67). Robert Schuman Centre for Advanced Studies, European University Institute.
Lindberg, L., & Scheingold, S. (1970). *Europe's would-be polity*. Prentice Hall.
Majone, G. (1998). Europe's "democratic deficit": The question of standards. *European Law Journal, 4*(1), 5–28.
Moravcsik, A. (2002). Reassessing legitimacy in the European Union. *Journal of Common Market Studies, 40*(4), 603–624.
Moravcsik, A. (2008). The myth of Europe's democratic deficit. *Intereconomics: Journal of European Public Policy,* (November–December), 331–340.
Murray, P., & Longo, M. (2018). Europe's wicked legitimacy crisis: the case of refugees. *Journal of European Integration, 40*, 411–425.
Reif, K., & Schmitt H. (1980). Nine second-order national elections: a conceptual framework for the analysis of European election results. *European Journal of Political Research, 8*(1), 3–44.
Scharpf, F. W. (1999). *Governing in Europe*. Oxford University Press.
Schmidt, V. A. (2013). Democracy and legitimacy in the European Union revisited: Input, output and 'throughput'. *Political Studies, 61*, 2–22.
Schmidt, V. A. (2015, September). *The Eurozone's crisis of democratic legitimacy: Can the EU rebuild public trust and support for European economic integration* (Discussion Paper 015). European Economy, European Commission.
Verney, S., & Katsikas, D. (2020). Eurozone crisis management and the growth of opposition to European integration. In B. De Souza Guilherme, C. Ghymers, S. Griffith-Jones, & A. Ribeiro Hoffmann (Eds.), *Financial crisis management and democracy*. Springer.

Weiler, J. H. H., Haltern, U. R., & Mayer, F. (1995). European democracy and its critique. *West European Politics, 18*(3), 4–39.
Wolff, S., & Ladi, S. (2020). European Union responses to the COVID-19 pandemic: Adaptability in times of permanent emergency. *Journal of European Integration, 42*(8), 1025–1040.
Zeitlin, J., Nicoli, F., & Laffan, B. (2019). Introduction: the European Union beyond the polycrisis? Integration and politicization in an age of shifting cleavages. *Journal of European Public Policy, 26*(7), 963–976.

Part II
Financial Governance and Resilience in the EU

Chapter 7
Financing Recovery and Development in the Post-pandemic EU: Issues of Strategy, Institutions and Implementation

George Andreou

Contents

Introduction

The budget of the European Union is very small in comparison to national budgets of both unitary and federal countries;[1] as a result, its funding capabilities are very limited. Historically, the EU budget has been essentially an investment-focused budget, with the bulk of its expenditure dedicated to the funding of the Common Agricultural Policy (CAP) and cohesion policy (a network of variable mixes of European and national sectoral policies serving the objective of economic, social and territorial cohesion). Between 2000 and 2019, the overall EU expenditure was confined at just one percentage point of EU GDP; at the same time, the share of

[1] During the 2014–2020 period, the EU budget accounted for only around 2% of EU public expenditure (European Commission, 2017: 6).

G. Andreou (✉)
Aristotle University of Thessaloniki, Thessaloniki, Greece
e-mail: gioandreou@polsci.auth.gr

D. Katsikas et al. (eds.), *Finance, Growth and Democracy: Connections and Challenges in Europe and Latin America in the Era of Permacrisis*, United Nations University Series on Regionalism 33, https://doi.org/10.1007/978-3-031-68475-3_7

agricultural and cohesion spending started to decline, with more resources transferred to areas such as research, trans-European networks and external action. At the level of ideas, this policy shift was founded on a logic emphasizing the need for maximizing the efficiency and added value of EU spending (European Commission, 2017: 6). At the level of interests, it reflected the unwillingness of EU member states to delegate enhanced budgetary power to the EU and to endow it with more financial resources (Begg, 2023:16). Taking into account this restrictive policy framework, it is no surprise that, during the last two decades, EU actors resorted to two main methods for mobilizing common financial resources in order to confront exceptional crises. The first method is to redirect existing fiscal instruments to new purposes; the second method is to create new, specialized financial instruments outside the institutional framework of the EU budget.[2] The 'galaxy' of EU public finances is thus becoming ever more diversified, raising new concerns about internal coherence, economic efficiency, financial sustainability and democratic control (Begg, 2023).

Between 2008 and 2019, the EU employed its cohesion policy as its major tool for growth-supporting investment (European Commission, 2017: 6). In 2020, attempting to mitigate the economic and social impact of the COVID-19 crisis, the EU established a new, temporary recovery instrument called NextGenerationEU. The centrepiece of the latter is the Recovery and Resilience Facility (RRF), which has been activated for a 6-year period through the implementation of National Recovery and Resilience Plans (NRRPs). RRF also aims at promoting the goal of cohesion but is also focused on strengthening economic and social resilience, mitigating the social and economic impact of the crisis and supporting the green and digital transitions. For 2021–2026, the RRF and the cohesion policy are operating in parallel, funding similar—though not identical—investment activities based on different terms and conditions, processes and mechanisms.

The goal of this chapter is to offer a comparative analysis of the activities of the RRF and cohesion policy in post-pandemic Europe. The first section provides an overview of the developments that shaped the terms of the symbiosis of cohesion policy and RRF. In the following two sections, the similarities and differences among these policies are discussed—firstly in terms of strategy, budget allocation and eligibility and subsequently in terms of governance, management and institutions. The last section concludes.

---

[2] The most prominent examples are the bailout funds during the debt crisis of the early 2010s, the Facility for Refugees in Turkey in 2016 and, most recently, the various instruments created in response to the COVID-19 pandemic.

EU Cohesion Policy and NextGenerationEU

Since 1987, the European Union has undertaken explicit policy assignments in the name of 'economic, social and territorial cohesion'. As defined in the Treaty on the Functioning of the European Union (TFEU), cohesion is an imprecise and nebulous concept that is open to multiple interpretations. Emphasis is placed on the reduction of levels of development between regions (and, since 1993, countries), whereas no definition of social and territorial cohesion is provided. It can be argued that the goal of cohesion is only marginally linked to the traditional notion of economic solidarity. Instead, stress is placed on improving economic efficiency by using a variety of fiscal and non-fiscal instruments. The community and member states accordingly seek to improve the allocation of resources across the territory of the European Union and, in the long run, to ensure equal opportunities for the various economic actors (Andreou, 2007: 1).

Following the inclusion of the principle of cohesion in the Single European Act (1987), the EU undertook to coordinate the sum of the European and national policies promoting all aspects of cohesion. In this context, the Union has developed its own cohesion-promoting policy instruments—the European Structural and Investment Funds (ESIF).[3] These funds have been operating in a multi-annual, periodically revised programming framework based on a set of common principles. The complex policy space[4] that is composed of the European, national and subnational policies aimed at promoting cohesion is commonly referred to as 'cohesion policy' (Andreou, 2022). At the time of writing, cohesion policy is going through its sixth programming cycle lasting from 2021 to 2027 (following the programming cycles of 1989–1993, 1994–1999, 2000–2006, 2007–2013 and 2014–2020).

The cohesion policy space emerged between 1985 and 1989. The landmark budgetary reform of 1988 introduced the concept of multi-annual fiscal planning and endowed the ESIF with a substantial budget and a multi-annual governance framework based on the principles of concentration, partnership, programming and additionality. Between the formative period of 1989–1993 and the outbreak of the pandemic, cohesion policy underwent four successive revisions. The first two revisions (which took place in 1994 and 1999 respectively) followed an incremental logic. By contrast, the 2006 and the 2013 revisions introduced a substantial change in the position of cohesion policy in the EU budget and policy frameworks, by aligning the activities of the ESIF with the 'Lisbon Strategy' and its successor 'Europe 2020' strategy. The aforementioned changes went hand in hand with significant changes in the size and the allocation of resources dedicated to cohesion.

[3] For 2021–2027, ESIF comprise the European Regional Development Fund (ERDF), the European Social Fund+ (ESF+), the Cohesion Fund (CF) and the Just Transition Fund (JTF).

[4] The term 'policy space' refers to a specific group of policies, as well as to the institutional embodiments of the latter. Each of the policies contained within this space is so closely interlinked with the rest that it becomes impossible to describe or analyze it without also examining the components of the whole set (Hooghe, 1996: 94–95).

Firstly, EU expenditure in the name of cohesion experienced a spectacular increase between 1989 and 2013, but in the period 2014–2020 the cohesion budget was reduced for the first time. Secondly, since 2006, the intensity of EU aid in less developed regions has declined. Thirdly, the share of cohesion funds for the rest of the EU regions has grown from 15.8% in 2007–2013 to 27.6% in 2014–2020 (Andreou, 2017).

In 2018, the European Commission presented a set of general proposals for the 2021–2027 Multiannual Financial Framework (MFF), which sets out the ceilings of the EU's annual expenditure, as well as of the expenditure for the period 2021–2027 as a whole. Significant cuts in the resources dedicated to cohesion policy were proposed: the allocation for the ESIF would decrease by around 10% in real terms and the share of cohesion policy in the total MFF would fall from 34.1% to 29.2% (Andreou, 2022: 78). The 2018 proposals were followed by a year and a half of negotiations in the EU Council, a fruitless European Council meeting in February 2020 and the outbreak of the Covid-19 pandemic which triggered radical changes in the EU's financial plans. In April 2020, the European Council asked the Commission to come up with a proposal for a recovery fund of 'sufficient magnitude'. This idea was taken up by a Franco—German proposal for a temporary European recovery instrument endowed with €500 billion of grants. In May 2020, the Commission presented a comprehensive recovery package that included amended proposals for the 2021–2027 MFF and the proposal for establishing a European Union recovery instrument—named 'NextGenerationEU'—for the years 2021 to 2024 (Andreou, 2022: 79).

Following two months of talks in the Council of EU Ministers and a five-day negotiation in the European Council, the EU reached a political agreement on the MFF and the NextGenerationEU, in late July 2020. This agreement was not changed by the subsequent negotiations between the European Parliament and the Council and was legally sealed in December 2020. The agreed plan introduced several new and ambitious elements that broke new ground, making it, potentially, a catalyst for further European integration. On the revenue side, NextGenerationEU is funded by EU-Bond issuances executed by the European Commission; on top of that, to repay this borrowing, the EU has agreed to boost its own resources system with a tax on non – recycled plastic from 1 January 2021, and to consider additional resources, such as a carbon tax, a digital tax and a financial transactions tax. These changes in EU's own resources system are likely to be retained after 2026 (when NextGenerationEU expires) and may have profound effects on the future steps of European integration (Katsikas, 2021). On the expenditure side, the size of NextGenerationEU would make a macroeconomic difference, offering vital support to member states at a time of acute financial need (Ladi & Tsarouhas, 2020: 1049). However, this plan is subject to serious limitations: it is in fact an *ad hoc*, temporary, and extraordinary strategy to deal with an emergency (Katsikas, 2022: 12) running in parallel with the 'old' rules and processes that continue to govern the rest of 2021–2027 MFF. Besides, the 2020 budgetary reform did not essentially affect the institutional architecture of the 'old' cohesion policy space and did not increase its budget (Andreou, 2022).

The 2020 reform led to the creation of a new major expenditure category for the EU budget. For the 2021–2027 period, the so-called 'Heading 2' has been renamed 'Cohesion, resilience and values' and contains almost the total sum of the combined expenditure under cohesion policy and NextGenerationEU (Andreou, 2022: 80–81, European Court of Auditors, 2023: 14). On the one hand, cohesion policy was endowed with an overall budget of €377.7 billion (2018 prices), a level comparable to the allocation under the 2014–2020 MFF. On the other hand, NextGenerationEU acquired a budget of €750 billion (2018 prices).[5] Taken together, cohesion policy and NextGenerationEU represent almost 60% of the total EU budget expenditure for the 2021–2027 period.

Comparing RRF and Cohesion Policy: Strategy, Budget Allocation and Eligibility

The flagship instrument of NextGenerationEU is the *Recovery and Resilience Facility (RRF)*. RRF concentrates 90% of the total resources of NGEU (€672.5 billion at 2018 prices) and provides *grants* (€312.5 billion) *and loans* (€360 billion) to EU member states to support public investments and reforms, as set out in *National Recovery and Resilience Plans* (NRRPs). The official mission of the RRF is 'to promote the Union's economic, social and territorial cohesion…, by mitigating the social and economic impact of that crisis…, by contributing to the implementation of the European Pillar of Social Rights, by supporting the green transition, by contributing to the achievement of the Union's 2030 climate targets and by complying with the objective of EU climate neutrality by 2050 and of the digital transition' (European Parliament and Council, 2021a: 31).

Officially, RRF and cohesion policy are both serving the cohesion objective (Andreou, 2022; Patrin, 2023).[6] However, the spending priorities of these two financial instruments are structured and presented differently. On the one hand, policy areas funded by RRF are structured around *six pillars*: (1) green transition, (2) digital transformation, (3) smart, sustainable and inclusive growth (including economic cohesion), (4) social and territorial cohesion, (5) health, and economic social and institutional resilience and (6) policies for the next generation, children and youth (including education and skills). On the other hand, the 2021–2027 cohesion policy

[5] It should be considered, however, that there is some overlap between the expenditure under cohesion policy and NextGenerationEU: under another financial instrument in the new recovery package, REACT-EU, roughly 8% of the financial envelope of NextGenerationEU was spent to complement actions under the ESIF by providing immediate assistance to the regions most affected by the crisis caused by the pandemic.

[6] This view is not universally accepted. For instance, Lopriore (2022: 1) argues that RRF and EU cohesion policy have different objectives: 'The first aims to help the recovery and resilience of our economies, while the second promotes economic, social and territorial cohesion among the Member States and regions of the EU'.

supports *five policy objectives*: (1) smarter Europe by promoting innovative and smart economic transformation; (2) a greener, low-carbon Europe by promoting clean and fair energy transition, green and blue investment, the circular economy, climate adaptation and risk prevention and management; (3) a more connected Europe by enhancing mobility and regional ICT connectivity; (4) a more social Europe implementing the European Pillar of Social Rights; and (5) a Europe closer to citizens by fostering the sustainable and integrated development of urban, rural and coastal areas and local initiatives (Bachtler & Mendez, 2020: 245).

Moreover, there are specific differences in how the EU funding can be allocated under the RRF and the cohesion policy. Regarding RRF, the first two of its six priorities take precedence over the rest: at least 37% of the RRF's total allocation must contribute to mainstreaming climate actions and environmental sustainability; furthermore, at least 20% of the RRF budget must be dedicated to digital expenditure that will contribute to accelerating digital transformation. The 2021–2027 cohesion policy, on the other hand, has a thematic concentration requirement: a minimum proportion of ERDF and CF resources must be allocated to innovation (at least 25%, rising to 85% for the most developed regions) and the green transition (at least 30%) for ESF+, to social inclusion (at least 25%), youth employment (at least 12.5%), tackling child poverty (at least 5%) and supporting the most deprived persons (at least 3%) (Court of Auditors, 2023: 15).

NRRPs should propose a congruent set of reforms and public investment projects to be implemented between 2021 and 2026 and are subject to both broad and narrow conditionality. At the strategic level, NRRPs are (expected to be) fully consistent with the country-specific recommendations (CSRs) issued by the Council to Eurozone member states on an annual basis in the context of the European Semester. Furthermore, they must comply with the National Reform Programmes under the European Semester, the National Energy and Climate Plans, the territorial just transition plans, the Youth Guarantee implementation plans and, finally, the partnership agreements and operational programmes under cohesion policy (European Parliament and Council, 2021a).

In the case of cohesion policy, investment priorities are defined during the programming process for the 7-year 2021–2027 period and should also take into account the CSRs. Nevertheless, according to the European Court of Auditors (2023), in the past, member states had often not implemented their CSRs in full, and the link between EU cohesion spending and CSR implementation was rather weak. In principle, RRF funding is linked with national structural reforms more directly than cohesion policy: firstly, the RRF regulation requires member states to address in their RRPs 'all or a significant subset' of challenges included in CSRs; secondly, the reporting requirements of the RRF were integrated into the European Semester: if thus the Commission judges that reforms in the RRPs do not sufficiently address the challenges that member states are facing, it can propose additional CSRs (Court of Auditors, 2023: 16–17). Patrin (2023) argues that earmarking attached to the RRF is also stronger when compared with earmarking under cohesion policy: RRF funds must be used for projects pertaining to specific sectors and areas, defined by the Commission (and approved by the Council and the European Parliament) on the basis of its policy agenda (Patrin, 2023: 14).

Owing to the 'n + 3 rule', the eligibility period for the 2021–2027 cohesion policy funds is 9 years, and it runs beyond the end of the programming period. In contrast, the RRF's eligibility period is only six years. During this period, the agreed milestones and targets must be attained, and the related payments can be made until the end of 2026. On top of that, cohesion policy and the RRF use different methods for allocating funding between member states

- The allocation of the cohesion policy financial envelope takes into account national and regional disparities and is based on a well-established formula applied since 1999 (the so-called Berlin method). In this context, the main allocation criterion for cohesion policy funds is *regional* GDP and gross *national* income (GNI) per capita, i.e. relative prosperity compared to the EU average, adjusted for purchasing power, while unemployment rates, education levels, net migration from outside the EU and greenhouse gas emissions are also taken into account (Court of Auditors, 2023: 18). Poland is the largest recipient of 2021–2027 cohesion policy funding (20%), followed by Italy (12%) and Spain (10%).
- The method for allocating funds under the RRF was agreed in July 2020. More specifically, 70% of RRF grants[7] are allocated for the period 2021–2022 and are distributed to member states according to three criteria: (1) the size of a member state's population, (2) the inverse of its GDP per capita and (3) the average unemployment rate in the years 2015–2019. For the remaining 30% of RRF grants allocated for 2023, the unemployment criterion is replaced by the change in real GDP observed over 2020 and by the aggregated change in real GDP over the years 2020–2021 (European Parliament and Council, 2021a). Spain and Italy are the two largest beneficiaries of the RRF grant component, together receiving 43% of the final RRF allocation.

To sum up, unlike cohesion policy, RRF is not aiming at reducing regional and national development disparities simultaneously, as it focuses exclusively on the latter. It is also worth noting that pre-pandemic disparities were a bigger factor in determining the allocation of RRF grants than the economic impact of the pandemic, even though mitigating the latter was one of the RRF's primary objectives. More importantly, the different allocation keys under cohesion funding and the RRF reflect the fact that, whereas cohesion policy is a place-based, regionally anchored long-term investment policy, with a focus on territorial development and ultimately

[7] A maximum RRF loan amount of 6.8% of 2019 GNI applies in each member state. However, the amount of the loan support can be increased in exceptional circumstances and subject to availability of resources (i.e. other member states have not used their loan component in full). In practice, RRF loans are most attractive to those states that borrow with an interest rate higher than that of the Commission. In effect, Italy, Greece and Romania were the only states which requested the maximum amount.

aimed at fostering economic convergence, growth and jobs, the RRF is a reform and investment-oriented instrument, operating predominantly at national level (Koopman, 2022: 29).

Comparing RRF and Cohesion Policy: Governance, Management and Institutions

Cohesion policy and RRF also differ significantly regarding the division of responsibilities between EU institutions and member states. Cohesion policy actions are implemented under shared management, through both national and regional programmes. Hundreds of national and regional authorities in the member states are involved in programming, implementation, monitoring and auditing. Beneficiaries of ESIF funds can be public or private bodies, entities without legal personality or natural persons that are responsible for initiating or both initiating and implementing operations (European Parliament and Council, 2021b). On the other hand, the RRF is implemented under direct management, and member states are officially the beneficiaries. At the same time, member states are responsible for ensuring compliance with key principles of sound financial management. At state level, a lead authority (the 'RRF coordinator') has overall responsibility and acts as the single point of contact for the Commission; national ministries or regional authorities may be entrusted with implementing projects and reporting to this coordinator on their progress.

Important differences between the two financial instruments exist also with respect to the division of powers and responsibilities between EU institutions. While in the case of cohesion policy it is the Commission (DG REGIO and DG EMP) that shares the responsibility with the member states for managing cohesion policy programmes, the situation for RRF is different. Before adopting the decision authorizing any disbursements under RRF, the Commission must submit its preliminary assessment and take into account the opinion of the Council's Economic and Financial Committee. A committee of member states' representatives must then examine the Commission's decision and can overturn it with a qualified majority. In addition, there is a differentiation in the policy responsibilities of the European Parliament. The Parliament's power to approve the annual expenditure of the EU budget—according to the EU terminology, to 'grant discharge to the Commission'—applies to both cohesion policy and the grants component of the RRF; this discharge, however, does not cover the loan component of the RRF (Court of Auditors, 2023: 24–25).

Comparing management processes, RRF programming is more centralized than cohesion policy. As it has already been mentioned, RRF implementation is based on a single programming document for each member state—the NRRP—approved by the Council. Each NRRP details the investments and reforms supported by the RRF grants and, where relevant, loans. It is assessed by the Commission, which provides a proposal for a Council Implementing Decision (CID) setting out a binding set of measures, the associated milestones and targets to be achieved and the number and amount of instalments. Once the CID is adopted, it is complemented by 'operational arrangements' dealing with technical implementation issues, the financing agreements on which the budgetary commitments are based and the loan agreements, if applicable (Bokhorst & Corti, 2023: 2). In the case of cohesion policy funds, each member state signs a partnership agreement with the Commission. This document sets out the strategic orientation of the funding and the arrangements for using it; it also contains details of national or regional operational programmes intended to address the main challenges facing the country or the region. The Commission adopts implementing acts to approve both the partnership agreement and each individual programme.[8] Any subsequent changes to cohesion policy programmes only require the assessment and approval of the Commission, whereas changes to NRRPs require the Commission's assessment and a Council's approval as well. This creates a safeguard to ensure that member states do follow their commitments.

Finally, it is important to note that the partnership principle—one of the organizing principles of cohesion policy—is not a prerequisite for the RRF. Member states must apply the partnership principle when implementing cohesion policy in accordance with the European code of conduct on partnership. Public authorities at regional, local and urban level, civil-society organizations as well as economic and social partners must thus all contribute to drawing up partnership agreements and to preparing, implementing and evaluating each programme. The procedure used for the RRF is different; when drawing up NRRPs, national authorities are required to consult local and regional authorities, social partners, civil society and youth organizations only to the extent this is required by domestic legislation. The applicable consultation procedure is summarized in the NRRPs themselves (Court of Auditors, 2023: 29–31).

Discussion

Developing policy complementarities between cohesion policy and RRF has become a key priority for the European Union and its members. Avoiding duplication and overlaps is a basic policy goal.[9] More specifically, there is a need to ensure an efficient and coherent allocation of funds to avoid double funding and 'crowding out' of cohesion policy. Increasing synergies between the two instruments may also

[8] 379 different cohesion policy programmes were adopted for the 2021–2027 period (European Commission, 2023: 27).

[9] Article 28 of the RRF Regulation provides for complementarity, synergies and consistency between RRF resources and other national or EU financial instruments. This article requires member states to make an optimization effort to avoid the duplication of instruments and cooperation between administrations. On top of that, the RRF regulation stipulates that consistency is 1 of the 11 evaluation criteria for the NRRPs (Lopriore, 2022:2).

have other significant benefits, including (a) effectiveness gains from articulating more coherent strategies and coordinating investments; (b) efficiency gains from sharing capacities, resources and knowledge across funding bodies; (c) strengthened transparency and accountability in establishing a more visible link between EU policies and needs at national and regional levels; and (d) promoting learning and exchange between policies and instruments to inform reform processes (Bachtler et al., 2022: 24–29; Ferry & Kah, 2021).

Achieving complementarity and avoiding overlaps is a difficult task at multiple levels. Firstly, regarding strategy, there is considerable overlap between RRF and cohesion policy. Member states must use the RRF to promote cohesion, as well as strengthening economic and social resilience, mitigating the social and economic impact of crises and supporting the green and digital transitions. Cohesion policy also pursues these priorities and is putting increasing focus on closing the digital divide, making progress towards the zero-pollution ambition and supporting resource efficiency and investments in green infrastructure and mobility. This strategic overlap is particularly visible in 'pillar four' of RRF (labelled 'social and territorial cohesion'), which is almost identical with objectives four and five of cohesion policy (Sapala, 2024: 2); there is also significant overlap between 'pillar three' of RRF ('smart, sustainable and inclusive growth, including economic cohesion') and objectives one, two and four of cohesion policy. This overlap risks duplication and rivalry between RRF and cohesion policy, particularly as RRF is perceived as offering stronger incentives for beneficiaries (e.g. in terms of timescale, aid intensity and financial management). This asymmetry may have significant implications for the absorption of cohesion funding and for the broad objective of cohesion (Bachtler et al., 2022: 23).

Secondly, the shared commitment of RRF and cohesion policy to the strategic objective of cohesion is not translated to a common programming approach. Although economic, social and territorial cohesions are explicitly in the scope and objectives of the RRF, cohesion does not appear to be a significant objective of NRRPs. For the most part, NRRPs follow a 'sectoral logic' with a focus on maximizing national economic recovery and growth. Primacy is given to investments that promote the green and digital transitions which require minimum thresholds of expenditure. While cohesion is in many cases mentioned among the general objectives and/or the expected impacts of the NRRPs, there is often a lack of detail on how this will be delivered, as well as a lack of performance and impact assessment information. Cohesion is sometimes interpreted as economic convergence arising from national economic growth (i.e. more growth and investment is beneficial to all regions) rather than the territorial meaning of cohesion and place-based approach understood under cohesion policy. In sum, the NRRPs are only partially addressing the territorial dimension of development (that is prominent in cohesion policy), and their programming coordination with cohesion policy leaves much to be desired (Bachtler & Dozhdeva, 2021).

Thirdly, at the implementation level, the simultaneous preparation of partnership agreements and operational programmes (under cohesion policy) and NRRPs (under the RRF) has complicated coordination and overloaded administrative capacity across member states. More specifically:

- Whereas some member states are using the same authorities to manage cohesion policy alongside RRF (enabling interventions to be coordinated), other states have separate governance structures for different funding streams with limited coordination.
- The sectoral or thematic focus of RRF is challenging to align with cohesion policy in terms of geographical targeting and resource allocation.
- The involvement of local and regional authorities in the governance of new instruments varies greatly, with minimal involvement under many NRRPs (Bachtler et al., 2022: 23).

At the level of governance and management, between 2021 and 2026, national governments and administrations have undertaken the multiple tasks of launching their NRRPs, absorbing the remaining cohesion funds from the 2014–2020 period, absorbing the extra funds granted under REACT-EU during 2021 and 2022[10] and launching the new cohesion programmes for the 2021–2027 period. It has been noted that the simplified planning and decision-making process under the RRF allowed for the quick initiation of NRRPs, with some notable exceptions. More specifically, by the end of 2023, all NRRPs were up and running[11]; however, only 19 EU member states had received one or more payments (Bulgaria, Czechia, Denmark, Estonia, Greece, Spain, France, Croatia, Italy, Cyperus, Latvia, Lithuania, Luxembourg, Malta, Austria, Portugal, Romania, Slovakia and Slovenia). On the other hand, the adoption of 2021–2027 cohesion policy programmes has been hampered by considerable delays; as a consequence, member states will have to absorb their allocated funds for the 2021–2027 in a shorter timeframe than in the previous programming periods (Court of Auditors, 2023: 37).

The global energy crisis caused by Russia's invasion in Ukraine was an unforeseen factor that triggered a series of revisions in the RRF and the NRRPs, further complicating the picture in terms of (re)programming and implementation. More specifically, in May 2022, the EU introduced the REPowerEU Plan, which aims at rapidly decreasing the Union's dependency on Russian fossil fuels. The establishment of REPowerEU had a direct and visible impact on the RRF legal framework, programming and implementation. Under the revised RRF regulation, which entered into force in March 2023, member states were obliged to revise their NRRPs to include an additional REPowerEU chapter focused on energy and listing reforms and investments that will deliver on the objectives of the latter. In exchange, they would have access to a total sum of €245 billion—of which €225 billion are loans still available under RRF and €20 billion are new grants, to be financed through the frontloaded sale of Emissions Trading System (ETS) allowances (40%) and the

[10] See note 3.

[11] The last NRRP to be adopted was Hungary's—it was approved by the Council on 15 December 2022.

resources of the Innovation Fund (60%). Member states were also given the opportunity to use existing resources under cohesion policy in order to support the objectives of REPowerEU (European Parliament and Council, 2023).[12] By the end of 2023, all but three member states had submitted modified NRRPs with new REPowerEU chapters to the Commission, and most of these plans were approved by the Council (D'Alfonso et al., 2023: 4).

At the time of writing, the official point of view of the EU institutions is that RRF implementation is broadly on track. In terms of effectiveness, a major concern is the quality of the plans, given the speed with which they were drafted and assessed. Regarding implementation efficiency, it is still unclear how and to what extent member states—particularly those hit hardest by the pandemic and those with weak administrations—will be able to absorb their allocated funds within the prescribed time limit (Schramm et al., 2022: 120–121). A further note of caution applies to administrative bodies which are involved in simultaneously implementing cohesion policy programmes through different management systems. Considering the issues of coherence between RRF and cohesion policy, the prioritization of the RRF over other EU funds has already had an impact on the absorption and capacity of cohesion policy; moreover, there is evidence of weak coordination between NRRPs and cohesion policy programmes with a risk of competition for projects and lack of exploitation of synergies.[13] Finally, two major issues may be raised regarding accountability. A first important question is how the Council exercises its role and whether member states are prepared to criticize each other's plans and their implementation (Bachtler & Mendez, 2023: 16–18). A second, broader, issue derives from the centralized nature of the RRF; the lack of engagement of subnational and non-governmental actors into the RRF policy process is highly problematic and may also undermine the multilevel nature of the cohesion policy process.

Conclusion

Over the past few years, in response to various crises, shocks and/or perceived new needs and priorities,[14] the EU has systematically resorted to the establishment of new off-budget spending instruments. While the European annual budget and the MFF remain the most important European financial instruments in terms of size, temporary new instruments have been created, most of which earmark transfers, in the

[12] The funding mechanism devised for REPowerEU is another example of the EU employing preexisting financial instrument to confront new crises.

[13] RRF may be perceived as offering an 'easier' management system, and a substitution effect could arise. There is also a risk of duplication as RRF, and cohesion policy payments may be subject to different levels of control and audit potentially involving the same beneficiaries. This may be unclear to beneficiaries and public authorities.

[14] As a reminder, the EU has set itself ambitious goals in the fields of climate, environmental protection, digitalization, industrial policy and security and defense.

form of grants or loans, to national governments to promote specific expenditures. The most prominent example of these new instruments is NextGenerationEU—a worthwhile, timely and potentially transformative initiative that demonstrated the Union's capacity to respond to crisis that is, however, *ad hoc* and temporary. At the same time, the EU actors continued to utilize cohesion policy as 'a wallet for other EU policies or goals' (Polverari, 2013), by aligning it with both with their short-term goals (i.e. combatting the economic effects of the pandemic) and with their strategic priorities (i.e. promoting the green and digital transitions).

RRF—the most important component of is NextGenerationEU—is established in the name of economic, social and territorial cohesion (a deliberately vague and ambiguous concept) and, from 2021 to 2026, operates in parallel with the Union's 'old' cohesion policy that is following the 2021–2027 programming cycle of the MFF. At first glance, cohesion policy and RRF appear to be two sides of the same coin: both are investment driven and with a macroeconomic impact, and both contribute to the EU's green and digital transitions. However, their design is intrinsically different, reflecting different purposes: whereas the core objective of cohesion policy is to promote economic convergence in the EU's territory, the RRF attempts to respond to the economic and social challenges posed by COVID-19 (Koopman, 2022) and to economic and geopolitical concerns raised by the Ukraine war and the global energy crisis. Harmonizing the core objectives of cohesion policy and RRF with the EU's green, digital and energy agenda is a challenge for both, albeit for very different reasons. Besides, as has been analysed in the previous sections, RRF and cohesion policy are functioning on the basis of distinct terms and conditions and are following different processes and mechanisms.

Avoiding duplication and overlaps and developing policy complementarities between cohesion policy and RRF are a key objective for EU and national policy-makers. Considering the limited timeframe, as well as the numerous delays and complications that have marked the launch of both RRF and the new cohesion policy, it is too soon to reach definitive conclusions about the success of this attempt. From a cohesion point of view, the most problematic element in the symbiosis of these financial instruments is the weak emphasis placed by RRF on regional and local disparities. In any case, fragmentation in implementation arrangements across instruments, funds and levels of governance is and will remain a persistent challenge for all stakeholders for the remainder of the current programming period and, most likely, for the foreseeable future.

References

Andreou, G. (2007). The New EU Cohesion Policy: Enlargement, "Lisbonisation" and the challenge of diversity. ELIAMEP- EU CONSENT Second Year Annual State of the Art Report, Hellenic Foundation for European & Foreign Policy (ELIAMEP).

Andreou, G. (2017). EU cohesion policy: A policy in search of identity. In S. Verney & A. Kontis (Eds.), *European integration: Multiple crises and challenges of the future* (pp. 493–512). Papazisis. (in Greek).

Andreou, G. (2022). Solidarity in the EU after 2020; prospects for the cohesion "policy space". *Region & Periphery, 13*(13), 65–90.

Bachtler, J., & Dozhdeva, V. (2021). *The Recovery & Resilience Fund: An economic stimulus at the expense of territorial cohesion?* European Policies Research Centre Blog, University of Strathclyde. https://eprc-strath.org/the-recovery-resilience-fund-an-economic-stimulus-at-the-expense-of-territorial-cohesion/. Accessed 10 Dec 2023.

Bachtler, J., & Mendez, C. (2020). Cohesion policy: Doing more with less. In H. Wallace, M. Pollack, C. Roederer-Rynning, & A. Young (Eds.), *Policy-making in the European Union* (8th ed., pp. 232–253). Oxford University Press.

Bachtler, J., & Mendez, C. (2023, December). Navigating stormy waters: crises and cohesion policy beyond 2027. EoRPA Report 23/3, European Regional Policy Research Research Centre, University of Strathclyde Publishing. https://eprc-strath.org/wp-content/uploads/2023/12/Cohesion-Policy-EoRPA-report-23_3-ISBN.pdf. Accessed 3 Jan 2024.

Bachtler, J., Mendez, C., & Ferry, M (2022). *Towards a green and digital transition: The new cohesion policy strategies and reform debate.* EoRPA Report 22/2, EoRPA Regional Policy Research Consortium, European Policies Research Centre, University of Strathclyde, Glasgow and EPRC Delft.

Begg, I. (2023, July). The EU's increasingly complex finances: A ticking bomb? *EconPol Forum, 24*(4), 16–20.

Bokhorst, D., & Corti, F. (2023). Governing Europe's recovery and resilience facility: Between discipline and discretion. *Government and Opposition, 2023*, 1–17. https://doi.org/10.1017/gov.2023.14

D'Alfonso, A. l., Höflmayr, M., & Sabbati, G. (2023, December). *Monitoring the EU's economic outlook; Seeking to avoid a hard landing*. Briefing, European Parliamentary Research Service (EPRS).

European Commission. (2017). *Reflection paper on the future of EU finances.* COM(2017) 358, Brussels, 28.6.2017.

European Commission. (2023). *Cohesion 2021–2027: Forging an ever stronger Union – Report on the outcome of 2021–2027 cohesion policy programming.* Commission Staff Working Document, SWD(2023) 134 final, Brussels, 28.4.2023.

European Court of Auditors. (2023). *EU financing through cohesion policy and the recovery and resilience facility: A comparative analysis.* Review 01/2023. https://www.eca.europa.eu/en/publications/RW23_01. Accessed 10 Nov 2023.

European Parliament and Council. (2021a). Regulation (EU) 2021/241 of the European Parliament and of the Council of 12 February 2021 establishing the Recovery and Resilience Facility. *Official Journal of the European Union*, L 057, 18.02.2021.

European Parliament and Council. (2021b). Regulation (EU) 2021/1060 of the European Parliament and of the Council of 24 June 2021 laying down common provisions on the European Regional Development Fund, the European Social Fund Plus, the Cohesion Fund, the Just Transition Fund and the European Maritime, Fisheries and Aquaculture Fund and financial rules for those and for the Asylum, Migration and Integration Fund, the Internal Security Fund and the Instrument for Financial Support for Border Management and Visa Policy. *Official Journal of the European Union*, L 231, 30.06.2021.

European Parliament and Council. (2023). Regulation (EU) 2023/435 of the European Parliament and of the Council of 27 February 2023 amending Regulation (EU) 2021/241 as regards REPowerEU chapters in recovery and resilience plans and amending Regulations (EU) No 1303/2013, (EU) 2021/1060 and (EU) 2021/1755, and Directive 2003/87/EC'. *Official Journal of the European Union*, L 063, 28.2.2023.

Ferry, M., & Kah, S. (2021). Pursuing positive interactions – Within structural funds and with the RRF. *IQ-Net Thematic Paper, 48*(2), European Policies Research Centre Delft.

Hooghe, L. (1996). Building a Europe with the regions: The changing role of the European Commission. In L. Hooghe (Ed.), *Cohesion policy and European integration: Building multi-level governance* (pp. 89–127). Oxford University Press.

Katsikas, D. (2021). Reforming under pressure: The evolution of Eurozone's fiscal governance during a decade of crises. In J. Caetano, I. Vieira, & A. Caleiro (Eds.), *New challenges for the Eurozone governance joint solutions for common threats?* Springer.

Katsikas, D. (2022). Health and economic responses to the COVID-19 crisis in the EU. *Region & Periphery, 13*(13), 7–21.

Koopman, G. J. (2022). Cohesion policy and the recovery and resilience facility: Not just two sides of the same coin. *European Court of Auditors Journal, 1/2022*, 27–31. https://www.eca.europa.eu/lists/ecadocuments/journal22_01/journal22_01.pdf. Accessed 13 Dec 2023.

Ladi, S., & Tsarouhas, D. (2020). EU economic governance and Covid-19: Policy learning and windows of opportunity. *Journal of European Integration, 42*(8), 1041–1056.

Lopriore, M. (2022, February). *Recovery plans and structural funds: How to strengthen the link?*. EIPA Briefing, Maastricht. https://www.eipa.eu/publications/briefing/recovery-plans-and-structural-funds-how-to-strengthen-the-link/. Accessed 11 Nov 2023.

Patrin, M. (2023, February). *Governance by funding: NGEU, solidarity and the EU institutional balance* (Rebuild Centre Working Paper, 4). https://papers.ssrn.com/sol3/papers.cfm?abstract_id=4361461. Accessed 11 Nov 2023.

Polverari, L. (2013, September 6). *The European Unions cohesion policy between equity, austerity and relaunch*. Presentation at Seminario International, Santa Cruz de Sol.

Sapala, M. (2024, January). *Social and territorial cohesion in the recovery and resilience facility*. Briefing, European Parliamentary Research Service (EPRS).

Schramm, L., Krotz, U., & De Witte, B. (2022). Building 'Next Generation' after the pandemic: The implementation and implications of the EU Covid Recovery Plan. *Journal of Common Market Studies, 60*, 114–124. https://doi.org/10.1111/jcms.13375

Chapter 8
The European Failure to Tackle 'Too-Big-to-Fail' Banks

Mikael Mäkipää, David Howarth, and Scott James

Contents

Introduction

The perception of inevitable crisis has long faced the banking sector. Crisis talk ranges from Marxist retorts of how conflictual features of capitalism will lead to its destruction to the general public's contempt of the boom-bust cycle. Regulatory responses to the global financial crisis (GFC) aimed to ensure that what happened would not be repeated, hence either preventing or at least discouraging those banking activities deemed to be excessively risky. However, failed and diluted pieces of key legislation in advanced economies have put into question whether or not this

Material in this chapter borrows in part from Howarth and James (2023).

M. Mäkipää · D. Howarth (✉)
University of Luxembourg, Belval-Esch-sur-Alzette, Luxembourg
e-mail: david.howarth@uni.lu

S. James
King's College London, London, UK

D. Katsikas et al. (eds.), *Finance, Growth and Democracy: Connections and Challenges in Europe and Latin America in the Era of Permacrisis*, United Nations University Series on Regionalism 33, https://doi.org/10.1007/978-3-031-68475-3_8

'never again' is as determined as the urgency of the post-GFC discourse suggested. This chapter sheds light on why and how banking regulation in the era of 'permacrisis' failed to address important structural problems linked to a pivotal group in European banking: too-big-to-fail universal banks.

Universal banks with notable investment banking operations were central to the international financial crisis that severely shook the US and European economies (Hardie & Howarth, 2013a). Labelled 'too big to fail' (TBTF) due to their structural economic significance, these banks were actively involved in the creation, sale and purchase of securitised assets, and many relied heavily on short-term interbank wholesale markets. Despite the increased appetite for a major regulatory overhaul of banking within many governments, the main issues of TBTF banks—excessive risk-taking and potential reliance on the public purse to cover losses—were in many respects inadequately addressed.

This chapter investigates national government and European Union (EU) regulatory approaches in the aftermath of the financial crisis and their contribution to mitigating TBTF risks. This chapter examines four European countries with large banking sectors both in terms of total assets and assets to GDP—respectively, the UK, Germany, France and the Netherlands—EU-level regulatory developments and, by way of comparison, the US. All five countries had banking systems that were severely impacted by the 2008 crisis, necessitating huge government bailouts and generating significant political pressure to tackle TBTF banks. However, only a select few of the post-crisis reforms—notably the US and UK structural reforms—had a significant impact in addressing the issue of TBTF. Nearly all EU and national level legislation on capital requirements, liquidity rules, resolution rules, resolution plans and structural reform fell short of the goals set by the G20's Financial Stability Board (FSB) and the Basel Committee of Banking Supervisors (BCBS).

While most regulatory efforts were preoccupied with 'stability'—preventing future financial crises of a similar magnitude—several other goals were at play. These included minimising the pressures to resort to government funds in TBTF bank bailouts, restricting the systemic impact of bank failure, securing lending to non-financial companies and preventing or at least containing the highest-risk market-based banking activities. Some national legislation—as with capital requirements—resulted from international commitments. Many national governments also adopted a number of unilateral changes to domestic bank regulation and supervision, often in anticipation of—or with the aim to shape—international and EU rules. More commonly, however, governments refrained from doing anything prior to agreement on international guidelines or EU regulation lest the international competitiveness of national banks be undermined.

The pre-crisis regulatory preferences of our case study countries ranged from long-standing German and French pleas for tougher financial market regulation to US, UK and Dutch government hostility to most international regulatory developments, preferring instead their domestic 'light-touch' approaches (Blitz, 2005; *Financieel Management,* 2004; Zimmermann, 2010). Germany and France had already pushed for several reforms at the international and European levels, often contested vocally by the British and less so by the Americans and the Dutch. In the EU, the ensuing debate surrounding post-crisis regulation and supervision reflected the very same rift (Posner & Véron, 2010; Quaglia, 2010). Despite apparent differences in national positions, this chapter argues that when it comes to their impact on the TBTF issue, many of the post-2007 regulations in the five case countries were similarly limited, while the UK and the US went far further in two important areas than the French, Germans and Dutch.

This chapter contributes to the vast literature spawned by the crisis on the transformation of financial regulation, much of it devoted to key national jurisdictions, including the US (e.g. Pagliari & Young, 2014; Young & Pagliari, 2017), the UK (e.g. James, 2018; James & Quaglia, 2020), France and Germany (Hardie & Macartney, 2016; Massoc, 2020) and the Netherlands (Ganderson, 2020). Studies examining bank structural and other reforms have increased in recent years, but these tend to be either single case studies (e.g. James, 2018) or typically only compare a few European countries (Bell & Hindmoor, 2015; Ganderson, 2020; Hardie & Macartney, 2016; Howarth & James, 2020; Quaglia & Spendzharova, 2017; Massoc, 2020). Hence there has been only limited academic effort to compare a wider number of countries or to contrast the US and European experience. Howarth and James' (2023) comprehensive study of structural reform is a noteworthy exception.

This chapter examines government regulatory responses that targeted directly or indirectly TBTF banks and were designed to constrain banking activities. Given limited space, this chapter does not examine regulatory responses focused on special bank levies, remuneration, governance, credit rating agencies or the reinforcement of bank supervision—which are potentially relevant but secondary to tackling TBTF. Specifically, this chapter considers regulatory changes on capital requirements, liquidity, resolution, resolution planning and structural reform. The analysis of this chapter considers the global-level Basel III guidelines, as well as the relevant national and EU-level policies, minding their complex interplay.

In most advanced economies, the banking sector had expanded significantly during the decade leading up to the global financial crisis. The growth of universal banks in Western Europe and the US was substantial until 2007 (Table 8.A1 in the appendix). During the decade after the financial crisis, the majority of advanced economies—including four out of the five in our sample—featured shrinking or stagnating banking sectors relative to GDP (Table 8.A2 in the appendix) or even in real terms. Despite this, the largest national banks mostly maintained or even increased their relative standing—measured by assets relative to total national banking assets and GDP—within the sector, and the number of systemically important banks remained high (Tables 8.A1, 8.A3 and 8.A4 in the appendix). TBTF banks thus largely retained their dominant positions—even in the face of a decade of regulation aimed at tackling their systemic importance and the potential consequences of their failure for national economies and banking systems.

Contested Capital Requirements

Capital requirements not only ensure a safety net for times of turmoil but also restrict the amount of leverage available to financial firms. Capital requirements are thus a key instrument to ensure banking and financial sector stability as well as to protect the government purse from necessary bailouts. For that reason, US Treasury Secretary Timothy Geithner proclaimed in connection to the financial crisis that the highest priorities should be 'capital, capital, and capital' (Leonhardt, 2010). Pre-existing international and EU-level agreements were under significant pressure to be overhauled. A cornerstone of the pre-crisis global framework was the Basel I Accord on 'International convergence of capital measurement and capital standards' issued in 1988 by the Basel Committee on Banking Supervision (BCBS) and updated and revised in 2004 and 2005 as the Basel II Accord. The 'soft' rules of the Basel Accords were then incorporated by countries into legally binding national legislation. The EU transposition of the Basel Accords into the EU law through the capital requirements directives (CRD) allowed a wide margin of manoeuvre in their national implementation (Howarth & Quaglia, 2013). The US had refused to implement Basel guidelines into national law prior to the 2008 financial crisis.

The Obama administration demonstrated global leadership with its calls for tougher capital requirements, stricter leverage rules for banks and a ban on 'hybrid' capital that in normal periods is considered loss absorbing but ceases to be so during crises. At the international level, the G20's Financial Stability Board (FSB) adopted a similar, albeit vaguer position on capital by committing to a deadline of 2010 for an agreement and voicing support for a leverage ratio to complement the Basel II framework. The BCBS took a surprisingly hard-line approach to capital requirements, agreeing to a new set of rules in December 2010, providing (1) a tightening of the definition of bank capital, (2) increased risk weights for several assets, (3) capital buffers, (4) a recommended, potentially obligatory leverage ratio and (5) international guidelines on liquidity management. This Basel III Accord increased the required proportion of capital with proven loss-absorbing capacity—known as core tier-1 (equity) capital—in comparison to Basel II. The requirements were to be phased in between 2013 and 2019. For systematically important banks in particular, Basel III proposed the adoption of a simple 3% leverage ratio (BCBS, 2010).

The US shifted its policy on Basel requirements. The Federal Reserve proclaimed in 2010 its willingness to comply with Basel III, applying its requirements to all institutions with over $50 billion in assets, be they banks or non-banks. In contrast to Europe, the US regulation agreed in July 2013 set additional requirements for the largest banks. These imposed an additional 2.5% capital conservation buffer on top of the 4.5% Basel III minimum common equity tier-1 (CET1) ratio, increased the minimum ratio of tier 1 to risk-weighted assets from 4% to 6% and imposed upon large globally important US banks an additional G-SIB surcharge from 2016 onwards. In addition, in comparison to the BCBS-proposed tier-1 leverage ratio of 3%, the largest US bank holding companies were required to hold a leverage ratio of 5%. To highlight the rare bipartisan political consensus on the matter in the US, capital requirements were left untouched during the Trump administration's efforts to unravel many of the regulations in the Dodd-Frank Act after 2017. However, the debate on capital requirements resurfaced in the United States in the wake of the 2023 Banking Crisis, with the Federal Reserve proposing a 19% increase to capital requirements for the largest US banks. By September 2024, the Fed revised its proposal downwards to 9% due to the fervent opposition of the banking industry — the latter's hostility partially explained by the strictness of the earlier implementation of Basel III rules (Smith et al., 2024).

Such consensus on Basel III rules along political—let alone national—lines did not exist in the EU where many banks would face significant pressures to raise equity or other eligible forms of capital or dramatically reduce their lending and higher-risk investment banking practices. The EU's take on Basel III transposition—the fourth Capital Requirements Directive (CRDIV)—crucially allowed for a national margin of manoeuvre by setting two distinct capital buffers. The first—the capital conservation buffer—was set commonly for all banks in the EU, whereas the second, the countercyclical capital buffer, was to be determined domestically. The directive was complemented by the Capital Requirements Regulation (CRR) which set a *maximum* capital level applicable to all EU-headquartered banks. The aim was to prevent governments from undermining competitiveness by taking 'unfair' action to prop up the capital buffers of national banks (Howarth & Quaglia, 2013).

Shortcomings became apparent in the FSB's report (2020) published a decade after Basel III, which concluded that four out of our five case study countries had failed in their implementation of important elements of the capital requirements guidelines. The US, except with regard to the net stable funding ratio (NSFR) (discussed below), was found either compliant or largely compliant in all the relevant categories. France, Germany, the Netherlands and the UK only received a (mostly) clean bill of health on the liquidity coverage ratio but were all deemed materially non-compliant regarding risk-based capital rules. None of these four countries succeeded in implementing the Basel III guidelines on large exposures (2019 deadline), leverage ratio (2018) or the NSFR (2018) on time (FSB 2018; Lambert 2016). Problems were thus EU-wide and can be attributed to efforts to water down the EU legislative transposition of the Basel III guidelines. On average, banks in these four countries had managed to improve their capital positions during the decade following the financial crisis. These figures, however, disguised many significant underlying issues within EU-headquartered banks, as well as the flaws in the newly implemented Basel III guidelines (Goldstein, 2012; Howarth & Quaglia, 2013).

The BCBS compromises did not survive the grinding mill of intra-EU negotiations. Not only EU member states—notably France and Germany—but also the Commission and the European Parliament reopened some of the wounds previously stitched up in the BCBS, citing the need to mind 'European specificities' in the implementation of Basel III rules into the CRDIV. The EU legislation was to apply to all banks, not exclusively to large institutions as in Basel III. This made the application of certain Basel III provisions—especially the calculation of tier-1 capital—impossible without major structural changes in many EU banks and national banking systems. The European Commission justified the broad application of Basel III rules using arguments linked to stability, the appropriate implementation of EU competition policy and the need to maintain an 'international level playing field' (Paulis, 2012; European Parliament, 2011). Jacques de Larosière, former Bank of France governor and IMF managing director, made the case that the application of Basel III rules risked punishing the relatively safe, 'diversified' continental European universal banks rather than the investment banks engaging in riskier activities (de Larosière, 2010, 2011, 2012).

Several observers and organisations criticised CRDIV for having watered down important elements of Basel III (see, e.g. IMF, 2011). The UK Chancellor of the Exchequer even stated in a meeting of EU economic and finance ministers that 'We are not implementing the Basel agreement, as anyone who will look at this text will be able to tell you' (Barker, 2012). The UK (Conservative-Liberal Democrat) government was among the most vocal European supporters of the full implementation of Basel III rules in the CRDIV (IMF, 2011) and repeatedly criticised the Commission's CRDIV draft for lacking ambition (see, e.g. Djankov et al., 2011). The British sought an obligatory leverage ratio and the option of adopting tougher national capital requirements (Guerrera & Pimlott, 2010).

The issue of hybrid capital—capital with both debt and equity features, notably silent participations[1] (*Financial Times,* 2010)—was a major preoccupation for French and German governments with regard to Basel III rules. It was standard practice for many European banks to count hybrid capital towards the tier-1 capital base—to the cap of 15% set by Basel II. Excluding hybrids altogether would greatly disadvantage a range of European banks of varying sizes. A hybrid ban would hit the German public law Landesbanken, in particular, but also the largest German private commercial banks that used hybrid capital to maintain regulatory capital reserves. Germany therefore made sure that 'silent participations' were explicitly allowed in the CRDIV to count toward tier-1 capital.

Basel III set the voluntary leverage ratio at 3% and thus an assets-to-tier-1 ratio of approximately 33. The European Central Bank (ECB), the US and the UK governments, among others, promoted a simple mandatory quantitative leverage ratio as the best means to prevent excessive risk-taking (Masters, 2012). However, many EU member state governments, including Germany and France, were opposed to a simple leverage ratio. National positions aligned largely with the post-crisis capital positions of domestic banks: US and UK banks decreased their leverage ratios quickly after 2008, whereas their French, German and Dutch counterparts maintained generally higher ratios. In 2015, the average US assets-to-equity ratio reached 9.5:1, the UK 14.4:1 and the euro area average of 19.5:1 (Bell & Hindmoor, 2015; Howarth & Quaglia, 2016).

There were a number of attempts to further reinforce bank capital requirements, but European efforts repeatedly fell short of international developments and US and UK efforts. Most recently, in December 2023, the European Parliament and the Council of the EU agreed upon the European Commission's 2021 proposal—commonly known as

[1] Silent participations are assets that can count as equity (core tier-1) for regulatory purposes but, in effect, become debt during crisis periods and thus must be repaid or written off.

the 'Banking Package'—to amend certain aspects of the CRD and CRR and implement some of the remaining elements of Basel III. The revised legislation included an 'output floor' restricting the use of the banks' own internal risk models in the calculation of their capital requirements and brought EU standards on credit, market and operational risk closer to Basel III. However, the revised legislation also included cautious wording, mentioned 'EU specificities', allowed for derogations and granted generous transitional periods—notably on the output floor which is to be phased in by 2032. These EU efforts can be contrasted with those of the Biden administration's proposal of July 2023 known as the 'Basel III endgame', which sought to apply uniform risk models on all banks with $100 billion or more in assets. In the meantime, the Bank of England announced that the Basel III risk and output floor requirements would start to be rolled out in 2025—their final form to be decided in 2024—with the final implementation deadline set for 2030. The Bank of England accepted a relaxed schedule in part because of the competitiveness concerns of UK-headquartered banks arising from the proposed EU phase-ins and derogations (Jones, 2023).

Strengthening Liquidity Rules

The freezing of the interbank markets brought to attention the importance of liquidity—the ability to convert assets quickly into cash—for banks to meet immediate short-term obligations. Liquidity quickly emerged as a key instrument for increasing banking sector resilience and addressing the TBTF issue in the BCBS and at the EU and national levels. Liquidity rules in Basel III were designed to discourage bank reliance on short-term wholesale funding (less than 1 year), the extent of which differed among our case countries. Short-term funding reliance was highest in the UK, but UK-headquartered banks also took the greatest initiative in reducing that reliance after the financial crisis. In 2007, UK bank reliance on short-term funding represented over 60% of GDP (own calculations based on central bank data), but by 2010 this had already been cut down to 30%. This notable reduction was facilitated by early and restrictive rules on liquidity adopted in 2009—which became the blueprint for Basel III and CRDIV liquidity rules—that gave British banks a head start (see Financial Services Authority, 2009: 6; HM Treasury, 2009).

The Basel III liquidity regime was in many respects less far reaching than the new UK rules. The Basel III regime relied on two components: the liquidity coverage ratio (LCR) focused upon ensuring that banks have enough high-quality liquid assets to be able to survive a 1-month 'acute stress' scenario (such as a credit rating downgrade or a series of collateral calls) and the net stable funding ratio (NSFR) which requires a level of 'longer'-term (1 year or more) funding to prevent maturity mismatches. Controversially, high-grade corporate bonds, not considered by UK legislation to count towards liquidity cushions, were included in the Basel III provisions. The British liquidity requirements also required domestic entities to hold enough liquidity on their own, without support from the parent or other parts of the same group.

The US moved swiftly to implement Basel III liquidity rules. The Federal Reserve's October 2013 proposal on LCR was ambitious, going beyond the original BCBS version. Crucially, US regulators signalled their intention to apply the full set of Basel requirements on *all* financial institutions with total assets above $50 billion and not just banks (Hamilton, 2013), justified given the role of investment banks and AIG in the crisis. Large bank holding companies (consolidated assets over $250 billion) and non-banks with the 'systemically important' label were required to maintain high-quality liquid assets (HQLA) to withstand 30 days of net cash outflows, while for institutions with assets between $50 billion and $250 billion, the HQLA coverage requirement was set at 21 days. The transition period had a deadline of 1 January 2017, 2 years earlier than that prescribed by BCBS.

The net stable funding ratio (NSFR), by contrast, faced controversy, and the US missed the implementation deadline. The original US proposal implied NSFR's application to holding companies and depository institutions larger than $250 billion in consolidated assets but also to those with over $10 billion in on-balance sheet foreign exposure or to depositories that are consolidated subsidiaries of holding companies with $10 billion or more in assets. A different modified NSFR was to be made applicable to certain mid-sized (between $50 billion and $250 billion) institutions (such as foreign bank intermediate holding companies) at which on-balance sheet foreign exposure was less than $10 billion (Forrester et al., 2020). However, a new 2019 'tailoring rule' limited the scope of both the LCR and NSFR and lightened the regulatory burden of institutions deemed less risky. The new threshold for both domestic and foreign financial institutions was set to $100 billion in total assets. Combined with further 'tailoring' on a number of factors, the USA delayed the implementation of NSFR, which entered into force on 1 July 2021.

In the EU, the watering-down efforts on Basel III liquidity guidelines were led by the French and Dutch governments (Masters, 2012), reflecting the reliance of their domestically headquartered banks on short-term (less than 1 year) funding. Bank reliance on short-term funding reliance in France and the Netherlands was higher than in most other EU countries, and not even the 2009 French and 2011 Dutch revisions of national liquidity rules could reduce this reliance significantly (French Government, 2009). French bank short-term funding reliance totalled 45% of GDP in 2007 and remained at 40% in 2010. The CRDIV watered down the Basel III LCR and postponed the introduction of the NSFR from the original 2015 deadline to 2018. The LCR was introduced in the CRR, but an observation and review period in 2015 was to determine its detailed structure.

The German government, however, was not vocal over Basel III liquidity rules due to low overall reliance on short-term funding within German banks. Instead, bank debt in the German financial system was mainly issued using '*Pfandbriefe*'—longer-term covered bonds—characteristic of 'patient capital' within the German financial system (Hardie & Howarth, 2013b). Short-term funding reliance among German banks hovered at around 10% of GDP before and after the crisis, decreasing only slightly (Bundesbank data). In July 2009, the German Finance Market Law set broad liquidity provisions above the previous Basel II requirements as well as binding limits on interbank exposures that had been relatively important to German bank funding (BaFin, 2009). However, the August 14 circular (*Rundschreiben* 15/2009) titled 'Minimum requirements for risk management' clarified liability rules with general requirements that were far less restraining than the new UK rules.

Therefore, the Basel III liquidity guidelines, with the potential to limit dependence on short-term wholesale funding and tackle possible TBTF-related issues, experienced derogations in the implementation stage at both the EU and national levels. The USA provided significant leadership in all but meeting the NSFR deadline of 2018. The UK imposed stricter liquidity rules in 2009 than those later formulated by Basel III. The revisions of liquidity rules in France and Germany in 2009 and in the Netherlands in 2011, however, did not match Basel III's scope. Instead, the three countries—France and the Netherlands in particular—moved to water down the European and national transposition and implementation of Basel III guidelines. While the adopted EU rules were restrictive for a range of large EU-headquartered universal banks, the CRDIV's definition of liquidity and its long implementation schedule contributed to a less ambitious effort overall. Banks in all five of the case study countries managed to improve their liquidity positions and decrease their reliance on short-term funding after 2008. However, the British head start over most other EU member states was clear a decade after the crisis, as UK banks held on average far more liquid assets. Implementing the NSFR by the 2018 deadline set in Basel III failed in all five countries (FSB, 2018, 2020), and the EU member states avoided adding a set deadline in the CRDIV directive (Howarth & Quaglia, 2013).

Resolution by 'Bailing in' Banks

In September 2009, G20 leaders held a summit in Pittsburgh and voiced their commitment towards a more effective bank resolution rulebook, starting work towards harmonising resolution practices. However, the results over the next decade were hardly optimal, as reformed or adopted resolution rules ended up being nationally distinct, resulting in very different resolution processes. As with most other measures discussed in this chapter, an effective resolution regime reduces the perceived need for a government-sponsored bailout—especially of a TBTF bank—and helps to stabilise the wider banking system (Asimakopoulos & Howarth, 2022). Financial stability and further market discipline are promoted by mechanisms favouring the internalisation of losses ('bail-in') over their externalisation to the taxpayer in a bailout. This is seen as leading to equitable risk pricing for bank liabilities.

A resolution regime for insured banks has been in place in the US since the 1950 Federal Deposit Insurance Act, which effectively ensures the smooth resolution of most failing or likely-to-fail banks without recourse to government bailout. The Federal Deposit Insurance Corporation (FDIC) leads the resolution process by first cooperating with the respective bank's main regulator to determine whether the bank has failed. Instead of filing for bankruptcy, the FDIC takes over the failed institution and ensures depositor protection up to the insured $250,000. FDIC then takes over and manages the remaining bank assets with the goals of taxpayer cost minimisation and depositor return maximisation. Resolution is paid by fees that the FDIC has collected from its insured banks, pooled into a pre-funded deposit insurance fund (DIF). The FDIC also holds access to US Treasury borrowing which other banks reimburse subsequently. By contrast, none of the EU member states had a comparable resolution regime in place. However, the limits to the FDIC's mandate and the existing US resolution regime became apparent as the investment bank Lehman Brothers went bankrupt, and investment bank Bear Stearns and insurer AIG had to resort to Federal Reserve emergency support (Klein, 2017). These institutions were ineligible for FDIC financial assistance, exposing the drawbacks and inadequacy of restricting the FDIC mandate to commercial banks. The US resolution regime, although path breaking, failed to deliver one of its important goals of protecting the government purse due to systematically important investment bank and insurance company failures.

In response to said limitations, the 2010 Dodd-Frank Act widened the FDIC mandate to include all systematically important non-banks and bank holding companies. Further important reforms were undertaken, aimed at solidifying the US resolution regime (Crabb, 2018). Central to this was the 'Orderly Liquidity Authority' (OLA) created to transfer special powers to regulators for the orderly resolution of complex financial institutions, with the possibility (subject to an agreement with the Federal Reserve Board and the Treasury Secretary) for temporary use of taxpayer funds to provide liquidity in emergency cases. A federal government bailout of covered entities is explicitly forbidden under Dodd-Frank; the OLA imposed fees on surviving institutions receiving resolution funds, requiring the repayment of all received funds. In December 2012, the FDIC together with the Bank of England published a joint paper promoting the single point of entry (SPOE) resolution method for complex banking groups (FDIC, 2013). The 'single' point referred to the top holding or parent company, to which all the losses from elsewhere in the banking group would be funnelled, then placing the parent holding into bankruptcy. The SPOE method—adopted in the USA in 2019 but not yet in the UK—was planned with the TBTF problem specifically in mind. SPOE would contribute towards a resolution regime enforcing market discipline and 'bail-ins' by imposing losses on creditors, not taxpayers. This would be achieved by first replacing senior managers and then 'wiping out' shareholders. In addition, the FDIC issued new regulations for large financial institutions to issue convertible long-term debt eligible for a 'bail-in' in a hypothetical resolution process, intending to facilitate resolution whenever bankruptcy would be unenforceable.

The EU's bank resolution package was agreed upon in 2014, comprising the Bank Recovery and Resolution Directive (BRRD) as well as the Single Resolution Mechanism Regulation (SRMR) exclusive to the Banking Union member states (European Parliament and the Council, 2014a, 2014b). National governments agreed on the wide remit of the new rules, including nearly all 'less significant' and 'significant' banks with few exceptions (SRMR, Article 4). The bail-in tool would be invoked under a justified clause of 'public interest' (BRRD, Article 32(5); SRMR, Article 18(5)), imposing losses on private shareholders and debt holders before resorting to support from resolution funds or the public sector. For EU member states, the new resolution legislation introduced a coherent, unprecedented regime with adequate rules and funds to fully exclude or at least minimise government support in bank resolution. No EU member state previously had a national resolution regime, making bank resolution both economically and politically sensitive. Publicly funded bank bailouts, forced liquidations or government-brokered mergers with other national banks had been the norm.

Furthermore, highly relevant to the euro area periphery where government debt loads were very high, new EU-wide resolution rules could, it was hoped, undo the worrying sovereign-bank doom loop. However, the application of resolution rules has not lived up to expectations, neither at the EU nor at the national level. The FSB observed in 2020 that within the G20 'substantial work remains to operationalise resolution plans for systematically important banks' (FSB, 2020). Its report concluded that the implementation of resolution guidelines remained 'still incomplete' in some jurisdictions. In the EU, six banks facing solvency issues fell under the Single Resolution Board's remit: ABLV Luxembourg, Banca Popolare di Vicenza, Banco Popular Español, Nord/LB and Veneto Banca. Out of these, only Banco Popular Español ended up in resolution, which was highly exceptional and largely owed to Santander's intervention and acquisition of Popular for one euro. The losses were partly covered by following the bail-in procedure of wiping out shareholders and then junior subordinated debt holders (Mesnard et al., 2017).

EU bank resolution rules suffered from national political pressures and reflected the weak capital position of many EU-headquartered banks, which lacked appropriate own funds and eligible liabilities (Asimakopoulos & Howarth, 2022). Political pressures were evident in the several unsuccessful attempts to apply EU rules to Italian banks. In these cases, it became apparent that the Italian government would prefer an old-fashioned bailout with public funds or a forced merger over forcing losses upon national bondholders through bail-in (Donnelly & Asimakopoulos, 2020). Political costs of imposing losses on voters have therefore taken precedence over financial stability concerns on several occasions.

Another issue with EU bank resolution is its ineffectiveness regarding banks with an in-between size for regulatory purposes: banks that are too small for corporate insolvency rules yet too large to hold significant reserves of high-quality 'bail-inable' capital, representing approximately 120 of the bloc's 200 largest banks in terms of assets (Asimakopoulos, 2019). The vast majority of EU-headquartered banks are retail banks which fund their lending largely with customer deposits (Ayadi, 2019). Much of the ineffectiveness of EU resolution rules vis-à-vis this group of banks stems from difficulties in access to (generally insufficient) resolution and deposit insurance scheme funds in the majority of EU member states, exacerbated by the relatively high minimum requirements for own funds and eligible liabilities (MREL) (Asimakopoulos & Howarth, 2022), which are restrictive and likely impossible to meet for a sizable group of EU-headquartered banks (Asimakopoulos, 2019).

The largest universal banks in the EU were capitalised well enough to withstand a bail-in process for bank losses. However, due to the interplay of German, French and Dutch national preferences on individual parts of the banking legislative package—capital requirements, MREL, resolution financing and deposit insurance schemes—it became impossible to apply bank resolution rules to most banks due to their lack of adequate bail-in-eligible capital which, to begin with, they were not required to hold per EU rules. This non-applicability to a range of banks represented a significant political problem, making the resolution rules likely less palatable to the largest TBTF banks in the event of failure. Compromises made in an environment characterised by the scarcity of (acceptable) liquid capital and non-existent functioning resolution mechanisms, therefore, produced an EU bank resolution framework that itself merited a 'failing' or 'likely to fail' tag.

Resolution Plans

Governments in all five case study countries enacted legislation on so-called living wills, requiring banks to compose resolution plans for the event that regulators were to deem them failing or likely to fail. Institution-specific resolution plans are intended to facilitate the potential resolution process and thus limit contagion effects and the likelihood of government involvement for larger banks. In the US, 'living wills' were mandated by Section 165(d) of the Dodd-Frank Act, obliging bank holding companies and foreign banks with $50 billion or more in consolidated assets, plus all systematically important non-bank financial institutions, to annually compose and submit their detailed resolution plans to the Federal Reserve. Separately from these Fed obligations, the FDIC further required resolution plans from all insured depository institutions larger than the $50-billion asset threshold. Even though further recovery plans on how to restore financial health after a period of hardship were not required in the Dodd-Frank Act, the Federal Reserve later required detailed recovery plans from several bank and non-bank systematically important financial institutions. These requirements on resolution and recovery plans were coupled with monitoring and sanctioning efforts. When in April 2016 the living wills of five of the eight largest US banks were rejected by the Fed and FDIC jointly, the five banks were given a deadline of 1 October to 'correct' the resolution plans and were threatened with higher capital requirements and limits on business activities if they failed to comply (Lambert, 2016).

The EU Bank Recovery and Resolution Directive (BRRD) of 2013 imposed a similar requirement upon systematically important banks to submit resolution plans. All four European case study governments had previously either recommended the adoption of resolution plans or in the Dutch case (Intervention Act of 2012) adopted such regulation. However, the impact of these requirements on discouraging higher-risk investment banking and short-term wholesale funding was indirect and limited at best. In addition to resolution plans, the obligation to draft detailed recovery plans annually was included in the BRRD (Articles 5–9), applicable to systemically significant institutions, and with powers given to competent authorities to require a revision of an inadequate plan within 2 months. If the revised version fails, the authority is empowered to request changes to the institution's business. A supplementary regulation was issued in 2016 ((EU) 2016/1075), specifying in detail the required content of the recovery plans. However, these plans, as with the resolution plans, are still largely irrelevant in achieving the wider objectives related to tackling the TBTF problem. As noted above, this irrelevance stems principally from the significant political pressures that have repeatedly prevented the full application of EU resolution rules to individual failing or likely-to-fail banks.

The Politics of Structural Reform

Officially, the principal goal of bank structural reform ('ringfencing') is to protect the depositors, borrowers and other nonfinancial company clients of large universal banks from suffering losses caused by their riskier investment banking activities (Howarth & James, 2023). The broader objective of structural reform is to limit the effects of a bank failure on the real economy (in the form of a credit crunch) and contagion effects on the banking system and, importantly for the TBTF problem, to eliminate pressures for public sector bailouts. By separating or 'ringfencing' investment banking activities from retail banking, structural reform could also force banks to raise loss-absorbing capital for their investment operations to meet regulatory requirements. Bank structural reform thus emerged as a popular topic in all five countries. However, the measures adopted and their impact upon banks varied significantly.

Broadly speaking, the countries can be divided into three camps: the USA and the UK, which introduced elaborate reforms with strong ringfencing; Germany and France, which introduced weak versions of ringfencing; and the Netherlands, where no reform took place. Furthermore, a stalemate ensued at the EU level, and no legislation on structural reform was adopted. The US administration and the UK government adopted major bank structural reforms. The US Volcker Rule involved a complete ban on proprietary trading—that is, using the bank's own money to fund investment banking activities (Dodd-Frank, 2010, Section 619). The UK government ringfenced retail banking which forced large UK banks to separate retail and investment banking arms (HM Treasury, 2012). Both the US and the UK imposed capital requirements specific to the ringfenced entities. In addition, both offered clear definitions of which activities count as proprietary trading.

By contrast, France and Germany were slow to move on bank structural reform and then introduced very weak ringfencing of investment banking activities and narrowly defined proprietary activities banned from retail banks—despite early promises by leading politicians to act (French Government, 2013; German Ministry of Finance, 2013). The French ringfence targeted high-frequency trading and commodity derivatives trading and the German counterpart the same plus hedge fund financing. Neither France nor Germany imposed additional capital requirements on ringfenced entities. This ensured that proprietary trading and a wide range of speculative activities—the conditions of which were vaguely defined—were still allowed in France and Germany. The Dutch government successfully deflected the issue of structural reform, focusing instead upon the adoption of voluntary measures related to bank standards. Major EU-level reform was proposed by a high-level group of experts led by the governor of the Bank of Finland (Liikanen, 2012), was drafted into legislation by the European Commission in a watered-down form (EU Commission, 2014), was diluted further by the EU member states in the Council of Ministers and then blocked in the European Parliamentary finance commission on the grounds that the proposed reform was excessively weak (Howarth & James, 2023).

Conclusion

By analysing the financial crisis-induced regulatory responses of three EU member state governments compared with the UK and the US, this chapter has demonstrated the inadequacy of most reforms adopted specifically to address the TBTF problem. There are serious doubts about whether changes to European banking regulation over the past decade and a half will suffice to shelter TBTF banks and the public purse from future turmoil in global financial markets. The concept of 'permacrisis' applies to contemporary, post-GFC banking regulation which leaves ample space for chronic uncertainty, unpredictability and volatility within EU and member state banking sectors.

While the US and the UK adopted wide-reaching bank structural reforms, France, Germany and the Netherlands did not, and the watered-down EU-level proposal was eventually scrapped. The Basel III guidelines were significantly diluted in their transposition into EU law. The aim of reducing reliance on short-term funding by setting liquidity rules was to strengthen bank capital buffers and decrease the likelihood of banks having to resort to government funds during a crisis, which was better achieved by the UK and US rules adopted in 2009 and 2013, respectively. Unwilling and unable, politically and economically, to match the reach of British and American liquidity rules, EU member states watered down Basel III liquidity guidelines. None of the five countries examined in this chapter met the net stable funding ratio (NSFR) deadline.

The limited interest in some countries for either unilateral, international or EU-level action reflected worries over the competitiveness and lending ability of domestic banking sectors. This chapter has argued that national and EU-level regulatory responses failed to address the TBTF problem to varying degrees. US and UK bank liquidity and structural reforms were among the most effective regulatory measures constraining higher-risk banking activities and addressing the systemic threat posed by TBTF banks. None of the German, French and Dutch measures examined in this chapter can be seen as significantly constraining for TBTF banks. At the end of the day—despite the frequently hostile discourse from a range of political actors—the German, French and Dutch governments defended their TBTF 'national champions'.

Appendix: Tables

Table 8.A1 Largest universal banks, total assets and as a percentage of national GDP (case study countries; total assets, national currency, billions), end 2000, 2007, 2011, 2014[a])

	2000	% of GDP (2000)	2007	% of GDP (2007)	2011	% of GDP (2011)	2014	% of GDP (2014)
USA								
JPMorgan Chase & Co.	715.0	7.0	1562.1	10.8	2274.4	14.6	2573.1	15.2
Bank of America Corp.	642.2	6.3	1715.7	11.9	2219.6	14.3	2104.5	12.4
Citigroup Inc.	902.2	8.8	2187.6	15.1	1936.6	12.5	1842.5	10.9
Wells Fargo & Co.	272.4	2.7	575.4	4.0	1313.9	8.5	1593.3	9.4
US Bancorp (USB)	164.9	1.6	237.6	1.6	330.1	2.1	402.5	2.4
UK								
HSBC	451.9	28.6	1 172.8	61.9	1649.8	88.1	1 689.9	84.6
Barclays (Group)	316.2	20.0	1227.6	64.8	1563.4	83.5	1269.5	63.6
RBS (Royal Bank of Scotland) Group	320.0	20.3	1900.5	100.3	1432.8	76.5	1045.4	52.4
Lloyds-TSB[b]	218.0	13.8	353.3	18.6	970.5	51.8	854.9	42.8
Standard Chartered	102.4	6.5	329.2	17.4	599.1	32.0	725.9	36.4
Germany								
Deutsche Bank	929.0	44.0	2020.3	80.8	2164.0	80.3	1708.7	58.4
Commerzbank	460.0	21.8	617.0	24.7	527.0	19.6	557.6	19.0
DZ Bank	364.6 (2001)	17.3	431.3	17.3	405.9	15.1	402.5	13.7
France								
BNP-Paribas	694.0	46.9	1694.5	87.3	1965.3	95.5	2077.8	96.7
Crédit Agricole	480.7	32.5	1414.2	72.8	1880.0	91.3	1589.1	73.9
Société Générale	455.9	30.8	1071.8	55.2	1181.4	57.4	1308.2	60.9
BPCE[c]	–	–	–	–	1138.0	55.3	1223.3	56.9
Natixis (BPCE investment bank)	116.2	7.9	520.0	26.8	507.7	24.7	736.0	34.2
Crédit Mutuel	–	–	395.9	20.4	382.3	18.6	428.2	19.9
Netherlands								
ING	650.2	143.8	1312.5	212.0	1279.2	196.7	992.9	147.8
Rabobank Group	342.9	75.9	570.5	92.1	731.7	112.5	681.1	101.4
ABN-AMRO Group	543.2	120.2	892.2	144.1	404.7	62.2	386.9	57.6

[a]The banks listed were, in order, the largest in their respective home country at the end of 2014. A number of the largest banks in 2000 no longer existed in 2011 (e.g. Dresdner Bank in Germany and HBOS in the UK)
[b]Halifax Bank of Scotland (HBOS) was merged into Lloyds-TSB from 2009
[c]BPCE consisted of two separate banking groups (Banques Populaires and Caisses d'Epargne) prior to 2009
Source: Author's calculations based on bank annual reports/bank financial statements; see Howarth and James (2023)

Table 8.A2 Banking system assets as a percentage of GDP, 2002–2016[a]

	2002	2004	2006	2008	2010	2012	2014	2016
France	238	257	326	384	392	402	395	388
Germany	292	294	300	311	324	301	268	250
Netherlands	239	289	300	345	358	386	375	368
UK	327	380	451	531	502	466	384	392
USA	74	78	83	94	86	87	92	91

Source: BIS (2018, p. 78); national data, for further details see: https://www.bis.org/publ/cgfs60/cgfs60_metadata.xlsx
[a]Banking system assets on a domestic or resident basis

Table 8.A3 Banking system concentration (percentage of total assets held by largest three/five banks), 2002–2016[a]

	2002	2004	2006	2008	2010	2012	2014	2016
France				54/77	58/81	58/81	58/81	56/82
Germany	18/26	21/29	21/29	20/27	33/40	31/38	31/37	28/35
Netherlands	71/82	71/84	71/84	72/84	69/82	73/82	76/86	75/89
UK	28/41	32/47	34/50	33/45	42/53	41/54	37/51	33/48
USA	21/25	25/31	30/35	32/38	33/44	33/45	33/44	32/43

Source: BIS (2018, p. 85); national data, for further details see: https://www.bis.org/publ/cgfs60/cgfs60_metadata.xlsx

Table 8.A4 Number of systemically important banks by country at end 2018[a]

	Global SIBs	Domestic SIBs	Total number of banks
France	4	2	424
Germany	1	12	1623
Netherlands	1	4	94
UK	3	12	347
USA	8	N/A	5415

Source: FSB (2020)
[a]The USA has not designated domestic SIBs. A bank that is a domestic SIB in one country may be a subsidiary of a global SIB in another country.

References

Asimakopoulos, I. (2019). Making retail banks resolvable. *European Banking Institute Working Paper Series*. https://doi.org/10.2139/ssrn.3471187

Asimakopoulos, I., & Howarth, D. (2022). Stillborn banking union: Explaining ineffective European Union bank resolution rules. *Journal of Common Market Studies, 60*(2), 264–282.

Ayadi, R. 2019. *Banking business models: Definition, analytical framework and financial stability assessment.* Palgrave Macmillan Studies in Banking and Financial Institutions.

BaFin. (2009, August 14). Mindestanforderungen an das Risikomanagement – MaRisk'. https://www.caplaw.eu/file_download.php?l=de&sect=ov&mod=Kapitalmarktrecht&type=grundlagen&c=36&q=&d=bafin_rundschreiben_marisk_090814.pdf

Barker, A. (2012, May 3). UK in furious rejection of EU bank plan. *Financial Times*. https://www.ft.com/content/82eab320-949c-11e1-bb0d-00144feab49a

Basel Committee of Banking Supervision (BCBS). (2010, December 17). Assessing the macroeconomic impact of the transition to stronger capital and liquidity requirements. *Final Report*. BIS.org. https://www.bis.org/publ/othp12.htm

Bell, S., & Hindmoor, A. (2015). Taming the city? Ideas, structural power and the evolution of British banking policy amidst the great financial meltdown. *New Political Economy, 20*(3), 454–474.

BIS (Bank for International Settlements). (2018). FSB, global shadow banking monitoring report 2016. May.

Blitz, J. (2005, April 14). Blair accentuates the positive after opening attacks. *Financial Times*. https://www.ft.com/content/c88e6998-ad14-11d9-ad92-00000e2511c8

Crabb, J. (2018, November 20). PRIMER: A comparison of EU and US bank resolution regimes. *International Financial Law Review*. https://www.iflr.com/article/b1lp1y1kscOnjt/primer-a-comparison-of-eu-and-us-bank-resolution-regimes

De Larosière. (2010, October 16). Financial regulators must take care over capital. *Financial Times*. https://www.ft.com/content/55c69966-b9cc-11de-a747-00144feab49a.

De Larosière. (2011, March 4). Don't punish the banks that preformed best: Basel III may create new risks. *Financial Times*. https://www.ft.com/content/1b085c0e-45e1-11e0-acd8-00144feab49a

De Larosière, J. (2012, September 26). Seductive simplicity of ringfencing. *Financial Times*. https://www.ft.com/content/28196dde-0705-11e2-92b5-00144feabdc0

Djankov, S., Ligi, J., Simonyte, I., Miklos, I., Salgado, E., Borg, A., Norman, P., & Osborne, G. (2011, May 19). *Letter to commissioners Michel Barnier and Ollie Rehn*. http://online.wsj.com/public/resources/documents/BASEL-Letter-20110519.pdf

Dodd-Frank Wall Street Reform and Consumer Protection Act H.R. 4173. 2010. Washington. https://www.cftc.gov/sites/default/files/idc/groups/public/@swaps/documents/file/hr4173_enrolledbill.pdf

Donnelly, S., & Asimakopoulos, I. (2020). Bending and breaking the single resolution mechanism: The case of Italy. *Journal of Common Market Studies, 58*(4), 856–871.

European Parliament and the Council. (2014a, May 15). Bank Recovery and Resolution Directive (BRRD). *Directive 2014/59/EU*. https://eurlex.europa.eu/legal-content/EN/TXT/?uri=uriserv:OJ.L_.2014.173.01.0190.01.ENG

European Parliament and the Council. (2014b). *Single Resolution Mechanism Regulation (SRMR). 2014*. Regulation (EU) No. 806/2014. 15 July 2014 Establishing uniform rules and a uniform procedure for the resolution of credit institutions and certain investment firms in the framework of a single resolution mechanism and a single resolution fund.

EU Commission. (2014, January 29). Proposal for a regulation of the European Parliament and of the Council, on structural measures improving the resilience of EU credit institutions. 2014/0020 (COD). https://eur-lex.europa.eu/legal-content/EN/TXT/PDF/?uri=CELEX:52014PC0043&from=EN

European Parliament. (2011). *Draft report on the proposal for a regulation of the European Parliament and of the Council on prudential requirements for credit institutions and investment firms*. Committee on Economic and Monetary Affairs.

Federal Deposit Insurance Corporation (FDIC). (2013). *Annual report 2013*. https://www.fdic.gov/about/financial-reports/reports/2013annualreport/AR13section1.pdf

Financial Services Authority (FSA). (2009, October). *Strengthening liquidity standards including feedback on CP08/22, CP09/13, CP09/14*. http://www.centerforfinancialstability.org/forum/fsa_liquidity_standards_transitional_measures_200906.pdf

Financial Stability Board (FSB). (2020, November 13). *Implementation and effects of the G20 financial regulatory reforms sixth annual report*. FSB. https://www.fsb.org/2020/11/implementation-and-effects-of-the-g20-financial-regulatory-reforms-2020-annual-report/.

Financial Times. (2010, September 9). Fears for German banks under new rules. https://www.ft.com/content/63677394-bc35-11df-8c02-00144feab49a.

Financieel Management. (2004, October 19). Code-Tabaksblat Beter dan Sarbanes Oxley. https://financieel-management.nl/artikelen/code-tabaksblat-beter-dan-sarbanes-oxley/

Financial Stability Board (FSB). (2018). *Implementation and Effects of the G20 Financial Regulatory Reforms Fourth Annual Report. 28 November*. Washington, DC: FSB. https://www.fsb.org/wp-content/uploads/P281118-1.pdf

Forrester, J. P., Hitselberger, C. A., Taft, J. P., Delaney, T. J., & Bisanz, M. (2020, October 30). US Bank regulators finalize net stable funding ratio rule. Mayerbrown.com. https://www.mayerbrown.com/en/perspectives-events/publications/2020/10/us-bank-regulators-finalize-net-stable-funding-ratio-rule.

French Government. (2013, July 26). Loi de Separation et de Regulation des Activités Bancaires. NOR: EFIX1239994L. https://www.legifrance.gouv.fr/jorf/id/JORFTEXT000027754539?r=SWaVINHLiJ

French Government. (2009, May 20). Arrêté du 5 mai 2009 relatif à l'identification, la mesure, la gestion et le contrôle du risque de liquidité. NOR: ECET0908654A. https://www.legifrance.gouv.fr/jorf/id/JORFTEXT000020635107

Ganderson, J. (2020). To change banks or bankers? Systemic political (in)action and post-crisis banking reform in the UK and the Netherlands. *Business and Politics, 22*(1), 196–223.

German Ministry of Finance. (2013, August 12). Gesetz zur Abschirmung von Risiken und zur Planung der Sanierung und Abwicklung von Kreditinstituten und Finanzgruppen [Trennbankengesetz]. *Bundesgesetzblatt Jahrgang, 47*. Bonn. https://www.bgbl.de/xaver/bgbl/start.xav#__bgbl__%2F%2F*%5B%40attr_id%3D%27bgbl113s3090.pdf%27%5D__1616501900172

Goldstein, M. (2012, May 27). The EU's implementation of Basel III: Deeply flawed compromise. *VoxEU, CEPR*. https://voxeu.org/article/eu-s-implementation-basel-iii-deeply-flawed-compromise.

Guerrera, F., & Pimlott, D. (2010, October 26). Pandit and King Clash over Basel III. *Financial Times*. https://www.ft.com/content/1d392ba0-e071-11df-99a3-00144feabdc0.

Hamilton, J. (2013, October 25). Fed liquidity proposal seen trading safety for costlier credit. *Bloomberg*. https://www.bloomberg.com/news/articles/2013-10-24/fed-weighs-liquidity-demands-aimed-to-keep-biggest-banks-safe

Hardie, I., & Howarth, D. (Eds.). (2013a). *Market based banking and the international financial crisis*. Oxford University Press.

Hardie, I., & Howarth, D. (2013b). A peculiar kind of devastation: german market-based banking. In I. Hardie & D. Howarth (Eds.), *Market-based banking and the international financial crisis* (pp. 103–127). Oxford University Press.

Hardie, I., & Macartney, H. (2016). Too big to separate? EU Ring-fencing and the defence of too-big-to-fail banks. *West European Politics, 39*(3), 503–525.

HM Treasury. (2009). Banking Act 2009. The Stationary Office. https://www.legislation.gov.uk/ukpga/2009/1

HM Treasury. (2012). Banking reform: Delivering stability and supporting a stable economy. The Stationery Office. https://assets.publishing.service.gov.uk/government/uploads/system/uploads/attachment_data/file/32556/whitepaper_banking_reform_140512.pdf

Howarth, D., & James, S. (2020). The politics of bank structural reform: Business power and agenda setting in the United Kingdom, France and Germany. *Business and Politics, 22*(1), 25–51.

Howarth, D., & James, S. (2023). *Bank politics: Bank structural reform in comparative perspective*, with Scott James. Oxford University Press.

Howarth, D., & Quaglia, L. (2013). Banking on stability: The European Union's new capital requirement directive. *Journal of European Integration, with Lucia Quaglia, 35*(3), 333–346.

Howarth, D., & Quaglia, L. (2016). The comparative political economy of Basel III in Europe. *Policy and Society, 35*, 205–214.

IMF. (International Monetary Fund). (2011, July). United Kingdom: Staff report for the 2011 Article IV Consultation – Supplementary information. IMF Country Report, No. 11/220, Supplementary Report.

James, S. (2018). The structural-informational power of business: Credibility, signaling and the UK banking reform process. *Journal of European Public Policy, 25*(11), 1629–1647.

James, S., & Quaglia, L. (2020). *The UK and multi-level financial regulation: From post-crisis reform to Brexit*. Oxford University Press.

Jones, H. (2023). Bank of England delays final Basel Bank capital rules to July 2025. *Reuters*. https://money.usnews.com/investing/news/articles/2023-09-27/bank-of-england-delays-final-basel-bank-capital-rules-to-july-2025

Klein, A. (2017, June 5). A primer on Dodd-Frank's orderly liquidation authority. *Brookings*. https://www.brookings.edu/blog/up-front/2017/06/05/a-primer-on-dodd-franks-orderly-liquidation-authority/.

Lambert. L. (2016, 13 April). *US Regulators Fail "Living Wills" at Five of Eight Big Banks. Reuters*. https://www.reuters.com/article/us-usabanks-idUSKCN0XA1B4

Leonhardt, D. (2010, March 25). Heading off the next financial crisis. *The New York Times Magazine*. https://www.nytimes.com/2010/03/28/magazine/28Reform-t.html

Liikanen Group (High-Level Expert Group on Reforming the Structure of the EU Banking Sector). (2012, October 2). Final Report. https://ec.europa.eu/commission/presscorner/detail/en/IP_12_1048.

Massoc, E. (2020). Banks, power and political institutions: The divergent priorities of European states towards "too-big-to-fail" banks: the cases of competition in retail banking and the banking structural reform. *Business and Politics, 22*(1), 135–160.

Masters, B. (2012, February 2). Strasbourg hears call for tougher rules for banks. *Financial Times*. https://www.ft.com/content/f1e4cdd8-4d8e-11e1-b96c-00144feabdc0.

Mesnard, B., Margerit, A., & Magnus, M. (2017). The resolution of Banco popular. European Parliament briefing. Economic Governance Support Unit. https://www.europarl.europa.eu/RegData/etudes/BRIE/2017/602093/IPOL_BRI(2017)602093_EN.pdf

Pagliari, S., & Young, K. L. (2014). Leveraged interests: Financial industry power and the role of private sector coalitions. *Review of International Political Economy, 21*(3), 575–610.

Paulis, E. (2012, March 14). *Deputy Director General, DGMARKT*. Presentation and after dinner discussion at the University of Edinburgh.

Posner, E., & Véron, N. (2010). The EU and financial regulation: power without purpose? *Journal of European Public Policy, 17*(3), 400–415.

Quaglia, L. (2010). *Governing financial services in the European Union*. Routledge.

Quaglia, L., & Spendzharova, A. (2017). The conundrum of solving 'too big to fail' in the European Union: Supranationalization at different speeds. *Journal of Common Market Studies, 55*(5), 1110–1126.

Smith, C., Gandel., S. & Frankin, J. (2024, September 10). Federal Reserve halves proposed capital requirement rise for largest US banks. *Financial Times*. https://www.ft.com/content/86fd9a80-bf46-4711-ab33-e4dcbef5eeb4

Young, K., & Pagliari, S. (2017). Capital united? Business unity in regulatory politics and the special place of finance. *Regulation and Governance, 11*(1), 3–23.

Zimmermann, H. (2010). Varieties of global financial governance? British and German approaches to financial market regulation. In E. Helleiner, S. Pagliari, & H. Zimmerman (Eds.), *Global finance in crisis: The politics of international regulatory change* (pp. 121–136). Routledge.

[illegible]

Chapter 9
From Bailouts to Bail-Ins: Political Economy Constraints to Effective Crisis Resolution in the EU

Dimitris Katsikas

Contents

Introduction

As noted in the introduction to this volume, structural transformations that have occurred in the international system in recent decades are a fundamental aspect of the permacrisis concept. Permacrisis does not simply denote a period marked by multiple crises but a period when structural transformations have created conditions where crises are far more likely to occur, effectively becoming a constituent feature of the system (Henig & Knight, 2023).

One area which has undergone such a process of structural transformation has been the global financial system. The global financial crisis (GFC) revealed its inherently destabilizing nature, shaped by decades of deregulation, supervisory forbearance, increased competition and unchecked innovation. The development of the European financial market mirrored—and to some degree shaped—the developments occurring globally. Years of negative integration led to an increasingly unified

D. Katsikas (✉)
National and Kapodistrian University of Athens, Athens, Greece
e-mail: dkatsikas@pspa.uoa.gr

D. Katsikas et al. (eds.), *Finance, Growth and Democracy: Connections and Challenges in Europe and Latin America in the Era of Permacrisis*, United Nations University Series on Regionalism 33, https://doi.org/10.1007/978-3-031-68475-3_9

European financial landscape, where, however, supervision remained fragmented along national lines, and there was no European emergency mechanism or lender of last resort (Lastra, 2003; Quaglia, 2007). The result of this asymmetric integration process was the unsupervised venture of many European banks into highly risky market segments rendering the European banking sector particularly vulnerable to the effects of the GFC.

These effects were amplified by other gaps and failures in the institutional architecture of the European Union (EU). Most important among them is the incomplete and unbalanced governance of the Economic and Monetary Union (EMU), which not only failed to coordinate the economic policies of member states but ended up amplifying previous asymmetries (Copelovitch et al., 2016; Baldwin & Giavazzi, 2015). The combined effect of institutional failures in the EU's financial and economic integration manifested in the form of the so-called doom loop, i.e. the close financial ties of domestic banking systems with their sovereigns, particularly in the troubled southern economies of the Eurozone. Their financial interdependence transformed banking crises into sovereign debt crises and vice versa, contributing, in the aftermath of the GFC, to the breakout of the Eurozone crisis in 2010.

The dynamics of structural transformations notwithstanding, the permacrisis perspective does not imply a deterministic approach to societal evolution. On the contrary, crises are considered pivotal moments which catalyse political, social or institutional change.[1] Accordingly, permacrisis could be seen as a period that offers opportunities for reforming unsustainable models of social organization, however sustainability is defined (e.g. in terms of economic efficiency and growth, financial stability, social justice and equality, environmental protection, etc.), at both the national and international levels.

For the European Union (EU), this point of view is particularly relevant, given its sui generis nature as an ongoing political project which, as one of its founders famously proclaimed, 'will be forged in crises' (Monnet, 1978:417). Indeed, the EU's reaction to the GFC was considerable, as it engaged in a multi-year re-regulatory effort, established new European agencies and ultimately proceeded, as the crisis deepened and the doom loop dynamics look set to derail large Eurozone economies like Spain and Italy, with a much more radical reform, the establishment of the European Banking Union. While the Banking Union introduced many new regulatory and institutional elements in the EU's economic governance, in this chapter we will focus on one particular aspect: the bail-in principle in banking resolution.

The bail-in principle was thought to be a radical new element that would prohibit publicly funded bailouts, contribute to breaking the doom loop and instil more discipline in financial market participants. However, as we shall see, in practice it has not always operated as planned. Beyond its intrinsic limitations, a significant cause for the difficulties encountered in its implementation, and the focus of this chapter,

[1] In the institutionalist literature crises are often considered 'critical junctures' which can lead to paradigm change and establish new historical paths (Thelen, 1999; Pierson, 2004).

is the political economy dynamics involved in the resolution of banking crises. These dynamics have become more complex and difficult to overcome due to some of the major transformations associated with financial capitalism, such as globalization, securitization and financialization (for a more detailed discussion of these changes, see Schulmeister's Chaps. 14 and 19, in this volume).

The chapter is organized as follows. First, we briefly review the connection of the GFC with the Eurozone crisis and the reform efforts undertaken to address the problems of the European banking sector, including the introduction of the bail-in principle in bank resolution. Then we discuss the bail-in principle in more detail and identify its limitations, particularly in the current financial market context. Then we demonstrate the political economy constraints to the implementation of the bail-in principle in the EU in recent years, by examining in more detail two cases: Cyprus and Italy. The final section summarizes and concludes the chapter.

Crisis, European Banking Union and the Bail-in Tool

The global financial crisis hit the European banking system particularly hard. According to estimates of the International Monetary Fund (IMF), asset write-offs for the period 2007–2010 for European banks stood at $1.3 trillion, while write-offs for the global banking system totalled $2.3 trillion (IMF, 2010). The size and intensity of the crisis in the European banking sector highlighted the extent of European banks' exposure to global financial markets and the inadequacy of the European regulatory and supervisory framework to detect risks in a timely manner prior to the crisis. As a result, a fundamental review of the financial regulatory and supervisory framework got underway. An ambitious reform programme was launched; by the end of 2010, more than 30 legislative interventions had already been proposed (Commission of the European Communities, 2010), while in total, up to 2018, more than 60 proposals were submitted, 42 of which had been adopted.

The most significant part of this reform wave was the establishment of the European Banking Union (Howarth & Quaglia, 2013). The Banking Union comprises three main pillars: the Single Supervisory Mechanism (SSM), a supranational institution located at the European Central Bank (ECB), responsible for the supervision of the European banking system;[2] the Single Resolution Mechanism (SRM), which is a mechanism for the orderly recovery and resolution of banks in times of crisis; and the European Deposit Insurance Scheme (EDIS). The first two pillars have been largely completed, while progress in the third pillar has effectively stalled (Högenauer et al., 2023). Finally, the so-called single rulebook, a set of common rules which applies to all EU member states, underpins the operation of the Banking Union.

[2] The SSM supervises directly the 'significant' banks (113 at the end of 2023) and indirectly the 'less significant' banks, which are directly supervised by the national supervisory authorities.

The Banking Union was agreed in stages between 2012 and 2014, and different components of its pillars have gradually been activated since 2014. Compared to other financial reform initiatives, the Banking Union was more directly linked to the Eurozone crisis and its challenges, primary among them the risk posed by the connection between weak banks and fiscally constrained sovereigns in the EMU periphery (Donelly, 2014; Quaglia, 2019). The focus of this chapter is on a particular aspect of the Banking Union: the bail-in principle, which has become embedded in its SRM pillar.

The bail-in procedure 'aims at letting investors participate in a bank's losses at time of bankruptcy' (Schäfer et al., 2017). Adopting the bail-in principle effectively means that private investors, including shareholders and creditors, must bear substantial losses before any public funding can be used to restructure a bank during a crisis. Bail-in was promoted internationally as the taxpayer-funded bailouts of major financial institutions during the GFC provoked public outrage. In Europe, public pressure was high given the extraordinary support given to banks and other financial institutions. From 2007 to 2009, 84 banks in the EU received government aid in various forms (Meehl, 2022). More specifically, according to the European Commission (2013:1), 'between October 2008 and 31 December 2012 Member States provided €591.9 billion (4.6% of EU 2012 GDP) of capital support (recapitalisation and asset relief measures) to the financial sector'. The overall support, including state guarantees, approved by the European Commission, reached €3.6 trillion, of which €1.6 trillion was effectively used (Philippon and Salord (2017:3). Burdening public budgets with bank bailouts in turn was a major cause for the derailment of public finances and the sharp increase of public debt in many EU member states, contributing directly to the breakout of the Eurozone crisis.

Bail-in was introduced with the Bank Recovery and Resolution Directive (BRRD) and the Single Resolution Mechanism (SRM) Regulation which became operational on the first of January 2016.[3] The SRM comprises the Single Resolution Board, a supranational agency responsible for the orderly resolution of failing banks, and the national resolution authorities.[4] In the resolution procedure other institutions are also involved, primarily the ECB and the European Commission. The role of the European Commission is related to the state aid rules, which determine when and how state authorities can support a bank in trouble, to avoid breaching competition rules.[5] The SRM also includes the Single Resolution Fund (SRF),

[3] In 2018 the EU adopted the 'Banking Package' which updated the EU resolution legislation.

[4] The SRB is responsible for the entities and groups directly supervised by the European Central Bank and a few other cross-border groups. As of 10 July 2023, there were 113 banks under SRB's remit. National Resolution Authorities are responsible for all other banks. When the use of the SRF is required, the SRB is responsible for the adoption of the resolution scheme for that bank (SRB, 2024).

[5] The rules are set out in the Commission's '2013 Banking Communication'.

which can be accessed under extraordinary circumstances; it is a supranational fund financed by contributions of the banks in the member states of the Banking Union.[6]

The resolution process begins when the ECB declares that a bank is failing or likely to fail. Then the SRB decides on the procedure to be followed. If private sector solutions (e.g. purchase of the ailing bank by another bank) are unavailable and there are no other supervisory actions that can remedy the situation, then the SRB considers whether the bank should be liquidated or restructured under the resolution process. When normal national insolvency proceedings (liquidation) are likely to adversely impact the economy and/or undermine financial stability, resolution is preferred to safeguard public interest. The resolution process includes four different tools (bail-in, sale of business, bridge institution, asset separation). The bail-in tool requires that access to the SRF is possible only after losses corresponding to 8% of the bank's total liabilities and own funds are borne by shareholders and creditors. To ensure that bail-in can be implemented at a time of crisis, under the Banking Union's resolution rules, banks must meet certain 'minimum requirements for own funds and eligible liabilities' (MREL).

Bail-in in Theory and Practice

In theory, the bail-in principle offers several advantages. First, it improves market discipline and reduces moral hazard, which lessens the risk of a banking crisis altogether (Halaj et al., 2016; Avgouleas & Goodhart, 2014). Also, when the introduction of bail-in is accompanied, as in the EU, with increased requirements for holding liabilities and own funds that can be bailed in, the resilience of banks and the effectiveness and credibility of a bail-in are enhanced, rendering disruptions more manageable and the use of public funds less likely. Finally, introducing a bail-in regime helps to level the playing field, as large banks, which are more likely to benefit from a public bailout, enjoy reduced cost of capital (due to the implicit public subsidy) (Acharya et al., 2014; Ueda & Weder di Mauro, 2012), which in turn reinforces the moral hazard problem (Alessandri & Haldane, 2009).

Beyond its ex ante market improving effects, the bail-in principle is also beneficial for the health of public finances once a crisis erupts. Bailing-out banks is a costly business, and when this cost is borne by the public budget, fiscal sustainability suffers, and the risk of a sovereign debt crisis rises; the example of Ireland during the Eurozone crisis is a paradigmatic case of such adverse dynamics. More generally, public bailouts are an integral part of the bank-sovereign doom loop, which threatens both financial and fiscal stability, particularly in countries where there is a

[6]The SRF has been built up over a period of 8 years (2016–2023) and reached its target level of at least 1% of the amount of covered deposits of credit institutions in all 21 Banking Union countries at the end of 2023. The national compartments of the SRF have now been fully merged in the supranational fund and have effectively ceased to exist. In July 2023 the fund had accumulated 77.6 billion euros (SRB Press Release, 6 July 2023).

strong financial connection between banks and the sovereign. Bail-in helps to break this link, at least partly,[7] as banking crises are less likely to cause fiscal derailment.

Its benefits notwithstanding, bail-in is not a panacea and can cause its own problems. Avgouleas and Goodhart (2014) provide a succinct theoretical discussion of the potential problems of bail-in. Some of the problems have to do with the process itself. Bail-ins are likely to involve more time-consuming and expensive proceedings compared to bailouts. Moreover, the process can lead to long and difficult litigation. Also, there are difficulties in determining the valuation of a bank, particularly when it is under stress; this can lead to multiple bail-in rounds with negative confidence effects for the bank but also the broader market. All these complications become even worse, when we consider that many banks, particularly big, systemically important banks, are part of broader corporate groups, comprising many legal entities, often operating across borders (Gleeson, 2012).

Beyond these more technical and legal complications, there are more substantial issues related to bail-in. They can be grouped under three broad categories: (a) reduced ex ante lending, (b) contagion risk and (c) political economy conflicts. First, although bail-in may lead to an ex ante reduction of risk-taking and improved market discipline, this comes at the cost of reduced credit provision to the economy. Under a bail-in regime, the risk and therefore the price of uninsured debt rise, inducing banks to borrow less; this in turn results in lower levels of lending (Meehl, 2022). Second, while bail-in resolution strategies are in theory suitable for idiosyncratic bank failures, the same cannot be said for systemic crises. Triggering a bail-in during a broader economic or financial crisis can function pro-cyclically, as it undermines confidence for weaker banks and for banks with direct linkages (cross-holdings of claims) with the bank in crisis. This in turn may lead to a reassessment of risk for the entire sector, in effect deepening the crisis (Avgouleas & Goodhart, 2014).[8] Finally, political economy conflicts are unavoidable under a bail-in regime. Losses will affect private investors, including depositors, who will react and try to shift this burden elsewhere. The relevance of such conflicts for the effectiveness of the bail-in process cannot be overstated, since the identity and type of the bailed-in creditors (e.g. wholesale vs retail, domestic vs foreign) can have significant political economic implications, affecting the authorities' handling of the crisis.

Although empirical studies focusing on the impact of bail-in resolution regimes are still scarce, what evidence there is seems to corroborate many of these concerns. Thus, Siebenbrunner et al. (2024) show that bail-ins produce lower social losses compared to bailouts, in cases of idiosyncratic shocks but not in cases of systemic crises. More generally, Beck et al. (2020) show that more comprehensive resolutions regimes, which include bail-in mechanisms, tend to amplify systemic shocks.

---

[7] Eradicating the doom loop altogether necessitates a more comprehensive approach which includes limits on the exposure of banks to their sovereign debt and a supranational deposit guarantee scheme.

[8] The European rules provide for a number of exceptions to the bailing-in of certain liabilities. One of these is the avoidance of widespread contagion, which however is examined on an ad hoc basis and for particular classes of liabilities (article 27(5) SRMR).

Moreover, Beck et al. (2021) find negative effects for businesses more exposed to the bailed-in financial institution, as their access to credit is impaired. Exposed small- and medium-sized enterprises (SMEs) with limited internal liquidity are particularly vulnerable to this effect and make up the loss of liquidity by reducing investment and employment.

In this chapter, we focus on the political economy dynamics of bank resolutions; accordingly, in the next section we will delve deeper into the political economy conflicts surrounding bail-ins through a more systematic analysis of two major crisis episodes in the EU in recent years: the Cypriot and Italian banking crises.

Bail-in Cases in the EU

The Cyprus Crisis

Although the Cyprus crisis precedes the introduction of the EU's transnational resolution regime, it is important for a number of reasons: (a) the crisis culminated in one of the biggest bail-ins in history, as the bailed-in liabilities (deposits and junior bonds) amounted to 9.4 billion euros (over 50% of Cyprus GDP) (Clerides, 2018); (b) many of the provisions introduced with the BRRD were first implemented in the Cyprus crisis (Demetriades, 2018); and (c) related to the second point, the Cyprus crisis is generally considered a pivotal moment for the introduction of new European framework (Philippon & Salord, 2017, Schäfer et al., 2017).

The first signs of worry for the Cypriot banks begun with the Greek crisis, as the two biggest banks, Bank of Cyprus (BoC) and Laiki, had significant exposure both to the Greek banking market through an extended branch network, and to the Greek public debt, as they held substantial amounts of Greek government bonds.[9] When, in 2011, it was decided to proceed with a restructuring of the Greek public debt, the losses foreseen for the two Cypriot banks were substantial (4.5 billion euros or 25% of GDP). In this context, failure to meet capital requirements resulted in a first 1.8-billion public bailout operation for Laiki in May 2012, while the BoC requested state aid for half a billion euros to meet the European Banking Authority's (EBA) requirements. The situation continued to deteriorate; an independent study commissioned by the central bank put the capital shortfall of the banking sector at 8.9 billion, for the adverse scenario. In November 2012 there was a preliminary agreement on a memorandum of understanding (MoU) with the official creditors: a 17-billion-euro package, with 10 billion earmarked for the recapitalization of the banking sector. However, the creditors would only supply the 10 billion, and the rest would have to be found elsewhere; the solution that eventually prevailed was bail-in. On the 16th of March 2013, the Eurogroup approved the 10-billion bailout agreement and proposed the imposition of a 'solidarity levy' on all (including insured) deposits in

[9] In 2006 Laiki came under the control of Greek Marfin Investment Group (MIG).

Cypriot banks. The decision was heavily criticized internationally as it undermined confidence not only in Cyprus but across the Eurozone and was rejected by the Cypriot Parliament. On the 25th of March the Eurogroup reached a new deal whereby Laiki would be resolved into a good and bad bank, with the former set to be absorbed by BoC and the latter to be gradually wound down; BoC would also need to be recapitalized through the imposition of bail-in on junior bondholders and uninsured depositors.

The Cyprus case reveals the complex political economy dynamics around the resolution of the crisis, which relate to the distribution of costs: (a) between Cypriot and Greek banks, (b) between depositors of EU and non-EU origin, (c) between European official creditors and the Cypriot state and (d) between commercial and cooperative Cypriot banks.

A crucial aspect of the Cyprus deal, and one which increased the cost of the resolution for Cyprus, was the ring-fencing of the Greek banking system (Clerides, 2018). The operations of the Cypriot banks in Greece were sold to Greek banks at a heavy discount to avoid imposing a bail-in on the depositors of the Cypriot banks' branches in Greece; this would lead to the implosion of the Greek banking system and economy more generally, which were already hanging by a thread. Obviously, excluding Greek depositors from the bail-in increased the amount of bail-in that had to be imposed on Cyprus-based depositors. The effect was compounded by the heavy discount of the sale, agreed in hurried negotiations between the Eurogroup meetings in March 2013; estimates suggest that the Cypriot banking system effectively subsidized the Greek banking system with roughly 2 billion euros (Clerides, 2018:199).

Another important parameter of the bail-in was that this was mainly imposed on non-nationals. Cyprus had long operated as an international business and financial centre, with low corporate taxes and a rapidly expanding banking sector, whose assets had grown to nine times the country's GDP by 2009. Much of the incoming funds were from Russian companies, often belonging to Russian oligarchs, who were seeking a safe haven for their wealth; it is estimated that up to 37% of deposits belonged to foreigners with Russian owing 60% of these deposits, which amounted to 19 billion euros in early 2013 (Fontevecchia, 2013). Opting for the imposition of the bail-in, therefore, had the unusual benefit of sparing domestic depositors, since most of the depositors with funds over the insured threshold of 100,000 euros were non-EU residents. This protected the local economy from a deep recession. Obviously, this was politically much more palatable, despite concerns about the impact on the international credibility of the Cypriot banking system.

The imposition of the bail-in costs on non-EU residents was an idea warmly endorsed by European leaders and institutions. The are several reasons for this; first, there was 'bailout fatigue' given the already agreed rescue packages for Greece, Ireland, Portugal and Spain's banking sector and accordingly limited appetite for the dispensation of more European funds. This reluctance was justified by framing Cyprus as an offshore financial centre used for laundering money of Russian (among others) oligarchs; this aspect caught the public' attention in European countries, particularly Germany, where a news report citing a secret intelligence report suggested that the EU's bailout would serve to save the Russian oligarchs (Dettmer &

Reiermann, 2012). This story was picked up by German politicians who wanted to limit their exposure to another potential debacle (like the one in Greece) and perhaps use the opportunity to push for tax harmonization in the EU (they had already tried this with Ireland's bailout). Accordingly, they portrayed themselves as guarantors of a fair and disciplined resolution of the crisis and ascribed blame for the crisis to Cyprus, much as they had done with Greece (Aspriadis et al., 2018), insisting on the bail-in solution.[10]

A final parameter worth mentioning is the distribution of the resolution costs between the different types of domestic depositors and investors. In contrast to the two big commercial banks, the cooperative banking sector in Cyprus was shielded from a bail-in; it was bailed out with 1.5 billion euros from the loan Cyprus received. Beyond the fact that the sector had few depositors over the insured threshold, some analysts believe that the sector was spared due to its traditional links with the political system and of course the fact that depositors in cooperative banks were overwhelmingly Cypriot (Clerides, 2018). As a result, cooperative depositors and investors were treated very differently compared to the customers of the two large banks. Also, there were other exemptions, for example, for pension funds, or public universities, with large deposits from EU-funded programmes, which point to further political calculations, at both the national and European levels.

The Italian Crisis

The Italian banking crisis evolved in different stages during the 2010s. It is an interesting case for the purposes of this chapter because it involves different types of banks, different resolution proceedings and outcomes and covers the period both before and after the introduction of the European resolution scheme.

The crisis of the banking system was linked to some of its core features, such as its high dependence on the domestic economy and its substantial exposure to Italian public debt; moreover, troubles travelled quickly through the system due to the high levels of interconnectedness among domestic institutions (Moschella & Quaglia, 2019; Donnely & Asimakopoulos, 2020). Problems started accumulating because of the prolonged stagnation of the Italian economy and the impact of the GFC, particularly since its transmutation into the Eurozone crisis; these developments led to a significant rise in the number of non-performing loans (NPLs), which became the sector's most important problem (Boccuzzi, 2022).

The first resolutions came in 2014 and 2015.[11] In the first case, a small provincial bank, Banca Tercas, was found to be insolvent, and following deliberations it was

[10] Presenting the narrative employed by the creditors of Greece and Cyprus is not meant as a dismissal of its validity; Cyprus was an international offshore centre, and Greece had indeed adopted a wholly irresponsible fiscal policy before the crisis. Rather the point here is to demonstrate the strategic use of this narrative to justify political economy choices.

[11] The analysis that follows is not meant to be exhaustive; it focuses on the more important and relevant cases for the purposes of this chapter.

agreed to be sold to Banca Popolare di Bari (BPB), following recapitalization and the provision of guarantees for potential risk and losses, by the Interbank Deposit Protection Fund (FITD), which is funded by bank contributions. However, the European Commission challenged the support provided by the FITD and, following investigation, in December 2015, concluded that the FITD's funding constituted public support and was therefore illegal. This sparked a judicial clash with Banca Popolare di Bari and the FITD, which, with the support of the Bank of Italy, appealed to the EU's General Court.

After several years the Italian authorities would be vindicated, but in the meantime, the Banca Tercas sale had to be reorganized. A Voluntary Intervention Scheme (SVI), funded by the Italian financial sector, was set up and used to provide the funds that would have been furnished by the FITD, a solution that was acceptable to the European Commission. Moreover, the European Commission's interpretation blocked another proposal in November 2015, to rescue four troubled Italian banks (Banca delle Marche, Banca Popolare dell'Etruria e del Lazio, Cassa di Risparmio di Ferrara and Cassa di Risparmio della Provincia di Chieti) with FITD support. The European Commission argued that FITD's intervention constituted extraordinary public financial support, and this could only be justified under the new European rules if the banks were deemed to be failing or likely to fail; in this case, they should be subject to the new resolution proceedings, which included bail-in (Boccuzzi, 2022).

Under the resolution scheme, four bridge banks were created, to be sold, and one bad bank to receive the banks' problematic assets. The newly created national resolution fund covered losses and recapitalized the bridge banks, after shareholders and bondholders incurred losses. This led to public upheaval as most bondholders were in fact retail depositors, who had been sold junior bonds as a higher-yield alternative to deposits. This was a common practice among Italian banks, as they sought to find a market-based solution to their liquidity problems without having to change their organizational or ownership structure (Donnely & Asimakopoulos, 2020). The potential political implications were made manifest when in December 2015 a pensioner committed suicide after learning that he had lost most of his savings invested in one of the banks' junior bonds. Several months later, legislation compensated the retail bondholders of the four banks. At the same time, other senior creditors were protected, as the resolution process begun before the first of January 2016, when the bail-in tool entered into force (Barbagallo, 2017).

The next episode concerned two Veneto banks: Veneto Banca and Banca Popolare di Vicenza. The two banks faced severe problems already since 2013, and following failed attempts to raise capital from the markets, the Atlante Fund recapitalized them, becoming their main shareholder.[12] In March 2017 the two banks filed a request for 'precautionary recapitalization', a process which allows state authorities

[12] The Atlante Fund was a fund set up in 2015 with contributions from financial institutions to help recapitalize ailing banks and buy the junior tranches of NPLs (senior tranches were guaranteed by the state), facilitating their removal from the banks' balance sheets. A second Atlante II Fund was set up in 2016 and was eventually replaced by the Italian Recovery Fund in 2017.

to support financially a bank without recourse to the standard resolution process,[13] which however was denied by the European authorities, unless additional private funding could be raised; despite efforts by the Italian authorities, private funds were not forthcoming. In the summer the two banks were deemed failing or likely to fail by the ECB. The SRB declared that resolution of the banks under the EU rules was not in the public interest, and therefore the banks should be liquidated under national law. The Italian government tried to avert this outcome and requested from the European Commission the approval of state aid to facilitate an 'orderly liquidation', which effectively meant selling the better parts of the banks to another financial institution. The European Commission, contrary to SRB's assessment, decided that there were public interest grounds on which to justify the provision of state aid. In the end, the Italian authorities furnished 4.875 billion euros for the recapitalization, restructuring costs and coverage of the losses of the two banks and offered guarantees for future losses of 12.4 billion; these measures made possible the sale of the two banks to one of Italy's biggest banks, Banca Intesa Sanpaolo, for the symbolic price of 1 euro. The transaction also involved burden sharing from private investors. Losses were mainly incurred by the shareholders, i.e. the Atlante Fund (approximately 3.4 billion euros), and to a lesser extent by subordinate shareholders (approximately 1.2 billion euros) (Boccuzzi, 2022). Retail bondholders were later compensated by FITD and Intesa (on a voluntary basis), for the losses suffered.

The final episode to be reviewed took place—partly—during the same period with the Veneto banks' crisis but was different in that it concerned Monte dei Paschi di Siena (MPS), the world's oldest and Italy's fourth biggest bank at the time. Following the publication of EBA's stress test in July 2016, which showed a significant capital shortfall under the adverse scenario, the bank sought to raise capital in the markets but was unsuccessful. As a result, the bank applied to the ECB for precautionary recapitalization. In July 2017, the European Commission approved the restructuring plan of the bank, which was a necessary prerequisite for the approval of the precautionary recapitalization. A few days later the Italian government issued a decree which stipulated the terms of the process. The recapitalization involved the injection of 5.4 billion euros by the Italian government and the contribution of shareholders and holders of junior bonds, which were converted into equity (4.3 billion euros). Part of the government's cash injection was meant to cover the compensation of retail bondholders who lost due to the conversion (1.5 billion euros). The recapitalization was accompanied by a plan for a substantial restructuring of the bank operations and the sale of a portfolio of 24.5 billion euros of bad loans at a discount of almost 80%, with the support of the Atlante Fund. Finally, it should be mentioned that the state had already provided guarantees for two bond issues from the bank, worth 11 billion euros, in early 2017. The operation was part of a new supportive scheme introduced with Decree Law 237/2016, which created a public fund of 20 billion euros to deal with the capital and liquidity needs of MPS but also those of other banks facing problems.

---

[13] Precautionary recapitalization is an exemption to the normal resolution rules; it refers to the injection of own funds into a solvent bank by the state when this is necessary to remedy a serious disturbance in the economy and preserve financial stability. It is an exceptional measure that is conditional on final approval under the European Union State aid framework (ECB, 2024).

The Italian case demonstrates both how the handling of different crises can differ within the same resolution regime and how authorities can exploit different rules—and even the transition period to new rules—to handle crises differently, depending on the political economic dynamics of each crisis. The Banca Tercas crisis was resolved with recourse to the SVI; the four banks resolution followed the new European resolution rules but without implementing the full bail-in provisions, as the decision was taken a few days before the new regime was enacted; the Veneto banks were liquidated in an 'orderly fashion', with the support of the public treasury and PMS underwent precautionary recapitalization, also with public support.[14] In all cases, retail bondholders were compensated for their losses.

Discussion and Conclusions

The GFC and the ensuing Eurozone crisis proved catalytic for the reform of the EU's financial regulatory and supervisory framework. One of the most important innovations of the Banking Union, EU's flagship reform, was the adoption of the bail-in principle in the resolution of failing banks. The bail-in principle was introduced to eliminate publicly funded bailouts, break the link between banks and sovereigns and instil discipline in financial market participants. The endorsement of bail-in undoubtedly constitutes a step forward in the management of banking crises and, perhaps more importantly, in the formation of banks' incentive structure. Nonetheless, by itself it is not enough to prevent banking crises and has its own operational limitations, both procedural and substantive.

In this chapter, we focused on the constraints imposed on bail-in implementation, by the political economy dynamics of banking crises. Our purpose was to show the difficulties of implementing bail-in, irrespective of the formal resolution regime in place. It was shown that after the introduction of the new resolution regime, the formal bail-in requirements were not fully implemented in any of the banking crises examined in Italy, and even in cases where some burden sharing did take place, certain investor categories were compensated. Even in the case of Cyprus, where an extensive bail-in was implemented, this was limited to certain categories of investors and banks. In both cases, public bailouts were not averted.

Although a detailed analysis of the reasons for the inconsistent implementation of bail-in is beyond the scope of this chapter, a tentative interpretation put forward here is that the political economy constraints analysed above are so difficult to overcome due to the transformation of the financial system in recent decades. Globalization, securitization and financialization have greatly complicated the resolution of banks, by creating new constellations of interests, which stand to lose from

[14] The problems with MPS continue to date; in October 2022, a new recapitalization of 2.4 billion euros took place, 64% of which had to be covered by the Italian government (1.6 billion euros). Following the sale of a 25% stake of the bank to the market in late 2023, 39% of the bank remains under public ownership.

the implementation of bail-in and employ their political and economic weight to avert it. Thus, for example, the increased exposure of retail customers and SMEs to uninsured debt securities, without the appropriate level of expertise and understanding, renders them vulnerable to risks. Once these risks are realized, they stand to incur losses, which can greatly affect their life and business prospects, respectively. The political implications are obvious as demonstrated by the decision of the Cypriot authorities to shelter the cooperative sector and the Italian authorities' attempts to either avoid burden sharing altogether or to compensate retail bondholders when burden sharing was unavoidable. Similarly, the emergence of Cyprus as an international offshore centre complicated the distribution of resolution costs between domestic and foreign constituencies. On the one hand, this proved beneficial for the domestic economy as most of the burden affected uninsured deposits of non-residents; on the other hand, it greatly increased the overall cost of the crisis for the Cypriot banking system, as Greek branches and depositors were spared.

What is more, these were not exceptional cases, which represent a rare deviation from the norm. Even after the introduction of the new rules, most of the choices that were made are allowed, as exceptions, in the regulatory framework, which renders it ex ante susceptible to political pressure and ad hoc solutions. The complex procedure which involves multiple actors and numerous exceptions, and allows significant leeway to domestic authorities, demonstrates that the complex political economic dynamics have been internalized in the design of the rules, rendering them an endogenous constraint in the implementation of the bail-in tool. It is not by accident that there has been only one successful resolution case since the introduction of the new EU regime, with full bail-in implementation.[15]

The failure to implement bail-in is indicative of a broader failure to effectively address the destabilizing features of the global financial system, despite a decade of reforms following the GFC. As long as banks are considered too difficult to fail or to be bailed in, because they are too big (see the chapter by Mäkipää et al., Chap. 8, in this volume), too interconnected or simply because their failure would raise politically costly distributional conflicts, the danger of new destabilizing banking crises is always present.

References

Acharya, V., Anginer, D., & Warburton, A. J. (2014). *The end of market discipline? Investor expectations of implicit state guarantees*. Working Paper. Retrieved January 30 from The End of Market Discipline? Investor Expectations of Implicit Government Guarantees by Viral V. Acharya, Deniz Anginer, A. Joseph Warburton: SSRN.

[15] This was Banco Popular in Spain in 2017. There has also been a decision for the resolution of the Croatian and Slovenian subsidiaries of the Russian Sberbank Europe AG, which, however, is not a typical banking crisis as it is related to the sanctions imposed on several Russian banks following Russia's invasion into Ukraine.

Alessandri, P., & Haldane, A. (2009). *Banking on the state*. Bank of England. Retrieved January 10 from: Paper by Andy Haldane from material presented at the Federal Reserve Bank of Chicago/ World Bank event – International Financial Crisis: Have the Rules of Finance Changed?, 24 September 2009 (bankofengland.co.uk).

Aspriadis, N., Papaioannou, A., & Samaras, A. N. (2018). Games of (de)legitimization and images of collective subjects at the management of a financial crisis: The Cyprus memorandum in the German political discourse. *Cyprus Review, 29*(1), 19–41.

Avgouleas, E., & Goodhart, C. (2014). *A critical evaluation of bail-in as a bank recapitalisation mechanism* (Centre for Economic Policy Research Discussion Paper, no. 10065). Centre for Economic Policy Research.

Baldwin, R., & Giavazzi, F. (eds.) (2015). *The Eurozone crisis: A consensus view of the causes and a few possible solutions*, A VoxEU.org eBook, CEPR Press. Retrieved January 30 from The Eurozone Crisis: A Consensus View of the Causes and a Few Possible Solutions | CEPR.

Barbagallo, B. (2017). *Testimony to the Hearing on Decree Law 237/2016*. Joint Session of the Sixth Committees of the Senate of the Republic (Finance and Treasury) and the Chamber of Deputies (Finance). Retrieved January 10 from: Bank of Italy – Urgent measures to safeguard investors in the banking sector. Testimony of Carmelo Barbagallo (bancaditalia.it).

Beck, T., Radev, D., & Schnabel, I. (2020). *Bank resolution regimes and systemic risk* (CEPR Discussion Paper No. DP14724). Retrieved January 10, from https://ssrn.com/abstract=3603954

Beck, T., Da-Rocha-Lopes, S., & Silva, A. F. (2021). Sharing the pain? Credit supply and real effects of Bank Bail-ins. *The Review of Financial Studies, 34*(4), 1747–1788. https://doi.org/10.1093/rfs/hhaa067

Boccuzzi, G. (2022). *Banking crises in Italy Giuseppe Boccuzzi an application and evaluation of the European framework*. Palgrave Macmillan.

Clerides, S. (2018). The political economy of Cyprus' financial sector reform. In P. Manasse & D. Katsikas (Eds.), *Economic crisis and structural reforms in southern Europe*. Routledge.

Commission of the European Communities. (2010). *Regulating financial services for sustainable growth*. COM (2010) 301, 02.06.2010. Brussels.

Copelovitch, M., Frieden, J., & Walter, S. (2016). The political economy of the Euro crisis. *Comparative Political Studies, 49*(7), 811–840. https://doi.org/10.1177/0010414016633227

Demetriades, P. (2018). *Failing banks, bail-ins, and central bank independence: Lessons from Cyprus*. VoxEU columns. Retrieved January 10 from: Failing banks, bail-ins, and central bank independence: Lessons from Cyprus | CEPR.

Dettmer, M., & Reiermann, C. (2012). Bailing out Oligarchs: EU aid for Cyprus a political minefield for Merkel. *Spiegel Online*. Retrieved January 30 from: German Intelligence Report Warns Cyprus Not Combating Money Laundering – SPIEGEL ONLINE (economicsvoodoo.com).

Donnelly, S. (2014). Power politics and the undersupply of financial stability in Europe. *Review of International Political Economy, 21*(4), 980–1005. https://doi.org/10.1080/09692290.2013.801021

Donnelly, S., & Asimakopoulos, I. G. (2020). Bending and breaking the single resolution mechanism: The case of Italy. *JCMS: Journal of Common Market Studies, 58*, 856–871. https://doi.org/10.1111/jcms.12992

European Central Bank (2024). *What is a precautionary recapitalisationand how does it work?* Retrieved January 30 from What is a precautionary recapitalisation and how does it work? (europa.eu)

European Commission. (2013). *State aid: Commission's new on-line state aid benchmarking tool shows less aid to banks*. Press Release. December 20. Brussels.

Fontevecchia, A. (2013). *EU takes shot at Moscow with Cyprus Bailout as Russians Own 22% of deposits*. Retrieved January 30 from: EU Takes shot at Moscow with Cyprus bailout as Russians Own 22% of deposits (forbes.com).

Gleeson, S. (2012). *Legal aspects of Bank Bail-Ins*. Special Paper 205, LSE Financial Markets Group Series.

Halaj, G., Hüser A. C., Kok, C., Perales, C., & van der Kraaij, A. (2016). Systemic implications of the European bail-in tool: amulti-layered network analysis. *Financial Stability Review, ECB* (May).

Henig, D., & Knight, D. M. (2023). Polycrisis: Prompts for an emerging worldview. *Anthropology Today, 39*(2), 1–6. https://doi.org/10.1111/1467-8322.12793

Högenauer, A. L., Howarth, D., & Quaglia, L. (2023). Introduction to the special issue: The persistent challenges to European Banking Union. *Journal of European Integration, 45*(1), 1–14. https://doi.org/10.1080/07036337.2023.2183390

Howarth, D., & Quaglia, L. (2013). Banking union as Holy Grail. *Journal of Common Market Studies, 51*, 103–123. https://doi.org/10.1111/jcms.12054

International Monetary Fund. (2010). *Global financial stability report: Meeting new challenges to stability and building a safer system*. Washington.

Lastra, R. M. (2003). *The governance structure for financial regulation and supervision in Europe*. The London Financial Regulation Seminar, London School of Economics, 19 May.

Meehl, A. (2022). *Bailouts, Bail-ins, and Banking Industry Dynamics*. Working Paper. Retrieved January 10 from: Bailouts, Bail-ins, and Banking Industry Dynamics (europa.eu)

Monnet, J. (1978). *Memoirs*. Collins.

Moschella, M., & Quaglia, L. (2019). European Banking Union to the rescue? How supranational institutions influenced crisis management in Italy. *South European Society and Politics, 24*(4), 421–440. https://doi.org/10.1080/13608746.2020.1728957

Philippon, T., & Salord, A. (2017). *Bail-ins and bank resolution in Europe: A progress report*. Geneva Reports on the World Economy, Special Report 4.

Pierson, P. (2004). *Politics in time: History, institutions, and social analysis*. Princeton University Press.

Quaglia, L. (2007). The politics of financial services regulation and supervision reform in the European Union. *European Journal of Political Research, 46*, 269–290.

Quaglia, L. (2019). The politics of an 'incomplete' banking union and its 'asymmetric' effects. *Journal of European Integration, 41*(8), 955–969. https://doi.org/10.1080/07036337.2019.1622541

Schäfer, A., Schnabel, I., & Weder di Mauro, B. (2017). *Bail-in expectations for European banks: Actions speak louden than words* (European Systemic Risk Board Working Paper Series, No 7).

Siebenbrunner, C., Guth, M., Spitzer, R., & Trappl, S. (2024). Assessing the systemic risk impact of bank bail-ins. *Journal of Financial Stability*. https://doi.org/10.1016/j.jfs.2024.101229

Single Resolution Board (2024). *What is the Single Resolution Fund?* Retrieved January 25 from Single Resolution Fund | Single Resolution Board (europa.eu)

Thelen, K. (1999). Historical institutionalism in comparative politics. *Annual Review of Political Science, 2*, 369–404.

Ueda, K. & Weder di Mauro, B.. (2012). *Quantifying structural subsidy values for systemically important financial institutions* (IMF Working Paper No. 12/128).

[illegible]

Part III
Economic Policy and Governance in Times of Crises: Evidence from Latin America

Chapter 10
Economic Policies Amid Political Instability in Latin America

Maria Antonieta Del Tedesco Lins

Contents

Introduction

Latin America's image is deeply intertwined with crises, whether stemming from the foreign debt crisis of the 1980s or various episodes of political instability throughout its history. The region weathered intense financial turmoil in the 1990s, prompting substantial shifts in economic policy, and has frequently grappled with currency crises. The notion of permacrisis, explored in this volume, finds a strong resonance within Latin American economies, particularly evident in the cases of Argentina, Brazil, and Mexico. Examining a broader timeframe stretching back to the 1980s, we observe a recurring pattern of economic crises, notably marked by currency crises (Kaminsky, 2003, 2006). This is not merely a matter of witnessing a series of crises unfold but also recognizing that unresolved issues resurface, exacerbating currency devaluations and frequently leading to inflationary pressures and declining real incomes, particularly impacting disadvantaged groups.

M. A. Del Tedesco Lins (✉)
Institute of International Relations, Universidade of São Paulo, São Paulo, SP, Brazil
e-mail: madtlins@usp.br

D. Katsikas et al. (eds.), *Finance, Growth and Democracy: Connections and Challenges in Europe and Latin America in the Era of Permacrisis*, United Nations University Series on Regionalism 33, https://doi.org/10.1007/978-3-031-68475-3_10

A theoretical framework commonly employed to assess the trajectory of emerging economies is the concept of the middle-income trap (Glawe & Wagner, 2016; Agénor, 2017; Bresser-Pereira et al., 2020, inter alia). This concept refers to countries that have undergone periods of robust economic expansion, resulting in a significant rise in average income yet subsequently struggle to sustain this growth trajectory, thus failing to surpass the middle-income threshold. Brazil is a typical example of this phenomenon. Discussing the vast literature related to experiments in Latin America, Middle East, North Africa, and East Asia, Agénor (2017: 2) proposes a specific perspective of analysis for the concept of middle-income trap: "a middle-income trap is best viewed as a 'bad' equilibrium among many—bad but nonetheless stable, in the sense of being a persistent state to which the economy gravitates unless some significant shock, structural or otherwise, occurs." It means that countries with similar characteristics may converge to diverse levels of growth "depending on their initial conditions." This approach appears intriguing for Latin American countries, given that, even though they faced similar types of crises, employed several comparable policy strategies during their development period, and implemented similar macroeconomic instruments for stabilization, some national disparities make them unique cases.

There is an intense debate in Latin America about the determinants of the chronic low growth in the region. From one perspective, the supply-side approach aims to pinpoint shortcomings in the productive and institutional framework, a perspective that aligns with the challenges posed by the middle-income trap. On the contrary, a demand-side viewpoint argues that policies emphasizing macroeconomic stability impede government intervention in the economy, thus obstructing the expansion of demand and overall growth. Both perspectives offer relevant insights and are not mutually exclusive.

In this regard, the concept of the middle-income trap can be incorporated into the notion of a permacrisis. Prolonged periods of steady but moderate growth serve as limiting factors in addressing long-standing challenges that are seldom overcome. According to Brown et al. (2023), a permacrisis is characterized by countries being unable to effectively address various structural issues, thus impeding growth and development. The authors (2023: 9) assert: "The greatest risk is that these challenges persist and interact with one another," a statement directly applicable to Latin America.

Despite persistent economic and social challenges, there is a discernible shift in the "quality" of crises in recent times. Since the 2000s, Latin America has been less susceptible to external shocks. Many countries have tightened regulations on their financial systems, maintained healthy levels of international reserves, and improved the balance of public accounts compared to the turbulent episodes of the late twentieth century. The region is more resilient to monetary and financial shocks (Canuto, 2022). However, although the region was less vulnerable during the global financial crisis (GFC), it did not achieve sustained growth or significant social progress. Therefore, the region accumulates different structural challenges that can potentially become triggers for new crises, in addition to possible external shocks, such as those generated by the pandemic and armed conflicts in other parts of the world.

The COVID-19 pandemic crisis has exacerbated Latin America's prolonged period of mediocre growth. The pandemic's devastating impact has magnified the region's structural asymmetries, including inequality, healthcare deficiencies, educational shortcomings, limited innovation capacity, and stagnant productivity. Mere post-pandemic GDP growth, while welcome, is insufficient to tackle these entrenched problems and lift countries out of the enduring middle-income trap, regardless of its form (Canuto, 2022). During the last 15 years, Argentina, Brazil, and Mexico shared unfavorable trends, including low growth, heightened poverty, and inequality, and, in the cases of Argentina and Brazil, periods of significant political instability.

This chapter aims to elucidate the intersection between economic strategies and political transformations over the past 15 years, emphasizing the repercussions of political instability on economic outcomes. By concentrating on the three largest economies in the region, the objective is to contribute to a comprehensive understanding of the relationship between politics and economics in times of crisis. The next section is devoted to providing an overview of the economic performance of the three countries to ascertain if they are stuck in the middle-income trap, experiencing longer-term economic stagnation. The following section will deal with the specificities of each case. The last section concludes with a brief analysis of the three cases from the perspective of recurring crises that feed into each other and interconnect, as discussed in this volume under the concept of "permacrisis."

Economic Performance Amid Political Instability

The performance of Latin America's largest economies—Argentina, Brazil, and Mexico—over the last 15 years has been characterized by various economic ups and downs influenced by both domestic and international factors (Lins, 2021). Figure 10.1 shows this volatile trajectory for the three countries with Argentina having the sharpest variations and Mexico exhibiting more stability in the annual rates. Are these trends enough to be considered "a crisis?" Although the deepest external shock was the one caused by the pandemic, growth rates throughout the period indicate at least evidence of stagnation by showing no persistent expansion. Apart from Mexico, which maintained a positive trend throughout the period, Argentina and Brazil exhibit inconsistent patterns. Taking the average annual growth of Argentina, Brazil, and Mexico between 2010 and 2023—1.3%, 1.6%, and 2%, respectively—one can say that it was a mediocre performance, with greater volatility in the case of Argentina and Brazil. Despite the mediocre growth of their economies, Argentina, Brazil, and Mexico did not face a sharp rise in unemployment. The unemployment rate increased in 2020, as predicted, but employment has been recovering in the years 2021 and 2022.

The numbers become even more concerning when we look at the average annual GDP per capita growth between 2010 and 2023: in this period, Argentina saw an average growth rate of 0.12%, Brazil of 1%, and Mexico of 0.83%. Data for per

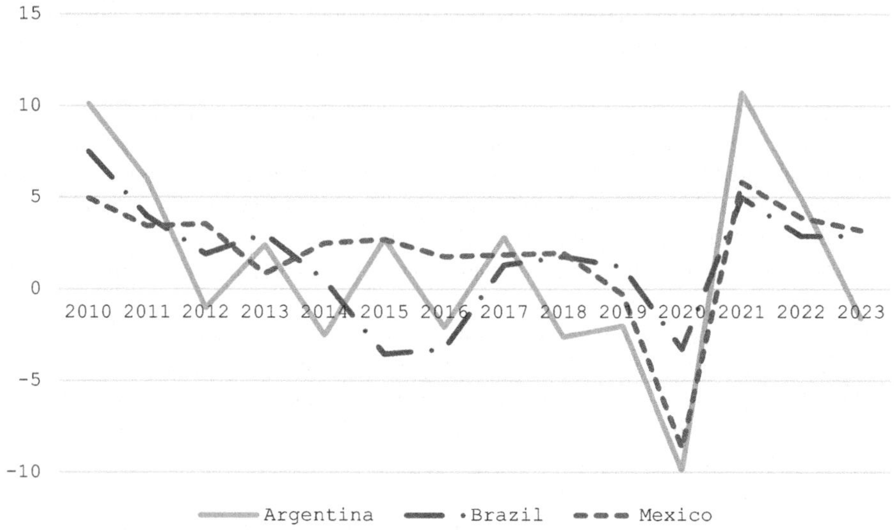

Fig. 10.1 GDP annual growth rates, %. (Source: World Bank database)

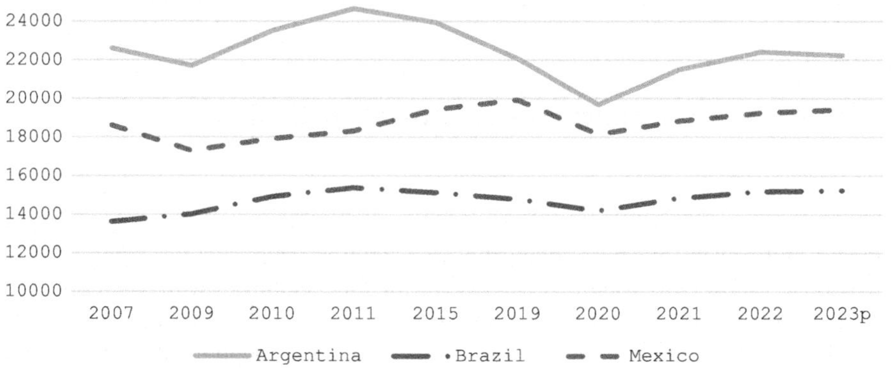

Fig. 10.2 GDP per capita, current prices (purchasing power parity; international USD per capita). (Source: IMF, World Economic Outlook, 2023 October report)

capita GDP show even more explicitly the dynamics of stagnant income in the three countries. Taking the data in comparable currency values (purchasing power parity) confirms that there was no significant real income gain for populations. Figure 10.2 shows this evolution through selected years. Argentina, despite the intensity of the crises it suffered during this period, remains the highest-income country among the three. For Brazil, the effects of the 2015–2016 recession are visible on per capita income, and for Mexico, there is a stubborn stagnation.

Bresser-Pereira et al. (2020), rather than identifying stagnation in Latin America as a typical case of middle-income trap, claim that it is a liberalizing trap, because the region adopted liberal reforms more intensively than emerging economies in other parts of the world, such as in Asia. According to the authors, among the major problems in Latin America was the decision to pursue trade liberalization before the industry was ready to face competition. Trade liberalization combined with an anti-inflationary policy based on managed exchange rates and high interest rates to attract foreign capital was a detrimental combination that led to a process of deindustrialization. This strategy resulted in excessive appreciation of these countries' currencies with little capacity to manage capital flows, in other words, a situation of Dutch disease, limiting the growth capacity of the industry. To what extent would the argument of the mistakes of the liberal reforms of the 1990s and the Dutch disease be sufficient to explain the stagnation in Latin America?

A comprehensive study by Agénor (2017) reviews empirical studies that focused on countries that are supposedly caught in the middle-income trap. Although there are many differences in the criteria used to define a middle-income trap situation, the priority factor—which gives the concept its name—is the evidence of a stagnation in per capita income, which may be a consequence of more structural variables, such as deficiencies in the education system, diminishing returns to physical capital, lack of access to technology, inequal income distribution, insufficient quality of human capital, or decreases in factor productivity.

Indeed, the three countries studied here have experienced an intense reduction in labor productivity during this period. Estimates from the International Labor Organization (ILO) show that the average annual growth rate of output per worker (GDP constant 2017 international $ at PPP) for Argentina decreased by 1.38%, for Brazil by 0.35%, and for Mexico by 0.11% between 2014 and 2023. In addition, the period was marked by a constant constraint of public resources to finance current expenditure and further stimulate investment. Focusing only on the primary government balance between 2010 and 2020, Fig. 10.3 shows that, while Brazil and Mexico largely maintained a positive balance, Argentina has consistently faced a primary deficit.

Notwithstanding the presence of structural shortcomings which inhibit the resumption of a growth process capable of getting these countries out of the trap, the recent crises have not led them again to the old, well-known nightmares of balance of payments crises. While Argentina faced very hard circumstances when negotiating its foreign debt, as Datz shows in this volume (Chap. 12), the three countries were significantly less vulnerable to balance of payment crises at this time, even with the economic stagnation experienced throughout this period. Despite experiencing low growth, the average current account balance for the three countries remained in the negative throughout the observed timeframe. Specifically, between 2010 and 2023, Argentina, Brazil, and Mexico recorded an average current account balance of −1.42%, −3%, and −1.25% of their GDP, respectively.

The liquidity buffer represented by foreign reserves was a crucial factor in reducing the external vulnerability of the three countries. Figure 10.4 shows the status of foreign reserves in absolute terms, in billions of dollars, and in relative terms,

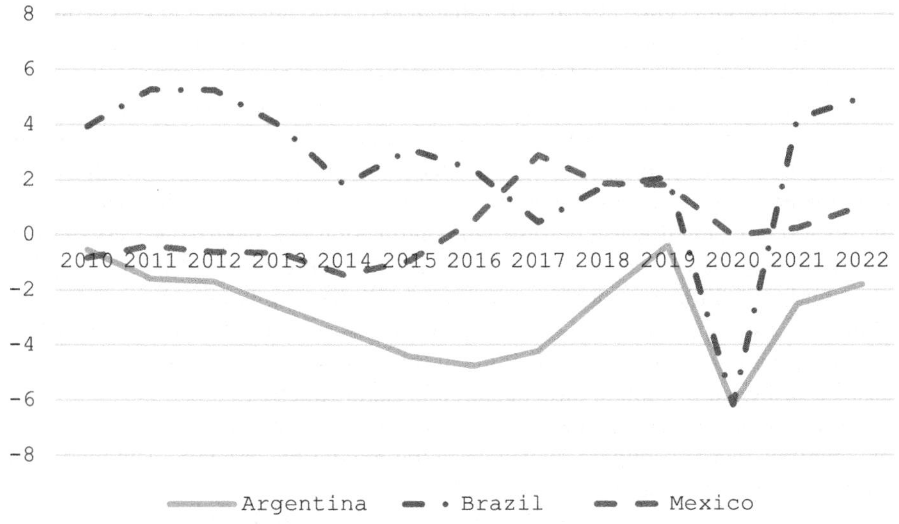

Fig. 10.3 Government primary balance, percent of GDP. (Source: IMF. Public Finances in Modern History Database. Available at: https://www.imf.org/external/datamapper/rltir@FPP/USA/FRA/JPN/GBR/SWE/ESP/ITA/ZAF/IND)

measured by the ratio of reserves to imports. Brazil stands out in both instances, albeit experiencing a decrease in the number of months that its reserves could cover imports as of 2022. This is mainly due to an improvement in GDP growth—leading to an increase in imports—and to the rise in import prices, which grew by about 24% compared to 2021.[1] Argentina's situation has been deteriorating since 2018, as the country has had more difficulty honoring its external debt and the debt stock increased substantially, as Fig. 10.5 shows.

Despite their reduced vulnerability to global shocks compared to previous periods, these countries underwent significant moments of political upheaval. While it is possible to discern shared elements in the trajectories of Argentina, Brazil, and Mexico, it is also imperative to analyze the particularities of the political dynamics of each country to get a better understanding of the intertwined relationship between politics and the economy and the dynamics of interdependence between the two domains. The next section explores the national experiences of these countries.

[1] Brazilian Ministry of Development, Industry, Commerce and Services. Available at: https://www.gov.br/economia/pt-br/assuntos/noticias/2023/janeiro/Balanca2022.pdf

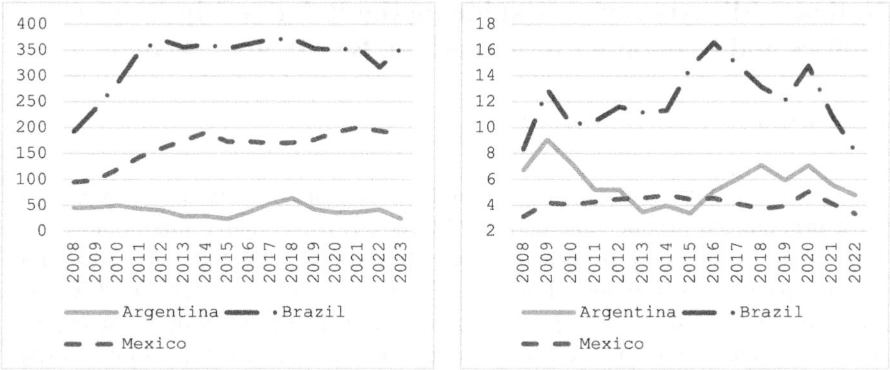

(a) Total reserves ex-gold, in USD billion (b) Total reserves in months of imports

Fig. 10.4 Foreign reserves (**a**) Total reserves ex-gold, in USD billion (**b**) Total reserves in months of imports. (Source: IMF—World Economic Outlook)

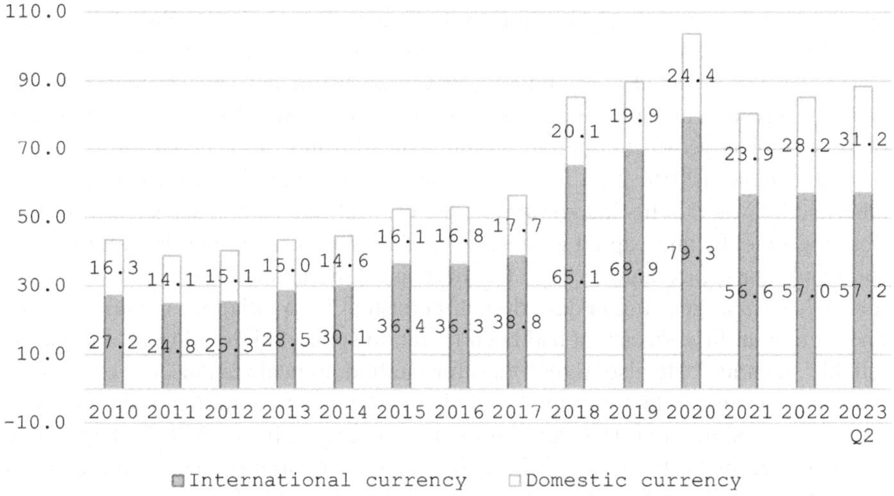

Fig. 10.5 Gross central government debt, in % of GDP. (Source: Argentine government. Ministerio de Economía—Finanzas. Available at: https://www.argentina.gob.ar/economia/finanzas/graficos-deuda/deuda-bruta-por-moneda-en-porcentaje-del-pbi)

National Idiosyncrasies: Exploring the Relationship Between Politics and Economics in Argentina, Brazil, and Mexico

Argentina

Argentina stands out as the country among the three analyzed here experiencing the most pronounced product fluctuations. Moreover, it has undergone notable shifts concerning the direction of its economic policies. Following the 2001–2002 crisis, the Peronist administrations of Presidents Néstor and Cristina Kirchner (2003–2007 and 2007–2015, respectively) pursued policies aimed at expanding public expenditure, alongside various heterodox measures, such as the nationalization of private pension funds (Lins, 2021), and controls over exports during the commodity boom to avert domestic prices to rise. Upon Mauricio Macri's election in 2015, the economy was already facing deceleration, escalating inflation, a public deficit hovering around 4.4% of GDP, and a substantial accumulation of public debt denominated in foreign currency (Pessoa, 2019).

Macri's economic policy rested on the premise that the primary cause of economic challenges stemmed from excessive state intervention by prior administrations. These interventions had primarily aimed at bolstering consumption through income transfers, ultimately leading to the country's isolation in the global economy. The proposed solution involved diminishing the state's influence through a series of reforms aimed at revitalizing private investments. This strategy aimed to facilitate a resurgence in economic growth. From the point of view of external relations, the objective was to open the country on all fronts of the economy.

Sturzenegger (2019: 2), a former central bank governor, emphasizes the legacy inherited by Macri at his inauguration: "the Central Bank's balance sheet was deteriorating quickly, and capital controls contributed to a rising gap between official and black-market exchange rates. The heritage also included four years of stagnation, a large and growing budget deficit, persistent high inflation, a dual exchange rate system, utility prices that had been frozen in spite of high inflation, and lack of reliable statistics." He also argues that, for methodological reasons, the official figures on government debt provided by Cristina Kirchner's administration should be reviewed. He shows the stark deterioration of the central bank (BCRA) net worth to a peak deficit of ca 93 billion USD during the third quarter of 2015 (Sturzenegger, 2019: 5). The Macri administration assumed the mantle of steering a politically contentious, albeit necessary, adjustment process. The liberalizing reforms introduced by the Macri government spurred an uptick in foreign investment. However, anticipated growth failed to materialize, resulting in increasing inflation and a dangerous hike in both the deficit and public debt. This significant deterioration in the economic landscape eroded government popularity.

A different perspective is presented by Amico (2020: 56–58), who identifies different phases in the economic policy of the Macri government. According to the author, the first was a shock phase: abolition of capital controls—with the aim of cooling the parallel dollar market and adoption of an inflation target system by the

BCRA combined with currency fluctuation. Liberalization of the foreign exchange market was expected to lead to adjustment of relative prices, which did not happen, and inflation rose, the peso depreciated, and BCRA had to raise interest rates. In June 2017, the government issued a 100-year debt bond, implying that the government deficit was lower than expected. In the same phase, the government made a debt payment to holdout creditors (see Datz, Chap. 12, in this volume).

The second phase was ironically named by Amico (2020) as "late populism." This is because facing the parliamentary elections that would partially renew the Chamber of Deputies and the Senate in a scenario of economic stagnation would pose a risk to the Macri government. Therefore, the elections marked a halt in the reform program. This phase constituted a deviation from the previous electoral program of the government and brought contradictions to the initial macroeconomic strategy. In 2017, changes were announced in the management of the inflation targeting regime, which had the immediate effect of currency depreciation. From there would come a third phase characterized by Amico (2020) as currency crisis and worsening of economic activity.

In September 2018, inflation targeting was abandoned in Argentina, having lasted only 25 months (Cachanosky & Ferrelli Mazza, 2021). According to the authors, two main factors help to explain the IT failure in Argentina: "The first one is the explosive growth of short-term bills, Letras del Banco Central (LEBACs), used to sterilize issued ARS.[2] The second one is a negative credibility shock that took place in December 2017. A perfect storm of foreign shocks in April 2018 only accelerated the failure of the BCRA policy inconsistencies" (Cachanosky & Ferrelli Mazza, 2021: 107).

Public debt appears to be a recurring issue in Argentina, almost like an unavoidable inheritance passed down from one government to the next. The data depicted in Fig. 10.5 vividly portray the substantial growth in debt during the period under examination. Just as Macri's administration denounced the legacy inherited from the Kirchner era, his successor, Alberto Fernández, could use a similar argument upon assuming office at the end of 2019, with Cristina Fernández de Kirchner as vice president. Furthermore, alongside the pronounced increase in debt as a percentage of GDP, it is essential to highlight the considerable portion denominated in foreign currency, significantly increasing the country's external vulnerability.

The Alberto Fernández administration will go down in history as synonymous with an economic catastrophe: consumer prices surged by approximately 408% over 4 years, the currency underwent severe devaluation, and the escalation of external debt, which had begun years before, resulted in increasingly challenging negotiations with the IMF, ultimately culminating in a period of profound destabilization. The president's popularity plummeted in tandem with the rise in inflation (Brasil & Pera, 2022). The government inherited a burdensome legacy from its predecessor, and the onset of the pandemic in early 2020 left few opportunities for a sound reformulation of economic policy. Fernandez's choice was for an unorthodox direction

[2] ARS is the symbol for Argentine pesos.

to the economy. Despite the unequivocal need to increase public spending to tackle the global health crisis, the government was elected as a clear alternative to the proposal brought by Macri. However, all relevant economic variables had deteriorated sharply, a trend which was further exacerbated by the pandemic. There was limited room for policy innovations, and the government lacked a proposal capable of addressing the inevitable deepening of the crisis.

The heart of the political instability laid within the Fernández government itself, marked by ongoing conflicts between the president and the vice president throughout their term. This discord stems from the internal dynamics of the Peronist electoral camp, which united to prevent Macri's reelection. This coalition brought together two distinct factions of the Peronist movement to create the *Frente para Todos*, with Alberto Fernández as president and Cristina Fernández de Kirshner as vice president (Lucca, 2022). While their alliance successfully ousted Macri in the elections, it also set the stage for internal division from the beginning, complicating consensus on any matter. This division reached a climax in May 2021 when a dispute led to the resignation of half of the cabinet members, sparking a political crisis. Furthermore, in September 2022, an assassination attempt on the vice president, though unsuccessful, exacerbated the government's unease and further destabilized the situation (Molino, 2021).

The worsening economic situation further eroded support for the government. Sergio Massa was appointed as the new economy minister with the hope of restoring credibility and predictability to the economic policy (Brasil & Pera, 2022). However, the level of disorder was so severe that his efforts saw limited success. This long history of economic instability led Argentina to elect, in October 2023, an outsider, far-right candidate, Javier Milei, defeating Minister Sergio Massa.

Brazil

When COVID-19 struck Brazil in February 2020, Jair Bolsonaro's presidency celebrated just 1 year in power, during which the main economic accomplishment was the pension reform passed by the congress in 2019.[3] The government's election campaign rhetoric blended nationalist and ultraliberal elements, but the government lacked ability to design and approve radical reform measures. Despite market expectations and the new government's belief in the necessity of reforms for economic recovery—before the pension reform, a legal control on public spending was approved in 2016, and a labor reform in 2017—these measures proved insufficient to stimulate economic activity (Lins, 2020). But the domestic crisis had begun back in 2013–2014. Political upheaval started with huge street demonstrations in June 2013 primarily highlighting social grievances, including concerns over the cost of public transportation, overcrowding in hospitals, and corruption. As the country was

[3] Emenda constitucional Nº 103 of November 12, 2019.

getting ready to host international sporting events, citizens questioned the justification of investing in stadiums amid the nation's significant social deficits. The political crisis intensified concurrently with the deteriorating economic conditions: inflation, since the global financial crisis (GFC), had consistently veered away from the central bank's target, and consumer prices were averaging annually 6.4% between 2008 and 2015, peaking at over 9% in 2014.

President Dilma Rousseff (2011–2014) adopted a strongly interventionist economic policy, which the government called the "new macroeconomic matrix"; its effects contributed to raising inflation further and were not effective in its central objective (Lins, 2022). This exacerbated macroeconomic instability and further fueled popular discontent. Upon her reelection, Rousseff attempted to pivot the direction of economic policy toward controlling inflation and decreasing fiscal deficits. However, her efforts came too late. Her failure to address both the 2013 street protests and opposition within Congress paved the way for an impeachment process, based on allegations of manipulating the federal budget (Winter, 2017). In short, Dilma Rousseff's second term deteriorated into a parliamentary movement aiming at the removal of the president under the allegation that she had acted against the law on public spending control, coinciding with a rapid deterioration in economic conditions.

Regarding political instability, a huge police and judicial investigation began in 2014. Initially, it was an investigation of a parallel exchange market operator based in the city of Curitiba, Paraná. As the investigations progressed, links between politicians and the investigated became apparent. So began the "Car Wash" operation. A group of public prosecutors in the state of Paraná initiated this operation that would evolve into a massive case implicating Brazilian politicians. Against the backdrop of political uncertainty and macroeconomic instability, an economic crisis broke out in 2014 (Guilherme & Ribeiro Hoffmann, 2021).

The recession of 2015–2016 marked the conclusion of an era of economic prosperity. As economic troubles deepened, discontent with the political system surged, paving the way for the rise of antiestablishment ideologies, particularly championed by far-right groups, as discussed by Herz and Ribeiro Hoffmann, Chap. 2, in this volume. This led to the election of Jair Bolsonaro in 2018. The 2018 elections must be understood in the light of the rupture of the political fabric from corruption scandals and a real deterioration of the economy with the recession that began in 2014.

Bolsonaro's 4 years in office proved to be far less favorable than his promises and the expectations of his ca 58 million voters in the second round. Following the previous years' slump, markets anticipated a robust recovery and the successful implementation of structural reforms from his tenure. However, 2019 already delivered disappointment with its poor growth, and the beginning of the pandemic in 2020 dashed hopes for a recovery. Political instability, emanating from within the government's inner circle, further compounded the situation. 2020 marked the convergence of three simultaneous crises: political, economic, and health. The roots of these crises can be traced back to 2013–2014, with the onset of the health crisis exacerbating and deepening existing issues.

As a result of all these political developments and the poor economic performance, the 2022 elections were marked by unprecedented polarization in Brazil. Even following the elections, democracy remained under threat. On January 8, 2023, thousands of supporters of former President Bolsonaro forcefully entered the centers of power in Brasília, invading the national congress, the supreme court, and the presidential palace. The elections were won by a coalition led by the Workers' Party (Partido do Trabalhadores), with former President Luiz Inácio Lula da Silva as the candidate, and composed of 16 center and center-left parties.

Mexico

Mexico is also a case of repeated crises and a long process of economic stagnation. Blecker (2022: 225) presents the situation clearly: "From 1975–76 to 1994–95, a crisis broke out about every 6 years, usually either right before or right after a presidential election. Each time, the balance of payments deteriorated, inflation accelerated, the peso was devalued, and a severe recession occurred." Between the late 1980s and the mid 1990s, a set of liberalizing reforms were implemented, and economic policy has remained relatively stable since then (Lins, 2021). Among the three economies, Mexico stands out as the most committed to economic stability. Since 1993, its central bank has been officially independent, a milestone Brazil achieved only in 2021, while Argentina is still far from making such a move.

In the intense scholarly debate about the causes of the weak growth of the Mexican economy, on the one hand, the supply-side approach seeks to identify deficiencies in the productive and/or institutional structure, an approach to which the contribution of the middle-income trap converges. Conversely, a demand-side perspective contends that policies prioritizing macroeconomic stability hinder the state's intervention in economic affairs, thereby acting as a barrier to demand expansion and growth. This clash of interpretations is highly prevalent in the analysis of the Mexican case. After about 35 years since liberalizing policies began to be implemented in Mexico and given that there has been no economic policy reversal during this the period, the main question that critics ask is why stable, more robust growth has not been observed (Ros, 2013; Nadal, 2020; Blecker, 2022). On the pro-stabilization side, a first set of responses was that reforms need time to produce growth. Time has effectively passed, and another way to explain low growth is to focus on supply-side shortcomings and other structural constraints.

Analyses from both sides are relevant. On the supply side, labor productivity has not grown for a decade and has even decreased in a few years as we saw above. According to ILO estimates, this indicator had an average annual variation between 2019 and 2023 of −0.9%, what is explained, among other factors, by the strong informality prevailing in the Mexican economy. On the demand side, economic policy is viewed as the main cause of low growth rates. The commitment to inflation control by the Mexican central bank, by administering interest rates—and keeping them high—would constantly limit investment incentives. So would the overvalued exchange rate in a country extremely open to trade with its richer neighbors. Conversely, a consistent and sometimes unexciting economic policy fosters high predictability in government actions, which in turn supports business planning. However, what about political stability?

A panoramic view of the Mexican political system might give the impression of stability. Since the transition to democracy in 2000, when there was a shift from a dominant party authoritarian rule to democracy (Álvarez Tovar, 2013), elections have occurred every 6 years, and there have been no reports of dramatic incidents such as candidate assassinations or electoral frauds. However, the fact that there have been few incumbent presidents since 2010,[4] that a president who is not a member of one of the two largest parties[5] was elected in 2018—Antonio Manuel López Obrador (AMLO), from the Movimiento Regeneración Nacional (Morena)—and that governments have maintained a commitment to macroeconomic stability does not mean that politics is stable. In defense of a more free-market approach and contrary to government policy, Rubio (2023) in a sharp critic to President López Obrador affirms: "Mexico undertook economic reforms largely in order to avoid reforming its politics. Therein lies the huge difference in results between Mexico and Chile, or between Mexico and its Asian peers."

Besides inequality and poverty, Mexico faces serious problems related to migration, corruption, drug traffic, and organized crime, despite the government's militarization of public security. Moreover, critics point to the lack of accountability for the government as a result of the president's control of parliament, weakening the system of checks and balances (Sánchez-Talanquer & Greene, 2021; Ellner, 2020). Sanchez-Talanquer and Greene (2021) highlight a notable trend of power concentration in the executive branch during the first half of AMLO's term. An instance of interference in institutions was witnessed in 2023 when the Senate approved alterations to the National Electoral Institute (INE), responsible for overseeing elections, resulting in a reduction of its resources. This move triggered large-scale demonstrations across the country, raising concerns about a potential regression of democracy, with fears looming of a slide back toward autocracy (Sánchez-Talanquer & Greene, 2021; Wirtschafter & Sarukhan, 2023).

As the 2024 presidential elections in Mexico approaches, the incontestable popularity of AMLO is expected to lead him to name his successor and retain control over the congress. Strictly considering indicators of public opinion, we can say that during the last two decades there was, and there still is, political stability in Mexico. However, given the deep social problems and those derived from the powerful structure of organized crime, the situation is much more complex.

---

[4] Since 2010, as the presidential mandate is 6 years, México had only three presidents: Felipe Calderón Hinojosa (2006–2012), Enrique Peña Nieto (2012–2018), and Andrés Manuel López Obrador (2018–2024).

[5] Vicente Fox of the Partido Acción Nacional (National Action Party—PAN) was elected in 1999, marking the end of a 70-year rule of the Partido Revolucionario Institucional (Institutional Revolutionary Party—PRI).

A Permanent State of Crisis, Both in the Economy and in Politics

This chapter explored the argument that political instability can be a determining factor in deepening economic crises. By analyzing the main political and economic trends of the three largest Latin American economies—Argentina, Brazil, and Mexico—it showed that the last 15 years have been a period of economic stagnation, during which these countries have been unable to address structural problems to overcome the middle-income trap. Besides mediocre growth rates, these countries have seen their social indicators worsen. The pandemic bears some of the blame for this.

Argentina's, Brazil's, and Mexico's responses to the COVID-19 pandemic were flawed, leading to significant loss of life and economic downturn, revealing that their healthcare systems and infrastructure were ill-equipped for such a crisis. While there were variations in their approaches, the Brazilian government's denial under Jair Bolsonaro and its lack of action represented the most harmful aspects of the pandemic's management in Latin America. Despite implementing isolation measures, income support, and distributing vaccines when available, the economic, social, and human toll of the health crisis hit these countries harder than many others worldwide.

This situation raises questions about whether the long history of crises in these countries contributed to the magnitude of the pandemic's impact and whether inherent factors within these economies and societies might precipitate or exacerbate future crises in response to external shocks. The evidence gathered in this chapter suggests a positive response to the query of whether past crises have influenced current outcomes. This is attributed to the fact that the underlying issues plaguing these societies have not been properly tackled. While certain institutions have weathered numerous storms—highlighted by the strain on democratic institutions in Brazil from 2019 to 2022—there remain significant social and economic challenges that demand resolution. Table 10.1 gathers information on some of the main variables discussed here to help compare these countries and provide an assessment of political instability's impact as an additional factor in deepening crises.

It was seen that the high approval ratings of the Mexican government did not shield the country from crises and that even a government with a strong interventionist tendency did not target institutions linked to macroeconomic stability, primarily the central bank. In Brazil on the other hand, when Luiz Inácio Lula da Silva returned to power in 2023, he publicly expressed his dissatisfaction with the central bank's interest rate policy, which was already protected by the autonomy law of 2021. Argentina is the most unstable among the three countries. Instability permeates its institutions and undermines predictability, which is detrimental to investment decisions. In all three cases, political dynamics have a profound effect on economic management. They are stories of multiple crises, whose elements intertwine and mutually influence each other, as discussed in this volume with the concept of permacrisis.

Table 10.1 The three cases summarized

	Argentina	Brazil	Mexico
Commitment with stability	No	Yes	Yes
External vulnerability	High	Low	Low
Gross capital formation annual average 2013–2022 (%GDP)	16,8%	17,4%	22,7%
Evidence of middle-income trap	Yes	Yes	Yes
Structural reforms	Inflation targeting later reversed Capital controls	Pension, labor and tax reforms, central bank autonomy approved	Social reforms proposed No substantial economic reforms
Government orientation	Left-wing populism (2007–2015 and 2019–2023) Right wing (2015–2019) Extreme right (2022–2027)	Center left (2003–2016) Center right (2016–2018) Extreme right (2019–2022)	Center right (2006–2018) Left-wing populism (2018–2024)
Political instability	High	High	Low to moderate

Regional cooperation could provide a platform for these countries to develop common responses to crises and provide economic and political effectiveness and stability. Argentina and Brazil are members of Mercosur, a regional bloc that aimed at a comprehensive and promising agenda but which suffered from the lack of consensus to deepen commitments; the most profound blow suffered by Mercosur originated precisely from the financial crises experienced by Brazil and Argentina in the late 1990s (Bouzas, 2001). Mexico has been a member of the North America Free Trade Agreement (NAFTA) and its successor, the United States-Mexico-Canada Agreement (USMCA), but these projects are more focused on fostering free trade. Other initiatives such as CELAC include these three countries, but it is only a space for political concertation; regional institutions in Latin America have failed so far to build a solidity which would allow them to survive and operate as national governments change, regardless of their political orientations. As a result, they end up relinquishing a powerful tool to politically construct alternatives to overcome the middle-income trap and tackle social problems.

References

Agénor, P.-R. (2017). Caught in the middle? The economics of middle income traps. *Journal of Economic Surveys, 31*, 771–791. https://doi.org/10.1111/joes.12175

Álvarez Tovar, J. A. (2013). Why has the transition to democracy led the Mexican presidential system to political instability? A proposal to enhance institutional arrangements. *Mexican Law Review, 5*(2), 277–304.

Amico, F. (2020). La macroeconomia de Macri: Adiós represión financeira, bienvenido nuevo default. *Circus Revista Argentina de Economía*, N°7, Verano de 2020, 52–89.

Blecker, R. A. (2022). Mexico: Unequal integration and "stabilizing stagnation". In L. R. Wray & F. Dantas (Eds.), *Handbook of economic stagnation* (pp. 225–249). Academic Press/Elsevier.

Bouzas, R. (2001). El Mercosur diez años después. ¿Proceso de aprendizaje o déjà vu? *Desarrollo Económico, 41*(162), 179–200.

Brasil, G., & Pera, M. (2022, September 22). What's ahead for Alberto Fernández's last year in office? *America's Quarterly*. Available at: https://www.americasquarterly.org/article/whats-ahead-for-alberto-fernandezs-last-year-in-office/

Bresser-Pereira, L. C., Araújo, E. C., & Peres, S. C. (2020). An alternative to the middle-income trap. *Structural Change and Economic Dynamics, 52*, 294–312. https://doi.org/10.1016/j.strueco.2019.11.007

Brown, G., El-Erian, M., & Spencer, M. (2023). *Permacrisis: A plan to fix a fractured world*. Simon & Schuster.

Cachanosky, N., & Ferrelli Mazza, F. J. (2021). Why did inflation targeting fail in Argentina? *The Quarterly Review of Economics and Finance, 80*(2021), 102–116. https://doi.org/10.1016/j.qref.2021.01.014

Canuto, O. (2022, October 24). *Will Latin America return to mediocre growth after shocks?* Centre for Macroeconomics and Development. Available at: https://www.cmacrodev.com/will-latin-america-return-to-mediocre-growth-after-shocks

Ellner, S. (2020). Introduction: Salient characteristics of Mexico's neoliberal turn and Andrés Manuel López Obrador's Critique. *Latin American Perspectives, 47*(6), 4–19. https://doi.org/10.1177/0094582X20953102

Glawe, L., & Wagner, H. (2016). The middle-income trap: Definitions, theories and countries concerned—A literature survey. *Comparative Economic Studies, 58*, 507–538.

Guilherme, B. S., & Ribeiro Hoffmann, A. (2021). The fall of a giant: Greed, corruption and abuse of power undermining democracy in Brazil. In *Financial Crisis Management and Democracy: Lessons from Europe and Latin America*. Springer Nature.

International Labor Organization – ILO. Database. Variable: SDG indicator 8.2.1 – Annual growth rate of output per worker (GDP constant 2017 international $ at PPP) (%). Available at: https://rshiny.ilo.org/dataexplorer58/?lang=en&id=SDG_0821_NOC_RT_A

Kaminsky, G. (2003, December). *Varieties of currency crises* (NBER Working Paper No. 10193).

Kaminsky, G. (2006). Currency crises: Are they all the same? *Journal of International Money and Finance, 25*, 503–527.

Lins, M. A. D. T. (2020). O Brasil mais isolado no mundo pós-COVID. In: L. E. G. Silva (Org.), *Perspectivas e desafios da economia brasileira no pós-pandemia* (1ªed, pp. 59–69). Konrad Adenauer Stiftung.

Lins, M. A. D. T. (2021). Latin American economic crises and populist bids: Argentina, Brazil and Mexico. In B. De Souza Guilherme, C. Ghymers, S. Grifiith-Jones, & A. R. Hoffmann (Eds.), *Financial crisis management and democracy* (1ªed., pp. 185–199). Springer International Publishing.

Lins, M. A. D. T. (2022). É urgente a inflexão nas curvas de degradação econômica. *Cadernos Adenauer, XXIII*(4), 27–41.

Lucca, J. B. (2022, jan.–abr.). Análise multinível do populismo argentino nas eleições de 2019. *Revista Debates*, Porto Alegre, 16(1), 96–120.

Molino, F. R. (2021, September 16). Briga entre Alberto Fernández e Cristina Kirchner paralisa o Governo argentino. *El País Brasil*. https://brasil.elpais.com/internacional/2021-09-16/briga-entre-alberto-fernandez-e-cristina-kirchner-paralisa-o-governo-argentino.html

Nadal, A. (2020). "Pensar fuera de la caja: la economía mexicana y sus posibles alternativas", serie Estudios y Perspectivas-Sede subregional de la CEPAL en México, N° 182 (LC/TS.2020/39-LC/MEX/TS.2020/10), Ciudad de México, Comisión Económica para América Latina y el Caribe (CEPAL).

Pessoa, S. (2019, May 24). Crise argentina: Macri tentou a receita liberal? Blog do IBRE-FGV. Available at: https://blogdoibre.fgv.br/posts/crise-argentina-macri-tentou-receita-liberal
Ros, J. (2013). *Algunas Tesis Equivocadas Sobre el Estancamiento Económico de México*. El Colégio de México and Universidad Nacional Autónoma de México.
Rubio, L. (2023, March 22). Mexico is killing its Golden Goose. *America's Quarterly*. Available at: https://americasquarterly.org/article/mexico-is-killing-its-golden-goose/
Sánchez-Talanquer, M., & Greene, K. F. (2021). Is Mexico falling into the authoritarian trap? *Journal of Democracy, 32*(4), 56–71. https://doi.org/10.1353/jod.2021.0052
Sturzenegger, F. (2019, September 5–6). *Macri's Macro: The Meandering Road to Stability and Growth*. Brookings Papers on Economic Activity Conference Drafts. Available at: https://www.brookings.edu/wp-content/uploads/2019/09/sturzenegger_conference-draft.pdf
Winter, B. (2017, March 1). Revisiting Brazil's 2013 protests: What did they really mean? *America's Quarterly*. Available at: https://www.americasquarterly.org/article/revisiting-brazils-2013-protests-what-did-they-really-mean/
Wirtschafter, V., & Sarukhan, A. (2023, March 16). *Mexico takes another step toward its authoritarian past*. Brookings. Available at: https://www.brookings.edu/articles/mexico-takes-another-step-toward-its-authoritarian-past/

Chapter 11
How Permacrisis Has Redefined EU–LAC Trade Governance

Julieta Zelicovich

Contents

Permacrisis as a Challenge for EU–LAC Trade Governance

Over the past decade, global trade has experienced numerous shocks, many of which originated in the political arena. Climate-related crises, financial shocks, health emergencies, and political controversies have impacted commodity prices and disrupted supply chain connectivity. Additionally, technology has brought about changes in the production landscape, significantly influencing trade-related decisions. As mentioned in the introduction to this volume, the co-existence and interaction of different shocks and crises create a more volatile and unpredictable context in which crisis becomes a fundamental system feature.

Trade is not immune to these developments. Under this era of "permacrisis," trade has undergone several significant changes: firstly, merchandise trade lost relevance in GDP growth, leading to the deglobalization debate (The Economist, 2019;

J. Zelicovich (✉)
National University of Rosario – National Scientific and Technical Research Council (CONICET), Rosario, Argentina
e-mail: julieta.zelicovich@fcpolit.unr.edu.ar

D. Katsikas et al. (eds.), *Finance, Growth and Democracy: Connections and Challenges in Europe and Latin America in the Era of Permacrisis*, United Nations University Series on Regionalism 33, https://doi.org/10.1007/978-3-031-68475-3_11

Baldwin, 2022). Secondly, new markets—China—have overpassed the traditional trade leaders. Furthermore, trade has become increasingly politicized and weaponized in many countries, raising awareness of the vulnerabilities implied in trade interdependence (Feldhaus et al., 2020; Narlikar, 2021). Lastly, new narratives on trade policy emerged, emphasizing the multipurpose nature of trade policy and the complexities of its governance in the multilateral arena (Zelicovich, 2020; Lamp, 2023).

Catalyzed by these processes, the interregional trade landscape between the European Union (EU) and Latin America has undergone profound transformations. The two regions have differentiated capacities in trade policy and disparate leverage in trade governance, but both have been vulnerable to external shocks. This chapter delves into the evolution of trade policy and trade governance in both regions between 2013 and 2023, aiming to show how trade flows, trade policies, and trade governance instruments between them were affected by the configuration of a scenario of permacrisis. In particular, we intend to understand how governments reacted to the ongoing shocks and adapted trade governance instruments to the new reality. We argue that the emergence of revised trade policies and renewed narratives on trade policy will lead to adjustments in interregional trade strategies. These adjustments, in turn, will prompt the revision of the existing trade governance tools and the enactment of new types of cooperation agreements.

Whereas the EU–Latin America trade relation has been a recurrent topic in literature (Bonilla & Sanahuja, 2022; Grieger, 2023), the effects of permacrisis on interregional trade relations have remained overlooked. To the best of our knowledge, a few recent studies have identified the adjustments and innovations introduced in European trade policy (Adriaensen & Postnikov, 2021; Babic et al., 2022). However, equivalent studies on the Latin American side are scarce (Cornick et al., 2022), and—even more so—on the interregional trade relations. This chapter, therefore, contributes to a needed understanding of how governments have adjusted their trade policies in response to crises (permacrisis) and, specifically, to the identification of innovation, asymmetries, and challenges in the interregional relationship during that process.

Trade between these regions has played an important role: Latin America (as a region) ranked as the EU's fifth-largest trading partner, whereas Europe stands as the third-largest market for Latin American goods (Grieger, 2023). Four trade agreements exist between the EU and some subregional partners (EU–Chile; EU–Mexico; EU–Andean Countries; EU–Central America), and a fifth is under negotiations (with Mercosur). Interregionalism has been fostered by these trade relations, as further shown by Bianculli, Brossa, and Jordana, Chap. 21, in this volume.

In analyzing the evolving changes in the trade scenario, it is important to consider that, unlike the EU, Latin America lacks a unified mechanism for its trade policies. Regulations concerning goods and services remain fragmented along sub-regional lines. Moreover, there is no singular voice in trade matters across the region. While countries in Latin America may share core values on trade and trade governance, their specific trade interests diverge (Zelicovich, 2024). In addition, the European Union has wielded larger rule-making power, as exemplified by Bradford's

"Brussels Effect" theory (Bradford, 2020). This has positioned Latin American countries as rule-takers in their international integration.

Trade patterns have affected Latin America's vulnerability, as well. Interregional trade has maintained an interindustrial pattern, exposing Latin American economies to the deterioration of international terms of trade. EU exports are composed mainly of manufactured goods, while those from Latin American countries are based on raw materials and crops (Bonilla & Sanahuja, 2022). EU's export basket to the region includes machinery, pharmaceutical products, vehicles, mineral fuels, and plastics. Latin America's export basket concentrates on mineral fuels, ores, slags and ashes, residues and waste from the food industries, coffee, tea, fruits, oil seeds, and vehicles (which supply chains are mainly dominated by European terminals).

After this introductory overview, the following section discusses trade policy changes in the EU and Latin America. Section "Trade policy changes in a decade of global transformations" moves to interregional relationships and the governance mechanisms in place. Firstly, the chapter evaluates the "old" instruments; then, it analyzes the innovations introduced in recent years as a response to external changes. It highlights the modernization of existing free trade agreements (FTAs), the emergence of new types of trade-related instruments, and the effects of unilateral EU regulations within the interregional framework. Lastly, we present our final remarks.

Trade Policy Changes in a Decade of Global Transformations

Trade Policy Changes in Europe

The EU's trade policy has been driven by the strategies set by the European Commission and the Directorate General for Trade (DG Trade). These strategies have reflected how the EU perceived the global trade landscape and the role of trade policy in Europe's relations with the rest of the world. From 2015 to 2023, many changes arose, showing an adaptation capacity to external crises.

In 2015, the release of the strategy "Trade for all. Towards a more responsible trade and investment policy" marked the first of a series of responses of EU trade policy to world crises. This document underlined the changes driven by technology and the expansion of global value chains over trade. Consequently, digital trade and services, public procurement, temporary movement of professionals, and regulatory fragmentation were prioritized as part of a series of new-generation agreements. As explicitly stated in the strategy paper, the EU aimed to use FTAs to establish rules for global governance in these topics. At the same time, the EU Commission stated its intention to use trade policy to promote its values, such as sustainable development, human rights, and good governance.

Two years later, the EU adjusted its policy in response to the political transformations in the international system and moved away from its initial optimistic view of globalization, as shown in the "Reflection Document on Globalization." European economic diplomacy emerged as a suitable mechanism to promote its regional economic interests and values. Further responses toward global transformations appeared in 2021 in "Joint Communication to the European Parliament and the Council on strengthening the EU's contribution to rules-based multilateralism" and in "Trade Policy Review – An Open, Sustainable and Assertive Trade Policy." These documents acknowledged the necessity of adapting trade policy to address challenges posed by climate change, on the one hand, and by the geoeconomic shift on the other.

Therefore, the EU trade policy adopted its available tools to combat "climate change" as a priority. This included unilateral measures (with "long-arm effects") like the Carbon Border Adjustment Mechanism (CBAM), as well as the reinforcement of the sustainability dimension of FTAs. Explicitly, the EU decided to promote sustainability through trade agreements (Tosun & Heinz-Fischer, 2022). In 2022, the EU established a series of priorities for sustainable development in FTAs, which entailed a more proactive cooperation approach, mainstreaming sustainability beyond the Trade and Sustainable Development chapters and increasing the monitoring and enforcement capabilities (European Commission, 2022a).

The EU also alluded to the concept of security and strategic use of the economic power of the European Union, leading to the alignment of EU's trade policy with its geopolitical interests (European Commission, 2021). Specifically, three main objectives were identified for EU trade policy: first, supporting the recovery and fundamental transformation of the EU economy in line with its green and digital objectives; second, shaping global rules for more sustainable and fairer globalization; and third, increasing the EU's capacity to pursue its interests and enforce its rights, including autonomously where needed (European Commission, 2021). The "European Economic Security Strategy," released in 2023, further extended these priorities to include promoting the EU's competitiveness, protecting against economic security risks through new trade policies, and fostering partnerships with countries that share concerns or interests in economic security (European Commission, 2023b: 2).

The Critical Raw Materials Act, the European Chips Act, and the Net-Zero Industry Act have been the main tools for these new goals in European economic and trade policy. At the same time, FTAs have been complemented with a larger "geo-economic toolbox" of thematic initiatives and partnerships (European Commission, 2023b).

In summary, as permacrisis set in as the main global scenario, the EU adjusted its trade policy and reframed its strategic goals. It embraced a new narrative recognizing trade policy as a multipurpose tool beyond its economic-technical aspects. Furthermore, EU market power was channeled through trade instruments to shape global governance according to European values and preferences, and to protect the European economy from external political, technological, and climate threats.

Trade Policy Changes in Latin America

In this scenario, trade policies among Latin American countries exhibited significant heterogeneity. Unlike the European experience, there is limited deep regional integration concerning trade issues. Regional trade policy coordination has been mostly fragmented and sporadic.

During the 1980s and 1990s, trade strategies in Latin America converged toward trade liberalization and neoliberalism. The so-called "Washington Consensus" set the template for domestic reforms that included trade policy. In this process, countries in the region became active members of GATT/WTO and embraced FTAs, both regionally and with partners outside the region. However, beneath these commonalities, individual national strategies retained their unique characteristics. This diversity became more pronounced in the 2000s when two competing models emerged: on the West Coast, a liberal regional integration model aiming for deep agreements; and on the East Coast, a post-hegemonic regionalism characterized by a multidimensional trade-related agenda and shallower trade commitments.

Despite experiencing various external crises and witnessing shifts in the global trade landscape, Latin American trade policies have seen relatively few changes in the past decade. According to previous research, "Some countries, such as Brazil, Chile, and Costa Rica, have trade policies that are quite consistent over time (albeit with a protectionist bent in the first case, and a liberalizing bent in the last two). Others, such as Argentina and Ecuador, are remarkable for frequent policy shifts" (Cornick et al., 2022, 13). There is little evidence of trade policy shifts driven by perceptions of external crises either because governments favored alternative policy tools or due to their limited fiscal capacity and policy space (UNCTAD, 2022).

The main goals in trade policy have remained focused on trade diversification, market access, and, occasionally, pursuing macroeconomic short-term balance policies. Tariffs have not been frequently employed as a trade tool in times of crisis. The Effectively Applied Simple Average Tariff (AHS Simple Average) has consistently followed a declining trend, remaining only a few points above the world average. According to World Bank data, the average tariff rate throughout the decade was 7.74%, peaking in 2016 and reaching its lowest point in 2020—at 6.6%.

In the realm of nontariff policies among Latin American countries, the primary transformations over the last decade have been driven by external actors. On the one hand, Latin American countries have pursued comprehensive FTAs with external partners, leading to substantial changes in various trade-related aspects. Notably, the countries in the region participate in 82 preferential trade agreements, including some deep arrangements like the Comprehensive and Progressive Agreement for Trans-Pacific Partnership (CPTPP). On the other hand, the region has implemented various customs and administrative trade procedure reforms as a result of the multilateral commitments of the WTO Facilitation Trade Agreement. These reforms have found further support and expansion through regional trade organizations, such as the ALADI.

In this way, it has been through foreign agreements that the region has exhibited a sensibility to emerging problems of global context. Digitalization, gender, infrastructure, and climate governance have been increasingly incorporated into national trade policy, regional integration efforts, and regional multilateral cooperation processes. It is important to notice that, in contrast to the European experience, these trade policy adjustments have not resulted from a regional strategic decision but rather a reflection of Latin America's position in the international arena as a "rule-taker."

Regarding geoeconomic trends, it is a fact that during these years Latin America established many partnerships with Asian countries. However, in contrast to the EU, this was not a consequence of a reasoned regional geoeconomic strategy but the consequence of the Asian countries' market growth and power of attraction.

Overall, despite being vulnerable to external crises, Latin American countries did not develop a strategic response in which trade or trade policy played a relevant role. On the contrary, there have been a few changes, mainly driven by external actors and agreements. Latin American countries have kept a rule-taker position in global governance and a reactive, non-coordinated position, lacking a regional strategy.

The Old and New Governance Instruments in Interregional Trade

As shown in the previous section, the contrast between EU and Latin American trade policy responses toward the permacrisis context has been significant. This asymmetry has affected how interregional trade has been governed. In this section, we compare and discuss the old and new instruments for interregional trade governance.

Old Trade Governance Instruments

Since the 1990s, the main trade governance instrument has been FTAs. The EU has pursued a sub-regional agreement strategy with the Latin American countries, with different results. For 30 years, these agreements have framed interregional trade and shaped bi-regional integration. Many of these were "Association Agreements," which have been deemed as FTAs "bolstered by broader political agreements" (Tosun & Heinz-Fischer, 2022). The "old" instruments include a "Global Agreement" with Mexico reached in 2000; an FTA signed with Chile in 2002; an agreement with the Andean Countries (with Peru and Colombia in 2012 and then the subsequent accession of Ecuador in 2017); and lastly, an agreement with Central America in 2012. Additionally, the EU negotiated an association agreement with Mercosur starting in 1999. In parallel, the EU–LAC dialogues were initially established and later replaced by EU–CELAC summits. While these agreements shared commonalities aligned with European strategic objectives, they also exhibited diverse scopes and commitments.

In terms of their depth, the "old" agreements exhibit variations, ranging from traditional trade agreements focused on tariffs and in-border measures—such as the 1997 Mexico–EC agreement, which lacks provisions on investment, services, or intellectual property rights—to rather deep agreements in the rest of the region. These latter agreements are considered WTO plus, with commitments in government procurement or property rights, among others. All the agreements share similar flexibility in their commitments and almost identical enforcement capabilities, as shown in Fig. 11.1.

Previous studies have underlined that, regarding sustainable development chapters, FTAs in the region differed: while the EU–Andean Community agreement and the EU–Central America agreement had deep commitments and adopted high standards, the agreements concluded with Mexico did not include a distinct chapter on trade and sustainable development, whereas the one with Mercosur—in the agreement in principle—did not refer to climate change or air pollution (Tosun & Heinz-Fischer, 2022). This reflects a very differentiated approach to the trade–climate change nexus in the interregional relation.

Regarding the promotion of values and the political cooperation related to trade, one last remarkable characteristic of this group of agreements is that, albeit including political dialogue and cooperation chapters, these provisions are not in force. Due to complexities in the European ratification process, there is a gap between the negotiated mechanisms and the commitments in place. As the recent assessment of

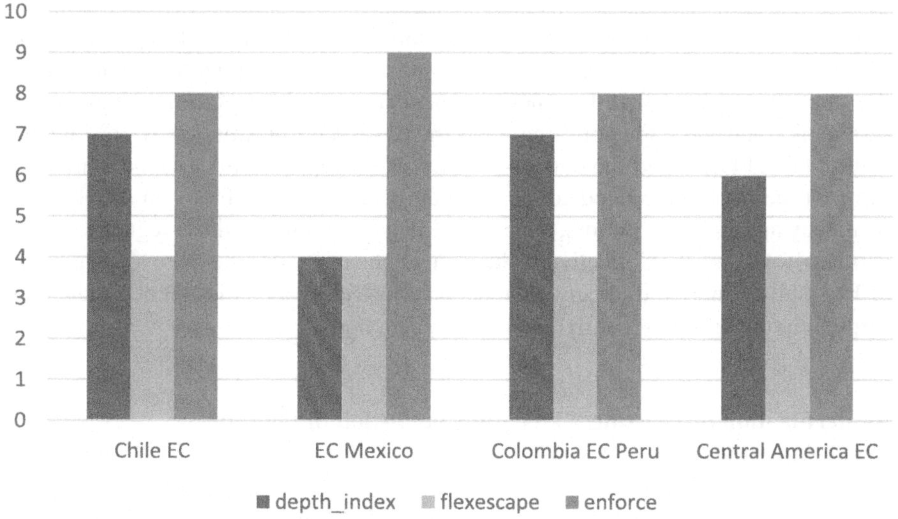

Fig. 11.1 Depth, flexibility, and enforcement in EU–Latin America FTAs. (Source: Author's calculations based on Dür et al., 2014; Baccini et al., 2015; Allee & Elsig, 2016)

EU–Latin American trade agreements shows, only the chapters from the trade pillar of the agreements are in force (European Commission, 2022b).

The old governance mechanisms also included interregional cooperation forums. Since the EU–LAC/EU–CELAC mechanisms were established in 1999, these summits have been utilized to reinforce shared values and goals on trade and to set common goals in bi-regional governance. Although the main focus of the mechanisms is political, trade has been part of the discussions. As Gardini and Ayuso show, "CELAC provides an umbrella framework for all the EU-LAC regional and subregional dialogues" (Ayuso & Gardini, 2018, 125).

Despite the expectations it had raised, the 2023 EU–CELAC summit was rather disappointing in trade governance matters. In the final declaration, countries introduced only one paragraph about the trade agenda. This paragraph underlined shared values, such as rule-based trade relations and the trade-sustainable development nexus. It invoked cooperation in strategic areas and clean energy supply chains, such as critical raw materials and technology transfer. Finally, the paragraph emphasized the need to fully implement the Association Trade Agreements between both regions. Overall, its impact has been limited.

To sum up, the old trade governance mechanisms provided tools for market access and created a thin layer of cooperation. They were driven by the EU strategy before the permacrisis era. As time passed, they presented limitations in dealing with a more complex context, highlighting the need for a more value-based and politically strategic trade policy.

New Trade Governance Mechanisms

In the last few years, the trade governance toolbox has broadened to provide room for integrating nontrade issues and geoeconomic concerns in interregional trade. In this section, we argue that three new mechanisms are taking place in the process of reshaping trade and trade policy between the EU and Latin America: (i) the modernization of old FTAs and the conclusion of previous agreements, (ii) the emergence of new types of trade-related cooperation agreements with a focus on supply chain resiliency and strategic sectors, and (iii) the launch of unilateral EU regulations with extraterritorial reach. Collectively, these mechanisms underline the evolving nature of EU–Latin America trade governance, demonstrating a commitment to adapt and respond to changing global dynamics and challenges.

Modernization of Existing FTAs and Conclusion of Pending Trade Agreements

In 2015, the EU outlined three key priorities for Latin America: modernizing the existing trade agreements with Chile and Mexico and concluding negotiations with Mercosur. These steps were intended to align the interregional trade governance mechanisms with the trade and values framework established by the European Commission. As discussed above, the agreements with Mexico and Chile marked the EU's first FTAs in Latin America. The existing commitments appeared outdated in light of the innovations and changes in trade and trade policy. Therefore, the EU authorities, in collaboration with their Latin American partners, anticipated the need for a revised agreement.

At the 2013 EU–CELAC Summit, Chile and the EU agreed to move forward toward the modernization of its standing agreement. The negotiations started in 2017 and were concluded in December 2022. The "EU-Chile Advanced Framework Agreement" combines a deep agenda of trade liberalization, with a large nontrade issue series of commitments. The 33 chapters include salient issues such as "Cooperation On Sustainable Food Systems," "Energy and Raw Materials," "Trade and Sustainable Development," "Trade and Gender Equity," "Good Regulatory Practices," and a special chapter on "Small and Medium-Sized Enterprises." Among other *avant-garde* commitments, the agreement incorporates chapters on the "Temporary Presence of Mutual Persons for Business Purposes" and "Mutual Recognition of Professional Qualification." "Delivery Services," "Telecommunication Services," "International Maritime Transport Services," and "Financial Services" are also included, and there is an important chapter on "Digital Trade." The agreement involves public procurement, as well. Overall, it is a comprehensive trade agreement with innovative clauses in nontrade issues.

In a similar timeline, the negotiations for the modernization of the agreement with Mexico started in 2016 and reached an agreement in principle in April 2018. The new text expanded the scope and depth of bilateral trade governance. It included several liberalizing commitments in trade goods and services, product-specific rules of origin, and stronger intellectual property rights and geographical indicators regulations. Being a "twenty-first-century regionalism" type of agreement (Baldwin, 2011), it also included chapters related to "digital trade" "capital movement," "cross-border services," "temporary admission," and "mutual recognition of professional qualifications." In addition, it referred to Delivery, Telecommunications, Maritime, and Financial Services. It included a chapter on Investments and a specific Investment Dispute Resolution Mechanism, which was innovative in interregional trade governance. Among the newest chapters that reflected the trade–values nexus, the nontrade goals, as well as the geoeconomic turn in trade policy, this agreement included specific chapters such as "Trade and Sustainable Development," "Cooperation on Animal Welfare and Antimicrobial Resistance," "Energy and Raw Materials," "Good Regulatory Practices," and "Anti-Corruption."

The result was an ambitious agreement, which, in turn, faced resistance. The technical negotiations continued for 2 years after the "agreement in principle" and are still pending. Some of the more critical issues are related to the European ratification process as the EU Commission considers splitting up the agreement, whereas Mexico prefers an integral ratification process (Moens, 2022).

The EU–Mercosur agreement differs from these two "modernized" agreements. The negotiations started in 2000 under the "framework agreement," following the mandate established by the European Parliament a year prior. After 20 years of negotiations, the parties reached an agreement in principle in 2019. The trade pillar included 17 chapters that deal with market access, trade disciplines, and services. It replicates many WTO commitments. However, it is rather limited regarding Intellectual Property Rights and new nontrade issues. It does not include an investment chapter, and the chapter on Trade and Sustainable Development was heavily criticized, both due to its scope and because it was kept apart from the dispute mechanism. The agreement is a hybrid between classical FTAs and a WTO plus agreement, without fulfilling the characteristics of a "new generation agreement" (Caetano, 2022).

While an agreement "in principle" was reached with Mercosur in June 2019, technical negotiations were prolonged over time. In March 2023, the EU introduced a side-letter with a joint instrument on sustainability, in line with European trade policies. This changed the balance of concessions that allowed the 2019 agreement and triggered a new negotiation process among parties, further delaying the conclusion of the negotiations.

Table 11.1 provides a comparison of old and new mechanisms included in the FTAS that frame interregional trade. Concluding the FTA with Mercosur seems a necessary step to drive bi-regional trade governance to an upper level, with new regulations. The agreements with Chile and Mexico show the many nontrade-related issues that the EU has promoted, in line with its strategic goals.

New Types of Trade-Related Cooperation Agreements

In the renewed EU–Latin America trade agenda, the supply of strategic minerals and raw materials became a strategic area. As the global push for achieving net-zero emissions gained momentum, ensuring a secure, sustainable, and ethical supply of critical minerals like copper, nickel, cobalt, lithium, and rare earth elements (REEs) became increasingly crucial for clean energy technologies (Vivoda, 2023). In this context, the EU launched a strategy to establish a Critical Raw Material Club for like-minded countries. Latin America stood as a key player for this "club" (BID-INTAL, 2023), alongside Canada, Ukraine, Kazakhstan, and Namibia.

Therefore, as part of the Latin American and the Caribbean Global Gateway Investment Agenda (2023), the EU has promoted a series of new cooperation mechanisms on raw materials and energy supply chains with several countries in the region. These mechanisms took the form of Memorandums of Understanding (MoUs). They contain guiding principles for the relationship and set the framework for future technical, financial, and political cooperation. In contrast to the traditional FTAs, they do not imply hard commitments since they do not give rise to any rights or obligations under international or domestic law. Between June and August 2023, the EU signed MoUs with Argentina, Chile, and Uruguay.

The MoUs with Argentina and Chile, both virtually identical, established a bilateral partnership on sustainable raw materials value chains, covering the materials crucial for the clean energy and digital transition. The partnerships identify five cooperation areas, encompassing joint development of projects, new business

Table 11.1 Nontrade issues in EU–Latin America FTA

	Trade and sustainable development	Protection of biodiversity and traditional knowledge	Cooperation on sustainable food	Cooperation on animal welfare and antimicrobial resistance	Energy and raw materials	Trade and gender	Transfer of technology	Anti-corruption	Good regulatory practices	Investment dispute resolution
Central America–EU FTA (2012)	Yes	No	No	No	No	No	No	No	No	No
Peru & Colombia–EU FTA (2012)	Yes	Yes	No	No	No	No	Yes	No	No	No
Chile–EU Modernized Agreement (2022)	Yes	No	Yes	No	Yes	Yes	No	No	Yes	No
Mexico–EU Modernized Agreement in principle (2018)	Yes	No	No	Yes	Yes	No	No	Yes	Yes	Yes
Mercosur–EU FTA in principle (2019)	Yes	No	No	No	No	No	No	No	No	No

models, promotion and facilitation of trade and investment linkages; cooperation on research and innovation along the raw materials value chains; cooperation to leverage environmental, social, and governance (ESG) criteria and align with international standards; deployment of hard and soft infrastructure for projects development; and strengthening capacities, vocational education and training and skills development.

Whereas the MoU with Argentina establishes that within 6 months the participants intended to develop a roadmap that identifies concrete actions in the five areas of cooperation identified, in the case of the MoU with Chile, no specific time lapse is specified in the development of the roadmap.

With Uruguay, the EU agreed to cooperate in renewable energy, energy efficiency, and renewable hydrogen. The MoU identifies several areas of cooperation, including promoting energy efficiency and exchanges regarding policies on renewable energy and renewable hydrogen. Uruguay and the EU recognize the importance of cooperation between the two sides, producing and consuming renewable hydrogen and a shared goal of reaching climate neutrality by 2050.

The EU–Uruguay MoU sets an intention to cooperate and promote the development of rules-based, transparent, and undistorted global hydrogen markets. Notably, the agreement encompasses specific trade policy commitments, including the avoidance of export restrictions such as "export licensing, export monopolies, dual pricing regimes, anti-competitive practices, as well as non-tariff barriers." Unlike the MoUs with Chile and Argentina, the MoU with Uruguay incorporates a clause addressing consultations to prevent safety hazards for infrastructure used in the transport of hydrogen, as well as potential environmental risks.

These new instruments introduce a novel mechanism for trade governance in the interregional relationship. Although they are not strictly trade policy tools, they create a framework for trade-related issues. Remarkably, these commitments are not integrated in FTAs but in new types of flexible instruments. This move might suggest an adaptation to the permacrisis scenario, in which political cooperation can be considered more resilient than juridical dispute settlement mechanisms (Roberts et al., 2019).

Unilateral EU Regulation with Extraterritorial Reach

Unilateral trade policy reforms also impacted interregional trade governance. We identify two parallel mechanisms. On the one hand, the EU domestic standards have influenced trade policymaking abroad, as illustrated by the "Brussels Effect" (Bradford, 2020). This induced a technical convergence on regulations (Christen et al., 2022). On the other hand, the "green deal" and the "European autonomy strategy" have led to the emergency of new trade regulations that have a direct extraterritorial effect. In this section, we argue that EU–Latin American trade relations are also being framed by these unilateral mechanisms, which are part of the European response to the permacrisis era.

Trade policy and climate action became increasingly intertwined as several pieces of legislation introduced limits and requirements for European exporters and importers. In these regulations, unilaterally the EU set standards that affected EU–Latin America trade relations.

One example of this "long-arm" legislative practice is the EU regulation on deforestation. In May 2023, the EU introduced a regulation on the availability, on the Union Market and the Export from the EU, of certain commodities and products associated with deforestation and forest degradation. This regulation extends to the production of commodities like soy, beef, palm oil, wood, cocoa, coffee, rubber, and some of their derived products, such as leather, chocolate, tires, or furniture, both in the EU market and outside the EU. The importers are requested to present a "due diligence" declaration concerning all relevant products supplied by each particular supplier. According to this legislation, they "must be able to prove that the products do not originate from recently deforested land or have contributed to forest degradation." Foreign countries are classified into three categories according to their risk of producing in deforestation-free areas. Latin American exporters face these requirements when trading with the EU, despite all the FTAs mentioned above.

In addition, in 2022, the EU Commission adopted a proposal for a "Directive on Corporate Sustainability Due Diligence." This legislation requires companies operating in the EU "to identify and, where necessary, prevent, end or mitigate adverse impacts of their activities" on human rights and on the environment. This requirement is applied to companies with more than 500 employees and 150 million euros in net turnover worldwide, or companies in defined high-impact sectors with 250 employees and net turnover of EUR 40 million worldwide.

The more striking measure among EU's unilateral legislation framing EU–Latin American trade relations is the Carbon Border Adjustment Mechanism. This measure introduces a "tax" for foreign exporters aiming to equal the carbon price of domestic production. The CBAM regulation entered into force in May 2023, with a transitional phase until 2026. The affected products include cement, iron and steel, aluminum, fertilizers, electricity, and hydrogen. Under the mechanism, "importers will need to declare each year the quantity of goods imported into the EU in the preceding year and their embedded [greenhouse gas] GHG. They will then surrender the corresponding number of CBAM certificates" (European Commission, 2023a, 1).

According to Conte Grand et al. (2023), 0.5% of Latin American exports could be affected by the CBAM, with Brazil, Chile, and Costa Rica as the ones with the highest exposure. In addition, Honduras, Brazil, Paraguay, Uruguay, and Argentina's exports show vulnerabilities toward the deforestation regulation, which affects 1.72% of regional trade (Conte Grand et al., 2023). In both cases, if the present list of products is expanded, the effects would be higher. Other researchers warned on the vulnerabilities of dependence on fossil fuel exports in the cases of Bolivia, Colombia, Ecuador, and Peru, in case of an expansion in EU "long-arm" climate regulation on trade (Cosbey & Vogt-Schilb, 2023). In response, several Latin American governments have implemented surveillance mechanisms over the European regulations. Some have expressed concern over discriminatory trade barriers (Moens & Mathiensen, 2023) while also evaluating their climate-trade-related tools (OECD et al., 2022).

Overall, European legislation, particularly in addressing the permacrisis aspect of climate change, has ultimately constrained Latin American options in interregional trade governance. Consequently, it emerges as one of the new trade governance mechanisms.

Final Remarks

The chapter contributes to identifying the evolving characteristics of interregional trade governance. It has identified external crises as conditioning factors that shape interregional trade policies and underscores the interconnectedness of global trade and the need for adaptive trade policies in Latin America and the EU.

The EU's response to an era of permacrisis has been strategically driven. Specifically, it has focused on addressing issues perceived as strategically relevant or threatening, such as geoeconomic risks related to supply chains and the imperative to combat climate change. In contrast, Latin America has been less responsive to external challenges. Two reasons stand out: on the one hand, there is no regional coordinated strategic trade policy, resulting in a lack of clear pattern of change; on the other hand, Latin American countries have had less policy space since they had weaker fiscal positions and more vulnerable and fragile economies.

In consequence, the EU has consistently demonstrated greater actorness and agenda-setting capability in these interregional trade relations. This dominance reflects the EU's ability to shape the discourse and direction of trade policy discussions in the EU–Latin America context.

We have identified three emerging mechanisms that frame interregional trade governance: the modernization of existing FTAs, the enactment of a new sectoral memorandum of understanding that sets cooperation mechanisms, and unilateral reforms, as well. This sets the stage for a time of innovation and creativity in trade regulation in a more uncertain global landscape. New priorities and new ways of cooperation emerge.

Among the new mechanisms in interregional trade, one remarkable feature is the partners' choice. The EU has prioritized bilateral relations above interregional or sub-regional. This shift has resulted in a more fragmented and asymmetric EU–Latin America trade relation, signaling the need for a more cohesive and inclusive approach to trade governance. Moreover, EU regulations have intended to shape interregional trade unilaterally.

The era of permacrisis highlights how relevant trade still is for interregional integration. At the same time, it underscores the asymmetries that frame EU–Latin America relations and the imperative for both regions to adapt to the evolving global landscape.

References

Adriaensen, J., & Postnikov, E. (2021). *A geo-economic turn in trade policy? EU trade agreements in the Asia Pacific*. Palgrave Macmillan.

Allee, T., & Elsig, M. (2016). Why do some international institutions contain strong dispute settlement provisions? New evidence from preferential trade agreements. *Review of International Organizations, 11*(1), 89–120.

Ayuso, A., & Gardini, G. L. (2018). EU-Latin American relations as a template for interregionalism. In F. Mattheis & L. Andreas (Eds.), *Interregionalism across the Atlantic Space* (pp. 115–131). Springer.

Babic, M., Dixon, A., & Liu, I. (2022). *The political economy of geoeconomics: europe in a changing world*. Palgrave Macmillan.

Baccini, L., Dür, A., & Elsig, M. (2015). The politics of trade agreement design: Revisiting the depth-flexibility Nexus. *International Studies Quaterly, 59*(4), 765–775.

Baldwin, R. (2011). 21st century regionalism: Filling the gap between 21st century trade and 20th century trade rules. *CEPR Policy Insight*, (56), 1–24.

Baldwin, R. (2022, August 31). *The peak globalisation myth*. Centre for Economic Policy Research. https://cepr.org/voxeu/columns/peak-globalisation-myth-part-1. Accessed 15 Sept 2023.

BID-INTAL. (2023). ALC tiene un rol clave en la provisión de minerales críticos para la transición energética global. *Connexa.*, (19), 1–9. https://publications.iadb.org/es/connexa-no-19-septiembre-2023-sintesis-de-informacion-y-datos-sobre-integracion-y-comercio. Accessed 25 Sept 2023.

Bonilla, A., & Sanahuja, J. A. (2022). *Unión Europea, América Latina y el Caribe: Cartografía de los Acuerdos de Asociación*. Fundación Carolina y EU-LAC Foundation.

Bradford, A. (2020). *The Brussels effect: How the European Union rules the world*. Oxford University Press.

Caetano, G. (2022). Análisis y prospectiva del Acuerdo de Asociación Unión Europea-Mercosur. Documentos de Trabajo Fundación Carolina – EU-LAC(FC/EU-LAC (4) ES), 1–37.

Christen, E., Meyer, B., Oberhofer, H., Hinz, J., Kamin, K., & Wanner, J. (2022). *The Brussels Effect 2.0. How the EU sets global standards with its trade policy*. Austrian Institute of Economic Research.

Conte Grand, M., Schultz-Antipa, P., & Rozenberg, J. (2023). Potential exposure and vulnerability to broader climate-related trade regulations: An illustration for LAC countries. *Environment, Development and Sustainability, 26*, 1–26.

Cornick, J., Frieden, J., & Stein, E. (2022). The political economy of trade policymaking in Latin America: An introduction. In J. Cornick et al. (Eds.), *Political economy of trade policy in Latin America* (pp. 1–32). Inter-American Development Bank.

Cosbey, A., & Vogt-Schilb, A. (2023). *Climate-related trade measures: Assessing impacts for Bolivia, Colombia, Ecuador, and Peru*. Inter-American Development Bank.

Dür, A., Baccini, L., & Elsig, M. (2014). The design of international trade agreements: Introducing a new database. *Review of International Organizations, 9*(3), 353–375.

European Commission. (2021). *An open, sustainable and assertive trade policy*. European Commission.

European Commission. (2022a). *The power of trade partnership: Together for green and just economy growth* (COM(2022) 409 final). European Commission.

European Commission. (2022b). *Individual Information sheets on implementation of EU Trade Agreements*. Commission Staff Working Document SWD(2022) 730 final.

European Commission. (2023a, October 30). *Carbon border adjustment mechanism*. European Commission Taxation and Customs Union: https://taxation-customs.ec.europa.eu/carbon-border-adjustment-mechanism_en. Accessed 15 Sept 2023.

European Commission. (2023b). *European economic security strategy*. European Commission.

Feldhaus, L., Huang, Y., Kim, S., Lee, J., Marechal, D., Sun, X., & Weiss, S. (2020). *The weaponization of Trade. A study of modern trade conflicts from the mid-1900s to present*. Columbia University.

Grieger, G. (2023). *EU trade with Latin America and the Caribbean. Overview and figures*. European Parliamentary Research Service.

Lamp, N. (2023, January 15). *Toward multipurpose trade policy? How competing narratives about globalization are reshaping international trade cooperation*. International Institute for Sustainable Development. https://www.iisd.org/articles/policy-analysis/multipurpose-trade-policy. Accessed 15 Sept 2023.

Moens, B. (2022, June 15). *Mexico pushes EU to get trade deal over the line*. Politico. https://www.politico.eu/article/mexico-pushes-eu-to-sign-off-on-trade-deal/. Accessed 23 Oct 2023.

Moens, B., & Mathiensen, K. (2023, January 16). *Trade partners see red over Europe's green agenda*. Politico. https://www.politico.eu/article/eu-green-agenda-has-its-trading-partners-seeing-red-climate-neutrality/. Accessed 15 Sept 2023.

Narlikar, A. (2021). Must the weak suffer what they must? The Global South in a world of weaponized interdependence. In D. Drezner, H. Farrell, & A. Newman (Eds.), *The uses and abuses of weaponized interdependence* (pp. 289–304). Brookings Institution Press.

OECD; CAF; ECLAC; European Union. (2022). *Latin American Economic Outlook 2022. Towards a Green and Just Transition*. OECD Publishing.

Roberts, A., Moraes, C., & Ferguson, V. (2019). Towards a geoeconomic order in international trade and investment. *Journal of International Economic Law, 22*, 655–676.

The Economist. (2019, January 24). The steam has gone out of globalization. *The Economist*.

Tosun, J., & Heinz-Fischer, C. (2022). Sustainable development in EU trade agreements: Different trade partners, different rules? In A. Karhu & E. Haaja (Eds.), *Global trade and trade governance during de-globalization. Transforming Trade Policy for Not-So-United World*. Palgrave.

UNCTAD. (2022, October 3). External constraints, sluggish growth cast long economic shadow over Latin America and the Caribbean. *UNCTAD Press Release*. https://unctad.org/press-material/external-constraints-sluggish-growth-cast-long-economic-shadow-over-latin-america. Accessed 18 Oct 2023.

Vivoda, V. (2023). Friend-shoring and critical minerals: Exploring the role of the Minerals Security Partnership. *Energy Research & Social Science, 100*, 103085.

Zelicovich, J. (2020). La Organización Mundial de Comercio. Entre las normas del siglo XX y la política comercial del siglo XXI. *Agenda Internacional, 27*(38), 81–104.

Zelicovich, J. (2024). Los países latinoamericanos y del Caribe en el sistema multilateral de comercio: desafíos y oportunidades bajo el multilateralismo de transición. In M. Alvarez, K. Inoue, & W. Weck (Eds.) *Retos y oportunidades de América Latina y el Caribe en el comercio mundial pospandemia* (pp. 105–154). Konrad-Adenauer-Stiftung.

Chapter 12
The Past as Insufficient Prologue: Sovereign Debt Restructurings in Latin America Since the 1980s

Giselle Datz

Contents

Introduction

Economic and financial crises are known to be cyclical. More recently, the notion that crises are not only recurring but feeding into one another in a seemingly permanent cycle of "cascading failures" has gained traction (Lawrence et al., 2023; Zuleeg et al., 2021). Economic, environmental, political, and social fragility reinforces prevailing uncertainty and renders it systemic. The resulting perma-or-polycrises defy extant knowledge and institutional apparatus in a world "of unprecedented and ever-rising interdependence" (Brown et al., 2023: 197; Tooze, 2022). Past solutions designed to solve isolated problems are ill-suited to address dysfunctions bound to produce negative spillover effects, whose scale and costs are not fully calculable ex ante.

G. Datz (✉)
Virginia Tech, Arlington, VA, USA
e-mail: gdatz@vt.edu

D. Katsikas et al. (eds.), *Finance, Growth and Democracy: Connections and Challenges in Europe and Latin America in the Era of Permacrisis*, United Nations University Series on Regionalism 33, https://doi.org/10.1007/978-3-031-68475-3_12

In this analytical context, where recurrent distress feeds into entangled upheavals, we explore a particular issue—area in which global public and private coordination have been ad hoc: sovereign debt governance. More specifically, given the lack of a statutory mechanism—akin to a global bankruptcy court for sovereign debt—which can render debt restructurings more predictable and expeditious, debt restructurings remain plagued by creditor coordination problems. Since the 1990s, but particularly after the Argentine default of 2001, the costs of default, already difficult to pin down given all their economic and political ramifications, have been compounded by the risks of litigation brought about by creditors in foreign courts (Datz & Corcoran, 2019, Makoff & Weidemaier, 2022, Grund, 2022).

Latin America, in particular, has not only been the site of many a debt crisis, but a veritable laboratory for debt restructurings, where "most of the main innovations (…) were tried and tested" (Ayres et al., 2023: 231) Argentina, Bolivia, Mexico, Peru, and Venezuela "have spent much of the last decades in periods of default or protracted re-negotiations" (Asonuma, 2016; Meyer et al., 2019). Members of the distinguishable group of "serial defaulters," these countries have had to contend with "substantial volatility, reflecting external economic shocks and dependency on often erratic short-term capital" (Reinhart & Rogoff, 2009; Faria et al., 2021: 3). Ecuador too has navigated repeated debt restructurings recently.

Since the 1980s, Latin American countries' debt restructurings have counted on an increasingly diversified group of creditors: from the commercial banks who counted on the support of the US government to arrive at a belated resolution to the defaults of the "lost decade," to unyielding bondholders (holdout creditors) suing sovereigns in foreign courts, and more recently to Chinese development funding institutions. The "creditor" category is increasingly diverse. Middle-income sovereigns (our focus here) borrow from bilateral (other countries), multilateral (development banks and the International Monetary Fund), and private sources. Yet none of these categories is necessarily homogeneous when it comes to preferences and strategies of engagement with debtor countries. Debt negotiations with China (a non-member of the Paris Club) are still novel and mediated by the creditor's long-term trade and geopolitical interests, often diverging from that of other country creditors (Kaplan, 2021). Private creditors also differ in their time horizons, appetite for risk, and willingness to push debtor countries beyond their restructuring offers. Indeed, those creditors who refuse to participate in debt restructurings and, rather, sue sovereign debtors in foreign courts are a minority who have been at the center of restructuring disruptions for middle-income countries from Argentina to Greece. They are thus the focus of the analysis developed in this chapter.

Rather than offer a compilation of lessons learned from debt restructurings past, in the spirit of the challenges posed by permacrisis, we argue here that "solutions" to debt restructurings in the past 40 years have proven limited to their temporal context, at times contributing—even if inadvertently—to making future restructurings more difficult. At other times, "solutions" targeted preemption of potential disruption to the debt restructuring process. Those were often second-best, "market-based innovations" that, nonetheless, have required incremental redesign and did not do away with (relative) instability. In a context of permacrisis, where calls for global coordination to solve lingering and new challenges of broad significance have remained mostly unheeded, solving debt crises will further expose the tenuous nature of the existing sovereign debt architecture and its role in the ever-more politicized twenty-first-century interdependence (Brown et al., 2023; Solana, 2023).

In section "Back to bonds: The Brady Plan as a resolution to the 1980s debt crisis", we briefly review the resolution of the 1980s Latin American defaults: the securitization of commercial banks' loans, creating a buyout bond market for emerging economies. Section "Minority rules: Creditor litigation in the 1990s" explains how the return to bond finance allowed for the advent of litigating bondholders in foreign courts, while section "Argentina's 2001 default and the proposal for a Sovereign debt restructuring mechanism" explains the ultimately failed proposal for a sovereign debt restructuring mechanism. In section "The changing tide that shakes all boats: Holdout creditors' victories against Argentina in US Courts, 2001–16", litigating bondholders' boldness (and judicial luck) is exemplified in the case of *NML v. Argentina* case, which played out in US courts from 2001 to 2016. Section "A market-based "solution": Collective action clauses (CACs)" explains the ways in which "market-based" solutions in the form of contractual innovations have attempted to limit the power of holdout creditors. Finally, the chapter concludes with a reflection on the limits to contractual ingenuity in debt restructurings that remain mired in the uncertainty of legal challenges and their outcomes.

Back to Bonds: The Brady Plan as a Resolution to the 1980s Debt Crisis

A resolution to the protracted negotiations of Latin American debts in default was finally arrived at when Nicholas Brady became the US Treasury Secretary in September 1988. His plan acknowledged the problem of debtor countries as one of insolvency, rather than illiquidity, and debt relief was finally provided. Commercial banks' loans were pooled together and repackaged as Brady bonds in a process known as securitization. Because these Brady bonds were issued at a discount in either principal or interest relative to the original commercial banks' loans, sovereign debt service obligations were reduced. A key feature of Brady bonds was that the payments of their principal used zero-coupon US Treasury securities as collateral, while interest payments were backed by high investment grade securities purchased with IMF funds directed at facilitating these debt restructurings (Power, 1996; Clark, 1994).

Seventeen countries carried out Brady restructurings on a case-by-case basis, from 1990 to 1998. Ten of those were Latin American debtors: Mexico, Costa Rica, Venezuela, Uruguay, Argentina, Brazil, the Dominican Republic, Ecuador, Panama, and Peru. Overall, the Brady Plan "successfully reduced emerging market debt burdens, restored market access, diversified the emerging market creditor base, took illiquid loans off of advanced economy commercial bank balance sheets and converted them into tradeable securities" (Shenai & Bolhuis, 2023: 5). An important positive spillover effect was the development of a secondary market for emerging market bonds, which later facilitated sovereigns access to new borrowing. Throughout the 1990s, Latin American countries—mainly Argentina, Brazil, and Mexico—issued the largest share of the total volume of emerging markets debt being traded, about 75%. As Bustillo and Velloso (2000: 5) explain: "investors were drawn by high growth potential and high yields in most Latin American countries, as well as by a general trend towards the implementation of economic and political reforms" under IMF guidance.

Therefore, on the one hand, the return to sovereign bond finance in a context of financial globalization facilitated emerging market countries' access to global credit, predictably accompanying booms in international credit cycles (Datz, 2009). On the other hand, countries issuing foreign bonds were exposed to seemingly inescapable financial volatility. "Disciplining" portfolio investors (many of which investors in sovereign bonds) were diverse yet prone to herding as they tracked common indexes and benchmarks, as well as replicated the actions of market leaders in a context of information asymmetry (Santiso, 2003). These private players operated much more swiftly than ever before, at times exaggerating "market adjustments" (despite or beyond fundamentals) and even contributing to "sudden stops" of capital flows because of financial contagion from currency crises (Calvo, 1998; Kaminsky & Schmukler, 2003a, b; Calvo et al., 2003).

Furthermore, beyond the macroeconomic turmoil linked to the wave of emerging markets' financial crises in the 1990s, the new era of bond finance made creditor coordination more challenging. In particular, creditor litigation against sovereign debtors in foreign courts would make substantial strides in challenging sovereign immunity and exacerbating default costs.

Minority Rules: Creditor Litigation in the 1990s

In 1992, two Panamanian corporations, Weltover Inc. and Springdale Enterprises Inc., along with a Swiss banking corporation, Bank Cantrade, refused to accept the Argentine restructuring of dollar-denominated bonds and took its lawsuit all the way to the US Supreme Court. To the benefit of the creditors, the Supreme Court confirmed that issuing debt in international capital markets is a "commercial activity" on the part of the debtor. This allowed US courts to have jurisdiction over sovereign bonds issued under US law despite the determinations in 1976 Foreign Sovereign Immunity Act (Lew, 1993).

Building on this precedent, in 2000, Elliott (a hedge fund active in lawsuits against sovereigns) took Peru to US courts, aiming to recover the full face value of its debt claims plus interest. The litigating creditor argued for a "novel interpretation" of the *pari passu* (or equal treatment) clause in foreign bond contracts. This standard clause in bond contracts since the mid-nineteenth century attests to the "borrower's promise to ensure that the obligation will always rank equally in right of payment with all of the borrower's other subordinated debts" (Blackman & Mukhi, 2010: 55). Elliott argued that *pari passu* in this case meant that Peru could not pay creditors of restructured debt without paying the hedge fund proportionally. A judgment of $56 million was issued in favor of Elliot. This was enforceable through Peru's assets used for commercial activity in the United States (IMF, 2001). Since Peru had no such assets to be seized, Elliott targeted the third parties involved with bond payments, that is, the sovereign's fiscal agents and clearinghouses (IMF, 2001: 12; Weidemaier & Gelpern, 2013). With insufficient time to appeal the orders obtained by Elliott, Peru settled so as to avoid defaulting on its Brady bond payments coming due (Blackman & Mukhi, 2010).

Elliott's success pursuing the *pari passu* strategy reverberated through sovereign debt litigation circles. Not only had a holdout creditor received a favorable judgment, but it was also able to obtain a restraining order to prohibit the payment of interest to other bondholders until payments were made to that holdout creditor. A chain reaction of hedge fund litigation followed, and other enforcement actions were brought to court exploring the same strategy. Nonetheless, most of these legal actions did not succeed. By 2003, the *pari passu* clause was no longer receiving favorable judgments in global courtrooms (Blackman & Mukhi, 2010). Even so, it was by then clear that sovereigns were not only exposed to exchange rate risk when issuing debt in foreign currency, but even more directly, they were subjecting themselves to the authority of foreign courts as commercial actors no longer shielded by sovereign immunity (Schumaker et al., 2021; Datz, 2021).

In this context, the Ecuadorian default was "a first" in three categories: the first in Latin America since the debt crisis of the 1980s, the first default on international sovereign bonds since the 1930s, and the first default on Brady bonds (governed by NY-law). In addition, the country's 2000 debt restructuring featured a number of innovative steps, among them, the use of so-called exit consents (or exit amendments). These allowed a majority of bondholders to modify the bond terms other than those relating to payment before they exited into the new (restructured) bonds. In this way, the old (defaulted) bonds became less attractive to potential holdout creditors (IMF, 2001, Ayres et al., 2023). Exit consents—which were later governed by the collective action clauses discussed below—thus amounted to an inventive use of bond clause amendments to prevent holdout creditors from not only inflicting pain on the debtor, but also deterring otherwise willing creditors to participate in restructuring deal for fear that holdout creditors would obtain a better offer later on (Gulati & Buchheit, 2000, Buchheit et al., 2019). Yet, by then it had become clear that the holdout problem was far from easily extinguishable. In the new era of bond finance, Latin American borrowers and their creditors would be put through harsher tests.

Argentina's 2001 Default and the Proposal for a Sovereign Debt Restructuring Mechanism

On December 23, 2001, interim president Rodriguez Saa announced to a cheering Congress that Argentina was defaulting on its $132 billion public debt. At the time, the country's debt-to-GDP ratio stood at 130%. Markets were unsurprised. The country's struggles with its fixed exchange rate, banking crisis, and recession had reached their peak. The Argentine default was not only the largest in history (involving $82 billion owed in principal and about US$20 billion in interests to private bondholders), but the debt restructuring to follow would become the most complex operation of its kind until that point in time. No less than 152 types of bonds in six currencies and under the law of eight different locations were to be swapped for new bonds (*Euromoney*, 2005; Guzman, 2020; Gelpern, 2005).

The Argentine default added fuel to the fire of concerns about debt restructurings in the post-Brady era. In 2001, then, IMF managing director, Anne Krueger, stated: "there is a growing consensus that the present process for restructuring the debts of a sovereign is more prolonged, more unpredictable and more damaging to the country and its creditors than would be desirable. Exploring ways to improve the sovereign debt restructuring process is a key part of the international community's efforts to strengthen the architecture of the global financial system" (Krueger, 2001: 1). Without such improvements, financially and politically costly private creditors' bailouts by the international community (through the IMF) were the only available, yet unsustainable answer (Miller, 2002).

The Proposal for a Sovereign Debt Restructuring Mechanism

In late 2001, the IMF moved forward with its proposal for a sovereign debt restructuring mechanism (SDRM), which would include international legal procedures like those stated in Chapter 11 of the US Corporate Bankruptcy Code, binding all countries in a treaty-based approach. The plan included four elements: (1) standstills and automatic stays to prevent a creditors' grab race in the event of a default; (2) preferred-creditor incentives for the provisions of new money by the private sector; (3) conditionality on the part of the debtor to negotiate in good faith and adopt policies that were deemed appropriate; and (4) supermajority voting to bind minority creditors to a restructuring agreement so as to lower the potential threat of litigating holdout creditors (Kruger, 2002).

Critics pointed to a serious conflict of interest on the part of the fund: it would be a creditor and agent of other official creditors, as well as the acting arbitrator of the process, overseeing the restructuring process and deciding when a debt standstill would be officially sanctioned (Langton, 2002). Creditors doubted that the IMF could make a politically neutral determination as to whether a distressed debtor was unwilling or unable to pay, and whether in the latter case this inability had been self-inflected or unavoidable (Committee on International Economic Policy Reform, 2013). In turn, debtor countries also objected to any compulsory system of debt resolution proposed by the fund, fearing that it would sharply raise their cost of financing in international markets (Helleiner, 2008).

The combined opposition to a change in sovereign debt arrangements materialized in November 2002 when finance ministers and central bank governors from the G-20 "failed to bridge the gap between widely opposing views of how best to resolve emerging market debt defaults" (*Financial Times*, November 25, 2002). In particular, the opposition of Latin American countries showed that countries well-versed in debt crises remained most strongly opposed to an IMF-coordinated debt restructuring mechanism. Ultimately, in 2003, the International and Financial Committee of the Board of Governments of the IMF conceded that it was not "feasible [then] to move forward to establish the SDRM" (IMF, 2003). Ever since, the fund has continued to support countries in crises. It has attempted (and at times failed) to provide accurate debt sustainability analysis that can inform debt restructurings (Setser, 2024), and has enhanced calls for greater transparency of public debt (IMF, 2023). More consequently, absent an SDRM, the IMF joined a growing chorus that saw in the promotion of foreign bond contractual changes—that is, the inclusion of evermore specific collective action clauses—a (limited) "market-based solution" to countering holdout problems (Hagan, 2020). The latter were never more evident than in the litigation involving a minority of private bondholders and Argentina in US courts, to which we turn next.

The Changing Tide That Shakes All Boats: Holdout Creditors' Victories Against Argentina in US Courts, 2001–16

The official debt restructuring of the bonds defaulted by Argentina in 2001 was opened by President Nestor Kirchner's team in February 2005 and ultimately counted on the participation of 76% of creditors. In 2010, Cristina Fernández de Kirchner (Nestor's wife and successor in office) presented an offer similar to the one put forth in 2005. This time, 93% of the total debt that had been defaulted on in 2001 was restructured. Yet that was not all. Among the 7% of creditors who did not accept either the 2005 or 2010 exchange offers was a particularly experienced hedge fund: NML Capital, a subsidiary of Elliott who had sued Peru and Brazil in the 1990s. These minority holdout creditors then sued Argentina in the Southern District of NY for repayment of the defaulted bonds that had been bought at a deep discount, even after the default was declared in 2001 (Guzman, 2020).

NML Capital got the upper hand when, in December 2011, a New York District Court Judge (Thomas Griesa) ruled in its favor, stating that Argentina violated the *pari passu* clause when it continued paying bondholders of restructured bonds while refusing to pay holdout creditors. Judge Griesa was, by that time, familiar with the litigants. In February 2012, expecting Argentina to defy his orders, the judge issued an injunction prohibiting the country from paying its restructured bonds and warning financial intermediaries against collaborating with Argentina in this endeavor (Gelpern, 2013). The lawyers for the debtor lost their appeal despite the US government's public support of Argentina (USA Amicus Curiae, December 2013).

The next step was the Supreme Court. Argentina's legal team challenged Judge Griesa's interpretation of the *pari passu* clause (a question of state law) and of federal law on sovereign immunity.[1] The outcome was, again, unfavorable to Argentina; the US Supreme Court refused to review Judge Greisa's decision on *pari passu* and held that the Foreign Sovereign Immunities Act did not immunize sovereign debtors against post-judgment discovery of its assets outside of the United States. The latter point empowered NML Capital to keep searching for nonimmune Argentine assets through the globe which it could claim as repayment. For its part, unable to pay the bondholders that had accepted the 2005 and 2010 debt restructurings, given how the injunction strong-armed financial intermediaries to not dare channel Argentine payments to these creditors, the country entered into a technical default in 2014.[2] For President Fernandez de Kirchner, who had made the litigation with the so-called "vulture funds" a political battle at home and abroad, there was no giving in (*UN News,* September 24, 2014). Yet, the stakes were extremely high. While not accepting to pay the holdout creditors, Argentina remained outside of international capital markets, not issuing new foreign bonds. Given the decision in favor of NML and the injunction that compromised the debtor's financial intermediaries, Argentina could not issue new foreign bonds.

The stalemate was finally broken when opposition president Mauricio Macri took office in 2016. Despite his minority in Congress, Macri counted on the support of the Legislative to repeal domestic laws (the Lock Law and the Sovereign Payment Law) that prevented the Argentine government from paying creditors that had rejected the 2005 and 2010 debt restructurings *(Cronista*, 16 March 2016*, Infoabe*, 30 May 2016). Soon after, Judge Griesa lifted his earlier injunction, and—in a significant show of market confidence—Argentina managed to sell $16.5 billion in new bonds to international investors to help fund its upcoming repayment of holdout creditors. This was "the largest emerging market debt sale on record" at the time (*Cronista*, 14 April 2016, *The Wall Street Journal*, 19 April 2016, *Forbes*, 30 April 2016). Ironically, even Elliott's founder and manager, Paul Singer (2016), called Argentina's April bond issuance a "record-breaking return to international capital markets" (*The New York Times*, 25 April 2016). In April 2016, NML Capital and its partners in litigation were paid $9.3 billion, making an astounding profit on their original investment in Argentine bonds[3] (*Financial Times*, 29 February 2016; *La Nación*, 23 April 2016).

---

[1] Transcript of Oral Argument, Republic of Argentina v. NML Capital, Ltd. 8232;573 U.S.___(2014).

[2] Technical default in this case meant that even though Argentina deposited the money due in a New York bank, no payment was ultimately delivered to bondholders.

[3] Other hedge funds that participated in the litigation against Argentina were Aurelius Capital Management, Dart Management, Blue Angel Capital, Bracebridge Capital, Olifant Fund, and Montreux Partners (Guzman, 2020).

Argentina's saga in US courts was far from a tale about a dismissible outlier (Datz & Corcoran, 2019). Creditors' demands met with legal support not simply when it came to the decision in favor of repayment. Through his injunction, Judge Griesa "produced the most potent remedy against a foreign government in recent memory" (Weidemaier & Gelpern, 2014: 190). What is more, as Guzman (2020: 728) concluded: "the anomalies that [the Argentine] case contained may be interpreted as symptoms of the current unhealthy state of the international architecture for sovereign debt crises resolution." Indeed, the Argentine experience revealed that US district court judges had significant "discretion for making decisions that exceed the US borders, and which can create coordination problems that undermine international lending markets" (*Ibid*: 731). How could debtors and (some) creditors protect themselves from the actions of litigation-prone bondholders (like NML and its peers)? To this answer we turn next.

A Market-Based "Solution": Collective Action Clauses (CACs)

After Argentina's legal ordeal, neither did debtor countries want to be the "next Argentina," nor did most bondholders wish to find themselves in the predicament NML imposed (however indirectly) on the holders of restructured bonds. Attention veered toward contractual changes already in motion as a means to deter holdout-driven dysfunction.

In foreign sovereign bonds issued under New York law, each bondholder had the contractual right to opt out of a restructuring, and instead demand a higher repayment than that on offer by the debtor, for instance. Aware of this threat even well-meaning bondholders could be unwilling to accept a debt restructuring that would not be final since a more favorable deal would have to be eventually cut between the debtor and the holdout creditors (Gelpern & Gulati, 2006). Yet, if restructuring decisions could be collectively binding for all creditors, then the problem of holdouts could be minimized (Weidemaier & Gulati, 2013). Collective action clauses (CACs) were seen as the device that could lead to this better outcome. The US Treasury became an enthusiastic proponent of CACs, which became a public signal that bailout policies were a thing of the past for the W. Bush administration. Furthermore, for whatever they were worth, the clauses were more appealing to creditors and debtors than the much-disliked SDRM. If only to put the latter to rest once and for all, CACs were worth the effort of contractual changes (Gelpern & Gulati, 2006). According to Mexican central bank president, Guillermo Ortiz: "We were worried because it [CACs] would increase our financing costs. The truth is we did it because it was a way to get rid of the SDRM" (*Latin Finance*, December 8, 2003).

Indeed, Mexico was the first major sovereign issuer to include CACs in bonds issued in 2003. Other countries followed suit, making it clear that "CACs ha[d] assumed pride of place as a key component of the official sector's response to sovereign debt crises" and gained center stage in discussions about the Eurozone debt crisis in 2009–10 (Weidemaier & Gulati, 2013: 54). Importantly, fears that CACs could signal to creditors that there was a veiled intention to default underlining the move to make restructurings more orderly were put to rest when Mexican bonds were oversubscribed, and prices were not affected (Helleiner, 2006). This was evidence that private bondholders valued the scenario in which debt restructurings would incur a lesser risk of holdout disruption (Chang and Papaioannou, 2020).

The experience of Argentina since the Griesa injunction of 2012 combined with the Greek debt exchange of 2012 added more fuel to the call for further contractual changes. In 2013, deliberations by the "Sovereign Debt Roundtable"—an informal grouping of creditors, bankers, lawyers, and public officials led by US Treasury—on contractual changes to international sovereign bonds were published by the London-based International Capital Market Association (ICMA) and backed by the IMF[4] (Sobel, 2016: 3; ICMA, 2014; IMF, 2014). The Greek experience revealed "the difficulties with using bond-by-bond CACs in comprehensive restructuring attempts, where blocking minorities in one issue cannot be offset by pro-restructuring majorities elsewhere" (Zettlemeyer et al., 2012: 26). Enthusiasts of market-based contractual reform had reason to both place renewed faith in these clauses and push for more strategic modalities that would prevent the bond-by-bond blocking disruption unleashed by tenacious holdout creditors. Enter: new aggregation rules to be incorporated in "enhanced CACs." The rules were meant to "reduce the scope for obtaining blocking positions, provide the sovereign with greater flexibility and at the same time protect against possible abuse or oppression of the minority by sovereigns"[5] (IMF, 2019: 3).

Enhanced CACs then became the norm for new bond issuances. As of 2019, 88% of all 510 international sovereign bond issuances since October 2014 (totaling US$620 billion) included the enhanced CACs that allow for a supermajority of creditors to determine the voting outcome on restructuring terms (IMF, 2019). As had been the case with the original CACs of the early 2000s, the inclusion of enhanced CACs did not increase the cost of credit for sovereign borrowers (Chang & Papaioannou, 2020).

Furthermore, since 2017, bond issuances that have, for the most part, included the enhanced CACs also included a clarification of the *pari passu* clause behind the

[4] In the Greek case, the vast majority of sovereign bonds (about 86%) had been issued under Greek law and required unanimous consent of bondholders. So to overcome this hurdle, the Greek legislature passed a law allowing a majority (votes representing 50% of the face value and a consent threshold of 2/3 of the face value taking part in the vote) to restructure all the sovereign bonds outstanding. As a result, blocking the restructuring became "near impossible" (Zettlemeyer et al., 2012: 7).

[5] The final proposal for an enhanced CAC contained "a menu of voting procedures, including a 'single-limb' aggregated voting procedure that enables bonds to be restructured on the basis of a single vote across all affected instruments, a two-limb aggregated voting procedure, and a series-by-series voting procedure" (IMF, 2019: 3). This was critical because recent empirical work and derived simulations show that CACs are effective in "minimizing the holdout problem" when single-limb aggregate voting is specified. CACs with bond-by-bond voting, in contrast, are insufficient to ensure high rates of creditor participation in restructurings (Fang et al., 2020).

NML vs. Argentina litigation. Even sovereign debtors who did not include enhanced CACs in their newly issued bond contracts (Azerbaijan and North Macedonia under English law, and Lebanon under New York law), added reviewed *pari passu* clauses. Despite "variations in the formulation of the modified clauses, they all specifically disavow the obligation to make ratable payments" (IMF, 2019: 6). Again, no one wants to relive Argentina's court struggles.

CACs were put to the test in 2020 with debt restructurings by Argentina and Ecuador. The aggregated voting mechanism (requiring a 75% majority) in CACs was first used in the Ecuadorian debt restructuring of September 2020. The innovation discouraged holdout creditors (IMF, 2020: 25). In the same year, Argentina restructured US$65 billion in debt in default (the country's ninth). Argentina had two series of bonds issued in 2005 and 2010 in connection with the 2010 restructuring and 17 series of bonds issued starting in the spring of 2016 during the administration of President Mauricio Macri, containing enhanced CACs. The country tried to "re-designate at any time—even after the exchange offer closed—which series of bonds would be aggregated together for voting purposes." That is, the Argentine government would manipulate the voting tally by taking those bond series that voted against the restructuring and place them in a different pool, guaranteeing hence its desired outcome (i.e., to go on with the offer it had made to all bondholders, claiming it counted on the consent of a majority of creditors). In addition, Argentina was said to restructure "a subset of bonds, and then sweeten the terms to try to convince an increasing proportion of creditors to play along. Each successive round snap[ed] up more approvals — a strategy nicknamed 'Pac Man,' which makes it more difficult for opposing bondholders to block a deal" (*Financial Times,* June 30, 2020; Buchheit & Gulati, 2020). This frustrated—to put it mildly—not only creditors but also officials and lawyers who had been supportive of the enhanced CACs featured in the exchanged bonds (Sobel, 2020, Gelpern, 2020). For them, debtors were in effect "gerrymandering ideal voting pools to maximize the cram down of holdout creditors" and thus undermining the "fairness and integrity" of the restructuring process (IMF, 2020: 25).

After negotiations between the Argentine government and a group of eligible bondholders, an agreement to regulate the ability of the debtor to manipulate the voting process to its favor was made. Once these amendments were put in place, at the end of August 2020, the Argentine government obtained the consent required under the CACs (93.5% of the bondholders) to restructure 99% of the eligible bonds (IMF, 2020; Silva et al., 2023).

These developments make clear that contractual changes are at best partial solutions to the kinds of challenges that (can) prevail in sovereign debt restructurings. Rather than granting the parties in debt restructurings the relief of *terra firma*, CACs and enhanced CACs have brought up further discussions after Ecuador and Argentina. As Ayres et al. (2023: 247) put it: "Experience with contract reform to date points to repeated cycles of innovation *in response* to shocks" (Ayres et al., 2023: 247, emphasis added). That is, the goal of preemption is constantly triggered by new disruptions, yet since the tools used (such as CACs in its many versions) can feed into new strategies to push for unilateral benefits, more orderly debt restructurings remain a moving target.

Conclusion

When the Brady Plan of 1989 finally offered a way to restructure the defaulted debts of many Latin American countries to international commercial banks, the formula of securitization of loans along with some debt relief finally proved acceptable to creditors and debtors. Far from an immediate process, however, these Brady restructurings were operationalized amid democratic transitions and iterated negotiations of structural adjustments with the International Monetary Fund (IMF). Yet by the mid-1990s, the ghosts of the 1980s defaults were finally put to rest. Yet, the securitization of commercial banks' loans into Brady bonds inadvertently opened the door to a (re)newed menace to sovereign debt restructurings in the 1990s and 2000s: private bondholders who refuse to participate in majority-accepted debt restructurings only to sue the sovereign in foreign courts for a large profit.

In the past three decades, sovereign debt restructurings of foreign sovereign bonds have had to contend with holdout creditors, preempt their (further) litigating instincts, and prevent them from undermining private debt restructuring negotiations altogether. When (protracted) debt restructurings came to an end, despite the settlement of legal disputes, room was still left for more dysfunction to come. Without a formal mechanism to rule over debt restructurings uniformly and predictably, contractual innovations have been the prevalent recourse to try and prevent protracted and costly debt deals for most of the actors involved.

Nevertheless, adaptability through "market-based solutions," however inventive, does not preclude some creditors from trying to leverage contract provisions to disrupt restructurings and extract larger repayments from debtors. Contractual changes may eventually lead to minimal room for dysfunction but seasoned students of debt restructurings past have long cautioned that "this is at best an uncertain process that will take several decades" since "adaptation is a long and winding road littered with institutional problems" that cannot do away with judicial "interpretive shocks" completely (Committee on International Economic Policy and Reform, 2013: 20). Insofar as existing institutions cannot offer commonly applicable solutions that may guarantee a smooth conclusion to future debt restructurings, these events are part of the permacrisis scenario conceived by Brown et al. (2023), in which not only bad luck, but missed opportunities continue to undermine national and global economic stability. In the absence of fundamental change brought about by global cooperation (such as would be required to create a new statutory mechanism for restructuring sovereign debts), ad hoc ingenuity has to make do. The past thus remains an insufficient prologue to a future where sovereign debt restructurings are a predictable part of permacrisis.

References

Asonuma, T. (2016). *Serial Sovereign defaults and debt restructurings* (IMF Working Paper No. 2016/066).

Ayres, J., Gelpern, A., & Powell, A. (2023). Sovereign debt restructuring: In need of a new approach. In A. Powell & O. M. Valencia (Eds.), *Dealing with debt*. Inter-American Development Bank.

Blackman, J. & Mukhi, R. (2010). The evolution of modern sovereign debt litigation: vultures, alter egos, and other legal fauna. *Law and Contemporary Problems* , *73*(4), 47–61.

Brown, G., El-Erian, M., & Spencer, M. (2023). *Permacrisis: A plan to fix a fractured world.* Simon & Schuster.

Buchheit, L., & Gulati, M. (2020). The Argentine collective action clause controversy. *Duke Law School Public Law and Legal Theory Series No. 2020-72.*

Buchheit, L., Chabert, G., DeLong, C., & Zettlemeyer, J. (2019). *How to restructure sovereign debt: Lessons from four decades* (Working Paper 19-8). Peterson Institute.

Bustillo, I. & Velloso, H. (2000). Bond markets for Latin America debt in the 1990s. *CEPAL, Serie Temas de Conyuntura No. 12.*

Calvo, G. (1998). Capital flows and capital-market crises: The simple economics of sudden stops. *Journal of Applied Economics, 1*, 35–54.

Calvo, G., Izquierdo, A., & Talvi, E. (2003). *Sudden stops, the real exchange rate and fiscal sustainability: Argentina's lessons* (NBER Working Paper No. 9828).

Chang, K., & Papaioannou, M. (2020). *Do enhanced collective action clauses affect sovereign borrowing costs?* (IMF Working Paper 20/162).

Clark, J. (1994). Debt reduction and market reentry under the Brady Plan. *Federal Reserve Board of New York Quarterly Review, 1993–94*, 38–62.

Committee on International Economic Political Reform. (2013). *Revisiting Sovereign Bankruptcy.* Brooking Institution.

Datz, G. (2009). What life after default? Time horizons and the outcome of the Argentine debt restructuring deal. *Review of International Political Economy, 16*(3), 456–484.

Datz, G. (2021). Placing Sovereign debt: Legal precedent and legislative preemption. In J. Flores & P. Pinot (Eds.), *Debt diplomacies: Rethinking Sovereign debt from colonial empire to hegemony*. Oxford University Press.

Datz, G., & Corcoran, K. (2019). Deviant debt: Reputation, litigation and the outlier effects of Argentina's debt restructuring saga. *New Political Economy, 25*(2), 300–313.

Euromoney. (2005, July 1). Argentina: Sovereign finally closes debt restructuring.

Fang, C., Schumacher, J., & Trebesch, C. (2020). *Restructuring sovereign bonds: holdouts, haircuts and the effectiveness of CACs* (European Central Bank Working Paper No. 2366).

Faria, R., McAdam, P., & Orrillo, J. (2021). *Serial sovereign default: The role of shocks and fiscal habits* (European Central Bank Working Paper No. 2629).

Gelpern, A. (2005). *After Argentina* (Institute for International Economic Policy Briefs in International Economics No. PB05-2).

Gelpern, A. (2013). Contract hope and sovereign redemption. *The Capital Markets Law Journal, 8*(2), 132–148.

Gelpern, A. (2020, June 10). *Keeping cozy by the dumpster fire: Argentina reads its contracts ... Twice ... Quel Scandale!*. Credit Slips.

Gelpern, A., & Gulati, M. (2006). Public symbol in private contract: A case study. *Washington University Law Review, 84*, 1627–1660.

Grund, S. (2022). *Sovereign debt restructuring and the Law*. Routledge.

Gulati, M., & Buchheit, L. (2000). Exit consents in Sovereign bond exchanges. *UCLA Law Review, 48*, 59–84.

Guzman, M. (2020). An analysis of Argentina's 2001 Default resolution. *Comparative Economic Studies, 62*, 701–738.

Hagan, S. (2020). *Sovereign debt restructurings: The centrality of the IMF's role* (Peterson Institute for International Economics Working Paper No. 20-13).

Helleiner, E. (2006). *The long and winding road: Towards a sovereign debt restructuring regime*. University of Waterloo: Manuscript.

Helleiner, E. (2008). The mystery of the missing Soveriegn debt restructuring mechanism. *Contributions to Political Economy, 2008*(27), 91–113.

International Monetary Fund. (2001). *Involving the private sector in the resolution of financial crises restructuring International Sovereign Bonds*. https://www.imf.org/external/pubs/ft/series/03/ips.pdf

International Monetary Fund. (2003, April 12). *Communiqué of the International Monetary and Financial Committee of the Board of Governors of the International Monetary Fund*. https://www.imf.org/en/News/Articles/2015/09/28/04/51/cm041203

International Capital Market Association (ICMA). (2014). *Standard aggregated collective action clauses for the terms and conditions of sovereign notes*. https://www.icmagroup.org/assets/documents/Resources/ICMA-Standard-CACs-August-2014.pdf

International Monetary Fund (IMF). (2014). *Strengthening the contractual framework to address collective action problems in sovereign debt restructuring*. IMF, Washington, DC.

International Monetary Fund (IMF). (2019). *Fourth progress report on inclusion of enhanced contractual provisions in international bond contracts*. IMF, Washington, DC.

International Monetary Fund. (2020, October). *Global financial stability report*.

International Monetary Fund. (2023). *Making public debt public – Ongoing initiatives and reform options*. IMF.

Kaminsky, & Schmukler. (2003a). *Sudden stops, the real exchange rate and fiscal sustainability: Argentina's lessons* (NBER Working Paper No. 9828).

Kaminsky, G., & Schmukler, S. (2003b). *The center and the periphery: The globalization of financial turmoil* (NBER Working Paper No. 9479).

Kaplan, S. (2021). *Globalizing patient capital: The political economy of Chinese finance in the Americas*. Cambridge University Press.

Krueger, A. (2001, November 26). *A new approach to Sovereign debt restructuring*. Address delivered at the National Economists' Club Annual Members' Dinner American Enterprise Institute.

Kruger, A. (2002). *A New approach to Sovereign debt restructuring*. IMF.

Langton, J. L. (2002). *Crisis management and sovereign debt restructuring: A market-based solution*. Mimeo.

Latin Finance. (2003, December 8). *What CACs Lack*. https://latinfinance.com/magazine/2003/12/08/what-cacs-lack/

Lawrence, M., Homer-Dixon, T., Janzwood, S., Rockström, J., Renn, O., & Donges, J. F. (2023). *Global Polycrisis: The causal mechanisms of crisis entanglement*. Cascade Institute. https://cascadeinstitute.org/technical-paper/global-polycrisis-the-causal-mechanisms-of-crisis-entanglement/

Lew, A. (1993). Republic of Argentina v. Weltover, Inc.: Interpreting the Foreign Sovereign Immunity Act's commercial activity exception to jurisdictional immunity. *Fordham International Law Journal, 17*(3), 726–775.

Makoff, G., & Weidemaier, M. (2022). Mass Sovereign debt litigation: A computer-assisted analysis of the Argentina Bond litigation in the U.S. Federal Courts 2002–2016. *UC Davis Law Review, 56*, 1233–1310.

Meyer, J., Reinhart, C. M., & Trebesch, C. (2019). *Sovereign Bonds since Waterloo* (NBER Working Paper No. 25543).

Miller, M. (2002). *Sovereign debt restructuring: New articles, new contracts – or no change?* (International Economics Policy Briefs, No. PB02-03).

Power, P. J. (1996). Sovereign Debt: The rise of the secondary market and its implications for future restructurings. *Fordham Law Review, 64*, 2701–2772.

Reinhart, C., & Rogoff, K. (2009). *This time is different. Eight centuries of financial folly*. Princeton University Press.

Santiso, J. (2003). *The political economy of emerging markets*. Palgrave.

Schumaker, J., Trebesch, C., & Enderlein, H. (2021). Sovereign Debtors in Court. *Journal of International Economics, 131*.

Setser, B. (2024, February 22). The IMF needs to focus on setting good targets for external debt sustainability. *Council on Foreign Relations Blog*. https://www.cfr.org/blog/imf-needs-focus-setting-good-targets-external-debt-sustainability
Shenai, N., & Bolhuis, M. A. (2023). *How the Brady Plan delivered on debt relief: Lessons and implications* (IMF Working Paper WP/23/258).
Silva, R., Campbell, M., & Ranieri, A. (2023, October 20). Lessons from Argentina's default on its international Sovereign debt. *Latin Lawyer*.
Singer, P., (2016, April 24). The lessons of our bond war. *The Wall Street Journal*.
Sobel, M. (2016). Strengthening collective action clauses: catalyzing change— the back story. *Capital Mar kets Law Journal, 11*(1), 3–11.
Sobel, M. (2020, June 30). Argentina and creditors enter new round. OMFIF.
Solana, J. (2023, February 22). Interdependence in the twenty-first century. *Project Syndicate*.
Tooze, A. (2022, October 22). Welcome to the world of the polycrisis. *Financial Times*.
UN News. (2014, September 24). *Argentina: los fondos buitre son una forma de terrorismo económico y financiero*. https://news.un.org/es/story/2014/09/1312401
Weidemaier, M., & Gulati, M. (2013). A people's history of collective action clauses. *Virginia Journal of International Law, 54*(1), 51–94.
Weidemaier, W. M., & Gelpern, A. (2013). *Injunctions in sovereign debt litigation*. UNC Legal Studies (Research Paper No. 2330914).
Weidemaier, W. M., & Gelpern, A. (2014). Injunctions in sovereign debt litigation. Y*ale journal on regulation, 31*(1), 189–218.
Zettlemeyer, J., Trebesch, C., & Gulati, M. (2012). The Greek debt exchange: An autopsy. Manuscript.
Zuleeg, F., Emmanouilidis, J. A., & de Castro, R. B. (2021, November 3). *Europe in the Age of Permacrisis*. European Policy Center.

Part IV
Digital Currencies and FinTech: Promised Benefits and New Risks

Chapter 13
Systemic Potential Aspects of CBDCs

Christian Ghymers

Contents

Introduction: CBDCs Are the Response to Crypto-Assets

The explosion of crypto assets is already well known and does not need further description here. Still, their pretention to be crypto-currencies, thanks to their underlying technology, deserves special attention. They are the origin of a genuine revolution in monetary systems, not for the probability of 1 day effectively playing the monetary functions, but rather for having provoked the sound, careful, and necessary reactions of central banks. These reactions have spurred the inevitable

C. Ghymers (✉)
Interdisciplinary Institute for the Relations between Europe, Latin America and the Caribbean (IRELAC), Bruxelles, Belgium

D. Katsikas et al. (eds.), *Finance, Growth and Democracy: Connections and Challenges in Europe and Latin America in the Era of Permacrisis*, United Nations University Series on Regionalism 33, https://doi.org/10.1007/978-3-031-68475-3_13

interest in Central Bank Digital Currencies (CBDCs) as the appropriate response to the threat of monopolistic private firms of global Internet platforms capturing monetary sovereignty. CBDCs are already operational in a growing number of countries, and active preparations are taking place in most central banks. Although the creation of interoperable CBDCs is the only efficient policy option, vested interests and retrograde ideologies try to impede their implementation by arguing the threat to individual freedom. On the contrary, CBDCs are a necessity for preserving collective freedom by warranting monetary sovereignty, improving the efficiency of monetary policies, and easing a systemic solution toward a multilateral agreement around the issuance of a multilateral currency that is not a debt of a national economy.

The potential coming revolution will not come from crypto assets but from these CBDCs because their underlying digital technology is not only an opportunity for improving the public good of a payments system and increasing financial inclusion but also for cutting the costs of cross-border operations spectacularly. Under the condition of universal interoperability between all CBDCs, this innovation would become a potential "game changer," under the assumption that the permacrisis creates the political pressures necessary for making the digital Special Drawing Right (SDR) the multilateral safe asset able to rebalance and stabilize the International Monetary System (IMS). This systemic aspect is the main purpose of this chapter, contrary to most central bank preoccupations directed primarily to domestic usage.

After a brief overview of the present (but moving) state (2023) of the digital money issues, this chapter presents shortly the domestic consequences on deposit banks and monetary policy before developing what should be the ideal option for maximizing the global benefits and, most of all, for preventing further fragmentation of international transactions.

What Is New with Digital Money?

The digitalization of monetary systems is not new. Money and finance account-based money have been digital for decades, with examples including electronic deposits on a digital ledger with commercial banks and nonbank financial service providers that have been digitalized since the introduction of informatics, as well as for central bank money. The financial firms have introduced many innovations and technological improvements in the underlying infrastructures, for example, the access instantaneous real-time prices on the Forex, or the real-time gross settlement (RTGS) systems organized by central banks. This is also true for retail operations, credit cards, prepaid cards, web-based services like PayPal, mobile-money accounts (over 400,000,000 users in Africa), or digital wallets such as M-Pesa in Kenya (processing payments equivalent to more than half of Kenya's GDP) and Alipay (Alibaba) and WeChatpay (Tencent) in China with more than 1 billion users for each of them (92% of mobile payments that represent more than two-thirds of all payments).

However, all these innovations are only efficiency improvements in the payment system and do not change the nature of money because they all remain a direct claim upon their official currencies through financial intermediaries. *Crypto assets, on the contrary, introduce a real change (and threat)* for monetary sovereignty and financial stability because they are created outside of the official monetary system in a decentralized way through the "distributed ledger technology" (DLT[1]), which allows for warranting the finality of transactions and payments through the network participants without any trusted authority. This innovation temporarily enjoyed an impressive success because blockchain technologies have provided operational alternatives to the liquid official assets at the very moment that central banks were obliged by the global financial crisis (2009–2009) to inject huge amounts of global liquidity. This abundance of liquidity favors financial speculative activities while creating fears for the monetary function of the store of value. Such an alternative became immediately attractive as a safe haven as well as for escaping fiscal, legal, and international controls (money laundering, trafficking, and terrorism). Also, some conspiracist, libertarian, and anarchist arguments support crypto assets as a means to contest public institutions and authorities. However, these assets that are not the counterpart of any debt and are not anchored to any official currency cannot be a currency but remain purely speculative assets subject to extreme price volatility. Their prices tend to behave cyclically as a complement to gold, like any other global financial asset, being directly correlated to global liquidity variations (Howell, 2022).

Another category of crypto assets—*the stablecoins*—appeared as an answer to the instability of the prices of these assets in order to develop their payment function by offering crypto assets backed by and pegged to real-world assets such as commodities, key currencies, gold, or sometimes other cryptocurrencies or even algorithms. Stablecoins typically should have a reserve of an equal amount of the currency or the assets to which they are pegged. However, no authority could warrant the appropriate fulfillment of this feature. Most of these stablecoins are demanded in countries suffering high inflation, like Turkey, where platforms allow easy access to stablecoins or other crypto assets. The project Lira (renamed Diem), proposed by Facebook, belongs to the category of stablecoins that stabilize their price by pegging their value to a basket of currencies issued by central banks (finally only pegged to the dollar). It failed, after strong reactions from monetary authorities, because its purpose was to become the world currency using the quasi-monopoly advantage of its global network of more than a billion users. Nevertheless, even anchored to an official currency these stablecoins remain out of the monetary system by being managed by some private interests without any clear regulation or public supervision.

The existing thousands of created *crypto assets are not currencies* because, even if they could fulfill some functions of money in some moments, they are inefficient

[1] Distributed Ledger Technology (DLT) is the supporting system of any blockchain, which can be permissioned (users need permission from a central authority) or permissionless (totally decentralized).

means of payments. They lack official support by definition, and their value cannot be predictable as a means of payment. Their monetary functions depend on the level of public trust they enjoy. The value of a crypto asset is only based upon the perception of its potential scarcity, being neither a claim upon an identifiable issuer nor on a real asset or project. Therefore, crypto assets cannot be used for fixing prices for payments; their value is submitted to the market's self-fulfilling processes, based only on the expectation of holders, that fluctuates wildly depending on many factors. Their ease of use for current payments is also lower than traditional money, depending on the service providers, and lower than that of credit cards (e.g., Bitcoin could only process five operations per second against Visa holding up to 24,000 payments per second). Furthermore, they are susceptible to inevitable regulations or future prohibitions, as in China. Their temporary attraction is based upon their restricted supply that deprives them of an intrinsic public good feature of money, which is the possibility to regulate liquidity through monetary policy. This deficiency makes them deflationary because their store of value function dominates, creating incentives for their hoarding. Furthermore, the main ones, such as Bitcoin, would be operationally too slow to support global payments and anyway too costly in terms of energy (CO_2 emissions) to become sustainable.

As regards *stablecoins*, they could provide more stability than speculative crypto assets or could even have own a partial monetary function. However, they remain susceptible to destabilizing runs, disruptions in the payment system, and concentration of economic power. They could never offer more stability and credibility than their anchor, and anyway, the indirect and uncertified claim upon the chosen reserves is necessarily less stable and less credible than the direct one provided by the use of a stable official currency managed by a credible lender-of-last-resort. They miss this essential monetary attribute that is trust, and they would need to be regulated and externally supervised to be able to sustain a sound monetary system.

From these developments, it appears that through the emergence of crypto assets and stablecoins digital technologies impact the monetary system directly by putting into question the issuance monopoly of central banks and, overall, monetary sovereignty by offering an apparently attractive global alternative. Indeed, through the link with global Internet platforms, the monetary ambition of big foreign, private actors is led by the profitable synergies given by access to or the capture of users' data, enabling them to be more competitive in supplying additional services. This leads to an additional high risk of increasing the market power and concentration of multinational FinTechs, with dangerous consequences for privacy, security, and democracy.

These risks explain the necessary reaction of central banks when they realize that not only their functions, but also monetary sovereignty itself is at stake, threatened by powerful private monopolies. Their inescapable answer has recently been to consider, analyze, and develop themselves some modalities ("permissioned") of the blockchain distributed ledger technology (DLT) for issuing the so-called Central Bank Digital Currencies (CBDCs). It will be the best way to preserve the public good nature of money while, in conformity with their mission, significantly improving the efficiency and scope of their payment systems. Especially important, CBDCs will promote financial inclusion thanks to the benefits of cheap digitalization for the users. Considerable efforts and attention have recently been deployed by central banks to analyze these opportunities and modalities.

What Is a CBDC?

A CBDC is an asset as safe and liquid as any banknote because, as a direct claim on the central bank, it would not carry either credit and liquidity risk or the risk of bank failure. In addition, CBDCs are a more efficient means of payment: significantly faster, safer, and cheaper than cash or bank accounts, particularly for cross-border payments using permissioned DLT.

A *retail CBDC* is an "e-currency," or "digital banknote," a means of payment issued by the national central bank equivalent to fiat money, but it would differ from existing digital money available to the general public (like debit and credit cards or e-payments) because this CBDC would be a direct liability of the central bank (like a note), not of a commercial bank. A *wholesale CBDC* refers to digital forms of central bank reserves whose access is limited to banks and other financial institutions. In this case, a CBDC plays a similar role as a bank deposit at its central bank, fulfilling the same universal functions as their money in cash or as bank reserves, but bringing the key features of cash into the digital era. The most probable architecture for creating CBDCs would be a hybrid form with a two-tier system combining retail and wholesale for outsourcing to banks and fintechs the services to the clients in a private–public partnership.

Contrary to a crypto asset or a stablecoin, a CBDC would be the safest digital liquid asset available to the public. It ensures the respect of national sovereignty and the existence of an anchor to the monetary system, preserving the public good character of money while enhancing financial inclusion and innovation in the means of payment. CBDCs would enjoy access to all the digital progresses, for example, by being preprogrammed to be used under warranted conditions or under prescribed circumstances. However, this modernization is not business-as-usual because CBDCs provide potential changes in the essence of money and of monetary policy, with important potential impacts for the International Monetary System (IMS) and currency competition and substitution, but also for the protection of freedom and privacy.

CBDCs' Impacts on Monetary Policies and the Banking Sector

It is obvious that the creation of a CBDC will result in a major change in the *composition of the monetary base and in the deposits in the banking sector*. The effects of the issuance of CBDCs on the balance sheets of central banks will be visible only in the composition of the monetary base and not on its total volume because a CBDC remains a form of central bank money. The substitution is only inside the monetary base: cash in notes against digital-cash and digital-cash against lower bank deposits (when customer deposits to the banks shift to CBDC deposits to the central bank). On the contrary, the potential effects on the banks are important: due to the advantages attached to CBDC with respect to traditional bank deposits, substitution of these deposits for CBDC will reduce the volume of their cheapest funding source. This bank disintermediation effect will depend on the characteristics of the CBDC but should be controlled. The risk of excessive substitution will be monitored and will be reduced by some modalities like imposing limits on the volume of CBDC holding, prohibiting companies from accumulating CBDC deposits, and accepting only non-remunerated CBDC current accounts. Anyway, central banks are in a position to make up for any excessive loss of deposit by lending back to the banks that suffer a significant loss of deposits. However, the probable effect would be a contraction of bank profitability as long as banks face higher costs of funding (in case they have to offer interest on deposits and borrow their funding on the wholesale market). Partial compensations could result from

- Financial inclusion leading to new activities and funding as available savings would increase (new clients opening accounts and acceding to credit and financial products)
- Reduction in dollarization and cryptoization as the use of local currency would increase (as far as domestic macroeconomic policies are credible)

On monetary conditions, the reduction of stable deposits in the banks, the higher competition for funding them, and their lower profitability will increase the effects of interest rate adjustments on the economy (higher efficiency of monetary policy). This might also imply somewhat tighter financial conditions through higher interest rates. Indeed, switching away from non-remunerated deposits to borrowing on the wholesale monetary market tends to push the lending rates to the banks upward. However, this tendency is limited since the central bank could compensate for this effect if the macroeconomic environment allows it.

CBDCs' Impacts on the Political Debates

CBDCs appear as a necessity for preventing the risks of losing monetary sovereignty and monetary policy efficiency while significantly upgrading the efficiency of the payment system. They will provide safer, cheaper, and faster services by combining liquidity security with instantaneous transactions, benefiting from all the advantages of digitalization. However, these important advantages for the citizens and the business sector present a potential risk for privacy. Indeed, contrary to some crypto assets, CBDCs must rely on a centralized technology ("permissioned DLT") to keep some possibilities of control at the central bank level in cases of illegal operations. Although technologies also allow for warranting protection of privacy, it is, of course, impossible to make sure that in the future, these guarantees will not legally be changed. This is the main argument used by several lobbies that understand that CBDCs are a direct threat to their profits or rents (bank associations, some FinTechs, crypto assets businesses, and some tax evaders), supported immediately by conservative political parties claiming that individual freedom would disappear. These critics argue that a digital currency would hand over too much power to the government, exposing citizens' use of money, sooner or later, to the inevitable temptation for the government to use it as a surveillance tool, targeting dissidents or minorities, prohibiting people to buy certain goods, or imposing negative interest rates. They also argue that this centralization would expose the currency and the citizens to cyberattacks. Furthermore, they pretend it would undermine the banking and crypto asset industries. These considerations have led to political pressures in the US Congress to prohibit by law the introduction of an e-dollar.

The Fed Board of Governors is also divided, with some governors, particularly Governor Neel Kashkari, associating CBDCs with the Chinese policy of totalitarian control of citizen transactions. Also, the banker lobby and the crypto asset business try to prohibit a CBDC dollar. Other voices, in a protectionist view, would want to reject multilateral coordination and interoperability for maintaining the weaponization of the dollar by cooperating discretionarily only with geopolitical allies. On the contrary, Fed Chair Jerome Powell said in June 2022 that "*an official digital version of the U.S. dollar could help safeguard its global dominance as other countries issue their own.*" As Powell acknowledged, there is a risk that the dollar will stay out of the development of CBDCs, that will give an advantage to alternative currencies. Furthermore, the development of stablecoins and crypto assets puts in danger the efficiency of monetary policy. A failure to issue an e-dollar or an e-euro would open the way to Chinese supremacy imposing its own technical standards in other emerging markets and developing economies (EMDEs).

The probability that a CBDC dollar would not be launched would present disadvantages both for the US economy and for the world. Nevertheless, the rest of the world would be in a better position to adopt interoperable CBDCs, increasing the possibility of using alternative vehicles, therefore weakening the international dominant status of the dollar, but exposing exchange markets to additional risks of unstable currency substitution. Additional global instability would result from the risk of creating more financial segmentation between monetary blocs. Furthermore, for the United States, the probable competition of stablecoins would weaken the FED monetary stance.

The Existing Projects for Implementing CBDCs

According to the Bank for International Settlements (BIS) survey in 2022, 93% of central banks are exploring CBDCs. Sixty countries are in an advanced stage of development, and over 20 central banks have launched their pilots, including Brazil, Japan, and Russia. Of this total, 25% would be limited to retail CBDCs only, while the rest considers both retail and wholesale CBDCs. In 2023, 18% of the central banks plan to issue a retail CBDC in the next three years and 16% plan a wholesale

CBDC. Fifty-eight percent consider doing it soon. Most central banks prefer to design a public–private partnership for their future retail CBDCs. The private sector would offer accounts or digital wallets to take charge of the relations with the clients and facilitate the management of CBDC holdings and payments, especially for the legal procedures of know-your-customer (KYC) and anti-money laundering/combating the financing of terrorism (AML/CFT). This kind of hybrid model would facilitate the use of the private sector's existing privacy and identity-management frameworks.

In early 2023, 115 countries were launching, experimenting, or analyzing CBDCs: 11 had already launched a CBDC, 104 others were experimenting with a pilot (17), had a CBDC in development (33), or were at the research stage (39), with others still considering (15) or canceling (2) it, representing over 95% of the global GDP.

China

China has clearly taken the lead in the works and pilot realizations of e-currencies with the *e-CNY*, which started in 2014 and was the first CBDC to be tested in 2020. The purpose of the e-CNY seems to be exclusively domestic, at least at the beginning, with the complementary purpose of controlling citizens since Article 28 of the Cybersecurity Law allows the government to acquire data from any Chinese entity in the name of "national security." The e-CNY is already operational in selected cities as an experiment, being progressively extended from four cities to 23 in 2022, and six more in 2023 to provide the e-CNY to the Asian games and test it with foreign users. Although the number of users is impressive, the volume of exchanges is below expectations. According to the central bank (PBOC), these numbers rose from 140 million users for an amount of US$9 billion in 2021 to 260 million users for US$15 billion at the end of August 2022. New extensions to densely populated regions were announced, as well as the connection of the e-CNY to the existing digital payments system, dominated by Alibaba Group's Alipay and Tencent Holding's WeChat Pay. Both have enabled the e-CNY as a payment option and will provide a potential extension to the equivalent of several trillions of dollars. In 2023, China has extended its pilot to most of its 1.4 billion population with the objective of reaching a volume of US$300 billion, which seems out of reach. Maybe the lack of privacy protection could explain this slower growth. In August 2022, the PBOC extended the tests to the Forex by joining a pilot project managed by the Bank for International Settlements (BIS) with Hong Kong, Thailand, and the United Arab Emirates in a cross-border digital currency trial. It used the BIS's prototype cross-border payments system, the "mBridge platform." The results show that direct Forex costs are cut by half but with the potential for further reduction of other remaining costs. In January 2023, China included the e-CNY in their currency circulation calculations where it represents only 0.13% of cash and reserves held by the central bank.

European Union

In the European Union, authorities had started in advance with their project to create a Pan-European debit card system in the Single Euro Payments Area (2007) to rival Visa and Mastercard, and the "Monnet Project" (2009) of a European Card. Amazingly, this project failed. Although not involving a CBDC at the beginning, this failure illustrates the difficulty of innovating on monetary issues. The ECB has long-floated the idea of a home-grown cross-border scheme capable of ensuring more monetary sovereignty and lower costs for international transactions through full interoperability. However, commercial interests have prevailed over a Pan-European solution, and disagreements on competition conditions between the European Commission and the main private stakeholders led to this project being abandoned in 2012.

In 2016, the e-euro project to implement a euro CBDC with technical analysis in the Stella project and the ECB pushing for a euro instant-payment system started being considered. The purpose is to handle all types of cashless payments, whether by card, transfer, direct debit or mobile, especially with the *Pan European Payment System Initiative* (Pepsi), associating 20 leading European banks, trying to base the system on the Sepa credit transfer instant (SCT Inst) scheme and the Eurosystem's TARGET Instant Payment Settlement (TIPS). In 2020, the project was confirmed under the name "*European Payments Initiative (EPI)*" for implementing an operational digital payment system for use anywhere in Europe, able to supersede the fragmented landscape that currently still exists.

Despite difficulties, in 2021, the ECB and the euro area national central banks launched a 24-month investigation phase for the e-euro. In October 2023, this investigation phase delivered its findings on the possible design and distribution models for a digital euro in the report "*A stocktake on the digital euro*" (ECB, 2023). The envisaged CBDC would be widely accessible to citizens and businesses through distribution by supervised intermediaries, such as banks, and there would be safeguards to protect privacy. On November 1, 2023, a preparation phase of 2 years was launched. Full-scale tests and experimentation will allow for meeting all the necessary requirements (privacy, inclusion, security, impacts on the banking sector, etc.). At the end of 2025, the Governing Council of the ECB shall take the decision when the European Union's legislative process is completed. This legal process was already started in June 2023 with the regulation proposals issued by the EU Commission. The e-€ will be a retail CBDC with a holding limit per account. It would be designed to have no material impact on financial stability or the transmission of monetary policy. Deposits would not be remunerated. Business holders and public authorities could operate in e-€ but could not accumulate holdings in e-€. Their payments would be immediately transferred to their commercial bank accounts.

The United States

The United States debate makes the dollar CBDC lag for political reasons. The republican Congress wants to prohibit it by law, and the FED is divided. No official plan is yet available at the end of 2023. The White House issued in September 2022 its technical evaluation, estimating the feasibility, setting the political guidelines, and presenting the different technical options, in case a CBDC for the dollar were decided by law, but without any recommendation for launching this e-dollar. While the Federal Reserve presented a white paper on digital payments in January 2022, it has not decided on whether or how to issue an e-dollar either, but is actively conducting technical investigations into both retail and wholesale CBDC design: *Project Hamilton,* at the Federal Reserve Bank of Boston with the MIT, focused on retail uses and payment channels, and *Project Cedar,* at New York Fed, dealt with wholesale payments. In phase 1, wholesale cross-border payments were tested for Forex spot transactions, showing that peer-to-peer settlements on Forex could occur in fewer than 10 seconds on average (against 2 days now) and with very low costs. In phase 2, it was examined whether distributed ledger technology could be used to improve the efficiency of cross-border payments in settlements involving multiple currencies. Each simulated payment scenario achieved an end-to-end settlement in under 30 s on average. In parallel, a nonprofit organization advocating for an e-dollar, the *Digital Dollar Project* (DDP), has launched several pilot projects with private retail companies.

The strategic growing gap between the progressing e-CNY and e-€ and the opposition to a possible e-dollar raises the key question of a risk of monetary fragmentation and of the future relations with the other reserve currencies, that could more easily become substitutes to the dollar for regional payments.

Other Countries[2]

Most central banks are also working on the feasibility and advantages of issuing CBDCs and more than 100 countries are considering issuing it. Seventeen countries have already launched their projects: the Bahamas since October 2020, Nigeria since 2021, the seven Eastern Caribbean States and Jamaica, India, Russia, Sweden, Australia, Britain, Brazil, and South Korea. In addition, others manage pilot projects, most of them in consortia (Canada, Ghana, Hong Kong, Kazakhstan, Malaysia, Mauritius, Saudi Arabia, South Africa, Singapore, Switzerland, Thailand, Ukraine, the United Arab Emirates, Uruguay). The rest are in a development or research stage, except for two that canceled their projects (Equator and Senegal).

[2] For Brazil, see Part IV, Chap. 15.

CBDCs and Their "Transmutation" Power of Central Bank Monies

Most of the attention of central banks in their preparation works was dedicated first to domestic aspects, like impacts on deposit banks, efficiency of monetary policies, security, privacy, inclusion, regulations, etc., which are indeed crucial for the sustainability of CBDCs. This quasi-exclusive focus on domestic aspects looks inadequate when understanding the systemic change CBDCs bring to the nature of money. The most essential advantage that CBDCs could deliver is the ability to eradicate most of the costs of cross-border payments. Indeed, CBDCs provoke a genuine transmutation of money by *eradicating the difference between resident and nonresident* agents.

Why is it so important? Why would a CBDC be any different from the "digital" money that the world spends in cross-border transactions with present credit and debit cards daily? The key difference is that holding a CBDC means holding a direct claim on a central bank—the most risk-less-liquid asset—while the claim with a credit card always remains the liability of a commercial bank. In the present exchange-rate transactions, a domestic bank only buys for its client a claim upon a foreign correspondent bank (or another intermediary). This means that the client has a less-safe-indirect claim on the Foreign central bank's money.

This feature is a radical change with important consequences for monetary policy, for the use of national currencies outside the borders, and, therefore, for the International Monetary System (IMS). This is why it should have been dealt with from the start, being taking on board when working on domestic aspects, regulations, and, overall, for choosing and designing technological options. Only recently, have pilot projects with multiple CBDCs been dedicated to evaluating the effects of CBDCs upon international transactions and the Forex, but the last ECB report (October 2023) on the e-€ does not deal at all with cross-border transactions.

In the present system, correspondent banks are necessary for cross-border payments. They duplicate all the processes and steps in the correspondent banking chain, implying high costs, low speed, operational complexities, blocked liquidity, limited access, and low transparency. These inefficiencies also introduce settlement risks into the system to the costly detriment of both financial intermediaries and end users. Only the direct intermediation costs are estimated for 2020 to be above US$120 billion, without including the costs for the risks, the liquidity needs, and the exchange-rate commissions, which would also decrease with the increase in competition introduced by the CBDCs. In April 2022, US$2.2 trillion of daily Forex turnover (Glowka & Nilsson, BIS, 2022) involved settlement risk. This cost has been rising since 2013 with a reduction of inter-dealer trading and an increasing share of transactions taking place outside the mechanism organized by the *Continuous Linked Settlement* (CLS) consortium of banks which includes only 18 currencies. Even this CLS, which enables simultaneous settlement of the payments on both sides of an FX transaction, implies significant intermediary and liquidity costs on top of only a 5-h window per day for simultaneous real-time gross settlement

(RTGS) systems across currency jurisdictions. The longer a foreign exchange transaction takes [typically, there is a 2-day settlement period but much more for least developed countries (LDCs)], the greater the "Herstatt risk" (settlement failure). According to Mandeng (2020), the settlement costs—that is, the "credit risk" when the payer or its intermediary default prior to final settlement plus the "liquidity risk" when the effective payment is delayed—are estimated to cost annually a minimum of US$130 billion.

The fundamental novelty of CBDCs is their technological power to simplify and eliminate most of the costs of cross-border payments thanks to some improved forms of "permissioned DLT," that is, not decentralized (contrary to Bitcoin). This modality allows for central control in the public interest while erasing resident-non-resident segmentation in international payments: DLT transfers instantaneously, peer-to-peer, payments or financial assets (like a "token"), digitally protected through a code. This safe technology not only could skip all intermediary interventions, eradicating their costs, risks (credit and liquidity risks), and delays required by the traditional sequencing of cross-border payments but even the verification of the legal requirements (AML, CLT, KYC[3], etc.) could be simplified with permissioned DLT networks which ensure a unique digital identity with smart contracts automating their execution on-chain. Forex transactions are transformed into operations equivalent to mere domestic payments, with much faster and more efficient conditions while benefiting from all the innovations brought by digital technologies. However, such progress requires a single condition: to be inter-operational across the different national payment systems thanks to the generalization of harmonized digitalized central bank money (CBDC) using the same "permissioned DLT." Therefore, a generalization of issuance of compatible CBDC opens the possibility to create a *genuine "transmutation" of central bank monies from a local to a potential, cheap, and safe multilateral means of settlements, in addition to the financial innovation and new functionalities provided by digital technologies.*

CBDCs' Social Impacts

For emerging economies and LDCs, all the present costs are much higher as they must transit through third-party currencies, supporting higher commissions, longer delays, and higher costs of liquidity and risks. This asymmetry takes an alarming dimension for smaller banks[4] and small amounts and retail operations, especially for lower-income or poor LDC migrants sending remittances to their countries. According to World Bank data (2023), global remittances toward low- and middle-

[3]ALM: anti-money laundering; CLT: combating the financing of terrorism; KYC: know-your-client,

[4]Since the global financial crisis, a fast decline (around 30%) in the number of active correspondent banks has been increasing the costs of cross-border transactions, especially for peripheral and poorer regions.

income countries were valued in 2022 at US$647 billion, triple the amount of overseas development assistance and double the value of foreign direct investment (US$259 billion). Although in decline, the global average cost for sending remittances of US$200 was 6.20% in 2023 (second quarter). This is a decrease from the more than 10% in 2009, thanks to the competition pressures from the fast development of digitalization payments, that operate in 2023 with an average cost of 4.60%, still higher than the 3% envisaged in the United Nations Sustainable Development Goals. The share of remittances paying total costs between 10–15% has regularly decreased from 29% in 2009 to 9% in 2023. The poorest regions have the highest costs. Six sub-Saharan African countries pay more than 20% in total costs, but the average costs for this region are also on a downward trend, at 8%. Latin America and the Caribbean's costs are 6.13%, East Asia's are 5.87%, and South Asia's are the lowest at 4.31%. This gives an indication that the major potential effect of digital currencies relies on these cross-border payments and will provide very important consequences for social inclusion and development.

The social positive impact of using CBDCs is enormous for the 1.4 billion people remaining outside of the formal financial system. These people are being discriminated against because it is too costly for banks, insurance companies, and other institutions to transact with low-income households. This handicap is an obstacle to development that CBDCs can eradicate allowing financially excluded populations to access efficient payment systems without needing a bank account, with low fees and less stringent identification requirements. These households could send and receive funds from other digital financial service providers more efficiently, easing their access to saving products and loans.

The Potential Transformation Effect of CBDCs for the International Monetary System (IMS)

Drawing on Ghymers' (2020) probabilistic exercise, this chapter argues that the most promising consequence of interoperable CBDCs is their capacity to put in motion a chain of changes, making easier—but also more necessary—a multilateral cooperation for ensuring more stable global liquidity as well as a more symmetrical IMS. The revolution of payment digitalization and its geopolitical and monetary policy consequences upon central banks and the Forex will open a historical opportunity to incentivize, or even oblige, authorities to move to a multilateral reserve currency, solving the costly Triffin Dilemma[5] and the macroeconomic dysfunctional asymmetry created by the use of a national currency as the main international one.

[5] The Triffin dilemma expresses the logical impossibility that the supply of global liquidity resulting from the domestic policies of the United States would be necessarily compatible with the need for liquidity from the rest of the world. The dilemma impedes the management of an optimal level of global liquidity, therefore generating international financial instability. See Ghymers, C. (2021).

This asymmetry confers to the dollar the so-called "*exorbitant privilege*" that creates very costly international spillovers leading to a global pro-cyclical instability of global liquidity. The systemic cause is the fact that global liquidity supply is functionally determined mainly by safe assets in dollars whose volume cannot adapt sufficiently to meet the needs for liquid safe assets of the world (Ghymers, 2022). This process creates destabilizing waves of global liquidity (Rey, 2013) and pushes the US economy into over-indebtedness. The permacrisis conditions should increase the absolute necessity to find the necessary investments for de-carbonization and could become an argument for making the IMS more symmetrical (see Ghymers, Chap. 18). The CBDCs could contribute to this objective, making it operationally feasible and more necessary for stability purposes.

Indeed, the ideal and definitive solution to the IMS flaw (RTI, 2015) is merely to make global liquidity determined collegiately through a new global safe asset, that is, a multilaterally controlled liability that is not a national debt anymore but a multilateral one. It is the simplest way to pursue global stability purposes according to objective indicators fixed collegiately by a committee of central banks. Operationally, the proposed reform consists in allowing the IMF to issue its existing Special Drawing Rights[6] (SDR, a basket made up of the five main reserve currencies) directly in digital form, which would become the multilateral best safe asset. This official e-SDR would be issued as the counterpart of central bank deposits or other national liquid official assets (sovereign bonds) from the five component currencies of the SDR. The variation of the issued volume of this multilateral safe asset would make operational a technical regulation of the global monetary base without resting on any national policy or by imposing international coordination of monetary policies.

Such an ideal and fundamental reform has been blocked since the rejection of Keynes' plan in 1944 and the numerous successive Triffin proposals. However, the technological properties of CBDCs in a context of permacrisis generating growing instability of global liquidity allows for considering the potential of a "game-changer" that they carry for tackling the key flaws of the IMS. Indeed, the emergence of CBDCs in a permacrisis context could lead to political pressures, making possible the following *potential scenario*:

- CBDCs would trigger three mutually supportive developments for a private e-SDR:
    (i) A strong increase in currency substitution, implying higher exchange-rate volatility (Kareken & Wallace, 1981), making the dollar less stable, reducing its competitiveness as a vehicle for Forex transactions and in its use by third countries.

[6] The present Special Drawing Right (SDR) is the legitim official multilateral reserve, created in 1969 with the legal purpose of becoming "*the principal reserve asset in the international monetary system*," according to the formal agreement enacted in the Article VIII, section 7, of the IMF statute.

(ii) In reply to this volatility, financial markets' appetite will quickly supply a "private e-SDR" more competitive than the dollar for two reasons: (a) bundling (and unbundling) the five CBDCs composing this private e-SDR becomes costless, and (b) it is the most stable vehicle since it is arithmetically immune by construction to exchange-rate fluctuations between its five components. This e-SDR will be highly demanded by the markets as the most competitive safe asset and the best vehicle for their Forex and "repo" transactions.

(iii) The costless e-SDR could automatically provide the missing global vehicle for transforming the global interbank market into a global "clearing union." All current transactions would have an interest to be converted immediately at zero costs and almost zero exchange-rate risk into deposits expressed in this most stable and multilateral reserve currency, making any deposits transferable into any other harmonized CBDC on a 24/7 operation at lower costs than by passing through the dollar.

- The resulting intense currency substitution with higher dollar instability will make US monetary policy less efficient and more uncertain, creating more negative spillovers and more fluctuations in global liquidity, impeding the capital inflows required by de-carbonization in LDCs.
- The growing worries among policymakers should provide strong incentives to bargain a multilateral monetary cooperation for endowing the IMF with the function to regulate the de facto clearing union by intervening in e-SDR, merging the private e-SDR with the official SDR.
- They would also agree that the e-SDR could be used as the cheapest and most flexible financial safety net, merging most existing facilities.
- Therefore, the CBDCs generalized use and their easy of convertion into e-SDRs will tend to incentivize, or even oblige, authorities to see the e-SDR as the missing tool for stabilizing global liquidity. Thus, by upgrading the IMF into global Lender-of-Last-Resort, which would issue or withdraw official e-SDRs for managing global liquidity as a public good, the IMS would officially move to a multilateral reserve system.
- CBDCs have thus the potential to lead to an IMS reform that solves the costly Triffin Dilemma, restores monetary stability, eases the financing of decarbonization, and provides a more efficient safety net.
  - So, in the context of permacrisis creating growing currency substitutions and thus pressures upon policymakers, CBDCs would force the merging of official and private e-SDR for regulating global liquidity. So, CBDCs could play the role of a powerful game-changer, forcing to solve the major systemic flaw of the IMS. The profitable systematic conversion into e-SDR, according to harmonized protocols ensuring interoperability, together with a multilateral regulation of (short-term) operational liquidity in e-SDR by the IMF would permit to dispense with the central role of the dollar in global liquidity; this would allow to escape from the Triffin Dilemma and to manage global liquidity not in function of domestic situations in the US economy anymore, but as a global public good in the interest of all economies.

Conclusion

CBDCs are indispensable for preserving monetary sovereignty and the efficient transmission of monetary policies. Furthermore, they have the potential to change the role of the national key currencies and ease the move toward a multilateral system as long as they are technologically compatible. The old Keynes/Triffin plans for establishing a rational system for global liquidity management to ensure macroeconomic stability could come to hand thanks to the inescapable technological revolution in payment systems, the benefits of which could only be realized with full interoperability. In these conditions, a costless e-SDR will emerge as the legitimate multilateral tool and the best safe asset able to manage global liquidity as a public good. It is nevertheless disappointing to see most central banks still focusing only on domestic aspects rather than on cross-border aspects. At the same time, vested interests and ideological beliefs could derail the implementations of CBDC in the United States. If CBDCs are not interoperable and universal, financial segmentation could worsen with a very high cost and massive financial instability. However, the resulting crisis could also provoke a reaction of rationality, forcing national authorities to be more cooperative, especially under the threat of global warming, which cannot be resolved without multilateral coordination and an IMS reform.

References

European Central Bank. (2023). *A stocktake on the digital euro: Summary report on the investigation phase and outlook on the next phase.* https://www.ecb.europa.eu/paym/digital_euro/investigation/profuse/shared/files/dedocs/ecb.dedocs231018.en.pdf

Ghymers, C. (2020). *The emerging revolution of digital currencies: A technological opportunity for the International Monetary System* (RTI Paper no. 13). Robert Triffin International & Centro Studi sul Federalismo, Louvain-la-Neuve & Torino.

Ghymers, C. (2021). *The systemic instability of ballooning Global Liquidity as a symptom of the worsening of the Triffin Dilemma* (RTI paper n°15). Robert Triffin International & Centro Studi sul Federalismo, Louvain-la-Neuve & Torino.

Ghymers, C. (2022). *The new form of the Triffin Dilemma and its built-in destabilizer: The process of relative shortage of dollar safe assets* (IRELAC Policy Working Paper 2022/06).

Glowka, M., & Nilsson, T. (2022). Forex settlement risk: An unsettled issue. *BIS Quarterly Review*. https://www.bis.org/publ/qtrpdf/r_qt2212i.htm

Howell, M. (2022). *Interview*. Cross Border Capital.

Kareken, J., & Wallace, N. (1981). On the Indetermination of Equilibrium Exchange Rates. *The Quarterly Journal of Economics, 96*, 207–222.

Mandeng, O. (2020). *Foreign exchange trading with instant settlement in central bank money*. Draft at https://www.economicsadvisory.com/comments/CBDC_and_foreign_exchange.pdf

Powell, J. (2022, June 17). Reuters. Fed's Powell: a U.S. digital dollar could help maintain international primacy | Reuters|Fed's Powell: a U.S. digital dollar could help maintain international primacy | Reuters

Rey, H. (2013). Dilemma not Trilemma: The Global Financial Cycle and Monetary Policy Independence. *Federal Reserve Bank of Kansas City Economic Policy Symposium*
RTI working party on SDR. (2015). Using the Special Drawing Rights as a lever to reform the international monetary system. *International Monetary Issues* n°2. Versant Sud.
World Bank Group. (2023). *Remittance prices worldwide.* http://remittanceprices.worldbank.org

Chapter 14
Bitcoin: Vehicle for Speculation and Fictitious Wealth Generation in the Age of Finance Capital

Stephan Schulmeister

Contents

Introduction

There already exists a huge body of literature on cryptocurrencies, in general, and the bitcoin, in particular, mostly dealing in detail with specific aspects of digital currencies.[1] In contrast to this body of literature, this chapter aims at a systemic analysis of the bitcoin phenomenon, that is, it deals with the origin, development, and price dynamics of the bitcoin in the context of finance capitalism, which has been shaping economic developments for almost half a century. The first part of this chapter recapitulates the history and core properties of bitcoins and most other cryptocurrencies (apart from stablecoins, which maintain a peg to fiat currencies). The

[1] For recent surveys, see Makarov and Schoar (2022), Fang et al. (2022), Aramonteand et al. (2021), and Liu and Tsyvinski (2020).

S. Schulmeister (✉)
University of Vienna, Vienna, Austria
e-mail: stephan.schulmeister@wifo-pens.at

D. Katsikas et al. (eds.), *Finance, Growth and Democracy: Connections and Challenges in Europe and Latin America in the Era of Permacrisis*, United Nations University Series on Regionalism 33, https://doi.org/10.1007/978-3-031-68475-3_14

next part elaborates on the pattern of bitcoin price fluctuations as a result of the interaction between news, technical trading systems ("algorithmic trading"), and optimistic or pessimistic market sentiments. Then it is shown how this phenomenon of "bullishness" or "bearishness"—being particularly pronounced in the bitcoin market—creates and destroys "fictitious" financial wealth and how it impacts the real economy. The final section deals with the growing importance of cryptocurrencies in the context of the currently predominant type of capitalism, for example, "finance capitalism," where striving for profits is focused on changes in the valuation of already existing assets (in contrast to the "real capitalism" of the 1950s and 1960s). Although they are often portrayed as a means to improve the efficiency and inclusiveness of the financial system, cryptocurrencies are in fact a product of the shift to finance capitalism and its destabilizing effects, itself one of the main structural transformations that have given rise to the permacrisis era.

History and Properties of Bitcoins

In October 2008, an anonymous person (or a group of persons) published the concept of a new cryptocurrency, the bitcoin, under the pseudonym Satoshi Nakamoto (Nakamoto, 2008). On January 3, 2009, the first 50 bitcoins were created through the "genesis block." By construction, the total number of bitcoins is limited to 21 million. "Mining" of bitcoins is done through a decentralized process of registering and verifying transactions in the form of data blocks ("blockchain"). The electrical power needed for the computational effort of creating a new block rises with the number of bitcoins already in circulation. Over the first two years of its existence, the price of one bitcoin remained lower than $1 and was rising only slowly over the following years (mining costs were negligible and demand for bitcoins was weak). Only in 2017 did the bitcoin price surpass $1.000 when the first bubble took off (Fig. 14.1): by the end of the year, one bitcoin was worth almost $20.000; afterward the bull market tilted into a bear market and the price of one bitcoin fell to roughly $4.000 by the end of 2018. In October 2020, a new bull market took off, and the price of one bitcoin rose from $10.000 to $63.000 in April 2021, then fell back to $30.000, boomed again and reached its all-time high in November 2021 (roughly $67.000). Over the following 12 months, a marked bear market caused the bitcoin price to fall drastically to roughly $15.000. Since then, it has been rising again in several persistent trends to roughly $70.000 (Fig. 14.1).

The main reason why mining costs rise with the scarcity of bitcoins still to be mined stems from the fact that the network operates without any central authority that would register and document all transactions (*centralized* blockchain technology). Instead, Satoshi Nakamoto wanted to create a payment system that would work without any central data control, motivated by his distrust of state institutions (Nakamoto, 2008). Hence, he had to rely on *decentralized* blockchain technology where the computational effort rises progressively the more bitcoins are already

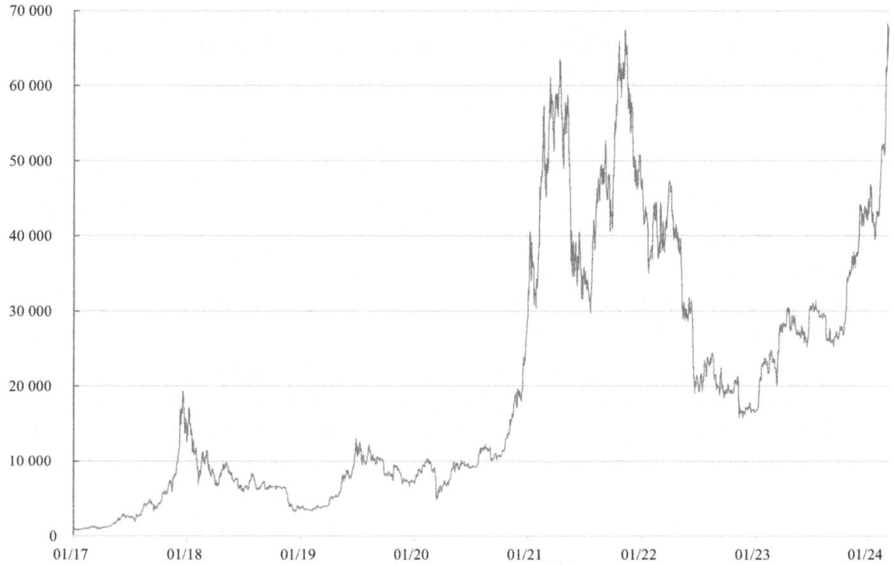

Fig. 14.1 Price of one bitcoin in US dollars. (Source: https://finance.yahho.com)

created (by July 2023, already 19.4 million bitcoins were in circulation, hence, there only remain 1.6 million to be mined). Therefore, a huge and rising amount of electrical energy is needed to generate a new block (as documented by the Cambridge Bitcoin Energy Consumption Index). Depending on the source of power production, the creation process of bitcoins and of cryptocurrencies in general raises carbon emissions significantly (see University of Cambridge—Judge Business School, 2022). In addition, also the electronic waste rises because increasing demands on the processing power of computers force the renewal of hardware 1–2 years after instalment (de Vries & Stoll, 2021). For both reasons, mining and trading bitcoins significantly burden the global environment.

Pattern of Bitcoin Price Dynamics

As with other speculative assets, bull and bear markets result from the interaction between news, technical trading systems ("algorithmic trading") and optimistic or pessimistic market sentiments ("bullishness" or "bearishness"). If new pieces of economic or political information trigger a price run, trend-following algo trading systems produce buy signals (in case of an upward run). The longer a run lasts (usually only some seconds, seldom some minutes), the more it loses momentum. Hence, contrarian models (they speculate on a change in the direction of a run) produce sell signals (at the end of an upward run). Together with negative news they bring about a tilt from an upward into a downward run. When the market is "bullish," upward runs last a little bit longer than counter-movements bringing about a short-term price trend in a stepwise process. Several of these trends accumulate to a bull market, lasting sometimes even several years, as, for example, in stock markets. Bear markets are brought about in an analogous manner when a pessimistic market sentiment prevails.[2] In the case of cryptocurrencies, runs and trends are much steeper so that bull and bear markets last much less and produce much bigger price changes compared to "normal" financial asset markets (Fig. 14.1).

There are two main causes for the exceptional volatility of cryptocurrency prices: the first is economic, the second psychological in nature. First, cryptocurrencies (besides stablecoins) lack any intrinsic or fundamental value that would serve as a "center of gravity" or as "attractor" as is the case of stock markets, foreign exchange markets, or commodities markets. In these cases, market fundamentals restrict the extent of "overshooting" (Schulmeister, this volume). Second, emotional factors like overconfidence, gambling addiction, greed and fear, bandwagon behavior—characteristics of "fast" speculation in general—seem to be particularly pronounced in the case of cryptocurrency trading, bringing about strong but short-lasting bullish or bearish sentiments. The related herding effects are then reinforced through the Internet via social media (Delfabbro et al., 2021). The economic as well as the psychological factors reinforce each other: the higher is the price volatility, the higher are the chances for excessive profits, and the more attractive fast speculation becomes, which then leads to higher volatility.

As in almost all speculative markets, most short-term trading is done in the respective derivatives markets, predominantly using futures contracts. Therefore, one does not need a "bitcoin wallet" but can easily buy or sell bitcoin futures (or options) on a derivatives exchange. In this case, one would also profit from a leverage of 2: at a margin requirement of roughly 50% of contract value (e.g., 1 BTC), one would cash in 20% of the margin payment if the bitcoin price changes by 10% (provided one has bet on the right direction of the price movement).[3]

Creation and Destruction of Fictitious Wealth

What are the effects of cryptocurrency price volatility on the creation and destruction of (fictitious) financial wealth and its distribution? How do these wealth effects impact the real economy, for example, through spending part of the additional wealth on goods and services?

[2] For a more detailed description of the general pattern of asset price dynamics, see Schulmeister, this volume (Chap. 19 of this book).

[3] Margin rates for a bitcoin future used to be lower but have risen due to the extremely high volatility of bitcoin prices. At the Chicago Mercantile Exchange (CME), e.g., margin rates increased from 35% to 50% (in other words, the leverage ratio declined from 2.9 to 2).

The introduction of cryptocurrencies, the growing diffusion of the belief that they constitute both a new, state-free digital money as well as a new form of wealth ("digital gold"), together with the limited amount of mineable tokens (in the case of bitcoins), "created" financial wealth out of nothing, that is, just through higher valuation ("fictitious capital"): in November 2021, the market value of all cryptocurrencies reached $2.830 billion, roughly 90% of the GDP of South America (12 countries). One year later, the market capitalization of cryptocurrencies declined to roughly $830 billion (by roughly 70%). Since then, however, bitcoin has been booming again, particularly since the beginning of 2024 when its price rose from $40.000 to $68.000 in early March (Fig. 14.1). This bull market was triggered by the fact that the US Security and Exchange Commission (SEC) approved Exchange Traded Funds (ETFs) tracking the price of the bitcoin in early January 2024.

During a bitcoin appreciation process, all holders and buyers of bitcoins make a valuation profit, and nobody suffers losses (sellers just do not profit from the appreciation). The opposite is the case when a decline in bitcoin prices depreciates the value of cryptocurrency wealth. Clearly, the same holds true for the revaluation or devaluation of any asset like real estate, stocks, or other kinds of financial assets. However, due to the exceptionally high price volatility of cryptocurrencies, the respective valuation changes are particularly pronounced in this case.

If market capitalization of cryptocurrencies would fall back to their initial value of zero, any net wealth effect would disappear (as in any zero-sum game). However, over the whole cycle of appreciation and depreciation, income would have been redistributed from mostly amateur "investors" to smarter and mostly already wealthy traders. Such an increase in capital income inequality is most probably even more pronounced in the case of trading and holding cryptos compared to other financial assets since the former calls for specific skills and financial means as regards the mining process, trading techniques, as well as keeping a capital buffer to weather sharp price declines.

This presumption gets support from the concentration of both the mining capacity and the ownership of bitcoins. As Makarov and Schoar (2021, p. 23) document, the top 10% of all miners control 90% and just 0.1% of miners control roughly 50% of mining capacity (about 50 miners). The authors also show that bitcoin balances held at intermediaries (i.e., holding bitcoins on behalf of many investors) have been rising steadily. "By the end of 2020 it is equal to 5.5 million bitcoins, roughly one-third of Bitcoin in circulation. In contrast, individual investors collectively control 8.5 million bitcoins by the end of 2020. The individual holdings are still highly concentrated: the top 1000 investors control about 3 million BTC and the top 10,000 investors own around 5 million bitcoins" (Makarov & Schoar, 2021, p. 30). Also, the—almost costless—mining of more than 1 million bitcoins by Satoshi Nakamoto himself after he (or she or they) had invented bitcoins must have contributed to ownership concentration even though the identity of Nakamoto is still unknown (Makarov & Schoar, 2021, p. 29).

Cryptocurrency Wealth and the Real Economy

What is the impact of an appreciation or depreciation of (non-stablecoin) cryptocurrency wealth on the real economy? To the extent that at least some part of the additional (valuation) wealth (in the case of an appreciation) is spent on goods or services, also the real economy profits from the creation of wealth out of nothing. By the same token, devaluations of crypto wealth will dampen the demand for goods and services. However, the—positive as well as negative—wealth effects on the real economy will be smaller in the case of cryptocurrencies compared to "normal" assets like stocks, bonds, or real estate because the valuation changes of cryptos are so much more extreme (Fig. 14.1), and, hence, perceived as less reliable. In other words: a rise (fall) of the market capitalization of, for example, bitcoins will stimulate (dampen) the real economy to a lesser extent than an equivalent change in the value of stocks, bonds, or real estate.

As regards the general relationship between asset inflation/deflation and inflation/deflation of goods and services ("flow inflation/deflation"), one can hypothesize the following: when (potential) investors expect a sustained appreciation of assets of many kinds (i.e., a bullish market environment), they will shift demand from the goods market to the asset market to profit from the expected valuation gain. This behavior will strengthen asset inflation and dampen flow inflation. By contrast, if assets are already highly valued and the goods market (i.e., flow) inflation is expected to rise, asset holders shift their demand from asset markets to goods markets for two reasons. First, they want to avoid losses from asset devaluation due to a decline in nominal asset prices as well as from a decline in real asset prices due to rising (flow) inflation. Second, the expectation of rising goods' prices motivates people to bring forward future consumption into the present.

This (hypothesized) inverse interaction between expected asset inflation and expected flow inflation contributes to a better understanding of inflationary dynamics in past decades, in particular in recent times: when ("normal") flow inflation of goods and services was low, asset prices boomed (as between the early 1990s and 2020/21), when flow inflation accelerated, asset inflation tilted into a deflation (as since 2021). Such an interaction also casts doubt on the promise or belief that bitcoins can serve as a hedge against inflation: when global inflation started to strongly accelerate in fall 2021, the value of bitcoins started to decline even more strongly (Fig. 14.1).

Value and Functions of Bitcoins

In general, one can state that the value of cryptocurrencies consists of the belief that they are valuable. Anchoring such a belief depends on three properties: the ownership of cryptocurrencies is clearly defined, while being secret at the same time, and the maximum number of cryptocurrencies is fixed. By construction, bitcoins do exhibit these properties. When a majority of (potential) bitcoin holders (measured by their "money votes") believe that its value will rise, it will rise and vice versa in the case of pessimistic expectations. Of course, that just a belief directly creates its own "reality" could not take place so easily if bitcoins had an intrinsic value and, hence, a benchmark to judge whether it is over- or undervalued.

As regards the essence of bitcoins (and other similarly constructed cryptocurrencies), one can conclude the following from the above considerations:

- Bitcoins represent a virtual or fictitious financial asset that serves as an optimal instrument for speculation but not for storing wealth. In other words, bitcoins do not constitute "digital gold" because they lack any intrinsic value. Precisely for that reason, bitcoins represent an optimal instrument for—primarily very short-term—speculation.
- Bitcoins are not an appropriate medium of exchange because their price is expressed in terms of the dominant fiat currency, that is, the US dollar, and fluctuates widely due to its function as speculation vehicle. In other words, bitcoins do not constitute "digital money" as any actor is forced to speculate before any payment. If a payer expects the bitcoin to appreciate, he will pay in dollars, at the same time the recipient will want to be paid in bitcoins and vice versa in the case of an expected bitcoin depreciation.

The second property of bitcoins as "non-money" can empirically be demonstrated using the experience of El Salvador with the adoption of bitcoins as legal tender in September 2021 (for a comprehensive documentation, see Alvarez et al., 2022). According to the "Bitcoin law," bitcoins must be accepted as a means of payments for all kinds of transactions in business, finance, and the tax system as second "national" money besides the (US) dollar. To promote the use of bitcoins, the Salvadorean government launched the "Chivo," a digital wallet to digitally trade bitcoins and dollars free of transactions fees. In addition, everybody who downloaded the Chivo app received a $30 bonus. Also, the COVID-19 pandemic should have incentivized the use of bitcoins as a means of payments.

In practice, however, this expectation did not materialize. Even though 68% knew about the existence of the Chivo Wallet, only half of the adult population downloaded the app, mostly in September 2021 and the subsequent months (virtually no downloads took place in 2022). The predominant motivation was the $30 bonus: after receiving and spending it, only 20% continued to use Chivo at least sporadically. Therefore, Alvarez et al. (2022) summarize their study on the bitcoin experiment in El Salvador as follows: "Our results show that, despite all incentives and the enhanced attractiveness of contactless payments in the midst of the pandemic, bitcoin is not widely used as a medium of exchange and usage of Chivo is low" (Alvarez et al., 2022, p. 19).

Bitcoins serve as a medium of exchange, that is, as "money substitute," only in two cases. In the first case, bitcoins are used to pay for illegal activities of all kinds, from trading drugs or illegal pornography to money laundering. In the second case, bitcoins serve as a means of money transfers in less developed countries where a (functioning) payment system does not exist or in countries where transfers should be hidden from (authoritarian) regimes (e.g., in Russia or China).

As regards the first case, a study by Foley et al. (2019) concludes: "… approximately one-quarter of all users and close to one-half of transactions are associated with illegal activity……Illegal users of bitcoins tend to transact more, in smaller sized transactions, often repeatedly transacting with a given counterparty…… These features are consistent with their use of bitcoin as a payment system rather than for investment or speculation. (Foley et al., 2019, p. 1847). However, this study excluded transactions on bitcoin exchanges (predominantly done for speculative purposes) as they wanted to focus on payments transactions. As Makarov and Schoar (2021) show, 90% of all bitcoin transactions are "spurious," that is, caused by strategies designed to impede the tracing of bitcoin flows. Out of the remaining "real bitcoin volume," 75% of transactions are carried out on bitcoin exchanges for trading and speculation purposes. In addition, Foley et al. (2019) overstated the role of bitcoin transactions for illegal activities (according to Makarov & Schoar, 2021) because their methodology could not discriminate sufficiently between "spurious" and "real" transactions. Therefore, Makarov and Schoar (2021) conclude that transactions not carried out on exchanges "such as illegal transactions or mining rewards, explain only a minor part of total volume" (Makarov & Schoar, 2021, p. 29).

Despite these—partly methodological—differences, both (and most other empirical bitcoin) studies agree on three facts: first, most bitcoin transactions are related to trading and speculation. Second, transactions for illegal purposes do constitute a serious problem. Third, bitcoins do not play any significant role in everyday transactions in the real economy.

Besides normal speculation, an additional opportunity to make (huge) profits stems from the fact that herding behavior rises with greed, gear, and the belief in fast profits, all of which is particularly pronounced in the case of bitcoin speculation: Internet "influencers" can trigger speculations of "bandwagonists" and exploit them by anticipation. For example, in February 2021, bitcoin prices jumped after Elon Musk had announced that Tesla would accept bitcoins as payments. By contrast, when he later in May announced the opposite because of the high-power consumption of bitcoin mining, bitcoin prices fell. It was or would have been easy for Elon Musk to buy or sell bitcoins (futures) in advance of these statements. An even more extreme case is that of the Dogecoin. This cryptocurrency was created by an IBM programmer (Billy Markus) and an Adobe programmer (Jackson Palmer) as a parody of bitcoins in December 2013. It was intended to be worthless. However, when Elon Musk made some enthusiastic comments about the Dogecoin in December 2020 and January 2021, its price rose by a factor of 15 within 6 weeks, and in April 2021 again by a factor of 10 (in total by a factor of roughly 150 within few months!).

The Bitcoin as an Incarnation of Finance Capitalism

The creation of cryptocurrencies, in general, and of bitcoins, in particular, fits perfectly into the main ideological, economic, and technological developments of past decades, that is, neoliberalism, finance capitalism, and digitalization. Already since the 1970s, these developments have gradually led to a transformation of the international financial system that has contributed to the comprehensive systemic crisis, which is referred to in this volume as Permacrisis.

Even though there exist different neoliberal "schools" like the Austrian School (Hayek and Co.), the Chicago School (Friedman and Co.), or the (specifically) German "Ordoliberals," they all have in common the preference for market solutions compared to policy interventions, irrespective of whether it concerns business cycle policy, the welfare state, (financial) market regulations, or monetary policy. As regards the latter, Hayek formulated in 1976 the most radical proposal that can also be interpreted as the theoretical foundation of cryptocurrencies: money should be privatized so that the governments would be deprived of their monopoly to create "fiat money" (i.e., not backed by some scarce and valuable commodity like gold). In such a way, the governments would no longer be able to enforce citizens to use this national money as legal tender (Hayek, 1976).

Under the growing influence of neoliberal theories, specifically of Chicago-type monetarism, the economic system was transformed from real capitalism as in the 1950s and 1960s to finance capitalism (Schulmeister, 2021). In the former, the framework conditions like a strict regulation of financial markets, building up the welfare state or full employment policy, directed striving for profit to activities in the real economy, to investment, production, and trade, and, hence, to the creation of real assets. In finance capitalism, by contrast, striving for profits focuses on financial, commodity, and real estate speculation, that is, on exploiting differences in the valuation of already existing financial and real assets (securities, derivatives, commodities, real estate, etc.).

The different intentions of investments in stocks and in real estate, respectively, illustrate the differences between the two types of capitalism: in real capitalism, one buys shares to participate in a company and to (co-)finance its real investments; in finance capitalism, one buys shares to profit from expected price increases. The profit from real estate investments in real capitalism comes from the creation of buildings, in finance capitalism increasingly from buying existing buildings expecting their revaluation.

The transition from real to finance capitalism took place between the early 1970s (transition from stable to unstable exchange rates and the related first oil price shock) and the early 1980s (high interest rate policy, dollar appreciation, Latin America debt crisis 1982). Over the four subsequent decades, the process of "financialization" has intensified more and more, driven by factors that have contributed also to the genesis of what is conceived as Permacrisis in this volume. First, the rising influence of the "free-market-paradigm" fostered a deepening of financial market liberalization together with an ever-rising variety of financial innovations (primarily derivatives of all kinds). Second, these developments facilitated financial speculation, at the same time, the slogan "Let your money work" became more and more widespread, spilling over from traditional financial institutions to shadow banks like hedge funds and amateur traders. Third, the process of digitalization in all its manifestations (hardware, software, the Internet) provided the basis for electronic trading platforms and for the global availability of price data at ever higher frequencies (up to microseconds), which in turn raised the speed of trading, in most cases automatically executed by algorithms. Fourth, because of these developments, financial instability has been growing over the short as well as over the long run.

The creation and diffusion of cryptocurrencies have taken the process of financialization to the extreme and can therefore be conceived as a final stage in the development of finance capitalism, its logic of profit-making has reached its (provisional) completion: virtual assets lacking any intrinsic ("fundamental") value enable profits that come exclusively from changes in the beliefs of their values.

Summary and Conclusions

This chapter showed that bitcoins and cryptocurrencies in general can be understood as the incarnation of finance capitalism, legitimized by neoliberal theories, and enhanced by digitalization. It advances six conclusions as preliminary answers to the questions raised in the introduction to this essay. First, the value of bitcoins (and of most other non-stablecoin cryptocurrencies) consists exclusively of the belief that they are valuable—in contrast to "normal" assets like stocks, real estate, commodities, or works of art that do have an intrinsic value. Second, bitcoin prices fluctuate much more than "normal" asset prices, in part because they lack any intrinsic value serving as some "center of gravity." Third, like other asset prices cryptocurrency prices move in a sequence of bull markets and bear markets, however, in a particularly pronounced extent. Fourth, bull markets create fictitious wealth, bear markets destroy it. Fifth, the effect of these valuation fluctuations on demand for goods and services is smaller than in the case of "normal" assets. Sixth, bitcoins and other cryptocurrencies neither serve as a medium of exchange ("digital money") nor as a store of wealth ("digital gold") but as an efficient vehicle for—predominantly short-term—speculation. In sum, cryptocurrencies add another element to the conditions of increased uncertainty and volatility, which are constitutive features of the permacrisis environment discussed in this volume.

References

Alvarez, F. E., Argente, D., & Van Patten, D. (2022, April). *Are cryptocurrencies currencies? Bitcoin as Legal Tender in El Salvador* (NBER Working Paper 29968). https://www.nber.org/papers/w29968

Aramonteand, S., Huang, W., & Schrimpf, A. (2021). DeFi risks and the decentralisation illusion. *BIS Quarterly Review.*

De Vries, A., & Stoll, C. (2021). Bitcoins growing e-waste problem. *Resources, Conservation & Recycling, 175*, 8–11.

Delfabbro, P., King, D. L., & Williams, J. (2021). The psychology of cryptocurrency trading: Risk and protective factor. *Journal of Behavioral Addictions, 36*(5), 686–697. https://doi.org/10.1556/2006.2021.00037

Fang, F., Ventre, C., Basios, M., Kanthan, L., Martinez-Rego, D., & Li, L. (2022). Cryptocurrency trading: A comprehensive survey. *Financial Innovation, 8*(13). https://doi.org/10.1186/s40854-021-00321-6

Foley, S., Karlsen, J. R., & Putnins, T. J. (2019). Sex, drugs, and bitcoin: How much illegal activity is financed through cryptocurrencies? *The Review of Financial Studies*, 1798–1853.

Hayek, F. A. (1976). *Denationalisation of Money*. Institute of Economic Affairs.

Liu, Y., & Tsyvinski, A. (2020). Risks and returns of cryptocurrency. *The Review of Financial Studies, 34*(2000), 2689–2727.

Makarov, I., & Schoar, A. (2021). *Blockchain analysis of the bitcoin market* (Working Paper 29396). National Bureau of Economic Research.

Makarov, I., Schoar, A. (2022, March 24–25). *Cryptocurrencies and decentralized finance* (Brookings Papers on Economic Activity, BPEA Conference Drafts).

Nakamoto, S. (2008). *Bitcoin: A peer-to-peer electronic cash system*. https://bitcoin.org/bitcoin.pdf

Schulmeister, S. (2021). Chapter 2: The road from prosperity into the crisis: The long cycle of post-war economic, social and political development. In B. De Souza Guilherme, C. Ghymers, S. Griffith-Jones, & H. A. Ribeiro (Eds.), *Financial crisis management and democracy*. Springer. https://doi.org/10.1007/978-3-030-54895-7

Schulmeister, S. (this volume). Chapter 19: Stabilizing asset prices through transition from continuous trading to electronic auctions. In D. Katsikas, M. A. Del Tedesco Lins, & A. Ribeiro Hoffmann (Eds.), *Finance, growth and democracy: Connections and challenges in Europe and Latin America in the era of permacrisis*. Springer.

University of Cambridge, Judge Business School. (2022). *A deep dive into Bitcoin's environmental impact*. https://www.jbs.cam.ac.uk/insight/2022/a-deep-dive-into-bitcoins-environmental-impact/

[illegible]

[illegible]

[illegible]

[illegible]

[illegible]

[illegible]

[illegible]

[illegible]

[illegible]

[illegible]

[illegible]

[illegible]

Chapter 15
Digital Currencies, Monetary Power, and Inequalities: Discussing the Potential Impacts of the Brazilian Central Bank Digital Currency (CBDC)

Maria Antonieta Del Tedesco Lins and Andrea Ribeiro Hoffmann

Contents

Introduction

In the different forms they can take, private or issued by central banks, digital currencies are becoming a reality around the world. In addition to the alleged advantages in terms of transaction cost reduction and agility gains, the creation of digital currencies can alter the distribution of monetary power among countries, and among the public and private sector, that is, states and markets, to paraphrase the title of Susan Strange's pioneering book in the discipline of international political economy (Strange, 2015). Both dynamics are relevant in the current global context marked by instability and crisis, referred to in this volume as Permacrisis.

M. A. Del Tedesco Lins (✉)
Institute of International Relations, Universidade de São Paulo, São Paulo, SP, Brazil
e-mail: madtlins@usp.br

A. Ribeiro Hoffmann
Institute of International Relations, Pontifical Catholic University of Rio de Janeiro, Rio de Janeiro, RJ, Brazil
e-mail: a_ribeiro_hoffmann@puc-rio.br

D. Katsikas et al. (eds.), *Finance, Growth and Democracy: Connections and Challenges in Europe and Latin America in the Era of Permacrisis*, United Nations University Series on Regionalism 33, https://doi.org/10.1007/978-3-031-68475-3_15

This chapter focuses on the creation of digital currencies by central banks; a recent report by the International Monetary Fund (IMF) states that the level of global interest in Central Bank Digital Currencies (CBDCs) is unprecedented and that "more than two-thirds of central banks are likely to issue a retail CBDC in the short or medium term (within the next six years)" (IMF, 2023, p. 6). As Ghymers (this volume) discusses, CBDCs are to a large extent responses by governments to threats of monetary sovereignty posed by crypto assets and monopolistic private firms. Another report from the IMF, produced to support central banks in this endeavor, states that "CBDC should therefore be approached with caution, and central banks should carefully assess whether and how it should be implemented. But the same uncertainty also calls for exploring CBDC proactively—there is a risk that central banks will find themselves unprepared in the future and increasingly unable to carry out their basic functions without CBDC. Central banks therefore also need to consider risks arising from not exploring CBDC" (Soderberg et al., 2003, p. 3).

The intensification of international financial flows and deregulation has precipitated numerous financial crises in the past, such as in Asia and Latin America, as well as the global financial crisis and the Euro debt crisis that followed. Moreover, as Bilotta (2024) argues in this volume, competition between the United States and China in the area of digital currencies may be already taking place; therefore, it is important to understand in more depth the potential economic, social, and political impacts of the creation of digital currencies at the domestic and international levels.

The huge success of the instant payment system set up by the Brazilian central bank in 2020 (Pix) and the launching of the Brazilian central bank digital currency (Drex) foreseen to take place in 2024 make Brazil an interesting case. Brazil's long and chronic inflationary history left the national currency with a legacy of low attractiveness and credibility for decades. Inflation was controlled in the mid-1990s, with a monetary reform that created a new currency, the Real, but despite more than 30 years of relative stability and the consolidation of Brazil as a large emerging economy, the Real is not a relevant currency in global exchange markets. The same inflationary past was, however, also responsible for financial innovations to protect the income of businesses, households, and the public sector. Such innovations included indexation, that is, the automatic overnight remuneration on deposits, that was adopted and quickly spread to contracts and payments. Innovations also allowed financial institutions to make immense profits, at the cost of the "bankless" population as discussed below. Brazil is also referred to as an "emerging market," and historically very active at the multilateral level, with a reformist agenda at the Bretton Woods institutions, including at the level of cooperation with the BRICS and the G20. Brazil has, however, not cooperated much at the regional level, that is, in Latin America, or with the European Union, the two regions addressed in this volume.

This chapter analyzes, therefore, the creation of a digital currency by the Brazilian central bank and discusses potential economic, social, and political effects at the domestic, regional, and global levels, with a focus on the cooperation in Latin America and with the European Union. The first section analyzes the historical process of digitalization in the Brazilian financial system and, therefore, the domestic conditions under which the project of a Central Bank Digital Currency was launched. The second section analyzes the project itself, its design, and implementation. The last section discusses the possible effects of the Brazilian CBDC.

The Path to Digitalization in the Brazilian Financial System

Since the establishment of the first banking institution to operate in the country, the Banco do Brasil, in 1808,[1] Brazil's economic history has been shaped by the presence and considerable influence of banking institutions as major players. One of the primary challenges of the Brazilian financial system, if not the foremost, has been the strong concentration in the banking sector that evolved over the years and still exists. The dominance of major banks in the Brazilian economy has long characterized the sector's landscape (Maia, 1999; Chang et al., 2008; Hordones & Sanvicente, 2021). The high and persistent inflation experienced in Brazil during the latter half of the twentieth century[2] reinforced this pattern of concentration, but, on the other hand, led to technological modernization so that banks could manage their operations effectively and safeguard deposits against inflation, such as the above-mentioned indexation, and the deployment of automated teller machines (ATMs). These investments in technology were implemented by contracting external firms or establishing subsidiary companies.[3]

After the 1994 monetary reform, known as the Real Plan, the gradual decline in inflation rates prompted banks to reassess their market strategies due to reduced revenue from inflation made with indexation. Throughout the 1990s, numerous financial institutions in Brazil encountered crises, prompting the government to implement extensive rescue measures spanning both private and public banks (Maia, 1999; Wise & Lins, 2015). This process spurred significant restructuring within the banking system, resulting in even higher concentration through a series of mergers and acquisitions. Graph 15.1 shows two decades of Brazilian bank concentration levels. In addition to highlighting the elevated concentration, the data reveals that periods of economic crises such as the global financial crisis (2008–2009) and the Brazilian recession (2013–2016) contributed to increased bank concentration, further consolidating power among the largest institutions.

[1] The bank was created at the request of then Prince Regent of the Portuguese Empire D. João, who arrived in Brazil that year fleeing from the Napoleonic wars. This first bank was liquidated but the name was used in the following banks, private and then public, and from 1905 it was the government's main instrument for monetary policies until the central bank, the current monetary authority, was created in 1964 (Westin, 2023).

[2] In 1990, the Brazilian monthly inflation rates for January, February, and March were 71.9%, 71.7%, and 81.3%, respectively, configuring a situation of hyperinflation.

[3] For example, one of the largest bank conglomerates, Itaú Bank, created in 1979 Itautec S.A., a Brazilian company that manufactured IT equipment, commercial automation, and banking automation. The company remained under the control of the conglomerate until 2013.

Graph 15.1 Bank concentration in Brazil, percent of total assets. (Note: (**a**) (blue line) Assets of the five largest banks as a share of total commercial banking assets. (**b**) (orange line) Assets of the three largest commercial banks as a share of total commercial banking assets. Total assets include total earning assets, cash and due from banks, foreclosed real estate, fixed assets, goodwill, other intangibles, current tax assets, deferred tax, discontinued operations, and other assets. Source: World Bank Global Financial Development Database. Available at: https://databank.worldbank.org/source/global-financial-development#)

The historical path of concentration, engagement of technological modernization and profitability, and therefore, power in the Brazilian economy and political system, has contributed to the active participation of the banking sector in the process of digitalization of finance alongside the Central Bank. Despite the Brazilian economy growth at an average rate of 0.53% between 2013 and 2022, the banking sector's profitability remained notably high, as shown in Graph 15.2.

Feld et al. (2021: 2.1) argue that the survival of banks is linked to the way they address the new opportunities derived from technological advancements and that they must rethink their strategies and adapt their ways of providing services. Still, according to them, the Brazilian central bank has been playing a tremendously important role in driving these changes forward in coordination with private financial institutions and in anticipation of market dynamics. These transformations can be seen in the advent of new banking transaction channels, which have swiftly changed the way customers engage with banking services. Graph 15.3 shows a significant shift in transactions over an 8-year period: digital banking accounted for a substantial portion in 2018, with mobile and Internet banking comprising 63%. By 2022, this figure surged to 77% of transactions for major banks, with mobile banking increasing from 41% to 66%.

To sum up, the Brazilian central bank and the public and private banking sectors have engaged intensively in the landscape of technological innovation spreading

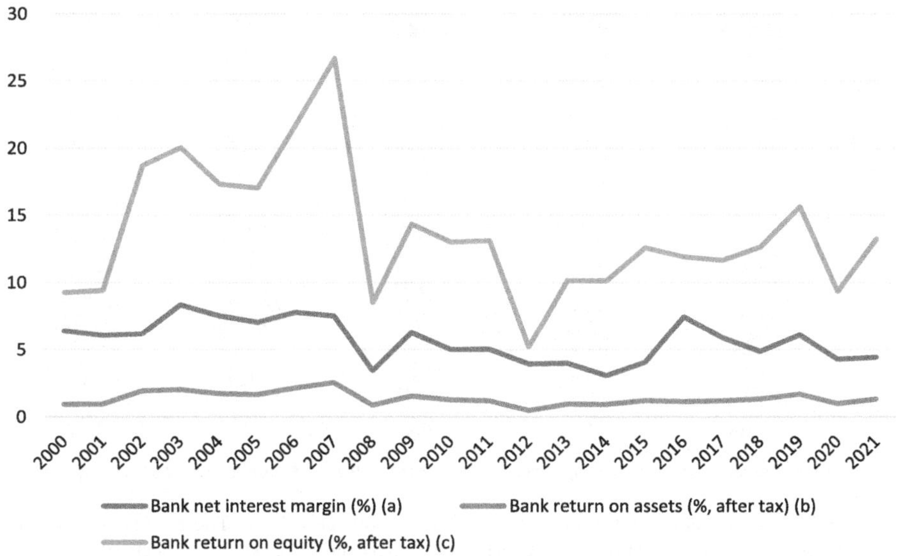

Graph 15.2 Bank profitability in the Brazilian banking system. (Note: (**a**) Accounting value of banks' net interest revenue as a share of their average interest-bearing (total earning) assets. (**b**) Commercial banks' after-tax net income to yearly averaged total assets. (**c**) Commercial banks' (totality) after-tax net income to yearly averaged equity. Source: World Bank Global Financial Development Database. Available at: https://databank.worldbank.org/source/global-financial-development#)

worldwide, favored by domestic characteristics that evolved historically. They have established strategies for reshaping domestic financial systems and facilitating cross-border transactions. The emerging dynamics between financial institutions and central banks encompass various dimensions, including regulation, technological infrastructure, market competition, and potential alliances or cooperation agreements with foreign and global agents.

Pix and Drex: What Has Been Done So Far in Brazilian Digital Banking?

A direct precursor of the Brazilian CBDC is the so-called Pix. Pix is the instant payment ecosystem that can be seen as a stage in the process of digitalization of finances and digital economy, but it is not a digital currency, it is only a modality of transfer with the defining characteristic of being instantaneous, and available anytime. Pix started to be developed officially in 2018 and was implemented in November 2020,

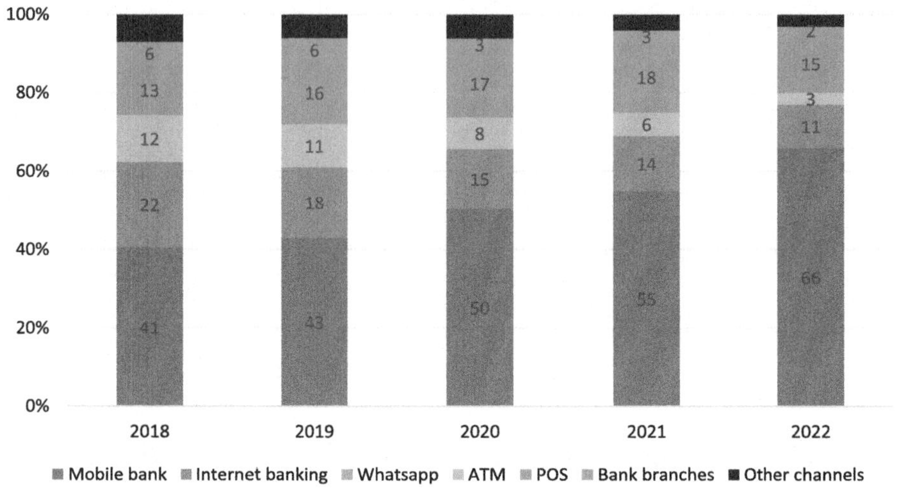

Graph 15.3 Distribution of transactions by channels, percent. (Note: The figures stem from a survey conducted between April and May 2023, encompassing 18 banks that collectively represent 86% of bank assets in Brazil. Source: FEBRABAN & Deloitte (2023), p. 7)

but the project started at the central bank as early as 2016.[4] The central bank defines Pix's rules and manages the operational platforms, providing the technological infrastructure, that is not based on blockchain, rather, a centralized digital platform among the Brazilian central bank, financial and payment institutions. Pix has been a success among the population; more than 158 million Brazilians use it, out of a population of ca. 200 million, and, from November 2020 to October 2023, ca. 66 billion transactions were concluded, with a value of almost 30 trillion BRL (ca. 6 trillion USD). In the first semester of 2023, Pix represented more than 90% of all banking transactions including transactions with debit and credit cards, other modalities of transfer (TED, DOC, TEC), and bills and checks (Sutto, 2023; Fluid, 2024). Despite this success in terms of the increase in the number of users and their apparent support of Pix, the inclusion of the population in the financial system combined with existing social and economic inequalities must be critically assessed as this could lead to vicious circles of indebtedness, depending on the regulatory framework (Lavinas, 2017).

In parallel to innovations in transfers, the Brazilian central bank is also working on the creation of a digital currency, the Digital Brazilian Real (Drex), to be launched in 2024. CBDCs are national currencies in digital format, issued on digital platforms operated by the central bank of the country. Traditional national currencies are the banknotes and coins issued by central bank, which are in circulation in the economy and can be deposited in banks, cooperatives, payment institutions, and

[4] The concept of establishing an instant payments system was initially introduced by the central bank in 2016 and during Ilan Goldfajn's tenure as the central bank governor, in 2018, the system started to be actively deployed and implemented.

other institutions authorized by the central bank. Digital currencies are issued by the central bank for wholesale transactions (settlement of transactions between authorized institutions) or institutions authorized by the central bank for retail transactions with their clients (BCB site). According to a report published by the Bank of International Settlements (BIS, 2021: 4), "if the CBDC is intended to be a digital equivalent of cash for use by end users (households and businesses), it is referred to as a 'general purpose' or 'retail' CBDC. In contrast to retail CBDC, 'wholesale' CBDC targets a different group of eligible users. It is designed for restricted access by financial institutions and is similar to today's central bank reserve and settlement accounts." CBDCs can also be classified according to whether they are based in accounts or values, if their validation and registration is direct (single-tier retail) or indirect (two-tier retail),[5] if they are centralized or decentralized, costly or not; the latter being a particular controversial point given that currency is not supposed to yield interest (Afonso et al., 2022: 461). Other relevant technical aspects are the technological options, that is, blockchain, the legal framework, including the question of privacy. The Brazilian central bank is following this topic for some years, and in August 2020 it established a Working Group to study the issuing of the Brazilian digital currency. The Working Group led to the creation of the "Guidelines of the Digital Real" in 2021, which was updated in 2023 (BCB, 2023a). A research laboratory in virtual collaborative space to assess the potential uses of the digital currency and its technological viability, called "LIFT Challenge Real Digital," was also established (BCB Site).

Regarding the legal framework, the central bank consistently fortified its role throughout each stage of the process. In 2022, Law No 14.478 was enacted (República Federativa do Brasil, 2022) establishing guidelines for the provision of virtual asset services and regulating virtual asset service providers. It also amended previous regulations pertaining to fraud involving virtual assets, securities, or financial assets, and expanded the scope of norms addressing crimes against the national financial system and money laundering to encompass virtual asset service providers within its provisions. In June 2023, the decree No. 11563 regulated Law No. 14.478 to bestow the central bank of Brazil with powers and competence to regulate and supervise all operations with virtual assets.

The key characteristics of the Drex were established by the 2023 guidelines as follows:

1. Emphasis on the development of innovative models with the incorporation of technologies such as smart contracts and programmable money,[6] compatible with the settlement of transactions through the "Internet of Things" (IoT).

---

[5] According to Sampaio and Centeno (2022, p. 13): "In the direct mechanism, the operationalization of the payment system (processing and recording) of all transactions with CBDC would be the responsibility of the central bank. In the case of indirect transactions, the intermediary may be a commercial bank or other financial institution."

[6] According to Lee (2021, not numbered): "Two natural components of the definition are a digital form of money and a mechanism for specifying the automated behavior of that money through a computer program" (this mechanism is termed "programmability" in this note). However, it is not

2. Focus on developing online applications, keeping in mind the possibility of offline payments.
3. Issuance of wholesale Drex by the central bank as a means of payment to enable the offer of retail financial services settled through retail Drex issued by participants in the National Financial System (SFN) and the Brazilian Payment System (SPB).
4. Application of current standards and rules for operations carried out on the Drex platform.
5. Ensuring legal certainty in operations carried out on the Drex platform.
6. Guarantee of the principles and rules of privacy and security laid down in Brazilian law, in particular the Banking Secrecy Act and the LGPD.
7. Technological design that enables full compliance with international recommendations and legal standards on the prevention of money laundering, terrorist financing, and the financing of the proliferation of weapons of mass destruction, including in fulfillment of court orders to trace illicit operations.
8. Adoption of a DLT[7]-based technological solution that enables registration of assets of different kinds, decentralization in the provision of products and services, interoperability with legacy domestic systems and with other systems for registering and transferring information and trading regulated digital assets, and integration with systems in other jurisdictions, with a view to making cross-border payments.
9. Adoption of resilience and cybersecurity standards equivalent to those applicable to critical financial market infrastructures (BCB, 2023a).

The legal structure for Drex will take into account the pilot phase conducted by the central bank since July 2023. Initially, participants from the financial sector were selected to test privacy and programmability features in certain types of transactions between institutions, followed by subsequent tests involving the general population (BCB, 2023b)

Positive elements of CBDCs highlighted in the literature are the potential for financial inclusion, reduction of costs of emission and maintenance, safety, and transparency. Fabio Araújo, then project leader of the Digital Brazilian Real Initiative at the central bank of Brazil, states that the main objective of the Brazilian CBDC is "to provide entrepreneurs with a safe and reliable environment to innovate through the use of programmability technologies, such as programable money and smart contracts," and that the potential inclusion of the population in terms of their access to the products is high (Araújo, 2022: 32). In a publication by the LIFT laboratory, Orestes and Townsend (2023: 4) state that the main goal of Drex is "to create a reliable and secure infrastructure for innovations that include but go beyond programmable money and enable smart contract technology, not just for payments but also for improved wholesale and retail financial infrastructure," but highlight that

clear whether these components alone are sufficient for a definition, given that various combinations of similar technology for payments automation have existed for decades. It was only after the advent of public blockchain cryptocurrencies that the term "programmable money" became common parlance.

[7] DLT is the acronym for Distributed Ledger Technology, a type of registration of information that is decentralized and distributed in a network, allowing for greater transparency. Blockchains are DLTs, but not all DLTs are blockchains as the latter are public and open source, having been developed in 2008 by Satoshi Nakamoto for the cryptocurrency bitcoin. DLTs are very similar to blockchains but they require permissions to be accessed and are developed to attend the necessities of specific groups (Exame, 2020).

while advanced economies often focus on improving the safety and efficiency, for emerging market economies financial inclusion is usually a priority too.

Despite the positive expectations advanced by the Brazilian central bank about the Drex, looking from a broader perspective, the digitalization of finances and the creation of CBDCs have significative distributive effects and geopolitical implications, which are extremely important, given the historical disputes surrounding claims for reform of the international monetary system, topics that are discussed below.

Discussing the Potential Effects of the Brazilian CBDC

The process of digitalization of monetary and financial transactions, in general, and the creation of a central bank digital currency in Brazil, in particular, is most likely to have a considerable impact both domestically and across borders, and gives rise to a multitude of economic, social, and foreign relations considerations. Orestes and Townsend (2023) extensively explore the potential impacts of monetary digitalization on consumers, small- and medium-sized enterprises, domestic asset transfers, and Brazil's cross-border operations. Profound changes are expected in the operational paradigms of financial institutions within national boundaries, redefining the landscape of competition and profitability for banks and other intermediaries. The impact is expected to be even more transformative on the international level as direct exchanges between countries might surge and bypass the need for intermediary currencies from third-party nations and diminish the dependence on the US dollar (Prasad, 2022; Kuehnlenz et al., 2023). This section explores, firstly, expected changes at the domestic level and then delves into considerations pertaining to international relations.

One of the economic consequences of the digitalization of transactions involves the restructuring of the functions and operations of financial institutions. In a hypothetical scenario where each citizen possesses an account with the central bank and transactions can occur directly between individuals and businesses digitally, banking disintermediation could be a potential outcome. Despite the widespread interest, there are concerns that a CBDC could potentially displace a significant portion of bank deposits. The question then arises as to what extent would a central bank digital currency compete with traditional banks. In Brazil, the ongoing initiatives by major financial institutions and the intense exchange that unfolds between them and the central bank suggest an impending adaptation process between banks and the monetary authority, which holds jurisdiction over standards and regulations. Araujo (2022) discusses the potential impacts of currency digitalization in Brazil and calls attention to the significance of the cooperation between private institutions and the central bank in the development of a regulated liability network to prevent financial disintermediation, which stands, in his view, as a fundamental pillar for the initiative's success. In his words: "In the case of Brazil, where the CBDC held by the general public will not bear interest, if risk perception is limited, the preference for a CBDC can be offset by rewards offered by banks or PSPs in order to generate demand for their tokens. Such rewards could, for instance, be a small yield on those holdings" (Araujo, 2022, p. 36).

Within the social realm, a central concern emerges around citizens' access to the totality of the digital financial infrastructure. On one hand, the experience with Pix has demonstrated a significant capacity for financial inclusion. Alongside the rapid growth of fintechs over the past decade (WEF, 2024), the expansion of digital banking and the capability to conduct transactions from checking and savings accounts, regardless of balance, have facilitated financial inclusion for lower-income segments of society. The possession of a mobile phone serves as the sole entry requirement for the Pix payment system. On the other hand, the rapid pace of technological advancement may leave less privileged groups lagging in accessing new opportunities.

Considering the societal impacts of making digital assets available to the population, regardless of its social and economic composition, a critical question is the privacy concerning citizens' financial affairs and spending habits. In a scenario where approximately two-thirds or more of the population conduct all their financial transactions through digital currencies, whether via individual accounts with the central bank or intermediated by private banking entities, transaction mediators would promptly possess comprehensive records of citizens' economic activities. While technology may enable some degree of anonymity and privacy in payment systems, it is foreseeable that individuals may face constraints in controlling financial institutions' access to their data.

From a political economy and geopolitical perspective, the digital revolution in general, and the innovations in the global monetary system will have effects in the distribution of power and therefore the global order (Prasad, 2022). Given the current context of Permacrisis, hegemonic disputes, and the leading role of China in the CBDCs, it is key to deepen the understanding of the implications of these changes for Brazil at the regional and global levels.

Cross-border payments through CBDCs need the interoperability between different systems to allow gains of speed and efficiency to transactions. There exist alternatives to creating technical and legal frameworks to facilitate exchanges between CBDCs. One option is to consider them as traditional currencies, recognized within their issuing nations and accepted for transactions with foreign countries. This approach would lead to minimal disruption to the existing system and would not depend on cooperation between central banks. Yet another possibility entails central banks collaborating to establish settlement arrangements and enabling agents to maintain diverse portfolios of CBDCs. Further levels of cooperation could lead to the development of multiple CBDC structures, empowering agents to manage distinct wallets (Kuehnlenz et al., 2023). Since in this volume we are particularly interested in the regional level and relations among the EU and LAC countries, this section will focus on the possible effects of the Brazilian CBCD to Mercosur and to interregional relations with the EU, that is, EU–Mercosur and EU–CELAC relations. Given their relevance to Brazilian positions, we also briefly discuss the initiatives under the BRICS.

As Sampaio and Centeno (2022: 18) note: "An interesting aspect about CBDC is that CBs are not working individually. There are currently seven cross-border CBDC projects. This cooperation is mainly related to the possible implications that CBDCs may have on international flows. The pioneer was the Multiple CBDC (m-CBDC) Bridge, a project with the central banks of China, the United Arab Emirates, Hong Kong, and Thailand in partnership with the BIS Innovation Hub15. The objective is to enable an international payments system that would work at any day and time and would use wholesale CBDC. With similar motivations, there are the Dunbar projects (Australia, Singapore, Malaysia, and South Africa); Helvetia (Switzerland and BIS), Jasper (Canada, UK, and Singapore); Aber (Saudi Arabia and the United Arab Emirates); Jura (France, Switzerland and BIS) and Onyx (France and Singapore)."

So far there are, therefore, no cooperation arrangements among central banks within LAC countries or promoted by LAC regional organizations. In a context of increasing competition between China and the United States, it would be in their interest to establish strategies, but the region is divided in terms of their interests, given that some countries have fully dollarized their economies, namely, Ecuador, El Salvador, Panama, Belize, Bermuda, in addition to the Free-Associated State of Puerto Rico, which is a US unincorporated territory. Cooperation in macroeconomic policy and finance has been hardly addressed in regional initiatives of cooperation (Lins & Ribeiro Hoffmann, 2021). Mercosur aimed to be a common market, including the free circulation of capital, and projects for a common currency were discussed, but this is the area that advanced the least over its 30 years of existence (Ribeiro Hoffmann, 2020). The proposals advanced by recently elected President Javier Milei in Argentina to adopt the US dollar would make this possibility even more remote, despite generalized skepticism about this proposal given the conditions of the economy.

LAC countries have also not engaged much with the EU; therefore, this could be an avenue for collaboration to strengthen the EU–CELAC bi-regional partnership, as also discussed by Billotta (2024) in this volume. One mechanism could be the incorporation of experts' dialogues at the EU–CELAC level, and, in the case of Brazil, a renewal of sectorial dialogues in the EU–Brazil Partnership. Despite the problems to Mercosur caused by the bilateral partnership, this could be important geopolitically, given the participation of Brazil in the BRICS and the enlargement of the BRICS to Egypt, Ethiopia, Iran, Saudi Arabia, and the United Arab Emirates. The latter is already collaborating with China in the Multiple CBDC Bridge, while Russia is also a leading country in digital currencies.

Final Reflections

The first section of this chapter argued that Brazil has a history of finance innovation due to its past economic instabilities and the characteristics of the domestic system such as high levels of concentration and profitability that made it possible for the banking sector to invest in technology. The second section showed how, in the context of the current worldwide process of acceleration of digitalization of finance, Brazil has created an instantaneous system for transfers, the Pix, in 2020, which is a major success with the population, and is expected to implement a central bank digital currency, the Drex, in 2024. The third section discussed possible economic, social, and (geo)political effects of these processes at the domestic and international levels in order to contribute to the incipient literature and debates with the public at large about these processes.

We argued that the effects at the domestic level include, firstly, the potential displacement of bank deposits, especially in light of the overall acceptance of the Pix by the population. Financial inclusion might increase as well, but in the absence of a robust regulatory framework and protection of clients, the gap with less privileged groups might increase in light of past experiences in the country, and the level of inequalities, that increased since the COVID-19 pandemic. More transparency and information as well as a proper regulatory framework are key, therefore, in order to ensure that the benefits overcome the risks, as also discussed by Barkas (this volume). Finally, privacy is another important matter to be considered, especially in the context of democratic fragility.

The effects of the adoption of central bank digital currencies are expected to be even greater at the international level given the current hegemonic competition between the United States and China at the global level, and the possible displacement of the centrality of the US dollar in the international financial and monetary systems. Despite the advancements in digital finance at the domestic level, Brazil has not done much at the international level. The reduction of the dependence on the US dollar could be a main benefit for the country, but only in a framework of collaboration with other countries and with the aim of increasing the legitimacy of the system and assuring stability. Also relevant in that regard is Ghymers' (this volume) discussion about the possibility, for instance, of the creation of digital Special Drawing Rights (SDR) to rebalance and stabilize the International Monetary System (IMS). However, so far Brazil has engaged only in initial discussions and collaborations about these matters in the context of the BRICS and the G20, but not at the regional level in Latin America, or with the European Union. In light of the objectives of this volume and the strengthening of the EU–CELAC Partnership, we believe that there is a considerable potential to improve exchanges and cooperation between Brazil and Latin American countries in the context of CELAC, as well as in the bilateral and interregional relations between CELAC and the European Union.

References

Afonso, J. R. R., da Nóbrega, M. A. R., & de Castilhos, N. N. A. O. (2022). Criptomoedas e Moedas Digitais dos Bancos Centrais–Desafios e Perspectivas da Tributação no Brasil. *Direito Público, 19*(102).

Araujo, F. (2022). Initial steps towards a central bank digital currency by the Central Bank of Brazil (pp. 31–37). *BIS Papers 123*. Available at: https://www.bis.org/publ/bppdf/bispap123_c.pdf. Access 08/03/2024.

Barkas, P. (this volume). Chapter 17: Financial innovation and consumer protection. In D. Katsikas, M. A. Del Tedesco Lins, & A. Ribeiro Hoffmann (Eds.), *Finance, growth and democracy: Connections and challenges in Europe and Latin America in the era of permacrisis*. Springer.
BCB. (2023a). *Diretrizes do Drex – 2023*. Available at: https://www.bcb.gov.br/estabilidadefinanceira/drex?modalAberto=diretrizes_realdigital. Access 08/03/2024.
BCB. (2023b). *Piloto Drex*. Available at: https://www.bcb.gov.br/estabilidadefinanceira/piloto-drex. Access 08/03/2024.
BCB Site, https://www.bcb.gov.br/estabilidadefinanceira/drex. Access 08/03/2024.
Bilotta, N. (2024). The weaponization of finance and digitalization: A cooperative approach between the EU and LAC. In D. Katsikas, M. A. Del Tedesco Lins, & A. Ribeiro Hoffmann (Eds.), *Finance, growth and democracy: Connections and challenges in Europe and Latin America in the era of permacrisis*. Springer.
BIS. (2021, January). Ready, steady, go? – Results of the third BIS survey on central bank digital currency. *BIS Papers* n° 114. Available at: https://www.bis.org/publ/bppdf/bispap114.pdf. Access 08/03/2024.
Chang, J., Guerra, S. M., Lima, E. J. A., & Tabak, B. M. (2008). The stability–concentration relationship in the Brazilian banking system. *Journal of International Financial Markets, Institutions and Money, 18*(4), 388–397, https://doi.org/10.1016/j.intfin.2007.04.004. Access 08/03/2024.
Exame. (2020, October 20). *As diferenças entre blockchain e DLTs*. Available at: https://exame.com/future-of-money/blockchain-e-dlts/as-diferencas-entre-blockchain-e-dlts/. Access 08/03/2024.
FEBRABAN & Deloitte. (2023). *Pesquisa Febraban de Tecnologia Bancária*. Available at: https://cmsarquivos.febraban.org.br/Arquivos/documentos/PDF/Pesquisa%20Febraban%20de%20Tecnologia%20Banc%C3%A1ria%202023%20-%20Volume%202.pdf. Access 08/03/2024.
Feld, M., Giacobbo, T. S. F. B., & Schuster, W. E. (2021). Technological progress and finance: The effects of digitization on Brazilian banking fees. *Economia, 22*(2), 85–99. https://doi.org/10.1016/j.econ.2021.09.001. Access 08/03/2024.
Fluid. (2024, January 11). Pagamento de tributos com Pix: as vantagens de ofertar essa facilidade na conta digital. *Fluid Blog*. Available at: https://dock.tech/fluid/blog/banking/pagamento-tributos-pix/. Access 08/03/2024.
Ghymers, C. (this volume). Chapter 13: Systemic aspects of Central Bank Digital Currencies (CBDCs). In D. Katsikas, M. A. Del Tedesco Lins, & A. Ribeiro Hoffmann (Eds.), *Finance, growth and democracy: Connections and challenges in Europe and Latin America in the era of permacrisis*. Springer.
Hordones, C., & Sanvicente, A. Z. (2021, Jan./Apr.). Structure, market power, and profitability: Evidence from the banking sector in Latin America. *Revista de Contabilidade e Finanças – USP, São Paulo, 32*(85), 126–142. https://doi.org/10.1590/1808-057x202010490.
International Monetary Fund (IMF). (2023). *Monetary and capital markets department IMF approach to central bank digital currency capacity development, 2023*(016). Avaliable at: https://www.elibrary.imf.org/view/journals/007/2023/016/article-A001-en.xml.(https://doi.org/10.5089/9798400240256.007)
Kuehnlenz, S., Orsi, B., & Kaltenbrunner, A. (2023). Central bank digital currencies and the international payment system: The demise of the US dollar? *Research in International Business and Finance, 64*, 101834. https://doi.org/10.1016/j.ribaf.2022.101834
Lavinas, L. (2017). *Takeover of social policy by financialization*. Palgrave Macmillan US.
Lee, A. (2021). What is programmable money? *FEDS Notes*. Available at: https://www.federalreserve.gov/econres/notes/feds-notes/what-is-programmable-money-20210623.html. Access 08/03/2024.
Lins, M.A.D.T. & Ribeiro Hoffmann, A. (2021). Regional governance and macroeconomic crisis management in Latin America. In *Financial crisis management and democracy: Lessons from Europe and Latin America,* co-edited with De Souza Guilherme, B., Ghymers, H. C., Griffith Jones, S. Springer Nature Switzerland AG.
Maia, G. (1999, August). Restructuring the banking system – The case of Brazil. *BIS Policy Papers No 6*. Avaliable at: https://www.bis.org/publ/plcy06b.pdf. Access 08/03/2024.

Orestes, V., & Townsend, R. M. (2023, April). Brazil's Central Bank Digital Currency: Improving Financial Infrastructure with Programmability. *LIFT Papers. Banco Central do Brasil N. 5*. Avaliable at: https://revista.liftlab.com.br/lift/article/view/120. Access 08/03/2024.

Prasad, E. (2022). Digital currencies carry threats as well as promises. *Financial Times*. Available at: https://www.ft.com/content/0ba1da77-cbec-48a3-84d2-9682a5d2f1c9. Access 08/03/2024.

República Federativa do Brasil. (2022). LEI N° 14.478, DE 21 DE DEZEMBRO DE 2022. Available at: https://www2.camara.leg.br/legin/fed/lei/2022/lei-14478-21-dezembro-2022-793516-publicacaooriginal-166582-pl.html. Access 08/03/2024.

Ribeiro Hoffmann, A. (2020). Mercosur between resilience and disintegration. In B. Weiffe, & D. Nolte. (Org.). *Regionalism under stress Europe and Latin America in comparative perspective*. Routledge.

Sampaio, A. V., & Centeno, V. (2022). Central Bank Digital Currencies: Considerations for a not-too-distant future. *Brazilian Keynesian Review, 8*(1), 10–33. https://doi.org/10.33834/bkr.v8i1.267

Soderberg, G., Kiff, J., Tourpe, H., Bechara, M., Forte, S., Kao, K., Lannquist, A., Sun, T., & Yoshinaga, A. (2003). How should Central Banks explore Central Bank digital currency? A dynamic decision-making framework. *IMF Fintech notes 008*. Available at: https://www.imf.org/en/Topics/fintech/central-bank-digital-currency/virtual-handbook#1.-How-Should-Countries-Explore-CBDCs%3F. Access 08/03/2024.

Strange, S. (2015). *States and markets*. Bloomsbury Publishing.

Sutto, G. (2023, November 17). Pix faz 3 anos com popularidade, R$ 29,7 trilhões movimentados e agenda a ser cumprida em 2024. *Infomoney*. Availalbe at: https://www.infomoney.com.br/minhas-financas/pix-faz-tres-anos-com-inegavel-popularidade-r-297-trilhoes-movimentados-e-agenda-a-ser-cumprida/. Access 08/03/2024.

Westin, R. (2023, July 7). Criado há 170 anos Banco do Brasil era privado e financiou a guerra do Paraguai. *Senado Federal. Arquivo S. Economia,* Edição 102. Available at: https://www12.senado.leg.br/noticias/especiais/arquivo-s/criado-ha-170-anos-banco-do-brasil-era-privado-e-financiou-a-guerra-do-paraguai#:~:text=A%20primeira%20experi %C3%AAncia%20banc%C3%A1ria%20do,financiar%20o%20imp%C3%A9rio%20luso%2Dbrasileiro. Access 08/03/2024.

Wise, C., & Lins, M. A. D. T. (2015). Macro-prudence versus Macro-profligacy-Brazil, Argentina and the global financial crisis. In C. Wise, L. E. Armijo, & S. N. Katada (Eds.), *Unexpected outcomes: How emerging economies survived the global financial crisis*. Brookings Institution Press.

World Economic Forum & Cambridge Centre for Alternative Finance. (2024, January). The future of global Fintech: Towards resilient and inclusive growth. *Insight Report*. Available at: https://www3.weforum.org/docs/WEF_The_Future_of_Global_Fintech_2024.pdf. Access 08/03/2024.

Chapter 16
Financial Technology in Global Context: Risks and Opportunities

Anastasia Kotovskaia

Contents

The Role of FinTech for the Financial System

In an era of permacrisis, the role of financial technology (FinTech) gains greater prominence. The term "FinTech" has become emblematic of the vast array of innovative business models emerging within the financial market. These innovative approaches encompass a multitude of technological advancements across various sectors within the financial industry. Although the new FinTech business models are heterogeneous, they all share a common trait: changing the market and driving new efficient products and services (Lerner & Tufano, 2011). Together, the diverse

A. Kotovskaia (✉)
Centres for European Policy Network, Berlin, Germany
e-mail: kotovskaia@cep.eu

D. Katsikas et al. (eds.), *Finance, Growth and Democracy: Connections and Challenges in Europe and Latin America in the Era of Permacrisis*, United Nations University Series on Regionalism 33, https://doi.org/10.1007/978-3-031-68475-3_16

entities considered as FinTechs are transforming the landscape of the financial industry and hold the potential to significantly influence the stability and resilience of the financial system (FSB, 2017). In recent years, FinTech companies have already demonstrated a significant impact on global finance (Stern, 2017).

FinTech solutions, born out of innovation and technology (Haddad & Hornuf, 2019; Tufano, 2003), offer new opportunities in the uncertainty of our times, and change the way to manage, access, and secure financial resources. In this context, exploring the multifaceted role of FinTech in addressing challenges and mitigating the effects of the permacrisis is of paramount importance.

The Disruptive Nature of FinTech

This transformative concept of FinTech exerts a disruptive force (Bower & Christensen, 1995) and harbors the potential to significantly reshape the global financial system (Claessens et al., 2018; Philippon, 2019). The need for innovation in the financial sector is driven primarily by customers (both commercial clients and consumers) who determine the trends of financial market development (Megargel et al., 2017). Their main requirements are acceleration of transaction execution, round-the-clock access to services, more convenient and understandable use of products and services, and the ability to obtain multiple products and services through a single interface. Using cutting-edge technologies, data science, and connectivity, FinTechs have revolutionized conventional financial transaction methods and introduced novel financial products and services that are now accessible worldwide. FinTechs have therefore contributed to the rapid growth of the financial market. The development of innovative products and services relies on a combination of interconnected factors such as access to funding, regulatory frameworks, technology, market demand, and the development of human capital (Nicoletti, 2017; Mention, 2019). For this reason, the progress of FinTech varies depending on the region and jurisdiction.

The emergence of the first FinTech companies in the late 2000s was catalyzed by the aftermath of the global financial crisis of 2008 (Koetter & Blaseg, 2015). The crisis eroded public trust in traditional banking institutions (Guiso et al., 2013), prompting the birth of startups and novel business models designed to address evolving customer needs and heightened demands. Simultaneously, regulatory changes in the banking sector, coupled with the deteriorating conditions in the financial market, compelled numerous banks across the globe to tighten their eligibility criteria for potential borrowers (Lopez de Silanes et al., 2015). Thus, the financial crisis exacerbated the challenges faced by enterprises seeking capital. All this opened the way for young FinTech startups to occupy new niches in the market. Crowdlending and crowdfunding platforms emerged as popular alternatives for individuals and businesses struggling to obtain financing from traditional financial institutions (Gierczak et al., 2016; Koetter & Blaseg, 2015; Klöhn, 2018). Through greater flexibility and the integration of innovative technologies, many startups have been able to offer more favorable terms to their customers compared to traditional financial service providers (Leboeuf & Schwienbacher, 2018).

In the times of permacrisis, FinTechs increase further their significance.[1] In recent years, there has been a substantial increase in alternative lending activities on a global scale.[2] This surge, however, has exhibited notable variations across countries, owing to distinct factors such as the level of economic development and the composition of the financial market. Specifically, the amplitude of FinTech lending operations tends to be more pronounced in nations characterized by higher national incomes and a less competitive landscape within the banking sector. Furthermore, jurisdictions with more lenient banking regulations have witnessed a heightened prevalence of FinTech-driven lending (IMF, 2023a).

Beyond lending, FinTechs also have a disruptive impact on the wealth management landscape. Historically, many wealth management providers were disinclined to serve clients with investments falling below a certain threshold. This landscape has undergone a transformation with the introduction of robo-advisors that have the capacity to rapidly assess and formulate appropriate wealth management strategies through algorithmic means (Maume, 2021; Papadimitri et al., 2021; Tertilt & Scholz, 2018). Consequently, such technologies have rendered wealth management services more accessible and adaptable to a broader clientele (Bakardjieva Engelbrekt et al., 2021). Furthermore, FinTech unveils a vast array of opportunities within the payments sector, characterized by cost-effectiveness, real-time transaction capabilities, and accelerated accessibility for consumers. Thus, FinTechs can enhance financial inclusion, particularly for individuals and small- and medium-sized enterprises (SMEs).

Initially, the focus of FinTech providers was on a key service, in the provision of which the startups aimed to achieve the greatest possible efficiency. However, current trends are shifting in favor of enterprises offering a diversified portfolio of products and services, with notable prominence afforded to industry giants, BigTechs,[3] and platform-based entities (Parker et al., 2017). BigTechs, a contraction of the term "big technology," encompasses significant multinational technology corporations that wield substantial influence and possess the capabilities to perturb the financial sector. These established market players already possess a substantial customer base, enabling them to swiftly attract customers for their new products and services. Owing to their formidable bargaining power, utilization of Big Data, and deployment of advanced analytical tools, these technology conglomerates have

[1] The trajectory of this trend is set by the dynamic and ever-evolving nature of the modern world, influenced by globalization and technological progress (see Chap. 1).

[2] Based on an industry analysis conducted by Allied Research in 2021, the size of the global FinTech lending market reached $450 billion in 2020 and is anticipated to soar to $4957 billion by 2030. By way of illustration, the FinTech lending market in Latin America witnessed an increase from $0.7 billion in 2017 to $6 billion in 2020 (IMF, 2023c).

[3] Beyond the widely acknowledged quartet of tech giants known as GAFA, which consists of Google, Apple, Facebook, and Amazon, BigTechs also encompass a more extensive range of influential players, including notable Chinese corporations like Alibaba and Tencent.

the potential to reshape the landscape of financial service providers. What is more, they can enjoy certain advantages, potentially distorting competition (Frost et al., 2019; Hornuf & Schwienbacher, 2017; Podszun, 2015). In addition to their core technological services, BigTechs extend their reach to encompass a wide spectrum of offerings, including financial services exemplified by proprietary payment systems like ApplePay and GooglePay. BigTechs are entering the financial market for a variety of reasons, but primarily to complement their own offerings and collect additional customer data. The extent of potential impact of BigTechs' activity on the financial industry is difficult to estimate and the possibility of occurrence of systemic risk is not excluded (Zetzsche et al., 2017).

In general, FinTech entities introduce groundbreaking solutions that improve service accessibility in the financial sector and intensify market competitiveness. In the age of digital technologies, traditional banking institutions are compelled to either engage in competitive rivalry with FinTech enterprises or undertake a fundamental restructuring of their own business models to maintain their competitiveness (Hornuf et al., 2018). The transformative impact of novel FinTech business models extends into the legal realm. Regulatory bodies play therefore a major role in striking a balance between fostering innovation and mitigating associated risks (Kern et al., 2006).

Regulation in the Digital Financial Ecosystem: Addressing Complexities

Throughout history, the dynamic interplay between innovation and state regulation has significantly shaped the trajectory of public welfare (Meissner et al., 2013). The successful digitization of the financial industry and its resilience during the permacrisis depends on effective and appropriate regulation (Brunnermeier et al., 2012). Unclear regulations, redundant requirements, as well as legal loopholes can lead to negative consequences, especially slowing down market development, opening the way to the black market, and allowing illegal activities (Campello et al., 2010). The law is generally based on existing market activity, which is why legislators mainly refer to existing traditional models when developing the legal framework. However, over time, business models change, and new market participants, products, and services emerge, which differ to varying degrees from their predecessors. Ignoring structural shifts in the financial system leads to a proliferation of new risks. In this regard, FinTech regulation involves many complex and evolving challenges for regulators around the world (Ehrentraud et al., 2020).

Given the high-risk nature of the financial market, encompassing significant monetary costs and potential losses, supervisors and regulators are forced to take into consideration the risk stemming from FinTech (Yadav, 2020). The rise of decentralized finance (DeFi), a financial ecosystem devoid of intermediaries, implementation of smart contracts, governed by computer code, usage of platforms, and artificial intelligence (AI) are not only transforming conventional financial system but require rethinking of the regulatory framework. These emerging risks cover, among others, cybersecurity and safeguarding personal data.[4] Managing and securing sensitive information also gives rise to numerous concerns, as any unauthorized disclosure to external parties elevates the risk of cybercrime and data manipulation. Remarkably, considerable progress has already been reached in addressing specific facets of these challenges, especially in the EU jurisdiction (see section "Operational resilience within the FinTech sector"). With ongoing digitalization continuing to reshape the financial sector, the collective actions of regulators and supervisors will assume a pivotal role in shaping the future of financial oversight and regulation.

Security Challenges in the FinTech Sector: Data Vulnerabilities, Cybersecurity, and Operational Resilience

The security of FinTech applications has emerged as a critical concern in the digital age. The FinTech sector, due to its handling of sensitive financial data, is a prime target for cyberattacks. Data breaches, if realized, can inflict substantial financial and reputational damage on the affected companies (Pawlak, 2017). Startling statistics reveal that the FinTech industry has been increasingly susceptible to cyber threats. Security vulnerabilities within this context can lead to severe repercussions for the entire financial sector, as evidenced by the staggering global losses of $8.4 trillion due to cybercrime in 2022, with an anticipated annual increase of 30% in 2023 (Statista, 2023). Against this background, the following question primarily arises: Why are FinTechs particularly vulnerable to such security breaches?

Data Security in FinTech: Intrinsic Vulnerabilities

The financial services sector safeguards a wide array of datasets, encompassing financial transactions, payment card details, credit reports, geolocation information, and various categories of personal and sensitive data. At the same time, those kinds of data represent an attractive target for criminals seeking unauthorized access. FinTechs face significant competitive pressure, driving them to continuously introduce innovative digital products and services to cater to their customer demands. However, the usage of cutting-edge, albeit less established, technologies in this pursuit can expose the financial sector to security risks. Involvement of emerging technologies such as the Internet of Things (IoT) or artificial intelligence (AI) is common

[4] Digitalization of the financial services sector also presents substantial challenges and unprecedented risks to consumers, necessitating vigilant monitoring and effective policy responses, particularly with respect to robust consumer protection measures (see Chap. 17).

for the FinTech industry, but it poses data threats and cybersecurity risks. Furthermore, it is not uncommon for these companies to integrate third-party software into their operations that potentially creates security bottlenecks. This practice opens avenues for malicious actors to exploit system vulnerabilities, gaining unauthorized access to sensitive information and conducting financial fraud and data theft.

To facilitate transaction processing and provide financial services, financial institutions need access to sensitive customer data, which they internally store. Potentially, security gaps emerge in their data storage solutions. Security vulnerabilities in FinTech are primarily intertwined with the architectural design of financial applications that act as digital conduits to financial institutions, communicating directly with the bank's back-end services through application programming interfaces (APIs). While these APIs are often open source, which benefits app developers, they can inadvertently introduce security threats. Usage of APIs often leads to a complex multifaceted data ownership structure, involving at least both an external owner and a FinTech institution. The absence of unified data ownership gives rise to significant security concerns, fostering an environment in which vulnerabilities may arise at various stages. Furthermore, the growing trend of hosting software systems and data in cloud environments has led to a notable surge in cloud-based cyberattacks that led to data breaches. Statistical data reveals that approximately 45% of global data breaches occur within cloud-based platforms (Thales Cloud Security Report, 2022). Given the sensitivity of financial data, secure storage solutions are imperative to avert vulnerabilities and defend against potential financial data breaches.

Cybersecurity Concerns for FinTech

The digital revolution has not only fostered the advancement of digital technologies in the financial sector but has also catalyzed the proliferation of cybercriminal activities. Especially a high level of interconnectedness across financial institutions and in particular their interdependencies of their information and communication technology (ICT) systems constitute a systemic vulnerability because localized cyber incidents could quickly spread from any financial entity to the entire financial system, unhindered by geographical boundaries. The evolving landscape of cyber threats demonstrates an increasing level of sophistication. In addition, the rise of remote workplaces, driven by global crises such as the COVID-19 pandemic, creates additional entry points for cybercriminals. That poses potential risks that could adversely affect the stability of the entire financial system, including the generation of liquidity runs and an overarching loss of confidence and trust in financial markets (Dieter, 2004).

Significantly, cybersecurity vulnerabilities are a heightened concern for FinTech startups, primarily stemming from potential inadequacies in their security protocols, particularly during the initial phases of their operations. However, the aftermath of succumbing to cybercrimes in the FinTech sector involves the comprehensive erosion of customer trust, substantial business losses to the extent of insolvency, and persistent legal and financial repercussions, which may prove challenging to overcome. Cybersecurity measures are necessary to protect sensitive financial data, ensure the integrity of digital transactions, and prevent cyber threats that could undermine the stability of FinTech platforms. Regulators in different jurisdictions start to address cybersecurity issues. For the purposes of illustration, in 2024, European Parliament adopted the Cyber Resilience Act[5] (CRA) to strengthen the overall level of cybersecurity. The CRA contains a cybersecurity framework for hardware and software products as well as for remote data processing solutions. The act does not impose rules on financial firms unless they manufacture hardware and software products and remote data processing solutions. However, those requirements address the security gaps in products with digital elements that FinTechs use to provide their services and thus have an immediate but significant impact on the financial market.

Operational Resilience Within the FinTech Sector

As financial crises tend to amplify vulnerabilities within the financial ecosystem, the FinTech sector is not exempt from the exigencies of operational resilience. Given the increased reliance of financial services providers on technological infrastructure, safeguarding operational resilience is getting to be one of the central priorities for regulatory authorities on a global scale. To provide a comprehensive international framework for addressing this pivotal concern, the Basel Committee on Banking Supervision released a set of foundational guidelines, "Principles for Operational Resilience," in 2021. Within the purview of regulatory oversight, the EU emerges as a noteworthy example of a jurisdiction that has introduced a comprehensive and all-encompassing regulatory framework addressing the concept of operational resilience specifically tailored to financial institutions.

Entered into force in January 2023, the EU Digital Operational Resilience Act[6] (DORA) represents a significant paradigm shift in the financial sector regulation ensuring the necessary safeguards within the financial system, mitigating the threats of cyberattacks and related risks. It establishes a pan-European regulatory framework for the oversight of ICT risks by European and competent national authorities, functioning distinctively from the conventional supervisory structure. In the scope

[5] Proposal for a Regulation of the European Parliament and of the Council on horizontal cybersecurity requirements for products with digital elements and amending Regulation (EU) 2019/1020 COM/2022/454 final.

[6] Regulation (EU) 2022/2554 of the European Parliament and of the Council of 14 December 2022 on digital operational resilience for the financial sector and amending Regulations (EC) No 1060/2009, (EU) No 648/2012, (EU) No 600/2014, (EU) No 909/2014 and (EU) 2016/1011 OJ L 333.

of DORA is a wide range of financial institutions, including, among others, payment institutions, e-money institutions, cryptoasset service providers, and crowdfunding service providers. Notably, DORA also extends its purview to encompass critical third parties offering ICT-related services[7] to financial entities.

To reinforce digital operational resilience and cybersecurity for the financial industry, DORA imposes far-reaching requirements on financial institutions. Thus, financial institutions are required to establish comprehensive ICT risk management frameworks. This encompasses the formulation of diverse ICT policies, procedures, and tools to facilitate early risk identification, ICT system protection, and the mitigation of cybersecurity threats. The regulation also asks financial institutions to regularly test their level of operational resilience. In the event of a cyberattack or security incident, companies must record and promptly report these occurrences to the relevant supervisory authority. Furthermore, financial institutions are compelled to integrate specific provisions into their contracts with third-party ICT providers. Consequently, financial institutions must undertake a comprehensive review of their strategies, policies, procedures, ICT protocols, and tools to ensure alignment with DORA's stipulations.

Data and cybersecurity as well as operational resilience for FinTechs have ascended to paramount significance, particularly in the era of permacrisis. The unprecedented shift toward digital financial solutions, combined with an environment where the financial sector faces over 1800 cyberattacks annually (Statista, 2023), spotlights the relevance of strengthening of security and resilience in the face of ongoing multifaceted threats. The ability to withstand operational disruptions and thwart cyberattacks becomes a litmus test for their viability and trustworthiness, especially during times of financial crisis. As financial crises can accentuate weaknesses, these companies should be prepared to navigate turbulent times with fortified cybersecurity measures and robust operational resilience frameworks in place.

FinTech and Its Implications for Financial Inclusion

The spreading of FinTech has ushered in a pivotal era in financial services, affording access to over 500 million individuals who were previously excluded from the conventional financial system. FinTech is promising to enable access to banking, lending, and investment opportunities to traditionally underserved populations. Concurrently, this transformative landscape has witnessed the entry of new stakeholders into financial markets, thereby accentuating the pressing need for regulatory oversight. Whereas acceleration of financial inclusion through digital means is a laudable goal, it necessitates a careful equilibrium between inclusion and prudent

[7] Third-party service providers offer various services that enable transactions and accessing the financial information without direct contact with a bank, for instance, providing payment initiation services through third-party platforms, account information, or credit scoring services.

regulation. The global financial crisis serves as a stark reminder that overly rapid inclusion, without adequate regulation and financial literacy, can engender financial instability.

Financial Inclusion: Global Imperative

An inclusive financial system is one in which citizens have access to and use financial services to cover their financial needs, such as savings, credit, or insurance services. Lack of access to such services can perpetuate income inequality and inhibit economic growth (Cihak & Sahay, 2020). Higher level of inclusion ultimately promotes entrepreneurship and private sector development (Demirguc-Kunt & Singer, 2017). Enhancing the availability of financial services has favorable effects on financial stability through the broadening of funding sources (Beck et al., 2014). A substantial rise of small depositors, resulting from increased financial inclusion, strengthens the robustness of banks' deposit base. Consequently, this makes financial system banks typically more resilient during periods of crisis (Hannig & Jansen, 2010).

However, roughly 1.4 billion individuals globally remain devoid of access to conventional banking services (World Bank, 2022). Likewise, SMEs experience challenges when seeking financing from conventional banks. In this environment, FinTech is poised to offer substantial opportunities, abetted by the increasing ubiquity of mobile phones and Internet connectivity (Boitan, 2016). This becomes especially significant in the context of permacrisis, where a considerable number of individuals are likely to encounter financial difficulties. The transformative potential of FinTech becomes evident through its facilitation of financial access for over 500 million previously excluded individuals.

The emergence of the COVID-19 pandemic further underscored the role of digital financial services in hastening financial inclusion, particularly within the constraints of social distancing measures, by broadening access to formal economic activities by means of offering new financial products, finance-related software, new forms of communication, and customer interaction (Gomber et al., 2017). FinTech has engendered opportunities for diverse segments of the population to partake in the financial ecosystem, thus unlocking its potential for societal and economic advancement. Moreover, through the digital transformation of financial services, FinTech firms have the capacity to reduce the expenses associated with delivering these services while expanding their reach to economically disadvantaged groups. Indeed, the cost of providing financial accounts digitally is generally 80–90% lower than the cost of the same services provided through branches of financial institutions (McKinsey Global Institute, 2013). This holds particular significance for developing countries, where a multitude of individuals and small enterprises face exclusion from conventional financial services.

Financial inclusion in a broader sense is regarded not only to the scale of the population's access to financial services, but also by their quality, convenience, efficiency, safety, population welfare, as well as the degree of impact on poverty and inequality reduction, including gender inequality. FinTech has ushered in a transformative wave in the global financial landscape, bringing with it the potential to address one of the most persistent and concerning disparities—the gender gap in financial inclusion.

Gender Gap in Financial Inclusion: FinTech as an Opportunity

The gender gap in financial inclusion has deep-rooted implications, limiting women's access to banking, savings, credit, and investment opportunities. Gender disparities in financial inclusion have been a persistent challenge across the globe.

Recent studies have illuminated the extent of this phenomenon. Globally, approximately 9% (The Global Findex Database 2021, 2022) fewer women than men have access to financial services. Moreover, this gender gap in financial inclusion is particularly pronounced in developing countries. Sub-Saharan Africa, for instance, illustrated a staggering 25% gender gap in access to formal financial services, with women disproportionately excluded from the financial ecosystem (UNDESA, 2021).

Since the FinTech solutions are inherently inclusive and accessible throughout geographical boundaries, FinTech presents an array of innovations and opportunities that can effectively reduce this gender gap. Mobile banking, digital wallets, and online payment systems allow women, especially in underserved regions, to access financial services conveniently, erasing the limitations posed by physical branch locations and hours of operation. Furthermore, traditional credit scoring mechanisms have often disadvantaged women due to gender-based disparities in access to assets and formal employment. FinTech allows for alternative data sources, enabling more comprehensive and equitable credit assessments, thus facilitating access to loans and other financial services for women.

FinTech firms, along with governments and nongovernmental organizations, can promote targeted financial inclusion campaigns that specifically address the needs and challenges faced by women (IMF, 2020). Especially in the time of permacrisis, those campaigns can leverage the digital nature of FinTech to engage and empower women economically, fostering their financial independence and thus contributing to the increasing economic activity that stimulates economic growth.[8]

[8] Beyond that, FinTechs possess potential to support other demographic groups marginalized within the financial system, including but not limited to individuals identifying as LGBTQ+, as well as those subjected to discrimination based on their race or ethnicity.

FinTech's Potentials for Financial Inclusion: Latin America's Emerging Landscape

The grade of the influence of FinTech on financial inclusion differs depending upon the region. While in Europe and Latin America, financial inclusion through the conventional financial institutions prevails, in Asia and Africa digital financial inclusion takes the lead (IMF, 2020). At the same time, the Latin American market has a potential to become one of the biggest FinTech markets in the near future, mainly through the efforts of Mexico, Brazil, and Argentina. The absence of a well-established financial infrastructure tailored to the broader consumer market may open new opportunities for the spread of FinTechs in the Latin American region. In the last years, Latin American economies, having weathered profound crisis disruptions (Centeno & Lajous, 2017; Machinea, 2010), demonstrated the emergence of new trends that hold the potential to reshape and strengthen the region's position within the global financial system. One of the central trends is the swift expansion of innovation and digitalization, among others, in the financial sector.[9]

In Brazil, only 70% of citizens have debit cards, 33% have credit cards, and a third of the country's citizens have no access to banking services at all. In other countries in the region, the level of financial inclusion is even lower. In Mexico, 90% of all transactions between the individuals are made exclusively in cash, which is far away from the trends of the modern global digital economy. It is noteworthy that more than 80% of Brazilians use instant payments within Brazil's Pix system (IMF, 2023b). In Mexico, around one-third of the population has credit and debit cards and only half of the citizens are clients of banks. At the same time, excessive bureaucratic requirements of conventional banks in Latin America may hinder the opening of bank accounts in some cases. Moreover, traditional banks do not necessarily offer mobile apps or web services. Simultaneously, consumer preferences are undergoing a profound transformation. Flexible FinTech startups in Brazil have sensed the widespread customer dissatisfaction with existing banks and have swiftly stepped in with a wide range of FinTech products available via smartphones.

For instance, Brazilian FinTechs are already reshaping the country's financial landscape and offering millions of Brazilians their first bank accounts.

Brazil's Neobank Nubank

Unlike traditional banks, Nubank offered its customers a convenient service through its mobile app, allowing customers to easily manage their finances, make payments, and track expenses. In addition, Nubank practiced data-driven decision-making. Using advanced analytics and machine learning algorithms, the company gained a deep understanding of customer behavior, preferences, and creditworthiness. The FinTech's business model demonstrates remarkable success (Kauflin et al., 2021). Nowadays, Nubank has established itself as the world's largest neobank with a customer base of over 80 million customers and market capitalization that is equivalent to one-fourth of that of Brazil's largest state-owned bank, Banco do Brasil.

In this environment, FinTech looks promising for the Latin American market (Pasquali, 2020; FinTech Argentina, 2021). Simplification of the regulatory framework is a further factor for the development of FinTech in Latin America. In the period between 2010 and 2020, a wave of streamlining national laws regulating FinTech swept across Latin America. For instance, Mexico adopted a decree enacting the FinTech Law in 2018, Chile approved its FinTech law in 2022, and Brazil adopted the Open Banking regulation in 2019. These laws established a clear regulatory framework for most types of FinTech activities, including crowdfunding, electronic payment funds, virtual assets, and digital asset exchanges. The Open Banking regulation, in turn, laid down the rules for financial institutions for sharing customer financial information and banking services with third-party providers (TPP) through the use of APIs aiming at enhancing competition, promoting innovation, and advancing financial inclusion. Peru and Argentina are planning similar legislation. Governments of almost all countries in the Latin American region declare their commitment to expanding access to financial services and introducing clear rules of operation.

Ensuring Secure Digital Financial Inclusion

Today, governments are pursuing deliberate policies to increase the population's access to financial services at both national and international levels. Despite the progress made in this area over the last decades, there are still many citizens and SMEs that lack access to basic financial services such as savings and credit. In the pursuit of financial inclusion, FinTech appears promising. By digitizing financial services, FinTech companies reduce costs, making these services accessible to a wider audience. This is especially critical in developing countries where traditional financial services remain out of reach for many due to geographical and financial barriers. Digital inclusion has the potential to become a driver of economic growth due to the democratization of investment instruments, reducing transaction costs and thus increasing the incomes of the population (Demirguc-Kunt et al., 2018). This digital transformation presents both opportunities and challenges that demand vigilant attention to ensure safe and sound digital financial inclusion through FinTech. The secure advancement of digital financial inclusion hinges upon the harmonization of various factors, each playing a pivotal role in safeguarding economic stability and trust within the financial ecosystem. The danger of rushed financial inclusion, lacking the oversight of prudent regulation and the bolstering of financial literacy, was starkly evident during the global financial crisis. Indeed, uncontrolled financial inclusion can adversely affect economic growth (Dabla-Norris, 2019). The quick transition necessitates watchfulness, with regulatory bodies sounding the alarm over emerging security risks and the possibility of inappropriate lending practices perpetuated by under-regulated financial institutions. One of the fundamental challenges is the unequal access to digital infrastructure and the disparities stemming from limitations in financial and digital literacy.

These disparities, if left unaddressed, can exacerbate existing inequalities, hindering the objective of financial inclusion. Additionally, novel data sources and data analytics, while promising, introduce the potential for biases. Hence, it is imperative to exercise caution and prudence when harnessing the power of data in the pursuit of inclusive finance. In the context of permacrisis, the need for secure and reliable digital financial inclusion has never been more evident.

Conclusions

FinTech encourages narrowing the gender gap in financial inclusion by reducing the barriers to access to financial services. By expanding access, reducing costs, enhancing financial literacy, fostering entrepreneurship, and employing more inclusive credit assessment methodologies, FinTech is playing a central role in promoting financial inclusion and economic empowerment among women worldwide. As this innovative sector continues to evolve, it has the potential to create a more equitable and inclusive financial landscape for all. At the same time, security risks associated with FinTech necessitate careful consideration of new solutions to cybersecurity and data protection challenges. To put it succinctly, the path to safe and sound digital financial inclusion through FinTech is marked by challenges that require a collective commitment to address them. Striking a balance between expansion, regulation, and digital literacy is crucial for realizing the promise of digital finance while safeguarding financial stability, trust, and inclusive financial access.

References

Bakardjieva Engelbrekt, A., Leijon, K., Michalski, A., et al. (2021). What does the technological shift have in store for the EU? Opportunities and pitfalls for European Societies. In *The European Union and the technology shift* (pp. 1–25). Palgrave Macmillan.

Beck, T., Demirguc-Kunt, A., & Levine, R. (2014). Bank concentration, competition and crises. *Journal of Banking & Finance, 30*, 1581–1603.

Boitan, I. (2016). Crowdlending and financial inclusion evidence from EU countries. *Economic Alternatives, 4*, 418–432.

Bower, J. L., & Christensen, C. M. (1995). Disruptive technologies: Catching the wave. *Harvard Business Review, 73*(1), 43–53.

Brunnermeier, M., Dong, G., & Palia, D. (2012). *Banks' non-interest income and systemic Risk.* AFA 2012 Chicago Meetings Paper. https://doi.org/10.2139/ssrn.1786738

Campello, M., Graham, J. R., & Harvey, C. R. (2010). The real effects of financial constraints: Evidence from a financial crisis. *Journal of Financial Economics, 97*, 470–487. https://doi.org/10.1016/j.jfineco.2010.02.009

Centeno, M. A., & Lajous, A. (2017). *Retos para America Latina en el siglo XXI.* Open Mind, BBVA. https://www.bbvaopenmind.com/articulos/retos-para-america-latina-en-el-siglo-xxi. Accessed 28 Oct 2023.

Cihak, M., & Sahay, R. (2020). *Finance and inequality*. IMF Staff discussion notes.

Claessens, S., Frost, J., Turner, G., et al. (2018). FinTech credit markets around the world: Size, drivers and policy issues. *BIS Quarterly Review*, 29–49.

Dabla-Norris, E. (2019). *Distinguishing constraints on financial inclusion and their impact on GDP, TFP, and the Distribution of Income*. IMF Staff discussion notes.

Demirguc-Kunt, A., & Singer, D. (2017). *Financial inclusion and inclusive growth: A review of recent empirical evidence* (World Bank Group Policy Research working paper WPS 8040). World Bank.

Demirguc-Kunt, A., Klapper, L., Singer, D., et al. (2018). *The Global Findex Database 2017: Measuring financial inclusion and the FinTech revolution*. World Bank Group.

Dieter, H. (2004). The stability of international financial markets: A global public good? In S. A. Schirm (Ed.), *New rules for global markets – Public and private governance in the world economy*. Palgrave MacMillan.

Ehrentraud, J., Ocampo, D. G., Garzoni, L., et al. (2020). *Policy responses to FinTech: A cross-country overview* (Bank for International Settlements, FSI Insights on policy implementation 23). BIS.

Financial Stability Board. (2017). *Financial stability implications from FinTech: Supervisory and regulatory issues that merit authorities' attention*. https://www.fsb.org/wp-content/uploads/R270617.pdf Accessed 10 Oct 2023.

FinTech Argentina. (2021). *Ualá busca llevar sus servicios financieros a toda la region*. America Economia https://www.americaeconomia.com/negocios-industrias/FinTech-argentina-uala-busca-llevar-sus-servicios-financieros-toda-la-region. Accessed 25 Oct 2023.

Frost, J., Gambacorta, L., Huang, Y., et al. (2019). BigTech and the changing structure of financial intermediation. *Economic Policy, 34*(100), 761–799.

Gierczak, M. M., Bretschneider, U., Haas, P., et al. (2016). Crowdfunding – Outlining the new era of fundraising. In O. Gajda & D. Brüntje (Eds.), *Crowdfunding in Europe – State of the art in theory and practice* (pp. 7–23). Springer.

Gomber, P., Koch, J.-A., & Siering, M. (2017). Digital finance and FinTech: Current research and future research directions. *Journal of Business Economics, 87*, 537–580.

Guiso, L., Sapienza, P., & Zingales, L. (2013). Determinants of attitudes toward strategic default on mortgages. *Journal of Finance, 68*, 1373–1515.

Haddad, C., & Hornuf, L. (2019). The emergence of the global FinTech market: Economic and technological determinants. *Small Business Economics, 53*, 81.

Hannig, A., & Jansen, S. (2010). *Financial inclusion and financial stability: Current policy issues* (Asian Development Bank Institute Working Paper 259).

Hornuf, L., & Schwienbacher, A. (2017). Should securities regulation promote equity crowdfunding? *Small Business Economics, 49*(3), 579–593. https://doi.org/10.1007/s11187-017-9839-9

Hornuf, L., Klus, M., Lohwasser, T., et al. (2018). *How do banks interact with FinTechs? Forms of alliances and their impact on bank value* (CESifoWorking Paper 7170).

International Monetary Fund. (2020). *The promise of FinTech: Financial inclusion in the post COVID-19 era.*

International Monetary Fund. (2023a). *Institutional arrangements for FinTech regulation: Supervisory monitoring* (Note 2023/004).

International Monetary Fund. (2023b). *Pix: Brazil's Successful Instant Payment System* (Western Hemisphere Dept 2023(289)). https://doi.org/10.5089/9798400249266.002

International Monetary Fund. (2023c). *The rise and impact of Fintech in Latin America* (Fintech Notes 2023(003)). https://doi.org/10.5089/9798400235474.063

Kauflin, J., Abreu, M., & Gara, A. (2021). How David Vélez built the world's most valuable digital bank and became a billionaire. *Forbes*. https://www.forbes.com/sites/jeffkauflin/2021/04/07/FinTech-billionaire-david-velez-nubank-brazil-digital-bank/?sh=272ad9116b27. Accessed 19 Oct 2023.

Kern, A., Dhumale, R., & Eatwell, J. (2006). *Global governance of financial systems: The international regulation of systemic risk*. Oxford University Press.

Klöhn, L. (2018). The regulation of crowdfunding in Europe. In D. Cumming & L. Hornuf (Eds.), *The economics of crowdfunding StartUps, portals, and investor behavior* (pp. 219–254). Palgrave Macmillan.

Koetter, M., & Blaseg, D. (2015). *Friend or foe? Crowdfunding versus credit when banks are stressed* (IWH Discussion Papers 8/2015).

Leboeuf, G., & Schwienbacher, A. (2018). Crowdfunding as a new financing tool. In D. Cumming & L. Hornuf (Eds.), *The economics of crowdfunding StartUps, portals, and investor behavior* (pp. 11–28). Palgrave Macmillan.

Lerner, J., & Tufano, P. (2011). *The consequences of financial innovation: A counterfactual research agenda* (NBER Working Paper Series 16780).

Lopez de Silanes, F., McCahery, J., Schoenmaker, D., et al. (2015). *The European capital markets study estimating the financing gaps of SMEs*. http://www.dsf.nl/wpcontent/uploads/2015/09/EuropeanCapitalMarketsStudy_2015_FINAL157.pdf. Accessed 17 Oct 2023.

Machinea, L.-J. (2010). *La crisis economica en America Latina. Alcances e impactos*. Fundación Carolina, XXV.

Maume, P. (2021). *Robo-advisors: How do they fit in the existing EU regulatory framework, in particular with regard to investor protection? Study requested by the ECON committee, European Pariament*. https://www.europarl.europa.eu/RegData/etudes/STUD/2021/662928/IPOL_STU(2021)662928_EN.pdf. Accessed 11 Oct 2023.

McKinsey Global Institute. (2013). *McKinsey global payments map. Fighting poverty, profitably: Transforming the economics of payments to build sustainable, inclusive financial systems*.

Megargel, A., Shankararaman, V., & Reddy, S. K. (2017). Real-time inbound marketing: A use case for digital banking. In D. Lee Kuo Chuen & R. Deng (Eds.), *Handbook of blockchain, digital finance, and inclusion* (pp. 311–328). Academic.

Meissner, D., Roud, V., & Cervantes, M. (2013). Innovation policy or policy for innovation? Search of the optimal solution for policy approach and organization. In D. Meissner, L. Gokhberg, & A. Sokolov (Eds.), *Science, technology and innovation policy for the future—Potentials and limits of foresight studies* (pp. 247–255). Springer.

Mention, A. L. (2019). The future of FinTech. *Research-Technology Management, 62*(4), 59–63. https://doi.org/10.1080/08956308.2019.1613123

Nicoletti, B. (2017). *The future of FinTech. Integrating finance and technology in financial services*. Palgrave Macmillan.

Papadimitri, P., Pasiou, M., Tsagkarakis, M.-P., et al. (2021). FinTech and financial Intermediation. In M. Pompella & R. Matousek (Eds.), *The Palgrave handbook of FinTech and blockchain* (pp. 347–374). Palgrave Macmillan.

Parker, G., Van Alstyne, M., & Choudary, S. P. (2017). *Platform revolution: How networked markets are transforming the economy and how to make them work for you*. W.W. Norton.

Pasquali, M. (2020). *El 'boom' del capital de riesgo en América Latina*. https://es.statista.com/grafico/17946/panorama-del-capi-tal-de-riesgo-en-latinoamerica. Accessed 9 Okt 2023.

Pawlak, P. (2017). *Cyber security woes: WannaCry?* EUISS.

Philippon, T. (2019). The FinTech opportunity. In J. Agnew & O. S. Mitchell (Eds.), *The disruptive impact of FinTech on retirement systems* (pp. 190–218). Oxford University Press.

Podszun, R. (2015). The More Technological approach: Competition law in the digital economy. In G. Surblytė (Ed.), *Competition on the Internet* (pp. 101–108). Springer.

Statista, (2023). *Number of cyber incidents in the financial industry worldwide from 2013 to 2022*. https://www.statista.com/statistics/1310985/number-of-cyber-incidents-in-financial-industry-worldwide/

Stern, C. (2017). FinTechs and their emergence in banking services in CESEE. *Focus on European Economic Integration, Q3/17*, 42–58.

Tertilt, M., & Scholz, P. (2018). To advise, or not to advise – How robo-advisors evaluate the risk preferences of private investors. *Journal of Wealth Management, 21*, 70–84.

Thales Cloud Security Report. (2022). https://cpl.thalesgroup.com/about-us/newsroom/thales-cloud-data-breaches-2022-trends-challenges

The Global Findex Database 2021. (2022). https://www.worldbank.org/en/publication/globalfindex/Data#sec3

Tufano, P. (2003). Financial innovation. In G. Constantinides, M. Harris, & R. Stulz (Eds.), *Handbook of the economics of finance* (Vol. 1, pp. 307–335). Elsevier.

UNDESA. (2021). *Financing for sustainable development report.* https://developmentfinance.un.org/sites/developmentfinance.un.org/files/FSDR_2021.pdf

World Bank. (2022). *The Global Findex Database 2021: Financial inclusion, digital payments, and resilience in the age of COVID-19* (Report 2022).

Yadav, Y. (2020). FinTech and international financial regulation. *Vanderbilt Journal of Transnational Law, 53*, 1109–1146.

Zetzsche, D., Buckley, R., Arner, D. W., et al. (2017). *From FinTech to TechFin: The regulatory challenges of data-driven finance* (EBI Working Paper 6).

Chapter 17
Consumer Protection and Financial Innovation: Microeconomic, Policy, and Behavioral Considerations for the Digital Era

Panagiotis Barkas

Contents

The views expressed hereby are privately held by the author and cannot be attributed to the European Securities and Markets Authority (ESMA) and/or the Hellenic Foundation for European and Foreign Policy (ELIAMEP).

P. Barkas (✉)
Greek and European Economy Observatory, Hellenic Foundation for European and Foreign Policy (ELIAMEP), Athens, Greece

Investor Protection and Sustainable Finance Division, European Securities and Markets Authority (ESMA), Paris, France

D. Katsikas et al. (eds.), *Finance, Growth and Democracy: Connections and Challenges in Europe and Latin America in the Era of Permacrisis*, United Nations University Series on Regionalism 33, https://doi.org/10.1007/978-3-031-68475-3_17

Technological Innovation, Regulatory Frameworks, and Consumer Protection

In today's rapidly evolving digital landscape, the realms of finance and technology are intertwining in an unprecedented manner. The emergence of new forms of financial innovation has ushered in a new era of convenience and accessibility, fundamentally transforming the financial services industry. It has empowered consumers to access a vast array of financial products and services with unprecedented ease. However, this transformative force also brings along a set of new and pressing challenges that demand consumer and policy attention.

The journey to explore the intricate interplay between financial innovation and consumer protection in the international economic and policy landscape requires delving into the critical role that each of these components plays in shaping the modern financial ecosystem. It also requires recognizing that they are not isolated concepts, but rather interconnected pillars upon which the financial industry stands. They also constitute driving forces that determine the future equilibrium that policy and politics shall strike in the efficiency–protection nexus. This is particularly pertinent in light of the current crises—and the permacrisis environment—as discussed in the introduction of this edited volume.

Financial innovation is important**.** Financial innovation has revolutionized the way people interact with and manage their financial resources, be they capital gains, labor income, or income from other financial assets. At its core, financial innovation encompasses three fundamental aspects: innovative financial products, advanced systems, and an expanding audience of retail investors. These three aspects respectively represent the object, the network, and the subject. The first facet brings forth a plethora of new digitally enabled financial products and services. It involves harnessing cutting-edge technologies and platforms that provide individuals with unprecedented access to investment opportunities. Gone are the days when financial markets were reserved for the elite; today, robo-advisors, peer-to-peer lending, crowdfunding, and cryptocurrency have democratized finance, making it accessible and affordable to the masses. Alongside innovative products, financial innovation has elevated the systems infrastructure that underpins the industry—a second component of the above three-aspects breakdown of financial innovation. This encompasses the seamless analysis of vast amounts of data, the power of big data, and the phenomenon of platformization. These systems enable quicker and more accurate decision-making, bringing sophisticated tools and analytical capabilities to both consumers and institutions. Retail investors are also using new investment vehicles, such as exchange-traded funds (ETFs) and cryptocurrency, which offer diversification and potential for higher returns. Furthermore, they facilitate internationalization, enabling cross-border transactions and investments, creating a globalized financial ecosystem. The third aspect of financial innovation is the outreach one, that is, the broadening of the audience participating in financial markets. The rise of fintech has empowered retail investors, allowing them to actively participate and seek opportunities by deploying financial innovation. This expansion of the investor base has unlocked diversification opportunities and the potential for higher returns, thereby reshaping the investment landscape.

Amid these opportunities, financial innovation also introduces new complexities. These complexities affect not only consumers, but also regulators tasked with overseeing this dynamic landscape. The necessity for consumer protection rules becomes thus evident. While financial innovation offers a myriad of opportunities in terms of efficiency gains, lower transaction costs, vanishing of intermediaries' rents, etc., it also poses significant challenges that demand robust consumer protection measures. The three abovementioned aspects of financial innovation also fence in three challenges originating from innovative financial products, advanced systems, and the expanding audience. The first pertains to the complexity for consumers and regulators. Innovative financial products, often driven by sophisticated technologies, can be challenging for both consumers and regulators to fully comprehend or utilize. As financial offerings become more intricate, ensuring that consumers make informed decisions and are safeguarded from risks becomes paramount. The second lies in the enhanced cross-border linkages and contagion risks. The increased connectivity brought about by advanced systems fosters cross-border linkages, potentially leading to contagion risks that transcend individual jurisdictions. Protecting consumers in this interconnected environment poses a significant challenge. The third challenge relates to the redress mechanisms, compliance requirements, and risk understanding, all of which have to evolve in order to meet the demands of digital finance. Regulators must strike a delicate balance between encouraging innovation and safeguarding consumers, all while ensuring that consumers have access to effective redress mechanisms when issues arise. In the ever-evolving landscape of financial innovation, the relevance and effectiveness of consumer protection measures hinge on a delicate balance between regulatory frameworks and their enforcement. It is important to recognize that this balance is not one-size-fits-all; it varies across countries and jurisdictions.

Financial innovation not only presents challenges, but also offers opportunities to enhance consumer protection. Innovative financial solutions can be harnessed to improve financial literacy and foster the development of consumer-friendly financial products. Moreover, to understand the interplay between financial innovation and consumer protection, one needs to also uncover the significance of collaboration. The synergy between financial institutions, regulators, and consumer advocacy groups emerges as a key element in the development of effective consumer protection measures that harmonize innovation and consumer welfare.

As we journey through the sections of this chapter ahead, we will examine how these two critical elements—financial innovation and consumer protection—can harmoniously coexist, whether they occasionally clash, and the microeconomic tools that can illuminate their intricate relationship. Moreover, we will emphasize the ongoing importance of research and monitoring in the realm of financial innovation, ensuring that regulatory frameworks remain not only relevant, but also effective, in addressing emerging—and often recurrent—challenges. In this complex, trial-and-error landscape of financial innovation, microeconomics provides invaluable theoretical foundations. It offers insights into market failures that can harm consumers while guiding regulatory interventions to mitigate these risks. Microeconomics complements other analytical perspectives presented in this edited volume, enhancing interdisciplinarity and complexity, necessary elements to understand the challenges societies face today, such as the crises of multilateralism, climate change, and democracy as discussed in the concept of permacrisis in the introduction of this volume. As we navigate this intricate terrain, we will gain a deeper understanding of the dynamics of consumer protection in the innovation economy. The next sections aim at exactly delving deeper into this enlightening journey to uncover the multifaceted relationship between financial innovation and consumer protection, drawing insights from microeconomics, policy intervention, global cooperation, and the fascinating realm of behavioral economics affecting digital finance.

Technological Innovations Challenging Consumer Protection Policies

This section brings together the core themes and insights garnered from our exploration of the intricate relationship between consumer protection and financial innovation. As we navigate this complex terrain, we aim to provide a detailed and insightful overview of how these two fundamental elements interact within the global financial landscape. Central to this discussion has been the understanding that consumer protection and financial innovation are not adversaries but rather symbiotic components of modern finance. This dynamic relationship is characterized by a delicate interplay where each element complements and reinforces the other, ultimately contributing to a more robust and inclusive financial ecosystem.

The advent of financial innovation, propelled by rapid technological advancements, has ushered in a profound transformation in the financial services industry. It has introduced a new era of digitally enabled products and services that have redefined the very essence of financial transactions. This innovation has transcended traditional boundaries, empowering individuals with unprecedented access to financial information, leveraging the potential of big data, and facilitating seamless cross-border transactions. In doing so, it has not only contributed to the democratization of the financial landscape, making it more accessible and affordable, but has also opened doors to diversified investment opportunities, potentially yielding higher returns for consumers.

At the heart of this intricate process lie the regulatory frameworks that orchestrate the harmonious coexistence of consumer protection and financial innovation. These frameworks serve as the guardians of equilibrium, responsible for fostering an environment where innovation can flourish while ensuring that consumers are shielded from potential risks and pitfalls. Regulatory bodies, spanning the globe, grapple with the formidable task of crafting regulations that strike a nuanced balance between nurturing innovation and safeguarding consumer interests. Achieving this equilibrium is a multifaceted challenge that demands a deep understanding of the ever-evolving financial landscape and the rapid pace of technological change.

Consumer protection emerges as a fundamental pillar of this equilibrium. It transcends its role as a mere legal requirement and assumes a central ethical and economic significance. Effective consumer protection is the bedrock upon which trust in financial markets is built. It is the linchpin that encourages wider participation and, ultimately, contributes to the overall stability and sustainability of the financial ecosystem.

A recurring motif that has threaded its way through our exploration is the indispensable role of collaboration. Safeguarding consumers and nurturing financial innovation is a multifaceted endeavor that cannot be borne by regulatory bodies alone. Rather, it necessitates a harmonized effort that unites regulators, financial institutions, consumer advocacy groups, and the consumers themselves. This collaborative approach is paramount for the development and implementation of effective consumer protection measures that can adapt and evolve in tandem with the ever-shifting landscape of financial innovation. It fosters an environment where best practices can be shared, vulnerabilities can be identified and addressed collectively, and innovations can be harnessed for the betterment of consumers.

To better illustrate the nature of innovation in its core dimension—that of constructive destruction—it is fitting to invoke the wisdom of Joseph Schumpeter, the eminent economist who would adopt the characterization of innovation as a process of "trial and error and error and error." This perspective underscores the inherent nature of innovation as an iterative journey, one marked by experimentation, adaptation, and occasional setbacks. It serves as a poignant reminder of the importance of designing financial products and services that are grounded in principles of transparency, accessibility, and inclusivity. While innovation propels us forward, it must always be tempered by a steadfast commitment to consumer well-being and a democratic society.

The Importance of Regulatory Frameworks

The foundation of consumer protection within the innovation economy lies in robust regulatory frameworks. These frameworks serve as the cornerstone for ensuring that financial innovations benefit consumers while mitigating risks. In this section, we will explore the pivotal role played by regulatory frameworks. Firstly, they ensure fair and transparent practices for market participants. Regulatory frameworks set the rules of the game for financial institutions and fintech companies. By establishing clear guidelines, they ensure that businesses operate fairly and transparently. This includes regulations related to fee disclosure, product terms, and risk communication. Secondly, a primary objective of regulatory frameworks is to maintain market integrity. This entails preventing market manipulation, fraud, and other illicit activities that could harm consumers. Regulations are designed to deter unethical behavior and hold wrongdoers accountable. Thirdly, they boost investor confidence, which is key to addressing market information asymmetries. Consumer protection extends to investors who participate in the financial markets. Regulatory frameworks provide a sense of security to investors, assuring them that their investments are made in an environment governed by rules that reduce the likelihood of exploitation or misconduct. Lastly, regulatory frameworks establish mechanisms for consumer redress. In cases of disputes or grievances, consumers have a structured path to seek resolution, ensuring that their rights are upheld. This helps maintain trust in the financial system, which becomes particularly crucial in times of structural changes such as those brought about by financial innovation.

Evolving Regulatory Approaches and the Role of International Bodies

The complexity and dynamism of the innovation economy have prompted regulators to adapt their approaches to consumer protection. The literature distinguishes two main ways in which regulatory approaches have evolved, the rule-based and the principle-based approach. Traditional rule-based regulation prescribes specific requirements that financial institutions must follow. In contrast, principle-based regulation sets out broader principles and guidelines, allowing for more flexibility and adaptability in the face of rapidly changing technology. Regulators are increasingly embracing principle-based approaches to accommodate innovation.

Uncertainties about the multiple outcomes that new regulation may cause in the financial markets domain have rendered regulation an object of testing. While laboratory-like testing environments are generally hardly reproduced in social sciences and policymaking, new techniques have enabled bodies drafting new regulation to adjust it in the aftermath of controlled tests. As the most typical example, regulatory sandboxes are employed tools where fintech startups can test their innovations in controlled environments under regulatory supervision. This approach allows startups to experiment and iterate while regulators monitor their activities closely. Regulatory sandboxes strike a balance between fostering innovation and safeguarding consumers.

Regtech solutions—that is, regulatory technology—are emerging to help both financial institutions and regulators keep pace with technological advancements. These solutions leverage automation, data analytics, and artificial intelligence to monitor compliance in real time, reducing the regulatory burden and enhancing consumer protection. Under these circumstances, collaboration among regulatory bodies from different sectors has also become crucial. The convergence of industries, such as finance and technology, necessitates coordinated efforts to regulate effectively and protect market participants against new forms of threats. Regulators are increasingly working together to address the challenges posed by digital finance. As the boundaries between sectors become more blur, financial market participants are not only faced with known forms of threats that emerge from market instability, liquidity risks, and other forms of financial risks. In parallel, they need to be protected from digital security issues, cybersecurity attacks, phishing and scam attempts, and other forms of cybersecurity threats that the increased level of connectivity engenders.

Consumer protection in the innovation economy often extends beyond national borders. International bodies play a vital role in harmonizing standards and fostering cooperation among nations. The significance of these international entities spans across areas of regulatory standardization, information sharing, cross-border dispute resolution, and financial inclusion. In recent years, international bodies like the Financial Stability Board (FSB) and the International Organization of Securities Commissions (IOSCO) work toward standardizing regulations across jurisdictions. This standardization ensures that consumers receive consistent levels of protection, regardless of where they engage in financial activities. In parallel, sharing information and best practices at the international level is essential. It helps regulators and industry stakeholders gain insights into emerging risks and effective consumer protection measures. Collaborative efforts enable the development of global strategies to address common challenges. As consumers increasingly access financial services from international providers, mechanisms for cross-border dispute resolution become critical. International bodies work on frameworks that enable consumers to seek redress even when dealing with foreign financial institutions. International cooperation can promote financial inclusion by ensuring that innovative financial services are accessible to consumers worldwide. This is particularly vital for consumers in developing economies, where access to traditional financial services may be limited.[1]

Balancing Innovation and Consumer Protection

One of the central challenges in regulating the innovation economy is striking the right balance between fostering innovation and protecting consumers. A number of complexities stand in the way of achieving this equilibrium. Fostering innovation in financial services is essential for economic growth and expanding access to financial products. Regulatory frameworks must provide a conducive environment for innovators to thrive, which, in turn, benefits consumers through increased choice and lower costs. While innovation offers substantial benefits, it also introduces new risks. Consumer protection measures must evolve to address these risks effectively. Regulators face the challenge of identifying and mitigating risks without stifling innovation. Regulatory frameworks must be adaptable to keep pace with the rapid rate of technological change. This adaptability involves continuous monitoring of the financial landscape, learning from emerging threats, and updating regulations

[1] See Chap. 20 discussing the possible cooperation between the EU and Latin America countries, and Chap. 16 for further relevant data on Latin America, Asia, and Africa.

accordingly. Empowering consumers with knowledge and awareness is a critical aspect of achieving the balance between innovation and protection. Informed consumers are better equipped to navigate the evolving financial landscape and make sound financial decisions.

To illustrate the interlinked above-discussed concepts of regulation and innovation in financial markets, the relevant literature often focuses upon case studies and regulatory successes from different regions and sectors. These examples shed light on how effective regulatory frameworks can foster innovation while safeguarding consumers. Often quoted in the literature, the Financial Conduct Authority (FCA) in the United Kingdom established a regulatory sandbox that has nurtured numerous fintech innovations. It provides a controlled environment for startups to test their products, receive feedback, and refine their offerings while ensuring consumer protection. In Europe, the General Data Protection Regulation (GDPR) has set a global standard for data privacy and protection. It empowers consumers with greater control over their personal data while imposing strict penalties on companies that fail to comply. The GDPR demonstrates the importance of robust data protection regulations in the digital age.

Case studies of regulatory approaches in various countries highlight the complexity of balancing innovation and protection in the crypto space. In fact, regulators worldwide have responded differently to the rise of cryptocurrencies by adopting different regulatory responses.[2] Some have embraced them as innovative financial assets, while others have imposed strict regulations to mitigate risks. China's central bank digital currency, known as the Registration counting for EU Survey Workshop (DCEP), represents a unique case study in the adoption of digital currencies at the national level. The regulatory framework surrounding DCEP emphasizes consumer protection, including safeguards against fraud and misuse.

The above sections underscore the critical role of regulatory frameworks in shaping consumer protection within the innovation economy. It emphasizes the need for adaptable, principle-based regulations that strike a balance between encouraging innovation and mitigating risks. International cooperation and information sharing, as well as case studies of regulatory successes, provide valuable insights into effective consumer protection strategies in the rapidly evolving financial landscape.

Microeconomic and Behavioral Economics Foundations of Consumer Protection in the Innovation Economy

Microeconomics provides the theoretical foundation and a powerful tool for understanding how market failures can lead to consumer harm and how regulatory intervention can help mitigate these risks. One key concept in microeconomics relevant

[2] See also Chaps. 13, 14, and 15 for more on this.

to consumer protection is asymmetric information. This occurs when one party in a transaction has more information than the other party. In the context of financial innovation, financial service providers may often possess more information about the risks and benefits of a new product or service than consumers do. This can lead to consumers making poor decisions that harm their financial well-being. A second concept applicable to the analysis of the intersection between consumer protection and financial innovation is that of welfare economics. Financial innovation can create new products and services that have the potential to improve consumer welfare by increasing choice, lowering costs, and enhancing access to financial services. However, it can also lead to new risks and challenges, such as increased complexity, opacity, and potential for exploitation. Another key concept in microeconomics relevant to consumer protection is market power. In some cases, financial service providers may have significant market power and use this dominant position, which can lead to harm to consumers. For example, if a financial service provider is the only provider of a particular product or service, it may be able to charge high prices or offer poor quality without fear of losing customers.

Overall, microeconomics provides a useful framework for understanding the importance of consumer protection in the context of financial innovation. By addressing issues such as asymmetric information, capturing of consumer surplus and market power, regulatory agencies can help ensure that consumers are protected from harm and can benefit from the innovative products and services that financial service providers offer.

In parallel, literature acknowledges a range of psychological and cognitive factors that also influence consumers' financial decisions and their ability to protect themselves effectively. The behavioral challenges in digital finance encompass these factors, which are increasingly incorporated into modern consumer and investor protection policies (UK FCA, 2013). Besides analyzing microeconomic aspects of consumer protection, the following sections explore the key policy aspects related to behavioral challenges by venturing into the realm of behavioral economics and cognitive aspects that shape consumer behavior within the digital finance landscape.

Understanding how psychological, social, and emotional factors influence economic decision-making is crucial in comprehending the challenges and opportunities within this rapidly evolving domain. It also provides researchers and policymakers with powerful tools to interpret economic behaviors typically considered unorthodox, complex, and intertwined decisions and "irrational" reactions of markets and economic agents. Given that consumer behavior in the digital finance era is not solely driven by rational decision-making, but also largely influenced by cognitive biases and social dynamics, recognizing and addressing these aspects is pivotal in enhancing consumer protection.

Microeconomic Challenges Requiring Consumer Protection Policy Intervention

Market asymmetry challenges in the digital finance environment are reflected in various forms. The rising number of retail investors participating in financial transactions through digital means also underlines the imperative for better, faster, and targeted information toward them, while ensuring the existence and adequacy of channels for complaints and redress mechanisms. This section sheds light on some key economic challenges in this domain.

Lack of Financial Literacy One of the fundamental challenges urging for consumer protection in digital finance is the widespread lack of financial literacy among consumers. Financial literacy, or the lack thereof, stands as a significant behavioral challenge in the digital finance era. Many consumers find themselves navigating complex financial products and services without a solid understanding of how these innovations work. They often lack the knowledge and understanding of how digital finance works, including the intricacies of financial products and services. This lack of knowledge leads to poor decision-making and renders individuals vulnerable to scams and frauds.

The digital finance landscape is filled with intricate investment platforms, robo-advisors, cryptocurrencies, and peer-to-peer lending platforms. While these innovations offer unprecedented opportunities, they also demand a certain level of financial acumen to navigate safely. Without adequate financial education, consumers may make uninformed choices that adversely impact their financial well-being.

Overindebtedness Digital finance has made accessing credit easier than ever before. While this is undoubtedly advantageous, it comes with the potential pitfall of overindebtedness. This seemingly straightforward ease of access to credit through digital finance channels can lead to overindebtedness, particularly among those who do not fully understand the terms and conditions of loans or credit products. As a result, consumers who do not fully grasp the terms and conditions of loans or credit products may find themselves accumulating unsustainable levels of debt.

The allure of quick and easy credit can be enticing, especially when facilitated by digital platforms. However, the ease of access may lead to impulsive borrowing without a clear understanding of the long-term consequences. Protecting consumers from overindebtedness is a paramount concern in the digital finance space.

Limited Access to Dispute Resolution Mechanisms Digital finance often transcends national borders, making it challenging for consumers to seek recourse when they encounter problems or disputes arise with financial service providers. Cross-border transactions and investments can blur the lines of jurisdiction, leaving consumers uncertain about where to turn when problems occur.

Consumers in the digital era demand to have access to effective dispute resolution mechanisms, irrespective of their geographical location. Ensuring that these mechanisms can address issues in a cross-border context is vital for upholding consumer rights and maintaining trust in digital financial services.

Limited Transparency Complexity and opacity often shroud digital financial products and services. The technical nature of these innovations can make it difficult for consumers to decipher the fees, charges, or terms associated with the products they are using. The lack of transparency can lead to consumer confusion and potentially harmful financial decisions.

Transparency is essential to building trust in the digital finance ecosystem. Consumers must have access to clear and understandable information about the financial products and services they engage with. Transparent pricing, terms, and conditions empower consumers to make informed decisions and protect themselves from hidden costs.

Cybersecurity and Data Privacy Risks The collection and storage of sensitive information in digital finance introduce cybersecurity and data privacy challenges. Consumers may not fully grasp the potential risks and vulnerabilities associated with these services. Digital finance involves the collection and storage of sensitive information, including personal and financial data. With the increasing prevalence of cyberattacks and data breaches, consumers face heightened risks related to the security and privacy of their data.

Cybersecurity breaches can have devastating consequences, leading to identity theft, financial loss, and reputational damage. Protecting consumers from these risks is a multifaceted challenge that encompasses robust cybersecurity measures, stringent data privacy regulations, and consumer education on safe online practices.

Behavioral Economics and Cognitive Aspects of Digital Finance

Exploring the intricate intersection of human behavior and financial decision-making in the digital age, researchers and policymakers have delved into the fascinating realm where psychology meets financial technology (see Hirschleifer, 2001; OSC, 2017; ASIC, 2016, etc.). This dynamic field unveils how our cognitive biases and emotions shape our financial choices in an increasingly digitized world. By deploying the theoretical tools of behavioral science, this section looks into the cognitive aspects that influence consumer behavior in the context of digital finance.

Limited Attention In the digital age, information overload can lead to consumers overlooking critical information, such as terms and conditions or risks associated with financial products. Consumers often fail to pay adequate attention to important financial details, leading to suboptimal decisions.

Loss Aversion Behavioral economics demonstrates that consumers tend to be more sensitive to losses than gains. By making them more sensitive to losses than gains, this psychological bias can make consumers cautious or risk-averse when engaging in digital finance activities. Digital financial services are often designed to prioritize and emphasize potential gains. To encourage responsible financial decisions, potential gains and potential losses should be exhibited in tandem.

Overconfidence When using digital financial services, some consumers overestimate their knowledge or ability to navigate their complexity, leading to overconfidence. This overconfidence can result in risky behavior and poor decision-making. The complex navigation of lack of user-friendly interfaces of digital financial services, along with the limited access to educational resources, can help lead to overconfidence and promote uninformed decision-making.

Present Bias A common behavioral pattern that can lead to irrational financial decision-making, present bias is the tendency for consumers to prioritize immediate gratification over long-term benefits. In digital finance, this bias can lead to impulsive decisions or excessive consumption.

Social Influence Consumers are influenced by the behavior and opinions of others, including peers, family, and social networks. This social influence can lead consumers to follow trends, even if those trends are not in their best financial interest. Influencers who are paid by financial service providers in order to serve as role models or direct retail investors toward specific products or categories or products are increasingly active in the era of social media. They are generally known are finfluencers. Finfluencers may simultaneously spread both opportunities and risks.

Policy Intervention Through the Lenses of Micro and Behavioral Economics

Addressing these policy challenges in the digital finance landscape necessitates a multifaceted approach that involves policymakers, regulatory bodies, industry players, and consumer advocacy groups. To address information asymmetry challenges, regulatory intervention can take several forms. Disclosure requirements can help ensure that consumers have access to information about the risks and benefits of a financial product or service.[3] Consumer education programs can also help consumers better understand the risks and benefits of financial innovation (IOSCO & OECD, 2018). In addition, regulatory agencies can require that financial service providers follow certain guidelines or standards to ensure that products and services are safe and reliable.

[3] However, as argued by North (2009), disclosure and information dissemination may not be sufficient for comprehensive investor protection, regardless of how well-designed or well-timed is their delivery.

To address issues of market power, regulatory agencies may impose price controls, forbid mergers and acquisitions that may lead to monopolistic or oligopolistic market structures or require financial service providers to offer certain quality standards. In addition, competition policy can help promote competition in the financial services industry, which can help reduce market power and ensure that consumers have access to a wide range of products and services at competitive prices. The cooperation between traditionally separated regulatory authorities becomes in light of these developments more important than ever.

Being inherent in digital finance and having far-reaching implications for consumer protection policy, understanding and addressing the behavioral challenges that are inherent in digital finance are essential for effective consumer protection. Policymakers, regulators, industry participants, and educators must work collaboratively to promote financial literacy, ensure responsible lending practices, establish robust dispute resolution mechanisms, enhance transparency, and safeguard consumer data from online frauds and cyberattacks. Leveraging insights from behavioral economics can help design digital financial services that align with the cognitive tendencies of consumers, fostering responsible financial behavior in the digital era.

Policy Responses to Address Microeconomic Challenges

Policy measures must prioritize consumer protection in each of the abovementioned areas of microeconomic inefficiencies or market failures along the following lines:

Financial Literacy Initiatives To address this challenge, policymakers must prioritize financial education initiatives. These may include public awareness campaigns, school curriculum enhancements, educational programs, online resources, partnerships with educational institutions, and online resources that empower consumers to make informed financial decisions. Policymakers should promote financial literacy initiatives that equip consumers with the knowledge and skills needed to navigate digital finance safely.

Responsible Lending Practices To combat over-indebtedness, regulators can enforce responsible lending practices within the digital finance sector. This could include imposing limits on borrowing, conducting thorough credit assessments, and ensuring that loan terms are transparent and fair. Policymakers must implement responsible lending practices and ensure that consumers receive clear and comprehensible information about the risks associated with borrowing. Additionally, regulations have the discretion to cap interest rates or limit the extension of credit to high-risk individuals.

Cross-Border Dispute Resolution Policymakers should explore international cooperation frameworks for cross-border dispute resolution. This may involve agreements that enable consumers to seek remedies even when dealing with foreign financial institutions. Collaborative efforts between regulatory authorities, industry stakeholders, and international organizations are essential to address cross-border dispute resolution challenges. Mechanisms for resolving disputes that transcend jurisdictional boundaries must be developed and implemented. Additionally, promoting standardized complaint-handling processes can enhance consumer protection.

Enhanced Transparency Regulatory bodies should mandate enhanced transparency in digital financial products and services. This entails clear and standardized disclosure of fees, charges, and terms to empower consumers to make informed decisions. Standardized formats for presenting this information can simplify comparisons between products. Additionally, regulatory oversight should ensure that financial institutions communicate product terms in plain language that consumers can easily comprehend.

Cybersecurity and Data Privacy Regulations Policymakers must enact robust data protection regulations that safeguard consumers' personal and financial information. Robust cybersecurity and data privacy regulations must be established and enforced to protect consumer data in the digital finance space. This includes measures to prevent data breaches and protocols for notifying affected individuals in the event of a breach. Penalties for data breaches and unauthorized access should serve as deterrents. In parallel, consumer education campaigns can also raise awareness about cybersecurity best practices.

Policy Responses to Address Behavioral Biases

In the realm of behavioral economics, crafting effective policy responses is a critical endeavor. Having investigated how cognitive biases influence decision-making, this section outlines the principles upon which policymakers can design interventions to mitigate these biases. Reflecting the behavioral challenges described above, the following paragraphs delve into the strategies and solutions that bridge the gap between human nature and effective governance of digital finance.

Attention to Important Information Regulatory frameworks can mandate concise and visually prominent disclosures to capture consumers' attention effectively. Designing user interfaces and financial products that prioritize essential information can mitigate this challenge. Moreover, the use of behavioral nudges, such as reminders or alerts, can encourage consumers to review and consider essential information before making decisions.

Adding Responsibility and Transparency in Loss Aversion Policymakers can design regulations that emphasize risk disclosure to counteract loss aversion. By highlighting potential losses or negative consequences, consumers may be more inclined to evaluate risks more objectively. Mandatory disclosure of comparative or absolute exhibition of incurred losses, potential loss of entire investments or examples of past performance aggregate loss statistics can help investors understand through illustrations their potential wins or losses from new forms of financial services.

Tackling Overconfidence Through Suitability Requirements Consumer protection policies should include measures that address investors' overconfidence, such as mandatory suitability assessments for complex financial products. Regulators can also require financial institutions to provide clear risk disclosures to counteract overconfidence. Moreover, certain categories of products may be banned, either horizontally, or through product intervention measures that restrict their sale and distribution to specific categories of investors.

Long-Term Investment Horizons Against Present Biases Policymakers can encourage the development of financial planning tools and apps that promote long-term financial goals. Digital finance platforms can leverage behavioral insights to encourage saving and investment for the future. Additionally, regulations may limit the accessibility of high-cost, short-term credit products to mitigate the negative effects of present bias. This is expected to yield positive repercussions, both in terms of financial well-being, as well as in the macroeconomic aspects of financial stability.

Leveraging Social Influence for Financial Education Socially responsible financial behavior can be encouraged through social networks and peer-to-peer interactions within digital finance platforms. Consumer protection policies can incorporate measures that promote financial literacy and critical thinking to counteract undue social influence. Providing consumers with the skills to evaluate financial decisions independently can mitigate the impact of peer pressure (see AFM, 2016; AMF, 2016; Kawanishi & Hashinaga, 2016, etc.).

Future Horizons in Consumer Protection and Financial Innovation

The intricate and harmonious symphony between consumer protection and financial innovation reflects the two facets that are not opposing forces, but rather interdependent elements. When in balance, they create a financial ecosystem that needs to be resilient, efficient, and equitable. Regulatory frameworks, guided by principles of transparency and inclusivity, are the linchpin of this delicate equilibrium. Collaboration among diverse stakeholders emerges as the cornerstone of success, enabling the crafting of consumer protection measures that evolve in step with the dynamic financial landscape.

This chapter argues that as we forge ahead into an era where financial innovation continues to reshape our world and the allocation of resources, we must do so with the spirit of Schumpeterian innovation, embracing progress while remaining vigilant in our commitment to safeguarding consumers. By doing so, we ensure that the benefits of financial innovation are shared widely, and the financial landscape continues to evolve in a manner that serves the interests of all, fostering a future where innovation and consumer protection walk hand in hand.

Looking forward and turning our gaze toward the future, the realms of consumer protection and financial innovation are destined to further co-evolve hand in hand. The path ahead is filled with exciting possibilities, new challenges, and an imperative to adapt and innovate in response to an ever-changing financial landscape. Technological advancements will effortlessly drive change; change will incur both opportunities and risks, and policymakers will need to remain vigilant in order to take into consideration the increased interdependencies that embed the human element into policy tools. Remaining relevant in all these areas requires ongoing monitoring and the strategic foresight skills in the present in order to envisage and better prepare our policy systems to cope with upcoming and arising challenges.

Technological Advancements: The Engine of Change

The future of consumer protection and financial innovation is inextricably linked to the trajectory of technological advancements. Emerging technologies, such as blockchain, artificial intelligence, and quantum computing, hold the promise of revolutionizing financial services. Blockchain, with its immutable ledger and smart contracts, has the potential to enhance transparency and security in transactions. Artificial intelligence, fueled by machine learning algorithms, can analyze vast datasets to provide personalized financial advice and detect fraudulent activities. Quantum computing, although in its infancy, may enable rapid, complex calculations that could reshape risk modeling and portfolio optimization. As these technologies mature, regulatory bodies and industry players must grapple with the challenges and opportunities they present. The delicate balance between fostering innovation and safeguarding consumers becomes more intricate as financial services become increasingly reliant on cutting-edge technology. Striking the right regulatory chords to harness the benefits of these innovations while mitigating risks will be paramount.

Technological and Ethical Challenges Amidst Digital Financial Globalization

The globalization of financial markets is an inexorable force that will continue to shape the landscape of consumer protection and financial innovation. Cross-border transactions and investments have become commonplace, thanks to the interconnectedness of the global economy. However, this globalization also introduces complexities in terms of regulatory harmonization, enforcement, and dispute resolution. Regulatory bodies worldwide face the formidable task of aligning their policies and standards to create a cohesive global framework. International collaboration, already a critical element in the realm of financial regulation, will need to evolve further. Bodies such as the European Supervisory Authorities (ESAs),[4] the Financial Stability Board (FSB), the International Organization of Securities Commissions (IOSCO), the Basel Committee on Banking Supervision, etc., will play pivotal roles in facilitating global cooperation. Moreover, the standard setting role of the EU in promoting the forefront of financial regulation incurs spillover effects in the form of standard setting and knowledge diffusion for other world regions.[5] This is becoming recognized in the relevant academic and policy literature as the "Brussels effect" (Bradford, 2020).

As financial services become increasingly digitized, the importance of data privacy and security cannot be overstated. The proliferation of personal and financial data necessitates robust safeguards to protect individuals from data breaches, identity theft, and unauthorized access. Regulatory frameworks, such as the General Data Protection Regulation (GDPR) in Europe, have set essential standards for data protection. However, as innovation in data analytics and artificial intelligence accelerates, ensuring that these frameworks remain effective and adaptable will be an ongoing challenge. Striking a balance between fostering innovation that leverages data and preserving individual privacy will be central to future regulatory discussions.

In parallel, and as technology continues to shape the financial landscape, ethical considerations become increasingly pertinent. Questions surrounding the ethical use of artificial intelligence, the responsible deployment of blockchain, and the equitable distribution of financial resources take center stage. Regulators and industry leaders must grapple with these ethical dilemmas to ensure that innovation benefits society as a whole. Frameworks for ethical AI, guidelines for blockchain

---

[4] The European Supervisory Authorities (ESAs) are three regulatory agencies established by the EU in 2010, to help facilitate the development and convergence of financial services regulation and supervision across the EU. The three agencies are the European Banking Authority (EBA), the European Insurance and Occupational Pensions Authority (EIOPA), and the European Securities and Markets Authority (ESMA).

[5] Including Latin America, as discussed in other chapters of this book.

governance, and principles for responsible lending are areas where industry standards are evolving. The advent of decentralized finance (DeFi) platforms, which operate outside traditional financial institutions, also poses unique ethical challenges, such as smart contract vulnerabilities and decentralized governance.

Innovative Policy Tools and the Human Element: Behavioral and Experimental Economics Enabling Financial Inclusion

In the quest for effective consumer protection and financial innovation, the human element cannot be overlooked. Behavioral economics, a field that explores how psychological, social, and emotional factors influence economic decision-making, holds the key to understanding consumer behavior in the digital age. Regulators and financial institutions are increasingly integrating behavioral insights into their strategies (OECD, 2017; European Commission, 2016; IOSCO, 2019). Personalized financial nudges, gamified financial education, and behavioral-driven product design are becoming common approaches to help consumers make informed decisions and avoid financial pitfalls.

To foster innovation while managing risk, regulatory sandboxes have emerged as a valuable tool. These controlled environments allow fintech firms to test their products and services with reduced regulatory burden. Regulatory bodies monitor these experiments closely, enabling them to understand the implications of emerging technologies without stifling innovation. The future will likely see an expansion of regulatory sandboxes, fostering an environment where experimentation can thrive while consumer protection remains a priority. Collaboration between regulators, industry participants, and consumer advocacy groups within these sandboxes can yield valuable insights and shape future regulatory frameworks.

Financial inclusion remains a global imperative, with millions of people still lacking access to basic financial services. The future of consumer protection and financial innovation must address this pressing issue. Fintech innovations, particularly in the realm of mobile banking and digital wallets, have made significant strides in increasing access to financial services in underserved regions. Regulators, in partnership with governments and private sector actors, must work toward creating an inclusive financial ecosystem. Initiatives like the World Bank's Universal Financial Access 2020 program seek to ensure that everyone has access to a transaction account and, by extension, a gateway to other financial services. Blockchain-based digital identities and mobile money platforms have the potential to bring financial services to remote and unbanked populations.

Ongoing Research and Monitoring in Financial Innovation

As the financial landscape evolves and technology advances, continuous assessment and adaptation are vital to ensure that regulatory frameworks remain relevant, effective, and capable of addressing emerging challenges. The elements that comprise the new financial landscape need to be at the epicenter of policy initiatives, while their simultaneous evolution is likely to determine the magnitude and direction of the financial innovation vector.

The Dynamic Nature of Financial Innovation Financial innovation is not a static phenomenon; rather, it embodies a dynamic and ever-evolving process. As new technologies emerge and consumer preferences shift, the financial industry responds with innovative products and services. Blockchain, cryptocurrencies, decentralized finance (DeFi), and artificial intelligence are just a few examples of technologies that have disrupted traditional financial models. To navigate this ever-changing landscape, regulatory bodies and market participants must engage in ongoing research to understand the implications of these innovations fully. Staying ahead of the curve requires vigilance and adaptability.

Regulatory Adaptation Regulatory bodies play a pivotal role in shaping the trajectory of financial innovation. However, the challenge lies in striking the right balance between fostering innovation and safeguarding consumers. The pace at which new technologies are introduced can sometimes outstrip the ability of regulatory frameworks to respond adequately. To address this, regulatory bodies must engage in continuous research to identify potential risks and assess the impact of new technologies. Regulatory sandboxes, pilot programs, and collaboration with industry stakeholders are mechanisms that enable regulators to monitor and adapt to emerging trends.

Risk Assessment and Mitigation One of the primary objectives of ongoing research is to promptly identify and assess risks associated with financial innovation. These risks can encompass a wide range of areas, including cybersecurity threats, data privacy concerns, market volatility, and consumer vulnerability. To mitigate these risks effectively, regulators need access to real-time data and insights. Collaboration with cybersecurity experts, data analysts, and risk management professionals becomes imperative. Proactive risk assessment allows for the development of targeted regulatory measures to protect both consumers and the stability of financial markets.

Consumer Protection and Empowerment Consumer protection remains a central pillar of financial regulation. Ongoing research in this domain focuses on understanding how financial innovations impact consumers. Do these innovations enhance financial inclusion, or do they pose risks of overindebtedness and predatory practices? Are consumers adequately informed about the products and services they engage with? Consumer empowerment is another critical facet. Research efforts aim to identify how consumers can make informed decisions in a rapidly evolving landscape. Financial education initiatives, digital literacy programs, and behavioral insights are leveraged to equip consumers with the knowledge and tools needed to navigate the complexities of the digital financial world.

Market Integrity and Fairness Maintaining market integrity and fairness is essential for fostering trust and confidence in financial markets. Ongoing research seeks to detect and address potential market manipulation, fraud, and unethical practices. With the rise of algorithmic trading, high-frequency trading, and decentralized platforms, monitoring market activities in real time becomes paramount. Regulators collaborate with market surveillance experts and data analytics firms to develop sophisticated tools for market monitoring. Artificial intelligence and machine learning algorithms are increasingly employed to detect irregularities and ensure that trading activities adhere to established rules and regulations.

International Collaboration and Information Sharing In an interconnected global financial system, international collaboration is indispensable. This holds true for distant regions with increasingly enhanced collaboration efforts. Regulatory bodies from different jurisdictions must work together to effectively address cross-border challenges. Ongoing research efforts facilitate the sharing of information, best practices, and lessons learned. Supranational organizations like the Financial Stability Board (FSB) and the International Organization of Securities Commissions (IOSCO) serve as platforms for global cooperation. These bodies conduct research, issue guidelines, and coordinate efforts to address systemic risks and ensure consistent regulatory standards across borders.

The Role of Academic and Industry Research Academic institutions and industry research play a vital role in advancing our understanding of financial innovation. Ongoing research projects conducted by universities, think tanks, and industry associations contribute valuable insights into the implications of financial innovation.[6] Regulatory bodies often collaborate with these research entities to access the latest findings and leverage academic expertise. This collaboration fosters an environment where evidence-based policymaking can thrive, leading to more effective regulatory frameworks.

Anticipating Future Challenges Ongoing research is not merely about addressing current issues, but also about anticipating future challenges. As financial innovation continues to accelerate, regulators and researchers must stay ahead of emerging trends. This proactive approach ensures that regulatory frameworks are agile and adaptable. The potential challenges on the horizon include quantum computing's impact on cryptography, the ethical implications of AI-driven decision-making, and

[6] One such project aspires to be the Jean Monnet Network "Crisis-Equity-Democracy for Europe and Latin America" in the context of which this edited volume is being published.

the evolution of decentralized finance. By staying vigilant and conducting foresight research, regulatory bodies can prepare for these challenges and make informed decisions.

Ongoing research and monitoring are the linchpins of effective consumer protection and financial innovation. As technology evolves and financial services become increasingly digital, the importance of continuous assessment cannot be overstated. Regulatory bodies, in partnership with academia and industry, must remain at the forefront of research to foster innovation while safeguarding the interests of consumers and maintaining the integrity of financial markets. The road ahead is dynamic and challenging, but with a commitment to evidence-driven regulation, it is a path that can lead to a more inclusive, secure, and innovative financial future.

Conclusion: A Dynamic Landscape

Financial innovation has revolutionized the financial services industry, making it easier and more convenient for consumers to access financial products and services. However, financial innovation has also introduced new risks and challenges for consumers, including complex financial products, cybersecurity threats, and predatory lending practices. In the context of the permacrisis discussion and the recent economic and geopolitical developments, this translates into enhanced financial interconnectedness and interdependencies, that bring along more contagion and consumer-related risks of transboundary nature.

To protect consumers, governments and regulatory bodies have introduced various consumer protection measures, such as mandatory disclosures, consumer education programs, and regulatory oversight of financial institutions. The effectiveness of consumer protection measures depends on the regulatory framework and the level of enforcement, which can vary across different countries and jurisdictions. Financial innovation also presents opportunities for enhancing consumer protection, such as the use of fintech solutions to improve financial literacy and the development of new consumer-friendly financial products. Collaboration between financial institutions, regulators, and consumer advocacy groups can facilitate the development of effective consumer protection measures that balance innovation and consumer welfare. Ongoing research and monitoring of financial innovation and consumer protection are necessary to ensure that regulatory frameworks remain relevant and effective in addressing emerging risks and challenges.

The future of consumer protection and financial innovation is a dynamic and ever-evolving landscape. Technological advancements, globalization, data privacy, financial inclusion, ethics, behavioral economics, and regulatory experimentation are all facets of this intricate tapestry. Regulators, industry participants, and stakeholders must approach this future with adaptability, collaboration, and a shared commitment to consumer well-being. The harmonious coexistence between consumer protection and financial innovation, as elucidated in this exploration, will continue to evolve, guided by the enduring principles of transparency, accessibility, and inclusivity. Each crisis in the path of the history will inevitably have repercussions that will threaten the balance and tilt it in one direction or the other. What is important is that each of these crises creates the necessary buffers for the system to restore its original resilience, with a human-centric objective of rendering finance a tool for innovative and inclusive economies.

Recent policy developments underscore the role of regulators, industry stakeholders, and consumers themselves in ensuring a secure and prosperous financial future. In the innovation economy, financial innovation holds great promise for expanding access, reducing costs, and increasing choice. However, this progress must go hand in hand with robust consumer protection measures to safeguard individuals from harm and ensure that the benefits of innovation are distributed broadly and equitably. Consumer protection within the innovation economy is an ongoing endeavor that requires adaptability, collaboration, and a deep understanding of both economic principles and behavioral dynamics. By addressing information asymmetry, promoting financial literacy, embracing technology, and fostering global cooperation, we can pave the way for a more secure and inclusive financial future for all.

References

AFM. (2016). *AFM and the application of behavioural insights*. Dutch Authority for the Financial Markets. https://bit.ly/2OhlcU2

AMF. (2016, June 20). *Financial education in the digital era: What challenges for Savings?* Scientific Advisory Board Conference of the Autorité des marchés financiers. Programme and conference papers available at, https://bit.ly/2pIpg10

ASIC. (2016). *ASIC and behavioural economics: Regulating for real people*. Australia Securities and Investments Commission. https://bit.ly/2sHwwfF

Bradford, A. (2020). The Brussels effect: How the European Union rules the world. *Faculty Books*. 232. https://scholarship.law.columbia.edu/books/232

European Commission. (2016). *Behavioural insights applied to policy*. https://bit.ly/1OrU8VO

Hirschleifer, D. A. (2001). Investor psychology and asset pricing. *Journal of Finance, 1533*(61).

IOSCO. (2019). *The application of behavioural insights to retail investor protection* (Final Report FR05/2019)

IOSCO & OECD. (2018). *The application of behavioural insights to financial literacy and investor education programs and initiatives*. https://bit.ly/2JrijOh

Kawanishi, S., & Hashinaga, M. (2016). *Application of behavioral economics to financial education: Shift in focus from behavioral bias to mindset bias* (JFSA Financial Research Center, Discussion Paper 2015-3). https://bit.ly/2Pod6pl

North, G. (2009). Efficiency, fairness & irrationality: Incompatible or complementary? *Banking & Finance Law Review, 311*(24).

OECD. (2017). *Behavioural insights and public policy: Lessons from around the world*. https://bit.ly/2JyTJ9X

OSC. (2017). *Behavioural insights: Key concepts, applications and regulatory considerations* (OSC Staff Notice 11-778). http://bit.ly/2ftNrP7

UK FCA. (2013, April). *Applying behavioural economics at the financial conduct authority*. (Occasional Paper No. 1). https://bit.ly/2xmvOXt

Part V
Learning from the Past and Looking to the Future

Chapter 18
Climate Crisis: Systemic Aspects of De-Carbonization and Macro-financial Requirements

Christian Ghymers

Contents

C. Ghymers (✉)
Interdisciplinary Institute for the Relations between Europe, Latin America and the Caribbean (IRELAC), Bruxelles, Belgium

D. Katsikas et al. (eds.), *Finance, Growth and Democracy: Connections and Challenges in Europe and Latin America in the Era of Permacrisis*, United Nations University Series on Regionalism 33, https://doi.org/10.1007/978-3-031-68475-3_18

Introduction

As developed in this Monnet Network, the global economy is trapped in the so-called "permacrisis," which means that a permanent state of crisis has been established because any given crisis in one of the components of the economic system engenders a crisis in all the others, making any solution more complex and costly. Nevertheless, since the other face of the permacrisis is a systemic crisis, the interconnections and causal links between the issues should also mean that cumulative causalities could be reversed as vicious circles could be turned into virtuous circles. Would it be naively optimistic to imagine the permacrisis being turned into a "perma-exit-crisis process"? Paradoxically, being deeply pessimistic about climate change might provoke such a reversal in the present chain of causalities of permacrisis because it is about to become a hierarchy of crisis, relying upon the irreversible one—climate change—which will force radical systemic changes anyway to prevent humankind extinction. Facing such a binary option, the permacrisis should inevitably trigger a rational survival reaction. Therefore, the permacrisis has the potential to go back to the original meaning of a crisis: "*when an event shakes the status quo, forcing us to consider new options for action*," that is, systemic changes. This reversed causality could be triggered by the apocalyptic gravity of climate change, whose solution would only be possible by solving the concatenation of the other crises. There is a case for considering that, as far as a growing consensus does exist for tackling the climate crisis—the worst threat to the welfare and survival of our democratic societies—the implementation of an effective de-carbonization would tackle most of the other systemic issues, solving in turn the main other crises in the global economy. Indeed, for making de-carbonization on time, multilateral cooperation is essential for focusing on radical changes in relative prices of fossil energies (carbon price increases), on the financing gap of Emerging and Developing Economies (EMDEs), therefore on tackling the asymmetric IMS, in turn, correcting the excessive yield in pure financial activities versus the yield in real investments, leading so to deal with the underdevelopment and the growing inequality in incomes and their resulting waves of populism. Such a rosy scenario is bound to emerge from the darkest scenario of exponential global warming.

After decades of procrastination, the degree of awareness of the risks posed by climate change has recently increased, and with it, the issue has finally become the subject of political concerns. However, implementation plans and funding are not only generally lagging but wrongly designed, giving the impression that changes would be manageable with minor costs. Due to this double policy mistake, it is already clear that the Paris Agreement objective of a 1.5-degree increase will not be respected, implying huge additional costs, making realistic the darkest scenario of a disorderly transition obliging to radical survival decisions. IMF acknowledges that current nationally determined contributions (NDCs) "*would only reduce emissions by about 12 per cent by 2030 compared with 2019. This is less than half of the emissions cuts needed for 2 °C and less than a quarter of the emissions cuts needed for 1.5 °C*" (Black et al., 2023).

Considering the huge amounts required by global de-carbonization and the important disparities across economies, this chapter assesses the capacity of the current International Financial System to efficiently close the estimated financing gaps, taking into consideration the structural handicaps of less developed economies. The "*Network for Greening the Financial System*[1]" (NGFS) recently concludes: "*... the risk of a lack of external financing from advanced economies (AEs) and local circumstances in emerging markets and developing economies (EMDEs) and low-income countries (LICs)* [is] *limiting the ability to transition globally in a time-line fashion*" (NGFS, 2023).

De-Carbonization as Global Systemic Change

The Evolution of Disavowal: From Climate Skepticism to "Greenwishing"

The disavowal observed up to recently has shifted from climate scepticism to a dominant belief that a combination of technologies, higher prices for carbon, and the dynamism of private finance could solve this issue smoothly and automatically with only minor macroeconomic costs. This position relies upon most econometric models and the so-called integrated assessment models (IAMs), which are especially shaped for estimating the social cost of carbon and the total negative externalities of climate change that are not captured by conventional markets.

The usefulness of the existing models for policymaking should be questioned because they are exposed to significant risks. The main reason is their high sensitivity to the precise specifications of the models, which make their results too uncertain in policymaking for tackling such an irreversible phenomenon and its resulting extreme risk for humankind. As underlined by Nicholas Stern (2022), the abusive use of IAMs in the United States led it to "*suggest relatively low levels for carbon taxes. And they have been used to argue that policy on climate change should be overwhelmingly dominated by carbon pricing.*" While carbon pricing is a necessary tool for de-carbonization, it is far from being sufficient. The reason is that, faced with extreme risks—as is the case with irreversible climate changes—financial markets and current economic models are unable to assess them properly ex ante. This is clearly shown by economic history and is formally demonstrated by Weitzam's "Dismal Theorem."[2] Weitzam (2009) explains the specific uncertainties in climate economics due to nonlinear evolutions (tipping points), implying that no market mechanism can induce rational behavior; for systemic reasons, markets are unable

[1] NGFS is a group of Central Banks and Supervisors willing to contribute to the development of environment and climate risk management in the financial sector. https://www.ngfs.net/en/liste-chronologique/ngfs-publications

[2] This theorem explains that the uncertainty of certain parameters—like climate sensitivity—associated with high damage functions increases the risk and therefore the precautionary effect. The Dismal Theorem says "*in a stochastic universe where the probability that the destruction of capital increases by an order faster than the net value produced, the social discount rate tends towards a negative one so that the discount factor tends to infinity*".

to assess the effective yields of cutting CO_2 emissions on time. Therefore, a generalized precautionary principle must be applied when facing a situation with exposure to a potentially unlimited risk. The required higher precautionary savings for facing extreme risks in conditions of uncertainty (Drèze, 1990) is not yet adequately incorporated in the existing models as they do not result from behavioral parameters but from policy measures.

In addition, de-carbonization implies deep structural changes because energy is not a standard input but a fundamental production factor (carbon) affecting the whole output and consumption, as well as because most of the current parameters are outdated. It means that a lot of nonlinear complex impacts will be difficult to capture without sufficient data, and for which existing macroeconomic parameters risk underestimating. Nonlinearities also result from interdependencies between climate risks and macro-financial developments. Furthermore, disparities and specificities across countries need to be tackled. To adapt its country programs to de-carbonization, IMF (Black et al., 2023) launched promising but time-consuming research in this direction:

> New tools are required to assist policy-makers in designing, assessing, and implementing reforms to accelerate a 'just transition'. Designing and implementing effective and sustained climate mitigation policies requires quantitative, evidence-based analysis, with country-level assessments of their impacts. This includes impacts on the energy system (supply, demand, and prices); CO_2 and other GHG emissions; revenues from existing and new energy taxes; economic output; as well as on household and industry incidence. It requires an assessment of the trade-offs among instruments including carbon taxes, emissions trading systems (ETSs), electricity or individual fuel taxes, emission rate and energy efficiency regulations, feebates, renewables subsidies, public investments, and other policies. However, no tool has previously allowed for such estimation with near comprehensive country coverage.

Economies will also be impacted differently by global interlinkages and international spillovers, which will add a further layer of complexity. Therefore, there is a risk of giving policymakers and citizens the illusion of scientific results from some scenarios, in particular by showing small costs of de-carbonization that would be easily compensated thanks to the dynamism of market mechanisms. The by-product of this illusion is the undermining of climate urgency and gravity through the fact that the collective awareness of the need for and feasibility of a transition would consequently be considered as being solved by existing technologies whose implementation would be automatic. This attitude was recently named "greenwishing[3]", that is, the collective illusion that there are solutions at hand that will be implemented later. We consider that this optimistic view reflects an undervaluation of the uncertainty that will affect financial markets and yields. These results will also depend on uncertain systemic changes and innovations in governance that must

[3] Not to be confused with "greenwashing," which is also part of the disavowal. See https://www.pwc.ch/en/insights/fs/greenwashing-and-greenwishing.html

occur on time to reach a successful net-zero emission (Mc Kinsey, 2023).[4] This tendency to underestimate the degree of uncertainty is an unconscious bias related to the general disavowal.

This "greenwishing" and built-in optimism manifest a collective illusion that reflects the unconscious denying of the de-carbonization costs and the risks of catastrophic irreversibility. Most of existing works on energy transition do not yet deal with the side effects of changes in production and consumption structures that are urgently required for a timely de-carbonization. The very low relative price of carbon has enduringly changed the whole structure of world output, the way of life, and entire cultures. De-carbonization is, therefore, a major shock for every society, but it tends to be hidden, either unconsciously by the human brain, which is biased toward present benefits (Bohler, 2019) or consciously by vested interests[5] that refuse to lose their immediate rents whatever the costs for societies. Therefore, the issue of global warming tends to remain unresolved and worsening.

This neglectful behavior not only indicates an implicit disavowal by most economists and economic agents, but also a clear incoherence that shows a myopic way of working in the profession of economists as well as in those of private investors and in the financial sector.

The Specific and Unprecedented Difficulties in Assessing a Net-Zero Strategy and Identifying the Costs and Efficiency of the Necessary Policy Measures

The issue organizing an effective net-zero strategy is probably the most complex policy challenge humankind, policymakers, and economists have faced in history. Moreover, it requires overcoming two perverse processes: first, the "*tragedy of the horizons*" (Carney, 2015), which impedes timely and significant actions due to the increased uncertainty resulting from the short-termism of the policymakers' electoral bias for dealing with the fatal irreversibility of global warming; and, second, the electoral populist constraint that traps policymakers into a "*prisoner dilemma*" status quo favoring procrastination and impeding the needed coordination both among nations and among sectors. This combination tends to impede longer-term collective rationality, but all the published quantitative works on the costs of energy transition leading to the net-zero result are based upon a naive collective rationality hypothesis. Therefore, by assuming that the key systemic failures have been resolved, the models show solutions with relatively minor macroeconomic costs.

[4] "*Net zero is an ideal state where the amount of greenhouse gases (GHGs) released into the earth's atmosphere is balanced by the amount of GHGs removed*" (Mc Kinsey, 2023).

[5] The huge disinformation strategy organized by the oil lobbies explains most of the climato-skepticism actions, see https://phys.org/news/2021-09-oil-companies-discourage-climate-action.html https://sustainabilitycommunity.springernature.com/posts/favorability-towards-natural-gas-relates-to-funding-source-of-university-energy-centers

All are utopian and misleading. They rely upon implicit assumptions that the key difficulties are solved:

- Necessary measures would be adequately prepared, correctly managed, without disorderly path and taken smoothly on time among the main economic areas.
- Electorates and their policymakers would respect the rational choice that the small direct economic costs of acting now are strongly overcompensated by avoiding climate damages, and that any postponement increases the transition costs and decreases the longer-term benefits.
- Governance issues do not exist.
- Neither political and geopolitical conflicts nor chaotic social reactions would occur.
- Economies' heterogeneities are minimal.
- Neither market failures nor public failures would increase the uncertainty of return for investments in de-carbonization.
- No bottleneck in specific commodities, technologies, equipment, and skills for moving smoothly to clean energies.
- No impact of the structural and behavioral changes on the parameters of the model.
- No gap between the decentralized supply of renewable energies and the infrastructures of electricity grids[6].
- Permanent coordination among most nations and key actors.
- Essential financial and macroeconomic conditions permanently fulfilled.

In short, by default, models make the disavowal worse by dealing improperly with de-carbonization, which is a complex systemic issue plagued by many uncertainties among which the main one comes from the difficulties to ensure the urgent coordination required for facing the deep structural changes in the whole word.

Macro-financial Aspects of De-Carbonization

A Macroeconomic Panorama of De-Carbonization

Reaching net-zero emissions for 2050 is supposed to allow for the fulfillment of the Paris Agreement's target (2015) of maintaining global average temperatures within 1.5° Celsius of pre-industrial levels. However, as most governments have not yet taken effective measures, the increase in temperatures has continued, already approaching, in 2023, the Paris target. This acceleration could also indicate the probable existence of tipping points in a nonlinear relation between CO_2 emissions

[6] "*Grids are becoming a bottleneck for transitions to net zero emissions... grid investment needs to nearly double by 2030 to over USD 600 billion per year after over a decade of stagnation*" op. cit. International Energy Agency (2023), Electricity Grids and Secure Energy Transitions.

and climate impacts. According to UN Secretary-General António Guterres (2023), "*The era of global warming has ended; the era of global boiling has arrived.*" Anyway, it is clear that delaying actions implies fast increases in costs and the need to accelerate later the implementation of tougher policies worldwide.

In the approach taken in this work, these probable additional costs are not taken into account in the available data[7] to prevent exaggeration by extrapolating too recent information. According to most models and research on global warming, cutting CO_2 emissions up to net-zero means, from a macroeconomic point of view, organizing an enormous effort of *investment in de-carbonization*. Global macroeconomic constraints relate this increase in the investment share in GDP to an inevitable contraction in the remaining share in GDP, that is, a sharp *reduction in consumption* share. By how much? The prudent estimations of the NGFS Net Zero 2050 scenario (2022) give some orders of magnitude for specific investments in the energy sector and land uses. Total annual capital investment in energy in the Net Zero 2050 should rise from around 2.5% of the world's GDP today to about 4.5% in 2030, falling back to 2.5% by 2050. From 2021 to 2050, the required global cumulative spending in these sectors is estimated to reach at least US$ 275 trillion for three decades, or a total average of US$ 9.2 trillion per year, for covering both the still necessary traditional fossil energies and the progressive shift from high-emission to low-emission equipment, plus the necessary increase in new types of energy and technologies, as well as in related grid infrastructures and storage solutions. According to McKinsey (2022), from these US$ 9.2 trillion of global spending in energy investments, US$ 3.5 trillion are the necessary new investments. The remaining US$ 5.7 trillion covers US$ 1 trillion of existing spending, which would be reallocated toward low-carbon energies, US$ 2 trillion, which already are spent on low-carbon assets, and US$ 2.7 trillion for the average spending on traditional fossil energies, which would be necessary for ensuring the soft transition up to 2050. In 2022, about US$ 2 trillion are spent on low emissions in the world, of which the Emerging Market and Developing Economies (EMDEs) represent US$ 773 billion. AEs are already spending about US$ 1.2 trillion on low-emission assets. The necessary increase of US$ 3.5 trillion would be split into US$ 2 trillion of new investments from the EMDEs and US$ 1.5 trillion from the AEs.

The EMDEs effort would be much bigger, moving from US$ 773 billion in 2022 up to US$ 2.8 trillion, a net increase of US$ 2 trillion or a multiplication by 3.6, whereas the AEs should increase investment by a factor of 2.3. For the global economy, these US$ 3.5 trillion of additional investments in clean energies represent a macroeconomic effort of 3.5% of the world's GDP and a 1.7-fold increase with respect to 2022. For example, the rhythm of installation of solar panels per month should be multiplied by eight, wind farms by a factor of five and grid investment needs to nearly double by 2030 to over US$ 600 billion per year (McKinsey, 2022).

---

[7] The Network for Greening the Financial Sector (NGFS) presents a scenario for a delayed transition, which increases the transition costs and the damages resulting from the global warming: https://www.ngfs.net/ngfs-scenarios-portal/explore

The annual amount of new investment in clean energies and land-use systems means an unprecedented jump equivalent to 13% of total investment, that is, almost half the global corporate profit (McKinsey, 2022). This strong financial effort, which will be added to the financial costs of scrapping important equipment and high-carbonized activities that have not yet been amortized, implies a severe contraction in global consumption to make room for the necessary jump in the investment rate. In addition, the important structural differences due to the heterogeneity of national situations, not only in energy supplies, but also in development levels and trade specializations, imply that huge and stable international financial inflows would be tailored in the right amount to each case. Important effects on growth, productivity, inflation, and external current account balances need to be assessed in relation to the net capital flows for each economy and group of economies. To integrate all these interdependencies is the task of modeling climate change for assessing and measuring policy effects. Due to the size and scope of de-carbonization, many technical difficulties have yet to be solved to properly take into account the differentiated effects and their feedback on the other variables and countries. Would existing models based upon parameters reflecting pre-de-carbonization behaviors and elasticities be capable of accounting for changes in both this large scope and sharp magnitude?

We do not have an answer to this epistemological question, although much research is presently dedicated to improving the models and the method. In particular, the coherent reactions, mainly from the Bretton Woods institutions, deserve to be mentioned[8]. At this point, relying merely on common sense, it already appears that the indicated macroeconomic order of magnitude combined with complex spillovers and inter-twinned parameters acting on the feasibility of the inescapable decarbonization constitute a major global shock, which leads to a "great transformation" of the whole economic system. Such a systemic change could not be automatically successful relying only on pure market mechanisms and private finance given all the unknown parameters. In such a context of uncertainty, it is also common sense to consider that the governance systems must be changed to ensure proactive management involving all stakeholders and social groups, as well as close international policy cooperation. However, the same common sense makes clear that recent geopolitical evolutions are not moving in the right direction. The choice is merely binary: either governance is changed to manage a fast energy transition or other changes will be imposed in chaotic conditions with unmeasurable higher costs.

[8]The 2017–2020 Climate Change Policy Assessment (CCPA) pilots (a joint IMF-WB climate diagnostic assessment for small vulnerable countries), continued by IMF with its Climate Macroeconomic Assessment Program (CMAP) with its macro-fiscal modeling; the 2022 IMF Fund's Resilience and Sustainability Trust (RST), the 2022 World Bank's Country Climate and Development Report (CCDR, which is one of the pillars for the World Bank Group Climate Change Action Plan to integrate climate and development and which complements the IMF's CMAP), IMF's toolkit Debt, Investment, Growth and Natural Disaster (DIGNAD) model, the IMF's Climate Policy Assessment Tool (CPAT), which is a tool to design, assess, and implement policies for accelerating decarbonization in 200 economies and to evaluate debt sustainability risks following natural disasters.

The Order of Magnitude of the Funding Gap in Emerging Market and Developing Economies (EMDEs)

Under the optimistic bias provoked by the universal disavowal, consensus views are that AEs, with their supposed capacity for taking adequate policy measures, should be able to finance the necessary investments for meeting their commitments to net-zero, estimated roughly to more than double their present investments in renewable energies. Despite the optimistic view of the officials, there is also a consensus for acknowledging that the group of EMDEs is not automatically in condition to finance these needs because the effort is almost twofold bigger than the effort in AEs while they face much higher structural difficulties for transforming their energy supply toward clean technologies. Solving these difficulties is necessary not only for reaching their de-carbonization objectives but also for ensuring their own sustainable development for fighting poverty and supplying the necessary collective goods in education and health.

According to the data of the International Energy Agency and the International Finance Corporation (2023), the average yearly financial needs for EMDEs to invest in clean energy should increase from US$ 770 billion in 2022 up to US$ 2.8 trillion during the period 2031–2035. More specifically:

- **EMDEs** invested in 2022 around US$ 770 billion in renewable energies, or only 2% of their combined GDP; this should rise respectively to 5.6% and 7% of GDP on average for the two periods 2026–2030 and 2031–2035 (i.e., a **3.6-fold** increase in the second period compared to 2022). However, the investment in China, India, and Brazil represents more than three-quarters of this figure. To respect the Paris Agreement, annual investment in clean energy in EMDEs would need at least to triple in the next decade and should continue to increase up to 2035, staying at a high level up to 2050. Without China, the investment effort in the other EMDEs must rise from US$ 260 billion to US$ 1.9 trillion, that is, an investment effort of 8.9% of their GDP, a **7-fold** increase!
- **China** is the fastest and most advanced investor among EMDEs, with US$ 511 billion (2.9% of its GDP) in 2022; it must rise to an annual US$ 853 billion (4.8% of its GDP) on average during 2026–2030, and to US$ 947 billion (5.3% of its GDP) on average during 2031–2035, that is, a **1.8-fold increase.**
- **In Latin America**, clean energy-related investments should move up from an annual US$ 66 billion (1% of its GDP) in 2022 to an annual average of US$ 243 billion (3.8% of its GDP) during 2026–2030 and continue to go up to US$ 332 billion during 2031–2035, a **5-fold** rise in comparison with 2022.
- **Asia** (without China, Japan, and Korea) should move up from US$ 112 billion (1.2% of its GDP) to US$ 533 billion (5.5%) and then to US$ 711 billion (7.4% of its GDP) for the respective periods, that is, a **6.2-fold increase.**
- **For Africa**, the energy-related investments should jump from US$ 32 billion (1% of its GDP) to US$ 203 billion (6.8% of its GDP) and then to US$ 265 billion (8.8% of its GDP), that is, an **8.8-fold increase**.

These estimated investment needs allow us to give some rough orders of magnitude of the challenges our societies have to take up immediately to ensure their survival. It appears first that the effort is disproportionately big for economies struggling with high poverty challenges. It is common sense, but also supported by technical evidence, that this jump in investment rates could not be financed by compressing much their consumption. This means that their domestic savings must be completed by external savings, that is, by inflows of public and private capital from AEs. These richer economies, in turn, should be able to ensure a strong increase in their saving rates to be able to cover both the big increase in their own investment in clean energies (2.5% of their GDP) and to generate a net saving surplus for closing the financing gaps in EMDEs (5% of their GDP) with capital outflows.

Given these magnitudes, de-carbonization dictates that in a very short term (a few years), clean energy investment rates in EMDEs would have to increase from 2% to 7% of the GDP, that is, an increase of five percentage points of their GDP. AEs would have to increase clean investments from 2.1% of their GDP in 2022 to 4.6% in 2035, that is, an increase of 2.5 percentage points of their GDP. AEs' macroeconomic effort would be half of the EMDEs' effort.

Examining the present (IMF, 2023) investment and saving rates in AEs and EMDEs gives an idea of the enormous size of the global challenge to meet: AEs saving rates are presently hovering around 22% of their GDP, close to their investment rate at 22.4% (small net dissaving) while EMDEs present together higher average rates, 32.4% for saving and 32% for their investment rate (small net saving). Of course, these group averages hide big disparities, with Asia registering much higher rates of respectively 39.4% and 38.7% (a current account surplus of 0.7%), while Latin America at much lower levels of respectively 18.4% and 20.2% (a current account deficit of 1.8%) clearly insufficient for ensuring its own development. Sub-Saharan Africa has in the same insufficient rate of saving and investment, with 18.9% and 21.5% repectively (saving deficit of 2.6%). For AEs, disparities exist also, namely the United States with extremely low rates of 16.3% and 20.6% (saving deficit of 4.3%). The Euro Area, in turn, shows an opposite surplus of savings, with respective rates of 25.7% and 23.3% (surplus of 2.4%).

Since the net savings of EMDEs are 0.4%, and their investment rate should rise by 5% of their GDP, their financing gap requires capital inflows of 4.6% of their GDP, some US$ 1.840 billion per year during many years coming from AEs, for which this amount represents 3% of their GDP. AEs should be in condition to increase their saving rate from 22% now to 27.5% of their GDP (+2.5% for covering their own increase in investment +3% for filling the EMDEs financing gap by their investments abroad).

Would Financial Markets Be Able to Overcome Their Inability to Provide Sufficient Investments for De-Carbonization?

Financial experts still believe that private finance will be able to provide capital inflows as long as investors' risks are matched by an increase in yield expectations for their investment in de-carbonization. However, the cost of capital for a typical utility-scale solar project is usually much higher in EMDEs than in AEs, reflecting higher perceived risks. It is true that if their profitability could be sufficiently higher than in the AEs, gross inflows to EMDEs could be significantly increased. As explained by Aglietta (2015), free financial markets are unable to allocate efficiently the resources to reorient the production system because climate changes create extreme uncertainty, which in turn implies that the market value of de-carbonization investments *today* would be too low. A financial international public intervention is necessary for complement to the progressive taxation of CO_2 emissions ("malus") for giving an immediate incentive ("bonus") to new investments that abate greenhouse gases in compensation for the too-high uncertainty ex ante. The reason is that the increases in carbon prices can only be progressive and too slow to attract sufficient investments *now* in clean production and cover both risks and upfront costs. Therefore, de-carbonization needs an additional nonmarket mechanism for giving a financial bonus *today* able to act on firm expectations for increasing the relative value of their low-carbon investments (or reducing the private financial costs of riskier CO_2 saving investments), that is, increasing risky private yield of de-carbonization toward its social yield[9].

Could the International Monetary System (IMS) Ensure the Adequate Geographical Allocation of Resources (Capital and Technology) for De-Carbonizing the Global Output?

At the global level, the most recent forecasts from the IMF World Economic Outlook (October 2023) seem at odds or worryingly incoherent with the committed plans of de-carbonization because the estimated investment increases and consequent adjustment in savings do not appear at all in the period 2024–2028. Observing the past, present, and future dis-saving by the AEs group, especially in the wealthiest economy, the United States, which currently absorbs the world savings for 4.3% of its GDP and is expected to maintain this deficit around an average of 3.7% up to 2028, leads to the key systemic question of how to reverse this resilient old disequilibrium. The answer lies in the asymmetries provoked by an International Monetary System (IMS) based upon a national currency, the US dollar, as the main international

[9] See Aglietta (2015) for a detailed proposal. A clear example of the need to include the huge upfront costs: "*if a renewable energy plant produces electricity at a cost 30% higher than a coal plant, the real amount of investment to replace coal-fired electricity is 130%.*"

reserve. Indeed, for playing this international function, the US economy, issuing this main reserve currency, is condemned to automatically become a growing net debtor (i.e., to absorb foreign savings) and remain one permanently as far as the rest of the world needs more reserves in dollar, which is an observed fact. The specificity of the current IMS forces a dis-saving in the US economy and biases the international saving flows against a smoother diffusion of development. Dollar assets held by foreigners correspond to automatic inflows of capital in the US economy. This inescapable aspect of the IMS, which is based upon the dollar, appears as a systemic obstacle to the increase in AE saving surplus since non-US AEs should make up for the huge dis-saving of the United States. This is indeed not the case in current forecasts since the AEs maintain a small savings deficit up to 2028. This recognizes the absence of policy measures for de-carbonization on time: "...an indicator of effective (no)policy change: the underpricing of fossil energies (market failures) worsened by the direct subsidies given to their production or consumption (government failures)" (Ghymers, 2024)[10].

To this macroeconomic incoherence, an additional corollary of the Triffin Dilemma, which is very damaging for global development, is the significant spillover of the US macro-monetary policy that generates destabilizing pro-cyclical waves in global liquidity. Once a national currency is used as a foreign reserve by many other countries, asymmetries result that create biases in the policy mix of the issuer of reserves not only by exempting it from external monetary discipline but also by provoking significant spillovers on global liquidity conditions, which tend to become suboptimal and unmanageable. This is also the result of the dollar's international status, which generates a global boom-bust cycle (Rey, 2013) with very damaging effects on the stability of EMDEs' capital inflows and macroeconomic policies.

What Is the Incoherence of the Present IMS That Creates an Obstacle to the Capital Inflows in EMDEs?

Due to the inner logic of a currency, being debt-at-sight, any system based mainly on the use of a national currency for supplying international reserve assets to the rest of the world is doomed to conflicting policy objectives, inevitably leading to global macroeconomic instability. The reason is the inescapable dilemma the issuer of this currency faces between either going ever deeper into external debt in order to smoothly satisfy the growing world demand for liquidity, with the danger that this could, at some point, either undermine its creditworthiness, or failing to satisfy this demand for preserving its creditworthiness, exposing the world to a reserve

[10] In Ghymers (2024), the increase in subsidies to fossil energies gives an indication of the contradiction between the "greenwishing" words of policymakers and the real world of fossil energies' rent-seekers.

shortage with a consequent deflation. This corollary—or other face—of the Triffin Dilemma remains a major obstacle to the necessary stability of the gross inflows for de-carbonization. The destabilizing global liquidity waves created by the constraints on the US monetary policies act as a "*built-in destabilizer*" (Triffin, 1959) of the global liquidity, that is, an endogenous generation of pro-cyclical global monetary waves that constitute a systemic cause for recurrent global crises. This phenomenon has increased during the last three decades with the structural evolution of global finance (Ghymers, 2021, 2022).

The instability and pro-cyclicality of global liquidity come mainly from the paradoxical structural scarcity of dollar safe assets, which produces the present form of the Triffin Dilemma and its built-in destabilizer. It is a process of circular cumulative causality provoked by the binary discrimination introduced by using a national currency as a international reserve currency, which endows the dollar with higher liquidity (or "moneyness degree") than other safe assets. This differentiation in the liquidity degree develops binary distinction between the dollar and non-dollar components of the global "high-powered-money" (monetary basis), which sustains the reversed pyramid of global liquidity. As soon as a liquidity squeeze is in view, the demand for dollar-safe assets jumps while the nonbank sector (namely the repo markets) cuts its supply of pseudo-safe assets in other currencies (non-dollar reserves), creating a systemic instability of the global liquidity. Contrary to any national liquidity "reversed pyramid," where the basis is homogeneous and could always be controlled by its national central bank, global liquidity has an unstable binary basis that cannot be stabilized to the same degree in the absence of a genuine international Lender-of-Last-Resort (LOLR). A cumulative causality explains a growing scarcity of dollar-safe assets as the flow of their demand increases much faster than what can be provided by the US debt capacity. This growing gap is the result of two evolutions:

(i) A structural shift in the founding sources by which non-bank financial intermediation (NBFI or "shadow banks") substitutes traditional bank loans based upon demand deposits for short-term loans secured with dollar collaterals, provoking a huge need for dollar safe assets
(ii) The relative shrinkage of the US economy, as a result of the fast expansion of EMDEs, which reduces the relative weight in the global finance of the issuance of US liquid debts, while most of the liquidity needs of the growing EMDEs are in dollar

This excess demand for dollar-safe assets pushes down the yields of the dollar. Encouraged by these too-low yields, a combination of risk appetite and financial innovations among the private operators on the wholesale financial markets generates an intermediation for supplying by securitization pseudo-safe assets with non-dollar assets and corporate debts usable as collaterals ("Repo" and asset-backed commercial papers). However, these developments correspond to an endogenous increase in the global monetary basis of global liquidity, which becomes pro-cyclical, that is, reversible for missing an international LOLR and being composed of safe assets of two different qualities: the dollar-safe assets and pseudo-safe assets in non-dollars. Therefore, the Triffin Dilemma—which expresses the impossibility of a single economy to ensure an adequate supply of safe assets able to stabilize global liquidity by issuing its own liquid debts—induces the wholesale markets to create an accumulation of systemic destabilizing factors:

1. They encourage the issuance of lower-grade debt through new collateral.
2. They develop mismatches in terms of maturity, currencies, and credit quality.
3. These pseudo-safe assets as collateral tend to co-vary more with the global financial cycle, provoking endogenous reversibility in the volume of the monetary basis, which amplifies the contraction in global liquidity.
4. National central banks are poorly equipped for intervening safely in repo markets, which, by definition are part of the shadow banking sector, have no direct access to their central banks.

This vicious circle of liquidity destabilization has not (yet) become a run-out-of-dollar but rather leads to its contrary "dash-for-dollar" liquid assets and creates a cyclical appreciation of the dollar, with an inevitable global recession and a growing pro-cyclicality of liquidity, generating increasing socioeconomic costs. This built-in destabilizer is doomed to lead to a big crash. The failure to generate the resources for de-carbonization will probably create this systemic crisis, which will force systemic change.

Why does the dollar's role remain so dominant and unique? Why other competitors do not appear? The answer is simple: the primary determinant for being the main reserve currency is the capacity to provide a fast-growing supply of high-quality (liquid) debt, that is, to be also the dominant debtor. But there is no other candidate able to issue so high a volume of perfectly liquid assets. Competing with the dollar means competing to absorb in consumption the world savings, that is, to accept the necessary huge dis-saving. This would oblige the rest of the world to an even higher saving surplus. Furthermore, the competition between two key currencies would provoke sharp unmanageable substitutions (Kareken & Wallace, 1981) between these two standards, unsettling global liquidity and generating additional catastrophic macroeconomic instability. An efficient and stable IMS cannot logically be based upon either one or several national currencies, but needs a multilateral one.

Amazingly, economists dealing with the conditions for de-carbonization seem to ignore this double systemic difficulty. The above analysis of the current IMS shows the existence of a resilient additional obstacle for solving the financing gap of the EMDEs. Anyway, the fast-rising costs of insufficient actions should create the necessary pressures for resolving the systemic lack of tools for stabilizing global liquidity and getting out of the permacrisis.

Outline of a Solution

The Principle

The most obvious and easiest technical way to solve the Triffin Dilemma requires a genuine $(n + 1)^{th}$ currency, which is no longer the net debt of one of the "n" national economies. This additional currency to the "n" existing ones allows the restoration of the missing degree of freedom to national policies because with "n" different currencies there remains only $(n - 1)^{th}$ exchange rates and current account balances, making it impossible to get "n" autonomous policies: one economy has to abandon its sovereignty for supplying the necessary safe assets to the $n - 1$ other economies.

This is precisely what a multilateral currency is made for. It is exactly like what happens at the national level, where the liability of the central banks is necessary as an additional liability to the liabilities of the deposit banks. At the global level, this multilateral liquid asset should be issued by a legitimate, representative multilateral institution (the IMF). This multilateral institution would create the currently missing global LOLR in charge of managing global liquidity as a public good by issuing (withdrawing) its own liability against buying (selling) the exact asset counterpart in eligible national and liquid bonds to national central banks. This LOLR or Multilateral Central Bank (MCB) would be in charge of optimizing the volume of global liquidity according to technical criteria fixed collectively (e.g., global output gap and commodity prices) for increasing or reducing liquidities, including fulfilling the role of safety net. The value of this multilateral liability would be fixed by the weighted average of the values of its counterparts in national assets. It would play the role of multilateral first-best safe assets because it will be necessarily less discretionary, safer, exempt from any geopolitical discrimination or weaponization[11], arithmetically the most stable, collegiately manageable for ensuring stability, and its issuance would not imply a growing indebtedness of any national economy. This formula means a "multilateralization" of the issuance of safe assets against national safe assets. Exchange-rate risk and external constraints would appear symmetrical for the dollar as for any other national currency. The result is the internalization of the dollar spillovers and the stabilization of the global liquidity without increasing any debt, that is, resolving the Triffin Dilemma in the interests of all countries. This is, in fact, close to the Keynes/Triffin plans.

It would be difficult to imagine a simpler, more coherent, and more symmetric solution. The systemic logic of moving from national reserve currencies to a multilateral one is the same as what was necessary to do at the national level when national central banks substituted private bank currencies for their own liability issued in order to ensure the stability of interbank liquidity. The reason is the same: the need for a neutral LOLR, which issues its own liquid debt as the most liquid and

[11] The political weaponization of the dollar is a dangerous infringement to the necessary universality of an international currency, and the same would probably apply to the projects to build an anti-dollar international standard.

safest asset required for the clearing among national deposit banks, above all the "n" others, according to the needs and without creating asymmetries among other assets issued by banks.

The Operational Modalities

Due to the pressures created by the inevitable exponential increases in catastrophic climate damages and the accompanying worsening of financial and social crises, both making clear that the system is unsustainable, policymakers will be obliged to turn to radical systemic reforms among which to implement the principle of the costless creation of a multilateral currency. The geopolitical nature of the present obstacle to a systemic reform, namely the US resistance[12] to losing its "exorbitant privilege" to finance its deficit with its own currency, is doomed to change soon due to the combination of the revolution in payment digitalization (CBDCs[13]) with the unprecedented crisis that will result from the impossibility to invest on-time as required by de-carbonization. The IMF reform will appear as beneficial to all for improving the macroeconomic stability necessary to mitigate the important costs of the delay in de-carbonization. The expected benefits for all are monetary and macroeconomic stability and the disposition of an automatic financial safety net that can create smoothly the liquidity in case of urgency or crisis, along strict technical conditionality.

The benefits for the United States far outweigh the short-term disadvantages, in particular by preventing future competition between key currencies (like the euro and the renminbi), which would generate major instability. For the rest of the world, the advantages of the reform would be much more significant, and the short-term costs generated by the US external adjustment much lower if the risks of financial and exchange-rate turbulence could be put under control through the management of global liquidity.

How to proceed concretely? The obvious and safest option is to build on what exists and is legitimate: the International Monetary Fund and its Special Drawing Right (SDR).

1. **The SDR** is an international reserve asset created by the IMF with the legal purpose of becoming "*the principal reserve asset in the international monetary system*," according to the formal agreement enacted in Article VIII section 7 of the IMF statutes (1969). Its value is equivalent to the value of a weighted basket of

[12] A decision to change the IMF statutes and the SDR requires a qualified vote of 85%; this requires approval by the United States, which owns a veto with a percentage of the total voting power of 16.5%. Furthermore, the US Congress has to approve any issue of SDR superior to the US quota of SDR 83 billion. Although the United States can block any reform of IMF, necessity is likely to force it to a "new monetary deal" in their own interests.

[13] Central Bank Digital Currencies, See in this book, Chap. 13 "Systemic Aspects of CBDCs."

world currencies. However, the SDR is not yet a genuine currency but an asset that holders can exchange for currency when needed. The concrete solution is to upgrade the present SDR into a genuine *Multilateral Reserve Currency* (MRC) by allowing the IMF to issue (or withdraw) MRC directly as the multilateral safe asset used by national central banks and markets, as the most stable monetary base supporting the creation of global liquidity.

2. **This Upgrading of the IMF** into a *Multilateral Central Bank* (MCB or IMF*) by allowing it to issue its own liability against asset counterparts in deposits in national reserve currencies or national bonds confers it the role of the missing multilateral LOLR able to manage the global monetary basis in MRC for stabilizing the volume of global liquidity without affecting the debt of any national economy. The technical aspects are presented in the Analytical Annexes with the balance sheet of the MCB.
3. Operationally, **Blockchain technology** and the coming generalization of interoperable **Central Bank Digital Currencies (CBDCs)**[14] will make bundling/unbundling the SDR basket costless. Therefore, the new e-MRC would become highly attractive to the private sector, contrary to the present SDR. At the same time, due to the same absence of conversion costs, the dollar could and should remain the primary operational vehicle on the day-to-day markets for logistical (and logical) reasons: only one working standard is feasible for intra-day or short-term operations of dealers. For the same reason, a multi-currency option would be even more unstable[15] without a superior (n + 1th) reserve currency above them as regulated by a (n + 1th) LOLR. This proposal does not pretend (or would not imply) to substitute for the US dollar's operational role in the interbank markets, but mainly across the main central bank operations, as a universal vehicle for exchange-rate transactions and for liquidity management in a collegial way for ensuring global stability. This CBDC feature allows for maintaining the operational vehicle role of the dollar, so keeping the acquired technical advantages and network practices of its use as the standard tool for the dealers, especially in the intra-day or day-to-day transactions.
4. **The need for a substitution** account between dollar reserves and the new MRC. The future ability of permanent costless conversion in e-MRC will provoke the end of the scarcity of dollar-safe assets, suppressing the dollar's "exorbitant privilege" and making the IMS symmetric. It will be necessary to absorb the overhang of dollar assets resulting from substituting the demand for dollar-safe assets for the most stable, costless, multilateral safe asset. An off-market mechanism will organize an orderly process, preventing a sharp fall in the dollar exchange rate with a conventional fixed rate between the dollar and MRC through a **substitution account** (see Analytical Annex 2 for technical aspects). This account should be open at the MCB (IMF*), where the holders of excess dollar

[14] See Chap. 13 in Part IV.

[15] Due to the massive unstable currency substitutions, see Kareken and Wallace (1981).

reserves could deposit them in exchange for their equivalent value in MRC (SDR*) at a guaranteed exchange rate. At the end of the 1970s, a similar idea for moving to SDR reserves failed miserably on the question of the burden sharing of the exchange-rate losses that the expected depreciation of the dollar with respect to the SDR could imply. According to witnesses of these negotiations, the final US offer was to support half of the losses, but France refused, wanting to impose to the United States supporting all the losses. However, this historical failure shows a wrong analysis. With this substitution considered a systemic change, the proposal means a definitive and institutional move to the MRC issued by the IMF*, that is, the global LOLR. This implies no possible exchange-rate losses on the MCB (IMF*) balance sheet where dollar sales would be registered at the same value as MRC purchase with a conventional fixed exchange rate: without an open position left on the MCB, bookkeeping cannot show any loss. Only in the theoretical case of dissolution of the MCB and its substitution account could losses or gains appear when the dollar assets would be returned to their initial depositors (Sobol, 1979; Icard, 2011). Therefore, this was a sterile conflict of the past led by politicians without a systemic view. Furthermore, the character of public good of this IMS reform would justify the multilateralization of the great benefits facing only hypothetical smaller losses anyway.

The MCB as a Substitute to Conflictual Monetary and Exchange-Rates Coordination An important benefit for all countries of this MCB/MRC plan is to restore symmetric forces that are able to constrain the set of "n" monetary policy stances automatically and multilateralize the bilateral credits and debits. MRC creates an automatic self-constraint that negates the need for any supranational power and/or transfer of monetary policy sovereignty. This reform tends to be viewed as utopian, but it is a priori the more realistic one (or, the less difficult to agree upon) because it is operated along the logic of *"subsidiarity"*: more respectful of national policies' autonomy than in the case of coordination deals, fitting better with the current populist mood against international cooperation. National policies are self-constrained by the technical nominal anchor fixed by the costless MCB (the neutral "n + 1th" agent). An overdraft facility allows the financing of specific liquidity needs of any country as a percentage of their quota. This means purely technical management focusing only on the world's general interests. This nominal anchor—or global constraint—represents the need for organizing this public good of a global monetary policy stance that would be transparent and dedicated to international prices and growth stability.

Such a public good is "a-political" as it is purely technical, but at the highest global level: managing collegiately the degree of liquidity in function of objective parameters is the most efficient lever that monetary authorities could ever dream. Overall, this is the smoothest way to cooperate while respecting each other's sovereignty. There is no more need for stronger coordination of policies interfering with national sovereignties or against central bank autonomy once the "n" countries accept the costless upgrading of the SDR in the IMF statutes. Each economy recovers more autonomy with the eradication of the monetary spillovers: they remain free to adopt their own policy stances as they want, no more need for dedicating resources to costly safety nets or piling up an excessive stock of reserves, no more waste of time for bargaining polemical burden sharing for safety net or loans to the IMF/MCB, since, in case of a liquidity need in an economy, there is the possibility to decide to inject costless liquidity under conditionality, and—the most important effect—*no more Triffin Dilemma* since the IMS would become automatically more symmetrical, and therefore there would be no "built-in destabilizer" from the dollar system anymore since the proposed multilateral currency would be managed in service of global stability and the general interest as defined technically by the central bank members of the IMF.[16]

Conclusion

There is a very urgent need to improve the integration of climate economics and energy transition into macroeconomics. The gravity of climate change will soon oblige our societies—either by collective rationality or under chaotic survival conditions—to solve the current permacrisis because the absolute need for de-carbonization would be impossible without resolving the concatenation of systemic crises that impedes, in the current horizon, the financing of the necessary investments. The sooner it happens, the higher the probability to save democracy and life.

The funding gap for de-carbonization cannot be fulfilled on time with the present financial system, particularly for EMDEs. Multilateral interventions are inevitable to correct two systemic flaws. First, to ensure that private yields converge toward social yields, something that CO_2 taxes cannot achieve soon enough, thereby increasing immediately the conventional cashable value of the ex ante return on investments necessary to reduce CO_2 emissions. Second, for creating a global Lender-of-Last-Resort issuing a multilateral safe asset able to stabilize global liquidity and, thus, to spur international capital flows to EMDEs.

[16] Of course, this technical responsibility must remain exclusively in the hands of independent central bankers. This supposes that the IMF board gives a mandate to central banks of the IMF members to set up a specific monetary committee in charge of managing the MDR with the same autonomy as the central banks with respect to their respective treasury.

Annexes

Analytic Scheme 1: Balance-sheet of the Multilateral Central Bank (MCB=IMF*) in Multilateral Reserve Currency (MRC=SDR*)

ASSETS	LIABILITIES
A1 + A2 + A3=total claims on n central banks in SDR*/MRC	**L1+L2 +L3= Global Monetary Base total MRC liquid liabilities**
A1. Counterpart of % of central banks reserves (assets in 5 components of SDR) converted in MRC (= SDR*) (=valorised at daily market-rates against the MRC "Multilateral Reserve Currency")	**L1. Deposits in 5 reserve currencies from « n » CB converted into MRC** (countervalue changing all days but assets = liabilities, no exchange-rate risks for IMF)
A1.1 Swapped Bonds (monetary base in national currencies diminishes and rises in MCR)	**L1.1 = counterpart of swapped Bonds with CBs (global monetary base unchanged)**
A1.2 Bought Bonds (= pure monetary creation) decided as multilateral open-market policy (with veto)	**L1.2 = net issuance of MRC** (= exogenous variation in Global Monetary Base according to global needs, collegial decision under IMF proposal and minority veto)
A2. stocks of SDR reserves converted in SDR*= MRC	**L2. Reserve Deposits in MRC (SDR*) from National CB** (countervalue of received SDR)
A3. Overdraft Facility in MRC (SDR*) to National CB from deficit economies = Global Safety net (according to objective criteria and minority veto)	**L3 Overdraft loan = GLobal Safety Net** = endogenous net variation in Global Monetary Base according to national deficit adjustment needs decided collegiately with minority veto

Note: **SDR*** = an upgraded SDR= Multilateral Currency **MDR**

IMF* = an upgraded IMF = the **MCB** enabled to issue MDR

Analytic Scheme 2: Substitution Account
Balance-sheet of the Multilateral Central Bank (MCB=IMF*) in Multilateral Reserve Currency (MRC=SDR*)

ASSETS	LIABILITIES
1) claims upon "n" central banks expressed in MRC for their US$ deposits exchanged at a conventional book-keeping fixed rate of MRC for $	**1) US$ Deposits by «n» central Banks expressed in MRC** exchanged for MRC at the same conventional book-keeping fixed rate of MRC for $
2) Investment of these US$ deposits in longer-term assets (yield) expressed at current exchange rates	**2) Interest rate paid to central banks for their holding of MRC** expressed at current exchange rates
With a permanent and indefinite Substitution account, no exchange-rate loss or gain could appear, but a positive net return should accumulate in long-term for the positive yield curve (Long r-Short r) **Note**: MCB = upgraded IMF* allowing to issue its liquid liability MRC = upgraded SDR* in a genuine currency but required changes in IMF Articles of Agreement	Only in case of dissolution of the IMF, could appear exchange-rate net losses or gains; in this case, the initial depositors in key-currencies would support the losses and receive the gains

References

Aglietta, M. (2015). What is the quality of growth? Sustainability and inclusiveness. In L. Haddad, K. Hiroshi, & N. Meisel (Eds.), *Growth is dead, long live growth. The quality of economic growth and why it matters*. AFD IDS JICA. https://www.jica.go.jp/Resource/jica-ri/publication/booksandreports/jrft3q0000002a2s-att/Growth_is_Dead_Long_Live_Growth.pdf

Black, S., Parry, I., Mylonas, V., Vernon, N., & Zhunussova, K. (2023). The IMF-World Bank climate policy assessment tool (CPAT): A model to help countries mitigate climate change. *IMF Working Papers*, 2023/128

Bohler, S. (2019). *Le Bug Humain: pourquoi notre cerveau nous pousse à détruire la planète et comment l'en empêcher*. Robert Laffont.

Carney, M. (2015). *Speech given at Lloyd's of London*. https://www.bankofengland.co.uk/speech/2015/breaking-the-tragedy-of-the-horizon-climate-change-and-financial-stability

Drèze, J. (1990). *Essays on economic decisions under uncertainty*. Cambridge University Press.

Ghymers, C. (2021). *The systemic instability of ballooning Global Liquidity as a symptom of the worsening of the Triffin Dilemma* (RTI Paper no. 15). Centro Studi sul Federalismo.

Ghymers, C. (2022). The new form of the Triffin Dilemma and its built-in destabilizer: The process of relative shortage of dollar safe assets. *IRELAC Working Paper,* Brussels, 2022/06

Ghymers, C. (2024). Fostering the Dynamics of the Bi-Regional Summit EU-CELAC for Spurring the Cooperation. In A. Ribeiro Hoffmann, P. Sandrin & Y. Doukas (Eds), *Climate Change. In Climate Change in A Regional perspective: European Union and latin American Initiaitves, Challenges, and Solutions*. Springer Nature

Gutteres, A. (2023, July 27). *UN press conference on climate*.

Kareken, J., & Wallace N. (1981). On the indeterminacy of equilibrium exchange rates. *The Quarterly Journal of Economics 96*(2), 207–222.

Mc Kinsey Global Institute. (2022). *The Net-Zero transition: What it would cost, what it could bring*. https://www.mckinsey.com/capabilities/sustainability/our-insights/the-net-zero-transition-what-it-would-cost-what-it-could-bring

Mc Kinsey Global Institute. (2023). *What is net zero?* https://www.mckinsey.com/~/media/mckinsey/featured%20insights/mckinsey%20explainers/what%20is%20net%20zero/what_is_net_zero.pdf?shouldIndex=false

Icard, A. (2011). Enhancing the Role of the SDR as a Reserve Asset. In J. Boorman & A. Icard (Eds.), *Reform of the International Monetary System, the Palais Royal Initiative*. Sage Publications.

International Energy Agency. (2023). *Scaling up private finance for cleaning energy in emerging and developing economies*, Report, Paris. https://www.iea.org/reports/electricity-grids-and-secure-energy-transitions

International Monetary Fund. (2023, October). *World Economic Outlook*.

Network for Greening the Financial System (NGFS). (2023). *Conceptual note on short-term climate scenarios*. https://www.ngfs.net/sites/default/files/medias/documents/conceptual-note-on-short-term-climate-scenarios.pdf

Network for Greening the Financial System. (2022). *NGFS Scenarios for central banks and supervisors* https://www.ngfs.net/sites/default/files/medias/documents/ngfs_climate_scenarios_for_central_banks_and_supervisors_pdf.pdf

Rey, H. (2013). Dilemma not Trilemma: The global financial cycle and monetary policy independence. In *Federal Reserve Bank of Kansas city economic policy symposium*.

Sobol, D. (1979). A substitution account – Precedents & issues. *Quarterly Review*, Summer.

Stern, N., Stiglitz, J., & Taylor, C. (2022). The economics of immense risk, urgent action and radical change: Towards new approaches to the economics of climate change. *Journal of Economic Methodology, 29*(3), 181–216.

Triffin's hearing before the Joint Economic Committee of the US Congress, 28 October 1959.

Weitzam, M. (2009). On modeling and interpreting the economics of catastrophic climate change. *The Review of Economics and Statistics, 91*, 1.

Chapter 19
Stabilizing Asset Prices Through Transition from Continuous Trading to Electronic Auctions

Stephan Schulmeister

Contents

Introduction

In postwar history, economic development as well as framework conditions differed substantially between the prosperity phase of the 1950s and 1960s and the subsequent period of multiple crises, which as a whole are conceived as Permacrisis in this volume.

In the prosperity phase, the framework conditions gave clear priority to activities in the real economy, the financial sector was conceived as its "servant." Hence, goods markets were liberalized, whereas financial markets remained strictly regulated. Those prices that are of fundamental importance for investment and trade like interest rates and exchange rates were stabilized by central banks and the International Monetary System ("Bretton Woods"), respectively. Under "real-capitalistic" incentive

S. Schulmeister (✉)
University of Vienna, Vienna, Austria
e-mail: stephan.schulmeister@wifo-pens.at

D. Katsikas et al. (eds.), *Finance, Growth and Democracy: Connections and Challenges in Europe and Latin America in the Era of Permacrisis*, United Nations University Series on Regionalism 33, https://doi.org/10.1007/978-3-031-68475-3_19

conditions, the "core energy" of capitalist dynamics, that is, striving for profits, was directed toward activities in the real economy.

Following the breakdown of the Bretton Woods system in 1971, two strong dollar depreciations triggered the "oil price shocks" in 1973 and 1979, which in turn triggered two global recessions. Inflation accelerated, fought by central banks through raising interest rates. Under the condition of widely fluctuating exchange rates and commodities prices, together with interest rates exceeding the rate of economic growth, financial as well as nonfinancial business shifted their activities from real to financial investments. Under these "finance-capitalistic" conditions, economic growth has slowed down from decade to decade.

As a contribution to the first round of the Jean Monnet Network "Crisis–Equity–Democracy for Europe and Latin America," I sketched an overall picture of the systemic causes of the different economic performance in postwar development (Schulmeister, 2021). In the second round, my work focused on one core component of a finance-capitalistic regime, namely, the instability of asset prices and its impact on the real economy. My first contribution argues that the fluctuations of fossil energy prices and of carbon emission permit prices prevent an anchoring of the expectation that the effective emission costs will steadily rise faster than target inflation. As anchoring such an expectation is necessary to sufficiently stimulate investments in avoiding CO_2 emissions, policy needs to fix rising price paths of crude oil, coal, and natural gas (Schulmeister, 2023).

The present contribution deals with the phenomenon of bull markets and bear markets, which shapes the dynamics of asset prices in general. The "long swings" of stock prices, exchange rates, commodities prices, or house prices impact the real economy mainly through three channels—the distribution channel, the valuation channel, and the incentive channel—with respect to the attractiveness of financial speculation relative to real investments.

The phenomenon of "long swings" of asset prices is closely related to the growing dominance of computer-based technical or "algo(rithmic)" trading systems that completely disregard market fundamentals. They exploit the phenomenon of "runs" (i.e., "mini trends") of exchange rates, stock and bond prices, and commodity prices, and reinforce them at the same time. The sequence of "runs" accumulates into bull or bear markets because runs in line with the dominant—bullish or bearish—market sentiment last longer than counter-movements.

Mainstream economics cannot take into consideration the systemic causes of long swings of asset prices: if prices in those markets that come closest to the optimal market of equilibrium theory (as regards the homogeneity of "goods," accessibility, low transaction costs, etc.) persistently deviate from their fundamental equilibrium, then the entire paradigm can hardly be preserved. Hence, "overshooting" of asset prices is conventionally attributed to "shocks." Whereas concepts like "bullishness/bearishness," "overbought/oversold," "algo trading," etc., shape mindset and trading behavior in asset markets, these concepts do not form part of mainstream economics.

The neglect of the actual trading behavior in mainstream economics was and still is facilitated by the lack of an alternative approach that would generalize the stylized facts ("concrete theory"). Therefore, the "bull-bear-hypothesis" (BBH) is presented as an alternative to the still prevailing "efficient market hypothesis" (EMH). It is then shown that the BBH can explain the actual pattern of asset price dynamics to a much greater extent than the EMH. This result implies the following: if (very) fast trading becomes less attractive, then also the long swings of asset prices would be dampened since bull and bear markets are mainly brought about through the accumulation of (very) short-term trends.

There are two different ways of reducing the (expected) profitability of short-term trading. The first method consists of a general financial transactions tax (FTT), which would render fast speculation unprofitable even at a tax rate as low as 0.01% (e.g., high-frequency trading would disappear). The second method consists of moving from continuous trading in milliseconds to electronic auctions, for example, every 3 h. In this way, all types of (super) fast technical or algo trading systems could no longer be applied as they are cut off their input, that is, the most recent high-frequency price data. At the same time, traders would need to consider market fundamentals when placing their orders for the next auction.

The remainder of the chapter is structured as follows. The next section sketches the most important channels through which the instability of asset prices, in particular exchange rates, commodities prices, and stock prices impact the real economy and how the fluctuations of fossil energy prices and carbon emission prices impede an efficient carbon pricing. Then the prevailing "efficient market hypothesis" is compared to an alternative model of asset price dynamics, the "bull-bear-hypothesis." The next section explains how technical trading exploits asset price "runs" and strengthens them at the same time. Then it is shown how these trends accumulate into long-term bull markets and bear markets. The final section explains why replacing continuous trading with electronic auctions would stabilize asset prices over the short run as well as over the long run.

Asset Price Instability and the Real Economy

This section sketches answers to the following questions: How do the fluctuations of exchange rates, commodities prices, stock prices, and interest rates impact the real economy? How has asset price instability contributed to the genesis of what is conceived as Permacrisis in this volume? Three different channels can be distinguished: the distribution channel, the valuation channel, and the incentive channel. Let us discuss first the distribution effect.

The distribution channel concerns the large shifts between the prices of commodities and industrial goods as well as their income and demand effects. Prices of the most important commodities are determined on derivatives—primarily futures—exchanges due to their high degree of homogeneity (in contrast to industrial goods). For the same reason, practically all commodities are priced in the same currency, that is, the dollar as world currency. Commodities prices fluctuate much stronger than the prices of industrial goods, primarily for two reasons. First, the price

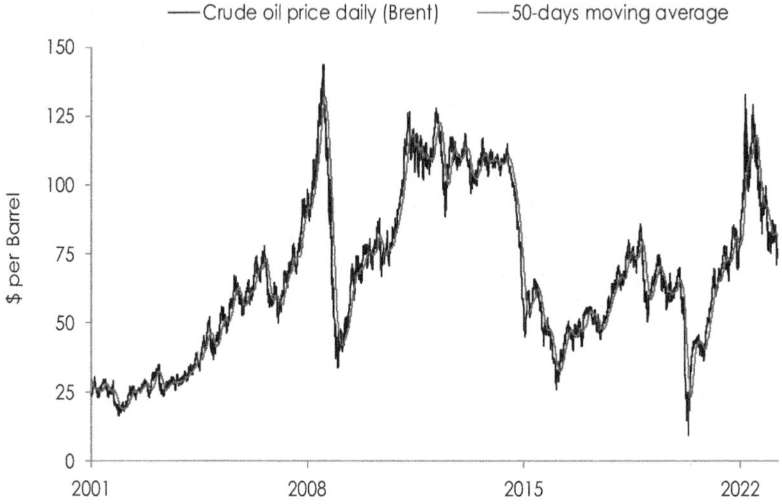

Fig. 19.1 Trending and speculation in the crude oil futures market. (Source: https://www.eia.gov/dnav/pet/hist/)

elasticities of demand for and supply of commodities are low and supply shocks occur frequently. Second, destabilizing speculation in derivatives markets has become increasingly important.

Crude oil is by far the most traded single commodity. At the same time, supply shocks are most pronounced in oil markets due to the concentration of market power (OPEC cartel, big single producers like Saudi Arabia or Russia) as well as due to political turbulences (from conflicts in the Middle East to Putin's war against Ukraine). The interaction of these factors causes oil price trends to be extraordinarily pronounced. Over the past 20 years alone, oil prices fluctuated in a sequence of (four) bull markets and (three) bear markets between \$20 and (almost) \$150 per barrel (Fig. 19.1).

The wide fluctuations of commodities prices induce massive redistributions in the global economy. Any commodities bull market shifts income from the net importers of commodities (mainly industrial countries) to net exporters. For example, the recent crude oil bull market that took off already in mid-2020 (Fig. 19.1) caused earnings of oil exporting countries to almost explode at the expense of net importers of crude oil. Similar redistributions took place over the 1970s due to the "oil price shocks" of 1973 and 1979, respectively. When oil prices strongly decline as in 1982/86 or 2014/15, income is redistributed in the opposite direction. The net effect of these redistributions on overall world trade is negative as the "winners" raise their import demand to a lesser extent than the "losers" reduce their imports.

Bull and bear markets of oil prices are often inversely related to strong and preceding changes in the dollar exchange rate (Fig. 19.2). For example, following the suspension of the Bretton Woods system in August 1971, the dollar lost roughly 25% of its value (relative to the four other reserve currencies). This development hit

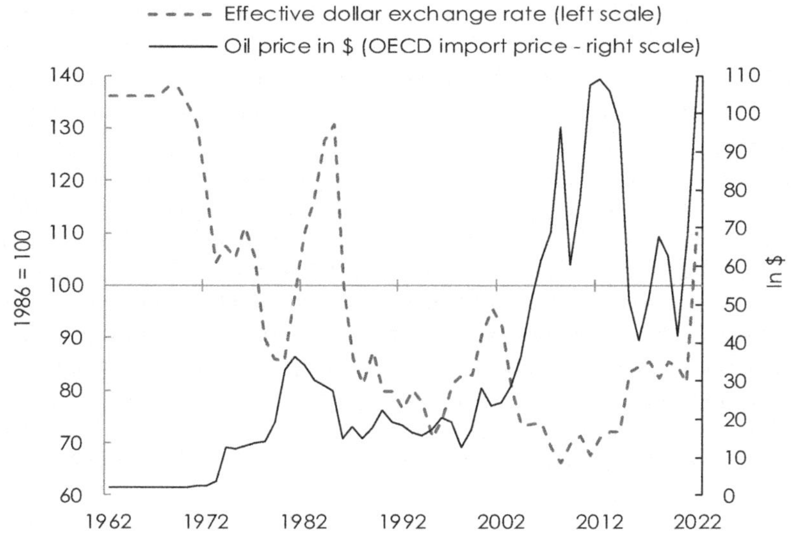

Fig. 19.2 Dollar exchange rate and oil price fluctuations. (Source: OECD, IMF)

most of those countries that exported exclusively oil, which is exclusively priced in dollars, that is, OPEC countries in the Middle East. This sequence repeated itself between 1976 and 1979. In both cases, OPEC took advantage of political turbulences to put through the "oil price shocks" of 1973 and 1979 (Yom Kippur War and turmoil in Iran, respectively). When the dollar boomed again between 1980 and 1985, oil prices fell. Also, over the last 20 years, the movements of oil prices and the dollar exchange rate were (approximatively) inversely related to each other.

The main systemic reason for the pronounced bull and bear markets of the dollar consists of its double role as national currency of the United States and as key currency of the world economy. As national currency, dollar exchange rate changes are influenced by national interests of the United States. The (stepwise) revocation of the Bretton Woods system between 1971 and 1973, for example, was mainly motivated by the interest of US policy to promote US exports. Ten years later, it became the predominant interest of US policy to fight inflation through increasing dollar interest rates, which induced a sustained dollar appreciation (Fig. 19.2). As world currency, (significant) changes in the dollar interest rate and dollar exchange rate impact the global economy since most international debts are held in dollars and practically all commodities are priced in dollars (for a more detailed analysis of the double role of the dollar, see Schulmeister, 2000).

Bull and bear markets affect the real economy also via the related wealth effects (valuation channel). In the international economy, the most important channel concerns the devaluation (revaluation) of dollar debts through any persistent depreciation (appreciation) of the dollar exchange rate. For example, the dollar declines over the 1970s incentivized countries to accumulate dollar debts (also fostered by low dollar interest rates). This effect was most pronounced in the then fastest growing economies, that is, in Latin America. However, when the dollar began to strongly appreciate in 1980, the burden of dollar debts was revalued, leading into the debt crisis of 1982. In a similar—though much less pronounced—manner, the dollar appreciation that took off in 1995 contributed to the debt crisis in East Asia (Schulmeister, 2000).

Of course, a rising dollar exchange rate raises not only the value of dollar debts but also the value of the respective assets (credits). The overall effect on world trade is, however, negative since the import reduction on behalf of debtor countries is higher than the (possible) increase in imports on behalf of the creditor countries.

Since "equity assets" like stocks, real estate, commodities, or cryptocurrencies are nobody's liability, any bull market raises the value of the respective asset, and nobody loses. Such a wealth effect will stimulate private consumption provided that the asset holders do trust in the permanent character of the revaluation (valuation channel). For that reason, the stock price boom in the United States over the 1990s did stimulate private consumption to a greater extent than the two bull markets following the bear markets in the early 2000s and after the financial crisis of 2008 (Fig. 19.3).

When a bear market devalues financial assets, the related negative wealth effects on demand can be compensated by a revaluation of real (estate) assets. Between 2000 and 2003, for example, the negative wealth effect of the stock bear market ("bursting of the internet bubble") was roughly compensated by the positive effect of the US house price bull market (Fig. 19.4). Afterward, stock prices started to boom again, and house prices continued to rise. The related appreciation of real as

Fig. 19.3 Stock prices in Germany, the United Kingdom, and the United States. (Source: Yahoo Finance)

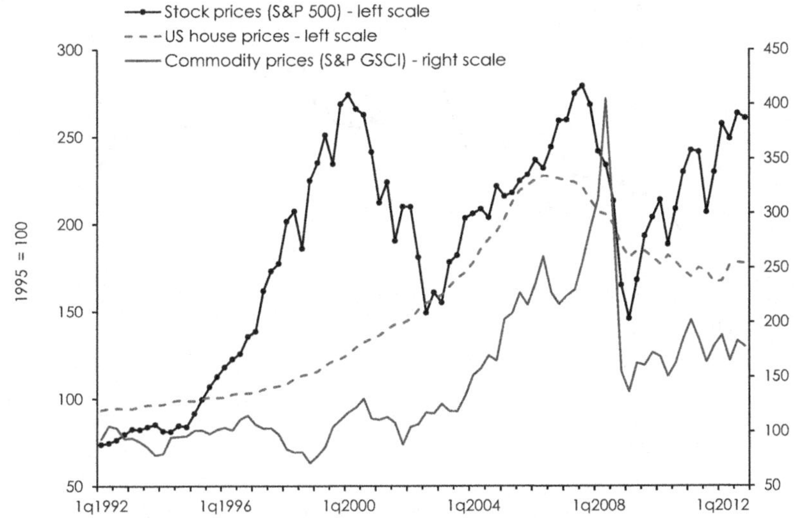

Fig. 19.4 Bulls, bears, and the financial crisis of 2008. (Source: Standard & Poors, Case-Shiller)

well as of financial wealth stimulated demand. At the global level, also commodities prices boomed. This "great moderation" let many economists believe in a stable capitalistic development without inflation and (financial) crises.

However, the three bull markets just paved the way for the three subsequent bear markets. For the first time since 1929, house prices, stock prices, and commodities prices declined almost simultaneously (Fig. 19.4). The negative wealth effects caused demand—nationally as well as globally—to decline strongly and banks' balance sheets to shrink, thereby wiping out their equity. Hence, the "synchronized" three bear markets can be conceived as the most important systemic cause of the financial crisis of 2008.

The third channel through which asset price dynamics affect the real economy concerns the incentive conditions for real relative to financial investments. Stable financial conditions as in the 1950s and 1960s focused on striving for profits to activities in the real economy as the latter yielded much higher returns than financial investments. This incentive effect was particularly pronounced in Europe, where also stock markets were "sleeping" (in contrast to the United States). In Germany, for example, the value of real assets (machinery, buildings, etc.) of nonfinancial business was roughly three times higher than the value of its financial assets. Over the 1970s, real accumulation of the business sector was dampened twice during the recessions of 1973 and 1979 (Fig. 19.5). Since the early 1980s, the value of its financial assets has risen much faster than the value of its real assets, the former exceeding the latter over the past 25 years (Fig. 19.5).

The shift from real-capitalistic to financial-capitalistic incentive conditions necessarily has dampened economic growth: on the one hand, financial speculation became more attractive, and on the other hand, real investments became more

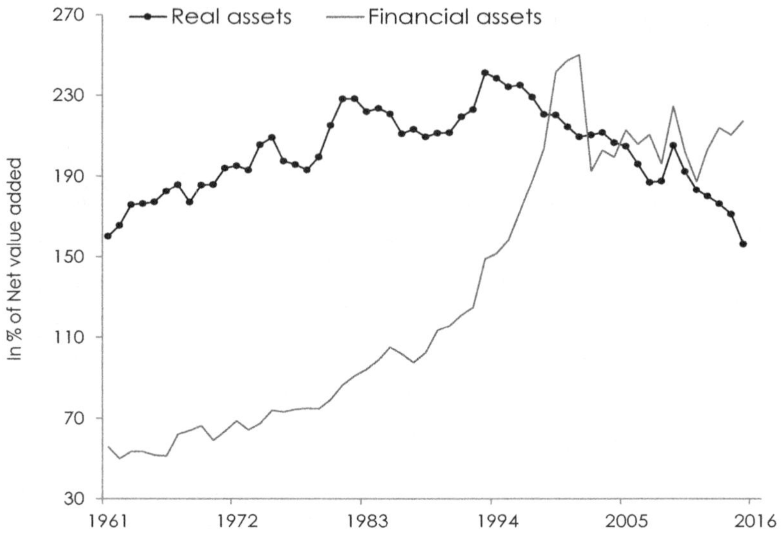

Fig. 19.5 Real and financial accumulation of nonfinancial business in Germany. (Source: destatis, Bundesbank)

uncertain and riskier. The two most important consequences of insufficient real capital formation were: first, the creation of "good" jobs has been slowing down, that is, jobs that are equipped with a substantial amount of capital. Instead, more and more working poor jobs were created, which need only little capital equipment. Second, the fiscal stance has been deteriorating as lower economic growth necessitates higher social expenditure, particularly for the unemployed and working poor, and yields lower tax returns at the same time.

Financial instability has not only contributed to the long-term development of important economic components of the Permacrisis but also to its most important ecological component. Schulmeister (2023) demonstrates in detail why the fluctuations of fossil energy prices and of carbon emissions permit prices impede an efficient carbon pricing. This is so because the latter would call for steadily rising carbon emission costs, and, hence, for steadily and reliably rising fossil energy prices as well as carbon prices. Only under this condition can profits of investments into reducing emissions be calculated (their most important component consists of the avoided costs of fossil energy and of emission permits, respectively). Over the long run, this condition does not hold due to bull and bear markets of fossil energy prices as well as of carbon permit prices. But even over the short run when neither a bullish nor a bearish regime dominate, carbon prices fluctuate much too much to provide a minimum of planning security (Fig. 19.6). The main reason for this instability is once again short-term speculation, in this case in the carbon permit futures markets (Schulmeister, 2023).

Fig. 19.6 Fluctuations of the futures price of EU CO_2 emission allowances. (Source: Intercontinental Exchange (ICE))

"Bull-Bear-Hypothesis" Versus "Efficient Market Hypothesis"

The "efficient market hypothesis" (EMH) still serves as the reference model of asset price dynamics. According to the EMH, asset prices are determined by the respective equilibrium conditions, that is, the "market fundamentals." The "pure" benchmark model is an ideal, frictionless market where all participants are equipped with perfect knowledge and where no transaction costs exist ("world 0").

The EMH model relaxes the assumptions of perfect knowledge and of no transaction costs. Also, in this "world I," actors are fully rational but do not know the expectations of other actors. Hence, prices can reach a new equilibrium only through a gradual price discovery process, driven by rational and therefore stabilizing speculation (Friedman, 1953). Any (temporary) deviation of asset prices from their fundamental equilibrium is due to exogenous shocks. The emergence of news and shocks follows a random walk and so do asset prices. Therefore, speculation techniques based on past prices cannot be systematically profitable (otherwise the market would not even be "weakly efficient"; Fama, 1970).

The "bull-bear-hypothesis" (BBH) perceives trading behavior and price dynamics in asset markets differently ("world II"). Imperfect knowledge and uncertainty are fundamental conditions of social interaction. Therefore, market actors use different models and process different information sets. Their expectations are governed not only by rational calculations, but also by emotional and social factors. In addition, they are mostly formed only qualitatively, that is, as regards the direction of an imminent price movement.

Upward (downward) price movements are triggered by news and then lengthened by "cascades" of buy (sell) signals stemming from trend-following technical trading systems. When the trend loses momentum, "contrarian models" produce sell (buy) signals, which contribute to a change in the direction of the price movement.

The trending behavior of asset prices is fostered by the dominance of either a "bullish" or a "bearish" bias in expectations. News that are in line with the prevailing "market sentiment" gets higher reaction than news that contradict the "market mood." Therefore, price runs in line with the "market mood" last longer than counter-movements. In such a way, short-term runs accumulate into long-term trends, that is, bull markets and bear markets.

The more an asset becomes over(under)valued ("overbought" or "oversold" in traders' jargon), the stronger become counter forces leading to a change in the market sentiment and finally to a tilt in the direction of the long-term trend (in this way, market fundamentals do matter).

The sequence of bull and bear markets shapes the pattern of long-term asset price dynamics: prices develop in irregular cycles around the fundamental equilibrium without any tendency to converge toward this level. It represents rather a "center of gravity" or an "attractor" (as in the theory of "chaotic systems").

Three (stylized) paths of asset prices clarify the differences between the EMH and the BBH (Fig. 19.7):

- In "world 0", new information at t = 1 causes the asset price to jump instantaneously from the old equilibrium at P = 100 (point A) to the new equilibrium at P = 104 (B). In t = 3, news causes the price to jump to P = 102 (at E), and in t = 5 the price jumps to P = 106 (at I).
- In "world I," it takes a series of transactions to move the price from P = 100 to P = 104 (from A to C). Since traders are rational, the movement will stop at the new fundamental equilibrium level and stays there until t = 3, when a new adjustment process takes off.

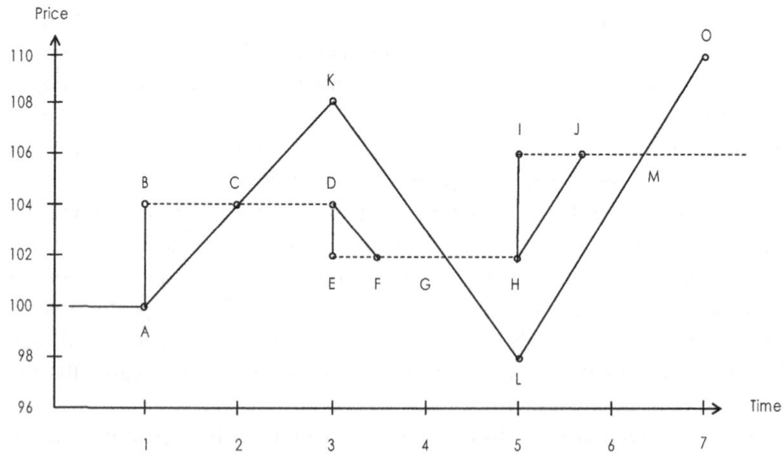

Fig. 19.7 Three stylized paths of asset prices

- In “world II,” traders form their expectations also according to the most recent price movements, that is, when prices move persistently up (down) they expect the respective short-term trend to continue. Hence, they buy (sell) when prices are rising (falling), causing the price to overshoot (from C to K, from G to L, and from M to O).

Profit-seeking traders will try to systematically exploit the trending in asset price dynamics through developing trend-following as well as contrarian strategies so that the conditions of “world II” will almost inevitably emanate from those of “world I”: if prices move smoothly from one fundamental equilibrium to the next, then actors will develop trading systems to exploit this trending behavior since they know that nobody knows exactly the “true” level of fundamental equilibria. Such trading rules based on price charts or on arithmetic transformations of price data have been developed for almost 200 years (“technical analysis”). Over the past 30 years, the trading algorithms have become more complex due to the digital revolution. All these trading strategies process only the information contained in the most recent price movements, and, hence, disregard market fundamentals.

Short-Term Trending of Asset Prices and the Role of Technical Trading

Technical analysis tries to exploit price trends (“the trend is your friend”). Hence, these trading techniques derive buy and sell signals from the most recent price movements that (purportedly) indicate the continuation of a trend or its reversal (trend-following or contrarian models).[1] Since “technicians” believe that the pattern of asset price dynamics as a sequence of trends interrupted by “whipsaws” repeats itself across different time scales, they apply technical models to price data of almost any frequency.

According to the timing of trading signals, one can distinguish between trend-following strategies and contrarian models. Trend-following systems produce buy (sell) signals in the early stage of an upward (downward) trend, whereas contrarian strategies produce sell (buy) signals at the end of an upward (downward) trend.

Technical analysis is omnipresent in financial markets (see, e.g., Cheung et al., 2004; Irwin & Holt, 2004; Gehrig & Menkhoff, 2006; Menkhoff, 2010; Menkhoff & Taylor, 2007). Many factors have contributed to the popularity of technical trading systems among practitioners. First, these systems can be “universally” used, that is, they can be applied to any kind of price data frequency. Second, these price data have become easily available. Third, computer hardware and software have become progressively more powerful. Fourth, the Internet has enabled traders to trade in real time on all important marketplaces in the world.

---

[1] Kaufman (2013) and Murphy (1999) provide an overview of the different methods of technical analysis. For a short description of the most important trading rules, see Schulmeister, 2009c.

Fig. 19.8 Trending and speculation in the US dollar/euro market. (Source: ECB)

Figures 19.1 and 19.8 show how the simplest moving average (MA) models operate in the oil futures market and in the dollar/euro market, respectively. The trading rule is as follows: buy (go long) when the current price crosses the MA from below and sell (go short) when the converse occurs (if a model uses two moving averages, then their crossing indicates a trading signal). The figures show that even these simple rules can exploit asset price trends; however, during "whipsaws," they produce a series of losses.

There exists a general pattern in the profitability of technical trading systems (Table 19.1):

- The number of profitable positions is always smaller than the number of unprofitable positions.
- The average return per day during profitable positions is lower than the average return (loss) during unprofitable positions.
- The average duration of profitable positions is several times greater than that of unprofitable positions.

This pattern characterizes technical trading in general (for a detailed analysis, see Schulmeister, 2008a, b, 2009b, c): make profits from the exploitation of relatively few persistent price trends and limit the losses from many small price fluctuations ("cut losses short and let profits run").

There operates an interaction between the trending of asset prices and the use of technical models. On the one hand, many different models are used by individual traders; on the other hand, the aggregate behavior of all models strengthens and lengthens price trends. Figure 19.9 documents this interaction; it compares the change in the aggregate position of 1092 technical models in the oil futures market (NYMEX) between January 2007 and June 2008 to the movements of the oil futures price (a value of +100/−100 of the net position index means that 100% of the models hold a long/short position).

Table 19.1 Components of the profitability of technical trading systems in various asset markets

	Number of models	Gross rate of return per year	Mean of profitability components					
			Profitable positions			Unprofitable positions		
			Number per year	return per year	Duration in days	Number per year	Return per day	Duration in days
Stock market, S&P 500[a]								
1960–2007, Spot, daily data	2580	1.5	6.5	0.09	42.1	11.7	−0.15	13.1
1983–2007, Futures, Daily data	2580	−3.7	6.5	0.09	40.5	13.5	−0.16	13.3
1983–2007, Futures, 30-minutes data	2580	7.2	87.4	0.40	2.6	138.7	−0.59	1.0
Foreign exchange market								
1973–1999, DM/dollar rate, daily data[b]	1024	7.9	6.0	0.07	55.0	8.1	−0.09	16.9
1975–2007, Yen/dollar rate, daily data[c]	1024	6.9	6.1	0.07	50.7	9.0	−0.09	16.3
1999–2006, Dollar/euro rate, 30-minutes data[d]	2466	1.1	139.5	0.31	1.7	223.5	−0.45	0.8
Commodity futures markets, 1989–2008 (June)[e]								
WTI crude oil, daily data	1092	12.7	3.3	0.15	84.4	5.7	−0.23	23.0
Corn, daily data	1092	3.8	3.0	0.11	89.8	6.5	−0.17	23.3
Wheat, daily data	1092	2.4	2.9	0.11	87.0	6.7	−0.16	25.0
Rough rice, daily data	1092	12.6	3.1	0.12	94.3	5.7	−0.17	23.5

Note: For any single trading system, the following relationship holds: GRR = NPP*DRP*DPP−NPL*DRL*DPL, where *GRR* Gross rate of return per year, *NPP(NPL)* Number of profitable (unprofitable) position per year, *DRP(DRL)* Return per day during profitable (unprofitable) positions, *DPP(DPL)* Duration of profitable (unprofitable) positions in days

[a]Schulmeister (2009c)

[b]Schulmeister (2006)

[c]Schulmeister (2008b)

[d]Schulmeister (2009d)

[e]Schulmeister (2009a)

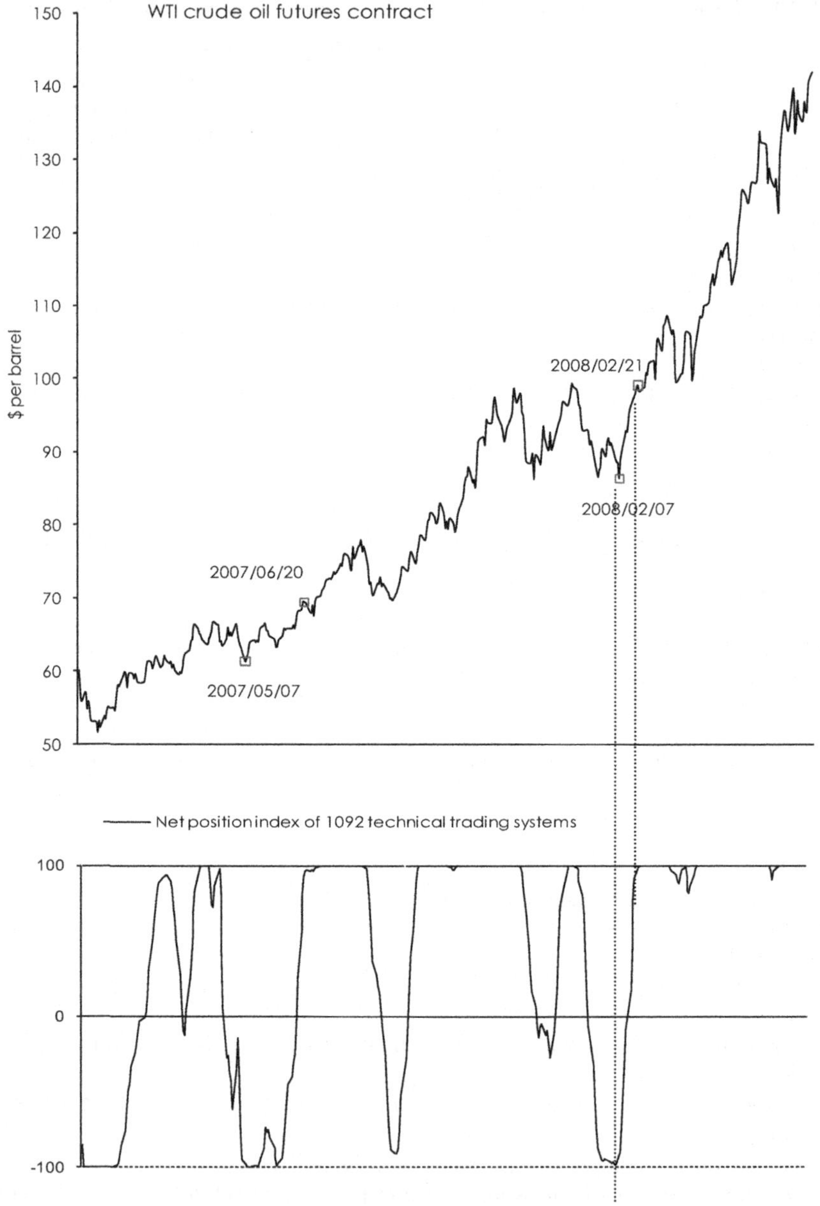

Fig. 19.9 Aggregate trading signals of 1092 technical models and the dynamics of oil futures prices, January 2007 to June 2008. (Source: Schulmeister (2009a))

Figure 19.9 shows the gradual adjustment of technical models to price movements. On February 7, 2008, for example, all models held a short position due to a preceding decline in oil futures prices. The subsequent price rise causes the models to gradually switch their position from short to long, the "fast" models at first, the "slow" models at last. On February 21, all models hold a long position. During this transition period from short to long, technical models exert an excess demand on oil futures since any switch implies two buy transactions, one to close the (former) short position, and one to open the (new) long position.

Studies on the aggregate trading behavior of the many different models, based on daily as well as on intraday data and operating in different markets, reveal the following (Schulmeister, 2006, 2009a, c):

- Most of the time the great majority of the models are on the same side of the market.
- The process of changing open positions usually takes off 1–3 days after the local futures price minimum (maximum) has been reached.
- It takes between 10 and 20 trading days to gradually reverse the positions of (almost) all models if a persistent price trend develops.
- After all technical models have adjusted their open positions to the current trend, the trend often continues for some time.

One can therefore conclude that the widespread use of technical trading systems strengthens short-term asset price trends ("runs").

From Short-Term Trends to Bull and Bear Markets

This section investigates the relationship between the following two phenomena:

- Stock prices, exchange rates, and commodity prices move in a sequence of upward and downward trends, which last for several years (bull and bear markets).
- Asset trading has become progressively "faster," mainly due to the use of algo trading based on intraday data. Consequently, transaction volume has expanded enormously.[2]

[2]Already in 2012, the volume of financial transactions in Europe amounted to roughly 120 times (nominal) GDP, in the United States it had declined from 106 times GDP (2008) to roughly 75 times (2012), mainly due to the Frank-Dodd Act, which aimed at limiting speculation in reaction to the financial crisis of 2008 (Schulmeister, 2015, fig. 11). However, these data underestimate the actual volume of transactions as they do not include trading CDS (credit default swaps) and "repos" (repurchasing agreements). Since 2012, transactions volume must have expanded further, mainly due to the unprecedented expansion of trading on "dark pools," the preferred marketplace of big players trading large blocks of stocks and other assets (as high-frequency traders). However, as data on dark pool transactions are not publicly available, one cannot quantify the recent rise in the volume of overall financial transactions (for dark pools, see Shorter & Miller, 2014).

The coincidence of both developments constitutes a puzzle. How can very short-term transactions generate asset price movements, which accumulate into long-term trends? The "Gestalt" of asset price movements indicates a hypothetical answer (see Figs. 19.1, 19.2, 19.3, 19.4, 19.6, and 19.8):

- Over the short run, asset prices fluctuate almost always around "underlying" trends.
- The phenomenon of trending repeats itself across time scales. However, the volatility of fluctuations around the trend rises with the data frequency (Schulmeister, 2009d).
- Over the long run, asset prices move in a sequence of upward and downward trends lasting several years in most cases ("bulls and bears").

These observations suggest that the pattern of asset price dynamics is shaped by the phenomenon of self-similarity: very short-term price trends ("runs") based on high-frequency data are embedded into comparatively longer-term trends based on data of lower frequency and so on. A bull market or bear market would then be the result of short-term upward (downward) trends lasting longer than counter-movements over an extended period.

To examine this hypothesis, the following exercise was carried out. First, the most pronounced bull markets and bear markets are identified, which occurred over the 1990s and 2000s in the stock market (S&P 500), in the foreign exchange market (dollar/euro rate), and in the oil futures market (NYMEX). Then it is elaborated on how the sequence of monotonic movements ("runs") of daily asset prices brings about long-term trends.

The tripling of stock prices between November 1994 and March 2000, their doubling between October 2002 and October 2007, as well as the rise by roughly 70% between March 2009 and January 2010 was mainly due to upward runs lasting on average by one-third longer than downward runs, and the average slope of upward and downward runs was roughly the same (Table 19.2). In the same manner, the bull market of the dollar/euro exchange rate and of oil futures prices was primarily brought about by upward runs lasting longer than downward runs.

The picture is somewhat different for bear markets. As the speed of price movements is generally greater during "bears" compared to "bulls," the differences in the slope of upward and downward runs contribute to a greater extent to the overall price change during bear markets than during bull markets. However, also the persistence of price movements matters: during "bear markets," downward runs last on average by one-third longer than upward runs.

The accumulation of monotonic price movements to long-term trends is particularly pronounced based on 5-day moving averages of the original price series (Table 19.3). This is not surprising: since there prevails almost always an "underlying" trend, smaller counter-movements are smoothed out even by a short moving average. For example, during the "Internet bull market" between November 1994 and March 2000, there occurred 637 runs based on the original S&P 500 data, but

Table 19.2 Asset price runs during "bull markets" and "bear markets" (Based on daily prices)

			Upward runs			Downward runs		
			Number	Average duration in days	Average slope[a]	Number	Average duration in days	Average slope[a]
S&P 500								
23/11/1994	24/03/2000	↑	319	2.35	7.28	318	1.87	−7.38
24/03/2000	07/10/2002	↓	167	1.73	12.92	168	2.05	−12.93
07/10/2002	09/10/2007	↑	341	2.04	7.08	341	1.65	−7.43
09/10/2007	09/03/2009	↓	103	1.69	15.93	103	1.74	−20.41
09/03/2009	19/01/2010	↑	57	2.25	10.28	57	1.56	−9.63
Dollar/euro exchange rate								
01/01/1999	26/10/2000	↓	113	1.79	0.47	113	2.38	−0.48
31/01/2002	30/12/2004	↑	209	1.96	0.56	209	1.66	−0.51
30/12/2004	14/11/2005	↓	57	1.74	0.53	58	2.16	−0.57
14/11/2005	22/04/2008	↑	168	2.03	0.49	167	1.65	−0.45
22/04/2008	27/10/2008	↓	31	1.74	0.71	32	2.31	−0.97
18/02/2009	03/12/2009	↑	57	1.81	0.88	57	1.68	−0.69
Oil futures prices (NYMEX)[b]								
21/12/1998	20/09/2000	↑	101	2.51	1.44	100	1.76	−1.43
20/09/2000	19/11/2001	↓	72	1.99	2.15	73	1.95	−2.68
19/11/2001	17/07/2006	↑	296	2.12	3.18	295	1.73	−3.43
17/07/2006	19/01/2007	↓	33	1.70	2.74	33	2.15	−4.01
19/01/2007	15/07/2008	↑	102	2.02	4.98	101	1.74	−4.07
15/07/2008	19/02/2009	↓	39	1.44	7.48	40	2.45	−8.43
19/02/2009	23/10/2009	↑	46	2.24	2.87	45	1.56	−3.12

Source: Own calculations; see Schulmeister (2009a, d). The sign ↑/↓ indicates bull/bear markets
[a]Average change in price level per day
[b]Most traded (front month) contract

only 244 based on 5-day moving averages. Of the latter, upward runs lasted on average 6.9 days, downward runs 4.1 days (Table 19.3).

The main (statistical) reason for why upward (downward) asset price runs last on average longer during bull (bear) markets is the following: during a bull (bear) market, there occur significantly more persistent, that is, long-lasting, upward (downward) runs than expected under the EMH. The main (behavioral) reason for this phenomenon is the following: when the direction of a short-term trend is in line with the prevailing market sentiment ("bullishness" or "bearishness," respectively), then traders put more money in their speculative position and hold it longer than during "counter-movements." At the same time, this behavior strengthens the trending of asset prices and, hence, the attractiveness of technical trading strategies.

Table 19.3 Asset price runs during "bull markets" and "bear markets" (Based on 5-day moving averages of daily prices)

			Upward runs			Downward runs		
			Number	Average duration in days	Average slope[a]	Number	Average duration in days	Average slope[a]
S&P 500								
23/11/1994	24/03/2000	↑	122	6.90	3.31	122	4.08	−3.52
24/03/2000	07/10/2002	↓	62	4.32	5.25	63	5.75	−5.79
07/10/2002	09/10/2007	↑	130	5.55	3.19	129	4.12	−2.93
09/10/2007	09/03/2009	↓	39	3.74	5.23	40	5.08	−8.01
09/03/2009	19/01/2010	↑	24	5.79	4.75	24	3.08	−3.27
Dollar/euro exchange rate								
01/01/1999	26/10/2000	↓	44	3.80	0.23	45	6.64	−0.24
31/01/2002	30/12/2004	↑	70	6.77	0.24	68	4.06	−0.24
30/12/2004	14/11/2005	↓	25	3.36	0.23	26	5.23	−0.27
14/11/2005	22/04/2008	↑	59	6.29	0.24	58	4.17	−0.19
22/04/2008	27/10/2008	↓	11	3.91	0.36	12	6.75	−0.54
18/02/2009	03/12/2009	↑	24	5.13	0.36	23	3.13	−0.28
Oil futures prices (NYMEX)[b]								
21/12/1998	20/09/2000	↑	36	7.64	0.70	35	4.29	−0.56
20/09/2000	19/11/2001	↓	30	4.40	0.89	28	5.14	−1.19
19/11/2001	17/07/2006	↑	98	6.81	1.42	98	4.73	−1.55
17/07/2006	19/01/2007	↓	11	3.27	1.14	12	7.25	−1.84
19/01/2007	15/07/2008	↑	40	5.95	2.18	39	3.59	−1.66
15/07/2008	19/02/2009	↓	12	2.83	3.08	13	8.92	−4.07
19/02/2009	23/10/2009	↑	17	6.41	1.37	16	3.75	−1.31

Source: Own calculations; see Schulmeister (2009a, d). The sign ↑/↓ indicates bull/bear markets

[a]Average change in price level per day

[b]Most traded (front month) contract

Transition from Continuous Trading to Electronic Auctions as a Means of Stabilizing Asset Markets

So far, the following stylized facts have been elaborated about the causes and consequences of asset price instability over the short run as well as the medium and long run:

- All important financial asset prices like exchange rates, stock prices, or commodities prices move in a sequence of bull and bear markets, and hence, in long-term irregular cycles.
- This "overshooting" dampens the real economy through changes in the global income distribution, changes in the real burden of (dollar) debts, changes in the valuation of financial wealth, related financial crises, and shifting striving for profits from activities in the real economy to financial speculation.

- The wide fluctuations of fossil energy prices as well as of carbon emission prices prevent anchoring the expectation that the effective costs of carbon emissions will rise steadily, and hence, that investments in emission reductions will be reliably profitable.
- Bull (bear) markets are brought about in the following way: when a bullish (bearish) market sentiment prevails, short-term upward (downward) price trends last a little bit longer than counter-movements, causing the asset to appreciate (depreciate) in a stepwise process.
- Turning points in price movements are triggered by news inducing trend-following systems to produce a series of buy (sell) signals. This lengthens the trend so that finally also amateur traders follow. When the trend loses momentum, contrarian systems produce sell (buy) signals, which together with some news trigger a tilt into a new downward (upward) trend.
- The phenomenon of trending repeats itself across time scales. It is strengthened by the widespread use of technical trading systems based on different data frequencies.
- The less market fundamentals are taken into consideration in asset trading (as with all types of technical or algo models), the greater is the extent of price overshooting. It is greatest when an intrinsic asset value does not even exist as in the case of cryptocurrencies.

It follows from this "diagnosis" that mitigating the extent of asset price "overshooting" calls for restricting short-term trending since "mini-runs" accumulate into short-term trends, which finally accumulate into bull and bear markets. This could be done in two different ways.

First, one could make short-term speculation less profitable by burdening the (notional) value of any financial transaction with a small tax (e.g., between 0.01% and 0.1%). Such an FTT would raise trading costs the more the faster transactions are carried out and the riskier they are (i.e., the higher is the leverage ratio in the case of derivatives trading). For example, if stocks or bonds are bought (sporadically) for holding them, an FTT of 0.01% or even 0.1% does not matter. If, however, a trading system carries out thousands of transactions per day to profit from minuscule price differences (as is the case with high-frequency trading), then even a tax rate of only 0.01% would render the whole business unprofitable (for the concept of a general FTT, see Schulmeister et al., 2008, and Schulmeister, 2015).

The second approach is theoretically more appealing, technically easy to implement, and has so far not seriously been discussed: moving from continuous trading in milli- or even microseconds to electronic auctions, for example, every 3 h (three times per—traditional—trading day). Like the FTT approach, the auction approach aims at restricting (super) fast technical or algo trading. However, it is more radical than the FTT approach in the sense that it does not restrict fast trading by making it more expensive but by making it impossible: if auctions are held only every 3 h, automated trading systems cut off their "food," that is, high-frequency price data.

There are several reasons why this idea should be seriously discussed. First, moving to electronic auctions would eliminate all transactions that are completely unrelated to market fundamentals. Second, asset trading would be slowed down and would become more fundamentals-oriented compared to the present "high-speed casino." Third, electronic auctions at certain intervals would organize a price discovery or "tâtonnement" process as envisaged by one of the founders of neoclassical economics, Léon Walras.

First, the auction model would eliminate all transactions stemming from automated trading systems that generate price movements from which they profit at the same time: high-frequency trading (HFT) systems anticipate large customer's orders through complex algorithms, jump in front of them by buying the assets and resell them within milli- or even microseconds to the customer at a miniscule higher price ("frontrunning").[3] Traditional trading systems based on tick, minute, or hourly data transform small price movements into short-term trends from which they profit at the same time.[4] As HFT as well as traditional technical trading generate liquidity that destabilizes asset prices, eliminating this excessive liquidity would reduce market inefficiency (liquidity per se is not a value in itself).

Second, replacing continuous trading with electronic auctions would shift the focus of trading to reducing the difference between the actual price and the expected fundamental equilibrium (as assumed by the EMH). A simple example illustrates this argument. Suppose a trader is specialized in Apple shares. He uses all available sources about firm-specific fundamental factors like (potential) innovations, marketing strategies, profit expectations, etc., about macroeconomic factors like expected GDP growth, etc., and watches also different technical trading systems. Even if he personally does not believe in these algorithms, he must take them into account as many other traders subscribe to them (Keynes' famous "beauty contest problem"; Keynes, 1936, p. 156). Suppose his fundamental analysis leads our trader to believe that the Apple stock is significantly overvalued. However, when the price starts to rise and (fast) trading systems produce buy signals, he would also buy to profit from the trend. However, if trading were restricted to electronic auctions, short-term trends can no longer be observed. At the same time, any trader must quantitatively gauge the extent of over- or undervaluation of the respective asset as a basis for his orders for the subsequent auction.

This example points at an extremely important feature of (modern) asset markets: trading is based on only *qualitative* expectations concerning the direction of imminent price *movements* (and not on *quantitative* expectations concerning the equilibrium or fundamental price *level*). If news hit the market, for example, that Pfizer acquired a new patent or that the trade deficit of the United States rose stronger than expected, traders will expect Pfizer share price to rise and the dollar exchange rate to fall without quantifying the extent of the imminent price movement. The reason is simple: there is not enough time and information to quantify

---

[3] The types of high-frequency trading and the related challenges for regulatory policy are documented in Shorter & Miller, 2016; Virgilio (2019) provides a survey of the literature on high-frequency trading.

[4] Figure 19.9 shows that when most simulated trading systems hold already a position in line with the current trend, the latter continues for some time, probably due to some "late coming bandwagonists" who—as a group—are the losers in this "game."

how strongly the Pfizer share price will rise, or the dollar exchange rate will fall and within which time. For making profits, it is in most cases sufficient to catch the direction of the imminent price movement.

The same is true for all technical trading strategies, chartism, as well as algorithmic models. For example, so-called "support lines" or "resistance lines" (purportedly) only indicate a continuation or a reversal of a prevailing price trend. In the case of moving average models, momentum models, or any other traditional (quantitative) technical model, a buy signal, for example, only implies that in most cases one will make a loss when following the signal (the number of single losses always exceeds the number of single profits; Table 19.1). However, persistent trends occur sufficiently often (even though one cannot know when) so that the profits from their exploitation overcompensate the smaller losses from "whipsaws," that is, smaller price fluctuations.

Whereas in the world of (super) fast continuous trading it is a waste of time to gauge the fundamental equilibrium level of an asset price, it would pay off to do so in the world of electronic auctions: the better one can approximate the extent of over- or undervaluation of an asset, the more profitable his auction orders will be. Also, other traders will have to focus on market fundamentals. Hence, when forming expectations about other traders' expectations ("beauty contest problem") fundamental factors will matter much more than "technical" factors.

Clearly, if three prices would be determined by electronic auctions per trading day, one could still apply technical trading systems based on the respective price series. However, as the speed of technical trading would be so much slower compared to continuous trading, one need not and will not blindly follow the trading signals as in the case of high-speed automated systems. Hence, one will take (also) fundamental factors into account.

The third argument in favor of moving from continuous trading to electronic auctions concerns auctions as a general method of organizing a fundamentals-oriented price discovery process, that is, as a means of approximating the "true" equilibrium price under "real-world conditions" (uncertainty, risk, nonrational factors, and their "bundling" to herding effects, etc.). In the context of asset prices, it is specifically important to shift the focus of expectations formations from "noise" to the market fundamentals.

Technically, such auctions are easy to implement, they would be conducted on electronic trading platforms in the same manner as the opening price is determined already today on organized exchanges: the computer calculates the equilibrium price based on all buy and sell orders, valid for the following 3 h.

At first glance, one could argue that such an auction model weakens market efficiency insofar as prices cannot react to news right away but only at the next following auction. Since immediate price movements to news almost always overreact (because traders must react as fast as possible without knowing the new equilibrium level), the slow-down of trading provides the time necessary to evaluate the possible price effect of all news that have hit the market since the last auction.

For all people who want to buy or sell stocks, bonds, foreign exchange, etc., for business purposes or for personal reasons, it is sufficient to be able to do so every 3 h. Hence, they would not be affected by replacing continuous trading with electronic auctions. By contrast, the environment of professional trading would change substantially: the many monitors for watching price movements at different data frequencies and the respective trading signals produced by different algorithms would become superfluous. At the same time, the ability to gauge the "true" value of an asset based on an analysis of its fundamental factors would become the most important prerequisite for successful trading.

Even though the idea to organize the asset price discovery process as electronic auctions is based on the empirical evidence of continuous trading over decades, it will hardly be discussed seriously very soon. The main reason for that is the following: what is "empirically evident" depends on the perception of the observer and, hence, on the theory he/she subscribes to. This in turn depends on the "Weltanschauung" or "paradigm" that dominates in academia, media, and politics: once a paradigm has been established, facts that fundamentally contradict the paradigm remain mostly unseen or are suppressed.

This issue was first analyzed in 1935 by Ludwik Fleck in his pathbreaking, yet for decades neglected monograph *Genesis and Development of a Scientific Fact*:[5] "Once a structurally complete and closed system of opinions consisting of many details and relations has been formed, it offers enduring resistance to anything that contradicts it……1) A contradiction to the system appears unthinkable; 2) What does not fit into the system remains unseen; 3) alternatively, if it is seen, either it is kept secret, or 4) laborious efforts are made to explain an exception in terms that do not contradict the system……" (Fleck, 1979, p. 27).

Since the late 1960s, general equilibrium theory completed with the assumption of "rational expectations" has been re-established in economics as a "structurally complete and closed system of opinions." Fleck calls such a system "harmony of illusions" (Fleck, 1979, p. 27), an expression that condensates the essence of the general equilibrium theory in two terms. Embedded in this model is the theory of the efficiency of financial markets that implies two assumptions: first, the prices of assets reflect their fundamental value, and second, speculation systems based only on the information contained in past prices cannot be profitable (otherwise, the market would not even be "weakly efficient"; Fama, 1970).

In line with Fleck's statement 1, it appears "unthinkable" (to mainstream economists) that asset prices move in "long swings" as a sequence of bull and bear markets and that trading rules derived only from past prices are (too) often profitable. Both phenomena would fundamentally contradict the prevailing "thought system": that precisely those markets that come closest to the perfect market of equilibrium theory (as regards market access, transaction costs, etc.) *systematically* generate "wrong" prices, for example, "overshooting," is "unthinkable" within the paradigm. The same holds true for destabilizing, yet profitable, speculation.

[5] Thomas S. Kuhn took the most original ideas from Fleck's monography for his bestseller *The Structure of Scientific Revolutions* (1962) as he himself noticed in the introduction ("an essay that anticipated many of my own ideas"; Kuhn 1962, p. VII). However, Kuhn did not quote Fleck's monography in the main text of his book. An English translation of Fleck's monography was published only in 1979 (including a foreword by Thomas Kuhn; Fleck, 1979).

For the same reason, technical trading is never considered as "profit-rational" (though not rational in the sense of "rational expectations") in theoretical models of asset price dynamics—"it does not fit into the system" and, hence, "remains unseen" (in accordance with Fleck's statement 2). In practice, trading rules have been used for more than 150 years but have been ignored also in empirical research (Fleck's statement 3). Only over the past 30 years have trading systems increasingly been analyzed, however, rather as some kind of useless "anomaly" ("noise trading")—although by now they generate most financial transactions (including HFT).[6] Therefore, also the following (dissolvable) contradiction has been neglected: if these models are useless, then the assumption of agents' rationality is untenable, and if they are (often) profitable, then the assumption of (weak) market efficiency is untenable.

Even though the empirical foundation of the proposal to replace continuous asset trading with electronic auctions contradicts directly the (still) prevailing economic paradigm, its documentation might be useful as part of preparing for a deepening of the present multidimensional crisis. As shown in section "Asset price instability and the real economy", bear markets can easily trigger a financial crisis via the negative valuation effects. For example, between February 17, 2020, and March 23, 2020, stock prices fell globally like never before in history (within roughly 5 weeks, the S&P 500 declined by 34% and the MSCI World by 33%). Only through an unprecedented intervention did the most important central banks succeed in stopping the decline and in convincing the "big players" to get back into the market (at much lower prices). As a result, the "fastest" bear market tilted into a mega bull market (stock prices more than doubled when the real economy suffered its deepest decline since 1945 due to COVID-19). A more recent example is the balance sheet contraction of US banks caused by falling bond prices, which in turn were caused by rising interest rates. Also in this case, policy had to intervene and thereby had to break its own rules.

Despite these turbulences, it seems still premature to deal with the technicalities of organizing electronic auctions. The respective guidelines, however, are clear cut: in each of the three global trading time zones (Asia and Pacific, Europa, America), there should operate one single and common exchange for each type of standardized assets. These comprise all assets already traded on organized exchanges like stocks, bonds, commodities derivatives, and carbon emission permits, as well as standardized assets that at present are still traded primarily over the counter like currencies (customized OTC instruments need not be traded in the form of electronic auctions as these instruments are not used for "fast" algo trading). "Dark pools" should be closed and other types of segmentation of markets for standardized assets need to be avoided.

---

[6] The same holds for the behavioral finance literature in general, which usually takes the EMH as the benchmark model and explores empirical deviations as "anomalies." By contrast, if one follows an inductive approach, then empirical phenomena like bull markets, bear markets, technical trading, etc., appear as characteristic properties of asset market dynamics ("benchmark") and prices oscillating around fundamental equilibria as idealistic imaginations ("anomalies").

Conclusions

Economic development over the last 50 years has been shaped by a structural financial instability. Its most important systemic component concerns asset price dynamics: exchange rates, stock prices, commodities prices, and bond prices move in a sequence of bull and bear markets, and hence, in long-term irregular cycles (in contrast to the 1950s and 1960s when financial markets were largely regulated).

This "overshooting" dampens the real economy through three channels: through shifts in the distribution of income from international trade (distribution channel), through changes in the real burden of international (dollar) debts and changes in the valuation of equity wealth such as stocks, bonds, commodities, real estate, etc., as well as through the related financial crises (valuation channel), and through shifting striving for profits from activities in the real economy to financial speculation (incentive channel).

In addition, the bull and bear markets of fossil energy prices as well as of carbon emission prices impede fighting global heating because they prevent anchoring the expectation that the effective costs of carbon emissions will rise steadily.

Bull (bear) markets are the result of the accumulation of short-term price trends lasting longer than counter-movements over an extended period. Short-term upward (downward) price movements are usually triggered by news and then lengthened by "cascades" of buy (sell) signals stemming from trend-following technical ("algo") trading systems. When the trend loses momentum, "contrarian models" produce sell (buy) signals, which contribute to a change in the direction of the trend. Short-term trending repeats itself across different time scales due to the use of algo trading systems based on different data frequencies (from tick data to daily data). Nowadays most financial transactions are triggered by automated trading systems that completely disregard market fundamentals (as all kinds of technical trading systems do).

In asset markets, most of the time there dominates either a "bullish" or "bearish" expectational bias. News in line with the prevailing market sentiment trigger more persistent price runs than oppositional news. In such a way, short-term runs accumulate into bull markets and bear markets. The more an asset becomes over(under) valued, the stronger become counter forces, leading to a change in the market sentiment and finally to a tilt in the direction of the long-term trend (in this way, market fundamentals do matter). Hence, asset prices move in irregular cycles around their fundamental equilibrium without any tendency to converge toward this level.

Dampening the "long swings" of asset prices calls for eliminating those (fast) transactions that strengthen short-term trending and that are completely unrelated to market fundamentals, that is, all transactions exclusively triggered by technical trading systems. This type of liquidity does not enhance the "price discovery process" but the "price distortion process."

A financial transactions tax could serve this purpose by making "fast" algo trading unprofitable. However, there is an alternative approach that is theoretically more appealing, technically easy to implement, and that has so far not seriously been discussed: replacing continuous trading in milli- or even microseconds with electronic auctions, for example, every 3 h. In this way, practically all types of (super) fast technical or algo trading systems could no longer be applied as they are cut off their input, that is, the most recent high-frequency price data. Asset trading would be slowed down and would become more fundamentals-oriented because traders need to consider market fundamentals when placing their orders for the auction.

Clearly, for now the idea to move from continuous asset trading to electronic auctions appears utopian at best. However, once the economic as well as the ecological unsustainability of the prevailing system of asset price formation becomes evident during a deepening of the present multidimensional crisis, discussed in this volume with the concept of Permacrisis, a serious discussion of the empirical foundation of this idea might help as one steps into the right direction. At the end of a dead end, one must turn around.

References

Cheung, Y.-W., Chinn, M., & Marsh, I. (2004). How do UK-based foreign exchange dealers think their market operates? *International Journal of Finance and Economics, 9*(4), 289–306.

Fama, E. F. (1970). Efficient capital markets: A review of theory and empirical work. *The Journal of Finance, 25*(2), 383–417.

Fleck, L. (1979). Genesis and development of a scientific fact, transl. by Fred Bradley and Thaddeus J. Trenn. In T. J. Trenn & R. K. Merton (Eds.), *"Foreword" by Thomas S. Kuhn*. The University of Chicago Press. (Originally published in German in 1935).

Friedman, M. (1953). The case for flexible exchange rates. In M. Friedman (Ed.), *Essays in positive economics*. University of Chicago Press.

Gehrig, T., & Menkhoff, L. (2006). Extended evidence on the use of technical analysis in foreign exchange. *International Journal of Finance and Economics, 11*(4), 293–284.

Irwin, S., & Holt, B. (2004). The impact of large hedge fund and CTA trading on futures market volatility. In G. N. Gregoriou, V. N. Karavas, F. S. L'Habitant, & F. Rouah (Eds.), *Commodity trading advisers: Risk, performance analysis and selection* (pp. 151–182). Wiley.

Kaufman, P. J. (2013). *Trading systems and methods* (5th ed.). Wiley.

Keynes, J. M. (1936). *The general theory of employment, income and money*. Macmillan.

Kuhn, T. S. (1962). *The structure of scientific revolutions*. The University of Chicago Press.

Menkhoff, L., & Taylor, M. P. (2007). The obstinate passion of foreign exchange professionals: Technical analysis. *Journal of Economic Literature, 45*(4), 936–972.

Menkoff, L. (2010). The use of technical analysis by fund managers: International evidence. *Journal of Banking & Finance, 34*(11), 2573–2586.

Murphy, J. J. (1999). *Technical analysis of the financial markets: A comprehensive guide to trading methods and applications*. New York Institute of Finance.

Schulmeister, S. (2000). Globalization without global money: The double role of the dollar as national currency and as world currency. *Journal of Post Keynesian Economics, 22*(3), 365–395.

Schulmeister, S. (2006). The interaction between technical currency trading and exchange rate fluctuations. *Finance Research Letters, 2*, 212–233.

Schulmeister, S. (2008a). Components of the profitability of technical currency trading. *Applied Financial Economics, 2008*, 1–14.

Schulmeister, S. (2008b). *Profitability of technical currency speculation: The case of yen/dollar trading 1976–2007* (WIFO Working Paper 325, 2008).

Schulmeister, S. (2009a, January). *Trading practices and price dynamics in commodities markets and the stabilizing effects of a transactions tax.* Study by the Austrian Institute of Economic Research (WIFO), supported by the Anniversary Fund of the Österreichische Nationalbank, Vienna.

Schulmeister, S. (2009b). Aggregate trading behavior of technical models and the Yen/Dollar exchange rate 1976–2007. *Japan and the World Economy, 21*, 270–279.

Schulmeister, S. (2009c). The profitability of technical stock trading: Has it moved from daily to intraday data? *Review of Financial Economics, 18*(4), 163–210, available online www.science--direct.com

Schulmeister, S. (2009d, November). *Technical trading and trends in the Dollar/Euro exchange rate*. Study by the Austrian Institute of Economic Research (WIFO), supported by the Anniversary Fund of the Österreichische Nationalbank, Vienna.

Schulmeister, S. (2015). The struggle over the financial transactions tax: A politico-economic farce. In *What future for taxation in the EU? Revue de l'OFCE, EUROFRAME 2014 Conference volume, 2015* (pp. 15–55).

Schulmeister, S. (2021). Chapter 2: The road from prosperity into the crisis: The long cycle of post-war economic, social and political development. In B. De Souza Guilherme, C. Ghymers, S. Griffith-Jones, & H. A. Ribeiro (Eds.), *Financial crisis management and democracy.* Springer.

Schulmeister, Stephan, "Fixing rising price paths for fossil energy – Basis of a 'green growth' without rebound effects", in Ribeiro Hoffmann, Andrea, Sandrin, Paula, Doukas, Janis (eds) , Climate change in regional perspective – European Union and Latin American initiatives, challenges, and solutions Springer, 2023.

Schulmeister, S., Schratzenstaller, M., & Picek, O. (2008, April). *A General financial transaction tax – Motives, revenues, feasibility and effects.* Study of the Austrian Institute of Economic Research (WIFO), Vienna.

Shorter, G., & Miller, R. S. (2014). *Dark pools in equity trading: Policy concerns and recent developments*. Congressional Research Service. Online: https://crsreports.congress.gov/product/pdf/R/R43739

Shorter, G., & Miller, R. S. (2016). *High frequency trading: Overview of recent developments.* Congressional Research Service. Online: https://sgp.fas.org/crs/misc/R44443.pdf

Virgilio, G. P. M. (2019). High-frequency trading: A literature review. *Financial Markets and Portfolio Management, 33*(2019), 183–208. Online: https://doi.org/10.1007/s11408-019-00331-6

Chapter 20
The Weaponization of Finance and Digitalization: A Cooperative Approach Between the EU and LAC

Nicola Bilotta

Contents

Introduction

As a global currency does not exist, international trade, transnational investments and cross-border payments require the intermediation of national currencies. An international currency fulfills the three main functions of money: medium of exchange, store of value, and unit of account. The global appeal of a currency depends on fundamental economic factors—such determinants include, for instance, the size of the issuing economy in terms of global trade and finance, the soundness of economic policies, financial market depth, and liquidity. A burgeoning literature also stresses that the choice is also driven by underpinning institutional and geostrategic factors (Eichengreen et al., 2018). As some national currencies are used disproportionately, any international currency holds global political and geostrategic value. States can use international monetary systems—and the leading role of their national currencies—as an instrument of power (Kirshner, 1995). Since the collapse of the Gold Standard, the US dollar has been the only truly global currency,

N. Bilotta (✉)
European University Institute – EUI, Fiesole, Italy

Instituto Affari Internazionali – IAI, Rome, Italy
e-mail: Nicola.Bilotta@eui.eu; n.bilotta@iai.it

D. Katsikas et al. (eds.), *Finance, Growth and Democracy: Connections and Challenges in Europe and Latin America in the Era of Permacrisis*, United Nations University Series on Regionalism 33, https://doi.org/10.1007/978-3-031-68475-3_20

providing the United States with a powerful tool for foreign policy. Nevertheless, three growing forces—economic dislocations, geopolitical tensions, and digitalization—might foster fragmentation in the global monetary system. The risk is the emergence of economic blocs, which could establish parallel, noncomplementary systems setting obstacles to the cross-border flow of capital and money.

In this scenario, the possible development of national Central Bank Digital Currencies (CBDCs) might provide the international monetary architecture with an underlying new tool to establish new ways to settle cross-border transactions. However, a future system of multi-CBDCs arrangements requires cross-country cooperation to make their infrastructure interoperable. As most countries are currently in the exploration phase of this new technology, the European Union (EU) and the Latin American and the Caribbean (LAC) have a unique opportunity to launch a cooperation exercise to develop experiments in the framework of CBDC systems. The EU and LAC have a shared interest in partnering up to shape the architecture of the next international monetary system to strengthen their autonomy from the United States and China.

The "Weaponization" of Finance

Following the invasion of Ukraine in February 2022, the decision by the United States and Europe to disconnect specific Russian banks from the Society for Worldwide Interbank Financial Telecommunication (SWIFT) and to freeze Russia's foreign reserves might have significant, long-term effects on the international monetary system. While transformations in this system have historically been slow to materialize, the range and scope of the recently deployed sanctions will likely catalyze a global push to diversify from the US dollar-centric global financial system. Whether the United States and European countries, as well as their allies, will strengthen or reduce financial sanctions against Russia in the future, the "weaponization" of finance against a G20 country like Russia sets a historical precedent that will amplify concerns that one day any country could be disconnected from Western-dominated financial infrastructure (Nicola Bilotta, 2022) (Figs. 20.1 and 20.2).

While it is true that no other contender could challenge the existing US-dominated dollar system in the short-to-medium term, the United States and its allies should strategically reflect upon the long-term implications if their leadership in the global monetary system is eroded. Debates on the US dollar's international dominance are nothing new. Even before the war in Ukraine, it was widely acknowledged that the current global monetary regime provided the United States with an extremely efficient bulwark to leverage and enforce its foreign policy internationally. As the global economy relies on the US dollar as the primary medium for cross-border transactions and foreign reserves, the United States derives significant economic and national security benefits from its central role in the global financial system (White House, 2022).

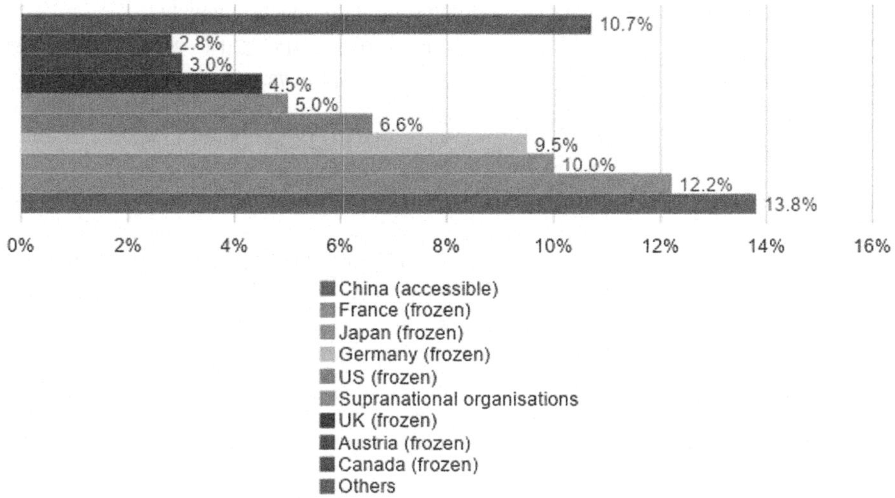

Fig. 20.1 Location of Bank of Russia foreign exchange reserves and gold assets in June 2021. (Source: Author's elaboration from *Bank of Russia Foreign Exchange and Gold Asset Management Report*, No. 1/2022, http://cbr.ru/Collection/Collection/File/39685/2022-01_res_en.pdf)

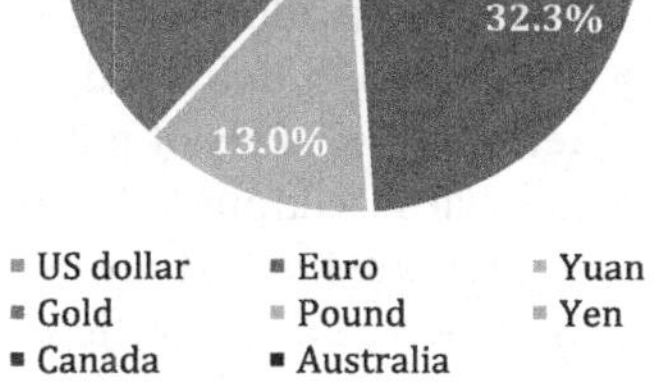

Fig. 20.2 Composition of Bank of Russia's assets in foreign currency and gold as of June 2021. (Source: Author's elaboration from *Bank of Russia Foreign Exchange and Gold Asset Management Report*, No. 1/2022, cit)

Over the past 20 years, several countries have been attempting to make their currency an attractive alternative to the US dollar. China has implemented significant efforts to globalize its national currency as, compared to its economic power, the yuan significantly underperforms as an international currency, making Beijing highly dependent and vulnerable to the US dollar (Reuters, 2020). Also, the European Union, one of the United States' closest allies, has set the goal of increasing the internationalization of the euro as a key dimension of its ambitions for

Table 20.1 The international status of the US dollar, the euro, and the renminbi

		2016	2017	2018	2019	2020	2021	2022
Share of global GDP (%)	The United States	21.38	20.94	20.73	21.39	21.61	–	–
	Euro	17.96	18.19	18.44	18	17.96	–	–
	China	12.84	13.23	14.03	14.29	15.19	–	–
Share of global FX reserves (%)	The United States	65.36	62.73	61.76	60.75	58.92	58.86	58.88
	Euro	19.14	20.17	20.67	20.59	21.29	20.58	20.06
	RMB	1.08	1.23	1.89	1.94	2.29	2.80	2.88
Share of forex trading[a] (%)	The United States	87.58	–	–	88.30	–	–	88.45
	Euro	31.39	–	–	32.28	–	–	30.45
	RMB	3.99	–	–	4.32	–	–	7.01
Share of global payments (%)	The United States	41.92	39.85	39.21	39.77	40.33	40.51	41.19
	Euro	30.69	35.66	34.32	36.32	43.10	36.65	35.49
	RMB	1.82	1.61	1.66	1.95	1.76	2.70	2.20

Source: Share of global GDP: World Bank Data; COFER: IMF Data; BIS: 2019; SWIFT: RMB Tracker, https://www.swift.com/node/11096

[a]Note: since each transaction involves two currencies, the sum of individual currency shares will also equate to 200%

strategic autonomy (Panetta, 2020). Countries have moreover tried to reduce their dependency on the US-controlled global payment infrastructure. For example, China, Russia, and India have repeatedly expressed their interest to jointly explore an independent alternative to SWIFT (Liu, 2022), while the EU launched (a rather unsuccessful) EU–Iran payment vehicle INSTEX in 2019 to get around US sanctions reimposed on Tehran by the Trump administration (Table 20.1).

Attempts to significantly erode the US dollar's dominance have failed thus far, yet there are—small but still relevant—signals of potential trends of fragmentation that could be accelerated by the war in Ukraine. The International Monetary Fund (IMF), for example, has already reported that some countries are renegotiating the currency used to settle their trade agreements in light of the sanctions applied to Russia. Moreover, foreign reserves in US dollars decreased globally from around 70% at the beginning of the 2000s to 59% in the third quarter of 2021. According to a recent IMF study, a quarter of this shift was allocated to the yuan while three quarters into the currencies of smaller countries (Arslanalp et al., 2022). Thus, central banks have been implementing a portfolio diversification strategy driven by market forces. In this context, the recent weaponization of the US dollar could accelerate this ongoing diversification process, a trend that may be further incentivized by a "de-risking management" strategy.

The key question, however, is where this shift could be diverted to, given that a credible alternative to the US dollar is currently lacking. The yuan does not seem to have the underlying characteristics to replace the US dollar. The yuan's

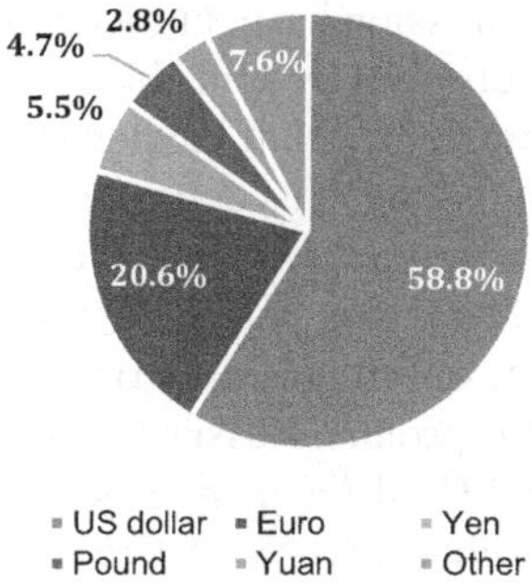

Fig. 20.3 World allocated reserves by currency for 2023, second quarter. (Source: Author's elaboration from: IMF Data, *Currency Composition of Official Foreign Exchange Reserve*, https://data.imf.org/?sk=E6A5F467-C14B-4AA8-9F6D-5A09EC4E62A4)

internationalization is weighted down by policy and institutional factors (like capital account controls or limited convertibility) that cannot be mitigated by geostrategic motivations. Furthermore, current trends of growing diversification in the composition of foreign reserves appear to be directed toward other Western countries and allies—such as the Canadian dollar, the Australian dollar, and the South Korean won—states that tend to align with the US foreign policy priorities (Fig. 20.3).

Despite their noteworthy operative constraints, alternatives to SWIFT are slowly emerging. China launched the Cross-Border Interbank Payments System (CIPS) in 2015, while Russia developed the System for Transfer of Financial Messages (SPFS) in 2014. The volume of transactions processed by the CIPS system grew by 83% in 2021 while SPFS doubled the number of processed messages (Shagina, 2021). However, today CIPS and SPFS together process less than 1% of SWIFT's volume of transactions. SWIFT is reported to carry around 140 trillion US dollars' worth of transactions—of which 40% in US dollars, 37% in euro, and 6% in UK pounds (The Economist, 2021). In the medium term, CIPS could be a more realistic and attractive option as the yuan has a stronger international status than the Russian rouble. Moreover, China could potentially foster CIPS' adoption through its extensive global trade links. Nevertheless, CIPS is constrained by the low internationalization of the yuan, which today is used for only 2% of global payments (Perez-Saiz & Zhang, 2023). Moreover, the CIPS system is directly linked with SWIFT as it can enable the transmission of information related to a transaction through either CIPS or SWIFT channels. Currently, CIPS and SWIFT are cooperating more than competing (SWIFT, 2016). What seems more plausible in the medium term is that new alternatives, like CIPS, could consolidate regionally and along trade links, ultimately leading to the establishment of different multilateral payment systems that cooperate and compete among each other.

In a situation similar to that experienced with SWIFT, countries have been trying to establish alternatives to VISA and Mastercard. The European Central Bank

(ECB) and the European Commission have, unsuccessfully, promoted several initiatives to create a domestic European system. In 2020, the European Commission published the "Communication on a Retail Payments Strategy for the EU" in which it stressed the EU's vulnerability due to its dependency on foreign payment systems. In 2021, 31 major European commercial banks launched the "European Payments Initiative" with the aim of developing a pan-European payment system by 2022. However, by December 2021, only French, German, and Belgium banks had confirmed their commitment to the project. Russia developed its own domestic payment infrastructure, called National Card Payment System (NSPK), in 2014, in light of Western sanctions following the invasion of Crimea. The Russian domestic card system, MIR, runs on the NSPK infrastructure. Today, more than 100 million MIR cards, 1/3 of the domestic market, are in circulation in the country. This sharp adoption has been also driven by the mandate for use by civil servants and pensioners.

China's UnionPay cards capture more than half of the global market. However, only 150 million out of the 9 billion cards issued are issued outside mainland China. The weaponization of Visa and Mastercard, which have suspended their activity in Russia, might incentivize the adoption abroad of UnionPay cards as it could appear a more reliable and less political alternative. However, both UnionPay and MIR have structural limitations in terms of scalability and usability. It will be extremely challenging—if not impossible—for these systems to reach a scale outside of their respective countries.

Future Scenario: Economic Dislocation, Geopolitics, and Digitalization

While prior attempts to reduce dependence on the US dollar were not successful, the confluence of geopolitical tensions, economic upheaval, and digital transformation may create a conducive environment for a gradual fragmentation of the global monetary system in the long term.

According to a recent article in *The Economist*, the 25 largest "nonaligned" countries—those that have neither imposed sanctions on Russia nor wish to take sides in the Sino-American conflict—now constitute 45% of the global population. Moreover, their share of global GDP has risen from 11% in the 1990s to 18% today, surpassing that of the EU (The Economist, 2023). Despite their substantial economic influence, the diverse national interests of these countries make it unlikely for them to act as a cohesive unit. However, they may find common ground on specific issues as exemplified by OPEC's recent decision to reduce oil production despite opposition from Western nations (Foroohar, 2023). The global oil trading market serves as a notable illustration of the distinct status of the US dollar. Since the early 1970s, major oil-producing nations, particularly those within OPEC, have consistently priced oil exclusively in dollars. Nevertheless, recent developments indicate modest efforts to diverge from the dollar in this sphere.

In December 2022, China extended an invitation to Saudi Arabia and other Gulf countries to consider settling their bilateral oil-trade transactions in yuan. Similarly, India and Russia are presently renegotiating to establish arrangements in rupees and rubles for settling their oil-trade transactions, driven by the repercussions of Western sanctions. Countries such as Russia, Iran, and Venezuela, collectively holding 40% of OPEC+ proven oil reserves, possess strategic incentives to contemplate a shift to yuan-denominated oil. Additionally, another 40% of proven oil reserves belong to the Gulf Cooperation Council, whose members, while historically close to the United States, have been increasingly assertive in articulating their own positions on vital regional and global issues. It is important not to overstate the potential impact, however. Even if all of China's oil imports were denominated in yuan, it would represent only 15–20% of future global contracts.

Nonetheless, it serves as a prominent example of a broader megatrend wherein countries are exploring alternatives to the US dollar in their trade agreements. Following this narrative, the world economy has experienced a growing number of bilateral and multilateral agreements to reduce dependency on the US dollar. For example, the People's Bank of China recently announced the signing of a Memorandum of Understanding (MoU) to establish Chinese yuan clearing arrangements with the Banco Central do Brazil. Furthermore, Brazil and Argentina have initiated discussions, seemingly improbable, about the development of a common currency, signaling their interest in closer economic integration. With the newly elected Argentinian government led by Milei, this development should be considered unviable. Of greater significance, the BRICS countries have announced their intention to engage in discussions regarding the launch of a new currency during the upcoming August 2024 summit. While it is probable that this announcement will remain primarily symbolic and abstract, it has the potential to encourage an enhanced trend among BRICS countries to facilitate trade settlements in their respective currencies.

In August 2023, the BRICS announced that Argentina, Egypt, Ethiopia, Iran, Saudi Arabia, and the United Arab Emirates have been invited to become new members. On the one hand, the enlargement of the BRICS group might further strengthen the geopolitical leverage of this parallel group of influence, consolidating a new voice in multilateral fora. On the other hand, it might damage the ability of a larger group of countries to find a common agreement in international affairs. Moreover, the new government in Argentina has already announced its intention to not join the BRICS while Ethiopia declared defaults on sovereign debt, making its global standing more fragile. If the BRICS have faced systemic weaknesses in the past, the future of this group of countries appears even more challenging.

Inertia and frictions are key forces that tend to consolidate the hegemony of the US dollar but, in this context of a growing politicization of money, the process of financial digitalization can be a crucial force of change in pushing diversification in both the composition of foreign reserves and cross-border payment systems. In the former area, with the advent of automated and electronic trading platforms that significantly lower transaction costs, central banks have gained a much easier and cheaper access to foreign currencies, incentivizing reserve diversification.

Furthermore, the possible introduction of Central Bank Digital Currencies (CBDCs) around the world has the potential to lower the costs of cross-border transactions (BIS, 2021). A recent survey of 50 central banks in the first quarter of 2021 explored initial thinking on CBDCs' cross-border use (Auer et al., 2021).

In a future scenario in which several national CBDCs are developed, bilateral and multilateral CBDC arrangements can promote establishing a new payment systems network based on multi-CBDCs arrangements in which exchange risks are drastically reduced and nodes are more independent from the US dollar. CBDCs could lower transaction costs, not incurring expensive interchange or foreign transaction fees as they would not require the multilayered clearance and settlement infrastructure behind credit card transactions (Auer et al., 2021). Moreover, a well-designed CBDC could facilitate the digitalization of information exchanges in alternative data, potentially connecting a CBDC system with higher value services provided at a lower cost (Ferrari & Mehl, 2021).

In line with this vision, digital networks and multi-CBDC arrangements could ease the empowerment of more efficient trade links with the application of smart contracts via distributed-ledger systems, programmable money, and programmable payments that could support increasingly complicated business logic. Finally, programmability can also automate processes that currently lead to cost frictions in the settlement of securities and can facilitate the orderly settlement of intra-bank reserves both domestically and cross-border via "currency corridors" such as multi-CBDC arrangements.

However, to enable this potential, there is the need for some degree of cooperation on shared standards and protocols to ensure interoperability between CBDC systems. CBDCs would then require countries to accept each other's currencies as the currency of trade. As China is the frontrunner in the global race for CBDC's issuance, Beijing is levering its first-mover advantage to influence the development of CBDCs globally. The People's Bank of China has already proposed a set of global rules to empower basic interoperability between CBDCs issued by different jurisdictions. It has been promoting experiments in cross-border transactions among CBDCs systems.

CBDCs: A New Bridge for EU–LAC Cooperation

Global economic power has been shifting over the last 40 years, leading to (slight) trends of fragmentation in the international monetary system. While the war in Ukraine might incentivize countries to seek new ways to reduce their vulnerability to the US-led global financial system, the US dollar is likely to maintain its primary role in the global monetary system. However, the battleground will be formed in the long run when digitalization could empower decentralization while undermining the unipolarity of the current system. In this scenario, the United States risks losing its leadership in the international monetary system if it fails to embrace and shape a new vision for a digitalized (and increasingly politicized) global monetary system.

The United States cannot however pursue its sole strategic interests when shaping the new system. Washington should coordinate and cooperate with other Western nations on equal ground. Otherwise, the United States risks fostering further fragmentation. While still in the early stages of CBDC development (Nicola Bilotta, 2022), the document *Public Policy Principles for Retail Central Bank Digital Currencies (CBDCs)* endorsed by G7 members under the UK Presidency in 2021 should only be the first step of a much more articulate exercise (G7, 2021).

There is space to further explore cooperation between the EU and LAC countries. In an increasingly polarized world economy, as in the current situation in the broader multilateral governance of digital space, where the major powers (the United States, China, and the EU) have different approaches and tend to pursue divergent interests, EU and LAC countries need to establish a cooperation on CBDCs in the framework of the EU–LAC Digital Alliance. As the EU's new digital agenda aims at reinvigorating its relationship with the LAC region by stressing their shared values and geopolitical strategic partnership (Hobbs & Ignacio Torreblanca, 2022), CBDCs' interoperability should be at the core of the current effort. With all the applications that CBDCs could have, from cross-border use to programmability for trade links, if their CBDC infrastructure is developed and designed to be interoperable, EU and LAC could indeed strengthen their commercial, economic, and financial ties. To promote such a vision, the EU and LAC countries should establish a strategic vision based on two key actions.

First, the ECB and LAC central banks should establish institutional dialogues on the latest developments of their CBDC projects. The aim is to further understand policy objectives and needs that central banks are pursuing to better assess potential synergies, common standards, and technology transfer. The purpose of establishing these dialogues goes beyond mere information-sharing: it should aim to facilitate a nuanced assessment of potential synergies that could arise from collaborative efforts. This includes identifying areas of mutual interest, such as common standards and best practices, which can contribute to the seamless integration and interoperability of CBDCs between the EU and LAC. Furthermore, the dialogues should serve as a platform for discussing the potential transfer of technology, fostering a spirit of cooperation and knowledge exchange. In essence, the establishment of institutional dialogues is a strategic step toward building a foundation of cooperation between EU and LAC central banks, fostering an environment conducive to effective collaboration in the realm of CBDC development.

Second, central banks should start cooperating in launching and developing experiments for cross-border transactions through CBDCs systems. Despite the existence of various CBDC projects, a noticeable gap remains in the absence of concrete experiments among the ECB and EU central banks and LAC central banks. This crucial phase of research and investigation demands a proactive approach, emphasizing the importance of cooperative efforts between EU and LAC central banks. By working together in these experiments, central banks can not only gain valuable insights into the practical challenges and opportunities of cross-border CBDC transactions but also foster a collaborative environment that accelerates the development and refinement of these initiatives. The collaborative experiments

Table 20.2 Cross-border CBDC experiments involving EU central banks

Project	Members
Project Jura	BIS Innovation Hub, Swiss National Bank, Banque de France
Project Stella	Bank of France, Monetary Authority of Singapore, J.P. Morgan
Experiment "Liquidity Management in a Multi-Currency Corridor Network"	European Central Bank, Bank of Japan
Experiment "Connecting digital islands: CBDCs"	SWIFT, Capgemini, Banque de France, Deutsche Bundesbank, HSBC, Intesa Sanpaolo, NatWest, SMBC, Standard Chartered, UBS, Wells Fargo
Project Venus	European Investment Bank, Banque Centrale du Luxembourg, Goldman Sachs Bank Europe, Santander, Société Générale

should serve as a testing ground for identifying potential obstacles and refining protocols for cross-border transactions. This hands-on approach will not only enhance the collective understanding of the nuances involved but will also pave the way for establishing common standards and protocols that facilitate seamless interactions between the European and Latin American CBDC ecosystems (Table 20.2).

In the pursuit of enhanced cooperation, the envisioned scenario should strive for the establishment of a set of common pillars. These pillars would be collectively adopted by a coalition of LAC and EU countries, forming a cohesive "club" that could serve as a guiding force for the formulation of CBDC-related legislations at the international level. This collaborative effort could trigger spillover effects, influencing and harmonizing CBDC policies across participating nations.

Drawing inspiration from the insights of legal scholars Hathaway and Shapiro (2020), the proposed approach aligns with the prevailing trend in international law. The concept of "shared interests and decentralized enforcement" has historically shaped many international legal frameworks. By forging a coalition of countries sharing common objectives in the realm of CBDCs, the proposed "club" model aligns with this established paradigm, seeking to influence and drive the development of global standards. Taking a cue from Buchanan's economic theory of clubs, LAC countries, and the EU could leverage the EU–LAC Digital Alliance to exert influence by controlling access to their network of CBDCs. The strategic use of network access as leverage could encourage compliance with established rules and standards. Nations unwilling to align with the guidelines set by the "club" would risk partial or complete exclusion from the shared CBDC network. This exclusion would not only limit their access to the economic benefits of participating in the CBDC ecosystem but would also create a compelling incentive for them to seek membership and adhere to the established rules.

This model of cooperation embraces a strategic and cooperative approach, leveraging the economic interdependence inherent in CBDC networks. By fostering a "club" mentality among LAC countries and the EU, this collaborative effort seeks to shape global standards through a combination of shared interests, decentralized enforcement, and the influential power of network access. This, in turn, creates a dynamic process where adherence to common rules becomes not just a matter of cooperation but a strategic imperative for nations aspiring to reap the full economic advantages of CBDC participation (Buchanan, 1965, 1–14).

Bibliography

Arslanalp, S., Eichengreen, B. J., & Simpson-Bell, C. (2022, March). *The stealth erosion of dollar dominance: Active diversifiers and the rise of nontraditional reserve currencies* (IMF Working Papers, No. 22/58). https://www.imf.org/en/Publications/WP/Issues/2022/03/24/The-Stealth-Erosion-of-Dollar-Dominance-Active-Diversifiers-and-the-Rise-of-Nontraditional-515150

Auer, R., Boar, C., Cornelli, G., Frost, J., Holden, H. & Wehrli, A. (2021). *CBDCs beyond borders: results from a survey of central banks*, (BIS Papers). https://www.bis.org/publ/bppdf/bispap116.pdf

Bank for International Settlement. (2021, July). *Central Bank digital currencies for cross-border payments (Report to the G20)*. https://www.bis.org/publ/othp38.html

Bilotta, N. (2022). *The weaponisation of finance and the risk of global economic fragmentation* (IAI Commentary, 29/04/2022). https://www.iai.it/it/pubblicazioni/weaponisation-finance-and-risk-global-economic-fragmentation

Buchanan, J. M. (1965). An economic theory of clubs'. *Economica*, New Series, *32*(125).

Eichengreen, B., Mehl, A., & Chiţu, L. (2018). *Mars or Mercury? The geopolitics of international currency choice*. VoxEU. https://voxeu.org/node/62433

Ferrari, M. & Mehl, A. (2021). *Central Bank Digital Currency and Global Currencies*. (in The International Role of the Euro, ECB). https://www.ecb.europa.eu/pub/ire/html/ecb.ire202106~a058f84c61.en.html#toc18

Foroohar, R. (2023). A new world energy order is taking shape. *Financial Times*. https://www.ft.com/content/d34dfd79-113c-4ac7-814b-a41086c922fa

G7. (2021). *Public policy principles for retail Central Bank digital currencies*. http://www.g7.utoronto.ca/finance/211014-documents.html

Hathaway, O., & Shapiro, S. J. (2020). *Welcome to the post- leader world*. Foreign Policy. https://foreignpolicy.com/2020/07/04/after-hegemony

Hobbs, C. & Torreblanca, J. (2022). *Byting back: The EU's digital alliance with Latin America and the Caribbean*. (ECFR Policy Brief). https://ecfr.eu/wp-content/uploads/2022/10/Byting-back-The-EUs-digital-alliance-with-Latin-America-and-the-Caribbean.pdf

Kirshner, J. (1995). *Currency and coercion. The political economy of international monetary power*. Princeton University Press.

Liu, Z. Z. (2022). Besides China, Putin has another potential de-dollarization partner in Asia. *CFR Blog*. https://www.cfr.org/node/240063

Panetta, F. (2020). *A digital Euro for the digital era, introductory statement at the ECON Committee of the European Parliament*. https://www.ecb.europa.eu/press/key/date/2020/html/ecb.sp201012_1~1d14637163.en.html

Perez-Saiz, H. & Zhang, L. (2023). *Renminbi Usage in Cross-Border Payments: Regional Patterns and the Role of Swaps Lines and Offshore Clearing Banks*. (IMF Working Papers No. 2023/077). https://www.imf.org/en/Publications/WP/Issues/2023/03/31/Renminbi-Usage-in-Cross-Border-Payments-Regional-Patterns-and-the-Role-of-Swaps-Lines-and-531684

Reuters. (2020, July 29). *Chinese Banks urged to switch away from SWIFT as U.S. sanctions loom*. https://reut.rs/309S59u

Shagina, M. (2021, April 28). *How disastrous would disconnection from SWIFT Be for Russia?* Carnegie Commentaries. https://carnegieendowment.org/publications/84634

SWIFT. (2016). *SWIFT offers secure financial messaging services to CIPS.* https://www.swift.com/de/node/21786

The Economist. (2021, October 23). *The geopolitics of money is shifting up a gear.* https://www.economist.com/leaders/2021/10/23/the-geopolitics-of-money-is-shifting-up-a-gear

The Economist. (2023, April 13). *Can the West win over the rest?* https://www.economist.com/leaders/2023/04/13/can-the-west-win-over-the-rest

White House. (2022). *Executive order on ensuring responsible development of digital assets, Presidential actions.* https://www.whitehouse.gov/briefing-room/presidential-actions/2022/03/09/executive-order-on-ensuring-responsible-development-of-digital-assets

Chapter 21
European Union–Latin American Interregional Relations: Taking Stock and Looking Ahead

Andrea C. Bianculli, Laia Brossa, and Jacint Jordana

Contents

Introduction

The European Union (EU) and Latin America and the Caribbean (LAC) have developed a long and deep-rooted history of relations, which operate across different agendas and at various governance levels over the last 50 years, or even longer. These interregional relations have fluctuated due to a diverse combination of

Andrea C. Bianculli would also like to acknowledge funding support through the project "Rethinking the fundamentals of regions and regionalism. The European Union and Latin America through the lenses of regional regulatory governance" (Reg-EULAC), funded by the Spanish Ministry of Science and Innovation (PID2019-105997GB-I00). Jacint Jordana also acknowledges support from the Institució Catalana de Recerca i Estudis Avançats (ICREA) (2020).

A. C. Bianculli (✉) · L. Brossa
Institut Barcelona d'Estudis Internacionals (IBEI), Barcelona, Spain
e-mail: abianculli@ibei.org

J. Jordana
Institut Barcelona d'Estudis Internacionals (IBEI), Barcelona, Spain

Universitat Pompeu Fabra (UPF), Barcelona, Spain

D. Katsikas et al. (eds.), *Finance, Growth and Democracy: Connections and Challenges in Europe and Latin America in the Era of Permacrisis*, United Nations University Series on Regionalism 33, https://doi.org/10.1007/978-3-031-68475-3_21

structural and agential variables in different historical periods. More recently, however, they have been immersed in a context of multiple crises, which confronted fundamental issues about the nature of such relations. From an EU perspective, difficulties in updating these relations range from the consequences of the 2007–2008 financial crisis, followed by weak economic growth in Europe, to the significant influx of migrants and refugees in recent times, the impact of Brexit, the rise of populism and far-right parties. Compounded with the COVID-19 pandemic, and with the more recent invasion of Ukraine by Russia, these critical challenges have put EU capacities to establish a sound regional foreign policy to the test. Moreover, the international system is going through a transitional phase, marked by the weakening of multilateral rules and institutions, the contestation of the international liberal order, and the consolidation of new global leaderships; all of which have deepened and amplified the effects of these various crises, which also pose greater tensions for regional governance and interregional dynamics (Meyer et al., 2019; Nolte & Weiffen, 2020). As put by the editors of this book, both the EU and LAC are facing the challenges of an era of permacrisis.

Certainly, assessing the challenges brought about by this new context on EU–LAC relations, based on a well-established set of instruments and policies, should provide a space for examining and assessing the need to reformulate the current status, which is of particular relevance. Yet, and to proceed with this assessment, we need to contextualize historically EU–LAC relations. To that end, this chapter looks back in time to then assess the current moment and future possibilities.

Currently, relations between the EU and LAC are complex and multilayered, and this framework is going back well beyond the 1990s and the interregionalism approach. Over the years, different mechanisms and strategies have been put in place, at different levels, ranging from bilateral dialogues to free trade agreements and interregional schemes. Moreover, relations revolve around three main agendas, including political dialogue, cooperation, and trade, and involve a wide array of state and nonstate, private and public actors.

EU–LAC relations have been explored and assessed both in policy and scholarly terms. The academic literature is vast and ever expanding and offers useful lenses through which to examine how the relationship between the EU and LAC has evolved. Though significant, to our knowledge, this body of research remains scattered across different fields and academic disciplines, including political science, international relations, and comparative regionalism. Also, it is limited to examining specific dimensions, either a particular policy area, analytical level (national, regional, or interregional) or period. Such fragmented approaches have prevented scholars from developing a comprehensive and overarching understanding of the mix of achievements and challenges of EU–LAC relations. Despite the potential of the current literature to produce relevant empirical insights, academic research has lagged in approaching these dynamics from a policy perspective while also assessing them through the various levels or arenas where they occur.

Building on these insights, this chapter investigates *how EU–LAC relations have evolved since the 1960s*. To this purpose, we make use of an analytical framework based on the notion of "policy instrument" taken as forms of action that governments (and international organizations) pursue to exercise some control and influence on individuals and organizations—including other governments—by means of applied knowledge encapsulated in specific interventions, usually codified and replicable (Howlett, 2019; Lascoumes & Le Galès, 2007). Based on this framework, we introduce a novel database, which provides a mapping of the policy instruments employed by the EU in its relations with LAC, which include the agreements governing the relations between the EU and LAC since the creation of the European Economic Community, and the cooperation programs funded by the EU in LAC. Our database has allowed for the compilation of information that so far has remained dispersed and scattered. Thus, the database is intended to provide some parsimony to the complexity observed in EU–LAC relations as it offers a relevant research tool to produce comparable and useful information on different policy instruments. Based on this, the chapter provides a more comprehensive assessment of these transatlantic relations across instruments, policy areas, analytical levels, and time. Furthermore, this assessment can provide not only scholars but also policymakers and various stakeholders with essential policy inputs to develop coherent and sustainable policies and strategies as a means to promote an effective and respectful interregional relationship.

The chapter is divided into four parts. First, we describe the general dynamics of the relations between the EU and LAC and how these have been addressed in the literature. The second part presents our methodological and analytical approach to understanding EU–LAC relations from a policy instruments approach. This is followed by an analysis of the data collected through our database for the period 1961–2022. The final section concludes and provides some reflections and recommendations regarding the future of EU–LAC relations.

EU–LAC Relations: Going Back in Time

During the second half of the twentieth century, relations between the EU and LAC developed significantly. These relations, which were practically nonexistent during the early years of the European Economic Commission (EEC), received an enormous boost with the entry of Spain and Portugal. Moreover, starting in the 1990s, interregional relations between the EU and LAC became especially relevant. Such EU's engagement with Latin America was expected to aid the region's pursuit of recognition as a global player (Gardini, 2021), and to promote regional cooperation and integration beyond its borders based on its own regional governance model (Bianculli, 2016; Ribeiro Hoffmann, 2016). Thus, the EU and LAC became enmeshed in a complex web of relations operating at various levels (bilateral, regional, interregional)—and primarily centered on three main policy areas (i.e., pillars): trade, political dialogue, and cooperation.

Political dialogue has operated at various levels. In the 1990s, the first bloc-to-bloc dialogues were launched, including those with the Common Market of the South (MERCOSUR) and the Andean Community (CAN). These dialogues were complemented with initiatives like the Euro-Latin American Parliamentary Assembly (EuroLat),[1] and various spaces to engage with business, civil society actors, academics, and other stakeholders. Furthermore, the EU would later promote more focused bilateral dialogues, as the one established with Chile in 2003, and the so-called strategic partnership with Brazil (2007). Yet, since 2014, interregional political dialogue would be weakened given that the EU would only occasionally reach out to LAC regional organizations and on very specific agendas, as illustrated by the initiatives on drugs with CAN, on the exchange of best practices in higher education with the Pacific Alliance, on tariffs and trade barriers with MERCOSUR, or on arms trade with the Union of South American Nations (UNASUR) (Selleslaghs, 2019).

Trade was and still remains a pivotal component of the EU strategy toward LAC. This trade agenda, which was part of a broader approach that also included political dialogue and cooperation, entailed the negotiation of comprehensive agreements encompassing industrial and agricultural goods, along with services, rules on government procurement, intellectual property rights, customs, trade facilitation, and technical trade barriers.[2] This strategy resulted in two interregional agreements, including the EU–Cariforum Economic Partnership Agreement and the EU–Central America Association Agreement, a multiparty free trade agreement (FTA) with three countries of the CAN (Colombia, Ecuador, and Peru), and bilateral association agreements with Chile and Mexico. The road to bloc-to-bloc negotiations proved bumpy and complex as shown by the negotiations with MERCOSUR (Bianculli, 2023; Sanahuja & Rodríguez, 2022), and the agreement with Colombia, Ecuador, and Peru, initially intended as an EU–CAN agreement (García, 2022). As of 2020, the EU has established a network of Association Agreements, comprising both bilateral and interregional agreements in LAC. This network includes a multiparty trade agreement involving three CAN countries (Colombia, Ecuador, and Peru) and an agreement with Chile. In June 2019, a political agreement was reached to sign the EU–MERCOSUR agreement, sparking meetings and negotiations between the two regions.

Cooperation, already part of the Rio Action Plan set during the 1999 Summit of Heads of State and Government of Latin America and the Caribbean and the EU, has evolved into a complex and multilevel agenda: it includes bi-regional cooperation through horizontal programs, subregional cooperation plans following a bloc-to-bloc approach, and bilateral programs with individual countries. Development cooperation was institutionalized through the Country Strategy Papers (CSPs) with individual countries and Regional Strategy Papers (RSPs) with CAN, Central America, and MERCOSUR, which were also complemented with Regional Indicative Programmes, establishing specific sector measures, periods, and planned financial engagement and expenses, with a focus on focal sectors. The year 2014

[1] EuroLat is composed by members of the European Parliament, the Latin American Parliament (Parlatino), the Andean Parliament (Parlandino), the Central American Parliament (Parlacen), the MERCOSUR Parliament (Parlasur), and of the Congresses of Chile and Mexico.

[2] For more on this subject, see Chap. 11 by Julieta Zelicovich.

marked a relevant change in the EU cooperation policy toward LAC as the new Multiannual Indicative Regional Programme for Latin America (2014–2020), moved away from the previous region-to-region strategy as RSPs were not renewed and bilateral cooperation ceased for five higher-income countries, leaving only Bolivia and Paraguay eligible for bilateral aid. Nevertheless, LAC countries continued to participate in various projects and initiatives under the EU Regional Program for Latin America, spanning areas such as social cohesion, digital connectivity, drug policies, and border management.

This intense and long history of relations fueled academic debates. The literature on EU–LAC relations is vast and ever expanding and offers useful lenses through which to examine how the relationship between these actors has evolved (Gratius, 2020; Sanahuja, 2015). Studies have also explored the relevance of the different instruments set up by the EU to approach LAC, including cooperation agreements with MERCOSUR and CAN (Bustamante & Giacalone, 2009; Doctor, 2007; Sanchez Bajo, 2005; Schade, 2022), and bilateral ones with Chile and Mexico (Dominguez & Crandall, 2019; Garcia, 2011). The literature has also highlighted the relevance of cooperation instruments and programs by the EU (Ayuso & Freres, 2010; Freres, 2000). Though significant, to our knowledge, this body of research remains scattered across different fields and academic disciplines, including political science, international relations, and (comparative) regionalism. This diversity is very much a consequence of the complex and multidimensional character of the phenomenon of interest: relations and dynamics between the EU and LAC comprise a wide array of different agendas (from higher education to health and climate change, among others) operating through the three pillars above identified, that is, cooperation, political dialogue, and trade, across various levels and involving a myriad of both state and nonstate, public and private actors, and networks.

Starting in the 1990s, interregionalism became a phenomenon of increasing relevance in international relations and international political economy: it turned out to be a natural corollary of the new or open regionalism (Rüland, 2010), which was based on the diffusion of the neoliberal ideal of free trade and economic liberalization. Simply put, interregionalism was seen as a "situation or a process whereby two or more regions interact" (Söderbaum, 2015, p. 175) and thus, characterized by triggering "widening and deepening political, economic, and societal interactions" (Roloff, 2006, p. 18) among them, either by means of their regional or sub-regional organizations, or by leading countries.

From a conceptual perspective, however, and despite the strong revitalization of regions and the expansion of both formal and informal relations between them, the field of interregionalism still remains a "fragmented field of study" (van der Vleuten & van Eerdewijk, 2020, p. 577). Theoretically, this is explained by the strong focus on definitions and the elaboration of typologies of interregional arrangements (Hänggi, 2006), but less on explaining drivers of success and failure. Even if consensus on conceptual definitions remains elusive (Ribeiro Hoffmann, 2016), from an empirical perspective, studies have remained too focused on the case of EU interregionalism given that the EU was the first regional organization to promote such strategies (van der Vleuten & van Eerdewijk, 2020).

In fact, taken as "region-to-region relations," interregionalism has progressively imbued the EU's external policies since the 1990s (Söderbaum & Van Langenhove, 2005). Whereas the EU has maintained relations with most world regions, including Africa, Asia, and LAC, interregionalism has been particularly strong within the EU's strategy toward the latter. Also, it can be argued that interregionalism proved to be a useful tool to push for regional integration worldwide, including LAC. The EU's interregional strategy clearly reflected its own commitment to regional market-building and global economic liberalization, on the one hand, and to the embedding of market economies in a framework marked by the support of political dialogue, cooperation and democracy, civil society participation, and social inclusion on the other. Furthermore, to the extent that the policy and institutional regulatory framework endorsed by the EU was based on its own experience, through these economic, political, and cooperation agendas, the bloc actively promoted its particular institutional model of regional integration (De Lombaerde & Schulz, 2009; Farrell, 2009).

Despite the potential of the current literature to produce relevant empirical insights, most existing approaches to interregionalism are based on an EU foreign policy approach, international relations theories, international political economy approaches, or diffusion processes (Ribeiro Hoffmann, 2016). This chapter adds to this discussion and draws on a public policy perspective to allow us to zoom in on the policy instruments devised by the EU to relate to LAC across policy areas and over time. In so doing, it also allows us to bring together two areas or agendas that so far have remained rather detached, namely, trade and cooperation.

Our Analytical and Methodological Approach

Our study provides a novel analytical framework to the study of the relations between the EU and LAC, which is focused on a policy approach. Thus, we attempt to assess the relations across sectors and their territorial dimensions. More specifically, we look at policy instruments that have been deployed by the EU to reach out, to relate with the region.

The notion of a policy instrument is crucial in this approach given that "policy tools represent the constitutive elements of public actions" and therefore, "they contain useful information on the nature and effects of public action" (Acciai & Capano, 2020, p. 118). In this case, we can examine the EU display of policy instruments in its relations to LAC over the years, discussing the purposes and aims they involved. Furthermore, we intend to assess the continuity and transformation of policy instruments over the years, their interrelation between sectors, and their territorial dimensions. We also intend to assess variation, including variation across time, across policy areas, and regions and countries in LAC. This will also allow us to discuss whether the instruments deployed reflect the objectives, structure the politics of regional interactions, and to what extent they have succeeded in generating the intended dynamics; yet we do not provide an evaluation of such instruments or its effects or impact.

To this end, we first define the type of instrument, which can be taken as "a device that is both technical and social, that organizes specific social relations between the state and those it is addressed to" (Lascoumes & Le Galès, 2007, p. 4) and that is intended to translate a policy problem/issue into effective action (Peters, 2005). Although it was argued that instruments attempt to correct the real and/or perceived defects in society or economy (Peters, 2005, p. 354), it can be said that they structure public policy and organize relations between citizens and states, but also between states, or between regions (Lascoumes & Le Galès, 2007). The notion of policy problem refers to how "society and/or its political system define and frame particular disconnections between current conditions and desired states as appropriate for pursuit of resolutions by government" (Hoornbeek & Peters, 2017, p. 369). Thus, whether EU–LAC relations concentrate on some policy problems, they also involve particular values and diagnoses about structuring interregional relations. For example, what is the problem about? Is it a problem of supporting development? Is it a problem of market creation in the region? Is it a problem of regional citizenship? Policy problem definition then affects the institutions that are established or charged with the responsibility of dealing with the policy problem as defined in the previous stage.

Our research is thus intended to offer a policy approach to assess how the relations between the EU and LAC have evolved across time, considering the transformations that the global order has experienced in recent decades. More specifically, we examine the policy instruments that the EU has deployed to reach out and relate to the region. Within the project, the notion of type of instrument is empirically translated into two categories: agreement and program.

First, agreements include those concluded by the EU member states and the EU (including the former European Communities—EC, EEC, ESCS) and/or the (EURATOM), with LAC countries and regional organizations. Thus, the final database comprises information on the agreements signed between the EU and regional organizations in LAC, including the (CAN), Caribbean Forum (CARIFORUM), Central American Common Market (CACM) and its successor, the Integration System (SICA), and the (MERCOSUR). Bilateral agreements between the EU and individual countries in the region include those with Antigua and Barbuda, Argentina, Bahamas, Barbados, Belize, Bolivia, Brazil, Chile, Colombia, Costa Rica, Cuba, Dominica, Dominican Republic, Ecuador, El Salvador, Grenada, Guatemala, Guyana, Haiti, Honduras, Jamaica, Mexico, Nicaragua, Panama, Paraguay, Peru, Saint Vincent and the Grenadines, Saint Lucia, Saint Kitts and Nevis, Suriname, Trinidad and Tobago, Uruguay, and Venezuela. In all, these countries are full members of the Community of Latin American and Caribbean States (CELAC). More specifically, agreements include, for example, bilateral agreements signed by the EU or other agencies, that is, EURATOM, and particular countries in the region in policy areas such as textiles, nuclear energy, food aid, visas, and in relation to the General Agreement on Trade and Tariffs (GATT), among others, and those involving various countries as in the case of the Multiparty Trade Agreement between the EU, Peru, and Colombia, also later Ecuador. It also involves region-to-region agreements as in the case of the Economic Partnership Agreement between the CARIFORUM States and the EC.[3]

Second, programs comprise those orderly project initiatives under cooperation and development and established by the EU to address different policy areas with a special focus on LAC and funded by the EU or in conjunction with other regional and international organizations and countries. Based on these operational definitions, we have collected information on a total of 237 agreements signed between 1961 and 2022, and 32 programs deployed between 1994 and 2023. Empirically, this is exemplified by programs including EuroSociAL+, ADELANTE, and EUROCLIMA.

Data on the agreements was collected through the careful exploration of different repositories available on the official websites of the Council of the European Union and the European Council (i.e., Consilium). This information was also contrasted with the EUR-LEX website, and with direct consultations with the EUR-Lex team, which provides access to EU legal documents. In the case of the programs, we conducted a first thorough revision of these through the website of the Department for International Partnership Directorate General (DG INTPA) of the European Commission, and which is responsible for the formulation of the EU's international partnership and development policy. Again, the information thus collected was contrasted and compared with similar information provided by the Fundación Internacional y para Iberoamérica de Administración y Políticas Públicas (FIAPP), the Spanish public international cooperation entity. This also included an interview with experts and officials at the FIAPP. Finally, the information both on the agreements and the programs was complemented by other relevant sources and documents, including secondary literature, publications and reports by the EU, regional organizations in LAC, and other relevant stakeholders, among others.

In all, the analysis of the data thus collected provides a comprehensive mapping and assessment of the policy instruments that have shaped the EU–LAC relationship over more than 60 years.

The EU and LAC: A Relation in the Making for Over 60 Years

Today's EU traces its beginnings to the signing of the treaty establishing the European Coal and Steel Community (ECSC) in 1951, along with the treaty creating the European Economic Community (EEC) and the European Atomic Energy Community (EAEC or Euratom) in March 1957. In a context marked by the Cold War and increasing protectionism, the first two agreements collected in our database are intended to promote "cooperation concerning the peaceful uses of nuclear

[3] Agreements with Caribbean countries as part of the African, Caribbean, and Pacific (ACP) Group of States and beneficiaries of the European Development Fund (EDF) since the 1960s have not been included as these were framed as part of a larger group including countries in other regions beyond LAC.

energy" as established by the accords signed between EURATOM and the governments of Argentina and Brazil. Only three years after the creation of the EEC, LAC regionalism resulted in the creation of the CACM and the Latin American Free Trade Association (LAFTA). Yet, agreements involving regional organizations in LAC would only start in the 1980s, slightly before the accession of Spain and Portugal. This was the agreement signed between the Andean Community (then Cartagena Agreement), including its five members, and the EEC in 1983. Two years later, a cooperation agreement was signed with the countries of the General Treaty on Central American Economic Integration (Costa Rica, El Salvador, Guatemala, Honduras, and Nicaragua) and Panama.

As shown in Fig. 21.1, between the 1960s and the mid-1990s, the main type of instrument used by the EU was agreements. This policy instrument underwent a relevant increase in the 1990s, the years of new or open regionalism and its corollary—interregionalism. Between 1999 and 2022, the EU signed 97 agreements with LAC, including bilateral agreements and interregional agreements (i.e., Andean Community, MERCOSUR), thus showing the flexibility of interregionalism as framed and practiced by the EU.

The mid-1990s is also the time for the more active deployment of programs as part of the EU's cooperation and development agenda. These remain in place during the early years of the new century, when agreements showed a slow decline, followed by a rise since 2007 and especially in more recent years.

With a focus on cooperation, between 1994 and 2021 the EU launched a total of 32 cooperation programs, which are exclusively funded by the EU, or funded by the EU in conjunction with other regional and/or international organizations and

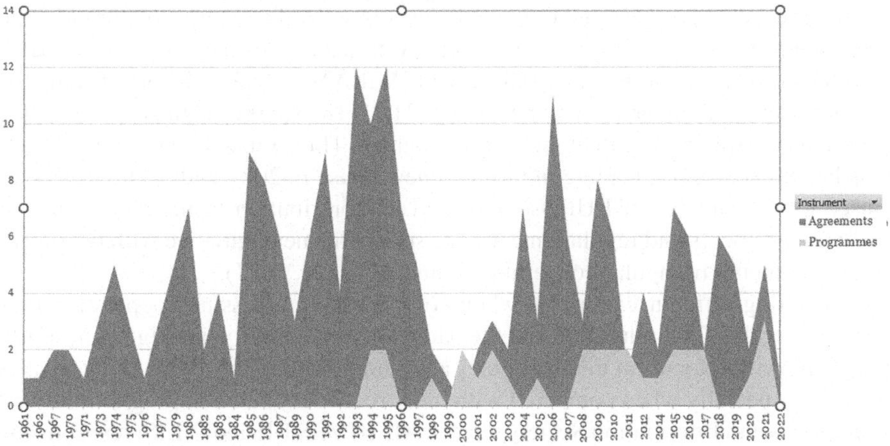

Fig. 21.1 Deployment of policy instruments by the EU: 1961–2022 (The "year" corresponds to the date when these two different types of instruments—agreements and programs—were signed or initiated, respectively). (Source: Own elaboration)

countries. These programs are intended to address specifically the region and are implemented in more than one country in LAC. In other words, we have not included cooperation programs where LAC countries can participate, but which are intended to address a wider geographical coverage, as in the case of Erasmus+, Horizon Europe, Copernicus, and Galileo.

The various agreements signed between the EU and LAC have been categorized according to the actors involved under three different categories or types: bilateral, interregional, and transregional. These include bilateral agreements such as those involving the EU and one LAC country. The second category refers to interregional agreements building on the most traditional definition of region-to-region agreements. Finally, transregional agreements refer to those deals signed between the EU and countries in LAC as part of that region.

Clearly, bilateralism remains a strong feature of the EU's strategy toward LAC: a total of 219 bilateral agreements have been identified in the database. This large number contrasts to the 16 interregional agreements signed, and the transregional ones which amount to two agreements. Table 21.1 depicts the list of agreements collected in the database and their distribution across time and level of agreement.

When assessing the evolution of these various types of agreements across time, bilateral agreements have been pursued throughout these 61 years and have remained in place even during the so-called golden years of open regionalism and interregionalism. In fact, interregional deals had a timid beginning in the early and mid-1980s and would see a relevant increase in the mid-1990s, followed by some brief reappearances during the first and second decades of the twenty-first century (Fig. 21.2).

The first cooperation programs identified in our project go back to 1994, as it is the case of ALFA, AL-INVEST I, ALLURE, and URB-AL I, and which were aimed at promoting higher education, the internationalization of micro-, small-, and medium-sized enterprises, and urban policies, respectively. In terms of duration, the three longest-standing programs are Latin American Investment Facility (LAIF), Caribbean Investment Facility (CIF), and ALBAN, which address sustainable development and higher education (see Fig. 21.3). The short time life of the last five programs is explained by their more recent launch. Thus, for example, ADELANTE was launched in 2015, leading in turn to a new phase in 2021 with ADELANTE 2. Based on the success of EUROsociAL and its contribution to the articulation of common protocols and regulations, the EC set up this new initiative with the objective of financing triangular cooperation (Jung Altrogge, 2021).

Interesting differences emerge when comparatively assessing cooperation programs in terms of their duration and the budget deployed in 1 year (Fig. 21.4). Early programs with a focus on urban policies and going back to the 1990s show smaller budgets, especially when compared with more recent cooperation programs around Enterprises and Information Society, that is, AL-INVEST II and @LIS, respectively.

Table 21.2 provides a categorization of the various cooperation programs according to the policy area they are mainly intended to address. These include climate[4]

---

[4] For more on this subject and more specifically climate crisis, see Chap. 18 by Christian Ghymers.

Table 21.1 Agreements: distribution of level of agreement across time. (Source: Own elaboration)

	Level of agreement			Total
Year	Bilateral	Interregional	Transregional	
1961	1			1
1962	1			1
1967	2			2
1970	2			2
1971	1			1
1973	3			3
1974	8			8
1975	3			3
1976	2			2
1977	3			3
1979	6			6
1980	7			7
1982	3			3
1983	2	1		3
1984	1			1
1985	8	1		9
1986	8			8
1987	6			6
1989	3			3
1990	6			6
1991	9			9
1992	4			4
1993	10	2		12
1994	11			11
1995	10	2		12
1996	7			7
1997	5			5
1998	2			2
1999	1			1
2001	2			2
2002	3			3
2003		2		2
2004	7			7
2005	3			3
2006	11			11
2007	6			6
2008	2	1		3
2009	8			8
2010	6			6
2011	1			1

(continued)

Table 21.1 (continued)

	Level of agreement			Total
Year	Bilateral	Interregional	Transregional	
2012	3	2		5
2014	2			2
2015	6	1		7
2016	4	1	2	**7**
2017	2			2
2018	6			6
2019	5	1		6
2020	1	2		3
2021	5			5
2022	1			1
Total general	**219**	**16**	**2**	**237**

and sustainable development, higher education, security and transnational crime, enterprises, urban policies, social cohesion, triangular cooperation,[5] and information society.

Thus, it becomes clear that 25% of the programs deployed were to address Climate and Sustainable Development, followed by Enterprises (Micro, Small and Medium Enterprises (MSMEs) and Security and Transnational Crime, with a total of 16% each. Thirteen percent of the programs were to address higher education.

Figure 21.5 shows which policy areas have been funded for longer periods of time. Based on this distribution, it becomes clear that the area of climate action and sustainable development has been funded for more than 40 years if we add the different programs involved, which are CIF, the various phases of EUROCLIMA, together with LAIF. Higher education is the second policy area that has received funding for the longest period. In this area, cooperation programs go back to 1994, starting with ALFA I, II, and III, and ALBAN. Finally, security and transnational crime cooperation is framed through various initiatives including COPOLAD, EL PAcCTO, and EUROFRONT. It has also received relevant funding for several years, starting in the 2010s, thus showing that this policy area has only recently become part of the cooperation agenda of the EU toward LAC.

The policy areas that have been funded for the shortest periods of time are those framed under projects addressing triangular cooperation and information society. As explained above, the EU only recently incorporated triangular cooperation as part of the cooperation programs with LAC. In the case of the so-called information

[5] According to the United Nations Industrial Development Organization (UNIDO) triangular cooperation involves "Southern-driven partnerships between two or more developing countries, supported by a developed country(ies) or multilateral organisation(s), to implement development cooperation programmes and projects," see https://www.unido.org/south-south-cooperation#:~:text=Triangular%20Cooperation%20is%20%E2%80%9CSouthern%2Ddriven,development%20cooperation%20programmes%20and%20projects.%E2%80%9D, last accessed 8 December 2023.

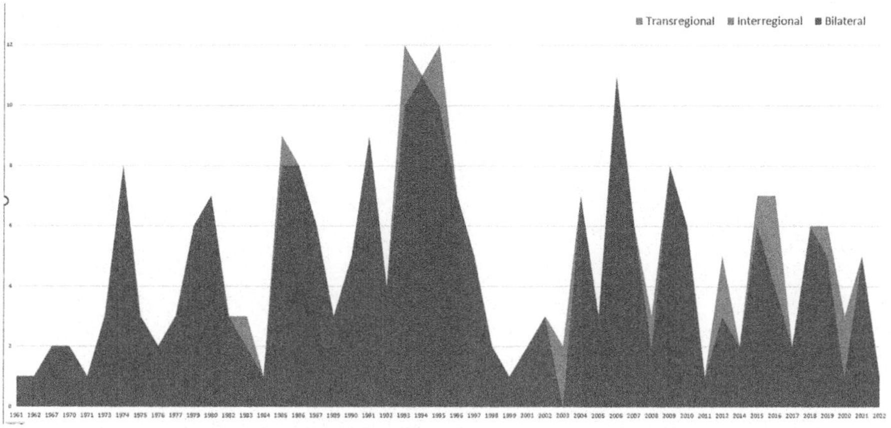

Fig. 21.2 EU–LAC agreements across levels: 1961–2022. (Source: Own elaboration)

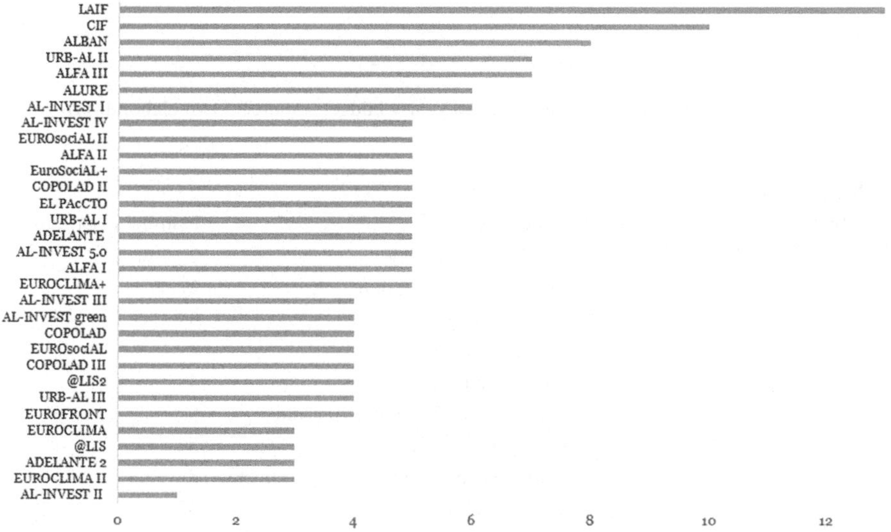

Fig. 21.3 Time life of cooperation programs. (Source: Own elaboration)

society, programs go back to the initial years of the twenty-first century and comprise two main cooperation initiatives. Thus, and building on the achievements of the Information Society Alliance (@LIS), the EU launched a second phase of the program called @LIS2 in 2009 with the objective of promoting further dialogue and cooperation on policy and regulatory frameworks in the area, while also strengthening interconnectivity, collaborative research, and regulatory convergence in LAC.

From a financial perspective, when comparatively assessing the total funding deployed across policy areas, higher education and enterprises are the areas most strongly funded. Cooperation programs in higher education have received the most

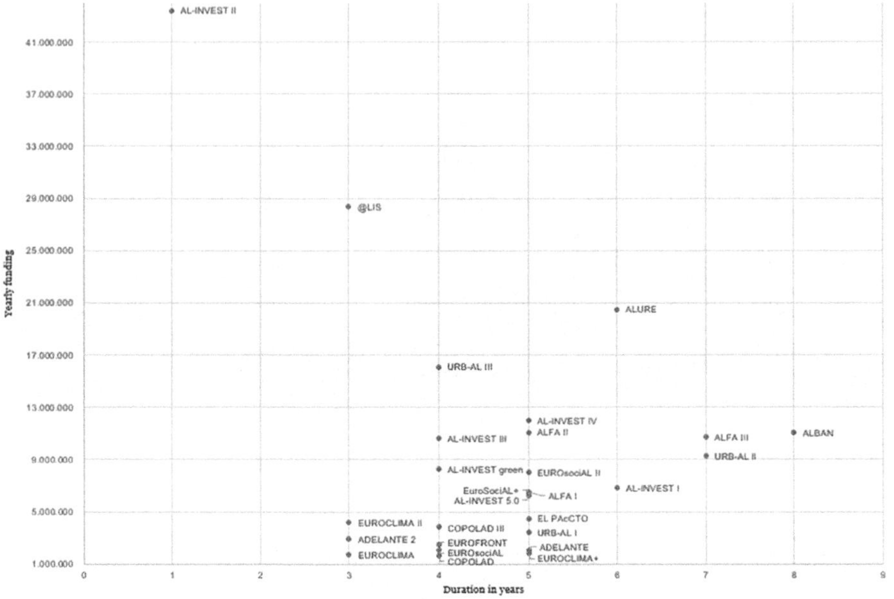

Fig. 21.4 Cooperation programs, time life, and yearly budget. (Source: Own elaboration)

Table 21.2 Number of programs across policy areas. (Source: Own elaboration)

Policy area	Number of programs
Information society	2
Triangular cooperation	2
Urban policies	3
Social cohesion	3
Higher education	4
Security and transnational crime	5
Enterprises (MSMEs)	5
Climate and sustainable development	8
Total general	32

funding, with a total of over 251 million euros. This policy area is closely followed by cooperation programs addressing enterprises (MSMEs) as framed under the different phases of AL-INVEST. Between 1994 and 2021, these initiatives received 218 million euros. Interestingly, programs addressing urban policies have also received relevant funding (almost 150 million euros), being this also an interesting policy area where cities and subnational governments are the key actors involved, and which also goes back to 1995.

The least funded policy area is triangular cooperation. This is more readily explained by the fact that only recently this policy area has been integrated in EU

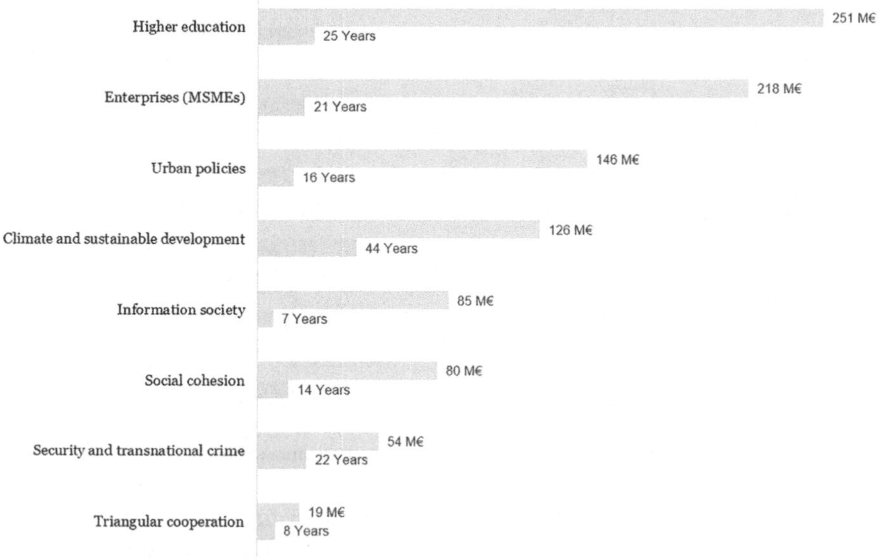

Fig. 21.5 Cooperation funding across policy areas and number of years funded. (Source: Own elaboration)

initiatives toward LAC, but also by the particular structure and dynamic of triangular cooperation, which can include more than one donor or financial supporter.

In all, whereas higher education stands out as the policy area receiving the highest amount of funding compared to other policy areas, it has received 26% of the total invested funds for 25 years (16% of the time). MSMEs follow with a total of 22% of the deployed funds for 21 years (13% of the time), while urban policies are the third area receiving the largest funds (15%) for 16 years (10% of the time).

Finally, we have assessed how funding has proceeded across policy areas and across time as depicted in Fig. 21.6.

Cooperation programs in policy areas such as higher education, climate, and sustainable development, or more recently, security and transnational crime, evince continuity in time, with funding growing and then decreasing, despite some interruptions or impasses. There is no clear pattern in the distribution. Still, and given that higher education, urban policies, and support to MSMEs concentrate 65% of the total funding, mostly during the 1990s and 2000s, it emerges that organizing networks at decentralized levels was a priority of the cooperation policy in that period. These policies were very much focused on direct collaboration with public organizations rather than larger state structures. However, after the global financial crisis, the focus concentrates on supporting key policies at the governmental level (security and climate change), probably aiming to strengthen state capabilities and structure a different type of interregional relations, strongly based on governmental cooperation.

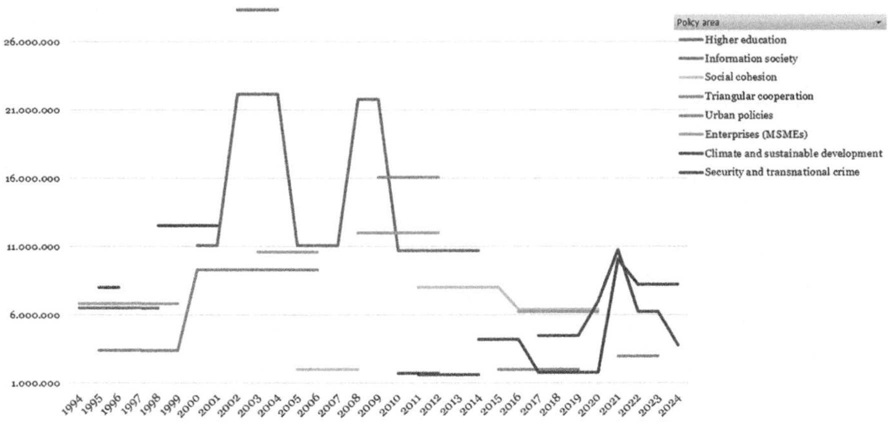

Fig. 21.6 Cooperation funding across policy areas and across time. (Source: Own elaboration)

This final graph (Fig. 21.7) shows how cooperation funding has varied across time. Whereas cooperation started quite timidly in the 1990s with a total of over 13 million euros, there was a notable increase by the end of that same decade. The peak was reached in the early 2000s with a peak of over 76 million euros. By 2007, as the financial crisis severely affected the EU, cooperation funds decreased accordingly, only to recuperate—though not to previous values as those of the initial 2000s—as the new decade of the twenty-first century was starting. Yet, today, cooperation funding seems to be just at the same levels of the mid-1990s. In all, EU cooperation funding has stagnated and declined due to the idea that most of the countries in the region should be graduated as aid recipients. More recently, the 2021–2027 Multiannual Financial Framework (MFF) merged many standalone EU external financing instruments into one, and thus established the single Neighbourhood, Development, and International Cooperation Instrument (NDICI). The graduation principle has been abandoned, thus allowing to finance cooperation with medium-high-income countries.[6] Yet, the allocation of funds established for LAC was the smallest of all funds directed to other regions. Furthermore, it entailed a decrease of 14% in real terms compared to the previous 2014–2020 financial framework (Jung Altrogge, 2021).

Similarly, within Team Europe, LAC received financial support of €927 million (United Nations Industrial Development Organization, 2020), which made it the region with the smallest budget allocated (Bianculli & Pascullo, 2022).

[6]The MFF 2021–2027 still differentiates LAC countries according to the level of development. Thus, a first group of countries is addressed through bilateral Multi-Annual Indicative Programme (MIP). This is the case of Bolivia, Belize, Colombia, Costa Rica (limited MIP), Cuba, Dominican Republic, Ecuador, El Salvador, Guatemala, Guyana, Haiti, Honduras, Jamaica, Nicaragua, Paraguay, Peru, and Suriname. A second group of countries without specific MIP is supported through the Pan-American window: Argentina, Brazil, Chile, Mexico, Panama, Uruguay, Venezuela, and Costa Rica.

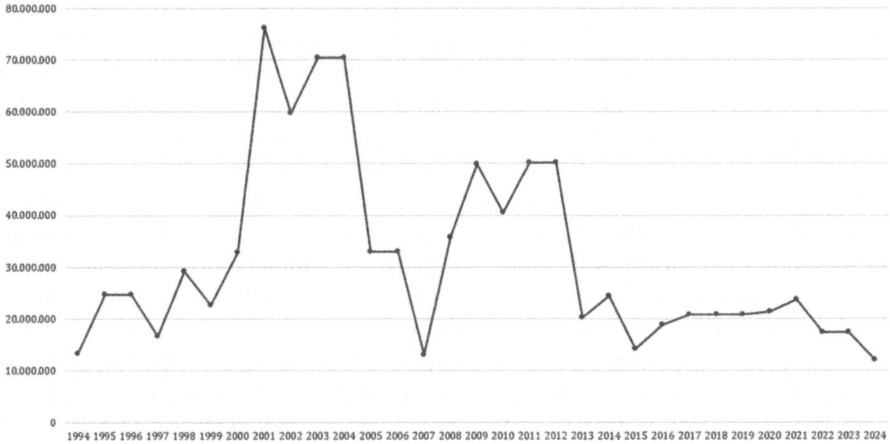

Fig. 21.7 Cooperation funding across time. (Source: Own elaboration)

Conclusions and Further Avenues for Research

This chapter has explored the relations between the EU and LAC through a policy approach. More specifically, it has investigated whether and how different policy instruments have been deployed for 61 years.

The EU and LAC, as well as the international community, have undergone changes that have affected the interregional dynamics over the years. While making causal claims about the drivers of policy change is far beyond our objective in this chapter, some of the developments and transformations observed through our analysis point to some specific critical moments.

Our comparative assessment shows that establishing agreements has been the most frequently used policy instrument since 1961. Agreements are instruments that usually have low direct costs for signatories and facilitate the establishment of more dynamic relations, either economic (trade, investment), or social and cultural. Furthermore, they can trigger closer relations among respective societies and economies, facilitating the circulation of people, services, and goods. These tend to be mostly deployed at the bilateral level, a trend that remains quite stable across time.

Interregional agreements were a key objective of EU foreign policy starting in the 1990s, and efforts were made in this direction, but this strategy never really took off and failed to become the main policy instrument. This type of agreement tends to be broader and deeper in terms of agendas and commitments, especially in trade, and involves a larger number of actors, all of which could explain the difficulties in reaching such agreements as negotiations may entail a larger number of preferences and incentives, making consensus more difficult and even elusive. Whereas the clearest example is the negotiation with MERCOSUR, even the finalization of the modernization process of the two trade pillars of the agreements with Chile and Mexico is also still pending at the time of writing. From a strictly trade perspective, this finding is in line with studies showing how and to what extent the negotiations of these deep trade agreements were related to developments at the multilateral level, as in the case of the negotiations under the World Trade Organization during the late 1990s, or years later, related to the decline of the multilateral trade order (see interalia Bianculli, 2023; Lamy, 2002; Sanahuja & Rodríguez, 2019).

Cooperation has triggered a dense agenda, involving a variety of actors at various governance levels. Cooperation programs are also a product of the world of the 1990s but were reconfigured after the global financial crisis and did not disappear. In so doing, these instruments aimed to strengthen administrative relations, rather than social and economic ties. In general terms, funding has varied across time, resulting in a temporal pattern with marked ups and downs. Certainly, the 2007–2008 financial crisis undermined the role and position of the EU on the international stage, and this could explain the reduction of funding during those years.[7] Yet, EU cooperation also stalled by the idea that most countries should be "graduated" as aid recipients (Dominguez & Sanahuja, 2023). Moreover, as we have shown in previous sections, the funding pattern is far from clear, and variation is observed not only across time, but also across policy areas. The cooperation agenda has also presented relevant changes as it attempted to adapt to new challenges and working methodologies, as shown by the implementation of triangular cooperation. The latter also talks to a learning process through long-standing programs as in the case of EUROsociAL.

Today, the EU confronts a multipolar world order, marked by the decline of multilateralism, new geopolitical realities, economic volatility, and democratic recession. The latest EU-CELAC meeting (Brussels, July 2023), after an 8-year hiatus, attests to the greater importance of LAC in this uncertain and challenging international scenario.

The comprehensive 41-point Declaration of the EU-CELAC Summit covers most of the topics already analyzed through our database, that is, climate change, sustainable development, social justice, and fight against corruption and crime. However, what is important is to calibrate which instruments are going to be implemented, and with what intensity. For example, the EU's renewed interest in the region resulted in the announcement of a €45 billion investment through the Global Gateway platform, with a strong focus on promotion of renewable energy and digital services. Through this platform, the EU aimed to achieve two objectives. First, to fill investment gaps that could not be met by traditional aid; and second, to respond to China's growing role in the region as a financier of development (Dominguez & Sanahuja, 2023). Additionally, while association agreements were

[7] In addition, and from a LAC perspective, the "EU was no longer perceived as a progressive actor, strongly advocating social cohesion, democracy, and human rights, or as a model for regional integration governance" (Bianculli & Pascullo, 2022). These were the years of the commodity boom in the region and important normative changes, especially in South America. Consequently, the EU's response to the crisis moved away from the expansionist policies pursued in LAC, mostly by South American countries, whereas the 2008 EU Return Directive, which created a "credible threat of forced return" (Acosta, 2009), was seen as seen as a counterexample to regional definitions and regulations on migration management in Latin America (Brumat & Acosta, 2019).

also part of the discussions, six Memoranda of Understanding (MoU) were signed, bilaterally with Argentina, Chile, Ecuador, El Salvador, Honduras, and Uruguay.[8] In all, the final outcome of the Summit showed some relevant continuities in terms of the agendas and policy instruments to be deployed, except for the new Global Gateway.

In sum, our chapter has contributed to developing a policy instrument approach to the analysis of EU–LAC relations, and thus, it has unraveled how policy dynamics evolve over time and the nature of the interregional relations they contribute to build and promote (Capano et al., 2015; Le Galès, 2011). Thus, we have attempted to provide a novel approach to the transatlantic relations, which can be of policy relevance for the development of coherent and sustainable policies and strategies as a means of promoting effective and respectful interregional relations. Further research could explore the factors underlying these changes over time, and the various combinations of policy instruments used and why.

References

Acciai, C., & Capano, G. (2020). Policy instruments at work: A meta-analysis of their applications. *Public Administration, n/a*(n/a). https://doi.org/10.1111/padm.12673

Acosta, D. (2009). Latin American reactions to the adoption of the returns directive. *CEPS Liberty and Security in Europe, November*, 1–8.

Ayuso, A., & Freres, C. (2010). La cooperación con América Latina: Hacia una estrategia europea comprometida con la calidad. In *Memorando OPEX: Vol. 138/2010*. Fundación Alternativas.

Bianculli, A. C. (2016). Regulatory governance regimes and interregionalism: Exploring the dynamics of EU-Mercosur negotiations. *Canadian Journal of Latin American and Caribbean Studies*. https://doi.org/10.1080/08263663.2016.1186393

Bianculli, A. C. (2023). Interregionalism, trade, and standardization: The Long Road to the EU-MERCOSUR trade agreement and the uncertainties ahead. In F. Duina & C. Viju-Miljusevic (Eds.), *Standardizing the world. EU Trade policy and the road to convergence* (pp. 171–194). Oxford University Press.

Bianculli, A. C., & Pascullo, M. (2022). Regional and interregional relations between EU and South America: Weathering the COVID-19 storm? In *Regional and international cooperation in South America after COVID: Challenges and opportunities post-pandemic*. https://doi.org/10.4324/9781003230403-4

Brumat, L., & Acosta, D. (2019). Three generations of free movement of regional migrants in Mercosur: Any influence from the EU? In A. Geddes, M. V. Espinoza, L. Hadj-Abdou, & L. Brumat (Eds.), *The dynamics of regional migration governance* (pp. 54–72). Edward Elgar Publishing. https://doi.org/10.1007/978-3-030-43942-2_7

Bustamante, M., & Giacalone, R. (2009). An assessment of European Union cooperation towards the Andean community (1992–2007). In *The EU and world regionalism: The makability of regions in the 21st century*.

Capano, G., Howlett, M., & Ramesh, M. (2015). Varieties of governance: Dynamics, strategies, capacities. In *Studies in the political economy of public policy*.

[8] For further details, see Press Release 'EU-CELAC Summit: towards a closer, stronger and renewed partnership between both regions,' available at https://ec.europa.eu/commission/presscorner/detail/en/ip_23_3929, last accessed 11 December 2023.

De Lombaerde, P., & Schulz, M. (2009). *The EU and world regionalism. The makability of regions in the 21st century*. Ashgate Publishing Ltd..
Doctor, M. (2007). Why bother with inter-regionalism? Negotiations for a European union-mercosur agreement. *Journal of Common Market Studies, 45*(2), 281–314. https://doi.org/10.1111/j.1468-5965.2007.00712.x
Dominguez, R., & Crandall, M. (2019). *Mexico and the European Union*. Oxford University Press. https://doi.org/10.1093/acrefore/9780190228637.013.1115
Dominguez, R., & Sanahuja, J. A. (2023). *Una asociación renovada. Balance y perspectivas de la Cumbre UE-CELAC y las relaciones euro-latinoamericanas*.
Farrell, M. (2009). EU policy towards other regions: Policy learning in the external promotion of regional integration. *Journal of European Public Policy, 16*(8), 1165–1184.
Freres, C. (2000). The European Union as a global "Civilian Power": Development cooperation in EU-Latin American relations. *Journal of Interamerican Studies and World Affairs, 42*(2), 63–85. https://doi.org/10.2307/166282
Garcia, M. (2011). Incidents along the Path: Understanding the Rationale behind the EU–Chile Association Agreement. *JCMS: Journal of Common Market Studies, 49*(3), 501–524. https://doi.org/10.1111/j.1468-5965.2010.02149.x
García, M. J. (2022). The EU–Peru/Colombia trade agreement. In *Latin America–European Union relations in the twenty-first century*. https://doi.org/10.7765/9781526136503.00010
Gardini, G. L. (2021). The European Union in Latin America. A 'neighbour' of values. In G. L. Gardini (Ed.), *External powers in Latin America. Geopolitics between Neo-extractivism and South-South cooperation* (pp. 29–43). Routledge.
Gratius, S. (2020). *The European Union, Latin America, and the Caribbean*. Oxford University Press. https://doi.org/10.1093/acrefore/9780190228637.013.1709
Hänggi, H. (2006). Interregionalism as a multifaceted phenomenon: In search of a typology. In H. Hänggi, J. Rüland, & R. Roloff (Eds.), *Interregionalism and international relations a stepping stone to global governance?* (pp. 31–62). Routledge.
Hoornbeek, J. A., & Peters, B. G. (2017). Understanding policy problems: A refinement of past work. *Policy and Society, 36*(3), 365–384. https://doi.org/10.1080/14494035.2017.1361631
Howlett, M. (2019). *Designing public policies: Principles and instruments: Second edition*. https://doi.org/10.4324/9781315232003
Jung Altrogge, T. (2021). *A new cycle in Euro-Latin American cooperation: Shared values and interests*.
Lamy, P. (2002). Stepping stones or stumbling blocks? The EU's approach towards the problem of multilateralism vs regionalism in trade policy. *The World Economy, 25*(10), 1399–1413.
Lascoumes, P., & Le Galès, P. (2007). Introduction: Understanding public policy through its instruments—From the nature of instruments to the sociology of public policy instrumentation. *Governance, 20*(1), 1–21. https://doi.org/10.1111/j.1468-0491.2007.00342.x
Le Galès, P. (2011). Policy instruments and governance. In M. Bevir (Ed.), *The SAGE handbook of governance* (pp. 142–159). Sage.
Meyer, T., de Sales Marques, J. L., & Telò, M. (2019). *Regionalism and multilateralism politics, Economics, Culture*.
Nolte, D., & Weiffen, B. (2020). *Regionalism under stress*. Routledge. https://doi.org/10.4324/9780429442186
Peters, B. G. (2005). The problem of policy problems. *Journal of Comparative Policy Analysis: Research and Practice, 7*(4), 349–370. https://doi.org/10.1080/13876980500319204
Ribeiro Hoffmann, A. (2016). Inter- and transregionalism. In T. Börzel & T. Risse (Eds.), *The Oxford handbook of comparative regionalism* (pp. 600–621). Oxford University Press.
Roloff, R. (2006). Interregionalism in theoretical perspective: State of the art. In H. Hänggi & R. Roloff (Eds.), *Interregionalism and international relations* (pp. 17–31). Cambridge University Press.

Rüland, J. (2010). Balancers, multilateral utilities or regional identity builders? International relations and the study of interregionalism. *Journal of European Public Policy, 17*(8), 1271–1283. https://doi.org/10.1080/13501763.2010.513586

Sanahuja, J. A. (2015). The EU and CELAC: Reinvigorating a strategic partnership. In E.-L. Foundation (Ed.), *Bi-regional relations/Reflection Fora Series*. EU-LAC Foundation. http://eulacfoundation.org/sites/eulacfoundation.org/files/PublishedVersion_EN.pdf

Sanahuja, J. A., & Rodríguez, J. D. (2019). Veinte años de negociaciones Unión Europea – Mercosur: Del interregionalismo a la crisis de la globalización. In *Documentos de Trabajo: Vol. 13/2019*. https://doi.org/10.33960/issn-e.1885-9119.dt13

Sanahuja, J. A., & Rodríguez, J. D. (2022). Twenty years of EU–MERCOSUR negotiations. In *Latin America–European Union relations in the twenty-first century*. https://doi.org/10.7765/9781526136503.00012

Sanchez Bajo, C. (2005). European Union-Mercosur interregionalism: Negotiations, civil society and governance. In M. Bøås, M. H. Marchand, & T. Shaw (Eds.), *The political economy of regions and regionalism* (pp. 33–57). Palgrave MacMillan.

Schade, D. (2022). *Interlinkages in EU–Andean community trade negotiations*. Manchester University Press. https://doi.org/10.7765/9781526136503.00009

Selleslaghs, J. (2019). The EU's engagement with Latin America: The changing nature of EU-Latin America interregional relations. In R. A. Wessel & J. Odermatt (Eds.), *Research handbook on the European Union and international organizations* (pp. 609–626). Edward Elgar Publishing. https://doi.org/10.4337/9781786438935.00040

Söderbaum, F. (2015). *Rethinking regionalism*. Palgrave Macmillan.

Söderbaum, F., & Van Langenhove, L. (2005). Introduction: The EU as a Global Actor and the Role of Interregionalism. *Journal of European Integration, 27*, 249–262. http://www.ingentaconnect.com/content/routledg/geui/2005/00000027/00000003/art00001

United Nations Industrial Development Organization (UNIDO). (2020). TEAM EUROPE. The EU Global Response to COVID-19. A Stronger Europe in the World. https://www.unido.org/sites/default/files/files/2020-06/BRO_Focus_TEAM_EUROPE_EU_Response_to_COVID19_JUNE2020.pdf

van der Vleuten, A., & van Eerdewijk, A. (2020). The fragmented inclusion of gender equality in AU-EU relations in times of crises. *Political Studies Review, 18*(3), 576–591. https://doi.org/10.1177/1478929920918830

SPRINGER NATURE

GPSR Compliance

The European Union's (EU) General Product Safety Regulation (GPSR) is a set of rules that requires consumer products to be safe and our obligations to ensure this.

If you have any concerns about our products, you can contact us on ProductSafety@springernature.com

In case Publisher is established outside the EU, the EU authorized representative is:

Springer Nature Customer Service Center GmbH
Europaplatz 3
69115 Heidelberg, Germany

The manufacturer's authorised representative in the EU is Springer Nature Customer Service Centre GmbH, Europaplatz 3, 69115 Heidelberg, Germany. If you have any concerns regarding our products, please contact ProductSafety@springernature.com

Printed and bound by CPI Group (UK) Ltd, Croydon, CR0 4YY
30/09/2026
02225599-0018

Lecture Notes in Production Engineering

Lecture Notes in Production Engineering (LNPE) is a new book series that reports the latest research and developments in Production Engineering, comprising:

- Biomanufacturing
- Control and Management of Processes
- Cutting and Forming
- Design
- Life Cycle Engineering
- Machines and Systems
- Optimization
- Precision Engineering and Metrology
- Surfaces

LNPE publishes authored conference proceedings, contributed volumes and authored monographs that present cutting-edge research information as well as new perspectives on classical fields, while maintaining Springer's high standards of excellence. Also considered for publication are lecture notes and other related material of exceptionally high quality and interest. The subject matter should be original and timely, reporting the latest research and developments in all areas of production engineering. The target audience of LNPE consists of advanced level students, researchers, as well as industry professionals working at the forefront of their fields. Much like Springer's other Lecture Notes series, LNPE will be distributed through Springer's print and electronic publishing channels. To submit a proposal or request further information please contact Anthony Doyle, Executive Editor, Springer (anthony.doyle@springer.com).

More information about this series at http://www.springer.com/series/10642

Ekkard Brinksmeier · Lars Schönemann
Editors

Ultra-precision High Performance Cutting

Report of DFG Research Unit FOR 1845

Springer

Editors
Ekkard Brinksmeier
Universität Bremen
Bremen, Germany

Lars Schönemann
Leibniz Institute for Materials Engineering
IWT
Bremen, Germany

ISSN 2194-0525 ISSN 2194-0533 (electronic)
Lecture Notes in Production Engineering
ISBN 978-3-030-83764-8 ISBN 978-3-030-83765-5 (eBook)
https://doi.org/10.1007/978-3-030-83765-5

This Springer imprint is published by the registered company Springer Nature Switzerland AG
The registered company address is: Gewerbestrasse 11, 6330 Cham, Switzerland

Foreword

Although precision manufacturing has a long history, the emergence of precision manufacturing optical surfaces using diamond tools was the result of multiple independent developments from the 1900s through the 1940s. By 1974, precision engineering, and the term nanotechnology, coined by Professor Norio Taniguchi and later quantified by Professor Patrick McKeown as manufacturing accuracy progressed from 1 part in 10^4 to 1 part in 10^8 (typically the ratio of the largest characteristic dimension to the form accuracy). Subsequently, the Royal Society and the Royal Academy of Engineering defined nanomanufacturing as production of structures with form accuracy essential to functional performance better than 100 nm.

Ultra-precision high performance cutting (UP-HPC) adds another critical constraint, which is cost-effective manufacture. Cost is one of the two basic limitations to future advances in ultra-precision manufacturing described by Erwin Loewen. Commercial applications have continued to drive the remarkable growth of ultra-precision machining over the last 80 years. Starting with aspheric Schmidt plate molds, commercial drivers progressed to aspheric camera lens molds, intraocular lenses, contact lens molds, and structured surface enhancing films. Today, molds for cell phone camera lenses, automotive head-up displays, and automotive lighting are just a few of the consumer applications with form accuracy better than 100 nm while exceeding 1 part in 10^5 tolerance ratios.

An indispensable force enabling this continued growth is the relationship between research institutes and industry. While industry must recognize new ultra-precision manufacturing opportunities, research institutes must accept the associated risk of developing new tools and processes with their deeper understanding and detailed analyses. Researchers must demonstrate feasibility of novel processes and allow industry to focus on implementations that satisfy the requirements of the market cost effectively.

Such is the case with this exemplary work funded by the German Research Foundation and directed by Professor Dr.-Ing. Ekkard Brinksmeier and Dr.-Ing. Lars Schönemann in collaboration with researchers from Bremen University and the Leibniz University Hannover. Beginning with an ingenious design using multiple diamond tools and thermal positioning, they have attacked the productivity problem at the source. Next, they have demonstrated the benefits of diamond machining metals and semiconductor materials at high speed. This is followed by an ambitious project to implement an electromagnetic linear stage for high precision machining. They have developed and demonstrated several tools which automatically balance a high-speed spindle to precision grades to eliminate time-consuming manual balancing. Finally, all of these improvements are enhanced by the development of a new control strategy to enable increased axis speeds for ultra-precision high performance cutting.

For more than 30 years, Professor Brinksmeier and his collaborators have addressed critical technology gaps in ultra-precision manufacturing. Their legacy includes unique solutions to some of our most difficult manufacturing challenges as well as producing an entire generation of precision engineers with contributions to international audiences at JSPE, ASPE, and euspen. Although it is difficult to predict what the driving markets for ultra-precision manufacturing will be in the coming years, it is clear that a cooperative relationship between research institutes and industry continues to be necessary.

March 2021

Byron R. Knapp
Senior Engineer

Preface

This book comprises recent results for increasing the performance of ultra-precision machining processes, focusing on diamond milling. It primarily serves as the final report of the German research unit FOR1845 "Ultra-precision High Performance Cutting" funded by the German Research Foundation (DFG) from April 2014 to June 2020, which is gratefully acknowledged by the authors. At the same time, the book also reveals remarkable results and potentials for further developments of ultra-precision machining and thus addresses both, scientists and industry.

The idea of increasing the performance of ultra-precision machining processes by the application of extremely high cutting speeds was forged by Prof. Ekkard Brinksmeier and Dr. Werner Preuß from the Laboratory for Precision Machining (LFM) in Bremen already in 2010. It quickly became clear that the research field for achieving this goal is not solely focused on the machining processes, but entails machine tool technology and software/control design as well. Thus, Prof. Berend Denkena from the Institute for Production Engineering and Machine Tools at the Leibniz University Hannover and Prof. Bernd Kuhfuss from the Machine Tool Department of Bremen University were asked to join the effort for proposing a joint research group. After several rounds of discussion, five relevant topics were identified and shaped into project proposals. After review by the DFG, funding was granted and the research began in the year 2014 under the technical leadership of Dr. Lars Schönemann, LFM Bremen. Detailed descriptions of the research results gained over the past 6 1/2 years can be found in this book. Some of the initial goals of the research unit were very visionary. Even if some limitations had to be accepted in the implementation, the results achieved clearly show promising paths for a more economical ultra-precision manufacturing. This should be an inspiration for all of us to build on what we have achieved and to continue to develop these advanced technologies.

During the course of the research unit, more than 20 researchers and technicians as well as numerous students were involved in the research work and contributed to the overall goal of increasing the performance of ultra-precision machining by writing their theses, presenting the work at numerous conferences, and publishing the results in relevant journals as well as this book. Their support and dedication to this work are highly appreciated.

April 2021

Ekkard Brinksmeier
Lars Schönemann

Contents

List of Contributors

Daniel Berger MAPEX Center for Materials and Processes, University of Bremen, Bremen, Germany;
Leibniz Institute for Materials Engineering IWT, Bremen, Germany

Benjamin Bergmann Institute of Production Engineering and Machine Tools IFW, Leibniz University Hannover, Garbsen, Germany

Ekkard Brinksmeier Leibniz Institute for Materials Engineering IWT, Bremen, Germany;
MAPEX Center for Materials and Processes, University of Bremen, Bremen, Germany

Berend Denkena Institute of Production Engineering and Machine Tools IFW, Leibniz University Hannover, Garbsen, Germany

Timo Dörgeloh Leibniz Institute for Materials Engineering IWT, Bremen, Germany

Johannes Hochbein Bremen Institute for Mechanical Engineering bime and MAPEX Center for Materials and Processes, University of Bremen, Bremen, Germany

Rudolf Krüger Institute of Production Engineering and Machine Tools IFW, Leibniz University Hannover, Garbsen, Germany

Bernd Kuhfuss Bremen Institute for Mechanical Engineering bime and MAPEX Center for Materials and Processes, University of Bremen, Bremen, Germany

Nasrin Parsa Bremen Institute for Mechanical Engineering bime and MAPEX Center for Materials and Processes, University of Bremen, Bremen, Germany

Oltmann Riemer Leibniz Institute for Materials Engineering IWT, Bremen, Germany;
MAPEX Center for Materials and Processes, University of Bremen, Bremen, Germany

Lars Schönemann Leibniz Institute for Materials Engineering IWT, Bremen, Germany;
MAPEX Center for Materials and Processes, University of Bremen, Bremen, Germany

Christian Schenck Bremen Institute for Mechanical Engineering bime and MAPEX Center for Materials and Processes, University of Bremen, Bremen, Germany

Per Schreiber Institute of Production Engineering and Machine Tools IFW, Leibniz University Hannover, Garbsen, Germany

Acronyms

42CrMo4	heat treatable steel type 1.7225/AISI 4140/42CrMo4
AE	acoustic emission
AFM	atomic force microscope
AlMg3	aluminium 3.3535/EN AW-5754/AlMg3
AlMg5	aluminium 3.3555/EN AW-5019/AlMg5
ARM	advanced RISC machines
ASPE	The American Society for Precision Engineering
CCLD	constant current line drive
CEEMD	complementary ensemble empirical mode decomposition
CHR	control parameter calculation method according to Chien, Hrones and Reswick
CIRP	The International Academy for Production Engineering (French: Collège International pour la Recherche en Productique)
CNC	computer numerical control
CPU	central processing unit
CuNi18Zn19Pb1	nickel silver CuNi18Zn19Pb1
CUPE	Cranfield Unit for Precision Engineering
CuZn30	brass 2.0265/EN CW505L/CuZn30
CuZn39Pb3	brass 2.0401/EN CW614N/CuZn39Pb3/MS58
CuZn40Pb2	brass 2.0402/AISI CW617N/CuZn40Pb2
DoF	degrees of freedom
EtherCAT	ethernet for control and automation technology
eu**spen**	The European Society for Precision Engineering and Nanotechnology
FEM	finite element method
FF	feed forward
FFT2	two-dimensional fast Fourier transformation
FOR1845	German research unit ("Forschungsgruppe") No. 1845 Ge germanium

HFIM	high-frequency-impulse-measurement
HPC	high performance cutting
HSC	high speed cutting
HSM	high speed machining
IPC	industrial PC
IR	infrared
IS	input shaping
JL	jerk limitation
JSPE	The Japan Society for Precision Engineering
LED	light emitting diode
LiPo	lithium-ion polymer
LLNL	Lawrence Livermore National Laboratory
MBSM	motion band sub-model
NiP	electroless nickel/nickel phosphorous
OFHC	oxygen-free high conductivity
PEM	predictive error method
PI	proportional-integral controller
PID	proportional-integral-differential controller
PLC	programmable logic controller
PSoC	programmable system on a chip
PWM	pulse width modulation
RBSM	residual band sub-model
RFM	radio frequency module
RISC	reduced instruction set computer
S355J2(+N)	low-alloy steel 1.0577/AISI A738/S355J2(+N)
Si	silicon
SSD	sub surface damage
TCP	tool center point
TP1	sub-project (German: "Teilprojekt") 1 of the FOR1845 on "Ultra-precision milling with multiple diamond cutting inserts"
TP2	sub-project 2 of the FOR1845 on "Ultra-precision high-speed milling"
TP3	sub-project 3 of the FOR1845 on "Electromagnetic ultra-precision linear guide"
TP4	sub-project 4 of the FOR1845 on "Balancing of spindles for ultra-precision high speed milling"
TP5	sub-project 5 of the FOR1845 on "Model-based toolpath correction for ultra-precision machining"
UDB	universal digital block
UP	ultra-precision
UP-HPC	Ultra-Precision High Performance Cutting
USM	ultrasonic motor
WLI	white light interferometer, a specific type of a coherence scanning interferometer
X40Cr14	stainless steel type 1.2083/AISI 420/X40Cr14

X5CrNi18-10	high-strength steel 1.4301/AISI 304/X5CrNi18-10
ZnS	zinc sulfide
ZnSe	zinc selenide
ZV	zero vibration
ZVD	zero vibration derivative

Symbols

$\overline{\Delta_y}$	µm	mean profile height deviation
α	°	angle of first unbalance mass for rotary redistribution
α	nm mm^{-1} K^{-1}	coefficient of thermal expansion
β	°	angle of second unbalance mass for rotary redistribution
χ_{act}	°	angular spacing of actuators
$\boldsymbol{\delta}$	m	magnetic air gaps
$\Delta\alpha$	°	difference in clearange angle of two tools
Δd	nm	depth difference of machined cutting marks
$\Delta\gamma$	°	difference in rake angle angle of two tools
Δh_{el}	nm	differential elastic springback of a grain
ΔL_{max}	nm	maximum thermal expansion at elevated temperature
ΔL_{min}	nm	minimal required thermal expansion for tool setting
ΔL	nm	thermal expansion of a beam
$\Delta \boldsymbol{q_{pos}}$	µm	vector of position offsets on q
Δr_{fly}	µm	difference in fly-cut radius of two tools
Δs	µm	difference in tool spur/track of two tools
ΔT	K	temperature difference
Δt	s	time interval
$\Delta \mathrm{T}_{max}$	K	maximum allowed temperature difference above ambient
$\Delta \mathrm{T}_{min}$	K	minimal temperature difference for a specific expansion
η	-	thermal absorption
γ	°	rake angle angle of a tool
γ	°	rotation angle of the USM
κ	W m^{-1} K^{-1}	thermal conductivity
λ	nm	wavelength of IR-LED
λ_c	Hz	cut-off frequency used in filters
ω	Hz	rotational frequency
ω	rad s^{-1}	angular velocity of the rotor
φ	°	half-angle of IR-LED
ϕ	°	effective angle of the resultant force
ϕ_{AB}	°	phase shift of travelling waves in the ultrasonic motor
Φ_e	mW	total radiant flux of IR-LED

(continued)

(continued)

ρ	gmm^{-3}	density
ζ	-	damping ratio
A	μm^2	surface area
$\boldsymbol{A}$	-	system matrix of state space model
A	m, *here* μm	(bi-directional) positioning accuracy (ISO 230-2)
a	nm	gain parameter for CHR method ($a = kL/T$)
a_e	μm	width of cut
AE_{max}	Mv	acoustic emission signal amplitude
A_1, A_2	-	input shaping gains
A_{max}	μm^2	cross section of the tool plunging into the material while cutting
a_{max}	ms^{-2}	acceleration limit
$a_{\max}$	ms^{-2}	acceleration limit
a_p	μm	depth of cut, infeed
$\boldsymbol{B}$	-	input matrix of state space model
C	JK^{-1}	heat capacity
c	ms^{-1}	propagation velocity of radio frequency signals ($\approx 3 \times 108\ ms^{-1}$)
$\boldsymbol{C}$	-	output matrix of state space model
c_H	-	coherence shock response spectrum
c_p	$J\ kg^{-1}\ K^{-1}$	specific heat capacity
d	mm	diameter of a fly-cutter
$\boldsymbol{D}$	N/(m/s), Nm/(rad/s)	damping matrix of the system model
d_c	nm	critical depth of cut
$\boldsymbol{d_S}$	m	position signals of the air gap sensors
E	Nm^{-2}	Young's modulus
e_{iRj}	μrad	inclination error around j-axis for i-movement
e_{iTj}	μm	straightness error in j-direction for i-movement
e_p	gmm	permissible specific unbalance
F	N	resultant force
f_0	Hz	carrier frequency of the RFM module
f	μm	(lateral) feed
f_{-3dB}	Hz	frequency at −3 dB (bandwidth frequency
$\boldsymbol{F_A}$	N	actuator force
f_c	Hz	commutation frequency of the ultrasonic motors
F_c	N	cutting force
$F_{c,\infty}$	N	constant cutting force at infinite speed
$F_{c,var}$	N	variable value of cutting force according to Ben Amor
f_D	Hz	Doppler shift
F_f	N	feed force
F_i	N	force of *i*-axis
F_{imp}	N	impulse force
$\boldsymbol{F_M}$	N	magnet pulling force
F_n	N	normal force
F_p	N	passive force
f_s	Hz	sample rate
F_u	N	centrifugal force
G	$mm\ s^{-1}$	balancing grade
$h_{cu,max}$	μm	maximum undeformed chip thickness

(continued)

(continued)

$H(f)$	μm N^{-1}	shock response spectrum
HV	N mm^{-2}	Vickers hardness
$\boldsymbol{i}$	A	coil currents of the electromagnets
i_{bal}	-	balancing iteration
I_e	W sr^{-1}	radiant intensity of IR-LED
I_f	A	forward current of IR-LED
j	ms^{-3}	jerk
$\boldsymbol{J_A}$	-	Jacobian matrix for the actuators
$\boldsymbol{J_S}$	-	Jacobian matrix for the air gap sensors
k	Nm^{-1} *here* Nm μm^{-1}	(dynamic) stiffness
$\boldsymbol{K}$	N m^{-1}, Nm rad^{-1}	stiffness matrix of the system model
K_c	MPa$\sqrt{m}$	fracture toughness
k_c	GPa	specific cutting force
K_D	N sm^{-1}	derivative feedback gain
K_I	N m^{-1} s^{-1}	integral feedback gain
K_P	N m^{-1}	proportional feedback gain
K_p	nm	proportional gain of of thermal actuator controller
K_u	nm	ultimate gain of thermal actuator plant model
L_0	mm	base length of a beam
L_c	km	effective contact length (cumulated)
L	s	delay time for CHR method
l_k	mm	contact length in milling
$\boldsymbol{l_n}$	mm	balance mass vector for rotary redistribution
l_{wp}	mm	workpiece length
$\boldsymbol{M}$	kg mass	matrix of the system model
M	m, *here* μm	(bi-directional) repeatability (ISO 230-2)
m	kg	mass
M_i	Nm	torque of i-axis
m_i	kg	balancing masses
m_p	kg	permissible residual unbalance mass
m_r	kg	rotor weight
M_u	Nm	torque generated by the USM
m_u	kg	unbalance mass
n_{act}	-	number of actuators
n	min^{-1}	spindle speed
$\boldsymbol{P}$	kg	parameter vector
P_1	nm	summation of low-frequency parts of the FFT2
P_2	nm μm^{-1}	summation of high-frequency parts of the FFT2
p_{ij}	kg	feed forward parameters axis i to axis j
P_n	-	commutation pulses sent to the ultrasonic motor
$P\_$	W	power of heat source (i.e. Laser or LED)
PV	μm	peak-to-valley
$\boldsymbol{q}$	m, rad	generalized coordinate vector
$\boldsymbol{Q}$	N, Nm	generalize force vector
$\boldsymbol{Q_{ff}}$	N	vector of generalized force offsets

(continued)

(continued)

Q	J	heat input
Q	mm^3 min^{-1}	material removal rate
q_n	µm	generalized coordinate in n of levitation guide
$\boldsymbol{Q_{set}}$	N	vector generalized set-point forces
$\boldsymbol{q_{z\_tol}}$	N	allowance for qz
r	mm	radial distance for calculation of Doppler shift
r_β	°	cutting edge radius
r_c	mm	correction radius
r_ε	µm	nose radius of a tool
r_{fly}	mm	fly-cut radius
r_i	mm	balancing radii
R_{kin}	nm	kinematic roughness (for optics usually in nanometers)
R	m, *here* µm	(bi-directional) mean positioning error (ISO 230-2)
R_2	-	coefficient of determination
s	µm	raster spacing
S_1, S_2, S_{eq}	mm^2	contact areas in schematic model of contact geometry between tool and workpiece according to Yan et al.
S_A	-	signal for first travelling wave motor
S_a	nm	arithmetic mean height (areal)
S_B	-	signal for second travelling wave motor
S_{p2p}	µm	peak-to-peak value
S_q	nm	mean quadratic height (areal)
S_{std}	µm	standard deviation
Sz	nm	maximum height (areal)
t	s	time
T_0	s	oscillation period
T_a	°C	actuator temperature
t_{acc}	s	acceleration time
T	s	time constant for CHR method
t_{dec}	s	deceleration time
t_{fade}	s	oscillation fading time
t_f	ns	fall time of IR-LED to zero
t_{heat}	s	heating time
$t_{heat,rev}$	s	heating time per revolution
T_i	s	integral time of thermal actuator plant model and/or controller
t_k	µs	contact time in milling
t_{res}	s	residual time
t_r	ns	rise time of IR-LED to full power
T_s	s	shaping delay
t_{total}	s	time per line for exemplary workpiece
$\boldsymbol{U}$	g mm	measured unbalance vector
U_c	g mm	counterbalance
U_f	V	forward voltage of IR-LED
$\boldsymbol{u}$	-	input vector
U	g mm	residual unbalance
v	ms^{-1}	relative spindle speed
v_c	mm min^{-1}	cutting speed
v_c^*	m min^{-1}	critical cutting speed

(continued)

(continued)

v_f	mm min^{-1}	feed velocity
v_{HG}	m min^{-1}	Speed limit, at which the variable part of the cutting force has decreased by 86.5%, according to Ben Amor
V	mm^3	volume
v_{rot}	m ms^{-1}	rotational speed (circumferential speed)
V_s	V	supply voltage of the USM
v_{set}	ms^{-1}	set-point velocity
w	mm	width of the thermal actuator
w_{est}	-	window size
w	-	set-point value
$\boldsymbol{x}$	-	state vector
$\dot{x}$	-	state vector derivative
$\boldsymbol{y}$	-	output vector
z_{ac}	m	acceleration distance
z_{dec}	m	deceleration distance
z_{fade}	m	oscilation fading distance
z_{res}	m	residual distance
$\ddot{z}_{set}$	m s^{-2}	set-point acceleration in z
z_{total}	m	total machining distance

Introduction to Ultra-Precision High Performance Cutting

Lars Schönemann

1 State of the Art in Ultra-Precision Machining

Over the past decades, Ultra-precision (UP) diamond machining has evolved to an established technology for generating complex optical surfaces as well as for producing parts with high mechanical accuracy [7] (see Fig. 1).

In principle, the technology of diamond machining originates from different strands of developments for manufacturing optics (lenses, mirrors and gratings), precision parts (e.g. automotive pistons) or nuclear weapons. For example, the ruling of diffractive gratings by a "diamond point" was accomplished by Rutherford in the 1860s [29], although there are other examples dating back even further. An excellent overview on the historical evolution on diamond machining can be found in the book "*Precision engineering: an evolutionary view*" by Christopher Evans [16]. Initially, precision coordinate measurement machines served as a basis for machine tools in the 1940s [30]. According to Evans, the earliest "well-documented" diamond turning of modern optics (Schmidt Plates for infrared rifle scopes) was carried out by Frank Cooke from Polaroid during World War II [16, p.142].

Fig. 1 Exemplary diamond milling (fly-cutting) setup for generating freeform optical surfaces with monocrystalline diamond tools, picture credit [40], License: CC BY 4.0

L. Schönemann (✉)
Leibniz Institute for Materials Engineering IWT, Bremen, Germany

University of Bremen, MAPEX Center for Materials and Processes, Bremen, Germany
e-mail: schoenemann@iwt.uni-bremen.de

E. Brinksmeier and L. Schönemann (eds.), *Ultra-precision High Performance Cutting*, Lecture Notes in Production Engineering, https://doi.org/10.1007/978-3-030-83765-5_1

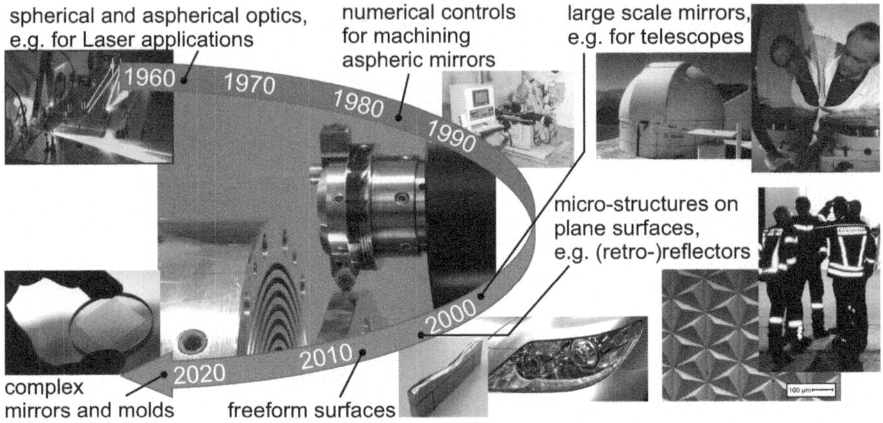

Fig. 2 The evolution of ultra-precision machining, according to [36], picture credits: [19, 33, 34, 37, 47], all other pictures ©Leibniz-IWT

Pioneering work in the 1960s was led by J.B. Bryan at the Lawrence Livermore National Laboratory (LLNL) in the USA (cf. [21]). Notable milestones (cf. Figure 2) were the application of reversal techniques to obtain mechanical parts with the highest degree of precision [31], the development of ultra-precision air bearing spindles [1] with minimal runout, the possibility to shape diamond tools with extremely sharp cutting edges and minimum waviness [17] as well as precision encoders for the exact position location in linear machine axes [9].

By the 1970s, ultra-precision machining had found use in manufacturing computer memory discs or optical components for photocopiers [10], although Saito stated that the greatest success of diamond turning was in generating flats [38]. He described that the applied diamond tools already featured a cutting edge sharpness of 250 Å (≡ 25 nm), which he deduced from the thickness of the generated chips of 750 Å [38]. He also highlighted balancing of the spindles as a crucial setup procedure and pointed out that the belts for connecting the spindles and their motors had to be carefully selected to minimize vibrations. The economic viability of diamond turning was already far superior to conventional techniques, as it enabled the reduction of machining times from several weeks for superpolishing to about one day [38]. Although numerical controls were already available at that time, those were not yet commonly applied.

In the 1980s, diamond machining was further commercialized, when more and more solutions for diamond machining equipment appeared in the market by manufactures in the USA, Germany and Japan [16]. The widespread application of computer numerical control (CNC) established the capability to generate complex surfaces in a fast and flexible way. At this time, Taniguchi published his well-known CIRP Keynote in which he described ultra-precision machining as "those processes/machines by which the highest possible dimensional accuracy is, or has been achieved at a given point in time" and predicted the development of machining accuracy until the 2010s [44].

Several noteworthy ultra-precision machine tools originate from this decade. The DTM-3 is a large diamond turning machine designed by [8] at the LLNL that allows for the machining of optics with a weight of up to 4,500 kg and a diameter of 2.1 m [8]. Therefore, it utilized a horizontally aligned hydrostatic spindle (in contrast to the more commonly applied air bearings) as well as a metrology frame isolated from the machine base and an oil shower for temperature control. It was succeeded by the Large Optics Diamond Turning Machine of the LLNL that utilized a vertical spindle orientation instead [39] and allowed for turning 1,400 kg workpieces with 162 cm diameter and 50 cm height. With its dedicated metrology frame, incorporating seven interferometers as well as capacitive gauges for position feedback, it enabled the generation of metal optics with 25 nm figure accuracy and 5 nm root-mean-square roughness. A large diamond turning machine was also developed at the Cranfield Unit for Precision Engineering (CUPE) by McKeown et al. [28, 48]. One distinct feature of this machine was the application of lightweight steel weldment filled with synthetic granite for the construction of the machine base. A dedicated control system allowed for axis speeds up to 10 mm s^{-1}.

In the 1990s, even more sophisticated control and actuator systems (fast tool servos) were implemented to increase the capabilities of diamond turning in terms of their achievable geometric complexity [15]. The idea behind this actually was much older (see [45, 48] or [14]), but could not be implemented without advanced electronics and microcomputer systems. Despite the advancements in machining performance, some physical principles were not yet completely understood and still relied on empirical knowledge [21]. To fill this gap, Lucca et al. investigated the energy dissipation during cutting [25] and the plastic deformations in the surface layer [27]. Lucca et al. are also the first to use atomic force microscope (AFM) for tool wear characterization [26], which is done in a similar fashion until today.

By the 2000s, developments such as direct drive linear slides, dedicated software and the availability of non-circular cutting edge geometries enabled the manufacture of optics with almost arbitrary freeform shape [36].

Despite the advances in achievable precision and complexity of the parts, the associated processes are still limited in their economic potential [6]. One reason for this is the limited choice of diamond-machinable materials. Typical substrates include copper, aluminum, brass and electroless nickel, whereas particularly steel and other iron-based substrates usually result in catastrophic tool wear [35]. While there are means to counteract this wear, such as vibration assisted machining [32] or chemical treatment of the surface and subsurface layer [4], these approaches are severely limited in their applicability. For example, elliptical vibration is frequently used for cutting molds for optical devices, however, it cannot be applied for high speed cutting applications due to the limited maximum vibration frequency.

Another reason for the limited machining speed is the very time-consuming cutting process with chip thicknesses of only a few microns. Typical circumferential milling tools for fly-cutting feature comparably large swing radii of $r_{fly} = 20\,\mathrm{mm}$ up to 60 mm [11], 95 mm or even larger [43]. Consequently, the inertia upon rotation generates dynamic disturbances [50], which are typically mitigated by limiting the applied spindle speeds between $n = 1,000\,\mathrm{min}^{-1}$, e.g. [49], and 5,000 min^{-1}, e.g.

[24, 50]. In addition, diamond milling is conducted using only a single diamond cutting edge (fly-cutting) to ensure a defined swing radius of the tool [51]. This along with the precision required for mirror surfaces (Sa < 10 nm and PV < 100 nm being typical thresholds) requires the linear machine axes to be moved at a particularly slow speed to achieve the required feed rate. Overall, the surface generation rate is only at around 2.5 $mm^2 min^{-1}$ [3] and even the manufacture of small optical surfaces may yield a machining time of multiple hours up to several days [12, 46].

The required precision and temporal stability not only affect the primary machining speed and time, but also all auxiliary processes required for setting up the machine tool, aligning tool and workpiece and balancing the rotor for the milling operation. Many of the concepts known from conventional machining, such as automated tool or part calibration within the machine, automated tool changing or balancing, do not offer the required precision. Therefore, time-consuming manual tool and workpiece setting procedures are required. For example, the spindles are balanced to an ISO balancing grade $< G0.04$ [2] to ensure the safe operation of the air bearings typically applied in UP-machining [20, 23]. Therefore, tiny oscillations of the rotor have to be detected and compensating masses have to be determined [5, 18, 20] and accurately placed at their respective locations on the rotor. So far, automated procedures to achieve this goal are not known. Instead, balancing an ultra-precision spindle is a tedious and time-consuming manual task in which weight is added at specific locations on the rotor until a satisfying balance can be assured. The smaller the masses are, the more difficult this task becomes.

2 The UP-HPC Approach

Ultra-Precision High Performance Cutting (UP-HPC) is a term coined by the German research unit ("Forschungsgruppe") No. 1845 (FOR1845) to subsume all activities around ultra-precision machining at elevated speeds, reducing the primary machining and auxiliary setup times as well as increasing the general process stability.

Both, high speed cutting (HSC) and high performance cutting (HPC) have been applied in conventional machining for several decades and are an essential part of precision machine design since the early 1990s [42] to increase the economic efficiency of milling processes and also to positively influence the material removal mechanisms [13, 41]. More recently, it has been shown that this also applies to micro milling [22]. An application of HSC in UP milling has not yet been approached and thus, the influences on material removal at this scale are not well-researched.

This was the reason for the initiation of the research unit FOR1845 in early 2014 by the Universities of Bremen and Hannover. It consists of five sub-projects (German: "Teilprojekte", TP), each targeting a specific approach to UP-HPC:

TP1 "Ultra-precise milling with multiple diamond cutting edges"
aimed to develop a tool setting mechanism based on thermal expansion to align multiple cutting edges in a fly-cutting setup to a common radius (Chapter 2).

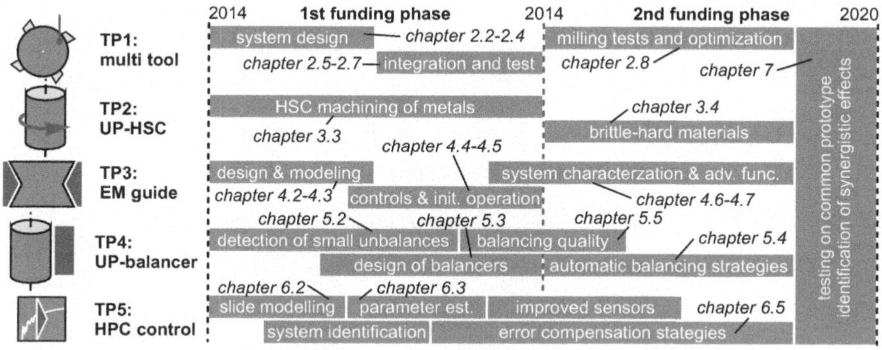

Fig. 3 Approaches of the Research Unit FOR1845 for achieving Ultra-Precision High Performance Cutting

TP2 "Ultra-precision high-speed milling"
focused on the scientific evaluation of high speed cutting with diamond tools, by analyzing its effect on the cutting forces, the resulting wear and, in the case of brittle materials, on the surface integrity (Chapter 3).

TP3 "Electromagnetic ultra-precision linear guide"
developed an electromagnetically guided and driven ultra-precise linear stage that allowed for extremely high feed velocities and enabled an in-process compensation of static and dynamic deviations (Chapter 4).

TP4 "Balancing of spindles for ultra-precision high speed milling"
targeted automated unbalance measurement and compensation techniques that supersede the speed and precision of manual weight-adding procedures by far (Chapter 5).

TP5 "Model-based toolpath correction for ultra-precision machining"
addressed the control-related aspects of UP-HPC by researching in-process analysis and compensation strategies (Chapter 6).

The topics addressed in the sub-projects are depicted in Fig. 3 along with a reference to the chapters of this book which deal with the respective topic.

3 Integration of Developments into a Common Test Stand

Actually, the development of individual measures to improve diamond milling is not sufficient. Rather, it is necessary to test the interaction of the individual developments in a joint test stand, in order to demonstrate the synergistic potential of the individual measures for economical UP machining. Thus, all developments of the FOR1845 were integrated into a common test stand (Fig. 4) which is designed to prove the viability of all approaches (Chapter 7).

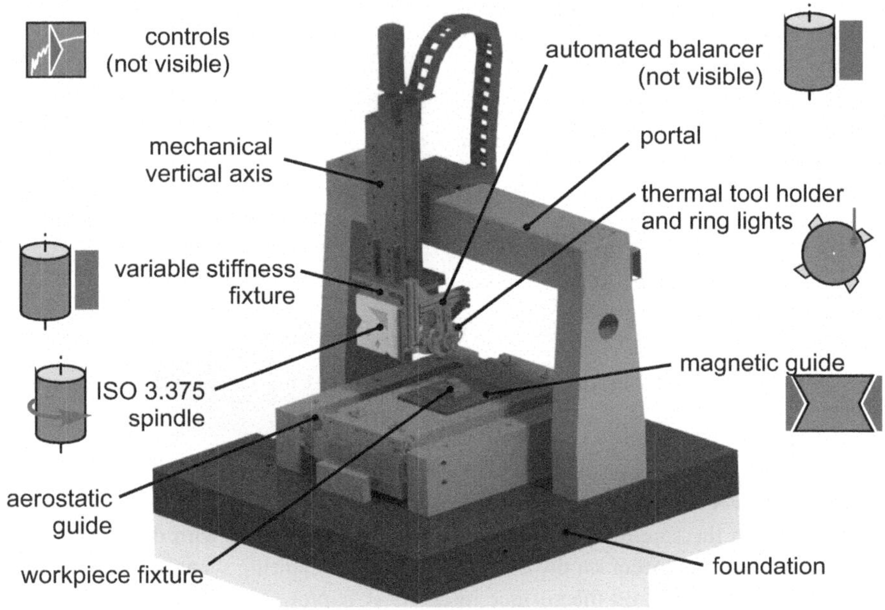

Fig. 4 Concept for the common test stand to integrate all developments of the FOR1845

Specifically, the test stand integrates the following components

a commercial ISO 3.375 air bearing spindle as the main tool spindle allowing for speeds $>5.000\,\text{min}^{-1}$,

the newly developed magnetic linear guide as a high-velocity feed axis,

a commercial aerostatic guide forming a cross-table with the magnetic guide for controls development and test,

the developed variable stiffness fixture to facilitate the unbalance detection,

the developed mechatronic balancers for automated UP-balancing,

the developed thermal tool setting mechanism for aligning multiple cutting edges to a common fly-radius, and

a mechanical vertical axis used for setting the depth of cut. This axis carries the load of many attached components and is only used for static positioning. Thus, a mechanical bearing technology was ranked to be sufficient in this case.

Further details concerning the test stand design and integration of individual components are introduced in Chapters 4 and 6.

The final Chapter 7 gives a retrospective on the highlight work of all projects within the FOR1845 and will also point out particular achievements over the past six years. Moreover, a brief outlook on potential future work will be given.

References

1. Arneson, C., Liebers, M.: History of the blockhead spindle. In: 33rd ASPE Annual Meeting. Las Vegas/NV, 4 November 2018
2. Brandt, C., et al.: Surface generation process with consideration of the balancing state in diamond machining. In: Denkena, B., Hollmann, F. (eds.) Process Machine Interactions. Lecture Notes in Production Engineering, pp. 329–360. Springer, Cham (2013)
3. Brecher, C., Lindemann, D., Merz, M., Wenzel, C., Preuss, W.: Freeform machining of molds for replication of plastic optics. In: Brinksmeier, E., Gläbe, R., Riemer, O. (eds.) Fabrication of Complex Optical Components. Lecture Notes in Production Engineering, pp. 41–52. Springer, Cham (2013)
4. Brinksmeier, E., Gläbe, R., Osmer, J.: Ultra-precision diamond cutting of steel molds. CIRP Ann. **55**(1), 551–554 (2006). https://doi.org/10.1016/S0007-8506(07)60480-6
5. Brinksmeier, E., Gläbe, R., Krause, A.: Precision balancing in ultraprecision diamond machining. In: Thornett, E.E (ed.) 8th International Conference on Laser Metrology, Machine Tool, pp. 262–269. CMM & Robotic Performance (Lamdamap 2007) (2007)
6. Brinksmeier, E., Preuss, W.: Micro-machining. Philos. Trans. R. Soc. A **370**, 3973–3992 (2012). https://doi.org/10.1098/rsta.2011.0056
7. Brinksmeier, E.: Ultraprecision machining. In: CIRP Encyclopedia of Production Engineering, pp. 1–5. Springer, Heidelberg (2018). https://doi.org/10.1007/978-3-642-35950-7_6403-4
8. Bryan, J.B.: Design and construction of an ultraprecision 84 inch diamond turning machine. Precision Eng. **1**(1), 13–17 (1979). https://doi.org/10.1016/0141-6359(79)90071-0
9. Carpenter, A.J.: Locating device for precision tools. U.S. Patent 2 948 817, 9 August 1960
10. Chapman, G.: Ultra-precision Systems; an Enabling Technology for Perfect Surfaces. Technical Report, Moore Nanotechnology Systems (2004)
11. Cheng, M.N., Cheung, C.F., Lee, W.B., To, S., Kong, L.B.: Theoretical and experimental analysis of nano-surface generation in ultra-precision raster milling. Int. J. Mach. Tools Manuf. **48**(10), 1090–1102 (2008). https://doi.org/10.1016/j.ijmachtools.2008.02.006
12. Davies, M.A., Dutterer, B.S., Suleski, T.J., Silny, J.F., Kim, E.D.: Diamond machining of diffraction gratings for imaging spectrometers. Precision Eng. **36**(2), 334–338 (2012). https://doi.org/10.1016/j.precisioneng.2011.09.006
13. Dewes, R.C., Aspinwall, D.K.: A review of ultra high speed milling of hardened steels. J. Mater. Process. Technol. **69**(1–3), 1–17 (1997). https://doi.org/10.1016/S0924-0136(96)00042-8
14. Douglass, S.S.: A Machining System for Turning Nonaxis symmetric surfaces. Ph.D. thesis. University of Tennessee, Knoxville (1983)
15. Dow, T.A., Miller, M.H., Falter, P.J.: Application of a fast tool servo for diamond turning of non rotationally symmetric surfaces. Precision Eng. **13**(4), 243–250 (1991). https://doi.org/10.1016/0141-6359(91)90001-y
16. Evans, C.: Precision engineering : an evolutionary view. Cranfield Press, Bedford, UK (1989)
17. Fernandez-Moran, V.H.: Diamond cutting tool having and edge thickness of 0.001 to 0.01 micron. U.S. Patent 30 60 781 (1954)
18. Grejda, R., Marsh, E., Vallance, R.: Techniques for calibrating spindles with nanometer error motion. Precision Eng. **29**(1), 113–123 (2005). https://doi.org/10.1016/j.precisioneng.2004.05.003
19. GT1976. KLF-A Weißenburg and fire station Weißenburg at Unterabschnitts- Übung at Tiefgrabenrotte, Frankenfels, Austria. CC BY-SA 4.0 (2018). https://de.wikipedia.org/wiki/Datei:2018-09-14_(708)_KLFA_Wei%C3%9Fenburg_and_fire_station_Wei%C3%9Fenburg_at_Unterabschnitts-%C3%9Cbung_at_Tiefgrabenrotte,_Frankenfels,_Austria.jpg. Accessed 25 Feb 2021
20. Huang, P., Lee, W.B., Chan, C.Y.: Investigation of the effects of spindle unbalance induced error motion on machining accuracy in ultra-precision diamond turning. Int. J. Mach. Tools Manuf. **94**, 48–56 (2015). https://doi.org/10.1016/j.ijmachtools.2015.04.007
21. Ikawa, N., et al.: Ultraprecision metal cutting - the past, the present and the future. CIRP Ann. **40**(2), 587–594 (1991). https://doi.org/10.1016/s0007-8506(07)61134-2

22. Jahanmir, S.: Surface integrity in ultrahigh speed micromachining. Procedia Eng. **19**, 156–161 (2011). https://doi.org/10.1016/j.proeng.2011.11.095
23. Knapp, B., Arneson, D., Oss, D., Liebers, M., Vallance, R., Marsh, E.: The importance of spindle balancing for the machining of freeform optics. In: ASPE Spring Topical Meeting, vol. 51, pp. 74–78. ASPE, Raleigh, NC (2011)
24. Kong, L.B., Cheung, C.F., To, S., Lee, W.B.: An investigation into surface generation in ultra-precision raster milling. J. Mater. Process. Technol. **209**(8), 4178–4185 (2009). https://doi.org/10.1016/j.jmatprotec.2008.11.002
25. Lucca, D., Rhorer, R., Komanduri, R.: Energy dissipation in the ultraprecision machining of copper. CIRP Ann. **40**(1), 69–72 (1991). https://doi.org/10.1016/s0007-8506(07)61936-2
26. Lucca, D., Seo, Y., Komanduri, R.: Effect of tool edge geometry on energy dissipation in ultraprecision machining. CIRP Ann. **42**(1), 83–86 (1993). https://doi.org/10.1016/s0007-8506(07)62397-x
27. Lucca, D., Seo, Y., Rhorer, R., Donaldson, R.: Aspects of surface generation in orthogonal ultraprecision machining. CIRP Ann. **43**(1), 43–46 (1994). https://doi.org/10.1016/s0007-8506(07)62160-x
28. McKeown, P.A., Wills-Moren, W., Read, R.F.J., Modjarrad, H.: The design and development of a large ultra-precision CNC diamond turning machine. Adv. Manuf. Processes **1**(1), 133–157 (1986). https://doi.org/10.1080/10426918608953160
29. Michelson, A.A.: The ruling and performance of a ten-inch diffraction grating. In: Proceedings of the National Academy of Sciences of the United States of America, vol. 1, no. 7, pp. 396–400 (1915)
30. Moore Tools. About Moore Tool: Precision Machining Technology, Precision Tools (2021). http://mooretool.com/about.html .Accessed 25 Feb 2021
31. Moore, W.R.: Foundations of Mechanical Accuracy. The Moore Special Tools Company (1970)
32. Moriwaki, T., Shamoto, E.: Ultraprecision diamond turning of stainless steel by applying ultrasonic vibration. CIRP Ann. **40**(1), 559–562 (1991). https://doi.org/10.1016/S0007-8506(07)62053-8
33. NASA. Rayon laser à travers un dispositif optique. public domain (2004). https://commons.wikimedia.org/wiki/File:Laser_optique.jpg. Accessed 25 Feb 2021
34. Negadrive. El Enano robotic telescope, Las Cumbres Observatory. CC BY-SA 3.0 (1999). https://commons.wikimedia.org/wiki/File:El_Enano_robotic_telescope.jpg. Accessed 25 Feb 2021
35. Paul, E., Evans, C.J., Mangamelli, A., McGlauflin, M.L., Polvani, R.S.: Chemical aspects of tool wear in single point diamond turning. Precis. Eng. **18**(1), 4–19 (1996). https://doi.org/10.1016/0141-6359(95)00019-4
36. Preuss, W.: A Guide to Diamond Machining. Shaker-Verlag (2019)
37. Pride, M.: 2010 Lexus LS 460 HID headlamp. CC BY-SA 3.0 (2010). https://commons.wikimedia.org/wiki/File:2010_Lexus_LS_460_Headlight.jpg. Accessed 25 Feb 2021
38. Saito, T.T.: Machining of optics: an introduction. Appl. Optics **14**(8), 1773 (1975). https://doi.org/10.1364/ao.14.001773
39. Saito, T.T., Wasley, R.J., Stowers, I.F., Donaldson, R.R., Thompson, D.C.: Precision and manufacturing at the Lawrence Livermore National Laboratory. In: NASA 2003 Conference, 1 November 1993
40. Schönemann, L., et al.: Synergistic approaches to ultra-precision high performance cutting. CIRP J. Manuf. Sci. Technol. **28**, 38–51 (2020). https://doi.org/10.1016/j.cirpj.2019.12.001
41. Schulz, H., Moriwaki, T.: High-speed machining. CIRP Ann. **41**(2), 637–643 (1992). https://doi.org/10.1016/S0007-8506(07)63250-8
42. Slocum, A.: Precision machine design. Prentice Hall, Englewood Cliffs, N.J (1992)
43. Takasu, S., Masuda, M., Nishiguchi, T., Kobayashi, A.: Influence of study vibration with small amplitude upon surface roughness in diamond machining. CIRP Ann. **34**(1), 463–467 (1985). https://doi.org/10.1016/S0007-8506(07)61812-5
44. Taniguchi, N.: Current status in, and future trends of, ultraprecision machining and ultrafine materials processing. CIRP Ann. **32**(2), 573–582 (1983). https://doi.org/10.1016/s0007-8506(07)60185-1

45. Thompson, D.C.: Theoretical tool movement required to diamond turn an off-axis paraboloid on axis. Technical Report, Lawrence Livermore Laboratory, 19 December 1975
46. Wang, S.J., To, S., Chen, X., Chen, X.D., Ouyang, X.B.: An integrated optimization of cutting parameters and tool path generation in ultraprecision raster milling. Int. J. Adv. Manuf. Technol. **75**(9–12), 1711–1721 (2014). https://doi.org/10.1007/s00170-014-6254-0
47. Werner, M.: Lytro-Light-field camera at Ars Electronica 2013 at Brucknerhaus, Linz, Upper Austria. CC BY-SA 3.0 (2013). https://commons.wikimedia.org/wiki/File:Ars_Electronica_Festival_2013_Lytro_lightfield_photography_03.jpg. Visited 25 Feb 2021
48. Wills-Moren, W., Modjarrad, H., Read, R., McKeown, P.: Some aspects of the design and development of a large high precision CNC diamond turning machine. CIRP Ann. **31**(1), 409–414 (1982). https://doi.org/10.1016/s0007-8506(07)63338-1
49. Wu, Y., Peng, W., Liu, Y.: A novel fabrication method for micro optical waveguide mold based on fly-cutting technology. Optik - Int. J. Light Electr. Optics **124**(9), 867–869 (2013). https://doi.org/10.1016/j.ijleo.2012.02.020
50. Zhang, S.J., To, S.: The effects of spindle vibration on surface generation in ultra-precision raster milling. Int. J. Mach. Tools Manuf. **71**, 52–56 (2013). https://doi.org/10.1016/j.ijmachtools.2013.04.005
51. Zhang, S.J., To, S., Zhu, Z.W., Zhang, G.Q.: A review of fly cutting applied to surface generation in ultra-precision machining. Int. J. Mach. Tools Manuf. **103**, 13–27 (2016). https://doi.org/10.1016/j.ijmachtools.2016.01.001

Diamond Milling with Multiple Cutting Edges

Lars Schönemann, Oltmann Riemer, and Ekkard Brinksmeier

Abstract Ultra-precision milling with multiple diamond cutting edges—which generally is favorable in terms of economic efficiency—requires an in-process tool setting system that allows for the compensation of alignment and fixation errors. Such a system was designed on the basis of thermal expansion as the main means of actuation. The heat input is generated by infrared light diodes which feed the respective energy to the rotating tool contactlessly. It is controlled in a way that ensures that only a specific portion of the tool holder is illuminated and therefore thermally expanded. By measuring the displacement at a reference plane with a capacitive measurement system and feeding it back to the control system, the actual position of the diamond cutting edge can be precisely set in nanometer range. This chapter gives an overview on the main technical developments for the respective prototype system and presents its performance when used in a machining environment.

1 Surface Generation in Diamond Milling

In general, ultra-precision machining with diamond tools (UP-machining) is an indispensable technology of optics manufacturing [6]. UP-milling processes, in particular, allow for the direct generation of complex geometries and freeform shapes with extremely smooth surface roughness and high form accuracy [7, 21]. The economic viability of these technologies is often increased by applying them in replication processes, e.g. by diamond machining the required molds for plastic or glass optics production [4, 18]. With this it is possible to manufacture a large quantity of optical parts from a single master form. Although comparably long processing times are acceptable in this case, the duration of diamond milling an optical mold is still a bottleneck in production, because the machining may require several minutes even for geometrically simple parts and up to multiple hours or even days for complex geometries [3].

L. Schönemann (✉) · O. Riemer · E. Brinksmeier
Leibniz Institute for Materials Engineering IWT, Bremen, Germany
e-mail: schoenemann@iwt.uni-bremen.de

MAPEX Center for Materials and Processes, University of Bremen, Bremen, Germany

E. Brinksmeier and L. Schönemann (eds.), *Ultra-precision High Performance Cutting*, Lecture Notes in Production Engineering, https://doi.org/10.1007/978-3-030-83765-5_2

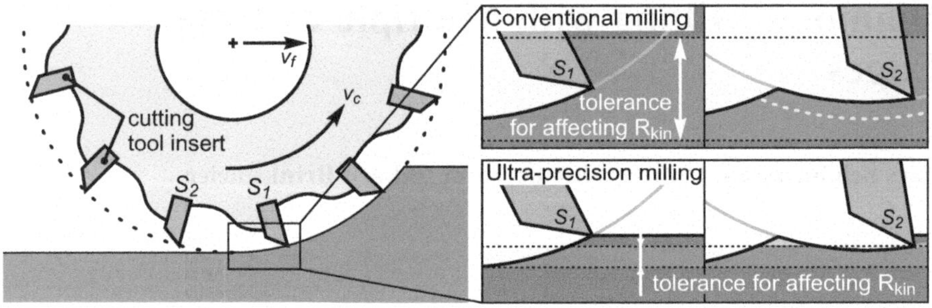

Fig. 1 Engagement conditions for multiple cutting edges in conventional and ultra-precision machining, cf. [11]

One of the reasons for these exceptionally long machining times is the limitation of diamond milling processes to the application of only one single cutting edge. Hence, these processes are also named "fly-cutting". The challenge of utilizing multiple cutting edges in diamond milling is their adjustment to achieve equal and predictable engagement conditions. Upon mounting the tool insert[1] on the tool holder, the manufacturing and assembly tolerances inevitably yield a deviation in fly-cut radius (Δr_{fly}), axial position (Δs, i.e. the subsequent cutting edges not running in the same "track"), and also in engagement angle ($\Delta\alpha$, $\Delta\gamma$). In particular, the axial and radial deviations may yield a magnitude of several micrometers.

Simply speaking, only if the fly-cut radii of all cutting edges feature a maximal difference below the kinematic roughness (in optics machining this typically implies $R_{kin} < 10$ nm), such a setup may be reliably used for machining (Fig. 1).

In reality, however, the associated surface generation is much more complex. When brought into contact with the workpiece, the radial and axial deviation of the cutting tools cause an irregular surface pattern which requires more describing parameters than just the simple formula to approximate the kinematic roughness in fly-cutting ($R_{kin} = f^2/(8r_\varepsilon)$). Instead, the differences in fly-cut radius Δr_{fly}, in axial direction Δs as well as all other geometric deviations such as the differences in shape and waviness of the cutting edge and the relative orientation of the cutting inserts have to be considered. A detailed analysis in 2D, i.e. for the kinematic roughness, can be found in [15]. A 3D-analysis of the generated surface is possible with numerical approaches, as presented in [16] and [17]. Ultimately, even the slightest deviation in any of these parameters results in new surface patterns that are generated and will lead to an undetermined surface roughness compared to fly-cutting with a single cutting edge (Fig. 2).

In summary, all cutting edges have to be aligned with as much precision as possible. The radial deviation Δr_{fly} has to be at least smaller than the maximum undeformed chip thickness $h_{cu,max}$ of the process, for all cutting edges to be involved in the material removal. Preferably, the remaining deviation of all cutting edges has to

[1] usually a carbide insert with a diamond soldered on top; the diamond is ground and lapped to form the actual cutting edge.

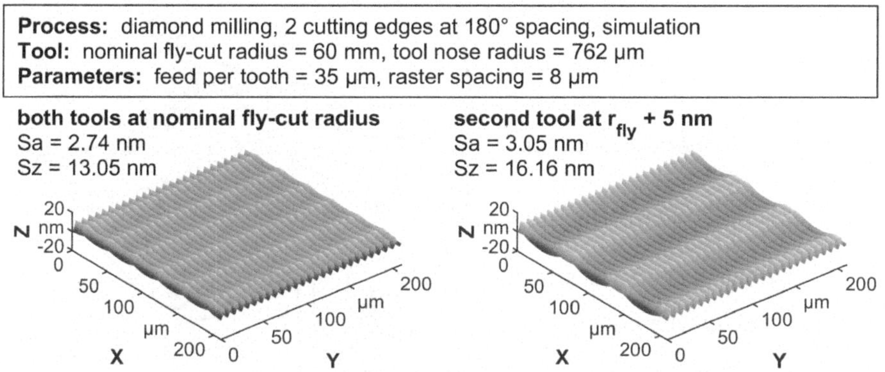

Fig. 2 Simulated surface of a two-tool diamond milling process with and without a deviation in fly-cut radius [17]

be lower than the kinematic roughness R_{kin}, i.e. <10 nm, in order to generate the final surface topography.

2 Tool Adjustment for Diamond Milling

For the compensation of positioning and guidance errors in machine tools, mechatronic components are applied to an increasing degree [8]. Despite the current progress of these technologies, the transferal of conventionally utilized concepts for tool alignment to ultra-precision machining is particularly challenging, as these systems should affect the general machining performance as little as possible. Thus, a combination of flexure hinges and highly precise actuators is commonly chosen [1, 19]. Implementing such alignment systems in milling operations, however, features the additional challenge of the milling tool rotating at high speeds on an air bearing. As a consequence, a lot of effort has to be put into the energy supply and data transfer systems, which ideally need to work contactless (for not disturbing the runout of the spindle) and be as lightweight and compact as possible (for maximizing the dynamics of the process). Systems that have been previously designed were not able to meet all of these requirements. The prototypes presented in [2] and [20] are based on purely mechanical tool setting and thus were not able to achieve the required tool setting precision. The mechatronic device presented in [9] achieves this, but is exceptionally voluminous and heavy due to the inclusion of wireless transmitters and control components on the rotor. This affects the spindle performance negatively and makes it effectively unusable for ultra-precision milling of optical surfaces.

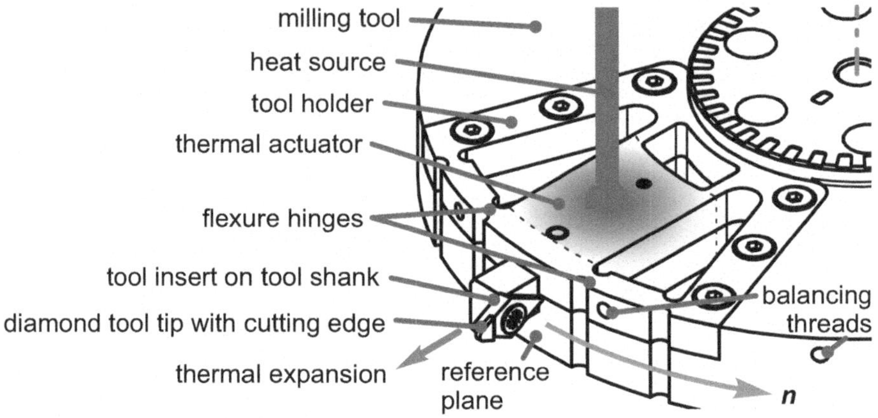

Fig. 3 Principle of an adjustable tool holder for generating a radial tool shift by thermal expansion [17]

2.1 Concept of Thermal Tool Adjustment

In the presented research work, the concept of defined thermal expansion was applied. This means that a specific portion of the tool holder is locally heated in order to expand it in radial direction (Fig. 3). Thereby, the tool that is fixed at the end of this "thermal actuator" changes its effective cutting radius. Using a dedicated control of the heat input, the expansion can be controlled in a way that the deviation between the subsequent cutting edges is minimized.

For minimizing the impact on the dynamic performance of the fly-cutter, e.g. the maximum spindle speed or the induced unbalances, the number of mechanical parts and electrical components that have to be integrated on the rotor has to be as low as possible. Heat input can be generated without mechanically contacting the substrate, e.g. by infrared radiation. This offers the unique possibility to place all heat-generating equipment on the static side of the fly-cutting process. In consequence, only very few mechanical parts are required on the rotor.

The required heat input may be calculated on the basis of material parameters and physical correlations. Thus, a mathematical model can be derived and used in the closed loop control of the thermal expansion. Moreover, thermal processes generally are elapsing slowly and thus, a specific thermal state can be maintained easily over a relatively long time by feeding only a minimum amount of heat into the system. This further facilitates the closed loop control. Thereby, it has to be ensured that the system is capsuled in the machine tool so that the delicate thermal state is not affected by coolant and forced convection due to the spindle rotation. This solution also ensures that the thermal state of the actuator does not affect the overall thermal stability of the machine tool. Generally, as only a small expansion of several nanometers is required, the proposed concept should not have a major effect on this issue.

Table 1 Calculations for thermal expansion and heating time

Actuator: steel 42CrMo4, $V = 10 \times 10 \times 30\,mm^3$				
$\alpha = 11.1$ nm mm^{-1} K^{-1}, $\rho = 7.850 \times 10^{-3}$ g mm^{-3}, $c_p = 461$ J kg^{-1} K^{-1}, $\eta = 0.4$				
ΔL	ΔT	Q	P	t_{heat}
10 nm	0.03 K	0.33 J	0.5 W 10 W	1.63 s 0.08 s
3.33 μm	**10 K**	108.57 J	0.5 W 10 W	542.83 s 27.16 s

2.2 Determination of Required Heat Input

Before actually designing holding mechanism for the tool inserts, the concept was validated, both analytically and numerically. A first approximation of the required heat input can be calculated by the standard physical equation of thermal expansion that takes the base length of a beam L_0, the coefficient of thermal expansion of the substrate α and temperature difference ΔT into account (Eq. 1).

$$\Delta L = \alpha \cdot L_0 \cdot \Delta T \quad (1)$$

Given the size of a typical fly-cutter to be approximately 150 mm in diameter, including a $L_0 = 30$ mm sized actuator into this seems reasonable. With the coefficient of thermal expansion being $\alpha \approx 11.1$ nm mm^{-1}K^{-1} for a 42CrMo4 type steel, the required temperature change for a $\Delta L_{min} = 10$ nm calculates to $\Delta T_{min} \approx 0.03$ K. On the other end, the maximum tolerable temperature change is set to $\Delta T_{max} = 10$ K above ambient. This yields a total thermal expansion of $\Delta L_{max} = 3{,}33$ μm.

In order to determine the required heat input Q for such a thermal expansion, the mass $m = v \times \rho$ and the thermal capacity c_p of the actuator have to be considered (Eq. 2).

$$Q = c_p \cdot v \cdot \rho \cdot \Delta T \quad (2)$$

Knowing the required heat input, it is possible to calculate the heating time t_{heat} required by a heat source with a power P and the thermal absorption η of the actuator surface (Eq. 3).

$$t_{heat} = \frac{Q}{\eta \cdot P} \quad (3)$$

In the following Table 1, the heat input and heating time for ΔL_{min} and ΔT_{max} is calculated for two kinds of heat sources, a laser with $P_{\text{Laser}} = 10$ W and an infrared-light emitting diode (IR-LED) with $P_{LED} = 0.5$ W. The calculation shows that the required expansion can be theoretically reached by both sources, though at different heating times.

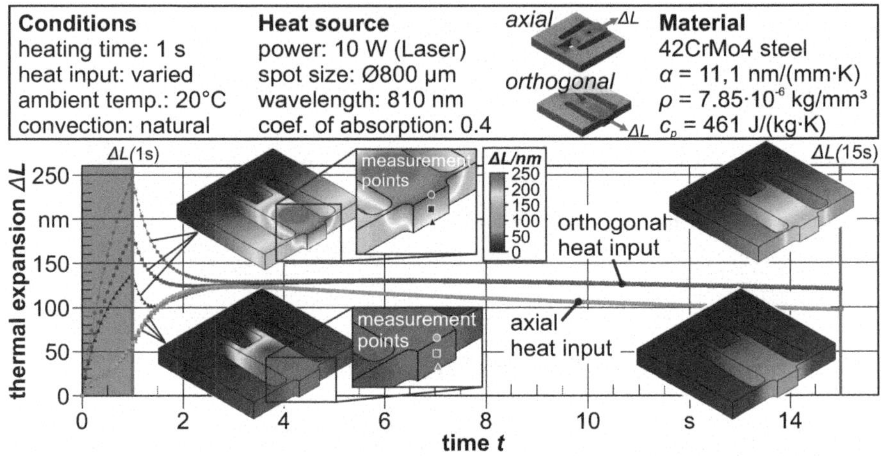

Fig. 4 Thermal expansion for heating an orthogonally and axially coupled thermal actuator with a Laser source ($P_{\text{Laser}} = 10$ W)

For the further analysis of the heat distribution and the 3D elongation of the material, numerical calculations were conducted using "Autodesk Simulation Mechanical 2016". Here, the actuator was modeled as a beam of the aforementioned size which was integrated into a setup for experimental verification. Therefore, the beam was connected to the base by two struts at the rear and two flexure hinges at the front. The setup offers two different setups for the coupling of the heat source: first, an orthogonal coupling in which the heat source is directed to the top (and possibly also the bottom) face of the actuator. Second, an axial coupling in which the heat is introduced to the rear face of the actuator. With the simulations it was investigated whether the orthogonal or axial coupling is preferable for a symmetric expansion and also if a high power (Laser) or low power (IR-LED) heat source is sufficient. For the simulation, the heat input was limited to a 1 s burst for all experiments.

The resulting expansion of heating the actuator by a Laser source is shown in Fig. 4.

Due to the high costs and complexity of integrating a Laser source in such a setup, the orthogonal coupling is limited to be one-sided, i.e. only on the top face of the actuator. This results in a tiling of the front face (at which the tool would be mounted) due to the inhomogeneous heat distribution within the actuator that is visible as a deviation in expansion of the three test points. After switching off the light source, this deviation is quickly reduced to a minimum as the heat distribution and thus the expansion becomes more homogeneous. Overall, an elongation of around $\Delta L = 125$ nm can be achieved without tilting after about 3 s in total using the orthogonal coupling. In contrast, the axial coupling shows a more homogeneous heat distribution from the start, as this setup serves the symmetry of the actuator. Furthermore, it is noticeable that the expansion of the actuator continues even after switching off the Laser due to the spreading of the heat (thermal conduction). After

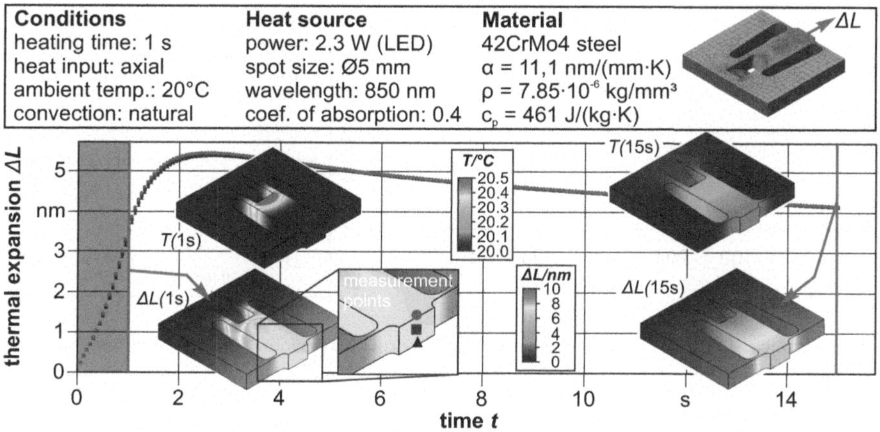

Fig. 5 Thermal expansion for heating an axially coupled thermal actuator with a IR-LED source ($P_{\mathrm{LED}} = 0.5$ W)

3 s of simulated time, the thermal expansion reaches a similar extent than that of the orthogonal coupling. However, the heat is dissipated more quickly in this case and therefore, the thermal expansion also decreases thereafter. Nevertheless, an expansion of 100 nm is still measurable after 15 s in total.

The simulated expansion for using an IR-LED with $P_{\mathrm{LED}} = 0.5$ W as heat source and axial coupling is shown in Fig. 5. The simulation shows that such a LED is capable of achieving an elongation in the nanometer range with a 1 s burst. The maximum expansion is again reached after 3 s of simulated time and measures about $\Delta L = 5.5$ nm. This implies that such an IR-LED might well be sufficient for driving the thermal actuator for the intended purpose of nanometer-precise tool setting. The benefit of this solution would be that a two-sided orthogonal setup could be realized as well, because LED are inexpensive and easy to integrate (both electrically and concerning operator safety).

In addition to the simulations with 42CrMo4 steel, the performance of other steel types has been evaluated as well. In particular, the stainless steel X40Cr14 has proven to deliver an increased thermal expansion (Fig. 6), because of its lower thermal conductivity ($\kappa_{\mathrm{X40Cr14}} = 22.6\ \mathrm{W\,m^{-1}\,K^{-1}}$ vs. $\kappa_{\mathrm{42CrMo4}} = 42.6\ \mathrm{W\,m^{-1}\,K^{-1}}$).

2.3 *Validation of the Thermal Mechanism in a Static Test Setup*

The concept of a thermal actuator was first evaluated in a static test setup. This offered the possibility to minimize the distortion from the rotation of the spindle (noise, centering and roundness error of the reference plane) and also facilitated the

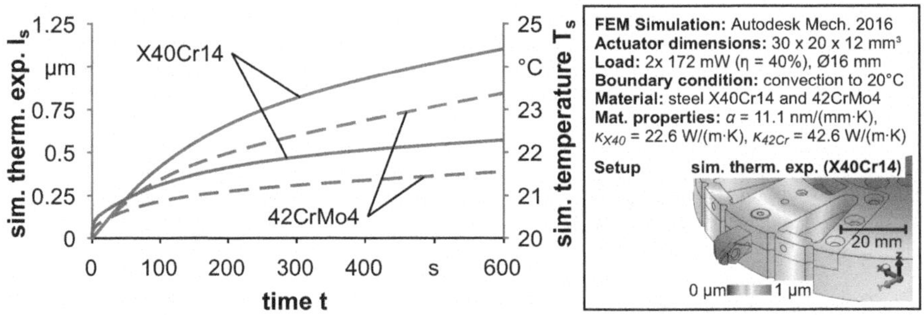

Fig. 6 Comparison of maximum temperature and thermal expansion for 42CrMo4 and X40Cr14 type steel

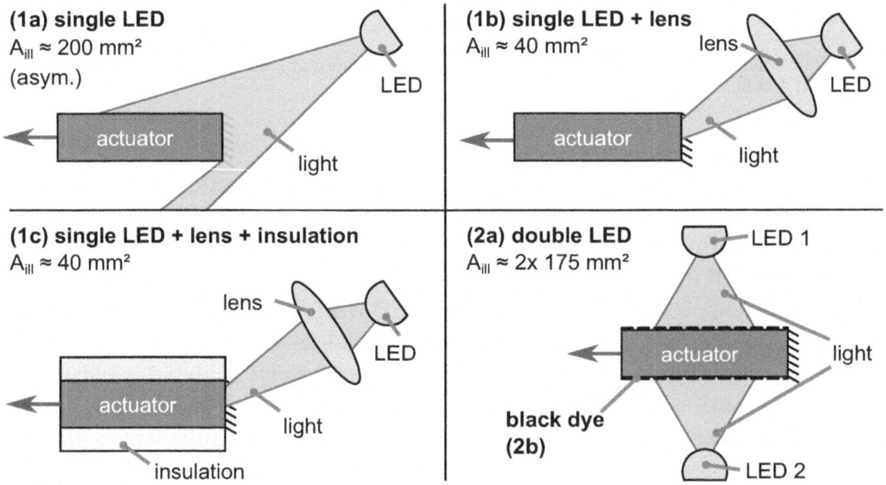

Fig. 7 Configurations of the static test stand for evaluating the thermal actuating principle

test of different heating setups. Four configurations were analyzed in this study: (1a) the illumination of the actuator's rear face with a single LED, (1b) the focusing of the LED radiation on the rear face with an additional lens, (1c) the addition of an insulating layer on the top and bottom face of the actuator to prevent heat loss by convection, and (2a) the illumination of both the top and bottom face of the actuator with two separate LED heat sources. The latter test was repeated with an additional coloring of the actuator faces with black ink (2b) to maximize the heat absorption (Fig. 7).

The results in Fig. 8 indicate that using only a single LED that is directed at the back of the actuator generates a thermal expansion of only ≈250 nm, which is not sufficient. Focusing the light does not generate a positive effect, but reduces the achievable expansion to slightly below 200 nm, which is probably caused by the absorption of the infrared radiation within the added lens. Isolating the actuator

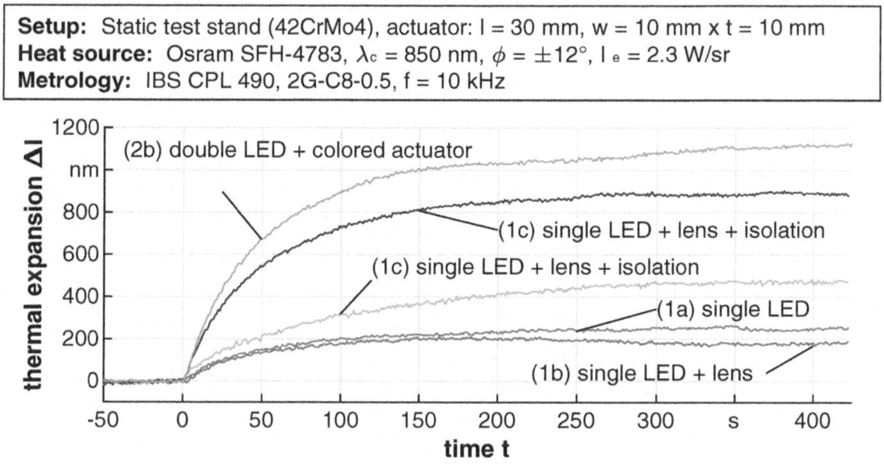

Fig. 8 Step response of the static test stand for the selected configurations

almost doubles the achievable expansion to about 470 nm. The best results can be achieved by using the double-sided LED setup that without any further modifications generates an expansion of 870 nm. When adding a black coloring to the illuminated actuator faces, the heat input is increased further, yielding an expansion of more than 1,100 nm.

Overall, these tests have shown that the general concept of using thermal expansion for tool setting in the nanometer range is basically applicable.

3 Determination of Tool Holder Geometry

The geometry of the actuator has been integrated into the design of a tool holder for diamond milling with two tools. As it is obvious from the calculations and simulations, a thermal tool setting mechanism would achieve the required precision, but with the given constraints on maximum temperature clearly lacks the capacity to achieve a maximal stroke that would suffice the typical tolerances of diamond tool inserts. Therefore, the thermal actuator was extended by a mechanical pre-setting mechanism for a coarse alignment of the cutting edges to the range of the thermal expansion. A detailed description of the initial designs can be found in [10]. These featured a mechanical mechanism that was mounted as an additional component at the front of the thermal actuator. Due to reasons of stability and overall size of the tool holder, this concept was discarded and replaced by an internal mechanism as an integral part of the thermal actuator. This novel design was first presented in [14] and later in more detail in [15].

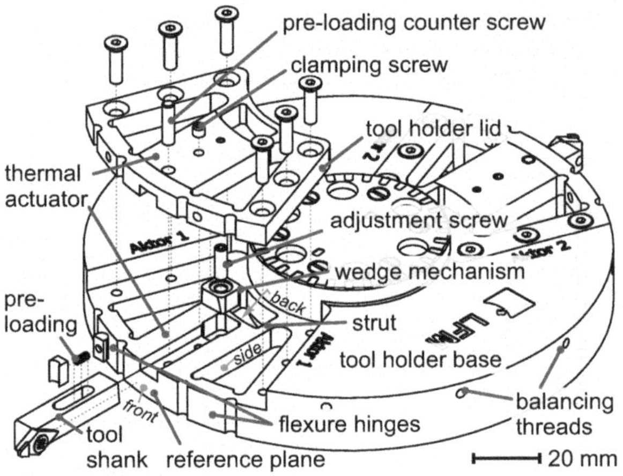

Fig. 9 Final design of a tool holder with two thermal actuators

Table 2 Technical data of tool holder and thermal actuator

Nominal engagement radius r_{fly}	65 mm
Number of actuators n_{act}	2
Spacing of actuators χ_{act}	180°
Dimensions of actuator $l \times w \times h$	$30 \times 20 \times 12$ mm^3
material	Steel X40Cr14
Thermal conductivity κ	22.6 W m^{-1} K^{-1}
Coef. of thermal expansion α	11.1 µm m^{-1} K^{-1}
Coef. of thermal absorption η	≈40%

The final design was made for a tool holder with a nominal diameter of 130 mm and features two beam-like thermal actuators (i.e. two tools) at 180° spacing which can potentially be increased up to four (Fig. 9). Each of the actuators is connected to the base of the tool holder by two struts at the rear and two flexure hinges at the front side while the rest is cut away to minimize thermal conduction to the base. The total dimensions of the actuator are 30 mm in length, 20 mm in width and 12 mm in thickness. The substrate material of the tool holder is X40Cr14 type steel which has shown the most promising results in the simulations. All relevant data are comprised in Table 2.

The mechanical presetting mechanism has been integrated into the thermal actuator and now features the tool shank as a slide. The tool shank is preloaded against a wedge mechanism with a 5° angle. When this wedge is moved by a precision screw, it shifts the tool shank in radial direction with a transmission ratio of $\tan(5°) = 0.0874$. In this way, the tool insert can be positioned across a range of ≈180 µm with a precision of <1 µm (Fig. 10) which is sufficient to compensate for all deviations from fixation.

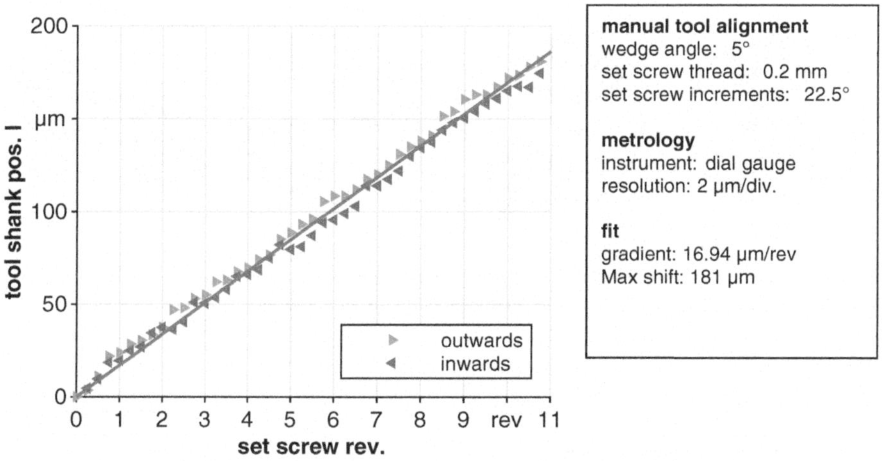

Fig. 10 Performance of mechanical presetting mechanism

4 Design of a Contactless Heat Input System for a Rotating Actuator

In a static setup, the heat input to the actuator is very simple, as both the heat source and the actuator remain at a fixed position. In contrast, the tool and hence also the actuator are rotating at several hundred revolutions per minute in an actual milling process. The heat transfer via an IR-LED is contactless per se and thus does not raise a problem here. However, the LED has to remain at a fixed position or otherwise the system design would get very complex. Thus, the heat can only be transferred to the actuator within a small timeframe, which is defined by the width of the actuator, circumference on which it is rotating and the spindle speed (Eq. 4).

$$t_{heat,rev} = \frac{w}{2 \cdot \pi \cdot r_{\text{act}} \cdot n/60} \tag{4}$$

At a typical spindle speed for diamond fly-cutting of $n = 1{,}000\ \text{min}^{-1}$, this calculates to $t_{heat,rev} = 4$ ms whereas for high speed cutting at $n = 20{,}000\ \text{min}^{-1}$ it is only $t_{heat,rev} = 200\ \mu\text{s}$. In combination with the forced convection due to the rotation, this timespan is not enough to generate a stable elevated temperature of the actuator. As a consequence, a device that allows the heat input to follow the actuator movement has to be devised.

A moving ring light system (patent pending) has been developed to serve this purpose [13]. It consists of multiple LEDs that are evenly distributed along a circle in a way that the peak intensity is directed at the actuator midpoint. All LED are powered by a common energy supply and each LED can be activated by a dedicated transistor, i.e. by a low-power signal line. One or more of these LED are used to

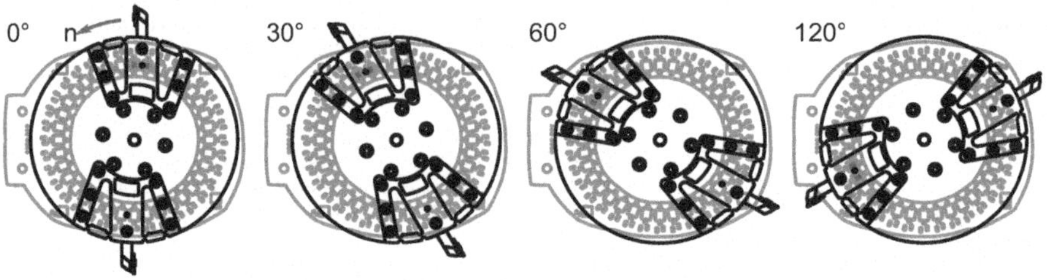

Fig. 11 Principle of the ring light system for a quasi-continuous heating of the thermal actuator. LEDs advance according to the angular position of the target actuator

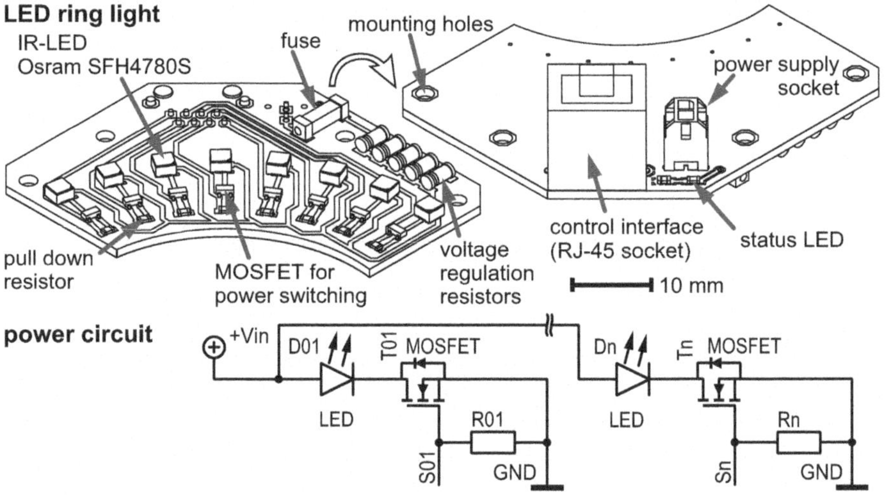

Fig. 12 Ring light (1/4) with 8 IR-LED, switching transistors and common power supply for all LED

illuminate the thermal actuator while the other LED are switched off. Upon rotation of the milling tool, the active LED are advanced along the ring to follow the position of the actuator (Fig. 11), while the body of the ring light stays stationary. In this way, a quasi-constant heating of the actuator is achieved.

For reasons of simplicity, handling and manufacturability, the current ring light system consists of four equal segments that cover a quarter of the ring and incorporate 8 IR-LED each (Fig. 12). In this way, the ring light can be easily dismounted even when enclosing the spindle shaft for illuminating the backside of the actuator. All technical specifications of the ring light systems are comprised in Table 3.

The switching of the LED is performed by a dedicated control electronics which was designed as a shield circuit board for an Arduino Mega 2560 board (Fig. 13). The Arduino evaluates the angular position of the spindle, either directly via the spindle encoder or via photo sensors that detect a scale on the tool holder, and generates the appropriate sequence of activated LED. As the use of LED also enables the

Table 3 Technical specifications of ring light system

Total number of LED	32
Element shape	¼ ring
IR-LED per element	8
IR-LED manufacturer and model	Osram SFH 4780S
Wavelength λ	820 nm
Radiant intensity I_e	2.3 W sr^{-1}
Half-angle φ	$\pm 10°$
Total radiant flux Φ_e	600 m W
Rise time t_r	8 ns
Fall time t_f	14 ns
Forward voltage U_f	3.3 V
Forward current I_f	0.5 A

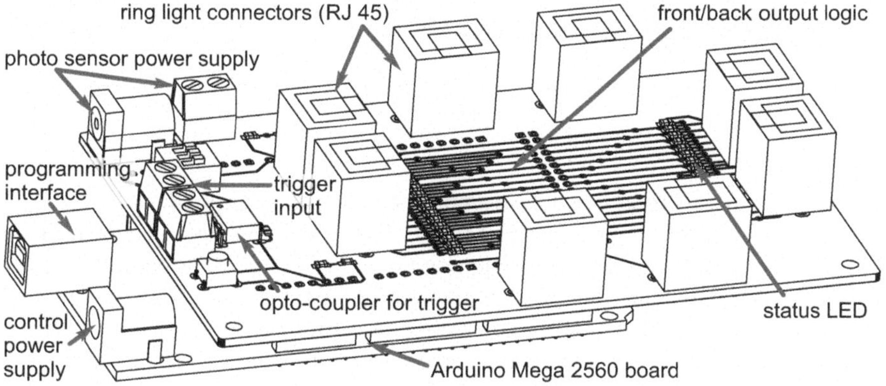

Fig. 13 Circuit board (Arduino Shield) for ring light control

application of double-sided heating, two separate sequences need to be generated for the front and back ring light, as one of them is running clockwise and the other one counter-clockwise to follow the spindle rotation. This is directly done on the circuit board by a hard-wired logic.

5 Experimental Spindle Setup for Tool Holder Evaluation

The evaluation of the finalized thermal tool holder was mainly conduced on two experimental platforms. First, an air-cutting spindle test stand was used on which the tool holder can be analyzed without cutting interaction (Fig. 14).

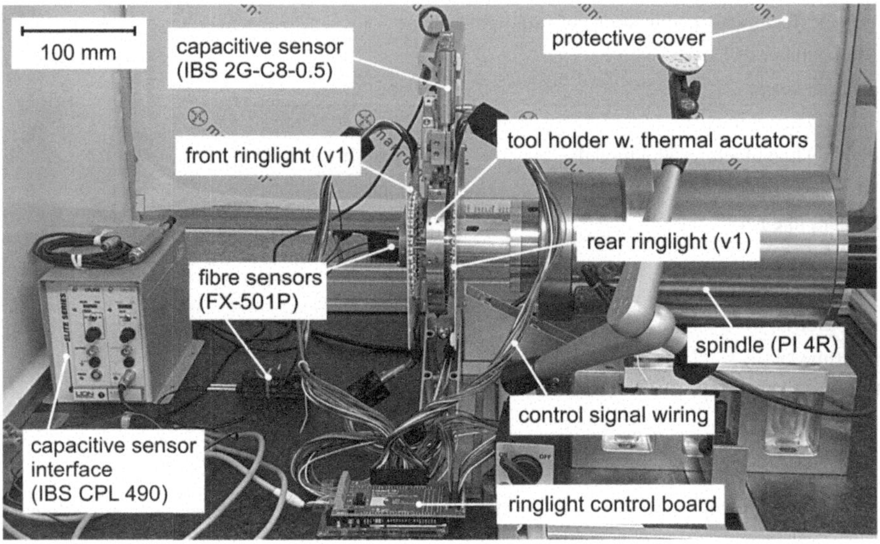

Fig. 14 Offline test stand for evaluating the thermal tool holder on an air-bearing spindle without cutting interaction

It consists of a Professional Instruments 4R air-bearing spindle on which the milling tool incorporating the thermal tool holder is fixed using an adapter which provides the needed clearance for mounting the rear ring light. Furthermore, a fiber sensor (FX-501P by Panasonic) is used to monitor the revolution of the actuator and determine the angular position for advancing the LED. The expansion is evaluated by measuring the position reference plane located below the tool shank on the circumference of the tool holder with a capacitive sensor (IBS 2G-C8-0.5 with a CPL 490 interface).

This setup was later transferred to a Nanotech 500FG machine tool for additional cutting experiments. The 4R air-bearing spindle is mounted on the B-axis table of the machine tool while the workpiece is fixed on the (clamped) main spindle of the 500FG. In addition to the test stand, a dynamometer was placed under the workpiece fixture to be able to measure the development of cutting forces during machining and to correlate this to the thermal expansion. The setup is depicted in Fig. 15 with the initial version of the ring light (v1: 36x LED type SFH4783, single board layout) shown in the left image and the revised ring light system (v2: 32x SFH4780S, quarter segment boards) shown on the right.

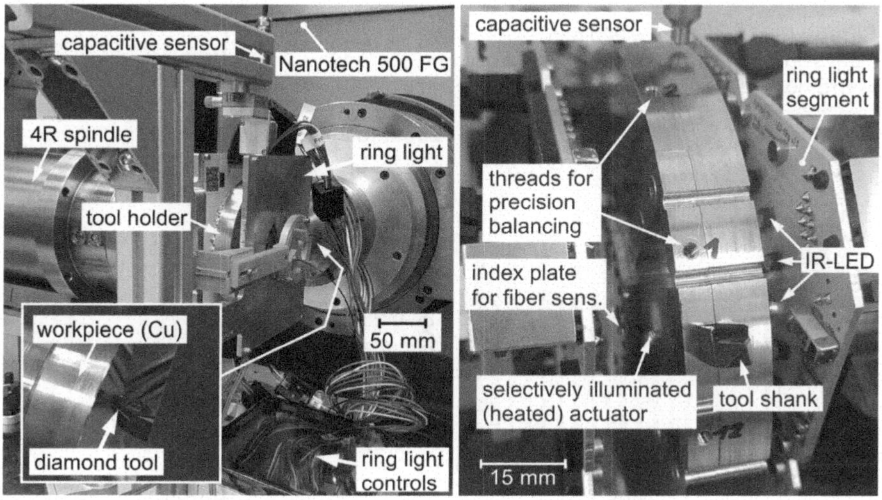

Fig. 15 Machine setup for evaluating the thermal tool holder on a Nanotech 500 FG. Left image shows the complete setup with ring light version 1 and the right image shows a closeup of the setup with the revised ring light (version 2)

6 Assessment of Actuator Performance

6.1 Results from Spindle Tests (No Machining)

When testing the actuator performance under rotation of the spindle, further processing of the measurement data is required. As the position of the reference plane is continuously measured during the process, the signal has to be segmented in order to reflect the position of the respective sections. A complete measurement of several revolutions as well as a zoom to a single revolution is shown in Fig. 16.

Due to the notches of the flexure hinges, the individual sections of the actuator are easily identifiable by the signal dropouts that occur when the capacitive measurements move out of the sensor's range at these points. Thus, they are utilized for the segmentation of the signal. The fully segmented signal consists of eight distinct sections: the two actuators, four flexure hinges (two per actuator) and two large portions in between. The latter should not be affected by the thermal state of the actuator and thus are used as reference. While the flexure hinges expand along with the thermal actuators, their position is of no relevance to the tool setting. However, their position could be evaluated to detect an asymmetry of the thermal expansion due to inhomogeneous heating as a result of misalignment between heat source and actuator.

In order to assess the temporal development of the thermal expansion, the mean position of each segment is determined for each revolution. Therefore, the noise of the signal is first reduced by applying a low-pass Butterworth filter with a cut-off

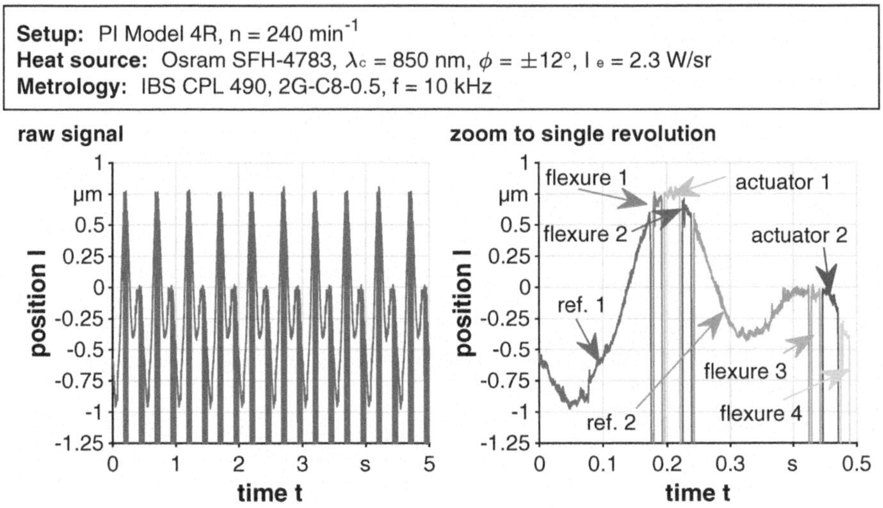

Fig. 16 Measurement of the reference plane with rotating spindle: raw data of 10 consecutive revolutions (left) and segmentation of a single revolution and association to actuator geometry (right)

frequency of $\lambda_c = 100$ Hz. Then, the mean signal of the first couple of revolutions is subtracted from each subsequent revolution in order to remove systematic deviations, like e.g. unbalances or runout errors, from the measurement. Finally, the segments are averaged into a single value which is recorded as the position of the respective segment. The temporal development of an exemplary test run at $n = 240$ min^{-1} is shown in Fig. 17.

Testing for the maximum thermal expansion that can be achieved at selected spindle speeds yields the following graph (Fig. 18).

This shows a clear dependence of the maximum expansion on the applied spindle speed that can be fitted to a logarithmic equation. The faster the speed is set, the more forced convection occurs on the actuator surface, resulting in a cooling of the thermal actuator and thereby a reduction of the maximum expansion. Nevertheless, up to a speed of $n = 1{,}500$ min^{-1} the achievable expansion is deemed sufficient to compensate most residual misalignment of the diamond tools after presetting.

6.2 *Open-Loop Performance in Cutting*

The tests in an test stand environment (i.e. without actual tool-workpiece interaction) have proven the general applicability of the selected method for tool setting on a rotating spindle. However, in this setup the location of the cutting edge is not determined directly, but measured as a shift of the reference plane situated slightly

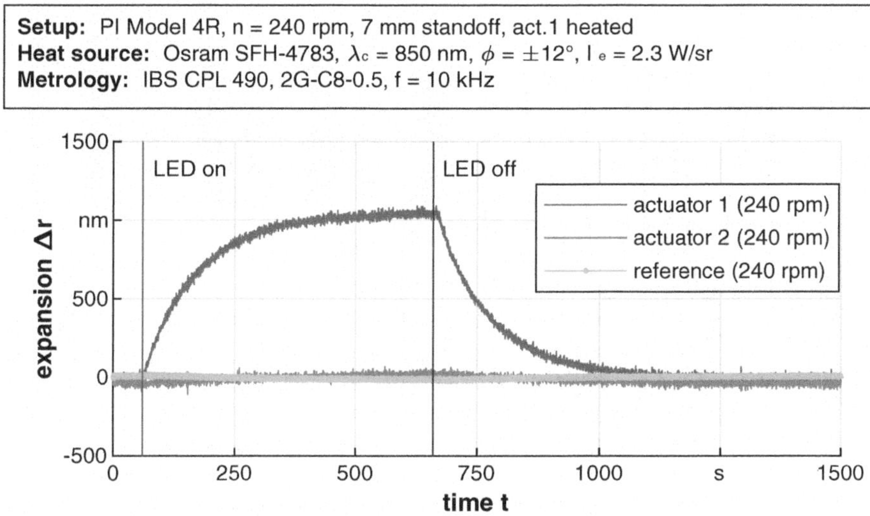

Fig. 17 Comparison of actuator expansion at 240 $\min^{-1}$ for a LED standoff distance of 7 mm; the light rings are switched to full power (1 A per active LED) between $t = 60$ s and 660 s

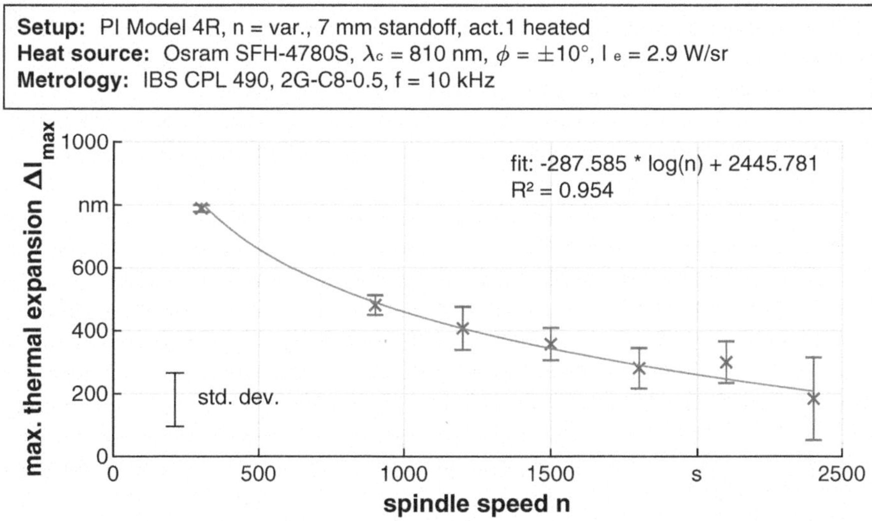

Fig. 18 Maximum thermal expansion for selected spindle speeds

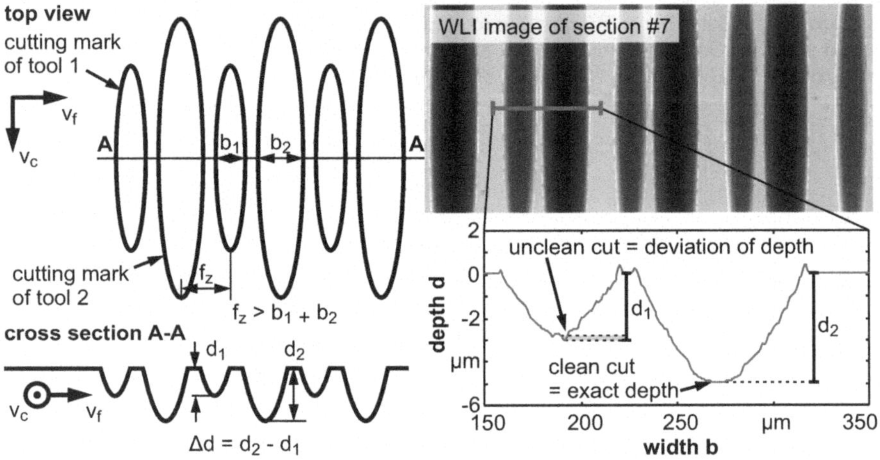

Fig. 19 Generation of isolated cutting marks from two engaged cutting edges by applying elevated cross feed velocity and measurement of generated marks with a WLI for evaluating the depth difference

below the tool shank on the circumference of the tool holder. Thus, it has to be verified whether the thermal expansion also affects the position of the cutting tool as a whole. This can only be analyzed in actual cutting experiments.

Therefore, a strategy was developed in which the tool inserts are mechanically pre-aligned. The infeed of the machine is set such that both cutting edges leave a mark on the surface of the workpiece (Fig. 19).

During cutting the cross feed velocity v_f is then set according to the selected spindle speed so that both tools leave separated marks on the workpiece surface. While heating the actuator with the LED ring light system, a set of these cutting marks is generated at selected time intervals (here: $\Delta t = 1$ s) to inscribe the respective state of the actuator expansion to the workpiece surface. This is later evaluated by measuring the cutting marks with a white light interferometer (WLI, a Talysurf CCI HD was utilized in this study) and determining the depth of the adjacent cutting marks. By comparing the development of the depth difference Δd to the initial state before heating the actuator, the thermal expansion $\Delta L = \Delta d$ of the tool holder is determined. The resulting measurements are shown in Fig. 20.

It can be seen that the mark depth changes according to the shift of the reference plane. However, the depth evaluation is prone to large deviations resulting from the depth measurements and the determination of the correct offsets. Furthermore, registration to the time-based measurements of the reference plane is done manually and thus associated with a deviation as well.

Nevertheless, a shift of the cutting edges along with the reference plane is observed for all measurements up to a spindle speed of $n = 1{,}800\ \text{min}^{-1}$. Higher speeds could not be applied as the maximum feed velocity of the Nanotech 500 FG (max. $v_f = 600\ \text{mm min}^{-1}$) is not sufficient to generate isolated marks in this case. Figure 21

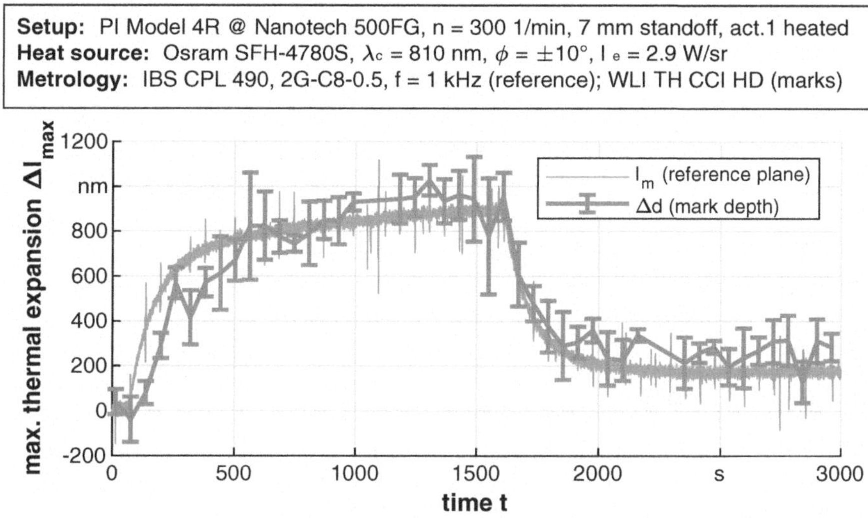

Fig. 20 Depth difference of cutting marks taken at 1 min intervals compared to the continuously measured expansion of the reference plane for $n = 300\ \text{min}^{-1}$

shows a comparison of the maximum measured difference in mark depth to the maximum expansion of the reference plane. It can be observed that both curves follow the same trend with the expansion measured via the mark depth being slightly below that of the reference plane. Nevertheless, this is considered to be a systematic deviation of the actuator.

7 Control of Actuator Position to Nanometer Precision

The previous measurement have shown that the thermal actuator is generally capable of achieving the required expansion for compensating residual tool misalignment. However, in order to apply the system for the milling of an actual optical surface, the thermal expansion has to be precisely set within its range and this position has to be maintained throughout the whole cutting operation. Thus, a closed loop control of the thermal expansion has been implemented.

7.1 Design of Control Loop

The schematics of the (PI) control loop are shown in Fig. 22. The location of the reference plane l is measured by the capacitive sensor and compared to an initially selected offset L_0 to determine the thermal expansion ΔL_{meas}. This is then compared

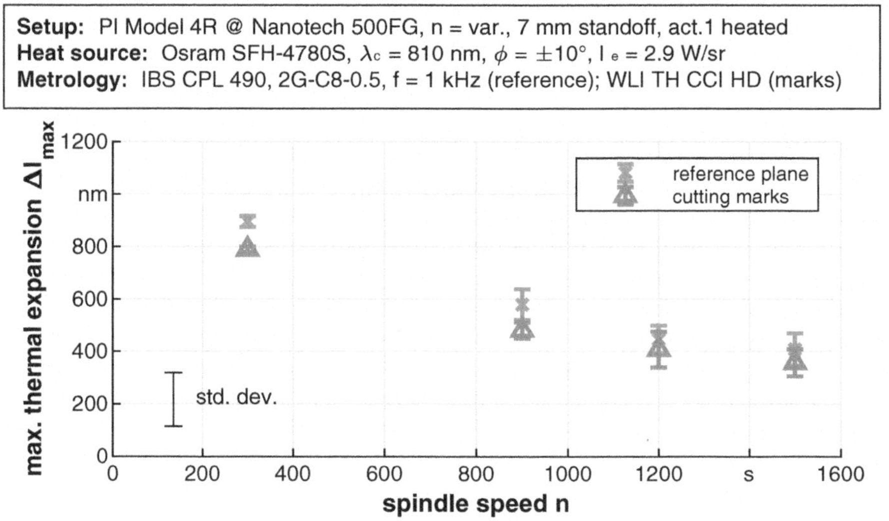

Fig. 21 Maximum thermal expansion of reference plane and depth difference of cutting marks for varied spindle speeds

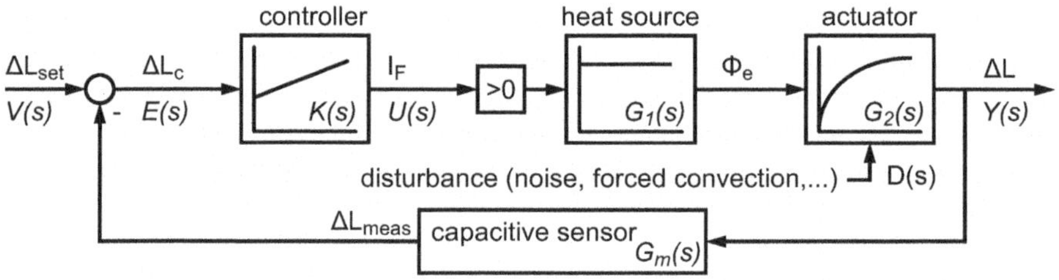

Fig. 22 Control loop for thermal expansion

to the set value of the expansion ΔL_{set} to determine the control offset ΔL_c. A proportional-integral-differential (PID)-controller is used to calculate the necessary forward current for the infrared LED I_f. This generates a radiant flux Φ_e that is directed on the actuator and causes a change of its temperature T_a. Due to the forced convection as a result of the spindle rotation, the actual temperature difference ΔT is reduced. Ultimately, this causes a thermal expansion ΔL of the actuator. Detailed explanations on the development of the control loop can be found in [12].

For the practical application, the sections of heat source, heat transfer, forced convection and actuator expansion are combined into a simplified model, i.e. a transfer function $G(s)$ of the whole system, which is derived from the step response $H(s)$ of the thermal actuator:

$$G(s) = \frac{Y(s)}{U(s)} = H(s) \cdot s \tag{5}$$

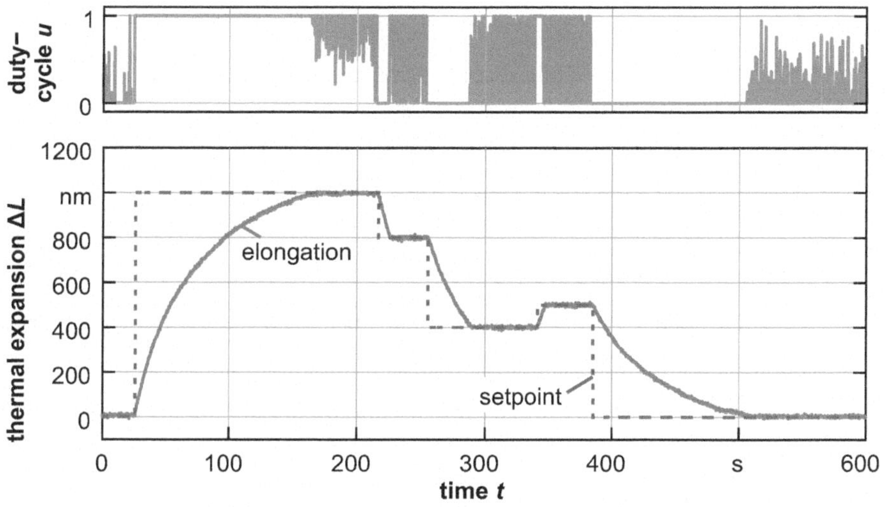

Fig. 23 Results for controlling the thermal expansion in a static setup

$$H(s) = \mathcal{L}\left\{\Delta L_{max} \cdot \left(1 - e^{-t/t_h}\right)\right\} \tag{6}$$

$$G(s) = \frac{\Delta L_{max}}{t_h \cdot s + 1} \tag{7}$$

7.2 *Performance of the Control Loop in a Static Setup*

Initially, the control loop was developed using a static setup of the actuator, to minimize disturbances from the dynamics of the spindle and to facilitate the acquisition of thermal expansion. With this setup it was verified that the thermal expansion may be controlled in the nanometer range and thereby be applied for tool setting. Figure 23 shows the system response for selected setpoints across the total range of thermal expansion. It can be seen that the targeted expansion is reached without overshoot and that a retraction of the actuator is possible by cooling the actuator (in this case by natural convection). The duty cycle of the LED still shows a lot of noise, which may be attributed to the not optimized control parameters chosen for this experiment.

In order to determine the minimum step size that can be set with the setup, a series of steps was fed to the control system, from ± 20 nm down to ± 1 nm. It is shown in Fig. 24 that steps down to ± 5 nm can be safely set within the system. While the 1 nm steps are also discernible in the graph, these set values cannot reliably be achieved, given the present measurement noise of approx. 6.5 nm.

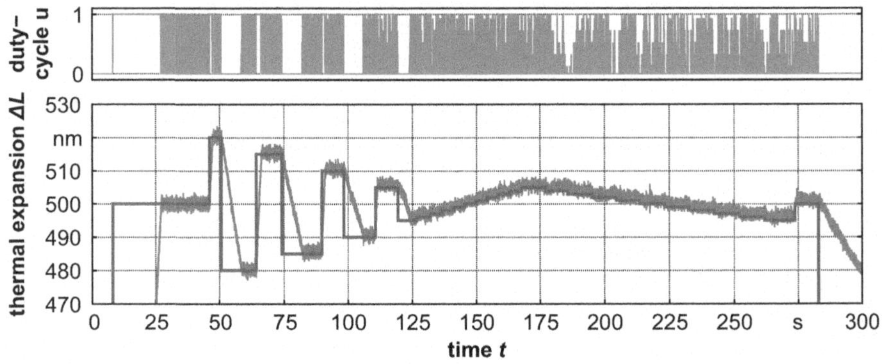

Fig. 24 Step series for determining the minimum control increments for the thermal actuator (static)

7.3 *Performance of the Control Loop in a Spindle Setup*

For control of the actuator during rotation of the spindle, its position has to be extracted from the roundness measurement of the reference plane. While this may be similarly done to the signal segmentation and analysis, the underlying approach is not suitable for real-time processing during the process. Instead, the position acquisition needs to be triggered per revolution so that only a small portion of the signal is processed (Fig. 25). In this case, the trigger signal is taken from the fiber optics measurement of the angular markings on the tool holder that are primarily used for advancing the LED of the ring lights.

On receiving a trigger signal, a finite number of samples with the selected frequency is acquired (Fig. 25, 1). For further processing and correct detection of all segments, the number of samples should be chosen so that one full revolution of the tool holder is obtained in one pass. For instance, at a typical sample rate of $f_s = 10$ kHz and a spindle speed of $n = 1{,}500\ \text{min}^{-1}$ (25 Hz), at least 400 samples are required. The measurement of a revolution is then aligned to a reference signal (2b), e.g. the mean of several revolutions with a defined heating state. After alignment, the signal dropouts are identified (3) and the data is split at these markers into sub-arrays representing each segment of the tool holder (4). To determine the average expansion of each segment, the difference between the current measurement and the reference is calculated (5) and the median of the resulting array is passed on (6). The median is preferred here over the mean of the segment, as it is more robust.

The extracted position of the actuator segment can then be utilized for building a control loop similar to that of the static setup. This has been done using a digital twin of the actual actuator that mimics its response (i.e. thermal expansion) to the control input (i.e. LED power) on the basis of a plant model (Fig. 26). In this way, the software implementation can be conducted truly independent of the availability of the setup on the machine tool. The internal plant parameters of the digital twin were calculated

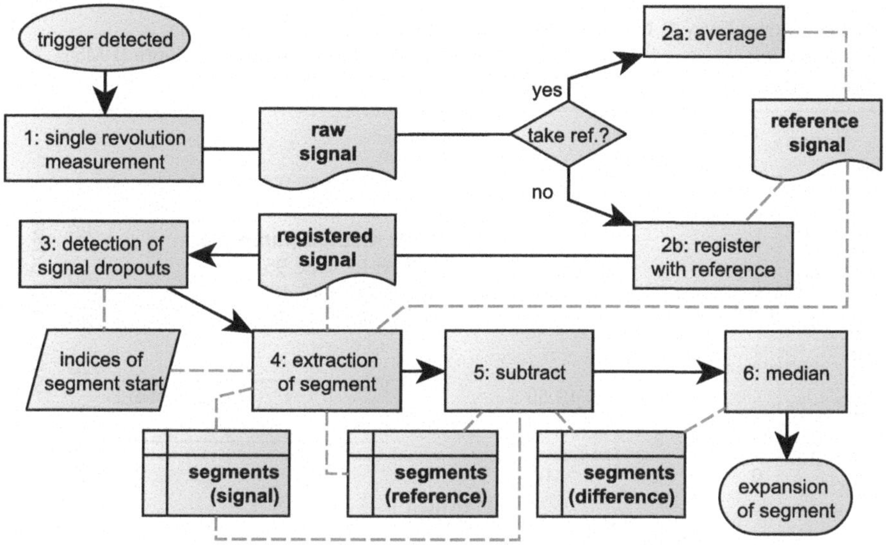

Fig. 25 Triggered data acquisition for determining position of actuator segment

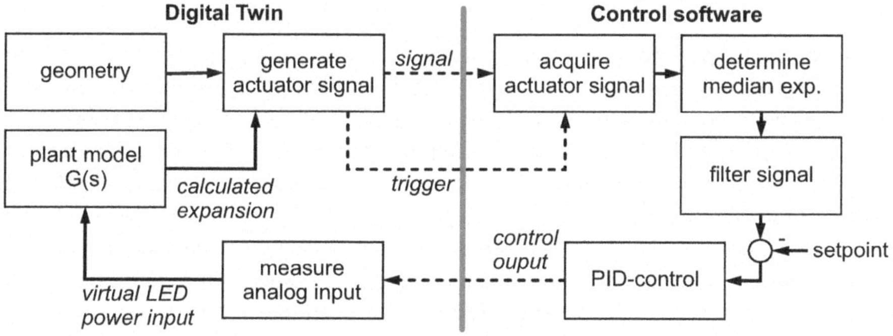

Fig. 26 Schematics of Digital Twin for the offline development of actuator controls

from the measurements obtained for the actual tool holder at $n = 240\ \text{min}^{-1}$, as shown in the previous sections ($K_{u,\text{DT}} = 1{,}102$ nm, $T_{i,\text{DT}} = 49.8$ s, $T_{d,\text{DT}} = 0.02$ s).

It has to be noted that while a spindle speed can be set within the digital twin, this only affects the frequency of the generated signal. The reduced maximum thermal expansion due to the forced convection is not considered in the current implementation, as it is not inherently necessary for the development of the control software. In the present evaluation, the plant model has been derived from a measurement of the actuator taken at low-speed, while the generation rate has been set to elevated spindle speed ($2{,}400\ \text{min}^{-1}$) to minimize the effective processing time of the simulations.

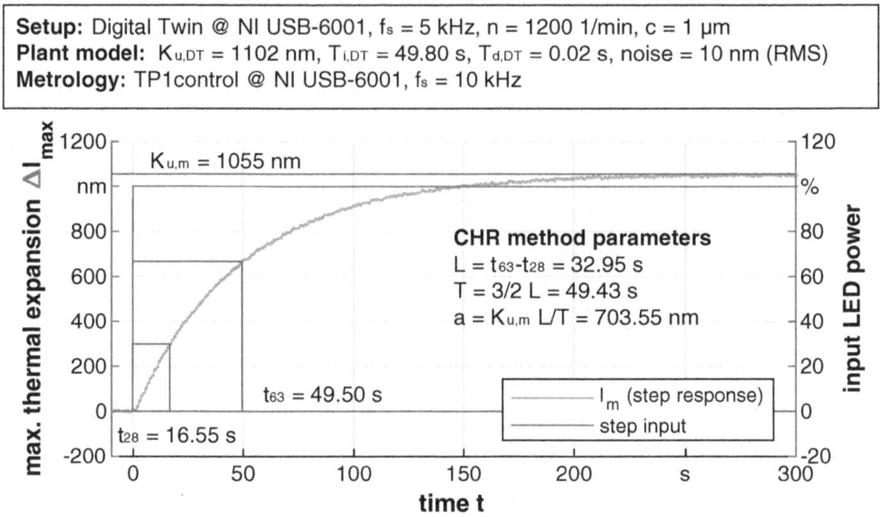

Fig. 27 Step response measured using a digital twin of the rotating tool holder and derived plant parameters

To account for possible deviations introduced by the signal splitting and the digital twin setup, the step response of the actuator is measured again with the adapted control software and the plant parameters of the actuator are determined (Fig. 27).

It can be seen that the measured plant parameters and are close to the respective parameters set in the digital twin ($K_{u,m} \approx K_{u,DT}$ and $T \approx T_{i,DT}$) with the dead time being significantly increased compared to the plant model $L \gg T_{d,DT}$. This is caused by expansion not being measured continuously, but once per revolution, i.e. at a significantly reduced frequency. Thus, the reaction of the system is measured later than the actual occurrence of the thermal expansion. Nevertheless, this is automatically considered by the control loop if the plant parameters are determined in this way.

The parameters for the PID controller are then calculated using different approaches. Initially, the method of (CHR) for setpoint accuracy with minimal overshoot was chosen and compared to the CHR calculation for disturbance rejection with minimal overshoot [5]. Additionally, the controller was tested with manually tuned parameters: K_p was chosen higher than the CHR values for potential decrease of rise time and steady-state error, T_i was set to a very long time constant as this is a major factor for decreasing the steady-state error and T_d was set to a small value for improved disturbance rejection. The calculated parameters are listed in Table 4.

The following Fig. 28 shows the response of the system with a closed control loop using the abovementioned PID parameters for a step-input of 500 nm. It can be seen that both parameter sets calculated according to the CHR method resulted in significant overshoot of the actuator position before settling to its final position. The method for setpoint accuracy yields less overshoot, but a significantly longer settling time than the other methods. With the parameters for disturbance rejection,

Table 4 Control parameters for the thermal tool holder (digital twin)

Parameter	CHR (setp. acc.)		CHR (dist. rej.)		Manually tuned	
	Calculation	Value	Calculation	Value	Calculation	Value
K_p	$0.6/a$	0.00085	$0.95/a$	0.00134	"High"	0.0064
T_i	$1 \cdot T$	49.43 s	$2.4 \cdot T$	119.16 s	"Very long"	1,200 s
T_d	$0.5 \cdot L$	16.48 s	$0.42 \cdot L$	13.9 s	"Short"	3 s

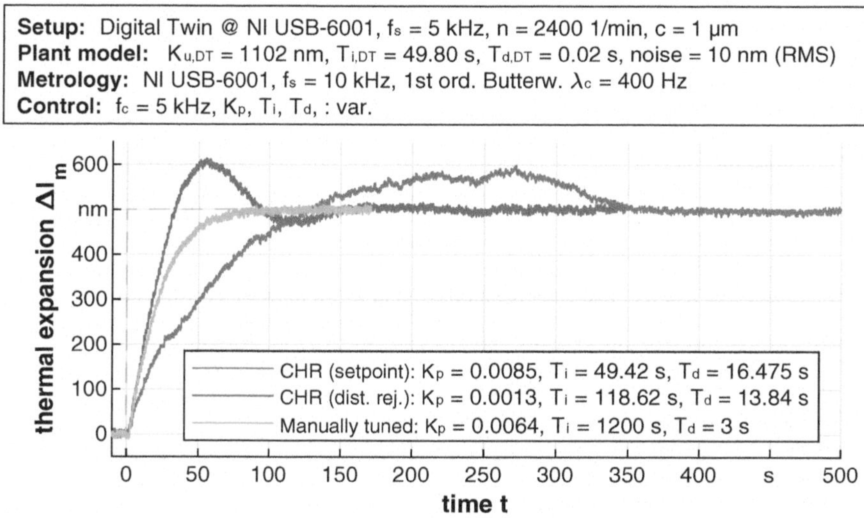

Fig. 28 Comparison of control parameters for a setpoint of 500 nm using a Digital Twin of the tool holder

the settling time is improved, but the overshoot is further increased. The self-tuned parameters yields the best results in terms of settling time, overshoot and setpoint accuracy and thus are chosen for further analysis.

The controlled response of the system using the self-tuned parameters is applicable across the complete stroke of the actuator as is shown in Fig. 29. As there is no overshoot with these parameters, the system may well be utilized for in-process re-setting of the tool, e.g. to compensate for gradual tool wear or low-dynamic disturbances.

With the given noise of the system (10 nm RMS), the system follows inputted setpoints down to ±5 nm, as depicted in Fig. 30.

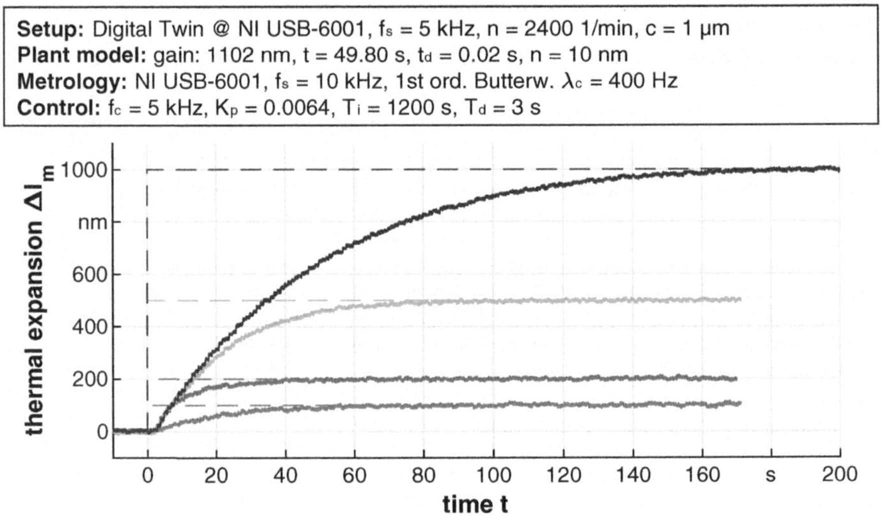

Fig. 29 Closed loop control of actuator position (Digital Twin) for selected setpoints

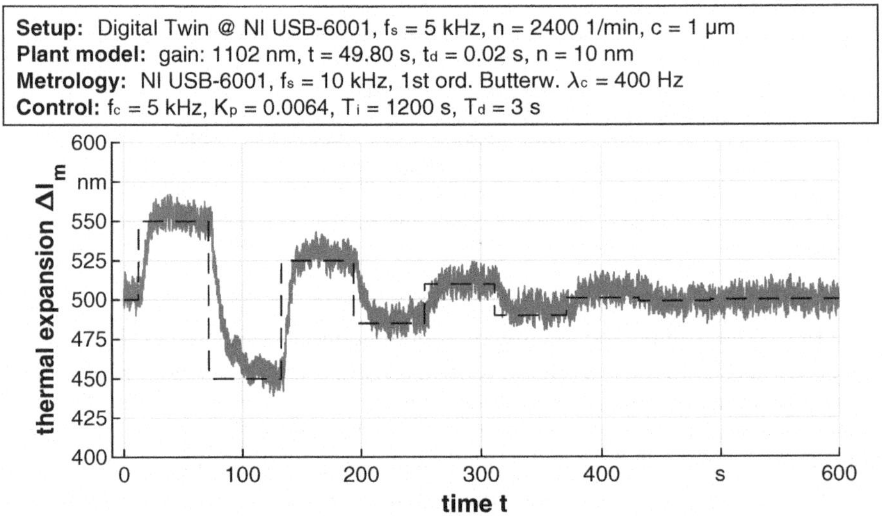

Fig. 30 Control response (Digital Twin) for selected small scale setpoints

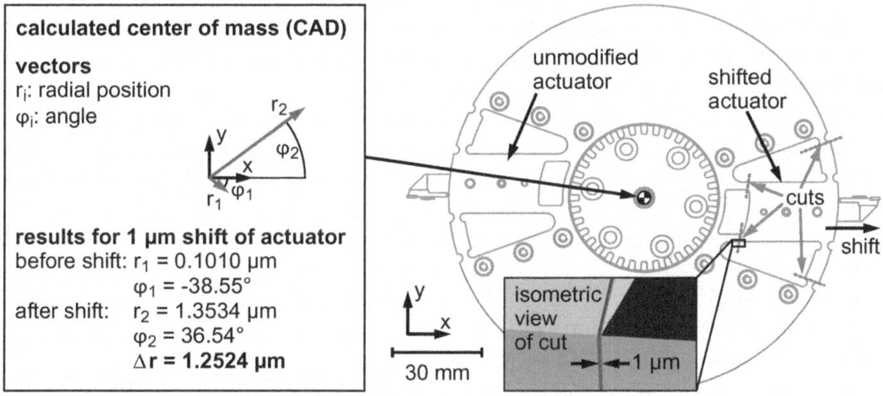

Fig. 31 Calculated unbalances for thermally expanded actuator

8 Influence Multi-tool-holder on General Machining Performance

After the control of the thermal actuator has been successfully demonstrated, this section will focus on potential influences of the tool-holding mechanism on the process itself.

8.1 Impact of Tool-Shift on Unbalances

First, it has been examined whether the tool shift induced by the thermal actuator results in a change of the balancing state of the rotor. Calculations based on the CAD model indicate that shifting one of the actuators by its maximum expansion (1 µm) moves the center of mass of the tool holder by approximately 1.25 µm (see Fig. 31). In theory, this results in a measurable change of the balancing state and could potentially be applied for ultra-fine balancing of the rotor, if a compensation mass is shifted in this way.

In order to verify this, the balancing state was measured experimentally for selected spindle speeds with the actuator at its base length ("cold") and at its maximum expansion ("heated"). The results are shown in Fig. 32. Generally, the measured unbalance is decreasing with increasing spindle speed. While the mean unbalance is approx. 5 g mm at 900 min^{-1}, it is below 0.31 g mm at 2,500 min^{-1}. Furthermore, no significant change of the unbalance could be detected when the actuator is at its maximum thermal expansion. This also implies that the system cannot be applied for balancing purposes in its current form.

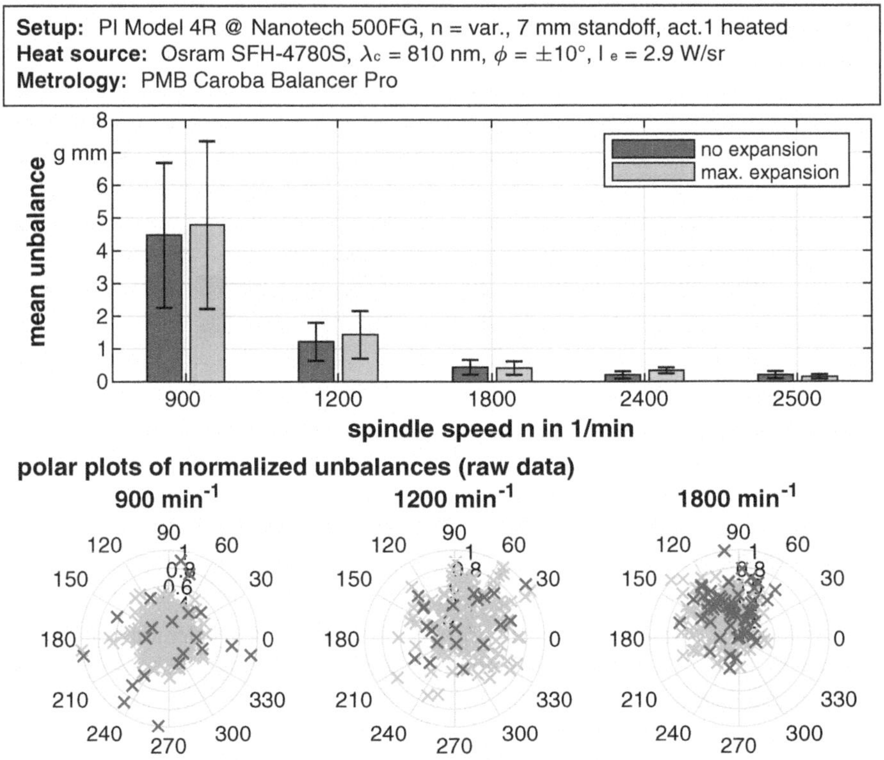

Fig. 32 Effect of tool setting on unbalances: mean unbalance and standard deviation for cold actuator and maximum thermal expansion (top) and normalized unbalances for selected spindle speeds (bottom)

8.2 Influence of Spray Mist Lubricant on Thermal Tool Setting

In the final experiments of this study, the influence of cutting fluid on the performance of the thermal tool setting was analyzed. For this, the cutting experiments described in Sect. 6.2 were repeated with minimum quantity lubrication directed at the cutting zone. The resulting spray mist potentially covers the heated faces of the actuator, thereby cooling the substrate in addition to the forced convection by the spindle rotation. Paraffin oil was selected as cooling fluid for these experiments, because it is electrically non-conductive and thus will not influence the electronics of the ring light system. In addition, it is only applied locally at the tool-workpiece contact point and therefore the influence of capacitive measurement of the reference plane is minimized. An exemplary analysis of both, the expansion measured at the reference plane and the cutting mark depth evaluated from the surface measurements, is shown in Fig. 33.

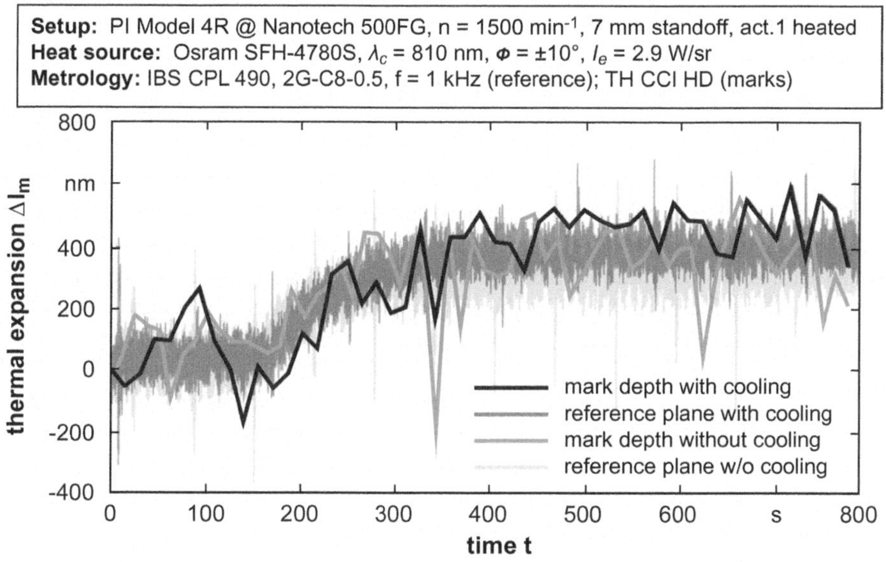

Fig. 33 Measured expansion of the thermal tool holder (reference plane) and depth change of cutting marks (actual tool shift) for cutting tests with and without cooling fluid

The analysis shows no measurable reduction in actuator expansion and tool shift for machining with cutting fluid. Both parameters indicate an expansion of 400 nm that is achieved after about 400 s.

9 Conclusion and Outlook

Diamond milling using multiple cutting edges offers the potential to significantly increase the productivity of diamond machining. Its broad application is averted by the lack of ultra-precision tool setting mechanisms that can be applied on rotating spindles. Hence, the possibility of a thermally induced tool setting was investigated in this study. By locally heating a specific section of the milling tool, i.e. the tool holder, an actuating mechanism was triggered that causes the attached diamond tool and its cutting edge to shift in radial direction. A closed loop control can then be applied to minimize the deviation between this tool's radius and that of other tools in the setup.

The thermal actuating mechanism was initially analyzed using finite element modeling and later evaluated a static test stand. Based on the findings obtained in these studies, a final design of a milling tool with thermally adjustable holders for two diamond tools was derived. The heat input is generated by a moving ring light with infrared LED which has been specifically designed for this purpose (patent pending).

Additional tests of the novel milling tool on spindle test stands and in machining experiments have confirmed the general applicability of thermal tool setting in diamond milling. It was possible to build a closed loop control of the thermal actuator that evaluates the position of a reference plane during rotation and drives the ring light according to the determined offset. The initial parameterization of the control loop yields acceptable results in terms of setpoint accuracy and speed, but still results in overshoot of the expansion. Thus, an optimized controller using manually tuned parameters has been derived using a Digital Twin of the system. The controller drives the actuator to its maximum expansion in about 200 s and achieved a setpoint accuracy of ±5 nm. Furthermore, it has been demonstrated that the thermal tool setting does not change the balancing state of rotor and even is unaffected by spray mist lubrication of the cutting zone.

In order to mature this concept to an industrially applicable solution, a further analysis of the position stability and repeatability as well as of the impact of the localized heating on the long-term thermal stability of the machine tool is vital. Furthermore, the electronics, software and (setup-)procedures have to be refined in order to be applicable in an industrial environment.

References

1. Bono, M., Hibbard, R.: A flexure-based tool holder for sub-μ positioning of a single point cutting tool on a four-axis lathe. Precis. Eng. **31**(2), 169–176 (2007). https://doi.org/10.1016/j.precisioneng.2006.03.007
2. Brinksmeier, E., Gläbe, R., Autschbach, L.: Novel ultraprecise tool alignment setup for contour boring and ball-end milling. In: 18th ASPE Annual Meeting, Portland/Oregon, USA, October 2013, pp. 271–274. American Society for Precision Engineering (2013)
3. Brinksmeier, E., Preuss, W.: Micro-machining. Philos. Trans. Roy. Soc. A **370**, 3973–3992 (2012). https://doi.org/10.1098/rsta.2011.0056
4. Brinksmeier, E., Riemer, O., Gläbe, R.M. (eds.): Fabrication of Complex Optical Components. Springer, Heidelberg (2013). https://doi.org/10.1007/978-3-642-33001-8
5. Chien, K.L., Hrones, J.A., Reswick, J.B.: On the automatic control of generalized passive systems. Trans. ASME **74**, 175–185 (1952)
6. Dornfeld, D., Min, S., Takeuchi, Y.: Recent advances in mechanical micromachining. CIRP Ann. **55**(2), 745–768 (2006). https://doi.org/10.1016/j.cirp.2006.10.006
7. Fang, F.Z., Zhang, X.D., Weckenmann, A., Zhang, G., Evans, C.J.: Manufacturing and measurement of freeform optics. CIRP Ann. **62**(2), 823–846 (2013). https://doi.org/10.1016/j.cirp.2013.05.003
8. Neugebauer, R., Denkena, B., Wegener, K.: Mechatronic systems for machine tools. CIRP Ann. **56**(2), 657–686 (2007). https://doi.org/10.1016/j.cirp.2007.10.007
9. Schönemann, L., Brinksmeier, E., Osmer, J.: A piezo-driven adaptive tool holder for ultraprecision diamond tool alignment. In: van Brussel, H., Brinksmeier, E., Spaan, H., Burke, T. (eds.) 9th Euspen International Conference, vol. 1, pp. 398–401 (2009)
10. Schönemann, L., Mejia, P., Riemer, O., Brinksmeier, E.: Design and evaluation of a thermal actuator for ultra-precision machining. In: Blunt, L. (ed.) 11th International Conference & Exhibition on Laser Metrology, Machine Tool, CMM & Robotic Performance (Lamdamap 2015), pp. 320–330. Euspen (2015)

11. Schönemann, L., Preuss, W., Riemer, O., Foremny, E., Brinksmeier, E., Kuhfuss, B.: Ultrapräzise Hochgeschwindigkeitsbearbeitung. Teil 1: Steigerung der Flächenleistung durch den Einsatz von Mehrfach- Werkzeugen und HSC-Spindeln. wt Werkstattstechnik **105**(6), pp. 366–370 (2015)
12. Schönemann, L., Riemer, O., Brinksmeier, E.: Control of a thermal actuator for UP-milling with multiple cutting edges. Procedia CIRP **46**, 424–427 (2016). https://doi.org/10.1016/j.procir.2016.03.194. Ed. by Wertheim, R., Ihlefeldt, S., Hochmuth, C., Putz, M
13. Schönemann, L., Riemer, O., Brinksmeier, E.: Arbeitsmaschine mit einem rotierenden Maschinenteilhalter, insbesondere Werkzeugmaschine mit rotierendem Werkzeughalter, Verfahren zum Justieren eines Maschinenteils, insbesondere Werkzeugs, sowie Ringlicht für eine derartige Arbeitsmaschine. German pat. req. 10 2017 119 828 A1. Leibniz-Institut fürWerkstoforientierte Technologien IWT, Universität Bremen, 29 August 2017
14. Schönemann, L., Riemer, O., Brinksmeier, E.: Recent advances in ultra-precision milling with multiple-cutting edges. In: 32nd ASPE Annual Meeting, Charlotte/NC, USA, 29 October–3 November 2017, pp. 175–179. American Society for Precision Engineering (2017)
15. Schönemann, L., Riemer, O.: Thermo-mechanical tool setting mechanism for ultra-precision milling with multiple cutting edges. Precis. Eng. (2018). https://doi.org/10.1016/j.precisioneng.2018.09.003
16. Schönemann, L.: Surface simulation for ultra-precision milling with multiple cutting edges. In: 69th CIRP General Assembly - Part 2, Birmingham, 22 August 2019
17. Schönemann, L., Berger, D., Dörgeloh, T., Riemer, O., Brinksmeier, E., Krüger, R., Schreiber, P., Denkena, B., Hochbein, J., Parsa, N., Schenck, C., Kuhfuss, B.: Synergistic approaches to ultra-precision high performance cutting. CIRP J. Manuf. Sci. Technol. **28**, 38–51 (2020). https://doi.org/10.1016/j.cirpj.2019.12.001
18. Sortino, M., Totis, G., Kuljanic, E.: Comparison of injection molding technologies for the production of micro-optical devices. Procedia Eng. **69**, 1296–1305 (2014). https://doi.org/10.1016/j.proeng.2014.03
19. Sze-Wei, G., Han-Seok, L., Rahman, M., Watt, F.: A fine tool servo system for global position error compensation for a miniature ultra-precision lathe. Int. J. Mach. Tools Manuf. **47**(7–8), 1302–1310 (2007). https://doi.org/10.1016/j.ijmachtools.2006.08.023
20. Transregionaler Sonderforschungsbereich TR4, ed. Prozessketten zur Replikation komplexer Optikkomponenten. Abschlussbericht. Berichtszeitraum 7/2008–8/2012 (2012)
21. Zhang, S.J., To, S., Zhu, Z.W., Zhang, G.Q.: A review of fly cutting applied to surface generation in ultra-precision machining. Int. J. Mach. Tools Manuf. **103**, 13–27 (2016). https://doi.org/10.1016/j.ijmachtools.2016.01.001

Ultra-Precision High Speed Cutting

Daniel Berger, Lars Schönemann, Oltmann Riemer, and Ekkard Brinksmeier

Abstract Today, the technology of high speed machining (HSM) is well understood and established for conventional turning and milling at high material removal rates. However, this is not the case for ultra-precision processes. Consequently, in this project the mechanisms of high-speed machining in the ultra-precision range were investigated for both, non-ferrous metals as well as brittle-hard semiconductor materials, by diamond turning and milling (i.e. fly-cutting). For both material classes, reduced tool wear, lower cutting forces and most important, superior surface quality were achieved. The reason for the advantageous material removal behavior when applying high cutting speeds is the transition to adiabatic shearing, occurring at high temperatures and beneficial pressure in the contact zone.

1 Diamond Milling and Fly-Cutting

Ultra-precision machining is well-known for achieving superior quality in surface and figure, but also for its time-consuming nature. This is particularly true for fly-cutting, as only one diamond tool is conventionally applied for milling [25]. So what is the advantage of fly-cutting, if optical components might be machined faster by diamond turning? A conceivable application is the machining of large mirrors, for which a fast rotational speed cannot be achieved in diamond turning due to weight of the part and acceleration of the work spindle. As a result, the process remains very slow. In fly-cutting, cutting speed only depends on spindle speed and diameter of the tool. Thus, a fast rotating tool spindle is beneficial in this case, making fly-cutting the preferable choice for the machining of large parts.

Also, the spiral tool path in turning operations leads to constantly changing crystal orientations when cutting monocrystalline semiconductors and other anisotropic materials. In turn, fly-cutting is cutting a straight line by definition so that a certain cutting direction on the material can only be guaranteed in milling.

D. Berger (✉) · L. Schönemann (✉) · O. Riemer · E. Brinksmeier
MAPEX Center for Materials and Processes, University of Bremen, Bremen, Germany
e-mail: schoenemann@iwt.uni-bremen.de

D. Berger
e-mail: berger@iwt.uni-bremen.de

Leibniz Institute for Materials Engineering IWT, Bremen, Germany

E. Brinksmeier and L. Schönemann (eds.), *Ultra-precision High Performance Cutting*,
Lecture Notes in Production Engineering, https://doi.org/10.1007/978-3-030-83765-5_3

As fly-cutting is the "simplest" of all diamond milling operations, the basic calculations of cutting speed and feed speed are straightforward. At first, the value for kinematic roughness R_{kin} is defined. In most cases, diamond machined surfaces should have optical features, i.e. values of $R_{kin} < 10$ nm need to be generated. Taking this value, a maximal feed f of 7.8 μm is allowed for achieving this surface figure when using a typical diamond tool with a corner radius of $r_\varepsilon = 0.78$ mm, according to Eq. 1.

$$R_{kin} \approx \frac{f^2}{8r_\varepsilon} \leq 10\,\text{nm} \rightarrow f \leq \sqrt{8r_\varepsilon \cdot R_{kin}} \tag{1}$$

The feed speed v_f directly correlates with the cutting speed v_c in milling operations, according to Eqs. 2–4.

$$v_f = n \cdot f \tag{2}$$

$$v_c = \pi \cdot d \cdot n \tag{3}$$

$$v_f = \frac{v_c \cdot f}{\pi \cdot d} \tag{4}$$

where n is the rotational speed of the tool spindle and d is the diameter of the fly-cutter.

In order to enhance ultra-precision fly-cutting operations, the most obvious approach to decrease main process times is the increase of feed speed. As feed f is already maximized by Eq. 1, the only way to increase feed speed is the increase of spindle speed. This approach is well-known for conventional, but not for ultra-precision machining. Thus, in this research the mechanisms of material removal of HSM on ductile and brittle materials were analyzed.

2 High Speed Machining

High speed machining (HSM) has its origins as early as the 1930s in a patent granted to Salomon [26]. However, due to a lack of suitable HSM machines and cutting materials, it was not possible to make use of this patent initially. However, from the 1960s onward, HSM was increasingly used in machining [33]. First in Japan, but also in Germany, the potentials were recognized and, above all, decisively influenced by the work of several researchers [24, 28, 29]. Today, particularly heat-distortion-sensitive and thin-walled components, such as those for the aerospace industry, are produced by high-speed machining. Compared to conventional machining, HSM is characterized by a higher material removal rate, lower cutting forces and better surface quality. A disadvantage is the decreasing tool life, which is due to the increasing thermal load on the cutting edge.

High-speed machining is currently not defined based on physical principles, although scientists have already provided several suggestions. For example,

Schneider proposed a fixed allocation of cutting speed ranges for conventional machining (0 to 500 m/min), for high-speed machining (500 to 10,000 m/min) and for ultra-fast machining (<10,000 m/min) [31]. Schulz mentioned the allocation of separate speed limits for individual materials [30]. Ben Amor succeeded for the first time in developing an analytically based definition for HSM based on experimental force and power measurements [3].

It was observed that for almost all metallic materials a typical force curve as a function of cutting speed is obvious. Interestingly, the cutting and feed forces run asymptotically against a constant value, which is designated Fc_{∞} in the case of cutting force. Ben Amor was able to show that the variable cutting force component can be well described by an exponential decay function (Eq. 5).

$$F_c\left(v_c\right) = F_{c,\infty} + F_{c,var} \cdot e^{\frac{-2v_C}{v_{HG}}} \tag{5}$$

For this purpose, a speed limit v_{HG} was introduced. v_{HG} is apparently the speed at which the variable part of the cutting force has decreased by 86.5% (exponent −2) according to Eq. 5.

During high-speed cutting of metallic (ductile) materials, a significant decrease in cutting force and other cutting force components can be observed for all materials investigated. Bäeker explains this decrease with a reduction of the flow stress, which is caused by an adiabatic chip formation [2]. During a cutting process, material compression and chip shearing occur alternately as a cycle. Initially, compression occurs along the contact zone, while shearing occurs near the surface. Furthermore, the material-specific strength values are exceeded with the following onset of shear localization and shearing of a segment. Shear localization occurs when thermal softening exceeds mechanical hardening so that softening leads to centralization of plastic deformation. As a result, the process itself accelerates as a further temperature increase with further deformation centralization sets in [1].

Even if for some materials the material separation mechanisms remain the same compared to conventional machining, the advantage of the increased material removal rate still exists, which is accompanied by superior economic efficiency.

The research unit Ultra-Precision High Performance Cutting (UP-HPC) aims at reducing primary and secondary process times while diamond machining, inter alia by high speed cutting (HSC).

Especially for the generation of complex freeforms, as needed for e.g. (IR) applications, diamond milling ("fly-cutting") and off-axis turning are frequently applied. In most cases, moderate cutting speeds (200 to 600 m/min) are set to avoid high thermal loads or high frequency excitation of structural loops [24]. As the final product is high-end equipment, long primary and secondary process times are acceptable, because the added value still exceeds the production costs by far. However, the reduction of primary and secondary process times is naturally desirable when manufacturing higher batch numbers [31]. Consequently, the influence of high (i.e. v_c = 4,000 m/min in this study) and conventional cutting speeds (i.e. $v_c = 4.00$ m/min) on the material removal mechanism of non-ferrous metals (ductile materials, Sect. 3) and semicon-

Table 1 Ductile materials processed by High Speed Machining

Metallic materials
OFHC copper
Brass CuZn30
Brass CuZn39Pb3
Aluminum AlMg3
Aluminum AlMg5
NiP (electroless nickel)

ductors (brittle materials, Sect. 4) were investigated in this study by off-axis diamond turning and fly-cutting.

3 Ultra-Precision High-Speed Cutting of Metallic Materials

In this section, the analysis of the material removal mechanisms while machining non-ferrous metals, listed in Table 1, at high cutting speeds is presented.

The impact of HSC on the transition to adiabatic shearing was examined by analyzing the cutting forces in on-axis turning and is presented in Sect. 3.1. The influence of HSC on mechanical abrasive and thermo-chemical tool wear in fly-cutting is discussed in Sects. 3.2 and 3.3, respectively. Eventually, the effects of high cutting speeds on surface topography are presented in Sect. 3.4.

3.1 Cutting Forces and the Transition to Adiabatic Shearing

In order to record the cutting forces with a continuous increase in cutting speed between 150 m/min and 4,500 m/min, a facing test was designed (Fig. 1).

Two tool types (carbide indexable insert and diamond radius tool) and three different infeeds ($a_p = 30$, 40 and 50 μm) were selected for machining. The tool holder was mounted to a Kistler force dynamometer MiniDyn 9256C1, which was fixed to the C-axis of the machine tool. The workpiece was mounted on a Professional Instruments spindle model 4R and rotated with 9,600 min^{-1}.

The feed speed was reduced inversely proportional to the distance from the turning center so that the material removal rate remains constant ($Q = 200\,mm^3/min$) in all tests. Feed direction was varied from the inside to outside and vice versa to exclude systematic influences. In the middle of the workpiece a hole was made to record the zero force level before and after cutting, allowing for drift compensation.

The recorded cutting force curves show excellent reproducibility, regardless of whether it is turned from the inside out or from the outside in (Fig. 2).

Further typical cutting forces for the three selected infeeds, when cutting brass CuZn39Pb3 with monocrystalline diamond, are shown in Fig. 3. A drop in the cutting

Fig. 1 Facing test with constant material removal volume for recording cutting forces as a function of cutting speed

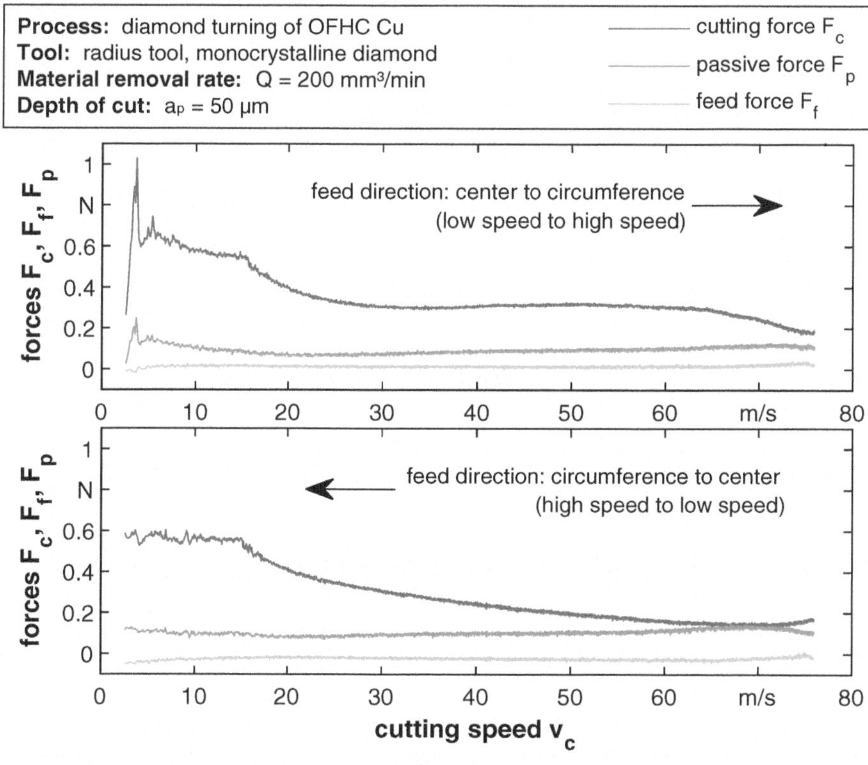

Fig. 2 Reproducibility of process force curves at inverse feed directions

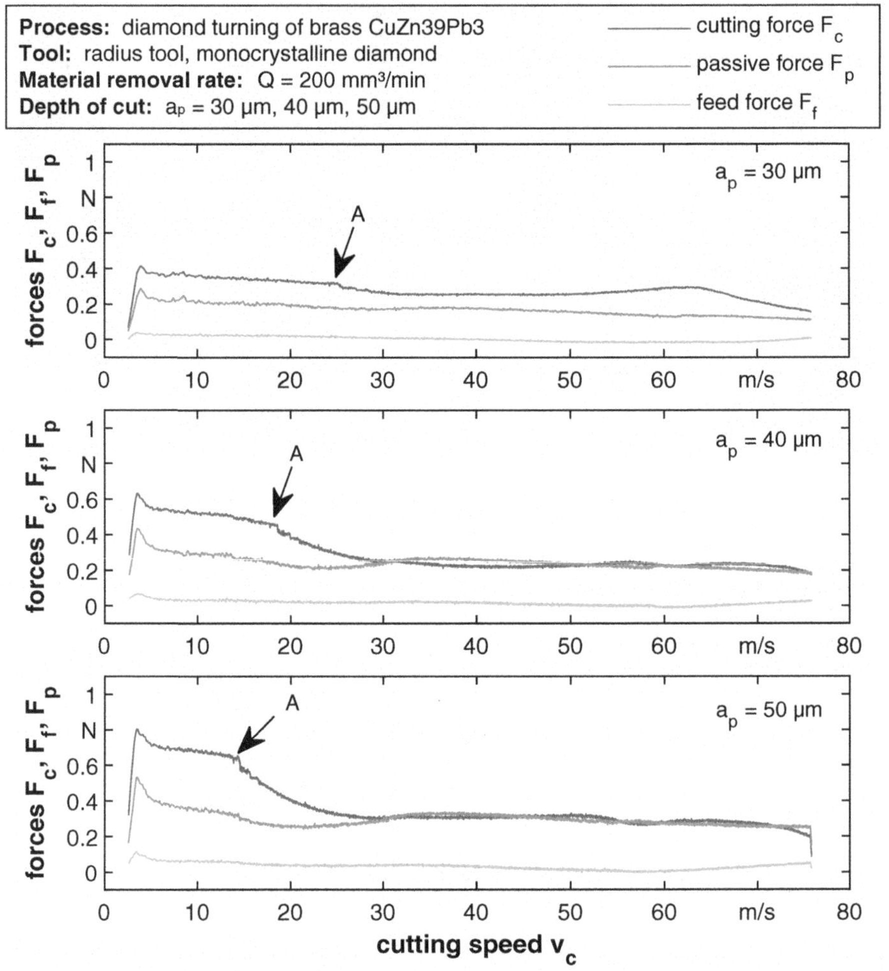

Fig. 3 Cutting forces as a function of the cutting speed at constant material removal rate. *A* denotes the transition to adiabatic shearing

force to a new, approximately constant level can be observed from a relatively clearly defined point (marked with "A" in Fig. 3). This starting point, which indicates the beginning of the transition to adiabatic shearing, has not been elaborated in literature before this investigation, as no continuous cutting force curves have been recorded up to this level of cutting speed.

With increasing cutting depth and decreasing hardness of the material, the starting point shifts to lower cutting speeds (critical cutting speed v_c^*, Table 2). More detailed results are shown in [5, 8, 27].

Exemplarily, a 3D simulation of the cutting force curve while diamond turning of OFHC copper with a radius tool was carried out. As can be seen in

Table 2 Ductile materials and the critical cutting speeds causing a transition to adiabatic shearing

Material	**Critical cutting speed v_c^* @a_p = 50 μm** [m/min]
Brass CuZn39Pb3	1,300
OFHC copper	950
Aluminum AlMg5	900
Electroless nickel	1,250

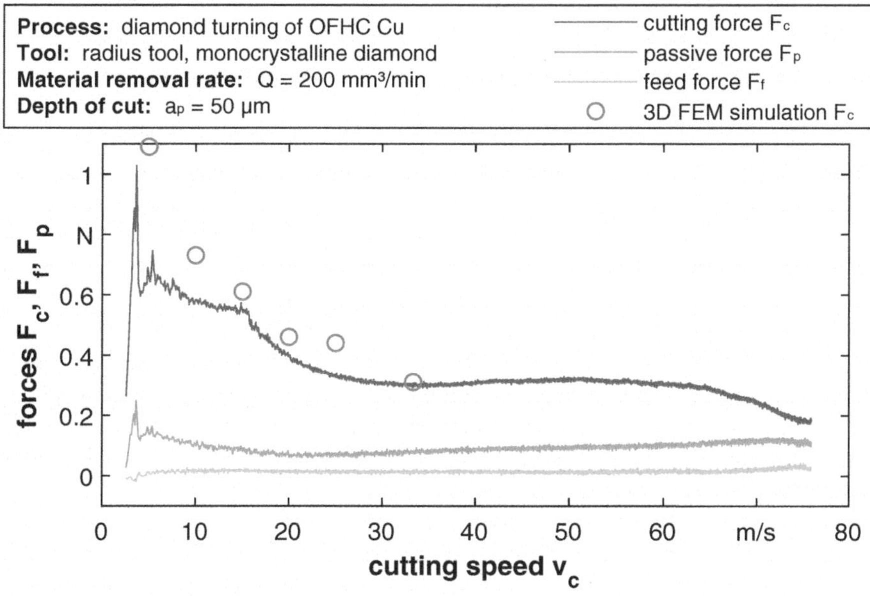

Fig. 4 3D simulation of the cutting force curve during diamond turning of OFHC copper and comparison with the forces measured in the experiment

Fig. 4, the simulation reproduces the measured cutting force in the range between $v_c = 600$ m/min and 2,000 m/min quite well. The starting point of the cutting force drop at $v_c = 800$ m/min can not be confirmed, however, probably due to the wide intervals of the cutting speed.

3.2 Investigation of the Dependence of Tool Wear on Cutting Speed

A quantitative investigation of the cutting speed's influence on diamond tool wear during the cutting of "diamond machinable" materials is very time-consuming, as very low wear occurs. Thus, a limitation to the two materials brass CuZn39Pb3

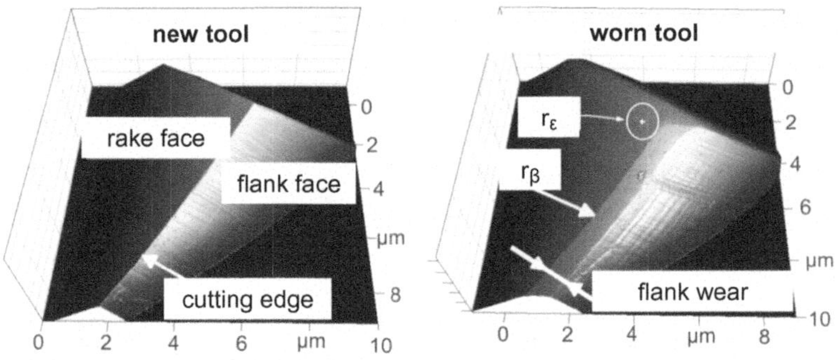

Fig. 5 AFM image of a V-shaped diamond blade before (left) and after (right) a wear test

with the Vickers hardness $HV130$ and electroless nickel with the Vickers hardness $HV530$ was made and wear experiments were only carried out with one low ($v_c \approx$ 380 m/min) and one high ($v_c \approx$ 3,800 m/min) cutting speed. In addition, relatively fragile V-shaped diamond blades with an included angle of 90° were used, as even minimal tool wear can be easily detected on this geometry.

A tool was slowly worn out by milling V-shaped grooves in alternating up- and down-milling mode into a 150 × 75 mm rectangular disc. The effective contact length L_c, defined as the distance accumulated up to a certain point in time at which the cutting edge was in contact with the workpiece, was chosen as the criterion for the load duration for the cutting edge. The width of flank wear land was selected as the criterion for wear evaluation.

After equal effective contact lengths, the tools were removed to measure the cutting edge geometry with an atomic force microscope and to determine the width of flank wear land (Fig. 5).

Plotting the wear land widths measured in the four tests against the effective contact length in Fig. 6 shows clearly that tool wear is reduced at high cutting speeds in comparison to lower speeds, possibly due to the shorter contact time at high cutting speeds. The diamond tool life is therefore longer in the HSC range when applying processes with interrupted cuts [5].

3.3 Investigation of Thermo-Chemically Induced Wear During HSC Diamond Milling of Steel

Steel is one the most important mold materials, but it is well-known that it is not capable for diamond machining according to catastrophic tool wear. The underlying mechanisms of the thermo-chemically induced wear of diamond tools during the processing of steel have not yet been conclusively clarified. In the recent past, ultrasonic machining was proven to be suitable for diamond machining of steel due to short contact times during tool engagement. Therefore, it seemed worthwhile to

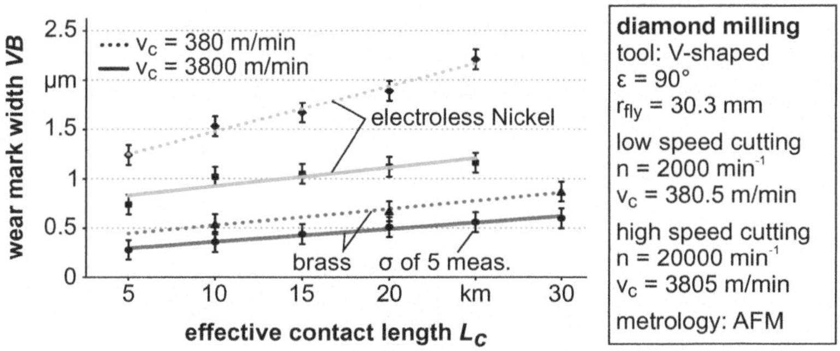

Fig. 6 Flank wear when milling electroless nickel and brass CuZn39Pb3 at low and high cutting speeds

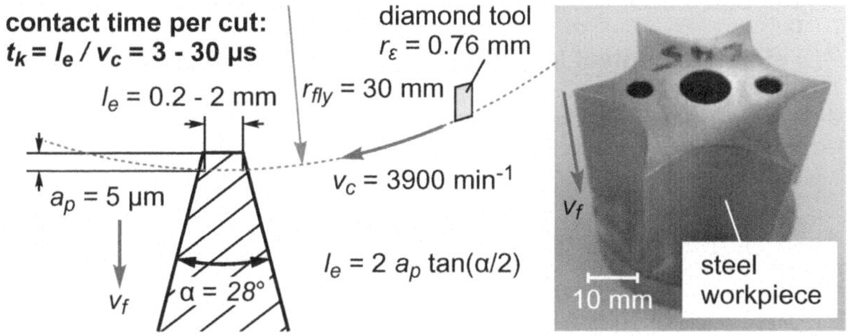

Fig. 7 Variation of the contact time t_k per intervention by varying the infeed a_p on a wedge-shaped steel substrate

investigate edge wear as a function of contact time during HSC milling. For this purpose, an experiment was designed in which the contact time could be varied by varying the infeed a_p on a wedge-shaped steel substrate (Fig. 7).

The flank wear land and cutting edge radius r_β as a function of the effective contact length L_c for different contact times are shown in Fig. 8.

With decreasing contact time, the wear of diamond tools is reduced considerably. This argues against a formation of an iron oxide layer on the cut surface of the steel substrate as assumed by Zhang et al. as an explanation for the reduction of tool wear observed in ultra-sonic diamond machining of steel [36]. Rather, the wear rate seems to depend only on the contact time. Figure 9 shows the flank wear land measured at the shortest contact time that could be realized in the experiment (3 µs) as a function of the effective contact length [7]. Although the rate of thermo-chemically induced wear could be reduced by a factor of 30 compared to the so-called "catastrophic" wear at permanent contact, this reduction is not sufficient to establish HSC diamond milling of steel as a practical method.

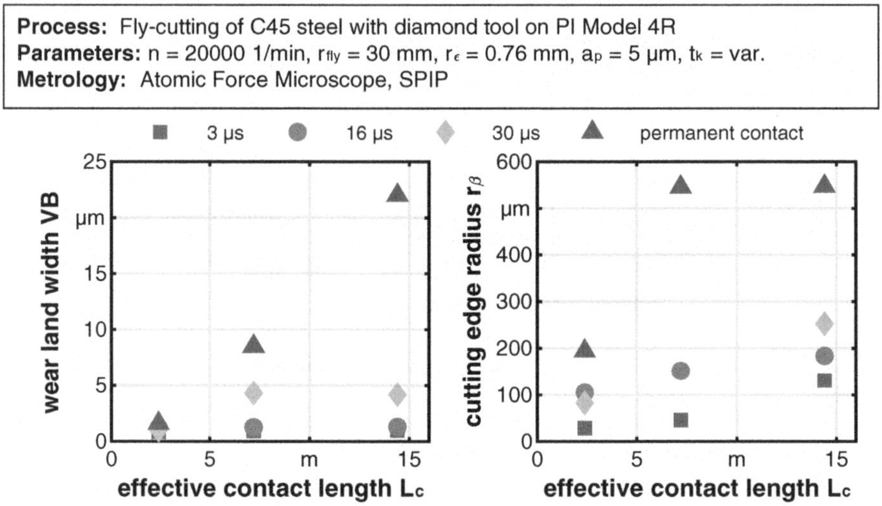

Fig. 8 Measured wear land width (left) and cutting edge radii r_β (right) as a function of the effective contact length L_c at different contact times t_k

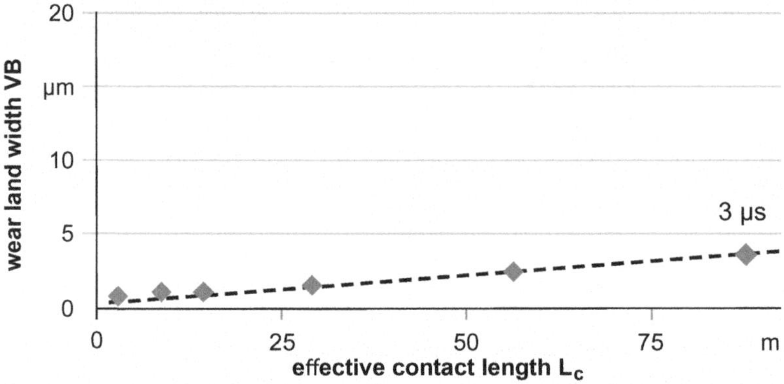

Fig. 9 Increase in wear mark width against effective contact length L_c for thermo-chemically induced wear at a contact time per intervention of 3 µs

3.4 Investigation of the Surface Topography of HSC Diamond Milled Surfaces

Almost all metal substrates suitable for diamond machining have a grain structure which, due to the differential elastic springback of the grain Δh_{el}, leads to a material-dependent surface roughness during machining. As the cutting forces are reduced during HSC diamond machining (see Sect. 3.1), it is to be expected that the differential

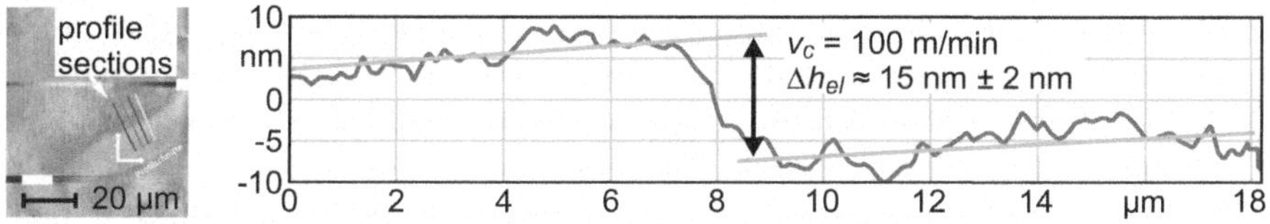

Fig. 10 AFM image and profile section of a cut grain boundary in OFHC copper

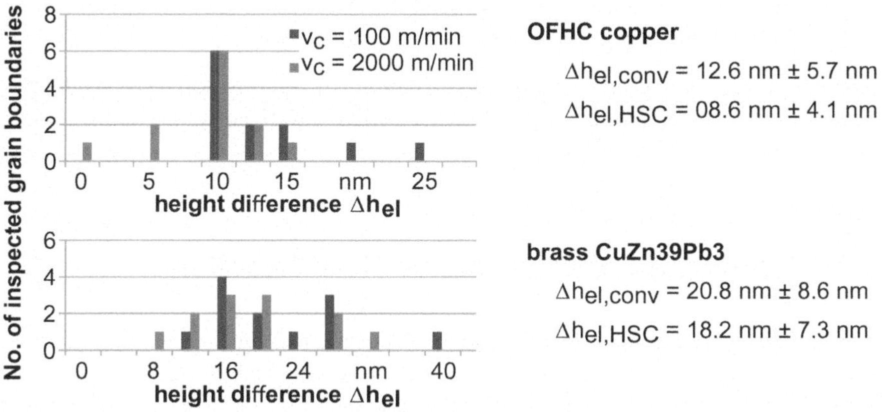

Fig. 11 Distribution of the measured grain height differences

elastic springback of the grains will also decrease so that an even better surface roughness may be expected.

In the experiments designed for this purpose, 12 grain boundaries were selected from approx. 120 grain boundaries identified on OFHC copper and brass CuZn39Pb3, which were then cut at a low cutting speed ($v_c = 100$ m/min). Subsequently, a very small shift by an infeed of 5 μs was applied before a second cut was made at high cutting speed ($v_c = 2{,}000$ m/min). The step heights of the cut grain boundaries were documented by an atomic force microscope (Fig. 10).

As the histograms in Fig. 11 show, it can be statistically proven that grain boundaries remaining after the application of high cutting speed have a slightly smaller height difference than those cut at low cutting speed. A more detailed presentation of the results is given in [7].

3.5 Conclusion on UP-HSC of Ductile Materials

In Sects. 3.1 to 3.4, the effects of high speed cutting were examined and have revealed the following essential results:

1. With increasing cutting speed, a transition to adiabatic shearing occurs in the chip forming zone, associated with an exponential decrease of the cutting force.
2. At high cutting speeds, abrasive tool wear is reduced due to low contact times during tool engagement. It could also be shown that thermo-chemically induced tool wear decreases too when cutting steel substrates. But despite this favorable effect in high speed cutting, the tool wear remains still too high for machining large sized optics.
3. The achievable surface roughness slightly improves with increasing cutting speed due to the reduced springback of the grains.

Accordingly, ultra-precise high-speed diamond machining offers considerable advantages in terms of process technology as well as significantly shorter machining times.

4 High-Speed Machining of Brittle-Hard Materials

Ductile regime machining of brittle-hard materials has received a great deal of attention from scientific studies around the world. It is well known that a prerequisite for plastic deformation is the presence of a hydrostatic pressure state in the contact zone, which was already stated by King and Tabor in 1954 [17]. The first researcher, however, to demonstrate the positive influence of the hydrostatic stress state on the deformability of brittle-hard materials, as predicted by Mohr's theory, was Theodore von Kármán in 1911 [16]. A review on the status of ductile regime machining was compiled by Neo et al. in 2012 [23]. Most importantly this review revealed that critical machining parameters to handle are feed, depth of cut and the tool geometry to maintain a process constantly with a chip thickness below a critical value. Concerning the tool, especially the negative rake angle and a large tool edge radius support ductile regime machining by inducing a hydrostatic pressure [23].

Diamond machining of semiconductor materials, like silicon or germanium, is well researched, but in most cases conventional cutting speeds are applied. High speed cutting (HSC) of semiconductor materials has not gained much attention in research. Liu et al. have investigated the characteristics of high speed micro-cutting of tungsten carbide and found that HSC could also be applied on brittle materials, when depth of cut and feed rate are low. They have applied a cutting speed of 741.4 m/min [20].

In this section, the application of high cutting speeds up to 4,000 m/min was investigated on elemental (Si, Ge) and compound semiconductors (ZnS, ZnSe). All experiments for investigations on high-speed machining of those materials were carried out on a Moore Nanotech 350FG ultra-precision machine tool. For the determination of critical chip thickness and surface integrity while high speed cutting, both off-axis turning and fly-cutting were investigated. In order to be able to reach high cutting speeds while turning, the radius of the workpiece mounting fixture on the work spindle was maximized (i.e. the radius of the workpiece's center was set

Table 3 Tool and workpiece specifications

	Specification	Value
Radius tool	Cutting material	Single-crystal diamond
	Corner radius	$r_\varepsilon = 0.76\,\text{mm}$
	Cutting edge radius	$r_\beta = 50$ to $150\,\text{nm}$
Workpiece	Materials	Monocrystalline silicon (Si), germanium (Ge), zinc sulfide (ZnS), zinc selenide (ZnSe)
	Orientation	(100) / (110) / (111)
	Geometry	$10 \times 10 \times 0.5\ \text{mm}^3$
	Cutting direction	<110> for all crystallographic orientations

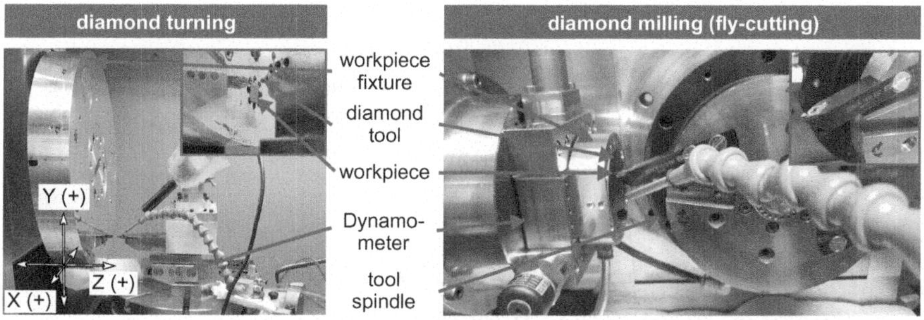

Fig. 12 Experimental setup for off-axis turning and fly-cutting

at 110 mm) and designed to adapt three square workpieces ($10 \times 10\ \text{mm}^2$ each), see Fig. 12. The resulting work spindle speed was 531 min^{-1} for low cutting speed (400 m/min) and 5,310 min^{-1} for high cutting speed (4,000 m/min). Plunging into the material (a_p) was enabled by moving the Z-axis, while the Y-axis generated the v_c-dependent feed speed (v_f).

The turning experiments were conducted using the main spindle of the 350FG while for milling (fly-cutting), a Professional Instruments ISO 3.375B air bearing spindle was mounted on the Z-axis of the machine tool and used as tool spindle.

Turning and milling experiments were performed with a single-crystal diamond radius tool. To exclude wear effects, a tool in fresh condition was applied for each set of cutting speeds. Process forces were measured on the tool side when turning, and on the workpiece side for milling. The specifications for tool and workpiece are shown in Table 3 and the experimental setups for both processes are illustrated in Fig. 12. Cutting direction was <110>, as this is the only direction existent on all crystallographic orientations. Additionally, this direction shows a beneficial behavior for ductile machining according to literature [9, 32, 37].

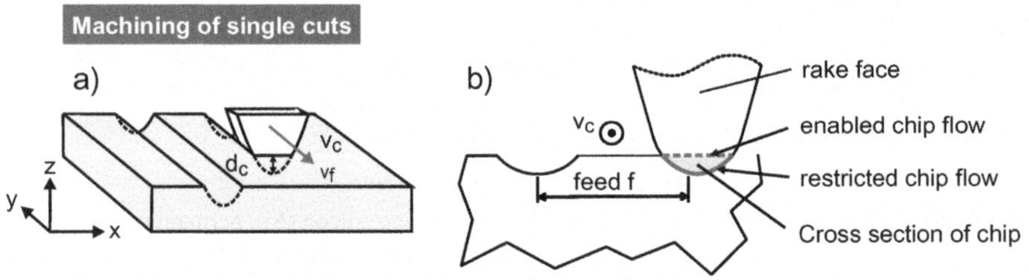

Fig. 13 Process strategy for high speed off-axis diamond turning and milling of single cuts for determination of critical depth of cut d_c

Table 4 Parameters for turning and milling of single cuts

Parameter	Values
Cutting speed v_c	400/4,000 m/min
Feed speed v_f	160/1,600 mm/min
Rake angle γ	0°/−20°/−30°
Depth of cut a_p	var. (0 to >500 nm)

4.1 Dependence of the Cutting Speed on Critical Chip Thickness and Surface Integrity

Maintaining the critical chip thickness is essential for the ductile machining of brittle-hard materials. The application of high speed machining is expected to increase critical chip thickness by amplifying the prevailing pressure in the contact zone. To test this hypothesis, the machining of single cuts by turning and milling aimed at investigating the dependence of the critical depth of cut (d_c) on process parameters. The process strategy is displayed in Fig. 13.

The feed rate was set to $v_f = 160$ mm/min when machining with a cutting speed of $v_c = 400$ m/min, while it was $v_f = 1{,}600$ mm/min for $v_c = 4{,}000$ m/min, resulting in equidistant cuts on each of the specimens. All relevant machining parameters are listed in Table 4.

The determination of the critical depth of cut d_c, which is the value where a transition from ductile to brittle machining takes place, was performed by analyzing the maximum height Sz in the center of the machined single cuts. Sz describes the difference between the highest peak and the deepest valley of the surface topography and is therefore a suitable parameter for describing the nature of the material removal mechanism (ductile/brittle). With increasing depth of cut, Sz also increases and the single cuts can be separated in ductile (a), ductile-brittle (b) and brittle (c) workpiece regions, as defined in Fig. 14. These regions can be separated by means of the Sz distribution. In ductile mode, Sz linearly increases. This trend continues in ductile-brittle mode, but scatter is present. Brittle mode starts when Sz varies widely and no linear trend is apparent anymore. The analysis has been performed by a MATLAB

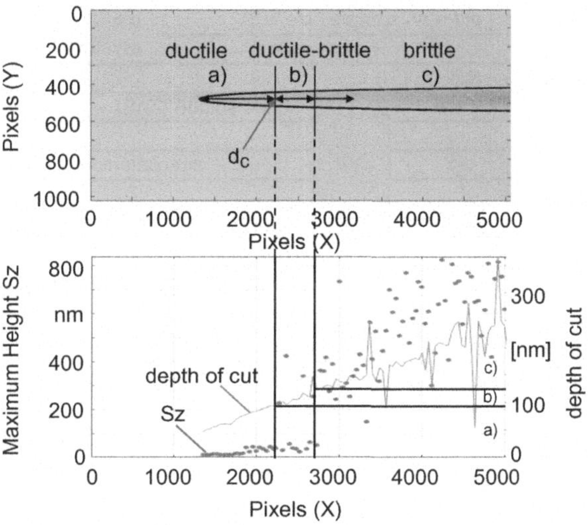

Fig. 14 Automated analysis of depth of cut a_p and maximum height Sz in single cuts to define ductile-brittle transition

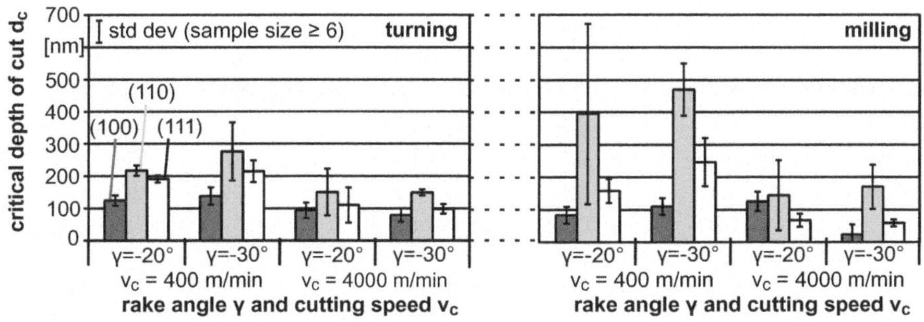

Fig. 15 Critical d_c for silicon, machined with low and high cutting speed

script, which runs through the single cuts and determines Sz on a 40 × 30 pixel area in intervals of 40 pixels. Pixel area and intervals have been chosen to maximize the covered area and minimize the offset of linearized area of curvature. 100 μm in X- and Y-direction corresponds to 306 pixels. The strong variation of a_p in the brittle region results from chipping.

Figure 15 shows the results for the critical depths of cut d_c, where the transition from ductile to ductile-brittle mode takes place, for both turning and milling. For low as well as high cutting speed, d_c increased with rising negative rake angles, especially for crystal orientation (110). However, the usual rake angles for the machining of brittle-hard materials (−20° and −30°) lead to minor values of the d_c when high cutting speeds are applied.

Fly-cutting was performed on the elemental semiconductors monocrystalline silicon (Si) and germanium (Ge) and additionally on the compound semiconductor materials zinc sulfide (ZnS) and zinc selenide (ZnSe). The latter materials are applied

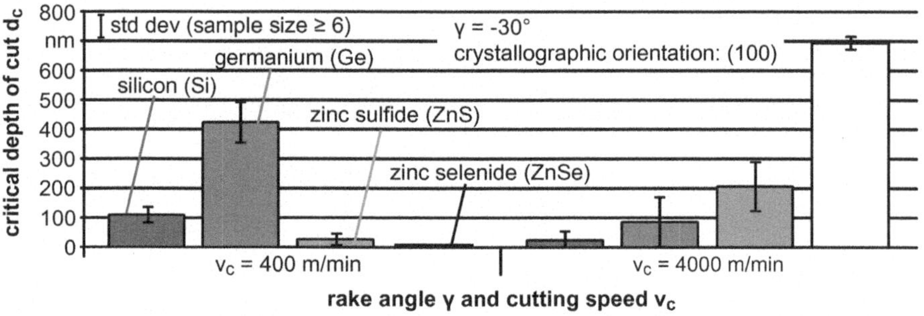

Fig. 16 Critical depth of cut d_c for silicon, germanium, zinc selenide and zinc sulfide, machined by fly-cutting with low and high cutting speed

Table 5 Detected specific cutting forces while machining of single cuts

v_c = 400 m/min	F_n [N]	F_c [N]	A_{max} [μm^2]	k_c [GPa]	d_c [nm]
Si 100	0.22	0.21	14.9	14.1	110
Ge 100	0.15	0.12	8.1		423
ZnS 100	0.44	0.27	18.1		27
ZnSe 100	0.86	0.83	56.0		1
v_c = 4,000 m/min	F_n [N]	F_c [N]	A_{max} [μm^2]	k_c [GPa]	d_c [nm]
Si 100	0.40	0.21	14.9	14.1	24
Ge 100	0.40	0.20	13.4		86
ZnS 100	0.45	0.18	12.1		206
ZnSe 100	0.42	0.22	14.8		694

for infrared optics and are experiencing a growing demand [14, 15, 19, 22]. Critical depths of cut are examined by the same procedure as for silicon and are displayed in Fig. 16.

While germanium shows the same behavior as silicon regarding the influence of the increased cutting speed, that is a reduction of d_c, the values of the two compound semiconductors zinc selenide and zinc sulfide behave in exactly the opposite way. At a cutting speed of $v_c = 400$ m/min, only a comparatively small critical chip thickness can be determined. Zinc selenide shows almost no signs of ductile cutting at conventional cutting speed. However, this changes when the cutting speed is increased to $v_c = 4,000$ m/min. Since this behavior occurs in both compound semiconductors investigated, it can be assumed that the ductile cutting ability is related to the bonding of the ions within the zinc blende structure.

To support this hypothesis, the measured normal and cutting forces (Z- and Y-direction, respectively) during machining are displayed in Table 5. Combined with the (constant) cross-section of the tool plunging into the material while cutting (A_{max}),

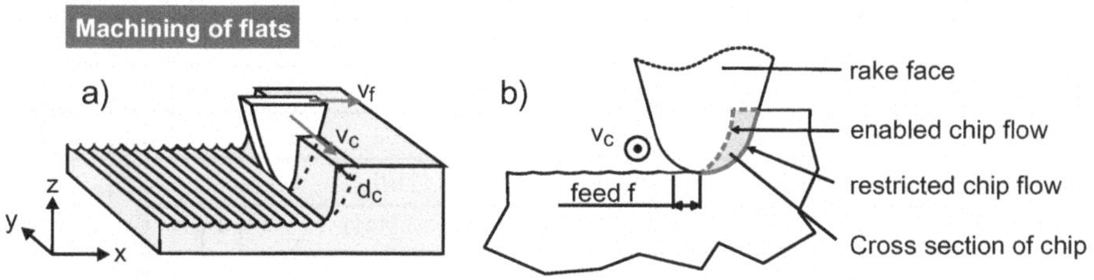

Fig. 17 Process strategy for high speed off-axis diamond turning and milling of optical flats

Table 6 Parameters for milling of flats

Parameter	Value
Cutting speed v_c	400/4,000 m/min
Feed speed v_f	5/7.5/10 μm/rev
Depth of cut a_p	3 μm
Rake angle γ	−30°

the specific cutting force k_c was calculated, giving an information on the prevailing pressure in the contact zone.

It is known from literature that the ductile machining of semiconductor materials required machining pressures of 8.8 to 16 GPa in the shear zone [12, 18]. The specific cutting forces for the machining of zinc selenide and sulfide with low cutting speed are beyond this range. Simultaneously, these are the only materials where no or only partly ductile material removal was present ($d_c < 27$ nm). For high cutting speed, all materials could be machined in ductile mode as the specific cutting forces remain in a range of 12 to 15 GPa. Obviously, the cutting of compound semiconductors requires a higher pressure in the contact zone for ductile machining.

4.2 *Process Window for HSC Machining of Optical Surfaces*

To analyze the capabilities of HSC milling optical surfaces, flats were produced by adding a feed movement in X-direction (Fig. 17). The machining of single cuts revealed that a rake angle of −30° is to be preferred for machining due to higher mean values for d_c at low cutting speed and lower standard deviations at high cutting speeds. Consequently, this angle was chosen for the machining of optical surfaces.

The parameters applied in experiments for machining of optical flats are shown in Table 6.

Subsequent to the experiments, surface roughness and subsurface damage were determined in order to evaluate the influence of cutting speed on the machined surface layer. Roughness was measured by a Taylor Hobson CCI HD white light interferometer. The arithmetic mean height Sa was chosen for analysis of the machined

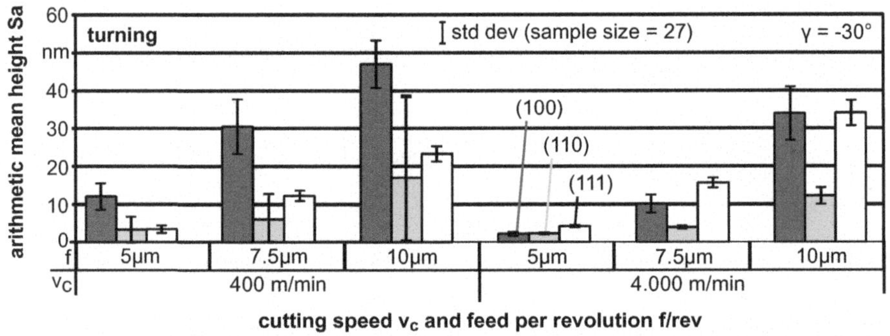

Fig. 18 Arithmetic mean height Sa for turned flats on silicon with different crystallographic orientations over cutting speed v_c and feed f for γ of $-30°$

flats in contrast to the single cuts (Sz), as this is a common parameter for areal characterization of optical surfaces.

Subsurface damage was investigated by polishing a wedge with a defined slope into the workpiece. Polishing was followed by an etching process with diluted hydrofluoric acid (0.1% HF) for exposing cracks.

Turning Experiments

Figure 18 reveals that only for workpieces with a crystal orientation of (111), a cutting speed of 400 m/min leads to superior surface quality compared to a cutting speed of 4,000 m/min, although the differences between roughness values are marginal, at least for feeds of 5 and 7.5 µm. When (100)-workpieces were machined, the arithmetic mean height for 7.5 µm feed per revolution differed between 10 nm ($v_c = 4,000$ m/min) and 30 nm ($v_c = 400$ m/min). By implication, ductile machining of this material is not possible when applying the selected parameters (Table 6) at low cutting speeds, while the high cutting speed at feeds per revolution of 5 and 7.5 µm leads to a surface roughness below 10 nm.

The reason for the superior surface quality when applying high cutting speeds in diamond turning is the evolution of high temperatures in the cutting zone. These could be observed by spark formation, as seen in Fig. 19.

Temperature measurements by infrared failed due to low resolution of the camera and a tool-sided temperature measurement could not be set up due to the tools' rotation. This is why the estimation was only made by comparing the sparking with a table for the emission of electromagnetic radiation (incandescence), as shown in Fig. 19. According to this, a temperature of 950 to 1,000 °C is present. These temperatures lead to a hardness decrease of silicon in the shear zone by a magnitude of 10 [34]. The decrease of hardness is accompanied by an indirect increase of the critical chip thickness d_c, which is a material based parameter and can be calculated by the following Eq. 6, which considers the Young's modulus E, the fracture toughness K_c and the Vickers hardness HV of the material [4]:

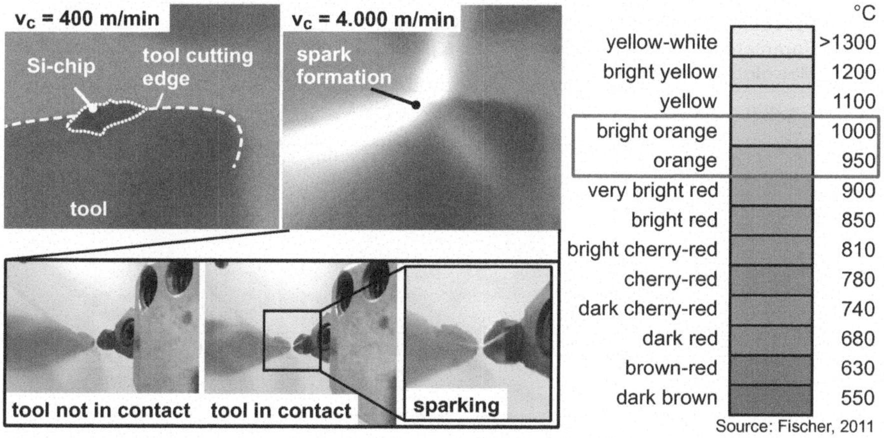

Fig. 19 Comparison between conventional cutting speed (400 m/min, top left) and high cutting speed (4,000 m/min, top middle), where sparking is present, estimated with temperatures up to 1,000 °C by annealing colors (right)

$$d_c \propto \frac{E}{HV} \cdot \left(\frac{K_c}{HV}\right)^2 \tag{6}$$

The decrease of hardness in high speed machining is relatable to the decrease of cutting forces, as shown in Fig. 20. Process forces were measured by a force dynamometer (Kistler Type 9119AA2) with a sampling rate of 20 kHz for the slower cutting speed and 50 kHz for v_c= 4,000 m/min. Because the natural frequency of the setup and the applied filtering have to be taken into account when determining force values, the natural frequency was experimentally determined by using an impulse hammer (Kistler Type 9722A) and a triaxial acceleration sensor (Kistler Type 8764B). Resulting natural frequencies were 2.8 kHz for the X- and Y-axis and 3.8 kHz for the Z-axis. It is recommended by Kistler to use only one third of these frequencies for filtering the force signals. Consequently, a 1st order Butterworth filter was applied with cutoff frequencies of 0.93 kHz for the X- and Y-axis (F_p and F_c) and 1.3 kHz for the Z-axis (F_f). The results in Fig. 20 show both the filtered and the unfiltered forces.

Although a reduction in cutting forces is discernible after filtering, this has to be attributed to the filter characteristics and the lack of datapoints for the higher cutting speed. The unfiltered values show similar peak heights for the cutting force. An on-axis turning operation was not performed due to the crystallographic orientation of semiconductor materials. The rotating workpiece would lead to varying cutting directions which result in a change of cutting force due to the occurring hardness variation.

Finally, sub surface damage (SSD) was detected for silicon on all machined crystallographic orientations by determination of the deepest crack which could be detected in the subsurface. Therefore, a wedge was polished into the machined

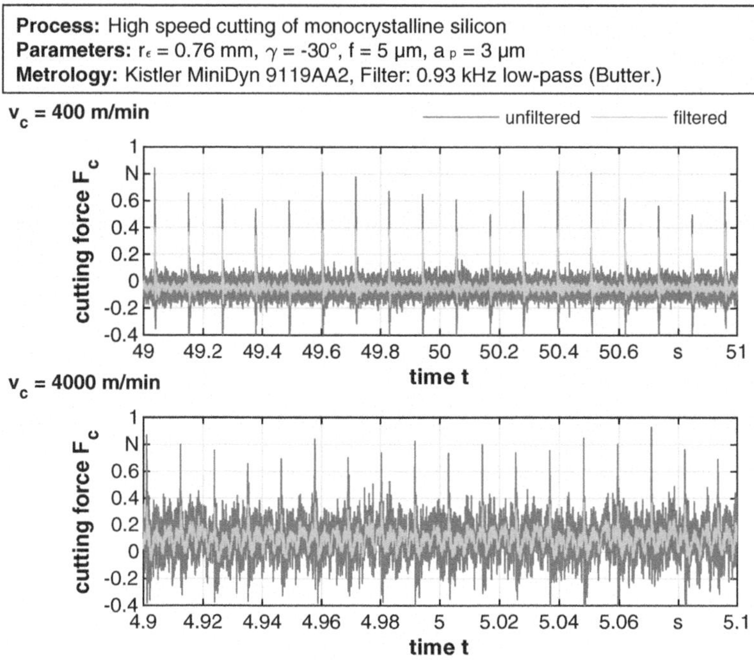

Fig. 20 Cutting Force F_c for off-axis turning of silicon with low and high cutting speed [27]

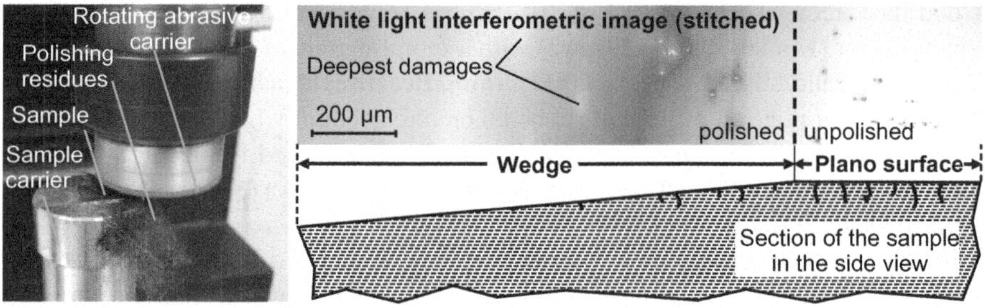

Fig. 21 Polishing procedure (left) and etching (not displayed) and subsequently performed sub-surface damage detection (right)

surface with an angle of 0.08°, which results in a linearly increasing depth up to 6 μm over a length of 4.5 mm. After etching with hydrofluoric acid, the damages were detected by white light interferometry, as illustrated in Fig. 21.

A correlation between the crack depth, shown in Fig. 22, and surface roughness (Fig. 18) can be drawn. This relationship has also been reported earlier in several investigations [11, 13]. For crystal orientations (110) and (111), the influence of cutting speed on crack depth was low, while it is pronounced for (100) specimens. In general, deeper cracks occur for this crystal orientation. For lower feed rates

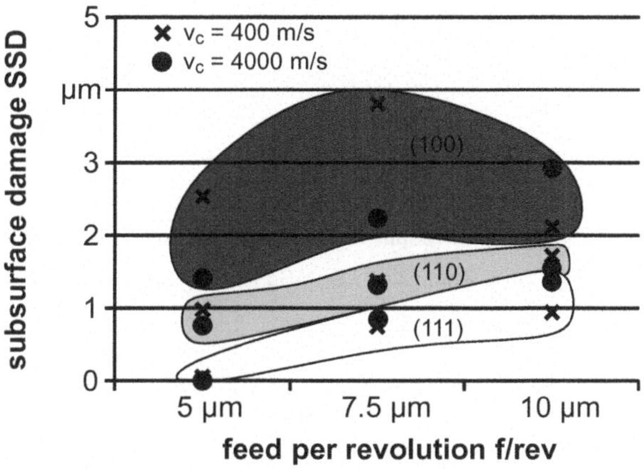

Fig. 22 Subsurface damage for turned and milled flats

(5 and 7.5 μm), higher cutting speeds are advantageous regarding crack depth, while this changes to the opposite for the high feed rate (10 μm). The crack depth varies strongly and does not follow the trend of the lower feed rates anymore. This could be explained by the brittle material removal, which occurred at such high feed rates when machining (100) specimens.

Milling (Fly-Cutting) Experiments

The milling experiments were again, like for the machining of single cuts, conducted on elemental and also on compound semiconductors.

In Fig. 23, the measurement results for surface roughness are shown by surface topographies from all machined materials in (100)-orientation. Cutting direction was <110>, respectively. In all cases, a high cutting speed leads to similar or even lower values for arithmetic mean height Sa. Additionally, Sq and Sz were measured (not displayed here), showing the same behavior.

The evaluation of the influence of different parameters on the critical chip thickness of germanium shows that it behaves similar to silicon with the same variations, though the order of magnitude of the respective critical chip thickness is higher. One hypothesis to explain this behavior is the heat capacity C and thermal conductivity k of both materials. Comparing the thermal conductivities of silicon (150 W/(m k)) and germanium (60 W/(m k)) yields a ratio of 2.5:1. The ratio for the heat capacities (silicon at 0.75 kJ/(kg K) and germanium at 0.31 kJ/(kg K)) is practically identical (2.4:1). This means that germanium reaches a higher temperature near the contact zone than silicon in a comparable process. A higher temperature can also be inferred from sparking that occurs at high cutting speeds. In the milling process used here, however, no spark formation could be observed, which is attributed to the short contact time between tool and workpiece.

While turning, the tool cuts through the whole width of the workpiece (10 mm), while the contact length l_k for milling is calculated using Eq. 7.

$$l_k = \sqrt{2 \cdot r_{fly} \cdot a_p} \tag{7}$$

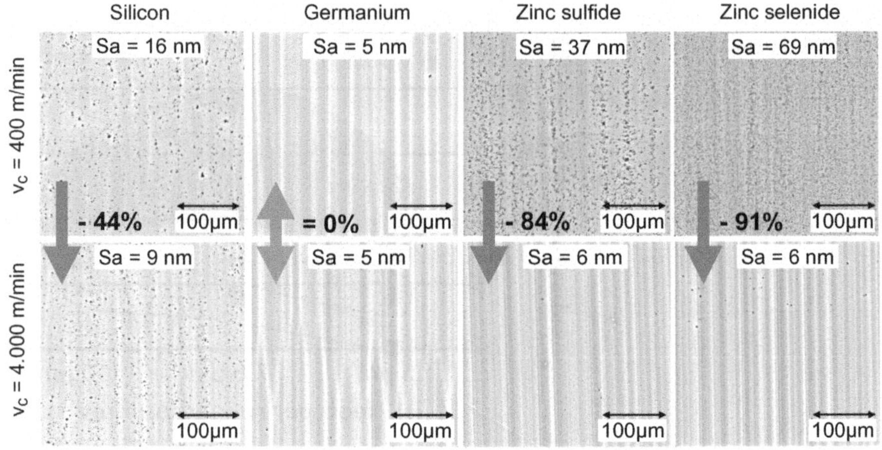

Fig. 23 Topographies of milled flat surfaces with low (top) and high (bottom) cutting speed

Table 7 Depths of last SSD occurrence for different semiconductor materials in (100)-orientation, machined by fly-cutting

Cutting speed [m/min]	**Silicon** [nm]	**Germanium** [nm]	**Zinc sulfide** [nm]	**Zinc selenide** [nm]
$v_c = 400$	500	60	730	930
$v_c = 4{,}000$	400	330	470	260

With the fly-cut-radius of $r_{fly} = 94.5$ mm and the depth of cut of $a_p = 3$ µm this calculates to $l_k = 0.75$ mm. Nevertheless, such thermal effects are also conceivable when milling germanium and would explain the observations here, because a decrease in hardness promotes ductile material behavior with increasing critical chip thickness.

The high amounts for critical cutting depths at high cutting speed for compound semiconductors zinc sulfide and zinc selenide are striking here in comparison to the elemental semiconductors. At a conventional cutting speed, hardly any ductile material behavior occurs due to the level of surface roughness, while high cutting speeds lead to an optical surface. An improvement by one order of magnitude of the roughness values between low and high cutting speed is promising, as this has never been revealed before and offers a chance to simplify the ductile machining of compound semiconductors only by increasing the cutting speed.

Subsurface damage was also analyzed after milling experiments with the same procedure as for the turning experiments (Fig. 21). However, only one specimen of each material could be examined due to the effortful procedure of polishing and etching. Results are shown in Table 7 for (100)-orientation for all materials.

Similar to the turning tests, the variation of the cutting speed had an inferior effect on the subsurface damage introduced in silicon. On germanium, on the other hand, at a cutting speed of $v_c = 400$ m/min, no major subsurface damage could be detected.

Table 8 Parameters for rough and fine cuts for examination of tool wear

Parameter	**Values**	
	Rough cuts	Fine cuts
Cutting speed v_c	400/4,000 m/min	400/4,000 m/min
Feed rate f	24.5 μm	7.5 μm
Depth of cut a_p	10 μm	3 μm
Rake angle γ	−30°	−30°

At the specified depth of 54 nm, there was only one final small noticeable feature within the surface without any major damage being detected. Other results could be observed regarding the influence of the cutting speed on the subsurface damage when machining zinc sulfide and zinc selenide. Here, an increase of cutting speed causes a reduction in the depth of damage introduced. Again, it is noticeable that the two materials with the ionic bond in the crystal lattice behave similarly to each other and in the opposite direction to the elemental semiconductors.

4.3 *Tool Wear as a Function of Cutting Speed*

The experimental setup for detecting wear as a function of cutting speed was similar to the setup shown in Fig. 12. The aim of the experimental investigations was the identification of a tool condition as a limit for ductile machining. The abort criterion was determined by the arithmetic mean height Sa, measured by white light interferometry after equidistant cutting lengths. Experiments were carried out on monocrystalline silicon with orientation (110) due to low acquisition costs for wafers and market availability. In diamond milling, with its short contact times between tool and workpiece and low chip thicknesses, tool wear is slowly progressing. In order to keep the experimental investigations in a reasonable time frame, cutting was classified into rough cuts and fine cuts, see Table 8.

Rough cuts were performed in order to generate material removal volume and provoke wear, while fine cuts were carried out to evaluate the tool's ability to cut in ductile-regime. Rough cuts were performed by raster milling on 2″ wafers with high width of cut a_e (Fig. 24, left). For the abort criterion, a finish cut was made on a $10 \times 10\ \text{mm}^2$ workpiece, like on the milling experiments in Sect. 4.2 (Fig. 24, middle). This criterion was set by measuring arithmetical mean height Sa after every 0.8 km of effective cutting length L_c by white light interferometry. The arithmetic mean height Sa was detected after fine cuts. The evolution of surface texture with rising contact length and accompanying tool wear is shown in Fig. 24, right.

Tool wear was determined by three wear parameters, e.g. flank wear land, dislocation of the cutting edge and cutting edge radius r_β. Those parameters were detected at the tool's cutting edge, as schematically shown in Fig. 25 (left), by atomic force

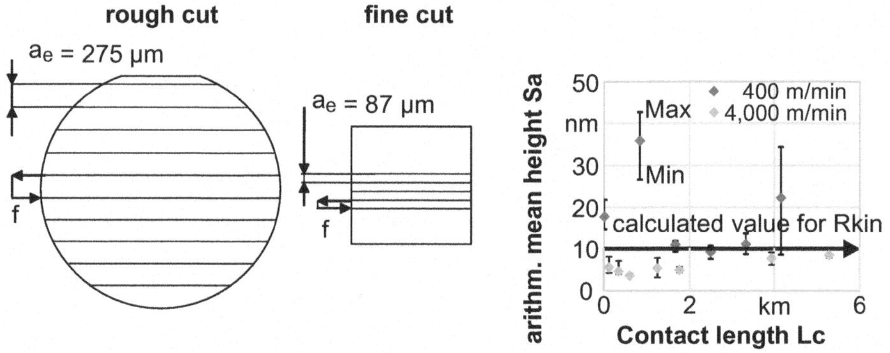

Fig. 24 Process strategies for rough and fine cuts and evolution of surface texture with rising contact length

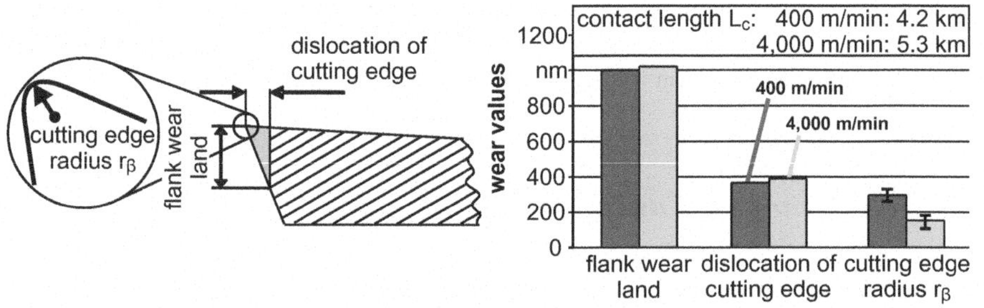

Fig. 25 Detected tool wear parameters (left) and measured values (right)

microscopy. Wear was determined after an effective contact length L_c of 4.2 km for low cutting speed and 5.3 km for high cutting speed, respectively. The different values represent the distance as long as ductile machining could be maintained. Once the values exceeded 10 nm, experiments were terminated and the final wear values were determined, as displayed in Fig. 25 (right).

Most importantly, high cutting speed does not decrease tool life. Moreover, the values for flank wear land and dislocation of cutting edge were almost the same for both applied cutting speeds, although the cutting length was 25% higher for high cutting speed. At the same time, certain values for flank wear land and dislocation of the cutting edge should not be exceeded for maintaining ductile-regime machining, which are 1,000 nm and 400 nm, respectively.

According to a schematic model of the contact geometry between diamond tool and workpiece (Fig. 26), proposed by Yan et al. [35], the cutting edge radius has an effect on the surface in contact with the workpiece material due to a change in the resultant force F. The resultant force F and its effective angle ϕ provide information on the extent to which the cutting edge radius causes a change in the machining pressure. Contact areas S_1, S_2 and finally S_{eq} are directly influenced by

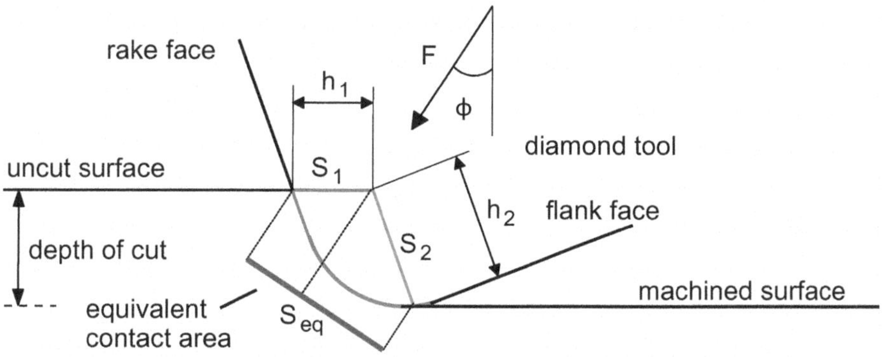

Fig. 26 Schematic model of the contact geometry between diamond tool and workpiece according to [35]

Table 9 Dependence of shear zone pressure on cutting edge radius and speed

Cutting speed v_c [m/min]	**Cutting edge radius r_β** [nm]	**Shear zone pressure k_c** [GPa]
400	28 (fresh)	1.9
	294 (worn)	3.2
4,000	64 (fresh)	13.8
	151 (worn)	8.3

this. A detailed description how the geometrical contact conditions are calculated can be found in [35].

By measuring the tangential and normal forces, the resultant force and its effective angle were calculated and set in relation to the equivalent contact area S_{eq}. The results for prevailing machining pressure, depending on the tool wear (fresh condition and abort criterion) for low and high cutting speed are shown in Table 9.

For the high cutting speed the stress decreased with increasing cutting edge radius, which is reflected in the higher roughness values with increasing machined volume, visible in Fig. 24. As only one measurement for the Sa-value exceeded 10 nm, it is assumed that the stress has not fallen below the limit value for maintaining a hydrostatic pressure and thus, no real transition to brittle machining has occurred. As already stated in Sect. 4.1, at least 8.8 GPa of pressure must be present in the shear zone to reach a ductile material removal [12, 18]. Here, the prevailing pressure while milling with conventional cutting speed remained below 8.8 GPa, which correlates with the higher Sa-values. In almost every condition the material removal was at least partly brittle, so that pressure could unload by crack propagation.

The dominant material removal mechanism was additionally analyzed by highfrequency- impulse-measurement (HFIM) with a QASS Optimizer 4D, utilizing a piezoelectric effect. The analysis is performed on structure-borne sound amplitudes, also known as acoustic emission (AE), which are plotted over time and frequency in

Table 10 Origins of emitted frequencies when cutting materials after [21]

Frequency [kHz]	Origin
0 to 32.3	Noise, elastic and plastic deformation
32.3 to 62.5	Microcavities
62.5 to 125	Shearing
125 to 250	Cleavage and microfractures
250 to 500	Inclusions
500 to 1,000	Intercrystalline microfractures

three-dimensional diagrams. Based on solid state vibrations, which cause frequencies in the audible sound range, acoustic emission is furthermore evoked by plastic deformation of the machined material. With its high sampling rates of up to 50 MHz, the origin of the emitted frequencies can be determined. According to Dhulubulu [10], the maximum values of structure-borne sound signals should depend on the strength properties of the materials and brittle failure as well as the rate of deformation, whereas the predominant frequency range can be traced back to the separation process caused in the workpiece material (see Table 10). Thus, low frequency ranges show a ductile cutting process, while the high frequency ranges are responsible for the initiation of fractures [21].

Exemplary sound amplitudes AE_{max} of the performed cutting experiments with high and low cutting speeds are shown in Fig. 27 and compared to the idle speed of the tool spindle.

Depending on the frequency range under consideration, the signal shows the interaction between tool and workpiece, as well as the background noise generated by the machine. During high speed cutting, amplitudes appear exclusively at frequency bands <125 kHz. According to Table 10, this indicates material removal in ductile mode. In contrast, the high frequency ranges, representative for brittle machining, do not show any significant signals. This is consistent with the surface characteristics and machining pressures from Fig. 24 and Table 9. Although it is not possible to distinguish between background noise and tool interaction, it can be assumed that no damage, such as microfracturing, was present.

In Fig. 28, the sums of the frequency ranges from Table 10 were calculated and the percentage of the total sum is displayed. The fine cuts in the performed sequence are shown for low and high cutting speed, respectively. The first four frequency ranges show a tendency to decrease their percentage share. In comparison, the remaining two frequency ranges tend to increase with increasing tool contact length and number of fine cuts.

Brittle material removal is characterized through the initiation and propagation of cracks into the machined material. The high amount of energy, released in very short time when cracks occur, leads to high propagation speed of the AE wave within the material. The immediate energy rise lets the atoms vibrate at high frequencies, while ductile machining generates a smoother distribution at different frequency

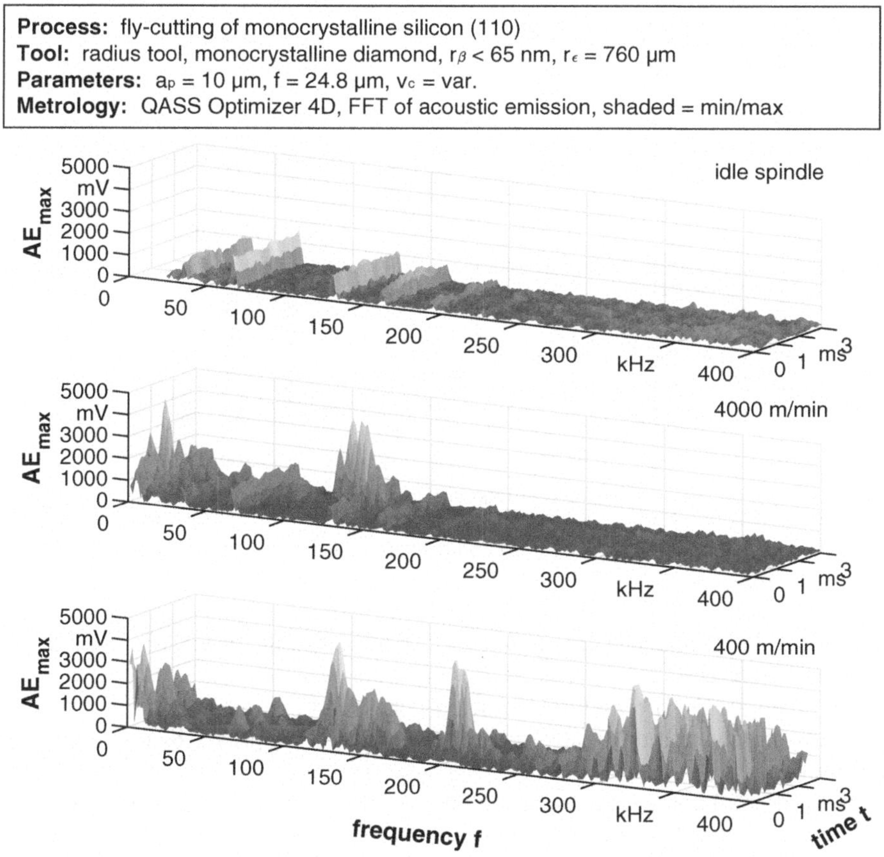

Fig. 27 Sound amplitudes of experiments with low and high cutting speed, compared to idle speed

ranges. These mechanisms are visible in Fig. 28, as the experiments with low cutting speed lead to a higher amount of brittle damage than high cutting speed and at the same time leads to a higher amount of AE signals in a high frequency range (250 to 500 kHz). Eventually, AE could not enable the in-process monitoring of tool wear, but it was capable for the characterization of the material removal mechanism.

4.4 Conclusion on UP-HSC of Brittle Materials

The aim of the study within this section was the fundamental investigation of the material behavior at high speed cutting of brittle materials, e.g. elemental semiconductors (Si, Ge) and compound semiconductors (ZnS, ZnSe). Off-axis diamond turning and fly-cutting were performed for the determination of critical depth of cut,

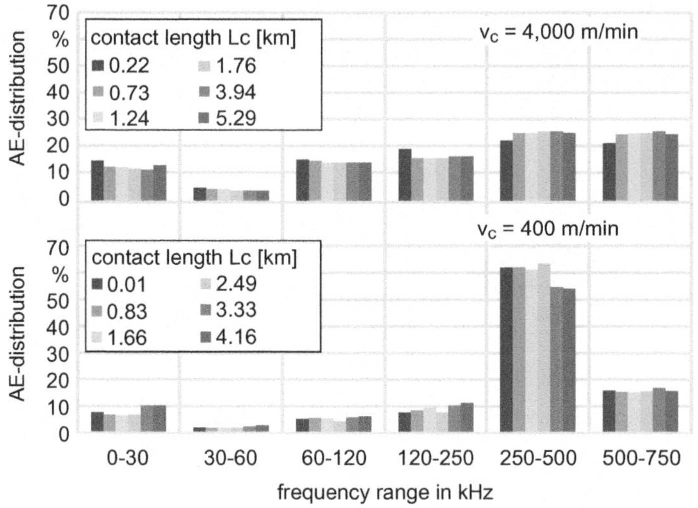

Fig. 28 Topographies of milled flat surfaces with low (top) and high (bottom) cutting speed

surface roughness and subsurface damage. Additionally, the progression of the tool wear was analyzed.

The main results are highlighted again below and prove for the first time that ductile machining of brittle materials can be significantly improved by just increasing the cutting speed.

The critical depth of cut for machining of single grooves is not increased by high speed cutting for elemental semiconductors, while it is for compound semiconductors. This circumstance is related to the ion bonding within the zinc blende structure of the compound semiconductors, which makes these IR materials brittle (lower hardness and similar fracture toughness compared to elemental semiconductors). While machining with conventional cutting speed, the machining pressure in the contact zone is not sufficient for ductile material removal (hydrostatic pressure) and results in brittle material removal. This changes with the application of HSC, where the machining pressure is in a range between 9 and 15 GPa, considered in literature as the suitable range for ductile machining [12, 18].

The achievable surface roughness when flat turning or milling improves with increasing cutting speed, which is related to the elevated machining pressure in the contact zone. In off-axis turning at high contact lengths per cut, temperature development plays a major role for the plasticization of the material, which promotes ductile chip formation instead of brittle material removal. The temperatures in the contact zone were estimated to 950 to 1,000 °C. These high temperatures were not detected while fly-cutting due to short contact lengths per cut, and consequently the reduction of surface roughness while the machining of elemental semiconductors was not as distinct as for off-axis turning. Still, all machined surface textures did not deteriorate in comparison to conventional cutting speeds so that the advantage of reduced machining times is valid without restrictions. For compound semiconductors, the reduction of surface roughness when HSC was 84% and 91% for ZnS and ZnSe, respectively.

Subsurface damage was detected by polishing and etching all machined materials and correlates to the surface roughness, particularly demonstrated in fly-cutting experiments.

For turning operations, tool wear increases with elevated cutting speed due to high temperatures in the contact zone, which lies above the thermal stability of the diamond tool. For milling operations, tool wear decreases by 25% when high cutting speeds are applied, which is related to the shorter contact times, as it has already been stated in Sect. 3.2 for ductile materials.

The process analysis by acoustic emission was not suitable for tool wear detection, but a procedure for the analysis of material removal mechanism (ductile/brittle) was proposed. When the signals are located in high frequency ranges, a brittle material removal occurs, while ductile machining is connected with an even distribution of frequencies over the whole analyzed range.

5 Conclusion and Outlook

It was shown in this research work that high cutting speeds are beneficial for ultra-precision machining, not only for reducing the required machining time, but also for improving the material removal behavior, by reducing the process forces and wear in metal cutting and facilitating a ductile-mode cutting of brittle materials.

Overall, this offers a great potential for improving the economic viability of industrially applied diamond milling, as long as the feed rates are increased as well (see Chap. 3) and the auxiliary processes for balancing are automated (see Chap. 4).

References

1. Abouridouane, M.: Bruchverhalten von Leichtmetallen unter Impact- Beanspruchung. Ph.D. thesis. RWTH Aachen (2005)
2. Bäker, M.: An investigation of the chip segmentation process using finite elements. Tech. Mech. **23**(1), 1–9 (2003)
3. Ben Amor, R.: Thermomechanische Wirkmechanismen und Spanbildung bei der Hochgeschwindigkeitszerspanung. Berichte aus dem IFW 03/2003 (2003)
4. Bifano, T.G., Dow, T.A., Scattergood, R.O.: Ductile-regime grinding: a new technology for machining brittle materials. J. Eng. Ind. **113**(2), 184 (1991). https://doi.org/10.1115/1.2899676
5. Brinksmeier, E., Ohlsen, I., Preuss, W.: Dependence of the cutting forces on cutting speed in high speed diamond turning. In: 29th ASPE Annual Meeting, Boston, USA, 9–14 November 2014, vol. 29, pp. 492–493 (2014)
6. Brinksmeier, E., Menten, A., Preuss, W.: Tool wear in high speed diamond milling. In: 29th ASPE Annual Meeting, Boston, USA, 9–14 November 2014, vol. 29, pp. 494–495 (2014)
7. Brinksmeier, E., Preuss, W., Riemer, O., Rentsch, R.: Ultraprecision high speed cutting. In: 30th ASPE Annual Meeting, pp. 58–63 (2015)

8. Brinksmeier, E., Preuss, W., Riemer, O., Rentsch, R.: Cutting forces, tool wear and surface finish in high speed diamond machining. Precis. Eng. (2017). https://doi.org/10.1016/j.precisioneng.2017.02.018
9. Chao, C.L., Ma, K.J., Liu, D.S., Bai, C.Y., Shy, T.L.: Ductile behaviour in single-point diamond-turning of single-crystal silicon. J. Mater. Process. Technol. **127**(2), 187–190 (2002). https://doi.org/10.1016/s0924-0136(02)00124-3
10. Dhulubulu, A.: Acoustic Emission (AE) monitoring of the milling process with coated metal carbide inserts using TRIM C270 cutting fluid. MA thesis. University of Toledo (2015)
11. Esmaeilzare, A., Rahimi, A., Rezaei, S.M.: Investigation of subsurface damages and surface roughness in grinding process of Zerodur® glass-ceramic. Appl. Surf. Sci. **313**, 67–75 (2014). https://doi.org/10.1016/j.apsusc.2014.05.137
12. Goel, S., Luo, X., Agrawal, A., Reuben, R.L.: Diamond machining of silicon: a review of advances in molecular dynamics simulation. Int. J. Mach. Tools Manuf **88**, 131–164 (2015). https://doi.org/10.1016/j.ijmachtools.2014.09.013
13. Hed, P.P., Edwards, D.F.: Relationship between subsurface damage depth and surface roughness during grinding of optical glass with diamond tools. Appl. Opt. **26**(13), 2491 (1987). https://doi.org/10.1364/ao.26.002491
14. Hodgson, B., Lettington, A.H., Stillwell, P.F.T.C., Baker, L.R., Masson, A.: Diamond turning of infra-red components. In: Infrared Technology and Applications. SPIE, May 1986. https://doi.org/10.1117/12.951967
15. Jasinevicius, R.G.: Influence of cutting conditions scaling in the machining of semiconductors crystals with single point diamond tool. J. Mater. Process. Technol. **179**(1–3), 111–116 (2006). https://doi.org/10.1016/j.jmatprotec.2006.03.106
16. Kármán, T.V.: Festigkeitsversuche unter allseitigem Druck (Strength tests under pressure from all sides). In: Zeitschrift des Vereines Deutscher Ingenieure 55 (1911). (in German)
17. King, R.F., Tabor, D.: The strength properties and frictional behaviour of brittle solids. Proc. Royal Soc. Lond. Ser. A. Math. Phys. Sci. **223**(1153), 225–238 (1954). https://doi.org/10.1098/rspa.1954.0111
18. Kovalchenko, A.M., Milman, Y.V.: On the cracks self-healing mechanism at ductile mode cutting of silicon. Tribol. Int. **80**, 166–171 (2014). https://doi.org/10.1016/j.triboint.2014.07.003
19. Li, S., Zhang, Y.: Application of single point diamond turning in infrared optics. In: 2016 International Symposium on Advances in Electrical, Electronics and Computer Engineering. Atlantis Press (2016). https://doi.org/10.2991/isaeece-16.2016
20. Liu, K., Li, X.P., Rahman, M.: Characteristics of high speed micro-cutting of tungsten carbide. J. Mater. Process. Technol. **140**(1–3), 352–357 (2003). https://doi.org/10.1016/s0924-0136(03)00758-1
21. Mian, A.J., Driver, N., Mativenga, P.T.: Chip formation in microscale milling and correlation with acoustic emission signal. Int. J. Adv. Manuf. Technol. **56**(1–4), 63–78 (2011). https://doi.org/10.1007/s00170-011-3185-x
22. Navare, J., Kang, D., Zaytsev, D., Bodlapati, C., Ravindra, D., Shahinian, H.: Experimental investigation on the effect of crystal orientation of diamond tooling on micro laser assisted diamond turning of zinc sulfide. Proc. Manuf. **48**, 606–610 (2020). https://doi.org/10.1016/j.promfg.2020.05.088
23. Neo, W.K., Kumar, A.S., Rahman, M.: A review on the current research trends in ductile regime machining. Int. J. Adv. Manuf. Technol. **63**(5–8), 465–480 (2012). https://doi.org/10.1007/s00170-012-3949-y
24. Nieminen, I., Paro, J., Kauppinen, V.: High-speed milling of advanced materials. J. Mater. Process. Technol. **56**(1–4), 24–36 (1996). https://doi.org/10.1016/0924-0136(95)01817-4
25. Preuss, W.: A Guide to Diamond Machining. Shaker-Verlag (2019)
26. Salomon, C.: Verfahren zur Bearbeitung von Metallen oder bei einer Bearbeitung durch schneidende Werkzeuge sich aehnlich verhaltenden Werkstoffen. DE523594C. Krupp AG, 27 April 1931

27. Schönemann, L., Berger, D., Dörgeloh, T., Riemer, O., Brinksmeier, E., Krüger, R., Schreiber, P., Denkena, B., Hochbein, J., Parsa, N., Schenck, C., Kuhfuss, B.: Synergistic approaches to ultra-precision high performance cutting. CIRP J. Manuf. Sci. Technol. **28**, 38–51 (2020). https://doi.org/10.1016/j.cirpj.2019.12.001
28. Schulz, H., Spur, G.: High speed turn-milling - a new precision manufacturing technology for the machining of rotationally symmetrical workpieces. CIRP Ann. **39**(1), 107–109 (1990). https://doi.org/10.1016/s0007-8506(07)61013-0
29. Schulz, H., Moriwaki, T.: High-speed machining. CIRP Ann. **41**(2), 637–643 (1992). https://doi.org/10.1016/S0007-8506(07)63250-8
30. Schulz, H.: Hochgeschwindigkeits-Bearbeitung - Technologie mit Zukunft. Werkstatt und Betrieb **127**(7/8), 539–541 (1994)
31. Schneider, T.: Aufwand, Nutzen und Grenzen des Hochgeschwindigkeitsdrehens. German. Darmstädter Forschungsberichte für Konstruktion und Fertigung. Shaker Verlag, Aachen, 25 July 1996
32. Shibata, T., Fujii, S., Makino, E., Ikeda, M.: Ductile-regime turning mechanism of single-crystal silicon. Precis. Eng. **18**(2–3), 129–137 (1996). https://doi.org/10.1016/0141-6359(95)00054-2
33. Tönshoff, H.K., Karpuschewski, B., Blawit, C.: Hochgeschwindigkeitszerspanung - Stand der Technik und Entwicklungstendenzen. VDI-Z **139**(9), 26–33 (1997)
34. Vandeperre, L.J., Giuliani, F., Lloyd, S.J., Clegg, W.J.: The hardness of silicon and germanium. Acta Mater. **55**(18), 6307–6315 (2007). https://doi.org/10.1016/j.actamat.2007.07.036
35. Yan, J., Asami, T., Harada, H., Kuriyagawa, T.: Fundamental investigation of subsurface damage in single crystalline silicon caused by diamond machining. Precis. Eng. **33**(4), 378–386 (2009). https://doi.org/10.1016/j.precisioneng.2008.10.008
36. Zhang, X., Liu, K., Kumar, A.S., Rahman, M.: A study of the diamond tool wear suppression mechanism in vibration-assisted machining of steel. J. Mater. Process. Technol. **214**(2), 496–506 (2014). https://doi.org/10.1016/j.jmatprotec.2013.10.002
37. Zhong, Z.W., Tok, W.H.: Grinding of single-crystal silicon along crystallographic directions. Mater. Manuf. Processes **18**(5), 811–824 (2003). https://doi.org/10.1081/amp-120024977

Electromagnetic Ultra-Precision Linear Guide

Rudolf Krüger, Benjamin Bergmann, and Berend Denkena

Abstract While electromagnetic levitation systems are already available for ultra-precision applications, they are limited to inspection or measurement tasks and non-mechanical processing due to their severely limited stiffness. This contribution introduces a novel electromagnetic linear guide, which was specifically developed for use in ultra-precision high performance machining. The active guide system features a position noise and a mean positioning error in the low nanometer range. At the same time, it provides sufficient dynamic stiffness for diamond machining. Furthermore, the actuator and sensor capabilities of the electromagnetic linear guide are applied to increase motion dynamics while reducing dynamic disturbances in motion phases by up to 75%. The capability of the new electromagnetic linear guide is finally shown for a reference diamond machining process.

1 Electromagnetic Bearings in Production Engineering

The performance of ultra-precision machine tools is largely influenced by the configuration of the feed and rotary axes. In particular, the implemented bearing solutions (including rotational bearings and linear guides) represent a limiting factor with regard to applicable motion dynamics and productivity. Conventional bearing technologies, such as roller bearings, typically rely on mechanical connections. Due to their high mechanical tolerances and considerable friction during operation, they are rarely used for the main axes of ultra-precision machine tools. Hydrostatic and aerostatic bearings, on the other hand, utilize fluid media for force transmission and

R. Krüger (✉) · B. Bergmann (✉) · B. Denkena
Institute of Production Engineering and Machine Tools IFW, Leibniz University Hannover, Garbsen, Germany
e-mail: bergmann@ifw.uni-hannover.de

R. Krüger
e-mail: Krueger_r@ifw.uni-hannover.de

E. Brinksmeier and L. Schönemann (eds.), *Ultra-precision High Performance Cutting*, Lecture Notes in Production Engineering, https://doi.org/10.1007/978-3-030-83765-5_4

allow for almost frictionless operation. Hydrostatic bearings in particular exhibit exceptional stiffness and damping due to the use of viscous fluids. However, with increasing motion dynamics, they become more susceptible to fluidic friction and thermal issues, which may ultimately affect accuracy or even dynamic transmission behavior (i.e. stiffness and damping). As a consequence, there is usually a trade-off between permissible motion dynamics and positioning accuracy.

In this context, electromagnetic levitation represents a promising technology for rotational bearings and linear guides in ultra-precision machine tools. Electromagnetic bearings provide contactless force transmission and truly friction-free operation, which, in turn, allows for extremely fast motion without sacrificing positioning accuracy or stiffness. Moreover, active control of the electromagnetic bearings provides additional functions that can be beneficial for the setup and operation of ultra-precision machine tools. The integrated air gap sensors enable continuous position monitoring of the levitating component in up to five degrees of freedom. At the same time, the integrated actuators can be used to manipulate the position (perpendicular to the feed direction) and orientation of the levitating component. Practical applications of these functions include the compensation of geometric errors, feed forward control of dynamic disturbance forces and active damping of structural vibrations, which may be introduced through the machining process or the feed drives [2–4].

Electromagnetic levitation systems for ultra-precision applications are already available, however, they are limited to inspection or measurement tasks and non-mechanical processing because of their severely limited stiffness [12, 13]. On the other hand, known electromagnetic bearings and linear guides for machining applications do not provide the required accuracy for ultra-precision machining processes [1, 4, 15, 16]. Hence, the first objective of the presented research project is the design of an electromagnetic linear guide that combines sufficient accuracy and stiffness for ultra-precision diamond machining. In this context, general requirements for ultra-precision machining include a form accuracy of 100 nm and a kinematic surface roughness of less than 10 nm. The second objective is to investigate the potential of electromagnetic linear guides for increased productivity in ultra-precision machining by applying the active guide system's actuator and sensor functions.

First, this chapter begins with design considerations for the new electromagnetic linear guide and its integration in a three-axis milling machine prototype (Sect. 2). Then, modeling and model-based control design are presented (Sects. 3 and 4). Following an initial proof of concept (Sect. 5), the distinct properties and functionalities of the electromagnetic linear guide are examined in more detail to obtain key performance figures (Sect. 6). In particular, the position noise (Sect. 6.1), the micro-positioning capability (Sect. 6.2) and the dynamic stiffness (Sect. 6.4) of the active guide system are determined. Next, advanced functions of the electromagnetic linear guide with regard to compensation of systematic errors and feed-forward control of dynamic disturbance forces are investigated (Sect. 7). Afterwards, the capability of the new linear guide is evaluated for the use in ultra-precision diamond machining (Sect. 8). The chapter closes with a conclusion, discussing the presented findings and research questions for future work (Sect. 9).

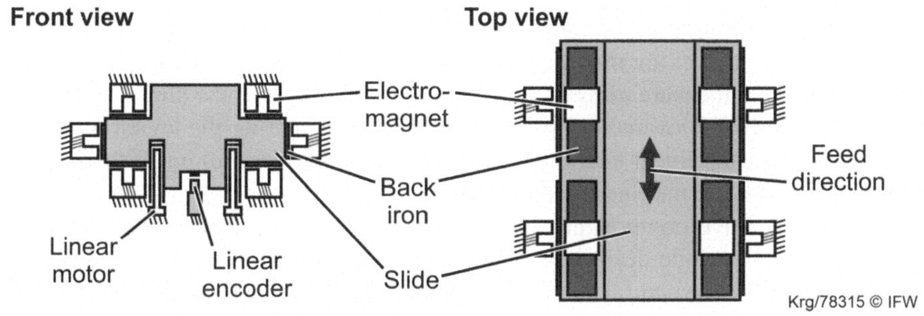

Fig. 1 Conceptual design for the electromagnetically guided feed axis [10]

2 Design and Assembly of the Electromagnetic Linear Guide

The following section introduces the fundamental design considerations for the new electromagnetic linear guide. Here, functional requirements of electromagnetic levitation systems as well as design principles for ultra-precision machines are considered. Furthermore, the implementation of the new guide system into a 3-axis milling machine tool as well as the layout of power, measurement and control electronics are considered.

2.1 Mechanical Setup

The design of electromagnetic levitation systems usually involves an iterative approach as the arrangement and specification of the electromagnets have a significant impact on the overall mechanical structure of the machine, which, in turn, may affect the requirements for the electromagnetic actuators. For this reason, a systematic approach is proposed in [5], which breaks down the complex design procedure into several work steps, including requirements definition, electromagnet arrangement and design, integration of feed drive and sensor systems, as well as material selection. With the proposed procedure, a set of twelve electromagnets in differential arrangement, with each two opposing magnets forming a bidirectional actuator, was selected for the functional basis of the new linear guide system, see Fig. 1. In comparison to a purely symmetrical arrangement with angled electromagnets, a differential arrangement requires more individual electromagnets. However, at the same time, the differential arrangement enables a more compact electromagnet design. Furthermore, it allows for a higher level of functional independence when controlling the levitating slide's five degrees of freedom.

In feed direction, the slide is actuated by two ironless linear motors with an optical scale for position feedback. Here, the use of two smaller motors instead of a single large one supports a compact, rigid and symmetrical design of the slide body. The linear motors are mounted recessed in the slide. Together with the magnet arrangement, this measure aims at a force application close to the slide's center of gravity to minimize unwanted tilting moments when actuating the levitating slide. In the same way, the linear encoder is recessed in the slide to minimize the impact of Abbe errors on the measured feed position.

Further, all active components are mounted to the guide frame to allow for a completely passive slide design, which avoids supply lines as potential sources of friction effects. The structural components of the linear guide are made from natural granite for improved material damping and thermal stability.

2.2 Electromagnet Design

The specific design of an electromagnet presents a challenging task due to highly non-linear properties and multiple parameter interdependencies. For the application at hand, a multi-stage design and optimization procedure utilizing a finite element simulation (FEM) and a multi-objective genetic algorithm was applied [7]. First, the electromagnet dimensions were estimated using an analytical force model with the specified force requirements. Then, a parametric finite element simulation was set up to validate the analytical model and to investigate the effect of electrical and geometrical parameters. Finally, the finite element simulation was coupled to a multi-objective genetic algorithm to identify a parameter set which satisfies the force requirements with minimum electrical losses.

The final design is based on a compact E-shaped magnet core made from laminated electrical steel (M250-35A) with a copper coil around the center pole (see Fig. 2 on the left). The design further incorporates aluminum fixtures and an integrated safety bearing made from brass. Moreover, a capacitive probe is mounted to the electromagnet in order to measure the air gap directly at the core. The spatial proximity of sensor and actuator aims to reduce the uncertainty for the identification of the control variable (i.e. the air gap). However, it also leads to considerable signal noise levels of the capacitive measurement system. In particular, the use of pulse width modulation (PWM) to adjust the referenced coil current can result in severe interference between the electromagnets and the capacitive probes [9]. Hence, the introduction of electrical isolation between electromagnet and probe, but also between back iron and measurement target, presents an imperative measure to reduce the signal noise levels. Accordingly, sensor holders made from a machinable glass ceramic (Macor) were used to attach the capacitive probes to the electromagnets. In combination with resolute grounding measures, the signal noise was reduced by more than 44% in average compared to aluminum sensor holders. Further, the use of the glass ceramic material reduced the thermal deflection of the sensor surface to less than 1 μm in the thermal steady state [9].

The electromagnet is complemented by a magnetic back iron made from low alloy steel (S355J2(+N)) to transfer the magnetic pulling force to the granite slide as

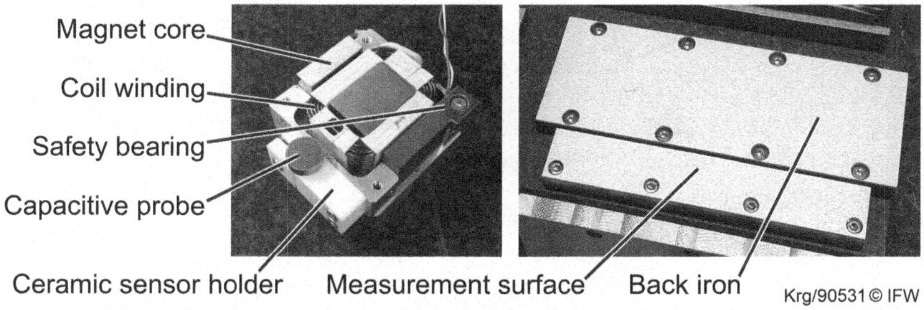

Fig. 2 Electromagnet and back iron design for the new guide system [9]

Table 1 Technical specification of the final electromagnet design

Specification	Value
Pole surface	8.25 cm^2
Air gap	0.2 mm
Number of turns	50
Coil inductivity (@ 1 T)	3.95 mH
Coil resistance	0.084 Ω
Coil current (nominal/maximum)	6.2 A/12 A
Flux density (nominal/maximum)	1 T/1.6 T
Magnet force (nominal/maximum)	300 N/700 N

well as a separate measurement surface made from high-strength steel (X5CrNi18-10, see Fig. 2 on the right). The measurement targets are electrically separated from the magnetic back iron and wired to a central grounding point, which connects to the reference ground input of the capacitive measurement amplifiers. The technical specifications of the final electromagnet design are summarized in Table 1.

2.3 *Specification and Assembly*

With the specification of the electromagnets, the initial concept was transferred into a detailed design which also considered additional components, such as linear motors and feedback systems, with their technical specifications. Figure 3 shows the components of the electromagnetic linear guide in an exploded view without the guide frame.

The final design includes capacitive probes with a dynamic resolution of 2.5 nm at 10 kHz (PISeca D-510.051 with E-852.10 signal amplifier). The ironless linear motors (Tecnotion UM9) provide a total maximum force of 600 N, which allows for an acceleration of up to 14 m s^{-2} for the slide with a mass of 42 kg. Additional motor filters (Copley Controls XTL-FA-01) are used to reduce current noise and

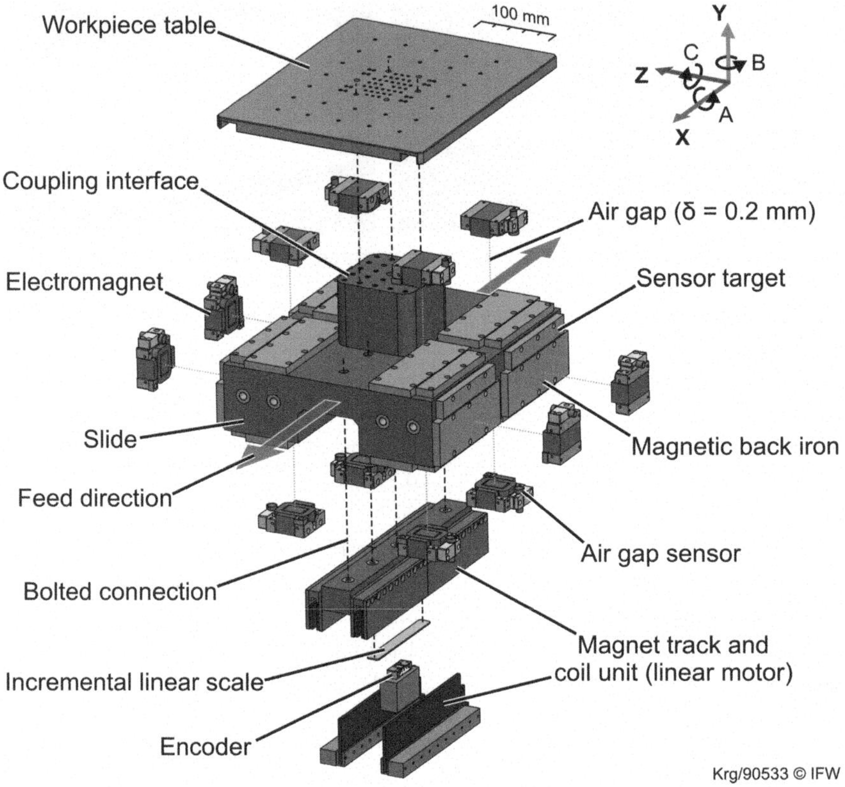

Fig. 3 Setup of the electromagnetically guided feed axis (exploded view without frame)

standstill jitter. Position feedback in feed direction is provided by an incremental linear scale (Renishaw RELM with TONiC T1011 encoder) with a resolution of up to 1 nm. Figures 4 and 5 provide further impressions of the actual design for the electromagnetic linear guide.

2.4 *Integration in a 3-Axis Milling Machine*

The desired fly-cutting reference process requires at least three controlled degrees of freedom in linear directions for feed, infeed and crossfeed [14]. Thus, the electromagnetically guided feed axis was combined with a secondary axis (Z-direction) guided by porous media aerostatic bearings for a 2-axis positioning stage. The stage features a box-in-a-box design for a minimum error budget and structural components made from natural granite. The 2-axis stage is complemented by a portal construction with a vertical axis (Y-direction) and a high-speed air bearing spindle (Professional

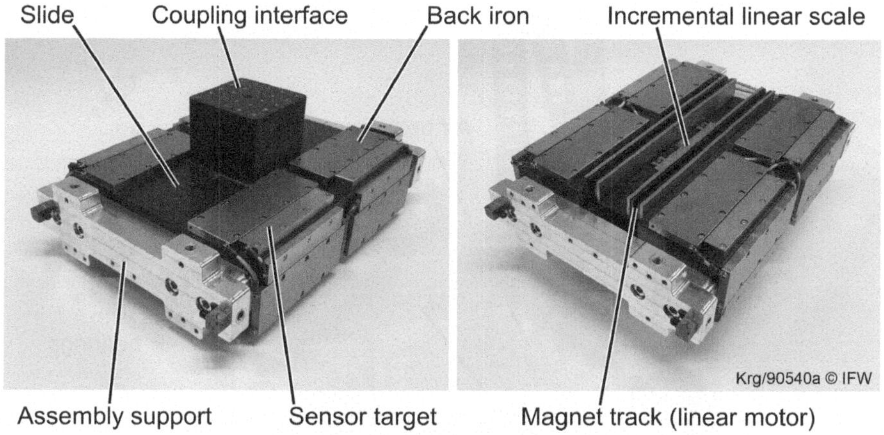

Fig. 4 Granite slide of the constructed test bench (top and bottom view) [14]

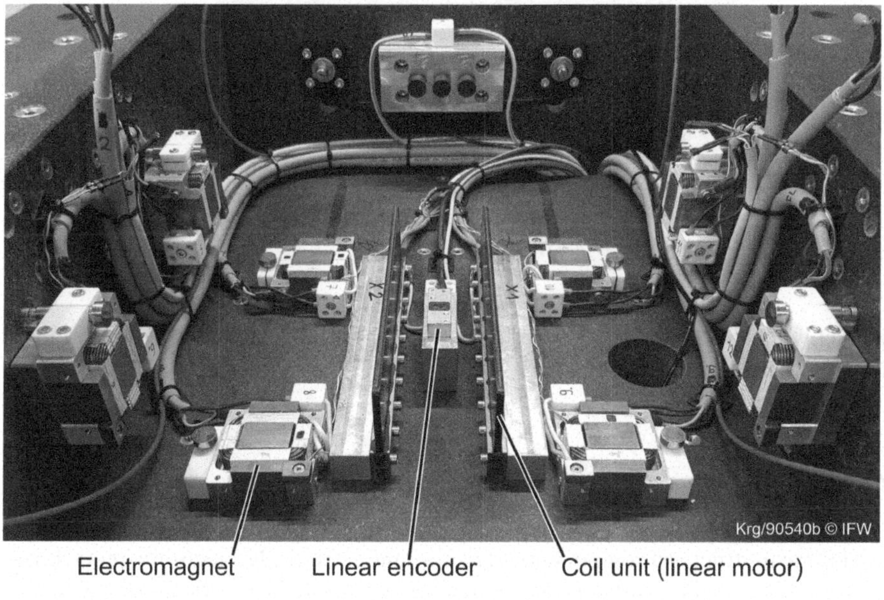

Fig. 5 Open guide frame (without top plate) of the constructed test bench [14]

Instruments Block-Head 4R). The vertical Y-axis features a servo motor, a reduction gearbox, roller bearings as well as two encoders for motor commutation and position feedback. The vertical Y-axis is primarily used for the infeed, which is static for the intended machining processes. Hence, motion accuracy of the Y-axis is of secondary importance and roller bearings are applicable in this case. The complete 3-axis milling machine tool prototype is shown in Fig. 6. Moreover, the machine tool design provides the flexibility for different configurations, e.g. to enable micro

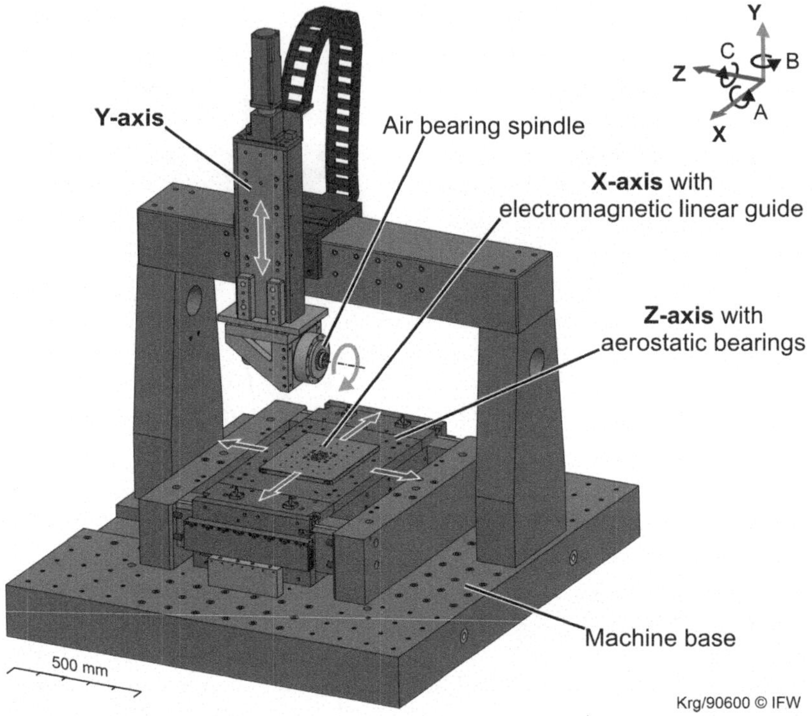

Fig. 6 3-axis milling machine prototype

milling with a vertically mounted spindle or high-precision planing with stationary diamond tools.

2.5 Power, Measurement and Control Electronics

In addition to structural components, actuators and sensors, the electromagnetic linear guide requires further hardware components, e.g. to evaluate sensor signals, calculate control variables and supply current to the electromagnets and linear motors. The complete hardware structure of the electromagnetically guided feed axis is illustrated in Fig. 7.

An industrial computer (Beckhoff C6930) is used as a central control system for the entire test bench. It provides a real-time control environment (TwinCAT) and an Ethernet-based real-time communication protocol (EtherCAT). Due to the large amount of data and the real-time requirements of the control application, an EtherCAT port multiplier is used for parallel data handling. Communication with the servo controller for the linear motors (Copley Controls XE2-230-20) is directly established via EtherCAT connection with a sample rate of 16 kHz (according to

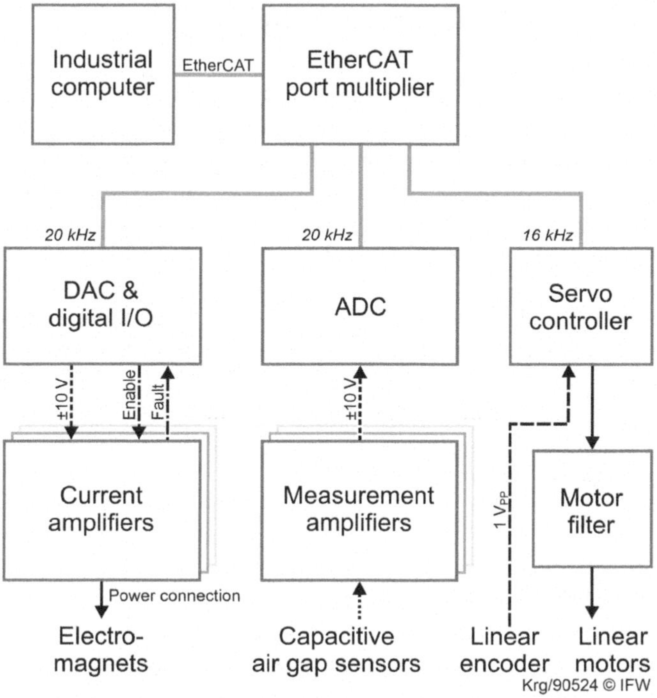

Fig. 7 Functional components as well as power and data connections of the magnetically levitated feed axis

the servo controllers PWM frequency). The servo controllers run in current control mode, the position and velocity control loops are implemented in the TwinCAT control environment. The signals of the capacitive measurement system are transferred to the control environment via analog-to-digital converters. Similarly, digital-to-analog converters provide reference values for the current amplifiers of the electromagnetic levitation system (Copley Controls JSP-180-020). Additional digital terminals control the current amplifiers' switch-on command, synchronization and fault detection. Communication between the industrial computer and the various terminals is established via EtherCAT with a maximum sample rate of 20 kHz, which corresponds to the current PWM switching frequency of the current amplifiers. The base time of the overall control system is set to 12.5 μs to cope with the different sample rates of the electromagnetic levitation system and the feed drives.

3 Modeling of the Mechatronic System

Electromagnetic bearings utilizing magnetic reluctance forces are inherently unstable systems. Accordingly, stable levitation requires a control system which continuously monitors the magnetic air gaps and adjusts the magnetic forces by calculating the appropriate coil currents for the electromagnets. However, due to the unstable and highly non-linear characteristics of electromagnets, commonly used heuristic control design methods cannot be applied for electromagnetic bearings and linear guides. Therefore, model-based control design methods present a purposeful way to determine stable control parameters without the risk of damaging or destroying the magnetic levitation system. For this, a simulation model is required that reproduces the fundamental properties and relationships of the real system [6]. The following section considers a mechanical model of the magnetic levitation system, coordinate transformation and force allocation mechanisms, as well as a model of the non-linear force characteristics of electromagnets.

3.1 Mechanical System

The mechanical system model of an electromagnetic linear guide usually consists of a single levitating object. The levitating component can be described by its equation of motion (1) with the matrices $\boldsymbol{M}$, $\boldsymbol{D}$ and $\boldsymbol{K}$, characterizing mass, damping and stiffness, as well as the generalized coordinates $\boldsymbol{q}$ and the generalized forces $\boldsymbol{Q}$, see Eqs. (2) and (3) The levitating slide's center of gravity is used as reference for the presented modeling approach.

$$\boldsymbol{M}\ddot{\boldsymbol{q}} + \boldsymbol{D}\dot{\boldsymbol{q}} + \boldsymbol{K}\boldsymbol{q} = \boldsymbol{q} \tag{1}$$

$$\boldsymbol{q} = \left[x \; y \; z \; a \; b \; c\right]^T \tag{2}$$

$$\boldsymbol{Q} = \left[F_x \; F_y \; F_z \; M_x \; M_y \; M_z\right]^T \tag{3}$$

Typically, a levitating component exhibits no significant friction or damping. In case of an electromagnetic levitation system, these properties are imposed by controlling the magnetic forces. Hence, the kinematic and dynamic properties of the magnetically suspended component can be described with the inverse mass matrix $\boldsymbol{M}^{-1}$ and a double integrator according to Eq. (4).

$$\ddot{\boldsymbol{q}} = \mathbf{M}^{-1}\boldsymbol{Q} \tag{4}$$

Using experimental modal analysis, the first natural frequency (i.e. the first eigenmode) of the slide was identified at approximately 1,600 Hz. This frequency value greatly exceeds the expected actuator dynamics. In this case, assuming a rigid slide body presents a valid approach and the structural dynamics can be neglected in the simulation model.

3.2 Coordinate Transformation

Using generalized coordinates, i.e. the translational and rotational degrees of freedom according to (2), presents an intuitive approach to describe the motion state of the electromagnetically levitated component. The generalized coordinates $\boldsymbol{q}$ can be obtained from the sensor values of the capacitive probes $\boldsymbol{d_S}$ using the Moore-Penrose inverse of the Jacobian matrix $\boldsymbol{J_S}$ according to Eqs. (5) and (6), where n is the number of electromagnets and sensors and m the number of generalized coordinates. The configuration of the Jacobian matrix only depends on geometrical considerations, hence, a reasonable estimation for the matrix entries can be obtained from available CAD models. Note that the entries of the Jacobian matrix (6) contain variable values that change with the feed position of the levitating slide as its center of gravity shifts in the fixed actuator coordinate system.

$$\boldsymbol{q} = \boldsymbol{J_S}^{+}\boldsymbol{d_S} = (\boldsymbol{J_S}^{T}\boldsymbol{J_S})^{-1}\boldsymbol{J_S}^{T}\boldsymbol{d_S} \tag{5}$$

$$\boldsymbol{J_S} = \left(\frac{\partial d_{S,i}}{\partial q_j^T}\right)_{i=1...n;\, j=1...m} \tag{6}$$

3.3 Force Allocation

Similar to the coordinate transformation of the sensor values, the actuator forces $\boldsymbol{F_A}$ can be calculated from the generalized forces and moments $\boldsymbol{Q}$ using the Jacobian matrix $\boldsymbol{J_A}$, see Eqs. (7) and (8). This approach also allows for a consistent force allocation for the overdetermined system. Note that for differential magnet arrangements, the actuator forces $\boldsymbol{F_A}$ have to be converted to individual pulling forces $\boldsymbol{F_M}$ of the involved electromagnets. Here, this is achieved by allocating positive actuator forces $\boldsymbol{F_A} > 0\,\text{N}$ to the electromagnets pulling in positive coordinate direction, and negative actuator forces $\boldsymbol{F_A} < 0\,\text{N}$ to the electromagnets pulling in negative coordinate direction.

$$\boldsymbol{F_A} = (\boldsymbol{J_A}^{+})^{T}\boldsymbol{Q} = \mathbf{J}(\boldsymbol{J_A}^{T}\boldsymbol{J_A})^{-1}\boldsymbol{Q} \tag{7}$$

$$\boldsymbol{J_A} = \left(\frac{\partial F_{A,i}}{\partial Q_j}\right)_{i=1...n;\, j=1...m} \tag{8}$$

The entries of the Jacobian matrices $\boldsymbol{J}_A$ and $\boldsymbol{J}_S$ depend on geometrical parameters of the magnetic levitation system, namely the distance of the sensors and actuators from the reference point, i.e. the levitating slide's center of gravity. Since a feed motion in X-direction results in a relative displacement of the center of gravity in the stationary sensor and actuator coordinate systems, individual entries of the Jacobian matrices will vary with the feed position. To ensure accurate coordinate transformation and force allocation, the pseudo-inverse of the Jacobian matrices must be updated according to the momentary feed position of the slide. For this, the Jacobian matrices as well as their pseudo-inverses include a symbolic variable for the feed position (i.e. the x-coordinate). The coordinate transformation and force allocation matrices are recalculated in consideration of the momentary feed position with each call of the control algorithm. Equation (9) exemplarily shows the force allocation matrix with the symbolic coordinate x and the geometrical parameters $l_X = 85\,\text{mm}$, $l_Y = 19.2\,\text{mm}$ and $l_Z = 86.5\,\text{mm}$, which represent the distance between the actuators and the slide's center of gravity in X-, Y- and Z-direction (see Fig. 3).

$$(\boldsymbol{J}_A{}^{+})^T = \begin{pmatrix} \frac{l_X + x}{4l_X} & \frac{l_Y}{4l_Z} & \frac{1}{4l_Z} & 0 & \frac{1}{4l_X} \\ \frac{l_X - x}{4l_X} & \frac{l_Y}{4l_Z} & \frac{1}{4l_Z} & 0 & \frac{1}{4l_X} \\ \frac{l_X - x}{4l_X} & -\frac{l_Y}{4l_Z} & -\frac{1}{4l_Z} & 0 & -\frac{1}{4l_X} \\ \frac{l_X + x}{4l_X} & -\frac{l_Y}{4l_Z} & -\frac{1}{4l_Z} & 0 & -\frac{1}{4l_X} \\ 0 & -\frac{l_X + x}{2l_X} & 0 & \frac{1}{2l_X} & 0 \\ 0 & -\frac{l_X - x}{2l_X} & 0 & -\frac{1}{2l_X} & 0 \end{pmatrix} \tag{9}$$

3.4 *Inverse Model of Non-linear Magnetic Force Characteristics*

The reluctance force (i.e. magnetic pulling force) of an electromagnet depends on the magnetic air gap and the flux inducing coil current. Variations of these values change the resulting pulling force in a non-linear fashion. A simple linearization for a working point of an electromagnet would severely limit its operating range. For the application at hand, a rather large operating range is required to account for varying loads (e.g. due to position-dependent bearing forces and dynamic feed forces) and air gap deviations (e.g. due to micro-positioning of the slide). Thus, it is not possible to define a single working point for all the electromagnets of the linear guide. Consequently, the application of linear control techniques requires the use of a model representation of the non-linear relationship $\boldsymbol{i} = f(\boldsymbol{\delta}, \boldsymbol{F_M})$ between the magnetic air gap $\boldsymbol{\delta}$, the required pulling force $\boldsymbol{F_M}$ and the respective coil current $\boldsymbol{i}$.

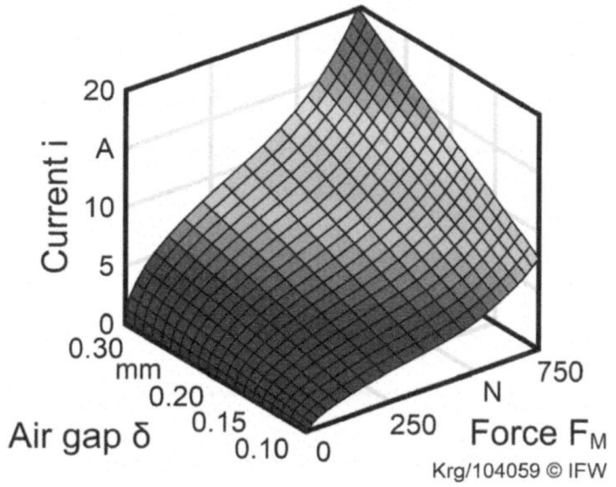

Fig. 8 Inverse function $i = f(\boldsymbol{\delta}, \boldsymbol{F_M})$ for the electromagnets of the experimental setup

The pulling force characteristics of the electromagnets $\boldsymbol{F_M} = f(\boldsymbol{\delta}, i)$ was initially obtained using numerical simulations (i.e. finite element methods) in the design phase. This approach produces reliable results if the magnetization curves of the involved magnetic materials are known with sufficient accuracy. While this information is available for a selection of common engineering materials, it may be necessary to identify the magnetization curves of specific metal alloys since changes of composition or thermal treatment can significantly alter the magnetic properties. For this reason, the pulling force characteristics of the electromagnets were directly measured using an experimental setup. Then, the characteristic diagram was mathematically inverted to obtain the inverse function for the calculation of the coil current reference (see Fig. 8). The inverse functional relationship was implemented as a 2D look-up table within the control environment.

4 Control Design for the Electromagnetic Linear Guide

This section proposes a systematic model-based control design approach for electromagnetic levitation systems using reluctance force actuators. In the following, a lean simulation model based on the model components from Sect. 3 is introduced. It allows for the identification of robust control parameters without the risk of unstable operation and damage to the actual electromagnetic levitation system. Furthermore, the final controller layout for the implementation in the industrial control environment is presented at the end of the section.

The mechanical model of the levitating component from Sect. 3.1 provides the basis for the simulation. Accordingly, the simulation is based on generalized coordinates and generalized forces. Assuming that the geometrical parameters for the Jacobian matrices and the characteristic diagram of the electromagnets are known with sufficient accuracy, it is feasible to neglect the coordinate transformation, the force allocation and the non-linear force characteristics in the simplified simulation model. This implies that the calculated reference force values are reliably transferred

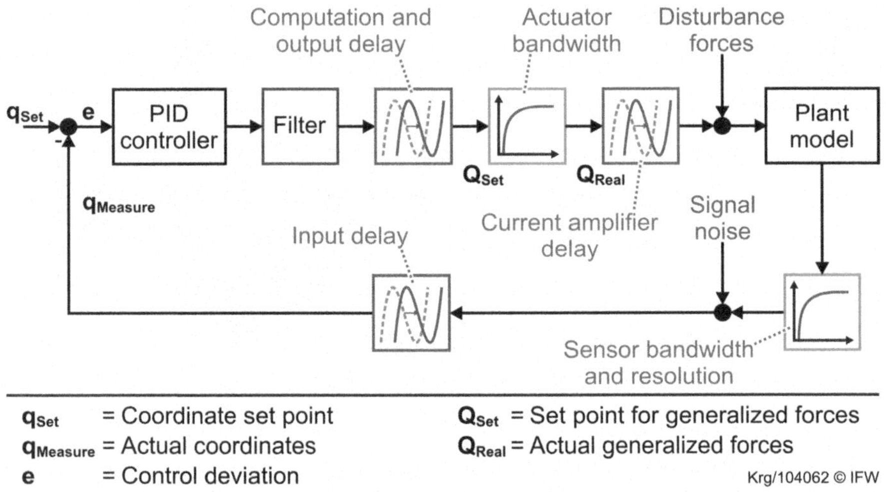

Fig. 9 Simplified simulation model for control parameter identification

into actuating forces with the correct amplitude and direction. Model deviations in this respect lead to minor amplitude errors of the regulated variables (i.e. the magnetic pulling forces), although no relevant impact in the control performance is expected. However, model components such as filters, signal delays and bandwidth restriction of actuators and sensors significantly affect the phase margin of the closed loop system and with this the control performance and stability. Thus, they are considered in the simplified model for a reliable real-world representation, see Fig. 9. The input delay of the control system corresponds to the cycle time of 50 μs. The computation of the control variables and the data output operation require another control cycle, which results in a further delay of 50 μs. The delay of the current amplifier amounts to 150 μs from the time a target current is set until the commanded current is reached.

For the application at hand, a set of five discrete proportional-integral-differential (PID) controllers is used to individually control the slide's five degrees of freedom. Each degree of freedom can be represented by a linear transfer function including the control parameters K_P, K_I and K_D (i.e. the proportional, integrative and derivative constants) for each PID controller. The simple simulation model allows for very fast computation, so that common optimization algorithms can be applied to efficiently identify control parameters for a desired performance objective (e.g. control bandwidth, reference tracking or disturbance rejection). Moreover, the simulation model allows for further testing of the identified control parameters in consideration of varying set point values or disturbance forces. For the implementation into the industrial control environment, the controller is extended by the coordinate transformation and force allocation mechanisms as well as the inverse model of the non-linear force characteristics from the previous section. The actual controller layout is depicted in Fig. 10.

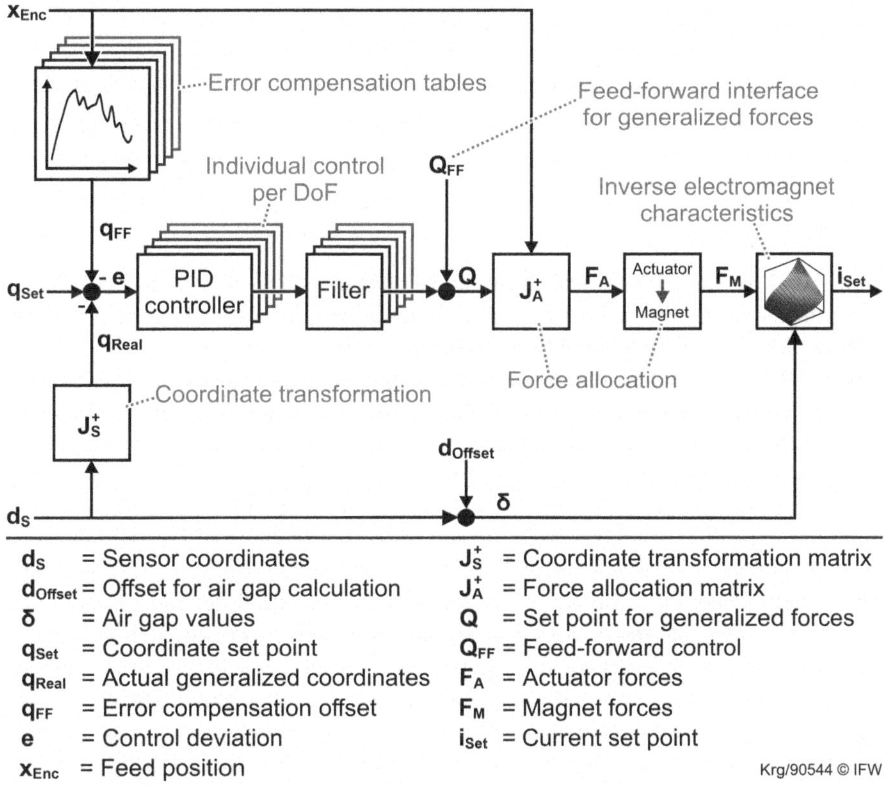

Fig. 10 Controller layout for implementation in the industrial control environment

5 Commissioning of the Electromagnetic Linear Guide

This section covers the procedure for the commissioning of the electromagnetic linear guide. First, a set of control parameters was identified using the approach from Sect. 4 for the initial start-up and operation of the electromagnetic levitation system. In operation, the system was subjected to a specified control deviation via a position reference step to evaluate robustness, reference tracking and decoupling of the generalized coordinates. The micro-positioning capability was explored in more detail to obtain preliminary results on the positioning accuracy of the electromagnetic levitation system.

The initial control parameters were set for a positioning bandwidth of 100 Hz in all five degrees of freedom according to the control design approach from Sect. 4. While the initial parameter set allowed for stable levitation, oscillations around 2,300 Hz occurred in the b-coordinate under external load—without causing instability though. Hence, a notch filter with a central rejected frequency of 2,300 Hz was implemented as a set point filter for the torque M_y. Consequently, the control parameters were then

Table 2 Control parameters for the electromagnetic linear guide

q	y	z	a	b	c
K_P	3,891,742	3,288,660	58,836	96,015	73,715
K_I	112,188,962	82,149,795	2,210,569	3,446,513	2,604,057
K_D	33,750	32,913	391	668	522

recalculated for the PID controller of the b-coordinate. The full control parameter set for the electromagnetic linear guide is summarized in Table 2. Further details on the commissioning strategy can be found in [8].

Note that the control system of the electromagnetic levitation system is initialized with non-variable matrices for coordinate transformation and force allocation. This is due to the fact that the incremental linear scale requires a homing procedure to provide absolute position information for the x-coordinate. For the initial launch of the electromagnetic linear guide, the feed position is assumed to be $x = 0$ mm, which does result in tracking errors in the rotational degrees of freedom but still allows for stable levitation (see Sect. 7.2). After the homing procedure, the coordinate transformation and force allocation matrices switch to position-dependent operation.

In order to evaluate the control performance of the electromagnetic linear guide, the control system was subjected to a reference step of 1 μm for the y-coordinate. The response was monitored with the integrated capacitive measurement system, see Fig. 11. Note that the control system was tuned for a practical compromise between reference tracking and disturbance rejection, thus, enabling high repeatability and accuracy when micro-positioning, as well as high stiffness and damping for the machining process. Since the control system is designed to react to small position deviations in the nanometer range, a reference step of 1 μm represents a rather excessive error for the position algorithm and results in a significant overshoot for the considered coordinate. Despite the extremely high excitation, the measurement data in Fig. 11 still shows a reliable decoupling of the five controlled coordinates.

The minimum step size for the micro-positioning motion is determined by the signal noise in the respective generalized coordinates. In the y-coordinate, for instance, the signal noise level allows for a reliable separation of 100 nm steps as demonstrated in Fig. 12. Note that the overshoot observed in Fig. 11 completely disappears for small reference steps in the submicron range.

6 Characterization of the Electromagnetic Levitation System

Following the commissioning process, the electromagnetic linear guide was investigated in more detail using additional measurement hardware to obtain reliable performance figures. First, position noise and positioning accuracy of the electro-

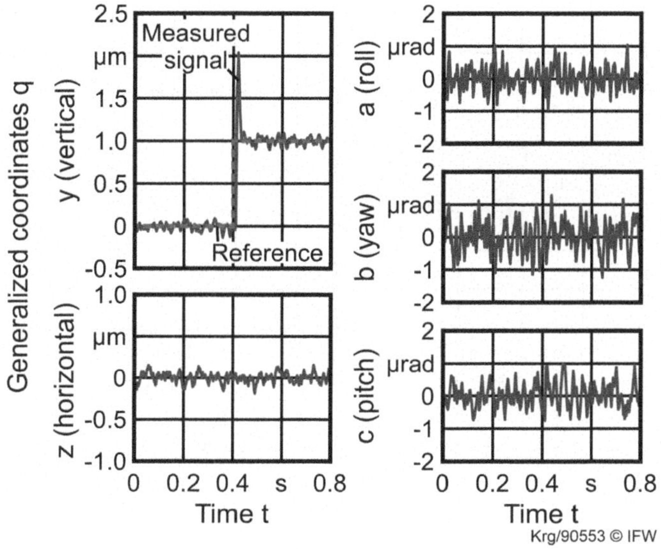

Fig. 11 Generalized coordinates for set point step in y-coordinate

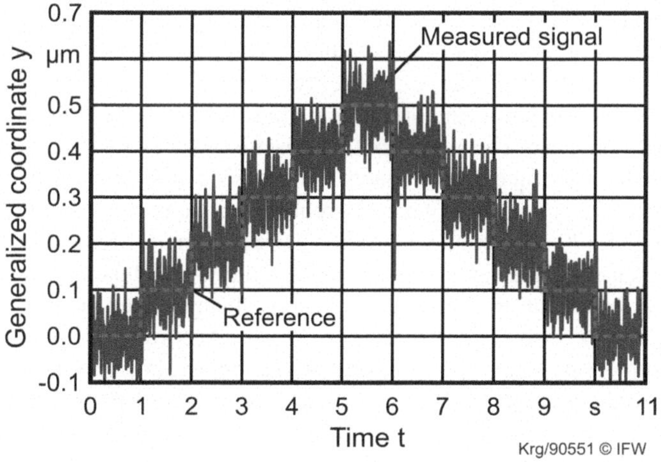

Fig. 12 Fine positioning in y-coordinate with 100 nm steps (measured with internal sensors)

magnetic linear guide were considered as they directly translate to surface and form deviations of the machined workpiece. In addition to the static positioning accuracy, the bandwidth of the micro-positioning motion was determined to assess up to which frequency position errors can still be compensated. Finally, the dynamic stiffness of the active guide system was investigated via an experimental modal analysis to evaluate its capability to reject dynamic disturbance forces. Other performance figures, for example those concerning the feed motion, are discussed in Sect. 7.

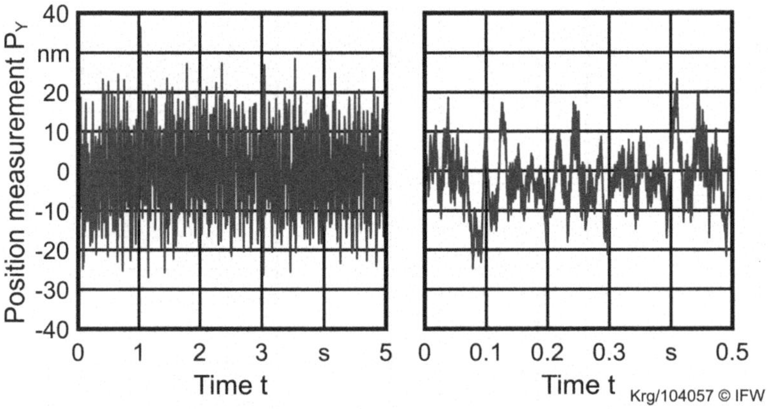

Fig. 13 Position noise of the levitating slide in the *y*-coordinate

6.1 Position Noise

Being a controlled system, the levitating slide of the electromagnetic linear guide exhibits a position noise at standstill. In a machining process, the position noise directly affects the generated workpiece surface and can ultimately compromise the surface quality. While the integrated capacitive measurement system provides information on the slides position and orientation, it cannot be used to reliably determine the actual position noise. The signals of the capacitive probes are susceptible to interference from the adjacent electromagnets and show increased noise levels as soon as the guide system is active. Hence, an external capacitive probe (Lion Precision 2G-C8-0.5 with CPL490 measurement amplifier) with a dynamic resolution of 0.33 nm at 15 kHz was used to measure position noise of the *y*-coordinate against the workpiece table of the levitating side. Figure 13 shows the measured position signal. The position signal has a standard deviation of 7.6 nm. According to the 3-sigma rule, 99.7 % of all measurements can be allocated to an interval of 22.8 nm.

The observed position noise occurs due to various disturbances within the closed loop system. For example, the sensor noise of the capacitive air gap measurement system propagates through the control loop and leads to noisy control variables (i.e. current set points). Moreover, time-discrete control algorithms and data processing delays introduce additional noise to the closed loop system. The measurement shown in Fig. 13 also includes the sensor noise of the external capacitive probe as well as possible vibrations of the additional sensor holder. Accordingly, the real position noise is probably even smaller than estimated with the measurement.

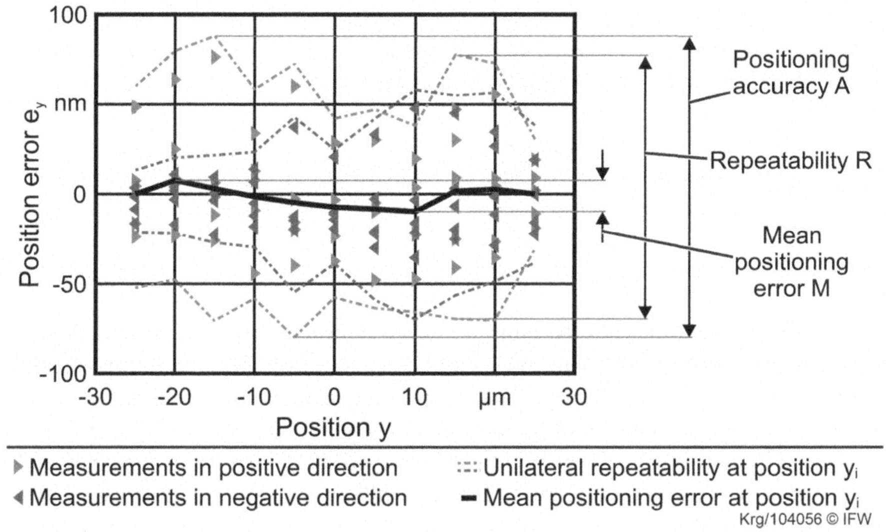

Fig. 14 Position error of the electromagnetic linear guide in y-direction according to ISO 230-2 (with the mean positioning error M, the repeatability R, and the position accuracy A)

6.2 *Positioning Accuracy*

Since the motion constrains of an electromagnetic linear guide are imposed by the control systems, it is feasible to specifically position the levitating slide within the air gap, i.e. in two degrees of freedom perpendicular to the feed direction, and in all three rotational degrees of freedom. In order to determine the static positioning accuracy of the electromagnetic linear guide, the micro-positioning motion was measured with a laser interferometer (Renishaw ML-10) according to ISO 230-2. Figure 14 shows the exemplary position error measurement for y-coordinate motion, which includes repeated position measurement for eleven positions over 50 μm (back and forth).

Compared to the initial results presented in [11], the overall positioning accuracy was further improved through an optimized sensor integration (i.e. improved electrical isolation of the capacitive probes and grounding of the measurement targets, compare Sect. 2.2) which reduced the signal noise significantly. Thus, the electromagnetic linear guide exhibits mean positioning errors below 50 nm for the linear and less than 0.3 μrad for the rotational degrees of freedom. Further, the repeatability mainly determines the absolute positioning accuracy due to the lack of friction and high linearity of the capacitive measurement system. The repeatability, in turn, is affected by the noise levels of the measurement system and the resulting position uncertainty.

Table 3 shows the accuracy parameters for all five controlled degrees of freedom (compare Fig. 14 for the statistical accuracy parameters). Different accuracy parameters for the individual degrees of freedom results from a different number of sensors

Table 3 Position accuracy of the electromagnetic linear guide according to ISO 230-2 over 50 μm for the y- and z-coordinates, and over 300 μrad for the a-, b- and c-coordinates (with the mean positioning error M, the repeatability R, and the position accuracy A)

q	y	z	a	b	c
M	0.017 μm	0.040 μm	0.30 μrad	0.25 μrad	0.23 μrad
R	0.134 μm	0.291 μm	1.85 μrad	1.14 μrad	1.56 μrad
A	0.168 μm	0.303 μm	1.87 μrad	1.31 μrad	1.78 μrad

for the respective coordinates. Notably, accuracy deviations in the rotational degrees of freedom can be attributed to the measurement accuracy of the interferometer, which is specified with ±0.5 μrad. The positioning accuracy in the submicron range indicates a general suitability of the new electromagnetic linear guide for precision application. In particular, the positioning accuracy of 0.168 μm for the y-coordinate is very close to the required form accuracy of ultra-precision workpieces which is generally specified with 0.100 μm. However, the positioning accuracy alone does not allow for a definitive statement regarding the final quality of the workpiece. The surface formation depends on further effects during the machining process, such as the interaction between cutting forces and the finite dynamic stiffness of the machine structure. Hence, a final evaluation of the electromagnetic linear guide's capability requires machining experiments (compare Sect. 8).

6.3 Positioning Bandwidth

In addition to the positioning accuracy, the positioning bandwidth of the electromagnetic linear guide was investigated. The positioning bandwidth indicates up to which frequency a specified displacement can be reliable set and determines the motion dynamics in the electromagnetic linear guide's controlled degrees of freedom. For the investigation of the positioning bandwidth, a stepped sine signal was used for the position reference and the system response was measured with the integrated capacitive probes. A set-point amplitude of 1 μm was used for the linear coordinates (y and z) and an amplitude of 10 μrad for the rotational coordinates (a, b and c). The frequency of the sine function was incrementally increased from 1 to 500 Hz. Figure 15 exemplarily shows the frequency response for the y-coordinate, while Table 4 summarizes the overall results of the experimental investigation. The identified bandwidths match the design specification from Sect. 5 of 100 Hz, except for the bandwidth of the b-coordinate. Here, the control parameters were increased with the implementation of the notch filter (see Table 2). While the filter effectively suppressed the oscillations around 2,300 Hz, the corresponding bandwidth limitation for the b-coordinate from the simulation was not observed for the real system. This indicates further potential to increase the positioning bandwidth of the other coordinates of the electromagnetic linear guide by further control parameter opti-

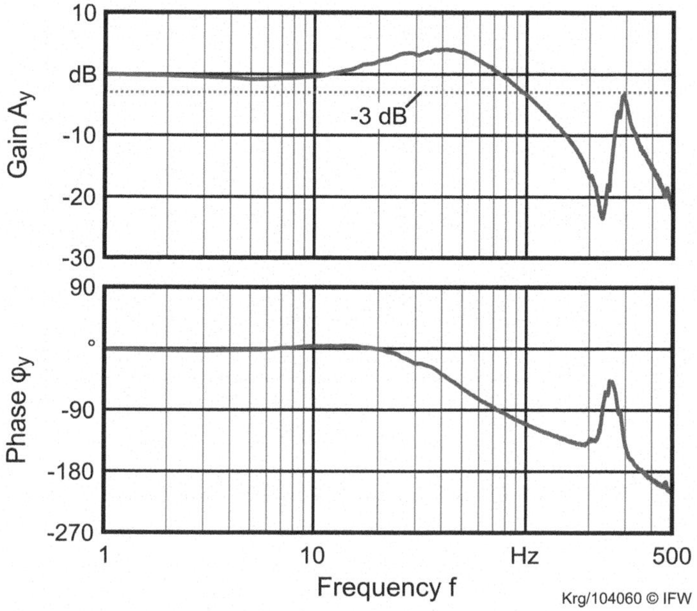

Fig. 15 Frequency response for reference excitation in the y-coordinate (for an amplitude of 1 μm with a frequency of 1 to 500 Hz)

Table 4 Positioning bandwidth of the electromagnetic linear guide in five degrees of freedom (for an amplitude of 1 μm in y and z, and 10 μrad in a, b and c)

q	y	z	a	b	c
f_{-3dB}	96 Hz	97 Hz	113 Hz	239 Hz	136 Hz

mization. However, increasing the feedback gain of the control system inevitably leads to a trade-off between positioning accuracy and bandwidth as the signal noise of the capacitive measurement system is also amplified by the control loop. While the use of digital filters allows for reduced signal noise levels, it also affects the phase margin and the electromagnetic linear guide's dynamic disturbance rejection.

6.4 Dynamic Stiffness

The dynamic stiffness represents a directional and frequency-dependent performance figure, which indicates the external force required to deflect the levitating slide by a certain distance. The dynamic stiffness of the functional prototype was determined through experimental modal analysis. For this, the levitating slide was excited with an impulse hammer (PCB-086C03) at the tool center point (TCP). The frequency-

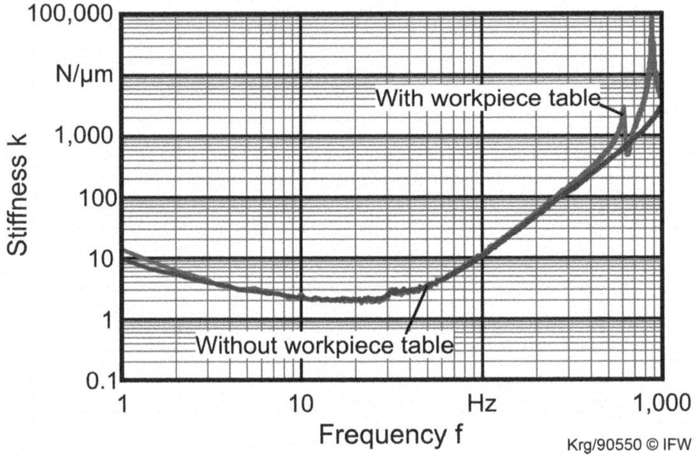

Fig. 16 Dynamic stiffness of the electromagnetic guide at the TCP in Y-direction (with and without workpiece table)

dependent response was measured in close proximity to the excitation point using a laser vibrometer (Polytec OFV-303 with OFV-3001 controller) and a three-axis accelerometer (PCB-356A16), both coupled to a modal analysis system of the type LMS Instruments SCADAS III. For the evaluation of the measurements, the signals of the vibrometer and the accelerometer were combined using sensor data fusion to obtain a broadband and low-noise signal. The frequency response function was measured for an excitation at the workpiece table and directly at the coupling interface of the slide. The measurement results are shown in Fig. 16. While the low frequency range is dominated by the control algorithm, the mass and structural dynamics of the electromagnetic linear guide become increasingly important for higher frequencies. As a result, the static stiffness is basically infinite, if the external load is smaller than 2,800 N (which is the load capacity of the electromagnetic levitation system). As expected, the lowest stiffness occurs near the control bandwidth limit, which is around 25 Hz for the experimental setup. Beyond that, the electromagnetic levitation guide does not show any critical natural frequencies up to 2,300 Hz. Adding the aluminum workpiece table (compare Fig. 3) introduces a natural frequency at 644 Hz, which is, however, very well damped, see Fig. 16.

The minimum stiffness of the electromagnetic linear guide is $1.9\,\mathrm{N\,\mu m^{-1}}$ at 25 Hz. Other relevant frequency and stiffness values result from the specified reference processes of the research unit. Conventional fly-cutting with a single diamond tool and a spindle speed of $2{,}000\,\mathrm{min^{-1}}$ results in an excitation frequency of 33 Hz ($2.6\,\mathrm{N\,\mu m^{-1}}$). Using the dual tool holder described in Chap. 2 for fly-cutting with $2{,}000\,\mathrm{min^{-1}}$ leads to a tool engagement frequency of 66 Hz ($5.0\,\mathrm{N\,\mu m^{-1}}$). Finally, the desired high-performance fly-cutting process with a single tool and $20{,}000\,\mathrm{min^{-1}}$ produces an excitation frequency of 333 Hz ($166.7\,\mathrm{N\,\mu m^{-1}}$). In consideration of the expected cutting forces of less than 1 N, the resulting deflection of the electromagnetic linear guide is estimated to be in the single digit nanometer range for the high-performance cutting process.

7 Advanced Functions of Active Magnetic Bearings

After the identification of the fundamental performance figures (see Sect. 6), advanced functions specific to the electromagnetic levitation system are considered. In order to minimize straightness and inclination errors for improved overall accuracy over the travel range, the capability of the electromagnetic linear guide system to compensate quasi-static errors was investigated. Afterwards, a feed-forward control mechanism was considered to reduce the levitating slides tilting motion in acceleration and deceleration phases, aiming at increased motion performance in combination with reduced tilting errors.

7.1 Compensation of Straightness and Inclination Errors

In case of the electromagnetic linear guide, the straightness and tilting errors over the travel path primarily result from shape deviations of the sensor targets for the capacitive air gap measurement system. Since the sensor targets were produced using conventional machining (i.e. milling and grinding), they show shape deviations in the single-digit micrometer range. These shape deviations translate to deviations from the ideal zero position and orientation of the levitating slide, which results in straightness and inclination errors over the travel path. However, since those errors occur systematically, the micro-positioning capability can be used to compensate the shape deviation of the sensor targets and effectively improve straightness and inclination errors of the feed axis.

A multi-axis calibrator (Renishaw XM-60) was used to obtain initial measurements for the error motion in all six degrees of freedom of the machine axis along the travel path (see Fig. 17). Again, ISO 230-2 was applied, using 19 measurement positions over a travel range of 90 mm. Naturally, inclination errors around the slide's main axes of inertia result in translational errors at the tool center point. Hence, a multi-stage approach was chosen for the systematic error compensation.

First, the position-dependent inclination errors from the initial measurement were used to calculate correction values for the a-, b- and c-coordinates. The correction values were stored in individual look-up tables, which provide corrective offsets depending on the momentary slide position in feed direction. With the first stage of the compensation activated, the measurement was repeated to identify remaining feed position and straightness errors. This measurement confirmed a significant correlation between the pitch angle error (c-coordinate or rotation around z) and the feed position (x-coordinate) due to the position of the electromagnetic linear guide's the linear encoder (compare Sect. 3.2) and the placement of the multi-axis calibrator's launch unit on the workpiece table. In fact, after the compensation of the inclination errors, the remaining position error in feed direction was in the range of the position uncertainty, hence, further compensation for the x-coordinate was not considered. The impact of the inclination errors on the straightness, on the other hand, is less pronounced. Since relevant straightness errors still occurred with the first compensation stage, look-up tables with corrective offsets for the y- and z-coordinate were derived from the measurement and implemented in the control environment. Finally, the measurement was repeated once again to evaluate the effectiveness of the compensation approach.

Figure 17 shows the measurement results of the fully compensated system in comparison to the initial measurement. The measurements indicate a mean straightness error of less than 1 μm and mean inclination errors smaller than 2 μrad (less than 0.4″) with systematic error compensation. These figures imply a general suitability of the electromagnetic linear guide for use in ultra-precision machine tools. While these errors were identified for a travel range of 90 mm, it is feasible to achieve the same straightness and inclination over larger travel paths if systematic error compensation is applied. For long travel paths, electromagnetic bearings offer the potential to exceed conventional bearings in ultra-precision feed axes with regard to the remaining straightness and inclination errors as well as the setup effort.

7.2 *Feed Forward Control of Dynamic Disturbance Forces*

Applying any kind of external force to the levitating slide results in position deviations due to the finite stiffness of the electromagnetic linear guide. The initial deflection ultimately results from the dead time of the controlled system, i.e. the time it takes to detect a disturbance, calculate appropriate control variables and supply the coil currents to counter the external load. In any case, the overall delay is primarily determined by hardware restriction and dictates the performance limit regarding the dynamic stiffness of the electromagnetic linear guide, which is basically its ability to reject disturbance forces (see Sect. 6.4). In view of the application at hand, i.e. ultra-precision diamond machining, random disturbance forces occur due to the cutting process and are relatively small with typical cutting force values of 1 N and less (especially for increased cutting speed as shown in Chap. 3). However, feed forces accelerating and decelerating movable components lead to considerable disturbances. Since feed forces are rarely applied in the exact center of gravity, they mostly introduce unwanted torque and, thus, unwanted inclination and position errors at the tool center point. Depending on the rotational stiffness of the implemented bearing technology, this effect limits the applicable motion dynamics of ultra-precision machine tools.

While feed forces present dynamic disturbances, they are highly systematic – especially for friction-free motion systems. The actively controlled electromagnetic linear guide provides sensory capabilities to identify and evaluate the error motion in acceleration and deceleration phases. Moreover, its actuator capabilities enable a

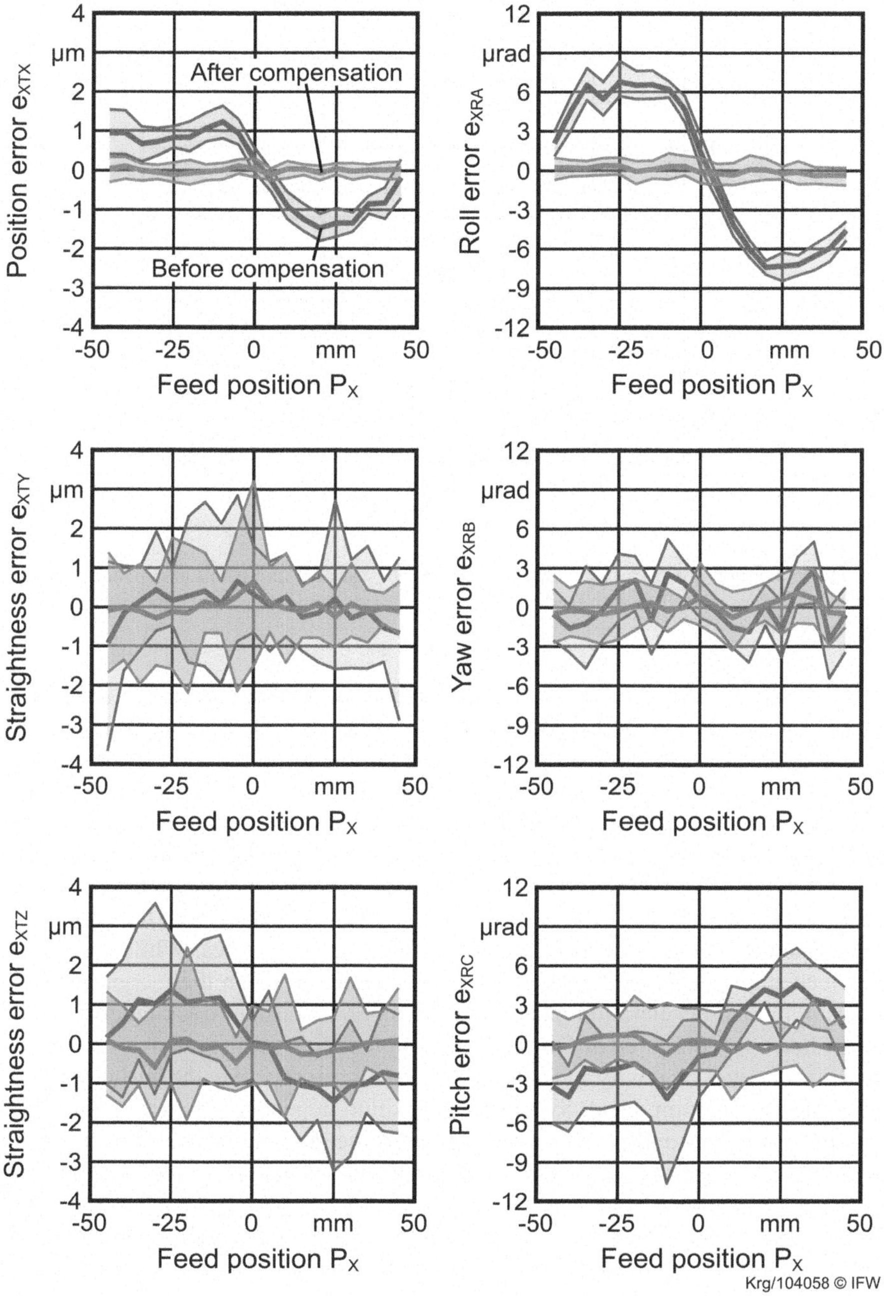

Fig. 17 Compensation of straightness and inclination errors over the travel path

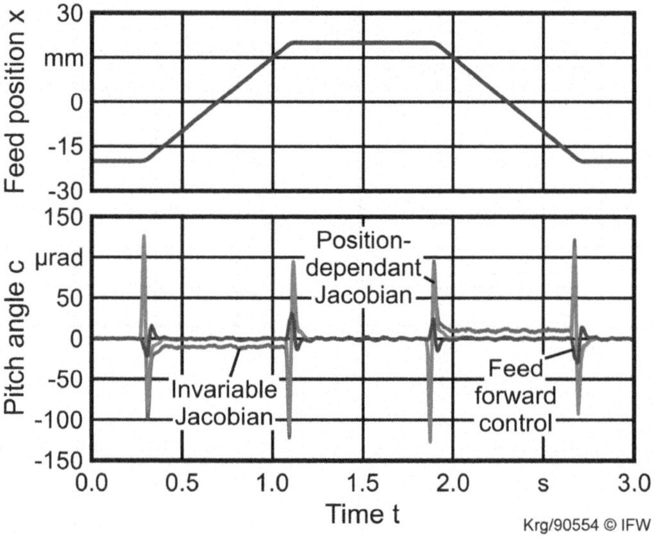

Fig. 18 Inclination errors during feed motion with non-variable and position-dependent inverse Jacobian matrices as well as with feed-forward control of dynamic disturbance forces

feed-forward control of systematically occurring disturbance forces. For a practical implementation of the feed-forward control mechanism, the acceleration set point for the feed drives was considered as a suitable reference.

In order to explore this approach, a reference motion over a stroke of 40 mm with the target velocity of 3,000 mm min^{-1} was considered. The acceleration was limited to 5 ms^{-1} to prevent damage to the test bench. The lateral displacement and inclination of the levitating slide were monitored with the integrated capacitive measurement system. First, the reference motion was carried out with the initial non-variable coordinate transformation and force allocation matrices. While the system remained stable, it showed considerable pitch angle errors (in the *c*-coordinate) in acceleration and deceleration phases. Furthermore, a constant tracking error in the *c*-coordinate was observed during the feed motion as the control system is unaware of the shifting center of gravity and adjusts the corrective forces over the fairly slow integrative feedback component. Switching to position-dependent matrices completely eliminates the constant tracking error, however, inclination errors still occur at the beginning and the end of the motion profile with the same magnitude (see Fig. 18).

Using an empirical approach, the acceleration was correlated with the observed disturbance torque M_z for the *c*-coordinate. Using a feedback gain of −4.455 kg m and a delay of 1.75 ms to calculate the corrective torque from the acceleration set point. The applied feed-forward control mechanism for systematically occurring disturbances has the same effects as an increased torsional stiffness of the electromagnetic bearing. Accordingly, maximum pitch angle errors in acceleration and deceleration phases were reduced by 75% as demonstrated in Fig. 18.

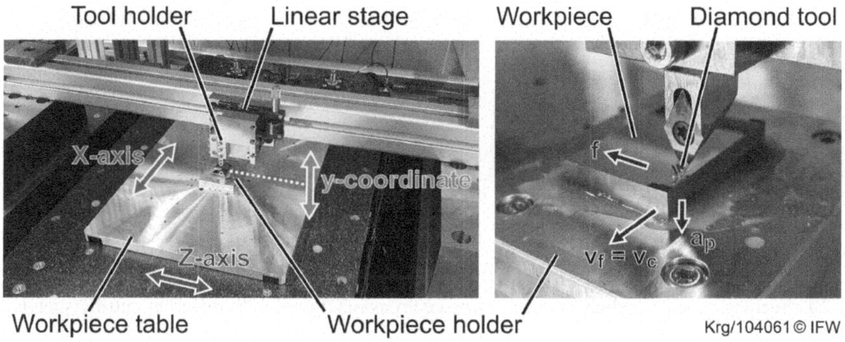

Fig. 19 Experimental setup for diamond machining (planing process with stationary tool)

8 Application in Diamond Machining

For the in-process evaluation of the new electromagnetic linear guide, machining tests were carried out to investigate the impact of the performance figures from Sects. 6 and 7 on the workpiece quality. The purpose of the machining tests was to identify the achievable surface roughness and form deviation at usual and severely increased feed rates. This should clarify whether electromagnetic bearings are basically suitable for ultra-precision machining, and whether they allow for increased productivity of diamond machining processes.

Ultra-precision planing with a stationary diamond tool was specified as the initial cutting process to minimize complexity and interdependencies which would be inevitably introduced with a spindle and a rotating tool. The planing process allows for the machining of single grooves and complete workpiece surfaces as well as individual pockets using the electromagnetic guide's micro-position capability. The experimental setup is shown in Fig. 19 and includes an additional portal with a custom holder for the diamond tool (C0.76mLFCi/0.25 by Contour Fine Tooling, NL) and a manually actuated miniature stage for the coarse adjustment of the depth of cut—fine adjustment of the depth of cut was done with the y-coordinate of the electromagnetic linear guide. The brass workpiece (CuZn40Pb2) was attached to the workpiece fixture with wax.

The cutting parameters for the machining experiments, i.e. line-by-line planing, were varied within the following boundaries:

1. Cutting velocity $v_c = 10 \ldots 6{,}000\,\text{mm min}^{-1}$,
2. depth of cut $a_p = 3 \ldots 15\,\mu\text{m}$,
3. lateral feed $f = 10 \ldots 50\,\mu\text{m}$.

First, machining of single lines with increasing cutting velocity and depth of cut were considered to confirm the stability of the cutting process. Note that the feed rate of the machine axis v_f is equivalent to the cutting velocity v_c for the planing process. Then, single line planing with the above-mentioned parameter range was

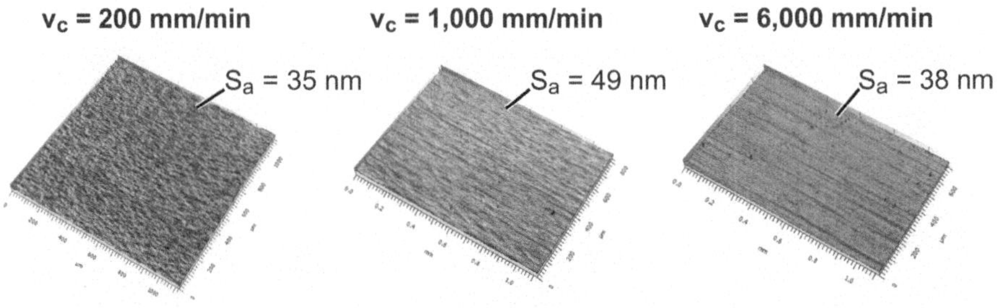

Fig. 20 Surface quality evaluation for workpiece areas machined with different cutting speeds v_c

used to generate individual surfaces on the brass workpiece. Here, the process was designed around the micro-positioning capability of the electromagnetic levitation guide: After the setting process, the levitating slide was raised by a specific amount to create the desired depth of cut a_p; after the cutting motion, the slide was lowered to allow for enough clearance to reposition the workpiece for the next cut. For this, the y-coordinate of the electromagnetic linear guide was configured as a NC-axis, which allowed for interpolated motion synchronized with the main feed axis in X- and Z-direction. With this approach, 3-axis machining was feasible, e.g. for the machining of individual pockets as shown in Fig. 21 on the left. The arithmetical mean height Sa was used to evaluate the surface quality. Figure 20 summarizes the results for three surfaces machined with different cutting velocities (for constant tool engagement conditions with $a_p = 2\,\mu m$ and $f = 10\,\mu m$). Notably, regenerative chatter was observed at some point for all cutting velocities. During tool engagement the impact of the process forces was visible in the generalized forces $\boldsymbol{Q}$ of the electromagnetic levitation system, however, vibrations of the levitating slide were not detected. Hence, the cause for the chatter effects rather lies in the structure on the cutting tool side. Since the chatter marks predominantly occurred at the boarder of the machined surface, sufficiently large surface patches without chatter were available to evaluate the surface quality using a confocal microscope of the type Confovis TOOLinspect. Here, the increase of the cutting velocity, i.e. faster slide movement, did not affect the surface quality in a negative way, as the measured mean height was in the same range between 35 nm and approximately 50 nm, see Fig. 20.

Finally, a complete workpiece surface of $20 \times 30\,mm^2$ was machined using rough cutting ($v_c = 3{,}000\,mm\,min^{-1}$, $a_p = 5\,\mu m$, $f = 10\,\mu m$) and finishing operations ($v_c = 200\,mm\,min^{-1}$, $a_p = 2\,\mu m$, $f = 10\,\mu m$), see Fig. 21 on the right. Again, the achieved surface roughness was approximately Sa $\approx$ 40 nm, which appears to be the limit for the experimental setup and conducted cutting investigations. However, it is not clear whether this limitation can be attributed to the electromagnetic linear guide or other machine components (such as the aerostatic bearings or the tool sided machine structure). This issue will be addressed in future machining experiments. Here, different processes (e.g. planing in Z-direction or fly-cutting) can be used to isolate the effects of individual components. Moreover, a reduced lateral feed f in

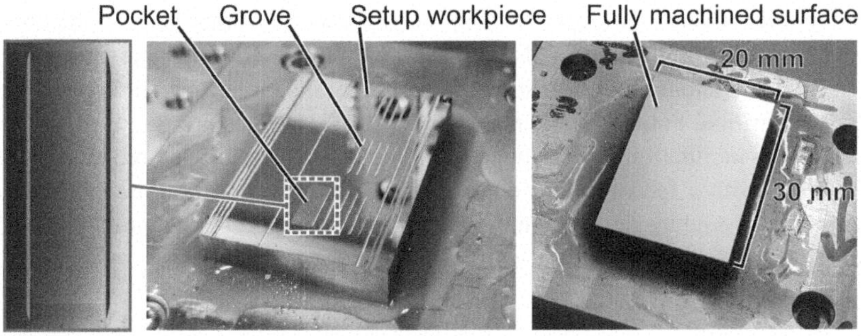

Fig. 21 Individual pocket (left) and fully machined surface (right) using high-precision planing (i.e. single line cutting)

combination with an even further increased cutting velocity v_c presents a promising approach to increase productivity without sacrificing surface quality.

9 Conclusion and Outlook

In the following, the presented content and main findings of this contribution are summarized. Also, the main results are discussed to derive further research question for future research activities.

9.1 *Project Summary*

This contribution introduced a novel electromagnetic linear guide, which satisfies both precision and stiffness requirements for high-precision diamond machining. First, design considerations were presented to combine functional requirements of electromagnetic bearings and fundamental design principles of precision machine tools. Then, a practical modeling and control design was proposed. After a basic proof of functionality, the new electromagnetic linear guide was extensively tested to obtain key performance figures. Moreover, the actuator and sensor properties of the electromagnetic linear guide were exploited to reduce straightness and inclination errors over the travel path as well as dynamic disturbances in acceleration and deceleration phases. Finally, the electromagnetic linear guide's capability in diamond machining was investigated.

The new electromagnetic linear guide displayed a position noise <23 nm and a positioning accuracy ≤ 300 nm or <1.9 µrad. Using a multi-stage compensation approach, mean straightness errors were reduced to less than 1 µm and inclination errors to less than 2 µrad over a considered travel range of 90 mm. The minimum dynamic stiffness is 1.9 N µm^{-1} at 25 Hz, however, it increases for the desired reference processes up to 166.7 N µm^{-1} at 333 Hz for the high-performance fly-cutting process. The frequency response function of the electromagnetic linear guide exhibits no critical natural frequencies up to 2,300 Hz. Despite the finite stiffness, the maximum inclination errors due to feed forces were effectively reduced by 75 % (to 31 µrad) with a feed-forward control algorithm. To conclude the experimental investigation, the new electromagnetic linear guide was used in diamond machining, achieving a surface quality of Sa $\approx$ 40 nm.

9.2 Discussion and Outlook

While the presented performance figures do not fully satisfy ultra-precision specifications, they are very close to the respective accuracy requirements for ultra-precision components (i.e. form deviations $\leq$100 nm and surface roughness $\leq$10 nm). Apart from the positioning accuracy in the sub-micron range, the new electromagnetic linear guide provides a sufficient dynamic stiffness for diamond machining. Hence, it represents the first electromagnetic levitation system for use in high-precision machining applications. In addition, the presented results demonstrate the capability of electromagnetic linear guides to reduce positioning errors which result from manufacturing or mounting tolerances or other deviations of the underlying machine structure. Also, a feed-forward control was applied to reduce the impact of dynamic disturbance forces while accelerating or decelerating the levitating component. Hence, it is feasible to improve the overall accuracy of the machine axes, e.g. with regard to straightness or inclination errors. In the present case, the travel range was limited to 100 mm. However, the presented compensation approach can be applied to any travel range and can also consider errors from subordinate machine structures, which helps to reduce the required manufacturing and setup effort, especially for long-travel motion systems.

The performance of the electromagnetic linear guide is mainly determined by the resolution and robustness of the integrated sensor system and the delays within the data processing system. Improving the signal-to-noise ratio of the position signal translates to increased position accuracy and reduced noise of the magnetic levitation system. Here, a decoupling of the air gap measurement (which is required to calculate the appropriate coil current based on the force reference) and the coordinate measurement of the levitating slide, e.g. by implementing an additional coordinate frame close to the tool center point) may proof beneficial. Reducing the delay of the data processing system results in faster reaction and increased dynamic stiffness.

Further measures include software-based optimization, e.g. the use of observer-based state space control to reduce the system-inherent signal noise and position uncertainty. The substitution of the PID controller's derivative component with an observer for velocity estimation allows for increased feedback gain, which, in turn, may further improve the dynamic stiffness within the control bandwidth. Note that above the control bandwidth, the frequency response function is mainly determined by the slide's mechanical properties, i.e. mass and structural dynamics. Here, a higher slide mass provides increased stiffness above the control bandwidth limit, but reduces the positioning bandwidth at the same time. Finally, the use of more elaborate models for the feed-forward control mechanism holds significant potential to further reduce systematic disturbances in acceleration and deceleration phases. This, in turn, allows to significantly increase motion dynamics while maintaining accuracy requirements for diamond machining.

References

1. Denkena, B., Kallage, F., Ruskowski, M., Popp, K., Tönshoff, H.K.: Machine tool with active magnetic guides. CIRP Ann. **53**(1), 333–336 (2004). https://doi.org/10.1016/s0007-8506(07)60710-0
2. Denkena, B., Hackeloeer, F., Neuber, C.-C.: 5-DOF harmonic frequency control using contactless magnetic guides. CIRP J. Manuf. Sci. Technol. **2**(1), 21–28 (2009). https://doi.org/10.1016/j.cirpj.2009.07.002
3. Denkena, B., Hackelo, F.L.: Multi-sensor disturbance force measurement for compliant mechanical structures. In:IEEE SENSORS. IEEE (2010). https://doi.org/10.1109/icsens.2010.5690446
4. Denkena, B., Guemmer, O., Floeter, F.: Evaluation of electromagnetic guides in machine tools. CIRP Ann. **63**(1), 357–360 (2014). https://doi.org/10.1016/j.cirp.2014.03.130
5. Denkena, B., Dahlmann, D., Krueger, R.: Electromagnetic levitation guide for use in ultra-precision milling centres. Procedia CIRP **37**, 199–204 (2015). https://doi.org/10.1016/j.procir.2015.08.008
6. Denkena, B., Dahlmann, D., and Krüger, R.: Control system for an ultraprecision electromagnetic linear guide. In: 16th Euspen International Conference & Exhibition. P. 2.16. May 30-June 3, Nottingham (2016)
7. Denkena, B., Dahlmann, D., Krüger, R. : Design and optimisation of an electromagnetic linear guide for ultra-precision high performance cutting. In: byWertheim, R., Ihlefeldt, S., Hochmuth, C., Putz, M. (eds.) Procedia CIRP, vol. 46. pp. 147–150 (2016). https://doi.org/10.1016/j.procir.2016.02.056
8. Denkena, B., Dahlmann, D., Krüger, R. : Experimental investigation of an electromagnetic linear guide for ultra-precision high performance machining. In: 17th Euspen International Conference & Exhibition. Hannover, GER, May 30–June 2, pp. 447–448 (2017)
9. Denkena, B., Bergmann, B., and Krüger, R.: LevitationHigh-performance machining. design & realisation – electromagnetic ultra–precision linear guide. In: Mikroniek, vol. 1, pp. 29–33 (2018)
10. Denkena, B., Bergmann, B., Krüger, R.: Enabling electromagnetic levitation technology for ultra-precision high performance machining'. In: 18th Euspen International Conference & Exhibition. P.2.15. Venice, IT, June 4-8, pp. 161–162 (2018)
11. Denkena, B., Bergmann, B., Krüger, R.: Elektromagnetische Linearführung für die hochpräzise Zerspanung. ZWF Zeitschrift für wirtschaftlichen Fabrikbetrieb **113**(7–8), 443–447 (2018). https://doi.org/10.3139/104.111938
12. Kim, W.-J., Trumper, D.L.: High-precision magnetic levitation stage for photolithography. Precis. Eng. **22**(2), 66–77 (1998). https://doi.org/10.1016/s0141-6359(98)00009-9
13. Lu, X., Dyck, M., Altintas, Y.: Magnetically levitated six degree of freedom rotary table. CIRP Ann. **64**(1), 353–356 (2015). https://doi.org/10.1016/j.cirp.2015.04.107
14. Schönemann, L., et al..: Synergistic approaches to ultra-precision high performance cutting. CIRP J. Manuf. Sci. Technol. **28**, 38–51 (2020). https://doi.org/10.1016/j.cirpj.2019.12.001

15. Stamann, M., Schallschmidt, T., Leidhold, R.: Electromagnetic rotary tables for mill and drill machining. WSEAS Trans. Syst. Control **9**, 199–207 (2014)
16. Weck, M., Wahner, U.: Linear magnetic bearing and levitation system for machine tools. CIRP Ann. **47**(1), 311–314 (1998). https://doi.org/10.1016/s0007-8506(07)62840-6

Spindle Balancing for Ultra-Precision High Speed Cutting

Timo Dörgeloh, Nasrin Parsa, Christian Schenck, Oltmann Riemer, Ekkard Brinksmeier, and Bernd Kuhfuss

Abstract Due to the high resulting centrifugal forces, high speed spindles require an extremely well balanced setup. Within this project, an automatic system for precision balancing of air bearing spindles was developed, which has the potential to supersede manual balancing completely and thus reduce setup times considerably. The scientific challenges of this approach are the measurement and compensation of extremely small residual unbalances, which lie below the detection threshold of conventional sensor systems.

1 Introduction to UP-Balancing and Motivation of the Research

Over the past decades, balancing has played a minor role in ultra-precision machining. The long non-productive times as well as the resulting high costs were accepted by industry, as there was no alternative for this process. However, due to the latest developments of high-frequency spindles, this topic gained new relevance for the performance and robustness of the production process in ultra-precision high-performance machining. The economic efficiency of ultra-precision (UP) processes is also becoming increasingly important due to the growing spread of UP machining in industry. Due to their physical principle, air-bearing spindles have a lower stiffness and load capacity compared to spindles with other bearing technologies. Therefore, air-bearing spindles have to be balanced exceptionally precise in order to prevent

T. Dörgeloh · O. Riemer (✉) · E. Brinksmeier
Leibniz Institute for Materials Engineering IWT, Bremen, Germany
e-mail: oriemer@iwt.uni-bremen.de

T. Dörgeloh
e-mail: doergeloh@iwt.uni-bremen.de

N. Parsa · C. Schenck · B. Kuhfuss
Bremen Institute for Mechanical Engineering bime and MAPEX Center for Materials and Processes, University of Bremen, Bremen, Germany
e-mail: parsa@bime.de

C. Schenck
e-mail: schenck@bime.de

E. Brinksmeier and L. Schönemann (eds.), *Ultra-precision High Performance Cutting*, Lecture Notes in Production Engineering, https://doi.org/10.1007/978-3-030-83765-5_5

damage to the air bearings due to unbalanced rotor displacement on the one hand and to avoid a negative impact on the production result due to vibration excitation of the machine structure on the other [25].

A rotor unbalance generally exists if the axis of mass inertia does not coincide with the geometric axis of rotation. This shift of the mass inertia axis is caused, for example, by imprecise assembly or manufacturing of the rotor. Tool wear also leads to a certain change in the mass inertia axis. An unbalance can be detected by different sensors based on the resulting vibrations. The most common sensors for measuring the vibration amplitude are displacement, velocity or acceleration sensors. The latter have become established in the field of unbalance detection and can detect even the smallest unbalance-induced vibrations of the rotor due to their high sensitivities. However, this sensitivity is not always sufficient. For example, relatively small unbalances at low speeds cannot be measured with sufficient precision. This is due to the low amplitude of the resulting vibration in this range, which is below the detection threshold of the sensors. A correct calculation of the amplitude and phase of the unbalance is therefore not possible.

Balancing of air-bearing spindles in industry is still done manually and requires several iterations, which is uneconomical and should be avoided [15]. Due to the high demands on the balancing quality for protection of the air-bearing, balancing masses in the range of a few μg have to be used. The conventional approach in ultra-precision machining—to use set screws as counterweights—is therefore limiting the achievable balance quality. This applies in particular to the fly-cutting process, in which the rotating tool has a much larger oscillation radius than in ball head milling, in which the same set screw has a much smaller influence on the balancing quality. The high spindle speeds required to achieve higher material removal rates and a reduction in production time in ultra-precision high-performance cutting therefore impose new challenges on the balancing process. Since the centrifugal force has a quadratic growth with increasing angular velocity and the balancing must be performed at operating speed, manual balancing is not suitable for high performance cutting applications in ultra-precision machining. An automatic balancing system with the ability to generate small counterbalances at operating speed is therefore desirable for achieving an optimal surface finish.

However, the common surface roughness parameters are not suitable to describe the finish of optical surfaces adequately and, moreover, do not allow any statement to be made about the influence of certain process variables and parameters on the balancing state [12]. The standard DIN EN ISO 25178 defines further parameters for surface characterization in addition to the classical roughness parameters [10]. Methods such as "Wolf pruning" were successfully used for an alternative description of surface quality. "Wolf pruning" segments a surface into individual regions on the basis of previously defined threshold values of height differences. The number and size of these regions allows the characterization of the investigated surface section. However, even with these additional values for characterization it is not possible to draw detailed conclusions on the influence of individual process parameters such as rotor unbalance [16]. As a result, there is a great need for research on the influences of rotor imbalance, structural and drive dynamics on the generated surface structures and finish in the area of ultra-precision machining [26].

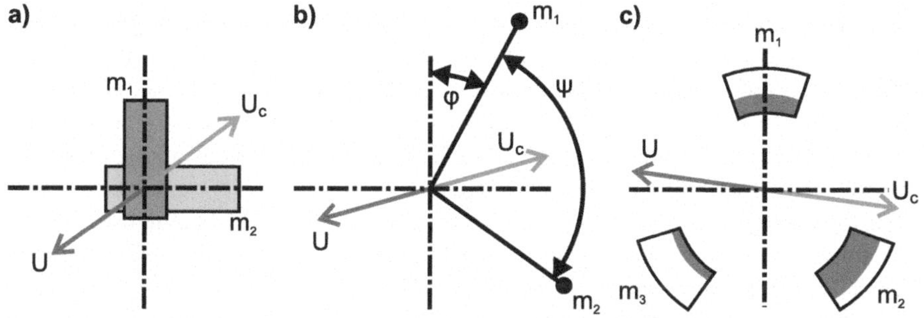

Fig. 1 Balancing an unbalance (U) by generating a counterbalance U_c with multiple masses (m_1, m_2, m_3) **a** by orthogonal mass redistribution (m_1, m_2) **b** by rotary redistribution (ψ, ϕ) of masses (m_1, m_2) **c** by addition or removal of mass (m_1, m_2, m_3) on defined circumferential positions

1.1 Balancing of Ultra-Precision Air-Bearing Spindles

Centrifugal forces and moments in a freely rotating system potentially lead to vibrations with transmission to the bearing. If this is the case, an unbalance is present. Unbalances can be represented graphically as eccentric masses in relation to the rotor axis. A distinction can be made between two types of unbalance, static and dynamic unbalance, whereby these two types usually occur in combination. A static unbalance is present if either the center of mass and the center of rotation or the center of mass and the unbalance of the rotor are in one plane. If center of mass and unbalance are out of plane, this is called a dynamic unbalance. While the static unbalance can be detected and compensated without operating speed of the rotor, the dynamic unbalance requires the rotor to be brought up to operating speed in order to be measured. In contrast, the compensation of the unbalance by adding a counterbalance usually requires the rotor to be stopped to zero speed.

The detection of unbalances of rotating spindles is usually achieved by measuring the resulting vibrations in amplitude and phase. Acceleration sensors are often used as a measuring instrument for this purpose, as they have a very high sensitivity and a high bandwidth. However, force or displacement sensors can also be used, depending on the requirements. If the unbalance in the individual measuring and compensation planes is known, a counterbalance can be realized by adding, removing or redistributing masses m_i on diverse radii r_i using various principles, as shown in Fig. 1.

The resulting vector of the counterbalance $\mathbf{U_c}$ should be as close as possible to the inverse of the measured unbalance $\boldsymbol{U}$ in order to balance the rotor (see Eq. 1).

$$\mathbf{U_c} = \sum m_i \cdot \mathbf{r_i} = -\boldsymbol{U} \tag{1}$$

Depending on the unbalance, the resulting centrifugal forces have a corresponding influence on the radial and axial rotor displacements of air bearing spindles [13].

In various manufacturing processes, these displacements can have a negative effect on the form accuracy and surface quality to a not negligible extent [21]. If the residual unbalance is excessively large, the air bearing of the spindle can be damaged. In order to minimize these negative influences, it is recommended to look into the standard DIN ISO 21940, in which the permissible unbalances for various applications are defined as balance quality grades (cf. Fig. 2).

The balance quality grade represents the maximum permissible angular velocity of the rotor center of mass over the entire speed range. For example, the balance quality grade $G0.16$ represents an angular velocity of $v_{rot} = 0.16\,\mathrm{mm\,s^{-1}}$. According to Eq. 2, the permissible specific unbalance e_p depends on the rotational frequency ω [11] and therefore decreases with increasing rotational frequency:

$$G = v_{rot} = e_p \cdot \omega = \text{const.} \tag{2}$$

whereas in conventional ultra-precision machining, the rotational speeds are in the range of $n = 100\,\mathrm{min^{-1}}$ to $2{,}000\,\mathrm{min^{-1}}$, Ultra-Precision High Performance Cutting (UP-HPC) is aimed at rotational speeds greater than $n = 10{,}000\,\mathrm{min^{-1}}$ in order to achieve increased productivity. If we assume a rotational speed of $n = 20{,}000\,\mathrm{min^{-1}}$, the permissible specific unbalance is $e_p = 0.076\,\mathrm{g\,mm\,kg^{-1}}$ at the balance quality grade $G0.16$ defined in the ISO standard. For the UP-HPC application, it was agreed that a balance quality grade of $G0.064$ should be achieved, which is close to the factory balancing quality of air-bearing spindles [14]. This is the next balancing quality grade after $G0.16$ according to the ISO standard and can be seen in Fig. 2.

At the reference speed $n = 20{,}000\,\mathrm{min^{-1}}$ the permissible specific unbalance for the balance quality grade $G0.064$ is $e_p = 0.03\,\mathrm{g\,mm\,kg^{-1}}$ and can be seen in Fig. 2. The permissible residual unbalance mass m_p according to Eq. 3 with a rotor weight of $m_r = 4.5\,\mathrm{kg}$ and a correction radius $r_c = 60\,\mathrm{mm}$ is therefore 2.25 mg.

$$m_p = \frac{e_p \cdot m_r}{r_c} \tag{3}$$

The most common method for balancing air-bearing spindles in ultra-precision machining is the manual adding or removing of set screws of known weight on the circumference of the rotor (see Fig. 1c). The fact that set screws, even in a size of M3 $\times$ 3, still have a weight of approx. 80 mg clearly shows that achieving a residual unbalance mass of 2.25 mg in the manual process is very challenging. Another method which is used is the relocation of two masses on a circular path and is based on the spread angle method shown in Fig. 1b). Since this method requires the use of larger dimensions in order to balance a wide range of residual unbalances, it requires very precise manual adjustment by a few angular minutes or seconds to achieve balancing quality level $G0.064$.

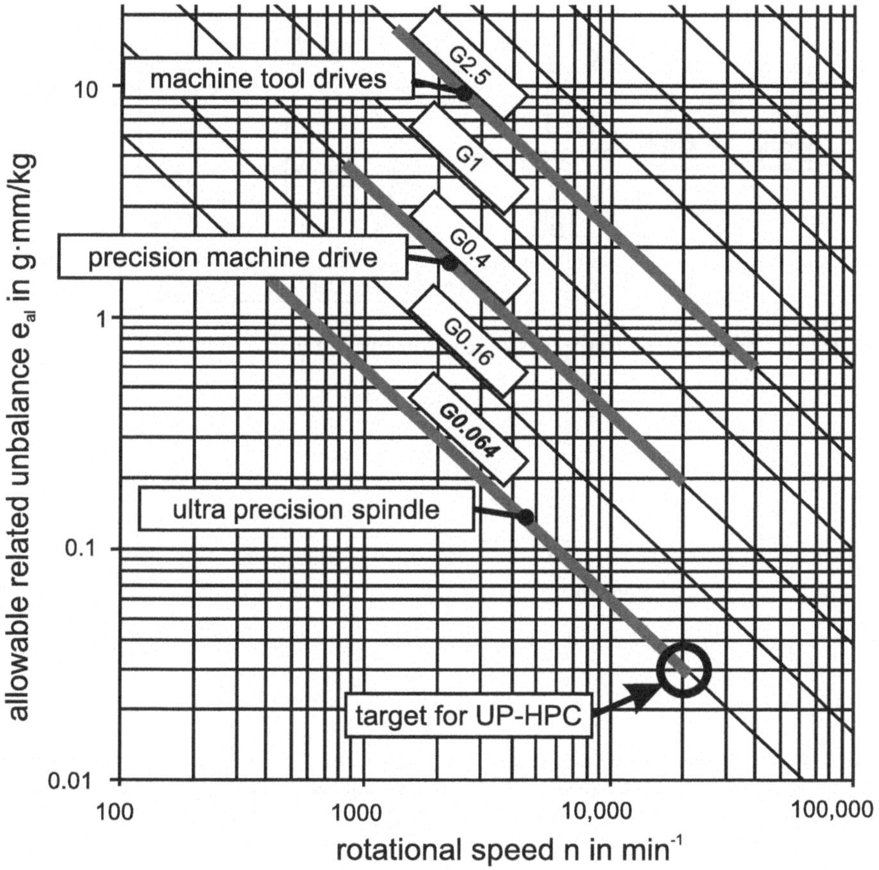

Fig. 2 Balancing grades following DIN ISO 21940 with an extended balancing grade of *G*0.064, in accordance to [11]

1.2 Shock Response of Spindle Rotor and Spindle Housing

Commonly, the unbalances are detected by measuring the vibrations that occur in the housing of the spindle. Due to the air bearing between the spindle housing and the rotor, the impact of unbalances on the rotor and the transfer of this effect to the spindle housing was investigated to verify the capability of unbalance detection by this method. Therefore, the transfer function of the rotating system was identified beforehand.

To remove the effect of feed axis on the vibrations, the spindle was mounted on a granite clamping table. The spindle was tested at different spindle speeds between 0 to 9,600 min^{-1} with 960 min^{-1} increments. To find out the transfer function of the system, the tool holder mounted on the rotor was excited with an impact hammer

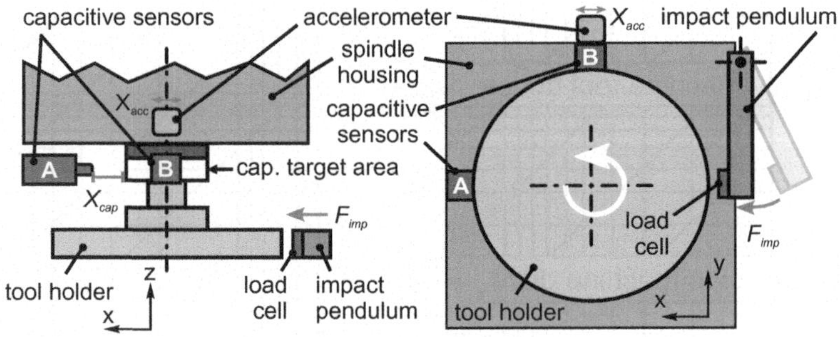

Fig. 3 Experimental setup for shock response measurements [7]

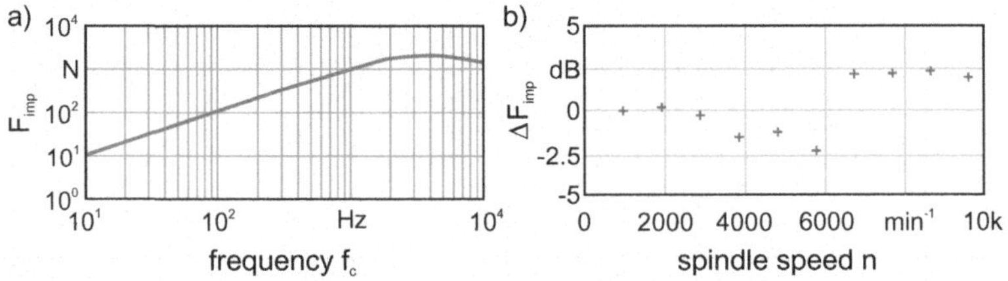

Fig. 4 Impulse signal response and variation of the peak impact force at different spindle speeds [7]

which was mounted on a pendulum. After exciting the spindle by the pendulum, the displacement of the spindle and also the vibrations of the spindle housing were measured.

Figure 3 illustrates the schematic procedure used for the excitation of the spindle. A load cell was used to measure the amount and duration of the impulse signal. To regenerate predefined impulse signals, the displacement of the pendulum was controlled by a mechanical stop. Thus, the resulting impulse duration was about 0.3 ± 0.01 ms and the impact force was approximately 1,200 N. To analyze the impulse signal, the frequency response of the signal was measured at 10 kHz sampling frequency for selected spindle speeds. Figure 4 shows the average impulse signal spectrum and the peak impact force at different spindle speeds.

The displacement of the rotor was measured by two capacitive sensors (see Fig. 3). The sensors which were used in the experimental setup were CPL490 probes from IBS Precision Engineering (Eindhoven, NL). The transfer function was calculated from the impulse signal and resulting vibrations of the spindle. In the next step, the transfer function between the impulse signal and the vibrations on the spindle housing was calculated. To measure the vibrations, two triaxial piezoelectric CCLD acceleration sensors type 4506 manufactured by Hottinger Brüel & Kjær GmbH (Darmstadt, Germany) were applied. They offer a sensitivity of $100\,\mathrm{mV\,g^{-1}}$ and were connected to a charge amplifier type 2692 by the same manufacturer. Sensor A, located in the opposite side of the impact direction, was used for measuring the actual

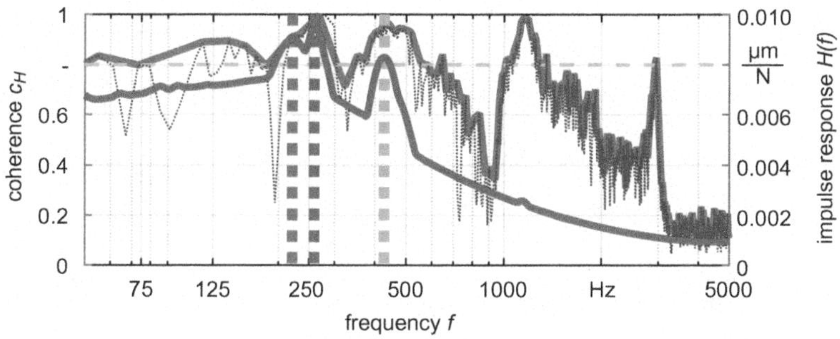

Fig. 5 Average normalized shock response spectrum $H(f)$ and the coherence c_H of sensor A with eigenfrequencies at 250 Hz, 260 Hz and 425 Hz. A minimum value of 0.8 (green dashed line) is accepted for the coherence function [7]

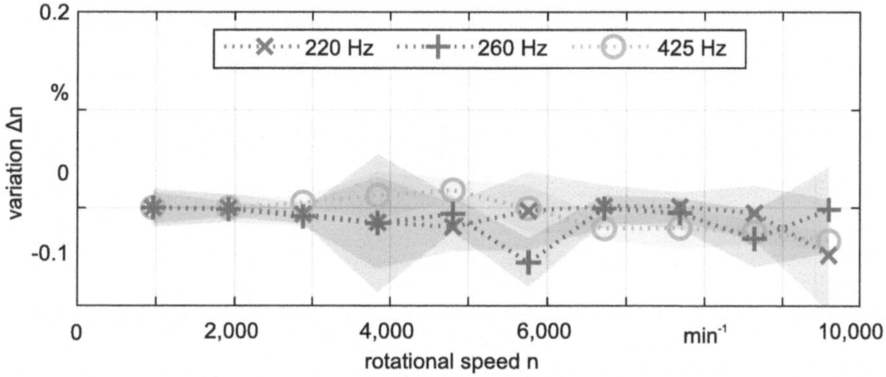

Fig. 6 Effect of spindle speed on impulse response. The spindle speed did not influence the dynamic behavior of the rotor [7]

impulse response, whereas sensor B, positioned perpendicular to the impact signal, was applied for identifying the direction of the vibration. The average shock response spectrum $H(f)$ of sensor A is shown in Fig. 5 together with the corresponding coherence function c_H and the identified eigenfrequencies.

A good coherence ($c_H \geq 0.8$) for the impulse response of sensor A was detected up to 600 Hz. In addition, three eigenfrequencies at 250 Hz, 260 Hz and 425 Hz, could be identified in the impulse response signal. In order to assess the effect of different spindle speeds on the impulse response the measurement was repeated for different spindle speeds while monitoring the amplitudes of the eigenfrequencies (see Fig. 6). As no significant dependency was found, this result suggests that the spindle speed did not influence the dynamic behavior of the rotor.

Furthermore, the impulse response of the acceleration sensor on the spindle housing was evaluated. The first analysis showed that the X-axis of the acceleration sensor was affected by the impulse signal due to the alignment of the sensor. The average impulse response and the coherence function of the X-axis is shown in Fig. 7.

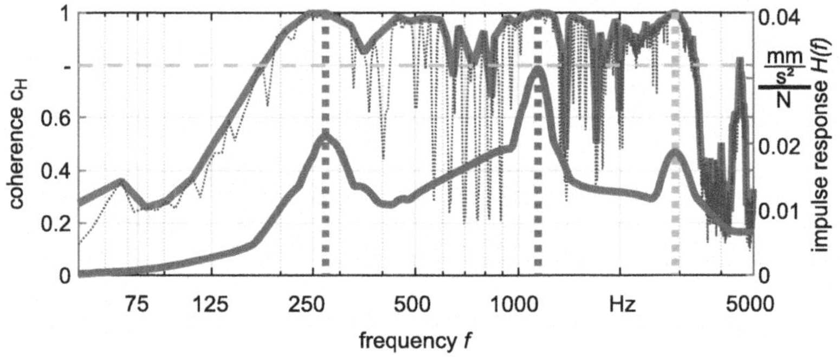

Fig. 7 Average normalized shock response spectrum $H(f)$ with eigenfrequencies at 274 Hz, 1,150 Hz and 2,900 Hz and coherence c_H of the accelerometer (minimum value of 0.8 is accepted for the coherence function) [7]

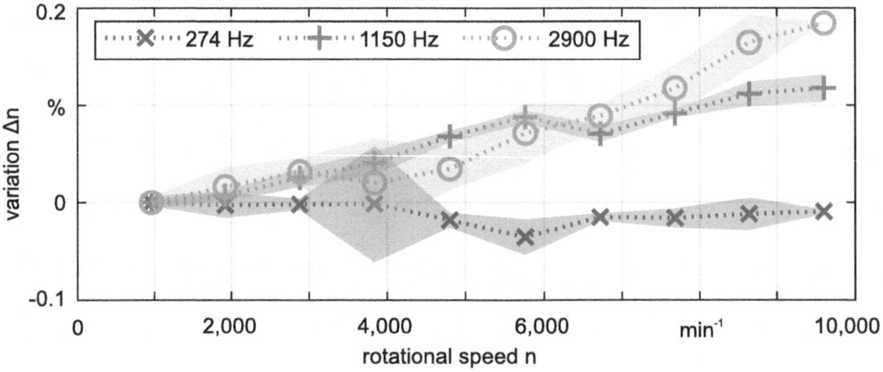

Fig. 8 Effect of spindle speed on the amplitude of three significant eigenfrequencies identified in impulse response measurements [7]

The coherence function exceeds 0.8 only at frequencies higher than 200 Hz indicating that the vibration of spindle housing in this range was caused by the excitation of the rotor.

The impulse signal shows three eigenfrequencies at 274 Hz, 1,150 Hz and 2,900 Hz. To check the effect of the spindle speed n on the impulse signal, the amplitudes of the eigenfrequencies were monitored after changing the spindle speed (see Fig. 8). It can be seen that the amplitude of the lower eigenfrequency (274 Hz) is nearly leveled off and remains unaffected by the spindle speed. However, the variation at higher frequencies increased and consequently the transfer function must be regarded as a function of the spindle speed n.

In conclusion, it can be stated from these experiments that the displacement measurement by capacitive sensors is suitable for frequencies lower than 425 Hz, while the typical setup of an accelerometer on the spindle housing is a better solution for the identification of unbalances at higher frequencies. Because measurement of the

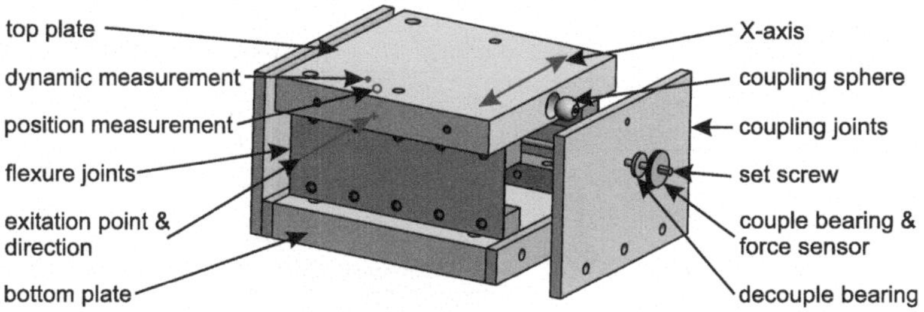

Fig. 9 Structure of the coupling system [6]

low frequencies is essential for balancing the spindle at typical operation speeds, the capacitive measurements would be the preferable choice. However, these measurements are significantly more expensive (in terms of equipment) and delicate in handling. Therefore, they are not generally suitable for industrial application [7].

2 Amplification of Vibrations for Measuring Tasks by Using Flexible Couplings

One possibility to improve the unbalance detection by using acceleration sensors is a temporary mechanical amplification of the unbalance excited vibrations at the spindle housing by changing the dynamic stiffness between spindle housing and machine frame. This approach was realized by a coupling system with tunable stiffness, based on a flexure joint concept (Fig. 9).

2.1 Experimental Setup

The coupling system basically consists of a top and a bottom plate connected via flexure and coupling joints (Fig. 10). The coupling joints are attached to the bottom plate and adjusted by set screws to switch between an operational state (coupled) and a setup state (decoupled).

In the operational state, the top plate is connected to the bottom plate by the flexure joints and clamped in place it via the coupling joints, effectively restricting a lateral motion along the X-axis. This connection resulted in a high stiffness state between spindle and the base. The dynamic behavior of the system changed in the setup state by disconnecting the coupling joints from the top plate. In this state, the bottom and top layer are only connected via the flexure joints allowing limited motion along the X-axis.

To ensure a repositioning with high precision, the coupling spheres are fixed to the coupling joints with individually shaped joint sockets using a polymer/metal

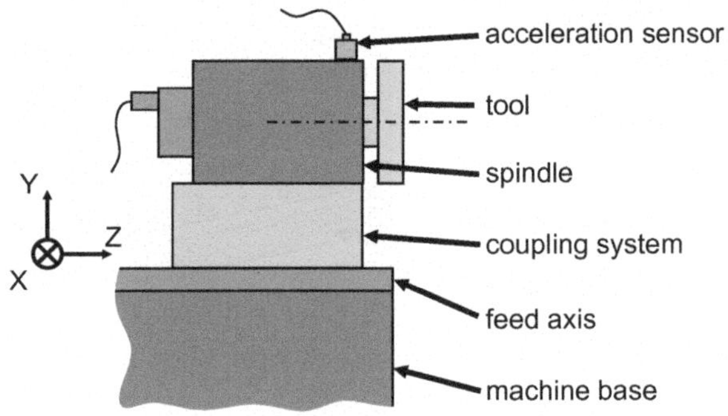

Fig. 10 Implementation of the coupling system [6]

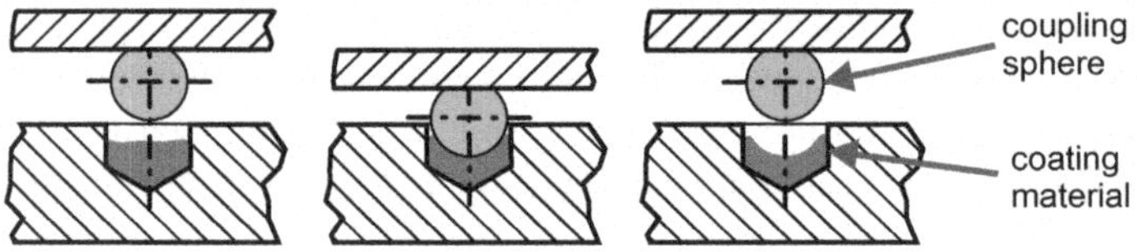

Fig. 11 Adjusting joint sockets to coupling spheres at the top plate by coating material (Moglice) [8]

compound (Moglice), see Fig. 11. For changing the coupling state, the coupling spheres are pressed into the joint sockets with a setscrew. The setscrew is additionally equipped with a force sensor to measure the applied clamping force.

The clamping force was measured by a piezoelectric sensor 1-CLP/62kN (Hottinger Brüel & Kjær GmbH, Darmstadt, Germany) with a sensitivity of $-4.3\,\mathrm{pC\,N^{-1}}$ and a maximal load of 62kN using a Kistler 5007 amplifier (Kistler Instrumente GmbH, Sindelfingen, Germany) with an uncertainty of about $\pm 50\,\mathrm{N}$. Dynamic properties of these two states were examined as well as the repositioning of the plates after each experiment. The displacement of the top plate along the X-axis was measured using a ML10 laser interferometer (Renishaw plc, Wotton-under-Edge, UK) with a resolution of 1 nm. An accelerometer sensor (Hottinger Brüel & Kjaer with sensitivity of $1\,\mathrm{mV\,ms^{-2}}$ and 2 to 7,000 Hz working frequency) was used to measure the vibration. The experiments were carried out in two phases. At first, the dynamic properties and feasibility of the designed structure was tested. Subsequently, the positioning accuracy during re-coupling was determined.

2.2 *Measurement of Dynamic Properties*

In both states, operational and decoupled, the system was excited by an impulse hammer at the same position. For analysis, the normalized frequency response was calculated. Figure 12 shows the final impulse response of the system in two different stiffness states.

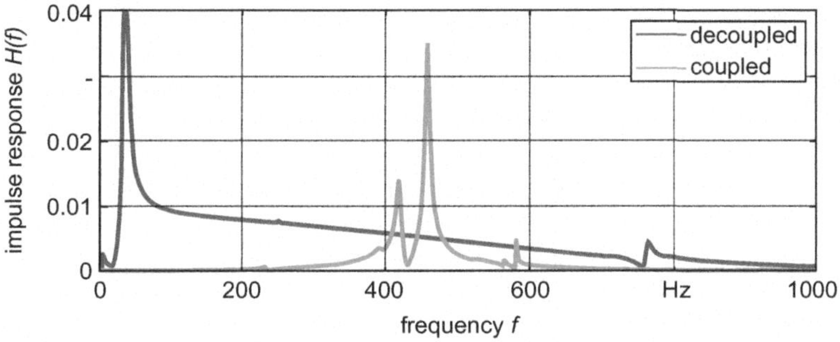

Fig. 12 Impulse response of two states of the system [6]

Three major characteristics were detected from the impulse response. First, the peak amplitude in the setup state is higher than the operational state by a factor of 28.3. Second, the frequency with the highest value in the operational state is about 485 Hz, however, in the setup state the frequency is shifted down to 35 Hz. And finally, in the setup state there are only two eigenfrequencies, whereas in the operational state three eigenfrequencies can be detected.

2.3 Repeatability of the Coupling

Two tests were carried out to analyze the state and dynamic performance of the system after each change of state. At first, different amounts of coupling forces were applied to detect their effect on the dynamic behavior and repositioning of the system (cf. Fig. 13a). It was found that the first and second eigenfrequencies remained relatively constant (cf. Fig. 13b); however, there is a considerable change in the third eigenfrequency at about 500 Hz, which is linearly dependent on the applied coupling force. In other words, instead of measuring the coupling force directly, it may be

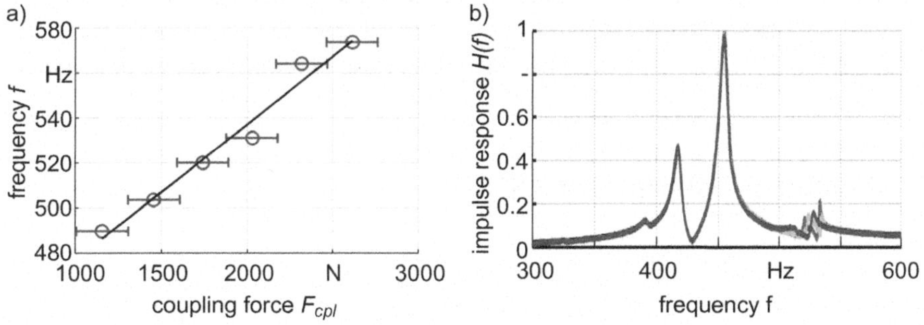

Fig. 13 Shift of the third eigenfrequency by changing the coupling force [8]

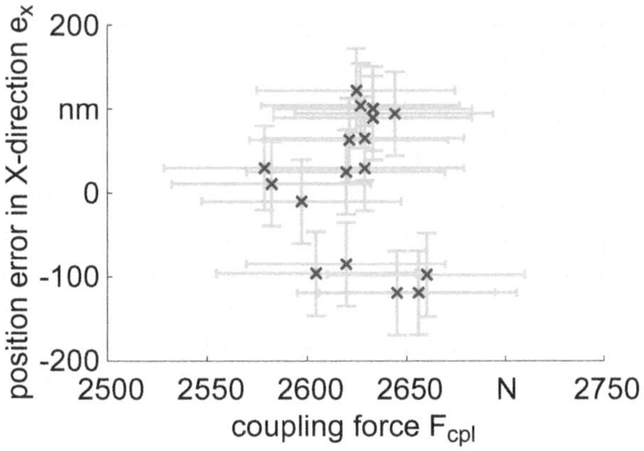

Fig. 14 Repositioning uncertainties of the plates with applying same amount of force [8]

controlled by tuning the third eigenfrequency to achieve more precise and more repeatable results (Fig. 13).

In order to test the repositioning to the operational state, the coupling force was kept constant within the uncertainty of the force sensor (2,600 N $\pm$ 50 N). The accuracy of the repositioning was determined by measuring the displacement between two coupled states to -12 ± 84 nm (Fig. 14). This precision should hold for many applications. Otherwise, the more sophisticated method by eigenfrequency controlled clamping is applicable.

2.4 Applicability of Coupling System for Spindle Balancing

In order to test the suitability of the coupling system for the balancing process, tests were carried out in the two operational states of the system. For this purpose, a spindle was mounted on the coupling system and regular balancing was carried out up to a point where the residual vibrations remained below the detection threshold of the sensors. The system was then changed to the setup state, which amplified the residual unbalance-excited vibrations. By further balancing in this state, the residual unbalance could be reduced even further, see Fig. 15. The results clearly demonstrate the suitability of the newly developed method for use in ultra-precision machining.

3 Balancing Concepts for UP-HPC

Automatic balancing systems are widely used in conventional milling or grinding operations. The conventional systems can balance the rotor within a few milliseconds sufficiently to achieve the required unbalance tolerances. However, these systems are unsuitable for ultra-precision machining, because they do not achieve the required

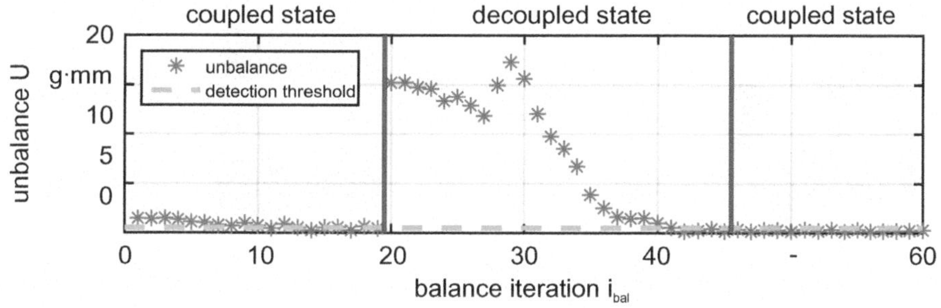

Fig. 15 Balancing process with application of the developed coupling system [6]

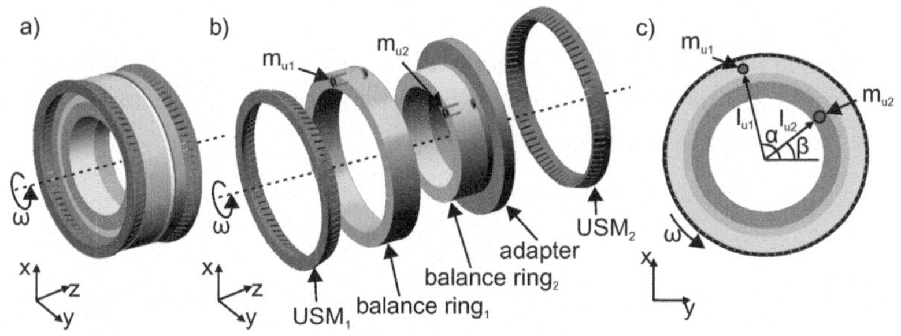

Fig. 16 Rotatory redistribution concept by two ultrasonic motors on the rotor of the working spindle; **a** exploded view, **b** assembly drawing, **c** angular positions of masses [9]

balancing precision or cannot be adapted without affecting the process. Since the most common systems in conventional machining are based either on the spread angle method or fixed-position correction via liquid media, these two methods were investigated with respect to their performance and balancing precision in two prototypes of a balancing system.

3.1 Rotary Mass Distribution via Ultrasonic Motors

The first concept of an automatic balancing system enables to balance the spindle with the use of a rotatory redistribution concept. In the designed setup, the position of the two masses m_{u1} and m_{u2} can be changed while the spindle is running without changing their distance from the center of the rotor. Therefore, a ring-shaped ultrasonic traveling wave motor was applied (Fig. 16).

The masses and their distance from the center were designed so that the following formula is satisfied:

$$|\mathbf{l_1}| \cdot m_{u1} = |\mathbf{l_2}| \cdot m_{u2} \tag{4}$$

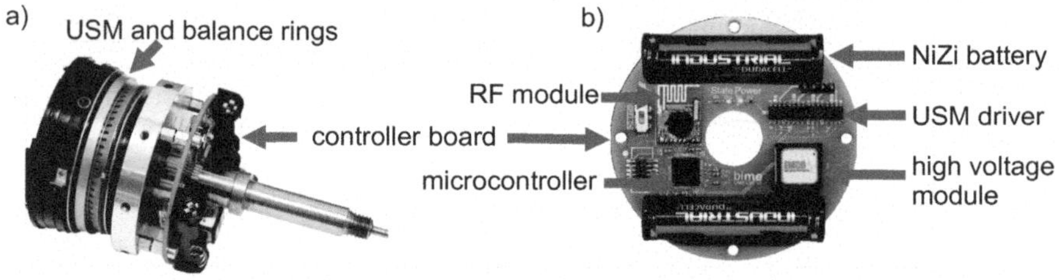

Fig. 17 Experimental setup with one ultrasonic motor: **a** assembled system **b** controller board [9]

where the specific masses m_{u1} and m_{u2} are connected to the respective balance rings at the specific vectors ($\mathbf{l}_1$ and $\mathbf{l}_2$) [17].

Each balance mass produces its specific centrifugal force. By changing the positions of the masses, the total centrifugal force can be varied. The balance force is calculated by the sum of the vectors:

$$F_u = \omega \sum_{n=1}^{2} \boldsymbol{l_n} \cdot m_u \tag{5}$$

where ω is the angular velocity of the spindle.

The balance masses can be shifted independently and by changing the position, the direction and amount of the resultant force vector can be adjusted for compensating the unbalances on the spindle. With an angular offset of $|\alpha - \beta| = 180°$ the centrifugal forces compensate each other, resulting in no effective unbalance. If both balancing masses are located in the same direction ($\alpha = \beta$), the maximum balancing force is generated [9, 23].

Setup and Operation Principle

The control board on the rotor consists of a microcontroller, a frequency module (RFM) for receiving signals from the operator, a driver responsible for controlling the ultrasonic motor rotation and a power supply (Fig. 17). In the following, a brief explanation about the major components which were used in the control board is presented.

The precision of the balancing system is determined by the smallest angular increment. Therefore, an ultrasonic motor from an autofocus camera lens was chosen for rotary distribution of the masses, i.e. to drive balance rings. This type of actuator already features a ring-shaped geometry with multiple piezoelectric elements working in two interleaved groups and allows for tiny rotational movements. By applying an electric voltage, the piezo elements are mechanically strained against the balance ring. Using two traveling wave signals provided by a microcontroller to drive the two groups of actuators, this strain is converted to a rotary motion. While the motor is powered off, the balance ring is self-locked by the preload force (see Fig. 18) [9, 22]. The amplitude and phase of the applied signals from the microcontroller regulate the

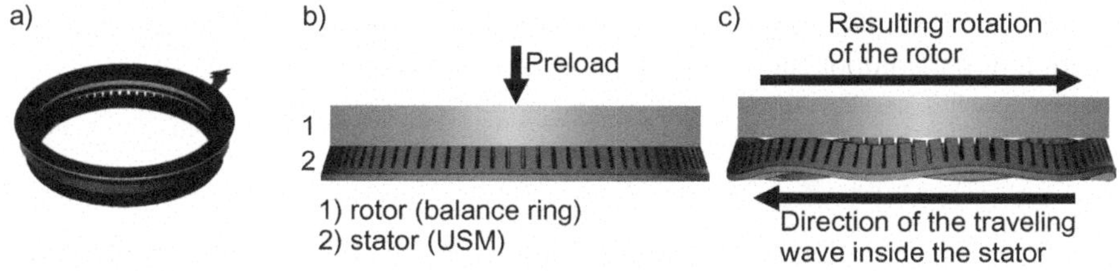

Fig. 18 Ultrasonic motor: **a** overview, **b** idle state, **c** in motion [9]

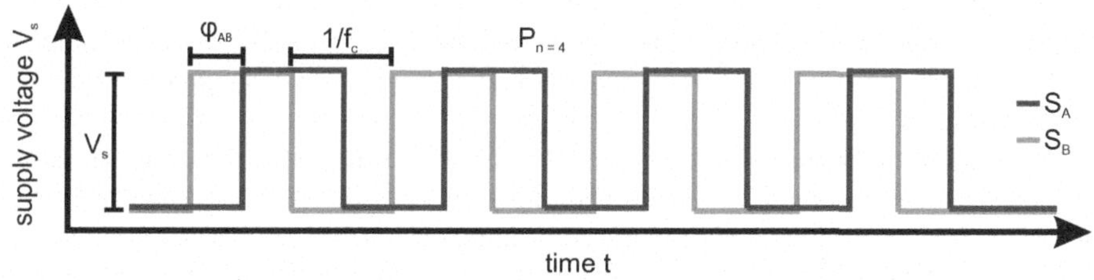

Fig. 19 The controlling signals from the microcontroller for motor driver [9]

mechanical strain of the piezoelectric elements on the stator and hence the rotational speed and direction of the rotor.

Two different signals are applied to the rotor to produce the traveling wave motion, SA and SB (Fig. 19). The traveling wave is generated in the piezoelectric elements due to the phase shift between these signals. This results in a rotational motion due to the frictional force, which pushes the rotor (balance ring) in opposite direction of the traveling wave propagation [20]. The phase shift ϕ_{AB} between the signals can be adjusted between 90° and −90° to change the direction of the rotation. Furthermore, some additional factors affect the operation of the motor such as the frequency of the signals f_c and the number of commutation pulses that are sent to the ultrasonic motor P_n [9].

The required supply voltage for the ultrasonic motor should be higher than 40 V. In the experiments, the generated signal from the microcontroller was adjusted by four operational amplifiers (LTC6090 by Linear Technology, Milpitas/CA, USA). These amplifiers were applied as motor drivers to transform the low current outputs of the microcontroller to the required supply voltage for the ultrasonic motor. Two NiZi-batteries were applied as basic energy supply. The required voltage was produced by a boost converter up to 100 V. Finally, the output of the boost converter was regulated and stabilized by eight 22 μF ceramic capacitors.

For sending and receiving signals from the operator to the motor, two RFM73 transceiver modules from HopeRF (HOPE Microelectronics CO., Ltd., Shenzen, China) were used for the experimental setup. This module works in the 2,400–2483.5 MHz frequency band. One RFM module was installed on the spindle. Due to the rotatory motion of the spindle, the Doppler effect to the sending and receiving signals should be taken into account. In general, the Doppler effect constraints the selection of the component to design the system and is defined as:

$$f_0 = \frac{v}{c} f_0 = r \cdot \frac{\omega}{c} f_0 \tag{6}$$

where v is the circumferential speed of the spindle, $c \approx 3 \times 10^8\,\mathrm{ms}^{-1}$ is the propagation velocity of radio frequency signals, $f_0 = 2.4\,\mathrm{GHz}$ is the carrier frequency, $r = 20\,\mathrm{mm}$ is the distance from the center of the rotor and $\omega = 470\,\mathrm{rad\,s}^{-1}$ is the angular velocity of the rotor. The maximum amount of calculated frequency shift which is produced by Doppler effect is equal to $f_{0\max} = 11.3\,\mathrm{Hz}$. This value is small compared to the operational frequency and therefore, the Doppler effect can be neglected.

The applied microcontroller was an ARM PSoC5 from Cypress Semiconductor. It controlled the ultrasonic motor by sending signals to the driver of the ultrasonic motor (USM) as well as controlling the communication between the operator and the USM motor. Producing of a pulse signal is time-consuming when the (CPU) of the microcontroller is engaged in the signal generation. Hence, it can affect the speed and the quality of the system operation. To avoid this problem, universal digital blocks (UDBs) of the PSoC5 were utilized which allowed for executing small operations and commands without using the CPU. Therefore, the pulse signals could be produced in UDB while CPU was busy with communication [9].

Experimental Validation of Balancing System

In order to verify the feasibility of ultrasonic motor for balancing the spindle, the generated torque by the USM (M_u) and its ability for shifting the balancing mass and the accuracy of the step size for the balancing system were analyzed. In addition, the ability of the ultrasonic motor to keep the balancing mass in the desired location during rotation of the spindle as well as capability of the USM to shift the balancing mass based on the defined step sizes were examined. The behavior of the ultrasonic motor was analyzed while changing different parameter values when the spindle was stationary. Figure 20 and Fig. 21 show the torque (M_u) and rotation angle (γ) for changing supply voltage (V_s), commutation pulse numbers (P_n) and commutation frequency (f_c). The rotation angle was measured with a laser triangulation sensor (optoNCDT 2300 by Micro-Epsilon Messtechnik GmbH & Co. KG, Ortenburg, Germany). During the measurements, one of the three parameters was varied while the others were kept constant. The standard parameters values were:

$V_s = 80\,\mathrm{V}$,
$P_n = 35$ and
$f_c = 31.5\,\mathrm{kHz}$.

The phase difference (ϕ_{AB}) remained constant at 90° during the measurements [9].

The effect of the supply voltage on the measured torque of the ultrasonic motor is illustrated in Fig. 20a. When the voltage falls below 40 V, the motor is not able to rotate and the resulting torque is 0. From 40 to 60 V, the torque increases considerably

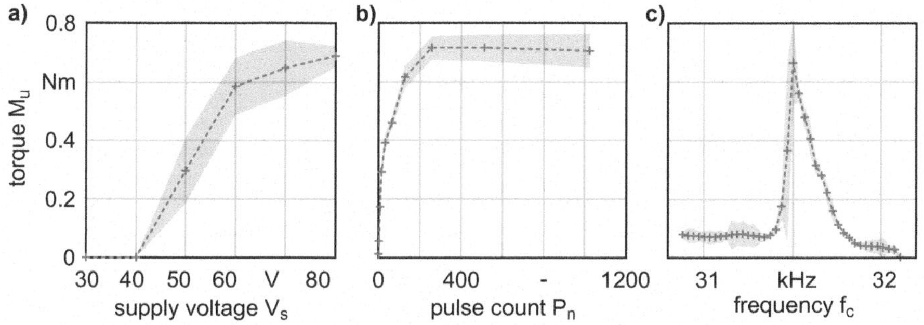

Fig. 20 Measurement of torque by changing the parameters with indication of threefold standard deviation: **a** supply voltage, **b** pulse number, **c** frequency [9]

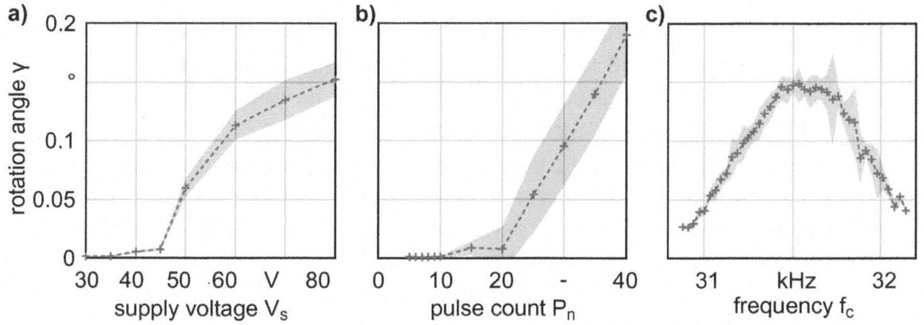

Fig. 21 Measurement of rotational angle by changing the parameters with indication of threefold standard deviation: **a** supply voltage, **b** pulse number, **c** commutation frequency [9]

from 0 to about 0.6 Nm. By increasing the supply voltage from 60 to 80 V, the curve eases off towards about 0.7 Nm torque.

The effect of commutation pulse number on the torque of the motor is shown in Fig. 20b. The commutation pulse number was varied from 2 to 1,024 pulses. At first, there is a sharp increase in torque when the commutation pulse number is increasing from 2 to 256. By further increasing the pulse number, the torque was stabilized to a constant value.

Finally, the effect of the commutation frequency can be seen from Fig. 20c. The frequency was varied from 29.8 to 31.4 kHz. The torque raises suddenly at 31.4 kHz, afterwards, it drops slightly to less than 0.1 Nm at about 31.8 kHz. The effect of parameters (V_s, P_n and f_c) on the step size is shown in Fig. 21.

When the supply voltage was lower than 40 V, there was no rotation of the motor. Increasing the voltage supply increased the rotation angle up to about 0.15° at 80 V. Investigating the commutation pulse number showed that very small step sizes (about 0.01°) could be achieved with $P_n \approx 15$. The curve shows a steep rise from $P_n = 20$ to $P_n = 40$ as it is illustrated in Fig. 21b.

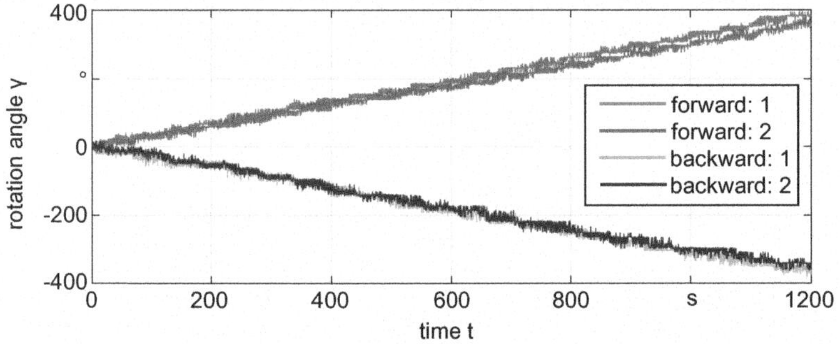

Fig. 22 Changing of angular position of the balancing mass during the rotation of the spindle [9]

To observe the effect of commutation frequency on the rotation angle, the frequency was varied from 29.8 to 32.2 kHz. By increasing the frequency to 31.5 kHz, the rotation angle was increased gently and reached its maximum value at about 0.17°. With higher values, the curve is decreasing again.

To analyze the capability of the ultrasonic motor for changing the balance state of the spindle and its accuracy, the operation of the ultrasonic motor was observed during the rotation of the spindle. The experiments were performed at $\omega = 150\,\mathrm{rad\,s^{-1}}$ (1,432 $\mathrm{min^{-1}}$). The balancing state was changed with a balance mass $m_u = 2.1$ g at a radius of 30 mm which provided a balancing capacity of 63 g mm. The position of the balance mass was detected by two external photoelectric sensors with one of the sensors detecting the angle of the balance mass (ϕ_b) and the other detecting the angle of the experimental setup (ϕ_e). As a result, at constant rotational speed, the angle of the balance mass could be measured ($\alpha = \phi_e - \phi_b$).

Furthermore, the supply voltage was set to $V_s = 64$ V, the commutation frequency to $f_c = 31.5$ kHz, the commutation pulse number to $P_n = 100$ and the phase of controlling signals was kept constant at $-90°$. The experiment was repeated four times and each time with 600 commutation pulse packages (each with $P_n = 100$). After every 30 packages, the motor was stopped for 10 s to test the ability of the motor for holding the balance mass in the desired position. In parallel, the balance state of the spindle was measured with a "Vibrobalancer 41" by SCHENCK RoTec GmbH.

Experimental Results

Figure 22 shows the rotational shift of the counter mass and the resulting balance state during rotation of the spindle. It can be seen that the ultrasonic motor is able to rotate the balance mass in both direction and hold it in its position during the rotation of the spindle.

Initially, the balancing process was performed with one USM to change the balance state by shifting one balance mass to change the direction of the unbalance force. Hence, the initial unbalance of the system could not be fully compensated. The measured vibration of the spindle relative to the rotor position is shown in Fig. 23.

Fig. 23 Measurement of changing balancing state in terms of amplitude and phase of the vibrations of the spindle during the rotational shift with one USM [9]

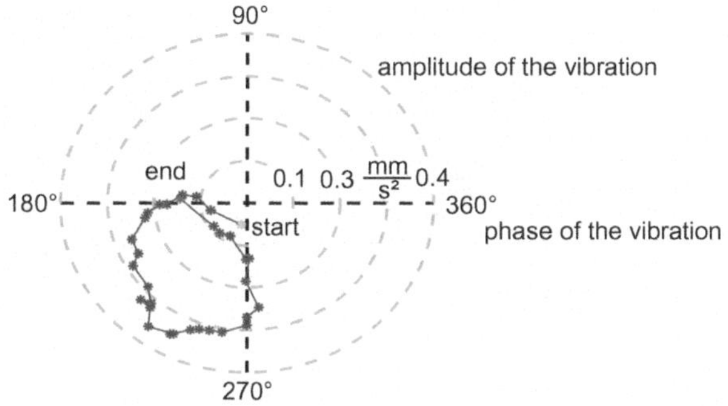

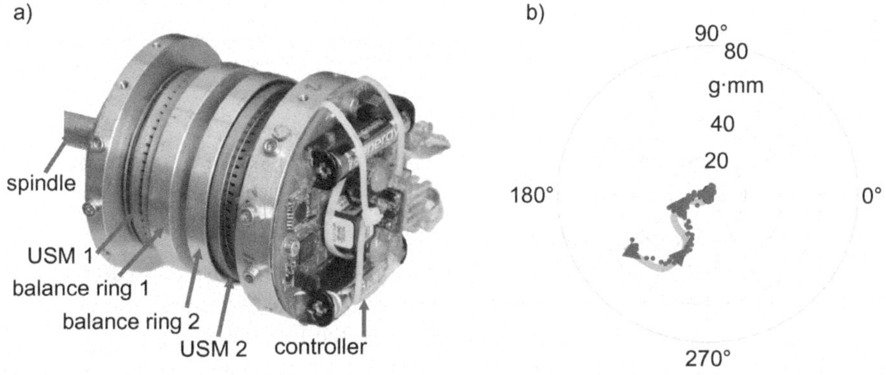

Fig. 24 Balancing with two ultrasonic motors: **a** setup, **b** measured balancing state

The experimental setup was able to change the balance state of the spindle by changing the position of the balance mass. In addition, the system was able to balance the spindle to 0.055 g mm by adjusting the balance mass with the amount of 2.1 g, which is better than ISO grade (0.064 g mm) [9].

In the next step, the experiment was applied with two USM to demonstrate the full balancing capability. In this setup, the balancing force could be adjusted more precisely due to the second balance mass (see Fig. 24a). The experimental results showed that the system was able to reach the balance state of less than 0.04 g mm.

3.2 *Mass Removal via Microfluidic Actuator*

A balancing concept used in industry for many years is based on adding fluidic masses to predefined tanks. This concept is realized, for example, in conventional grinding applications by patented fluidic balancing systems [1]. For this purpose, the cooling lubricant required in the grinding process is injected into the balancing system in a controlled amount via nozzles during rotor rotation. As soon as the spindle stops, the

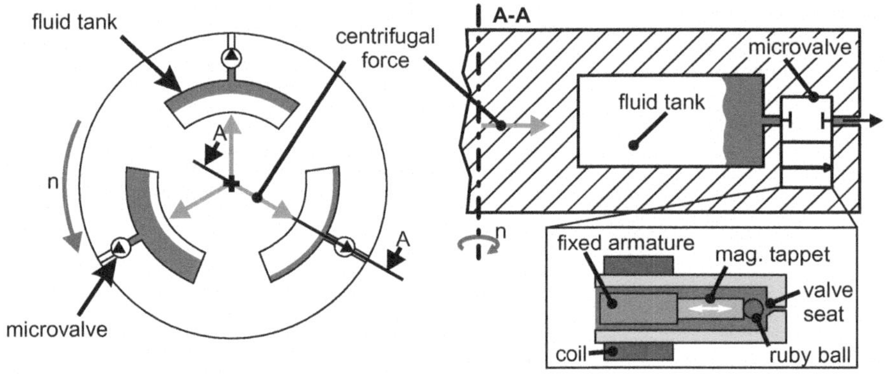

Fig. 25 **a** Scheme of a face-mounted microfluidic balancing disk, **b** working principles for the microvalve during spindle rotation

fluid is released via the open design of the system and must be re-injected during a re-balancing process.

Concept and Preliminary Analyses

In general, such balancing systems are primarily designed for use on hydrostatic or roller bearing spindles in order to compensate large unbalances as quickly as possible. Due to the large installation space of the systems, the low balancing precision and the inability to keep the balancing state, however, they are unsuitable for use on air-bearing high-frequency spindles in ultra-precision machining. In contrast, a spindle-mounted subtractive balancing system, in which a fluid is evacuated from pre-filled chambers, has not been utilized or considered in both conventional and ultra-precision machining. In addition, by using sealed tanks, the balancing condition could be kept for future use, eliminating the need for re-balancing after spindle restart.

For the above-mentioned designated balancing grade of $G0.064$ for UP-HPC machining, a subtractive balancing system has to be able to extract masses in the order of approx. 1 mg. Therefore, the concept of a microfluidic balancing system is presented below, which achieves this balancing precision by means of microvalves [3]. In order to open the selected microvalve, which is based on the principle of electromagnetism, a magnetic tappet inside the valve has to be pulled against a fixed armature, thus retracting a ruby ball positioned in a sapphire glass insert (valve seat). As soon as the electromagnetic field can no longer hold back the tappet, the valve closes as an integrated spring pushes the ruby ball back into its seat. This mode of operation has the advantage that the valve is additionally pressed into the seat by the fluid and centrifugal force acting during rotation. Therefore, an increased leak resistance is expected. The schematic design of the microfluidic balancing system with three evenly distributed microvalves on the circumference is shown in Fig. 25. In the three fluid tanks located behind the valves, the fluid forced outwards by centrifugal force is shown schematically.

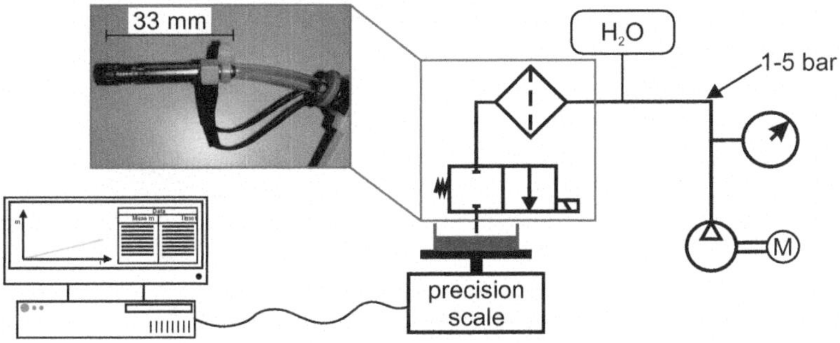

Fig. 26 Schematic drawing of the experimental setup and devices applied for the microvalve

To determine the achievable balancing precision of the microfluidic balancing system, the minimum amount of transported fluid was measured under different experimental conditions in a static test setup. Distilled water was used as fluid to be transported in the experiments, as this should have a negligible effect on process safety. The microvalve was connected to a tube filled with distilled water and supplied with compressed air (see Fig. 26). By varying the pressure of the compressed air from 1 to 5 bar in the experiments, centrifugal force conditions at different rotation speeds which act on the fluid are simulated. The opening times of the microvalve were varied from 0.1 to 50 ms in the experiments and the transported fluid mass was detected by a digitally readable precision scale (see Fig. 26).

Figure 27 shows the average values of the transported masses of 1,000 valve openings over the varying opening times. The results show that a precise dispensing of <1 mg can be achieved with the valve under all test conditions. With an opening time of 0.1 ms to 0.5 ms and a supplied air pressure of 1 to 5 bar, a mass of minimum 0.065 mg to maximum 0.21 mg per valve opening was transported. Starting with a valve opening time of 1 ms, a linear behavior with a proportional increase of the opening time can be recognized at all air pressures. It can also be seen that a proportional increase in air pressure is not accompanied by a proportional increase in the transported mass. This suggests that a saturated state would result if the air pressure continues to increase. These properties simplify the creation of a characteristic curve in the control concept. The results in Fig. 27 imply that an automatic balancing system with the tested microvalves has the potential to achieve a balancing quality of at least $G0.064$ for air-bearing spindles.

Prototype Design for an Automated Precision Hydrobalancer

Based on the previous findings, a prototype of an automatic balancing system was designed [4]. Various boundary conditions were defined for the suitability of the balancing system for use in ultra-precise high-speed cutting. Three main conditions should be fulfilled:

1. Wireless communication with a master computer, which sends the commands to open the individual valves to create a defined counterbalance in amplitude and phase.

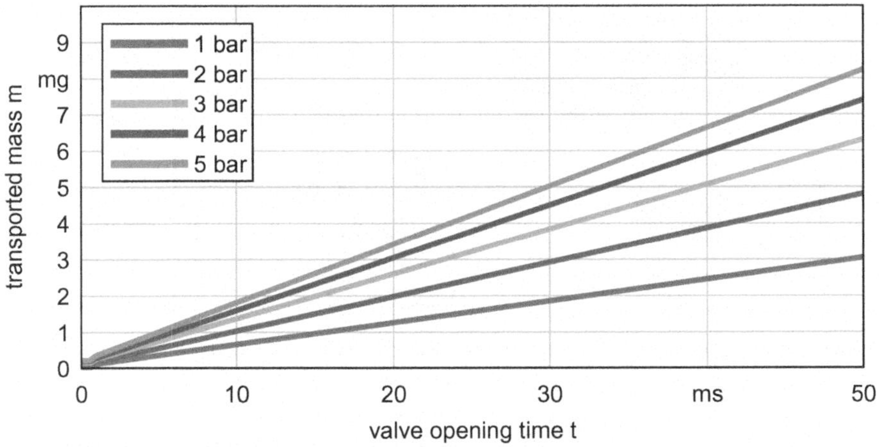

Fig. 27 Measurement of the transported fluid by varying the applied pressure and the release time of the electromagnetic valve

2. Integrated power supply, e.g. in order to avoid sliding contacts or mercury baths for the power supply. These systems would not have a tolerable influence on the rotor behavior and would also mean increased installation costs.
3. Achieving a balance grade of $G0.064$ at a cutting speed of $v_c > 2{,}000\,\mathrm{m\,min^{-1}}$ to enable in-process balancing in ultra-precise high-speed cutting.

In Fig. 28 the prototype of the automatic balancing system is shown. The balancing system uses three microvalves, which are evenly distributed at 120° intervals on the circumference of the outer surface. This minimum number of valves is sufficient for balancing due to the dosing precision shown in Fig. 27 and saves both weight and installation space. Nickel-zinc accumulators are placed on the circuit board, which supply the valves and the microcontroller with defined voltage and current via voltage converters. The microcontroller based on an ATMEL ATmega328 chip receives the opening commands of the valves from the master computer via a wireless 2.4 GHz radio interface. In addition, three tool holders were mounted on the base plate, one of which can be used in the machining process while the other two are implemented to maintain symmetry and will not contain a cutting edge. In comparison to the USM system, low voltages are sufficient to control the valves, which leads to a longer operating time due to the lower power consumption.

Experimental Validation

The performance of the balancing system was investigated by semi-automatic balancing experiments. Based on the calculated amplitude and phase, the corresponding valve was opened to discharge a certain amount of fluid from the tanks. The execution of the tests is based on the manual balancing process, i.e. the spindle speed was gradually increased in order to protect the air bearing from damage due to large unbalance-induced centrifugal forces. However, in contrast to the manual

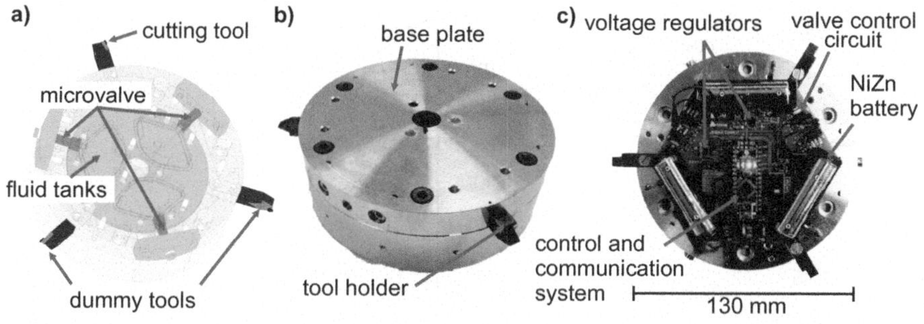

Fig. 28 Prototype of the automatic balancing system based on electromagnetic microvalves: **a** CAD design, **b** fully assembled system, **c** PCB inside the balancing system with mounted components

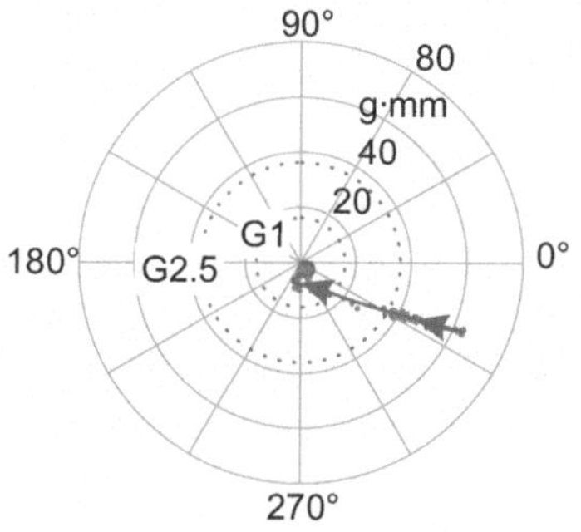

Rotational speed	3,000 min^{-1}
Rotor weight	4.5 kg
Balancing concept	fixed position
Initial balance state	G4.4
Final balance state	G0.02
Initial unbalance	63.22 g·mm @ 337.14°
Final unbalance	0.29 g·mm @ 325.44°

Fig. 29 Balancing protocol of a semi-automatic balancing procedure, achieving a balance state of $< G0.064$ at $n = 3{,}000\,\text{min}^{-1}$

balancing process, it is no longer necessary to stop the spindle in between balancing steps. This semi-automatic procedure already allows time savings of up to 75% compared to manual balancing (manual: 60 min; semi-automatic: 15 min). At $n = 3{,}000\,\text{min}^{-1}$, the defined balancing quality level of $G0.064$ is already overachieved with the present prototype balancing system, which can be seen in Fig. 29.

Both of the investigated balancing concepts proof to be sufficiently suitable for the automatic balancing of air-bearing spindles. The balancing concept with the ultrasonic motors convinces by its speed and the elimination of the application of any additional masses. However, the high voltage power supply for the ultrasonic motors is not yet sufficient to guarantee their use in a fully functional system.

The microfluidic balancing system convinces by its superior balancing precision and the easier control by low voltage. It is on the other hand limited in its total balancing capacity as the pre-filled tanks ultimately will be depleted after a certain number of procedures. Nevertheless, due to its precision and practicability, the concept of the microfluidic balancing system will be further investigated in the following chapter and transferred to a fully automatic balancing system.

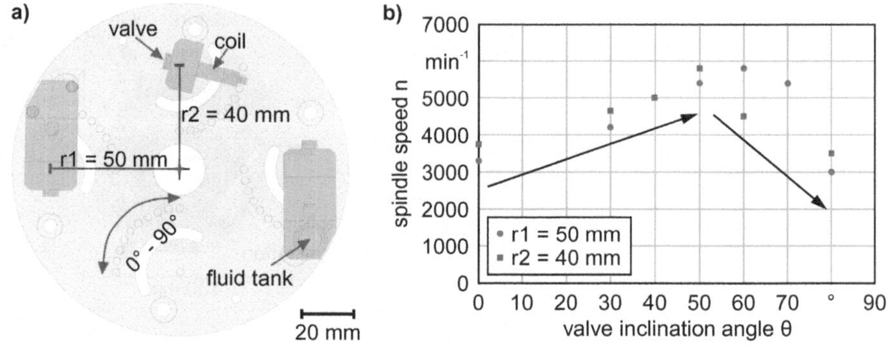

Fig. 30 **a** Concept drawing of the test tool with multiple possible valve inclination angles and two radii, **b** Maximal achievable rotational speed n at specific valve inclination angle θ

Fully Automatic Balancing with Microfluidic Actuators

Preliminary tests have shown that the valves of the microfluidic balancing system can only be opened up to a spindle speed of 3,000 min^{-1}. At higher speeds, the centrifugal force acts against the force provided by the electromagnetic field of the coils and thus the mobile armature for opening the valves can no longer be pulled back, leaving the valves closed. Possible solutions are either to increase the magnetic field, to reduce the balancing speed or to reduce the centrifugal force acting on the opening behavior of the valves. Since an increase of the magnetic field would not be possible without a development of new coils and a reduced balancing speed is not appropriate, the best approach was seen in the reduction of the centrifugal force acting on the mobile armature.

Therefore, it was investigated at which angle of inclination, relative to the lateral surface, the valve still opens and closes reliably. For this purpose, a test base plate was used in which the angle of inclination of the valves can be varied from 0–90° on two different radii (see Fig. 30a). The results of the test displayed in Fig. 30b show the maximum achievable speed at which the valve at a given inclination angle reliably opens and closes. It can be seen that the maximum speed of $n = 5{,}800\,min^{-1}$ is achieved at an angle of inclination of 50° for $r_2 = 40$ mm and at 60° for $r_1 = 50$ mm. At an angle of inclination ≥60° the valve could be opened, but it did not close after the voltage was removed. Presumably, the centrifugal force caused the mobile armature to lock up so that it could no longer bounce back.

Revised Hydrofluidic Balancing System

For a revised version of the balancing system a radius of 40 mm and an angle of inclination of 50° was therefore specified for the placement of the valves in order to maximize the achievable speed. Furthermore, additional requirements were defined for the second version of an automatic balancing system with the aim of easier handling and an increased performance.

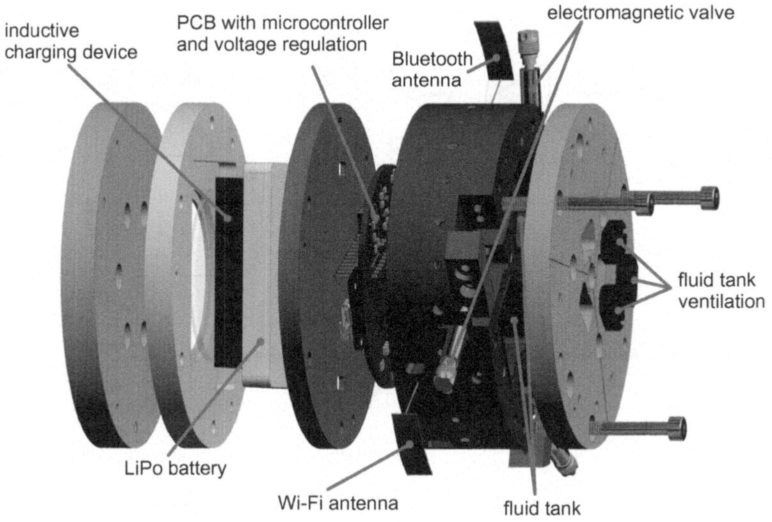

Fig. 31 Explosion drawing of the automatic balancing system for air-bearing spindles

1. Replacement of the nickel-zinc accumulators with a lithium-ion polymer (LiPo) battery, which requires less installation space.
2. Integration of a charge controller and wireless charging station so that the system does not need to be opened to change or charge the battery.
3. Connection of the balancing system to a cloud-based service in order to facilitate the exchange of measurement data.
4. Control and monitoring of the balancing system via an application for mobile devices to improve usability in a shop floor environment.

The implementation of the requirements in the hardware can be seen in Fig. 31. The explosion drawing shows the valves positioned in 50° angle, the new LiPo battery, the contactless charging interface, as well as the Bluetooth and Wi-Fi antenna for communication with the cloud based service.

By connecting the balancing system to the Internet, data can be exchanged between several systems. Figure 32 shows the schematic structure of the interface control. After the user has started the balancing process, the unbalance is measured, evaluated and the corresponding control commands are sent to the cloud. Here the microcontroller, which is mounted on the spindle, picks up the data and opens the corresponding valves. While the valves are open, the unbalance is continuously monitored and the measured data is graphically displayed to the user in the computer application and his mobile device. If the balancing process fails, the user can stop the balancing process and stop the spindle.

To ensure a smooth data transfer between both microcontrollers, a data structure based on semaphores is used. Data is only transmitted or retrieved if a corresponding signal is transmitted. As long as, for example, the valves in the automatic balancing

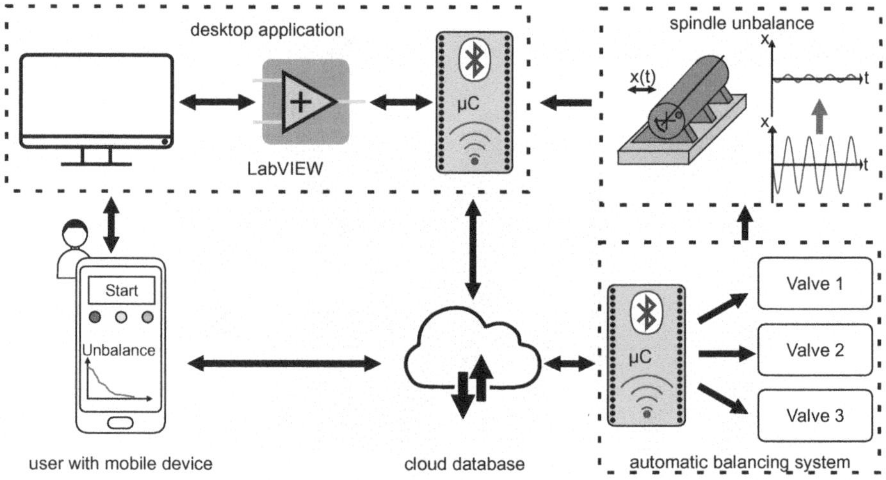

Fig. 32 Schematic structure of the interface control between balancing device and operator

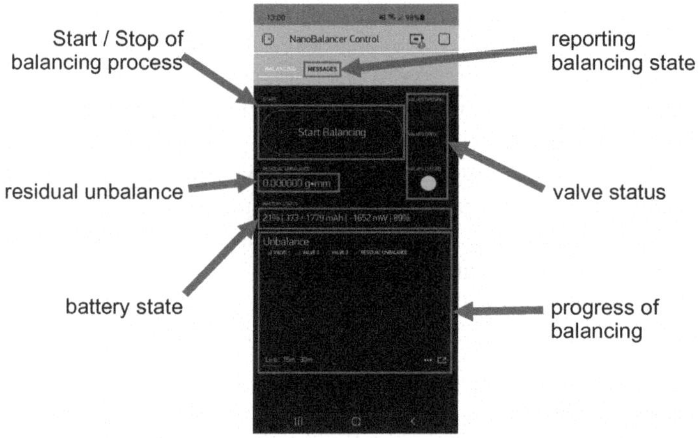

Fig. 33 Application interface displaying the operator the balancing state and further information e.g. the battery status

system are open, no new opening commands are requested, as the microcontroller of the balancing system does not issue a permission. These states are signaled to the user via a traffic light display in the application as seen in Fig. 33. The user can also monitor the state of charge, discharge rate and battery health in the application.

The complete balancing process will be started by the operator by pressing the “Start Balancing” button and can be stopped by pressing the same button with the switched caption “Stop Balancing”. When the balancing process is finished, a report function can be used to send the balancing result and history to the operator by mail.

4 Control System for Automatic Balancing Systems

The control system is a decisive component in the automatic balancing process. The goal is that the balancing process takes place with as little user intervention as possible that and the risk of bearing damage is avoided. For these reasons, a control system based on the graphical programming system LabVIEW from National Instruments was developed, which also offers the possibility to communicate with the systems of the other developments within the FOR1845 and thus provides an easy integration into the overall system. Due to the design principle of air-bearing spindles and the assumption of a rigid rotor behavior in the intended speed range as presented from Cao et al. [2], the influence coefficient method can be used to determine the unbalance. Furthermore, due to the design of the existing spindles, it is only possible to balance in one plane, as no access to the rear part of the rotor is provided.

To determine the influence coefficients for conventional balancing in one plane, two test runs must be carried out, between which the spindle must be stopped and accelerated again. During the first test run, the spindle is accelerated to operating speed and a measurement of the vibrations generated is carried out by the balancing measuring system. Then the spindle is stopped and a test mass is applied at a defined location. The amount and the position of the attached test mass is then transferred to the measuring system and a measurement is done at operating speed again. The influence coefficients can then be calculated from these two measurements. Using these coefficients, it is known how much mass must be attached or removed at which position on the rotor to compensate the unbalance.

In addition to this method, the control system enables a determination of the influence coefficients at runtime without stopping the spindle to be used with the automatic balancing system (see Fig. 34). This method uses the defined release of fluid to generate the required trial mass. The time advantage of this method is obvious, since the spindle does not have to be stopped to generate the test mass and calculate the coefficients. Once the coefficients have been calculated, they are stored in a file and loaded into the control system when required. Since the influence coefficients only include the system state at a certain speed, a new influence coefficient matrix must be calculated for a changed speed. In conventional balancing, this would imply multiple manual starts and stops of the spindle and the application of test masses. With the control system in automatic balancing, the rotational speed can easily be adjusted and the generation of the influence coefficients can be carried out automatically if no influence coefficient matrix has been previously generated.

A special feature of the control system is that it enables a fully automatic balancing process up to the desired operating speed. In Fig. 35 the flowchart of an automatic balancing process is displayed. If it is possible to control the rotational speed of the air-bearing spindle via an interface, the target operational speed for the machining process can be directly entered. The automatic balancing process then starts at a low speed for pre-balancing and the speed is incrementally increased until the operational speed is reached, while the unbalance is monitored in the individual intermediate steps and any required adjustments are automatically carried out.

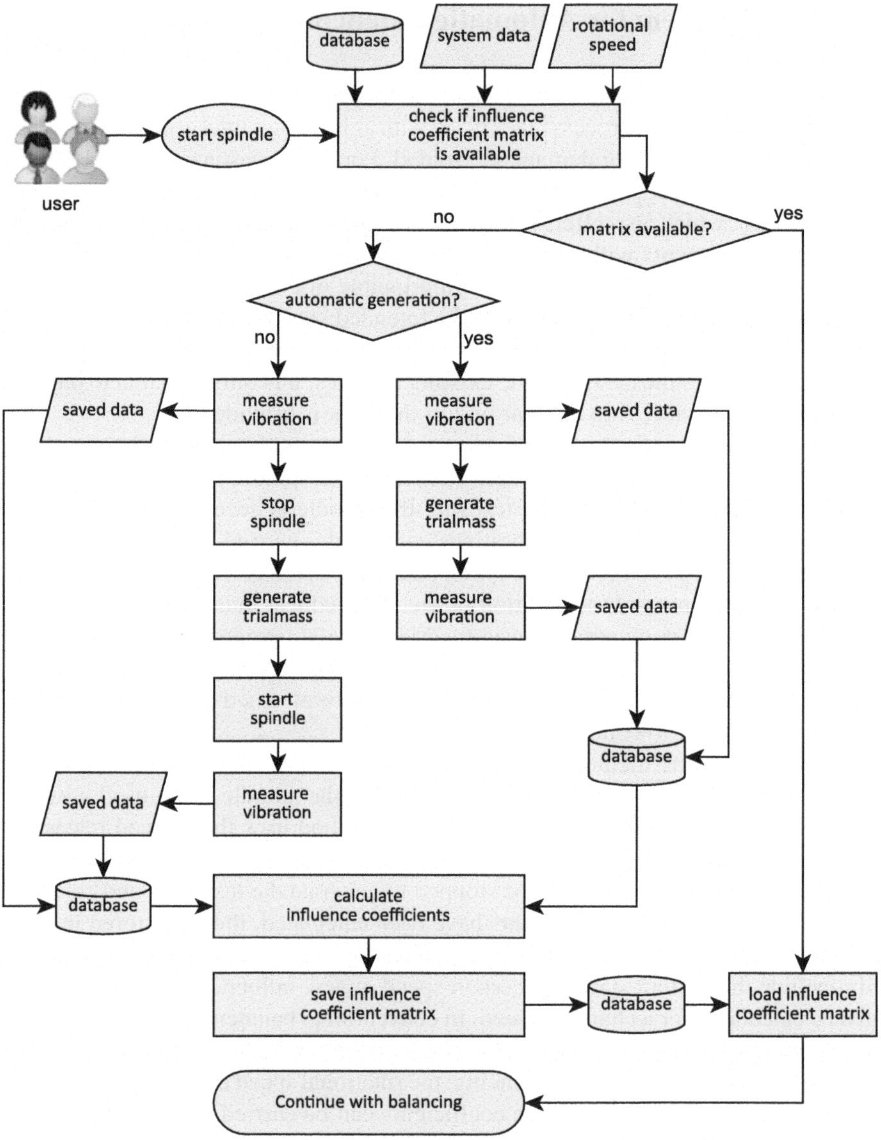

Fig. 34 Flowchart of an automatic generation of influence coefficients

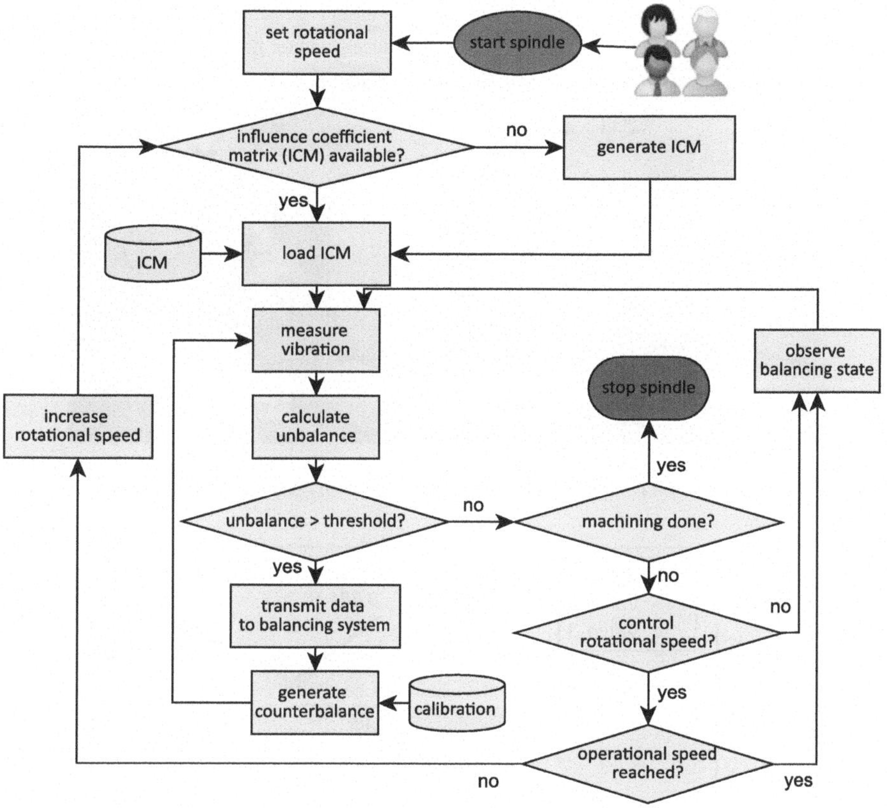

Fig. 35 Flowchart of an automatic balancing process for static or variable rotational speed

4.1 Validation of the Automatic Balancing Process

The validation of the system was separated into multiple parts. For testing the functionality and precision of the microvalves at different speeds, the automatic balancing system was mounted on a 4R air-bearing spindle by Professional Instruments Company (Hopkins/MN, USA). This spindle is able to provide a maximum rotational speed of 7,500 $\min^{-1}$ at a radial and axial bearing stiffness of approx. 80 N μm^{-1} and 230 N μm^{-1}, respectively. The experimental setup is displayed in Fig. 36. As in previous investigations, the unbalance-induced vibrations are detected by acceleration sensors with a sensitivity of 1,000 mV g^{-1} and forwarded to the measurement system. The assignment of the measurement data to each revolution is enabled via a trigger sensor. A high system stiffness is achieved by mounting the air-bearing spindle to a granite measuring table via fixtures.

In Fig. 37 the resulting unbalance changes ΔU for varying rotational speeds are displayed for each electromagnetic valve. These data were used to calculate a regres-

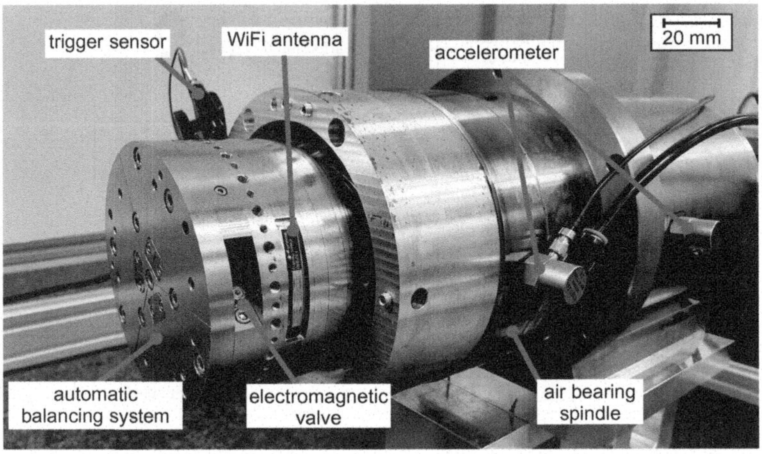

Fig. 36 Experimental setup for testing the automatic balancing system on an air bearing spindle

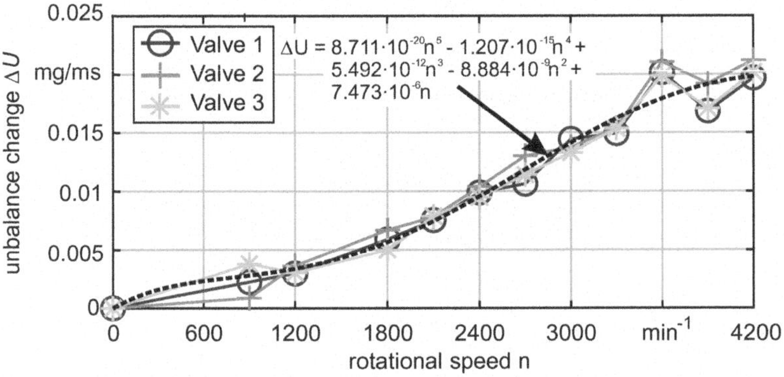

Fig. 37 Resulting unbalance change at varying rotational speeds for each electromagnetic valve and the calculated regression function

sion function for the valves to be saved in the control system. Due to the proximity of all results, a single regression function is sufficient and can be used for all valves in the automatic balancing procedure. This function enables an assignment of the mass to be removed with respect to a rotational speed and is taken as the reference for calculating the valve opening time.

4.2 Results

The results of the balancing tests of the new control system with the new automatic balancing system are shown in Figs. 38, 39 and 40 as residual unbalance U versus the

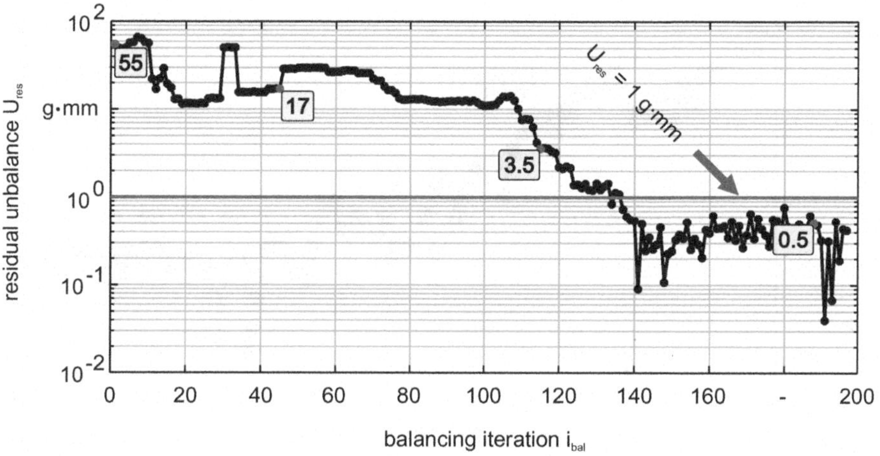

Fig. 38 Automatic balancing of a Professional Instruments 4R air-bearing spindle at 1,800 min^{-1}

balancing iteration i_{bal}. The first test was a pre-balancing at low speed. At this point, it is essential that large unbalances are reliably reduced to an acceptable value. The limits of the rotational speed and the unbalance to be achieved depend on the spindle used, since the bearing stiffness is the decisive factor here. For the spindle used in the experimental setup, a rotational speed of $n = 1{,}800\,\text{min}^{-1}$ and a permissible residual unbalance of $U \leq 1$ g mm were defined. With this residual unbalance, it is possible to safely accelerate to higher rotational speeds and perform precision balancing. The results of the first test are shown in Fig. 38.

As the results in Fig. 38 illustrate, pre-balancing is possible in a process-safe manner. Even if an incorrect measurement leads to an overcompensation of the unbalance, this is eliminated in the subsequent balancing iterations. After the pre-balancing was carried out at $n = 1{,}800\,\text{min}^{-1}$, the next step was to select a speed that was significantly higher than that of the pre-balancing. Therefore, the next test was an automatic balancing at a rotational speed of $n = 4{,}200\,\text{min}^{-1}$. The target for the residual unbalance to be achieved was chosen to be $U < 0.065$ g mm. The results of this test are shown in Fig. 39.

After a residual unbalance of $U = 0.88$ g mm was detected, the residual unbalance was successively reduced to $U \approx 0.046$ g mm. When this value of the residual unbalance is reached, it is possible to accelerate the spindle up to the operating speed without any risk of damage to the air bearing.

The next test is to investigate up to which maximum rotational speed the automatic balancing system can reliably operate. In the preliminary tests in paragraph 3.2, it has been shown that the microvalves can operate at 50° up to a rotational speed of $n = 5{,}800\,\text{min}^{-1}$. However, in Fig. 40 it can be seen that at a rotational speed of $n = 4{,}500\,\text{min}^{-1}$ the functionality is no longer given.

The results show the measured residual unbalance while a valve opening between the seventh and eleventh measurement iteration at which the valve was unable to

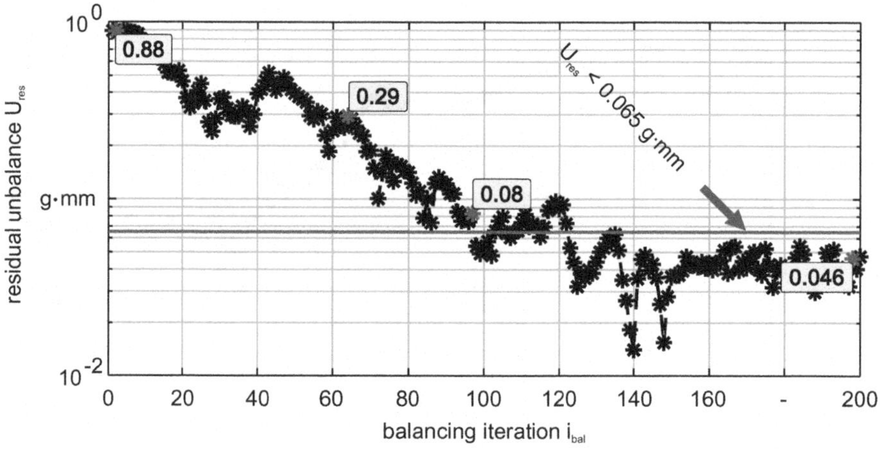

Fig. 39 Automatic balancing of a Professional Instruments 4R air-bearing spindle at 4,200 min^{-1}

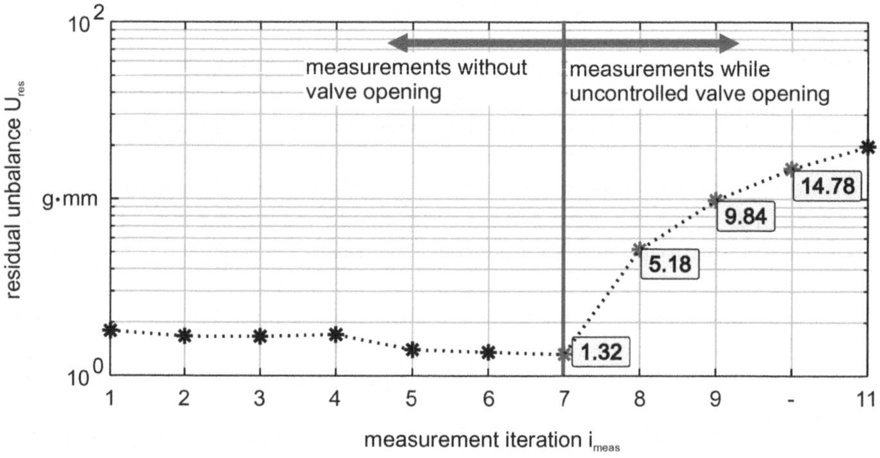

Fig. 40 Valve opening with the automatic balancing system at 4,500 min^{-1} on a Professional Instruments 4R air-bearing spindle

close. This result is surprising since the angle and radius of the preliminary tests were adopted in the final system. However, this is not a problem for reliable balancing the air-bearing spindle, since the unbalance-induced vibrations can already be detected safely and reliably with the acceleration sensors at $3{,}000\,\text{min}^{-1} < n < 4{,}500\,\text{min}^{-1}$.

The results of the balancing experiments show that a safe balancing is possible with the automatic balancing system in combination with the control system.

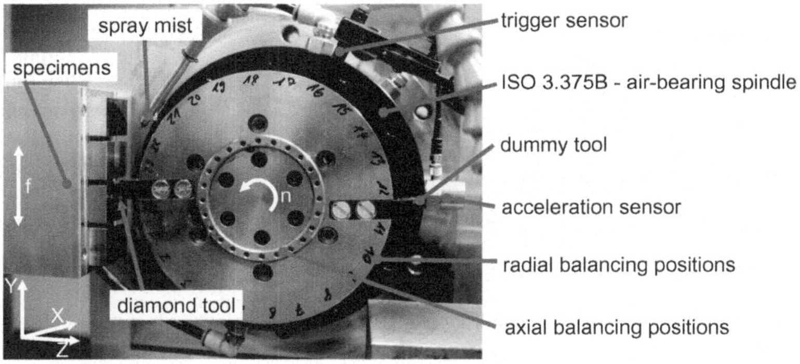

Fig. 41 Experimental setup for fly-cutting experiments with ISO 3.375B spindle on Moore Nanotechnology 350 Freeform Generator

5 Influence of Unbalance on Surface Generation

In order to be able to evaluate which balance grade is sufficient for ultra-precise high-speed machining with multiple tools, the rotor behavior of an air-bearing spindle was analyzed more closely. Of particular interest here is how the rotor behaves with varying rotor unbalance ($U = 0.1$, 1 and 10 g mm) and cutting velocity ($v_c = 1,000$ and $4,000\,\text{m min}^{-1}$). A proven method is to measure the displacement of a measurement artifact with several sensors in order to extract the rotor behavior from these measured data. In these investigations, however, only the measurement artifact was mounted on the spindle and set in rotation. Since the dynamic behavior is of particular interest for the process, a tool was mounted in addition to the measurement artifact to analyze the rotor behavior not only in the static case (without machining) but also in the dynamic case (during machining). The dynamic case can also be used to investigate how the rotor behavior is reflected in the workpiece surface. Therefore, investigations were carried out on a Moore Nanotech 350FG ultra-precision milling and turning machine (Moore Nanotechnology Systems, LLC, Swanzey/NH, USA) with a mounted ISO 3.375B air-bearing spindle from Professional Instruments Company (Hopkins/MN, USA) on the Z-axis.

Four non-ferrous metals were selected as workpiece materials for the machining experiments (aluminum AlMg3, OFHC copper, brass CuZn39Pb3 and nickel silver CuNi18Zn19Pb1). All specimens were simultaneously mounted in a clamping device on the main spindle of the machine (see Fig. 41, left) and face-turned ultra-precisely to ensure a uniform surface plane and thus a constant cutting depth of $a_p = 20\,\mu\text{m}$ for the subsequent cutting tests. The fly-cutter (swing radius $r_{fly} = 82$ mm), which was mounted on the ISO 3.375B spindle for machining the plane surfaces, was equipped with a monocrystalline diamond tool with a cutting edge radius $r_\varepsilon = 0.797$ mm. For precise balancing, the fly-cutter offers 24 evenly distributed axial M3 and radial M4 screw threads in the front or lateral surface respectively.

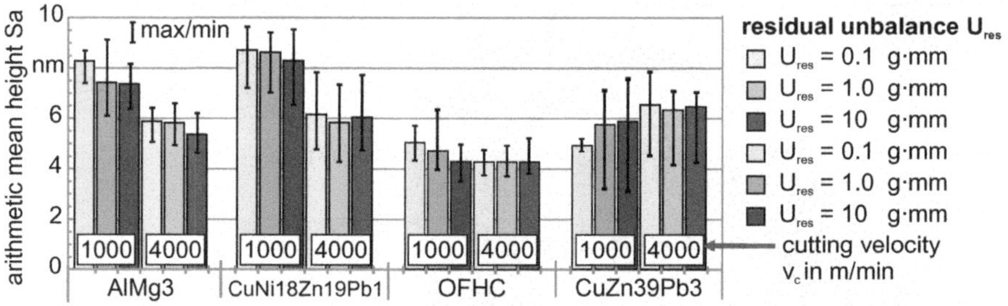

Fig. 42 Arithmetic mean height Sa resulting from cutting experiments with various cutting velocities and unbalance states

A balancing measurement system based on the influence coefficient method in combination with highly sensitive accelerometers with a sensitivity of 1,000 mV $g^{-1} \pm 10\%$ enabled a precise measurement of the balancing condition. Due to is inherent independence from the spindle specifications, the residual unbalance U was used as a parameter for setting the unbalance states instead of the balance quality grade from the DIN ISO 21940-11:2017 standard [11]. For the machining tests, the residual unbalance U was intentionally set to 0.1, 1 and 10 g mm for the cutting speeds $v_c = 1{,}000\,\mathrm{m\,min^{-1}}$ and $4{,}000\,\mathrm{m\,min^{-1}}$.

5.1 Cutting Experiments

The machined surfaces were measured with a white-light interferometer and afterwards analyzed using the image processing software "SPIP". Figure 42 shows the arithmetic mean height Sa (applied L-filter of 80 μm) for all materials over the residual unbalance and the cutting speed. Each column represents the mean value of four measurements along the machined surface. The error bars represent the maximum and minimum of the respective measurement series.

The results from high speed milling (cf. chapter 3) suggested that the values of the arithmetic mean height Sa in Fig. 42 decrease with increasing cutting speed. However, a negative influence of the residual unbalance on the Sa value cannot be determined in the results. At the same cutting speed the Sa values can be considered constant if the error bar is taken into account. The reduction of the Sa values with increasing unbalance, which can be seen in the results for AlMg3, CuZn39Pb3 and OFHC Cu, can be considered negligible, as the change of the values is much smaller than the error bar. The same applies to the increasing Sa values for CuZn39Pb3.

These results are surprising at first sight because usually vibrations in the machine system, caused by the rotor unbalance, have an influence on the surface topography. On closer inspection, however, the fly-cutting process presented here involves the surface being machined with only one cutting edge and this cutting edge periodically oscillates at almost the same circumferential position to cut the workpiece. Neverthe-

Fig. 43 Experimental setup for measuring the rotor displacement in X- and Y-direction by two capacitive sensors

less, it could be interesting to consider the situation when several tools are used, as the tools cut the workpiece at different phase positions. For an improved evaluation of the achieved results it is essential to know the rotor behavior during cutting.

5.2 Rotor Behavior Analysis

The rotor behavior under varying unbalance and rotational speed was analyzed by measuring the rotor displacement without a machining process. To measure the rotor displacement in the X- and Y-axis, two highly sensitive capacitive displacement sensors of the type CPL490 from IBS Precision Engineering (Eindhoven, NL) were positioned against a measurement artifact, as shown in Fig. 43.

The measuring artifact was manufactured on an ultra-precise machine tool and mounted between the spindle and an additional element, which was used to adjust the defined residual unbalance. The adjusted residual unbalance and rotational speeds are identical to those of the milling experiments to ensure comparability.

The recorded measurement data of the rotor displacement display a superimposed noise and were therefore filtered by the complementary ensemble empirical mode decomposition (CEEMD) method [24] as described in [5]. Through this method, it is possible to extract the frequency components from the measurement signal for evaluation, which have a significant influence on the signal amplitude and are related to the rotational frequency of the rotor. The data processed by this method were used to determine the position deviation of the contact point between a hypothetical tool cutting edge and the workpiece surface. For this purpose, the position data were read out at the point where the signal of the trigger sensor switches to high. In this way, the rotor position deviation can be reliably read out at identical angular positions for each revolution of the rotor. The detected position deviation in X-direction are displayed in Fig. 44 at the same residual unbalance but for a varying cutting velocity.

The acquired measurement data support the findings of the surface measurement data. At a lower cutting velocity, higher position deviations are evident at the contact point between the cutting edge of the tool and the surface of the workpiece. For example, the average position deviation in the measured X-direction decreases from

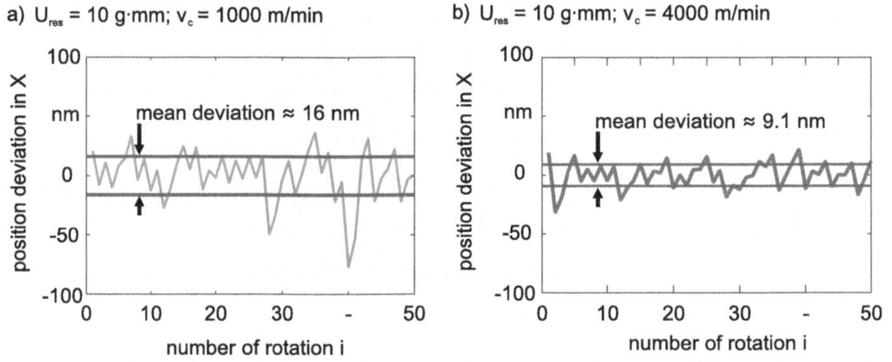

Fig. 44 Measured deviation of the tool contact point in x direction for **a** $U = 10\,\mathrm{g\,mm}$; $v_c = 1{,}000\,\mathrm{m\,min^{-1}}$ and **b** $U = 10\,\mathrm{g\,mm}$; $v_c = 4{,}000\,\mathrm{m\,min^{-1}}$

16 to 9.1 nm at a residual imbalance of $U = 10\,\mathrm{g\,mm}$ and $v_c = 1{,}000\,\mathrm{m\,min^{-1}}$ as well as $v_c = 4{,}000\,\mathrm{m\,min^{-1}}$, respectively. A varying residual imbalance of the rotor has no significant influence in this context (cf. [5]).

The results of the rotor displacement study show that the positive effect of an increased spindle speed on the surface topography during the machining tests also has a positive effect on the rotor behavior.

5.3 Surface Characterization

In order to verify the impact of the unbalance induced rotor displacement on the machining process, the resulting surface was calculated numerically using a geometric model of a milling process (the 3D-analysis of the generated surface is presented in [18] and [19]). For this, the milling tool was modeled as a torus, featuring the swing radius of the milling tool ($r_{fly} = 82\,\mathrm{mm}$) as its primary and the nose radius of the tool ($r_\varepsilon = 0.792\,\mathrm{mm}$) as its secondary radius. This torus was positioned to intersect with a planar surface at equidistant intervals defined by the feed and the raster spacing ($f = 80\,\mathrm{m}$ and $s = 8\,\mathrm{m}$, respectively) while the difference to the previous result was kept for the subsequent iteration.

To analyze the optical surfaces, the arithmetic mean height value Sa was used. To get a deeper insight, some signal analysis based on two-dimensional Fourier transform/spatial frequency analysis was performed. In order to apply the spatial frequency analysis to the surfaces quality examinations, a two-dimensional fast fourier transformation (FFT2) was applied to the simulated surface and the magnitude of the result was analyzed in lower and higher frequency domains by the characteristic values P_1 and P_2. To separate the lower and higher frequency effects on the quality of the surface, the FFT2 results around $0\,\mu\mathrm{m}^{-1}$ with $\pm 5\,\mu\mathrm{m}^{-1}$ deviation were

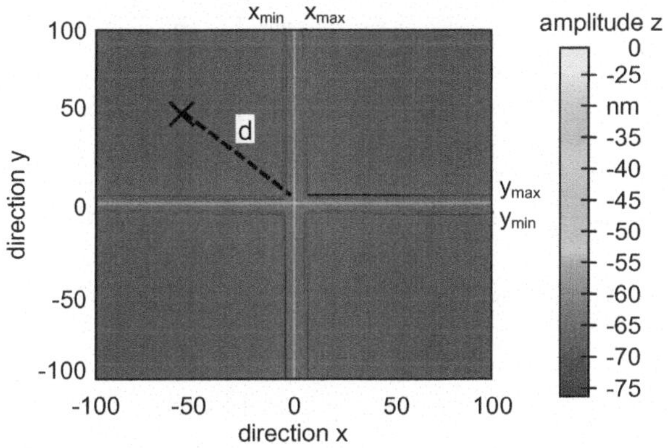

Fig. 45 Basic definitions of parameters in the FFT2 coefficient domain for calculation of the characteristic values P_1 and P_2

considered as low frequency result (see Fig. 45). For an improved evaluation of the FFT2 results, the logarithmic function was applied to the FFT2 values.

The parameter P_1 is defined by summing up the low frequency content of the FFT2 results of the optical surface (see Eq. 7). For the higher frequencies, based on the distance from the center, the value of each point is weighted and all the values of all calculated FFT2 coefficients are summed up to build the P_2 parameter (see Eq. 8).

$$P_1 = \sum_{x=x_{\min}}^{x_{\max}} \sum_{y=L}^{R} \mathrm{fft2}(S) + \sum_{y=y_{\min}}^{y_{\max}} \sum_{x=L}^{R} \mathrm{fft2}(S) - \sum_{x=x_{\min}}^{x_{\max}} \sum_{y=y_{\min}}^{y_{\max}} \mathrm{fft2}(S) \tag{7}$$

$$P_2 = \sum_{x=L}^{x_{\min}} \sum_{y=L}^{y_{\min}} \mathrm{fft2}(S) \times d + \sum_{y=L}^{x_{\min}} \sum_{y=y_{\max}}^{R} \mathrm{fft2}(S) \times d + \sum_{x=x_{\max}}^{R} \sum_{y=L}^{y_{\min}} \mathrm{fft2}(S) \times d + \sum_{x=x_{\max}}^{R} \sum_{y=y_{\max}}^{R} \mathrm{fft2}(S) \times d \tag{8}$$

Within the formulas, S is a matrix that represents the height values in Z-direction of the optical surface. The limits of the integration area to calculate P_1 are defined by $(x, y)_{\min}$ and $(x, y)_{\max}$ respectively (see Fig. 45). In addition, L ($-100\,\mu$m) and R ($100\,\mu$m) define the left and right margin of the square surface in X- and Y-direction and d is the distance of each surface point to the center.

For the surface simulation generation, the following parameters were set: feed $f = 7\,\mu\text{m}$ in cutting direction, fly-cut radius $r_{fly} = 60 \times 10^3\,\mu\text{m}$, raster spacing $s = 60 \times 10^3\,\mu\text{m}$ and size of the simulated surface $A = 210 \times 210\,\mu\text{m}^2$.

The characteristic values for the first simulated surface (surface 1) were calculated to Sa = 2.7 nm, $P_1 = 1.9 \times 10^8$ nm and $P_2 = 4.8 \times 10^{-3}$ nm μm^{-1}.

For the next step (surface 2), the deviation of the eccentricity is applied to the simulation with 40 dB signal-to-noise ratio. This deviation leads to the fol-

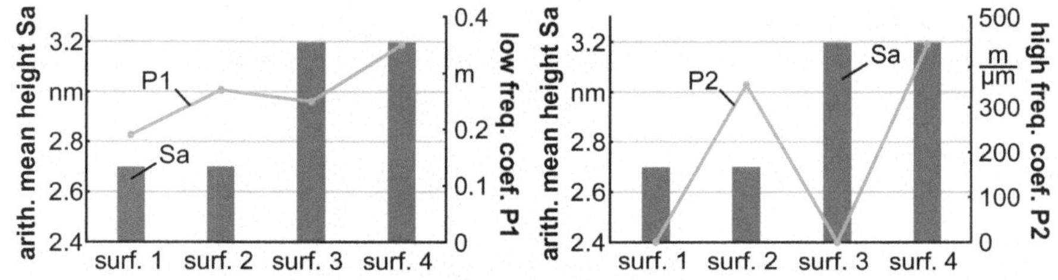

Fig. 46 Calculated Sa, P_1 and P_2 values for simulated surfaces

lowing surface roughness parameters: Sa = 2.7 nm, $P_1 = 2.7 \times 10^8$ nm and $P_2 = 3.5 \times 10^{11}$ nm mm^{-1}. Although the Sa value revealed to be not sensitive to this change of the surface, the characteristic value P_2 , which is related to the effect of higher frequencies, increases significantly.

By adding 0.1 nm deviation in fly-cut radius in the surface simulation (surface 3), the values change to Sa=2.7 nm, $P_1 = 1.9 \times 10^8$ nm and $P_2 = 4.9 \times 10^{-3}$ nm µm^{-1}. The effect of this deviation is identifiable by the P_1 and P_2 parameters.

A change in feed rate in cutting direction from 70 to 100 µm and an additional noise level of 40 dB in the simulation (surface 4) led to the following surface roughness parameters: Sa = 3.2 nm, $P_1 = 3.5 \times 10^8$ nm and $P_2 = 4.4 \times 10^{11}$ nm µm^{-1}.

This indicates the efficiency of using spatial frequency analysis in surface quality measurements, including additional information about the morphology of the optical surfaces (Fig. 46).

6 Conclusion

The precise balancing of high-speed air-bearing spindles is a challenging but necessary task in ultra-precision machining to avoid vibrations and damage to the bearing. While many processes in production technology are already automated, it was not yet possible to automatically and precisely balance an ultra-precision air-bearing spindle. Therefore, the possibility of automatic balancing of air-bearing spindles was investigated in this study. Two balancing systems in combination with a system for more precise measurement of unbalance-induced vibrations at low speeds enabled highly accurate balancing down to a balancing grade of $G0.064$. In addition, a monitoring and control system could significantly increase system safety. Two prototypes based on the spread angle principle and on the fixed position method have been developed, which use ultrasonic ring motors and microfluidic actuators for balancing, respectively. Both systems proved the ability to perform the required balancing grade of $G0.064$. Furthermore, the system for increasing the measurable unbalance-induced vibrations significantly improved unbalance detection. As a result, it was possible to measure unbalances below the detection threshold of conventional accelerometers. It was also shown that an unbalance measurement on the rotor, and not as usual on the stator, enables a measurement up to a spindle speed of $n \leq 1{,}800\,\text{min}^{-1}$. In combination with the implemented control system, the final automatic balancing system is capable of balancing an air-bearing spindle up to a rotational speed of $n \leq 4{,}200\,\text{min}^{-1}$ to a desired unbalance in magnitude and phase. Additionally, two characteristic values were introduced that could enhance the analysis of optical surfaces with relation to unbalances in machining.

References

1. Birkenstack, D., Jager, O.: Multi-chambered fluid balancing apparatus. U.S. Patent 3 950 897. Gebr. Hofmann KG, 20 April 1976
2. Cao, H., Dörgeloh, T., Riemer, O., Brinksmeier, E.: Adaptive separation of unbalance vibration in air bearing spindles. Procedia CIRP **62**, 357–362 (2017). https://doi.org/10.1016/j.procir.2016.06.069
3. Dörgeloh, T., Beinhauer, A., Riemer, O., Brinksmeier, E.: Microfluidic balancing concepts for ultraprecision high speed applications. Procedia CIRP **46**, 185–188 (2016). https://doi.org/10.1016/j.procir.2016.03.174. Wertheim, R., Ihlefeldt, S., Hochmuth, C., Putz, M. (eds.) 7th CIRP Conference on High Performance Cutting (HPC 2016)
4. Dörgeloh, T., Riemer, O., Brinksmeier, E.: Automated microfluidic balancing system for high speed air-bearing spindles. Procedia CIRP **77**, 263–266 (2018). https://doi.org/10.1016/j.procir.2018.09.011. 8th CIRP Conference on High Performance Cutting (HPC 2018)
5. Dörgeloh, T., Schönemann, L., Riemer, O., Brinksmeier, E.: Analysis of rotor behavior in ultra-precision high speed cutting. In: 34th ASPE Annual Meeting, pp. 69–74. American Society for Precision Engineering (2019)
6. Foremny, E., Schenck, C., Kuhfuss, B.: High precision coupling system. In: Annoni, M., Fassi, I., Wiens, G.J., Dimov, S. (eds.) 10th International Conference on Micromanufacturing (4M/ICOMM 2015), Milan, Italy, pp. 205–208 (2015)
7. Foremny, E., Schenck, C., Kuhfuß, B.: Dynamic behavior of an ultra precision spindle used in machining of optical components. Procedia CIRP **46**, 452–455 (2016). https://doi.org/10.1016/j.procir.2016.04
8. Foremny, E., Schenck, C., Kuhfuss, B.: Coupling system for ultra precision machining. J. Mech. Eng. Autom. **6**(6), 301–306 (2016)
9. Foremny, E., Schenck, C., Kuhfuss, B.I.: Integrated ultrasonic driven balancer for ultra precision high speed machine tools. Procedia Technol. **26**, 316–323 (2016). https://doi.org/10.1016/j.protcy.2016.08.041. 3rd International Conference on System-Integrated Intelligence: New Challenges for Product and Production Engineering
10. ISO: Geometrical product specifications (GPS)—surface texture: areal—part 2: terms, definitions and surface texture parameters. Standard ISO 25178-2 (2012)
11. ISO: Mechanical vibration—rotor balancing—part 11: procedures and tolerances for rotors with rigid behaviour. Standard ISO 21940-11 (2017)
12. Jiang, X.J., Whitehouse, D.J.: Technological shifts in surface metrology. CIRP Ann. **61**(2), 815–836 (2012). https://doi.org/10.1016/j.cirp.2012.05.009
13. Knapp, B., Arneson, D., Oss, D., Liebers, M., Vallance, R., Marsh, E.: The importance of spindle balancing for the machining of freeform optics. In: ASPE Spring Topical Meeting, vol. 51, pp. 74–78. ASPE, Raleigh (2011)
14. Levicron GmbH. Coorporate Website (2017)
15. Moon, J.-D., Kim, B.-S., Lee, S.-H.: Development of the active balancing device for high-speed spindle system using influence coefficients. Int. J. Mach. Tools Manuf **46**(9), 978–987 (2006). https://doi.org/10.1016/j.ijmachtools.2005.07.048

16. Rebeggiani, S., Rosén, B.G., Sandberg, A.: A quantitative method to estimate high gloss polished tool steel surfaces. J. Phys: Conf. Ser. **311**, 012004 (2011). https://doi.org/10.1088/1742-6596/311/1/012004
17. Riemer, O., Schönemann, L., Dörgeloh, T., Beinhauer, A., Foremny, E., Brinksmeier, E., Kuhfuss, B.: Balancing concepts for high speed aerostatic spindles. In: 30th ASPE Annual Meeting, pp. 273–274 (2015)
18. Schönemann, L.: Surface simulation for ultra-precision milling with multiple cutting edges. In: 69th CIRP General Assembly - Part 2, Birmingham, 22 August 2019
19. Schönemann, L., Berger, D., Dörgeloh, T., Riemer, O., Brinksmeier, E., Krüger, R., Schreiber, P., Denkena, B., Hochbein, J., Parsa, N., Schenck, C., Kuhfuss, B.: Synergistic approaches to ultra-precision high performance cutting. CIRP J. Manuf. Sci. Technol. **28**, 38–51 (2020). https://doi.org/10.1016/j.cirpj.2019.12.001
20. Smith, G.L., Rudy, R.Q., Polcawich, R.G., DeVoe, D.L.: Integrated thin-film piezoelectric traveling wave ultrasonic motors. Sens. Actuators A Phys. **188**, 305–311 (2012). https://doi.org/10.1016/j.sna.2011.12.029. Selected papers from The 16th International Conference on Solid-State Sensors, Actuators and Microsystems
21. Tauhiduzzaman, M., Yip, A., Veldhuis, S.C.: Form error in diamond turning. Precis. Eng. **42**, 22–36 (2015). https://doi.org/10.1016/j.precisioneng.2015.03.006
22. Uchino, K.: Piezoelectric ultrasonic motors: overview. Smart Mater. Struct. **7**(3), 273–285 (1998). https://doi.org/10.1088/0964-1726/7/3/002
23. Wallaschek, J.: Piezoelectric ultrasonic motors. J. Intell. Mater. Syst. Struct. **6**(1), 71–83 (1995). https://doi.org/10.1177/1045389X9500600110
24. Yeh, J.-R., Shieh, J.-S., Huang, N.E.: Complementary ensemble empirical mode decomposition: a novel noise enhanced data analysis method. Adv. Adapt. Data Anal. **02**(02), 135–156 (2010). https://doi.org/10.1142/S1793536910000422
25. Zhang, S.J., To, S.: A theoretical and experimental study of surface generation under spindle vibration in ultra-precision raster milling. Int. J. Mach. Tools Manuf. **75**, 36–45 (2013). https://doi.org/10.1016/j.ijmachtools.2013.08.003
26. Zhang, S.J., To, S., Zhu, Z.W., Zhang, G.Q.: A review of fly cutting applied to surface generation in ultra-precision machining. Int. J. Mach. Tools Manuf. **103**, 13–27 (2016). https://doi.org/10.1016/j.ijmachtools.2016.01.001

Ultra Precision High Performance Axis Control

Per Schreiber, Johannes Hochbein, Benjamin Bergmann, Christian Schenck, Bernd Kuhfuss, and Berend Denkena

Abstract Axis controls of ultra-precision machine tools have to fulfill demanding requirements regarding position and velocity tracking accuracy, disturbance rejection, and avoidance of vibration. Within this project, an axis concept for ultra-precision machining utilizing an electromagnetic linear guide is investigated. The axis concept offers additional, redundant degrees of freedom for error compensation and sensory information for monitoring tasks. It is shown that input shaping and feed forward control of disturbance forces allow for significant improvement in machining performance. To investigate the axis behavior of the multi-axis motion, an external measurement device with sufficient travel range and sub-micron resolution is needed. This task is solved with a novel speckle position sensor that is described in this chapter as well.

1 Introduction

Ultra-precision (UP) machining requires guiding the workpiece and tool with sufficiently high accuracy and low vibration such that high form accuracy and low surface roughness can be achieved. Often axis dynamics are limited deliberately in order to reduce the excitation of vibration and dynamic path errors from tilting slides or lacking trajectory tracking performance. Hence, a new motion system is required to allow for UP-machining at significantly increased axis dynamics. Characteristics of

P. Schreiber (✉) · B. Bergmann · B. Denkena
Institute of Production Engineering and Machine Tools IFW, Leibniz University Hannover, Garbsen, Germany
e-mail: Schreiber@ifw.uni-hannover.de

J. Hochbein · C. Schenck · B. Kuhfuss
Bremen Institute for Mechanical Engineering bime and MAPEX Center for Materials and Processes, University of Bremen, Bremen, Germany
e-mail: hochbein@bime.de

E. Brinksmeier and L. Schönemann (eds.), *Ultra-precision High Performance Cutting*, Lecture Notes in Production Engineering, https://doi.org/10.1007/978-3-030-83765-5_6

the feed motion are largely determined by trajectory planning, axis controls, and the applied bearing and drive technology and its transmission characteristics. The Ultra-Precision High Performance Cutting (UP-HPC) machine concept, which is described in Sect. 2 and shown in Fig. 1 is a three-axis machining concept. It incorporates an electromagnetic guide which adds five additional degrees of freedom (DoF). They are partly redundant and can be utilized as additional fine positioning axes. The dynamic properties of those redundant axes differ significantly from the other machine axes. Also, axis dynamics are subjected to variations of the system setup such as changing mass from the workpiece or the workpiece fixture. Thus, system models used for instance for model based control or controller tuning not only need to be accurate but also adaptable. Therefore, in order to obtain a model that fulfills the requirements of UP-machining, Sect. 3 of this work presents an approach to estimate actual parameters of a state-space model during runtime. The proposed approach is able to learn and adapt to varying conditions even if these conditions are not implemented in the initial model. Moreover, the section addresses how substantial differences of sub-system dynamics can be handled by the use of residual sub-band models.

Besides online parameter adaptation, another prerequisite for designing and optimizing a complex axis control system is a feasible, external system to gain comparable data on multi-axis positioning behavior [6]. Available systems such as laser tracker and grid encoders lack either resolution or range. Therefore, in Sect. 4 a new approach is introduced which combines the precision of laser speckle measurements with a suitable measurement range. This contactless system operates without a corporal solid measure and can easily be adapted to different kinematic set-ups and machine tools.

Dynamic errors that are induced by the acceleration and jerk of axis feed motion can affect machining quality. Thus, in UP-machining feed velocity, acceleration, and jerk values are commonly limited to a large extent. However, in order to achieve the targeted performance within the UP-HPC approach other measures to mitigate dynamic errors are required. In Sect. 5, the capabilities of an active guide in combination with vibration avoidance in order to improve process performance and productivity are shown. In order to mitigate the excitement of vibration, input shaping is investigated for the feed axis system. Altintas and Khoshdarregi [1] and Sencer et al. [14] showed that input shaping can effectively suppress vibration in conventional machining. The use of this approach in ultra-precision machining has not been investigated in depth. Secondly, the input shaping is investigated in combination with a force feed forward control of acceleration loads. It is shown that both approaches can improve productivity significantly. Further it is shown that the preferable choice of compensation approaches in order to improve productivity depends on the aimed cutting velocity and form deviation. To further support process and compensation parameterization the capability of internal sensor data in order to predict workpiece form deviations is evaluated. Finally, the results of this chapter are concluded and an outlook on future work is given in Sect. 6.

2 System Description

Central element of the research group is a machine prototype for ultra-precision high performance cutting. The prototype supports fly-cutting as well as planing with stationary tool. This section describes the kinematic axis structure of the prototype, the structure of the control system as well as the experimental setup for initial cutting tests.

2.1 Prototype Axis System Description

This section concerns the axis controls of the machine prototype which was developed and set up in the project. The design of the prototype is shown in Fig. 1. The kinematic design comprises three macro axes X, Y, Z. Another five fine-positioning DoF are contributed by the electromagnetic guide of the X-axis. Those DoF are denoted with their generalized coordinates $\boldsymbol{q}_y$ and $\boldsymbol{q}_z$ for the redundant linear DoF and $\boldsymbol{q}_a$, $\boldsymbol{q}_b$, and $\boldsymbol{q}_c$ for the angular DoF. The X-axis is placed within the slide of the Z-axis as a box-in-a-box design. Details on the design of the electromagnetic guide are given in Chap. 4. The Z-axis is guided by conventional porous media aerostatic bearings. Both, the X- and Z-axis are driven by two iron-less linear drives. The Y-axis utilizes a conventional roller guide, driven by a rotary motor with a mechanical brake. The Z-axis position is acquired by two linear encoders. The X- and Y-axis are equipped with one encoder each.

In a machining process, the macro axes X, Z provide the motion for feed and crossfeed and vice versa. Infeed is provided by the fine-positioning axis $\boldsymbol{q}_y$, while the macro Y-axis is used for pre-adjustment of the spindle and tool position in advance of the machining process. The Y-axis clamped and kept stationary with the brake during the process. The Y-axis can carry a fly-cutting spindle or a stationary tool for planing. Figure 1 shows the setup with the fly-cutting spindle.

2.2 Real-Time Control Architecture

The controllers of all motion axes as well as acquisition and processing of the sensor data are executed on an industrial PC (IPC) system (Beckhoff). To this end, a modular control framework was developed. The basic structure of the framework is shown in Fig. 2. Modularity concerns flexible involvement of the prototypes' nine DoF in motion and machining as well as modularity of each of the axes' controller and compensation modules. Online change of axis configuration as well as change of controller and compensation properties, was a fundamental requirement. This is due to the fact that an offline change and recompilation of modules would require shutting down the levitating axis. Shutting down the levitating axis however can

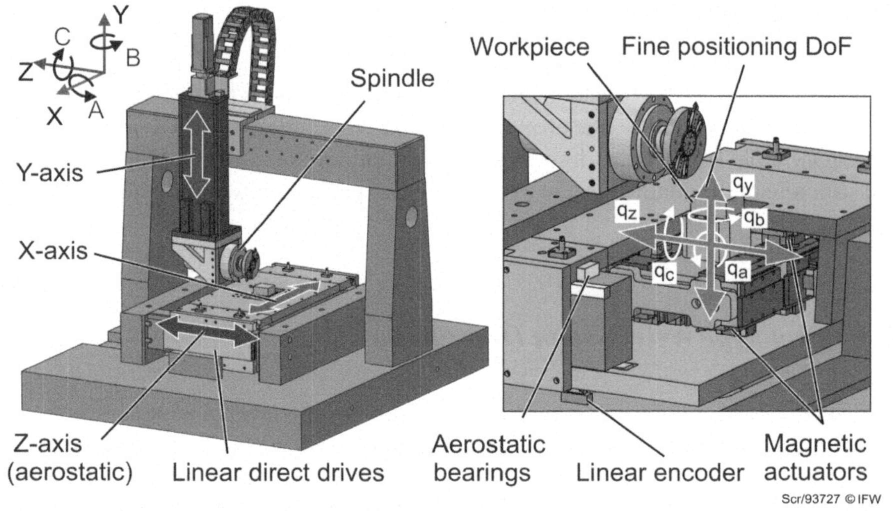

Fig. 1 Machine prototype for UP-HPC-cutting

lead to diverging from a thermostatic state and is thus not feasible for conducting repeatable experiments. A state machine module handles system and module states such as macro axis clearance depending on the levitation axis state or activation of compensation parameters depending on axis states. Also base functionalities such as homing are coordinated by the state machine. Set-point values for the axes are generated by a G-code interpreter which also handles interpolation for up to three linear axes. The modular system allows for flexible multi-axis interpolation with the fine-positioning DoFs of the magnetic levitation guide in any combination with the macro axes. Additional signals can be linked onto the output of the interpolation system for compensation applications. The individual axis controller modules are developed in Simulink and exported as IEC-61131 structured text using the Matlab PLC-Coder extension. The controller modules, which control position and velocity, are executed at 16 kHz on the IPC. The controller output, the drive current set-point value is transferred to the servo drive controllers via an ethernet for control and automation technology (EtherCAT) bus system. The current control is executed by the servo drive controllers. They also connect the position encoders to the system and transfer actual position and velocity to the IPC. For details regarding the control structure of the magnetic guide system please consider Chap. 4, Sect. 4.4.

2.3 Setup for Cutting Experiments

Cutting experiments were conducted, in order to evaluate the behavior of the axis and control system and compensation approaches in terms of their impact on the

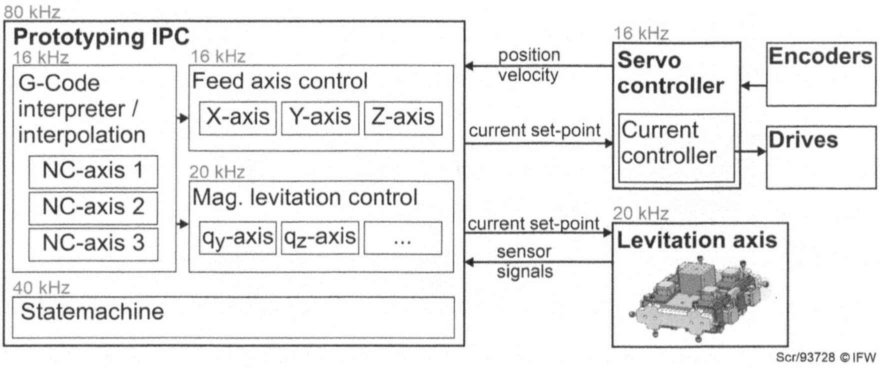

Fig. 2 Structure of the realtime control system

machining quality. For the experiments a planing process with stationary tool attached to the Y-axis was implemented. A planing process was chosen in order to evaluate the axis control system. In contrast to a fly-cutting process planing allows to exclude certain effects from the machining result. Those effects are for instance vibrations from spindle imbalances. Another disadvantage of fly-cutting in terms of investigating axis controls is that it leads to a form of "undersampling". For a typical fly-cutting spindle speed of 1,500 min^{-1} and a single cutting edge there is a short tool-workpiece contact at a frequency 25 Hz. Hence, axis and prototype behavior above 12.5 Hz would already be distorted by aliasing effects in the machining result. The setup for planing experiments is shown in Fig. 3. The stationary tool, is attached to the Y-axis such that the tool center point (TCP) is close to the TCP for the fly-cutting set-up. Thus, a part of the effects from structural dynamics of the Y-axis can be expected to be apparent in both, the fly-cutting and planing set-up. A manual linear stage was used for presetting the tool position while the depth of cut (a_p) is set by the fine positioning DoF q_y of the electromagnetic axis. The direction of cut corresponds to the Z-axis. For avoiding tool-workpiece contact during the retracting movement of the Z-axis, the q_y-axis was lowered to maximum extent while resetting the workpiece. In advance of the actual cutting experiments workpieces were planed entirely in this setup without re-clamping in order to achieve the best possible parallelism of the workpiece surface to the machine axes.

2.4 *Process and System Capability*

This section gives an overview over the system capability of the described axis and control system as a reference for further experiments. Figure 4 shows an exemplary machining result of a planing process with the above described setup. The workpiece (aluminum EN AW 5754) was machined in multi-axis interpolation with at a cutting speed $v_c = 500\,\text{mm min}^{-1}$ in Z-direction. Regarding axis control settings, the static

Fig. 3 Setup for cutting experiments (left and center) with the shaping process (right)

compensations and position-depended Jacobians from Chap. 4 were activated. An overlaying motive pattern was realized by varying the depth of cut between 3 μm and 7 μm in the process. The workpiece was lubricated with paraffin oil. Measurements of the workpiece show that a mean deviation $(\overline{\Delta_y})$ from the set point height difference of the pattern (4 μm) amounts to 54 nm. The surface roughness, determined as the arithmetic mean height Sa amounts to 42.8 nm. The theoretical limit of achievable surface roughness for the given tool nose radius r_ε and lateral feed f under otherwise ideal conditions $Sa_{lim} \approx 3f^2/64r_\varepsilon)$ amounts to 6.1 nm in comparison. Thus, the residual surface roughness of the aluminum workpiece can be assumed to be the current limit of the experimental setup. This is supported by the finding that it reflects the values that were archived in Sect. 4.8 with a brass workpiece and cutting in X-direction instead of Z-direction. Limiting factors and influences are, among others, tool-sided compliances, effects from chip formation, introduction of external vibration from the non-decoupled foundation, and remaining control deviations of the axis and guiding system.

3 Adaptive Parameter Estimation

Model based axes control for high speed UP-operations demands for high complexity and associated computational costs to represent the machine behavior within the required resolution and accuracy. To reduce the computational costs for realizing real time application, the complexity can be reduced by in-process parameter estimation and adaption that ensures the required precision [5].

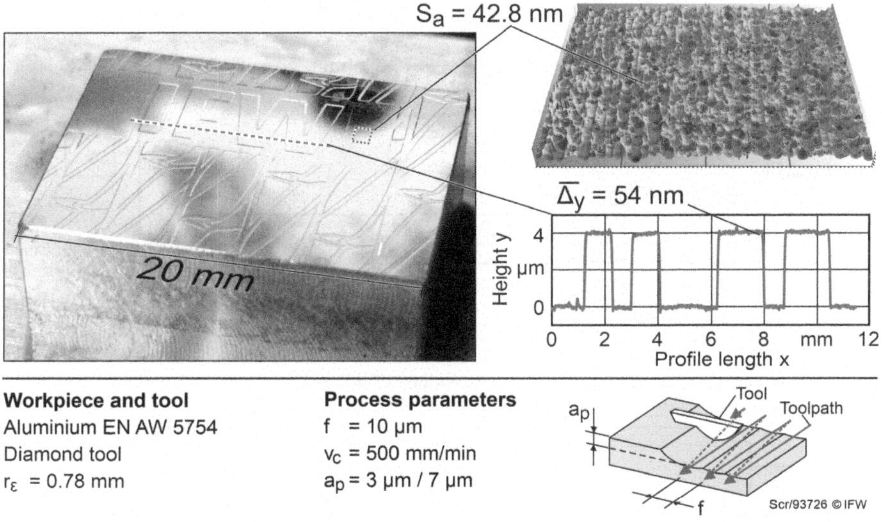

Fig. 4 Overview over system capability with exemplary surface and profile measurement

3.1 Model Structure

The model consists of two sub-models, the motion band sub-model (MBSM) and the residual band sub-model (RBSM). While the MBSM calculates the larger scale motion of the feed axes, vibrations and discrepancies are represented by RBSM. Due to this reduction, the parameters of both sub-models can be estimated separately and in individually suitable cycle times.

Each sub-model is represented as state-space model. In such models, the system is expressed by the state vector $\boldsymbol{x}$ with n state-variables. n was chosen to 8 (MBSM) and 6 (RBSM). Each state variable behaves as energy storage and records the influence of past inputs to the actual state. A state vector at a time t for an input vector $\boldsymbol{u}$ can be calculated as

$$\dot{\boldsymbol{x}}(t) = \boldsymbol{A}\boldsymbol{x}(t) + \boldsymbol{B}\boldsymbol{u}(t) \tag{1}$$

Hereby, $\boldsymbol{A}$ is the state matrix which defines the single state variables interaction and $\boldsymbol{B}$ is the input matrix that defines the input influence on the state variables. The output $\boldsymbol{y}$ of the model can be calculated from the state vector with the output matrix $\boldsymbol{C}$.

$$\boldsymbol{y}(t) = \boldsymbol{C}\boldsymbol{x}(t) \tag{2}$$

The output of both sub-models must be phase corrected and added to the final result. The complete process is shown in Fig. 5.

The parameters of the sub-models were separately estimated based on the predictive error method (PEM) [11]. Therefore, the future model output is estimated with

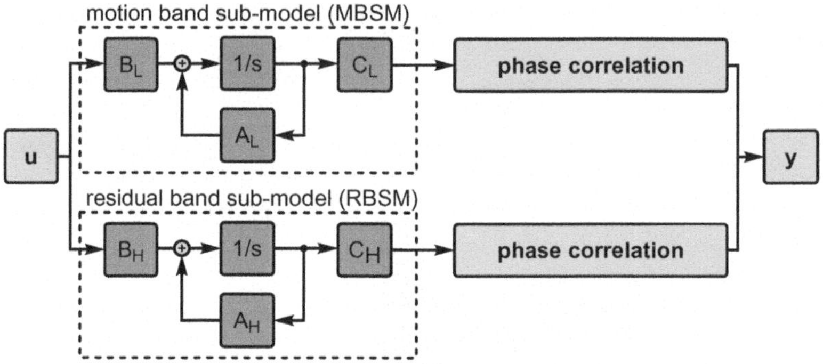

Fig. 5 Model structure with two reduced sub-models; cf. [5]

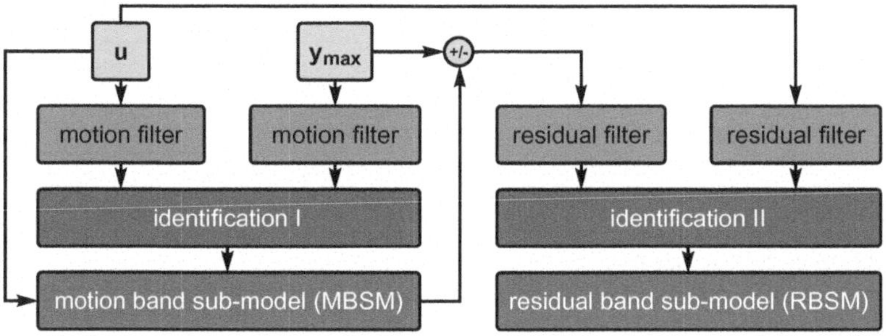

Fig. 6 Parameter identification procedure; cf. [5]

Eq. 2 and compared to the measurement at that time. The lowest deviation was then found with the Levenberg-Marquardt method [10]. The separation of the estimated and the measured data was realized with equiripple low-pass finite impulse response filters due to their constant group delay. This feature ensures that the unavoidable distortion of the motion data in time domain is independent of the velocity. For the MBSM parameter estimation all frequencies 20 Hz while for the RBSM parameter estimation all frequencies 200 Hz were suppressed. The procedure is shown in Fig. 6. A window of the measurements with a fixed size of w_{est} samples and the input $\boldsymbol{u}$ is used as input for the parameter estimation. The window lengths were heuristically chosen as 83.33 ms (MBSM) and 50 ms (RBSM). To react to parameter variation of the system, the parameters are estimated in each window individually. After this estimation and a comparison with the previous parameter, the parameters with the lower deviation are chosen as new model parameters. To get a robust system, the parameter changes were limited to 15% of the actual value.

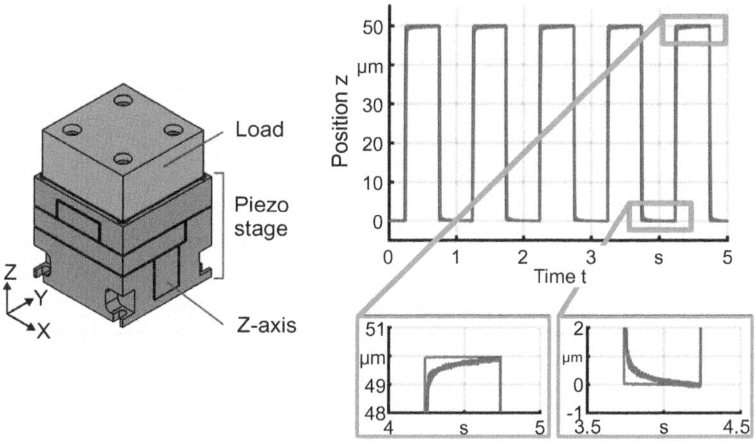

Fig. 7 Model parameter identification **a** Setup **b** Z-position with set-point values (blue) and actual values (red); cf. [5]

3.2 Experimental Setup

The identification algorithm was tested with a piezo stage "NanoCube" (P-611.3, Physik Instumente) in open-loop control mode. After initial identification, an additional load on the NanoCube in z-direction (0, 22, 31, 52, 77 g) as variable parameter simulated a change in the system and hence its behavior. Both the input to the piezo stage (set-point values) and the internal position sensor of the piezo stage (actual values) were used for the in process parameter estimation. As demanded motion in Z-direction a step function with an amplitude of 50 µm was applied to emulate a positioning task. This demanded trajectory was performed five times in a row with each load. The waiting time between positioning was one second. An example of the set-point trajectory and the corresponding actual trajectory is shown in Fig. 7.

The estimation error as difference between the measured actual position values and the estimated position values calculated by the model is illustrated in Fig. 8. Mean values were calculated during the stand still in the target position. The initial model parameter estimation gains a quite good prediction with an estimation error less than 1 nm. Nevertheless, changing the physical system by additional load increases the estimation error about several nanometers.

4 2D Speckle Position Sensor

To judge the effects of parameter estimation and path control a measuring device based on speckle pattern was developed. This sensor works without a corporal solid

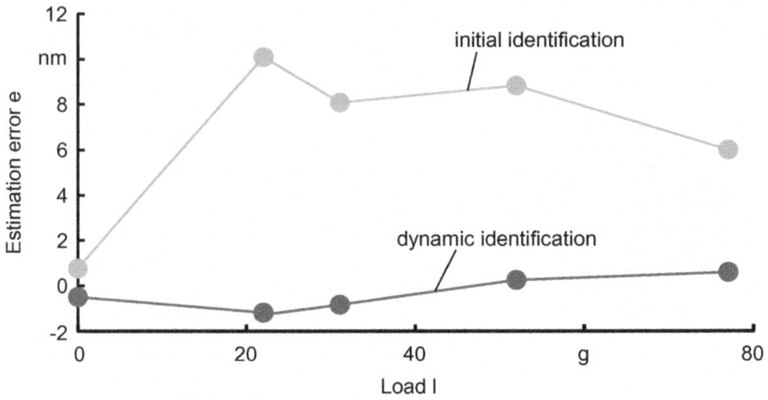

Fig. 8 Mean model estimation error during positioning tests with different loads with static and dynamic parameter estimation

measure and can easily be adapted to different machine tools. The following sections describe the principle of the measurement, the range extension procedure and results.

4.1 Laser Speckle

Laser speckle occur when a surface is illuminated by a laser. Imperfections in the surface cause interference effects that can be monitored by a digital camera as a pattern of light intensity. The distribution of these imperfections is of stochastic nature and unique to the respective surface. Common fields of application are robotics, consumer electronics, deformation analysis and machine tools [7, 12, 16]. A basic sensor setup to track the positions of ultra-precision machine tools was introduced in [3]. The principle of this sensor is shown in Fig. 9.

Due to the uniqueness of the pattern, a displacement of the test surface can be traced by tracing the displacement of the speckle pattern. As long as the displacement is short enough to ensure an overlap of two consecutive images, this shift can be calculated by means of image correlation (see Fig. 10).

4.2 Algorithm for Displacement Calculation

As general procedure, the first image is assumed to be the reference that is placed in a known reference position. All displacements are calculated in respect to this reference. The method to calculate the displacement consists of two steps. In the first step, the position is roughly estimated by two-dimensional cross correlation of the

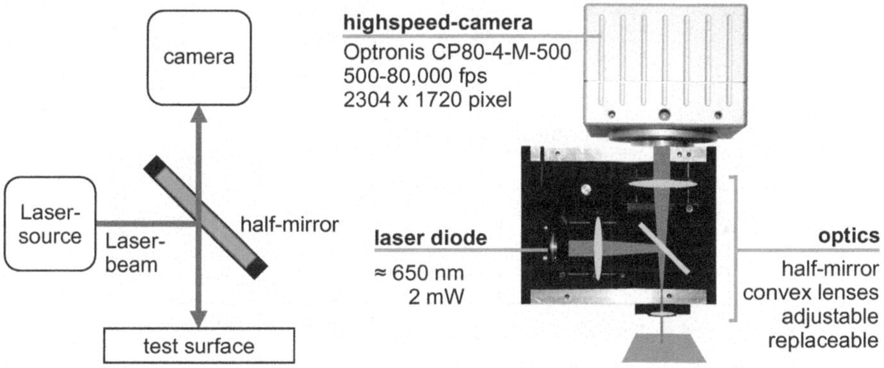

Fig. 9 2D Speckle Sensor; principle (left), experimental setup (right)

Fig. 10 Displacement between images

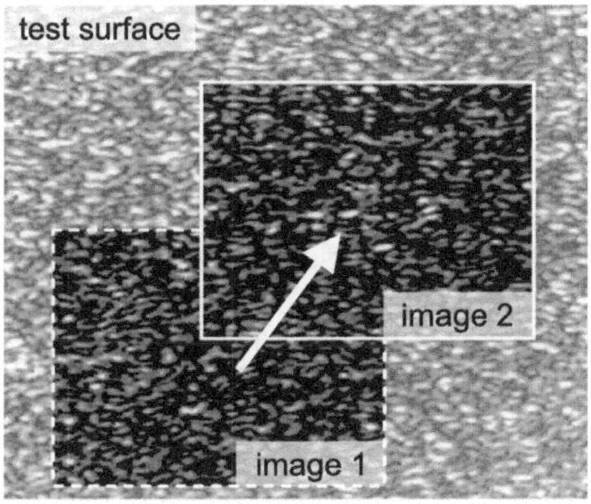

actual image (test pattern) with the reference. These results are highly affected by the boundary values. Therefore, a rectangular window function was applied to set the values at the window margins to zero. These margins were fit to be larger than the maximum expected displacement between two consecutive captures to guarantee an equal amount of summands in the cross correlation calculations. As a result, the displacement is presented as a two-dimensional vector of integer values that represent the number of acquired digital pixels. To enhance this limited resolution a sub-pixel interpolation was applied in a second step. Therefore, a Gaussian function is fitted onto the position of the maximum value of the correlation function and its neighboring pixels. The maximum of the fitted curve represents a better estimation of the displacement. This method of sub-pixel interpolation is performed for both dimensions independently.

For higher displacements, the overlap of the images becomes too small for a precise calculation. To handle this issue, the algorithm was extended with a function for reference pattern changing. Therefore, a threshold value was introduced. In case the displacement exceeds this value, the reference pattern is exchanged with the

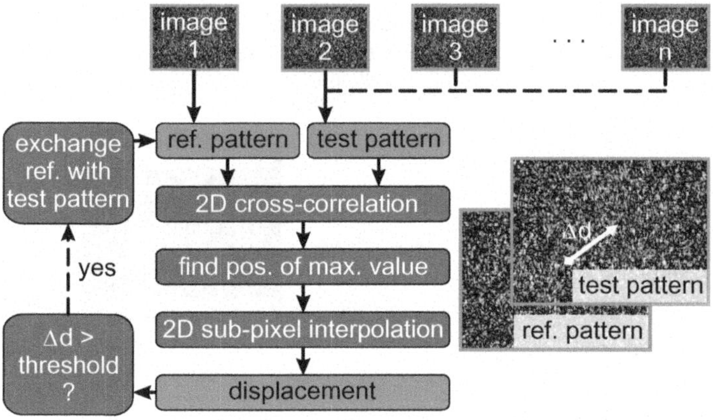

Fig. 11 Algorithm with reference pattern change, picture credit: [13], CC BY 4.0

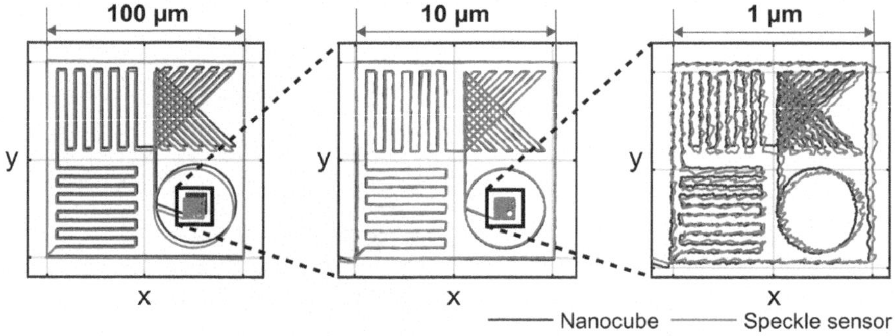

Fig. 12 Test pattern (blue) traced with speckle sensor (orange) in 100 μm, 10 μm and 1 μm scale (cf. [4]), picture credit: [13], License: CC BY 4.0

actual test pattern. For defining an adequate threshold value, divergent effects must be considered. These are basically the effective pixel size that defines the ratio of acquired pixel size and its real dimension [2] and the size of the images [3]. The complete algorithm is shown in Fig. 11.

A test pattern was traced with a piezo stage "NanoCube" (P-611.3, Physik Instrumente) and measured with the speckle sensor in different scales see Fig. 12. Sufficient path accuracy was verified by the internal measuring system. The speckle sensor performed best in the middle scale with a moderate number of pattern changes. In the large scale, the high number of pattern changes reduced the accuracy whereas in the small sub-μm scale the whole system is limited by noise.

A significant reduction of the number of pattern changes could be achieved by a cross-referencing algorithm. For that purpose, mapping of all images that were used as reference patterns allowed for defining the shortest connection between each actual pattern and the initial reference by Dijkstra algorithm for recalculation of the measured shift. Especially for long paths in small areas, the tool center point crosses

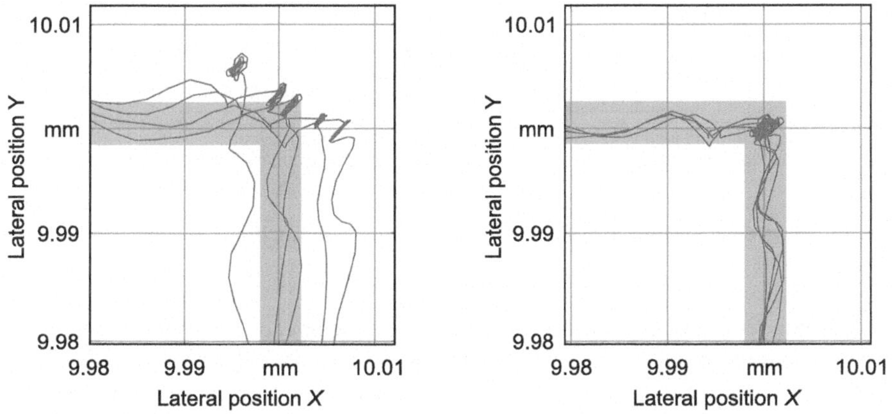

Fig. 13 Deviation of axis movement from test pattern. Left: without cross-referencing; Right: with cross-referencing

its own trajectory several times and the cross-referencing significantly shortens the path that is used in calculations. The effect is illustrated by tracking an edge of a repeatedly covered rectangle, see Fig. 13.

5 Axis Control for Performance Improvement

The following section investigates the application of vibration avoidance and feed forward compensation of dynamic deviations caused by axis motion. Emphasis of the investigation is the impact of the proposed methods on productivity.

5.1 Acceleration Force Feed Forward

Dynamic and static path errors can influence workpiece quality in machining. Due to finite stiffness of components and bearings, the acceleration of machine tool axes lead to displacements and rotations in DoF that are supposed to be locked. In case of the active electromagnetic workpiece slide, such displacements can be measured continuously and actively compensated in order to increase accuracy. Here, position offsets as well as force offsets can be imposed upon the electromagnetic guide set-points. Figure 14 illustrates the basic structure therefore. Position offsets $\boldsymbol{\Delta q}_{pos}$ can be added to the set-point values $\boldsymbol{q}_{\mathrm{set}}$ of the magnetic guide in order to account for static errors such as straightness deviations of the guides. A force feed forward $\boldsymbol{Q}_{ff}$ is added on the output of the electromagnetic guide control adding up to the set-point vector of generalized forces $\boldsymbol{Q}_{set}$. Force feed-forward is utilized to counteract

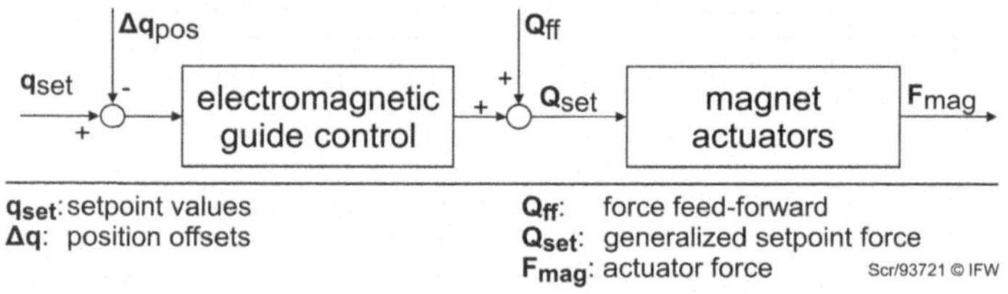

Fig. 14 Block diagram of the dynamic error feed forward, based on [9]

disturbance forces acting on the guide before they can cause a displacement. This requires that these disturbance forces can either be measured with low delay or be predicted. Here, force-feed forward is applied to loads from acceleration of the Z-axis as these are the dominating disturbance forces on the workpiece slide and can be derived from the acceleration set-point.

It was shown in simulation in [9] for the given setup that an acceleration force feed-forward can significantly reduce the tilting error q_a of the magnetic slide's A-axis for accelerated motion of the Z-axis. Empirical analysis showed that significant deviations also appear in q_z. Thus, for feed forward a force vector $\boldsymbol{Q}_{ff}$ is set based on the set-point acceleration $\ddot{z}_{set}$:

$$\boldsymbol{Q}_{ff} = -\ddot{z}_{set}\boldsymbol{P} \tag{3}$$

With the parameter vector $\boldsymbol{P}$:

$$[p_{zx}\ p_{zy}\ p_{zz}\ p_{za}\ p_{zb}\ p_{zc}]^T \tag{4}$$

The elements of $\boldsymbol{P}$ can be interpreted as the masses and inertia respectively. In comparison to [9], an empirically identified $\boldsymbol{P}$ vector was used instead of an analytical vector inferred from the Jacobian and masses. The identified values are $p_{zz} = 46$ to compensate for the deviation q_z in the feed direction and $p_{za} = 1.2$ to reduce a rolling movement of the X-axis. The remaining parameters p_{zx}, p_{zy}, p_{zb}, p_{zc} are set to zero as no significant acceleration response is induced in the corresponding DoF.

As described in Sect. 4.6 it can be necessary to apply a time delay on the $\boldsymbol{Q}_{ff}$ value in order to synchronize the magnetic feed forward force with the axis acceleration. However, this was not required as the Z-axis control loop itself features an acceleration force feed forward. This enables a precise acceleration following behavior of the feed axis. Moreover, since both feed forward values are calculated in the same thread of the control system and are subjected to a similar transport delay from the EtherCAT bus system, force onset of the axis linear drives and the levitation magnets is already sufficiently synchronized without additional delay.

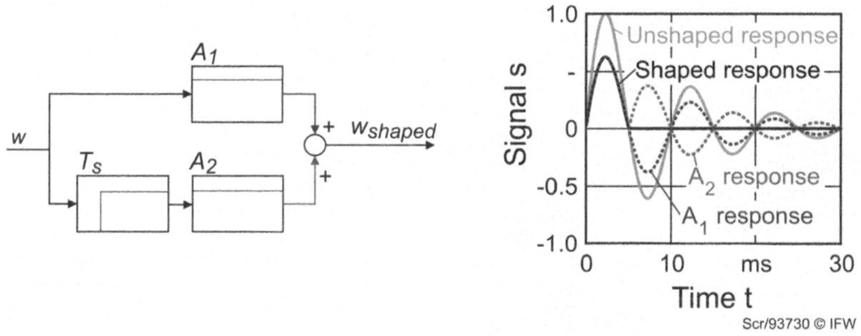

Fig. 15 Block representation of a zero vibration input shaper (left) and impulse response (right) based on [15]

5.2 *Vibration Avoidance with Input Shaping*

Input shaping is an approach to avoid the excitation of certain vibration modes by modification of the set-point trajectory. The concept is described in [15] and shown in Fig. 15. To illustrate the concept of input shaping, a system is assumed which responds as a second order oscillator with an oscillation period T_0 and damping ratio of ζ. To suppress excitation of this vibration, the set-point value w is split into two paths one of which is delayed by $T_s = T_0/2$. This leads to two oscillation responses with a shift of $\pi/2$. If the gains A_1 and A_2 are chosen correctly according to the damping value, those oscillation responses can cancel each other out completely. The gains are chosen as:

$$A_1 = \frac{1}{1+K} \tag{5}$$

and

$$A_2 = \frac{K}{1+K} \tag{6}$$

where,

$$K = e^{\frac{\zeta\pi}{\sqrt{1-\zeta^2}}} \tag{7}$$

This definition of an input shaper is referred to as zero vibration-shaper (ZV-shaper). In academia, various extensions to a ZV-shaper approach are known. In most cases they aim at increasing robustness towards parameter change. Those extensions, such as a zero vibration derivative (ZVD)-shaper suppress vibration in a wider frequency range, result however in an increased delay. Since parameter variations can be handled by the parameter adaptation (3), a ZV-shaper is preferable in this case.

Analysis of the structural behavior of the prototype was conducted using finite element modeling and experimental modal analysis [8]. In the case of Z-axis acceleration, the most prominent oscillation response is seen at 9.2 Hz. This resembles a rigid body motion of the entire machine prototype as identified in experimental

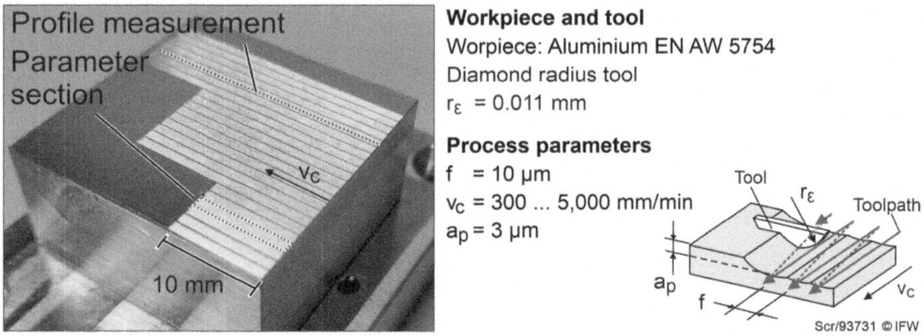

Fig. 16 Workpiece for cutting tests

modal analysis. This oscillation is also present as an oscillation of the electromagnetic X-axis slide relative to the Z-axis slide such that an impact on the workpiece form deviation can be expected and is evaluated in the following.

5.3 *Evaluation of Feed-Forward and Input Shaping in Cutting Tests*

In order to evaluate the effect of input shaping (IS) and acceleration feed forward (FF), cutting tests with stationary tool according to the setup above were conducted. As shown in Fig. 16 separate sections were planed with three different cutting velocities v_c, two jerk values j and three compensation settings. The acceleration profile of the Z-axis was set as a trapezoidal jerk-limited acceleration profile with an upper acceleration limit of $a_{max} = 5\,\mathrm{m\,s^{-2}}$. This value was however not reached for the jerk and velocity values. As lowest cutting respectively feed velocity, 300 mm min^{-1} was chosen as reference velocity for a typical UP-cutting process. $5,000$ mm min^{-1} was chosen as a benchmark velocity for an UP-HPC-cutting process and $2,000$ mm min^{-1} as a medium velocity. For each of these velocities, sections were planed with jerk values of 5 m s^{-3}, 50 m s^{-3}, and additionally 20 m s^{-3} for medium velocity. The lower jerk values serve to benchmark the performance of IS and FF with the conventional approach of limiting axis dynamics. To reduce the effect of cutting forces on the resulting profile, a narrow diamond tool with $r_\varepsilon = 0.011$ mm was applied. For each of the jerk-velocity combinations one section was planed with both, IS and FF activated, both deactivated, and one section with only IS activated. A summary of the process and trajectory parameters can be found in Table 1.

The planed sections were each measured with a tactile profilometer with a spherical probe with 500 µm radius since the focus of this investigation is on the profile deviation rather than roughness. For each section a median profile was calculated from five profile measurements. Figure 17 shows an exemplary median profile for $v_c = 5,000\,\mathrm{mm\,min^{-1}}$. It can be seen that the mentioned rigid vibration mode at

Table 1 Parameter overview for the cutting tests

Section set	Cutting speed v_c mm min^{-1}	Jerk j m s^{-3}	Compensations 1st, 2nd, 3rd section
1	300	5	FF+IS, -, IS
2	300	50	FF+IS, -, IS
3	2,000	5	FF+IS, -, IS
4	2,000	20	FF+IS, -, IS
5	2,000	50	FF+IS, -, IS
6	5,000	5	FF+IS, -, IS
7	5,000	50	FF+IS, -, IS, FF

For all sets: $f = 10\,\mu\text{m}$, $a_p = 3\,\mu\text{m}$, $r_\varepsilon = 0.011\,\text{mm}$, $a_{max} = 5\,\text{m s}^{-2}$

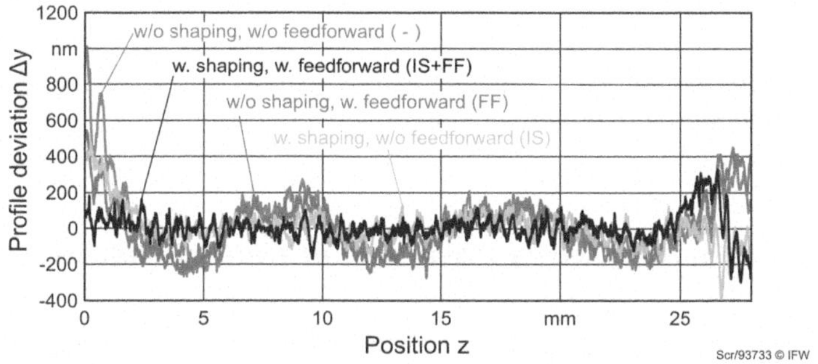

Fig. 17 Exemplary profile measurements of the machined surface for $v_c = 5,000\,\text{mm min}^{-1}$

9.2 Hz results in the dominating waviness in the planed profile with ca. 9 mm wavelength and over 300 nm in amplitude. The waviness is eliminated in the profiles with activated IS, thus showing that the compensation is effective. Regarding FF, it can be seen within the first millimeters of the profile that FF does reduce profile deviation here, since it reduces the tilting of the X-axis. However, quantitative evaluation is not conducted for FF as the spherical probe cannot probe the whole length of the profile and some uncertainty is associated with the alignment of the tactile measurements to each other in Z-direction.

Due to the limitations regarding the quantitative evaluation of FF, only IS is considered below. The analysis focuses on the overall profile deviation. Therefore, the range at the beginning and end of the profile, where the effect from axis acceleration is visible, are cut from the profile measurements for the following analysis. For the remaining part of the profile, the standard deviation S_{std} is calculated as well as the peak-to-peak value S_{p2p} of the profile after filtering with a linear Gaussian profile filter (according to ISO 16610-21) with a cut-off wavelength of 2 mm. S_{std} and S_{p2p} are shown in Fig. 18 for both, profiles with and without IS. It can be seen that for all velocity and jerk combinations, a S_{p2p} value of less than 100 nm is achieved with the use of IS while for deactivated IS S_{p2p} exceeds 100 nm significantly for the higher

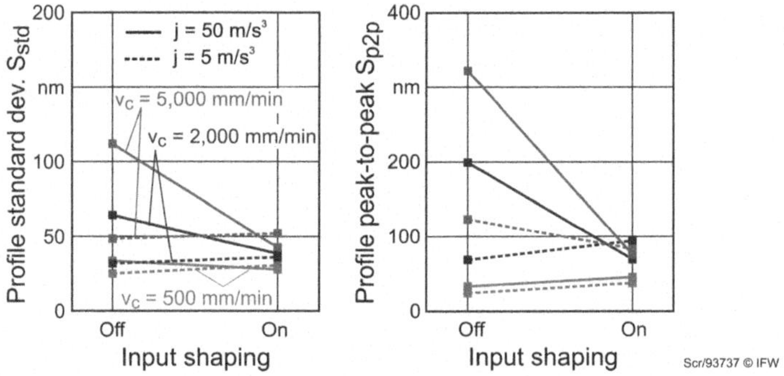

Fig. 18 Profile standard deviation S_{std} (left) and filtered profile peak-to-peak value S_{p2p} (right) for different cutting velocities v_c and jerk values j with and without input shaping

jerk and velocity combinations. This shows that IS can serve to allow for significantly higher feed velocities in UP-cutting applications.

5.4 *Internal Sensor Based Prediction of Cutting Quality*

A major feature of an active guide is that displacements of the slide position, in this case workpiece-slide position, are available to the control system during the process. Laser Doppler vibrometer measurements at different components of the machine prototype were conducted. They confirmed that the position signal of the levitation guide in Z-direction, which is known from the internal guide displacement sensors, can provide a sufficient estimate for relative tool-workpiece displacements. Therefore, an obvious approach is to predict the resulting form deviation of the workpiece based on the internal sensor signals in order to monitor and predict whether process and controller settings are viable to achieve a specified quality. This can either be done during a cutting process or before the actual process in an air cutting. Given a sufficient reliability of such a prediction, productivity of UP-cutting processes could be improved significantly as scrap parts could be avoided or axis dynamics could be increased with lower safety margins resulting in shorter process times. Furthermore, regarding the assessment of productivity impact, use of internal sensor data allows for analysis over a larger parameter range.

In the following the viability of such an approach is investigated. Figure 19 shows the generalized guide coordinates q_z (feed direction), q_a (roll angle) and x (crossfeed direction) for a feed velocity of 3.000 mm min^{-1} and all combinations with and without FF and IS. It can be seen that the relative effect of IS ad FF can be evaluated more comprehensively by the sensor data than by profile measurements. This is due to higher signal-to-noise ratio as the amplitude is more pronounced in the slide deviation than in the workpiece surface profile. Moreover, disturbances associated with profile measurement are not present. Also, alignment of the profiles is included

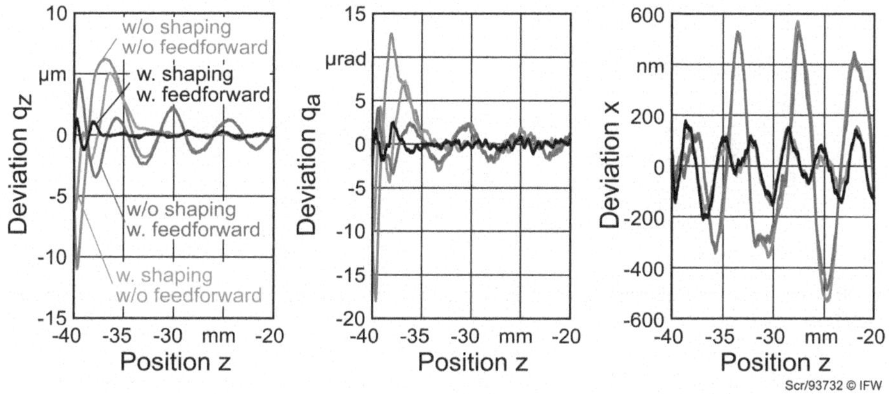

Fig. 19 Internal sensor values for deviation in q_z (left) and roll angle q_a (right) for with and without input shaping and feed forward acceleration compensation for $v_c = 3,000\,\text{mm min}^{-1}$

per se as the Z-position is captured in the same measurement. The discussed effect at 9.2 Hz is also strongly present in all three coordinates and reduced by the use of IS to a large extent.

To the end of evaluating the feasibility of predicting profile deviation based on internal sensor data, the standard deviation S_{std} of the planed sections profiles Sect. 5.3 is compared to the standard deviation values of internal guide sensor data. Figure 20 shows how the S_{std} values for internal guide coordinates q_z and q_a during an air cut correlate with S_{std} values of the measured profiles. The range in z, which is directly affected from axis acceleration, was excluded from evaluation. It can be seen that both, the standard deviation of the q_z and the q_a coordinate show a correlation to the resulting workpiece profile with R^2 values of 0.86 and 0.89 respectively. As expected, the correlation is clearer for higher deviations since the smaller values are more affected by noise and measurement uncertainties. The result shows, that at least for the given vibration mode, the sensory capability of the guide has the potential to predict critical form deviations in the workpiece. The observation that deviations in the guide coordinates are more than a magnitude higher than deviations in the workpiece also highlights the potential of guide position data in terms of sensitivity. However, additional modeling and a higher number of experiments has to be conducted in order to validate the correlation.

5.5 Analysis of Impact on Productivity by Input Shaping and Feed-Forward

This section focuses on evaluating the effect of IS and FF on productivity. The latter section showed that monitoring deviations of the internal guide coordinate

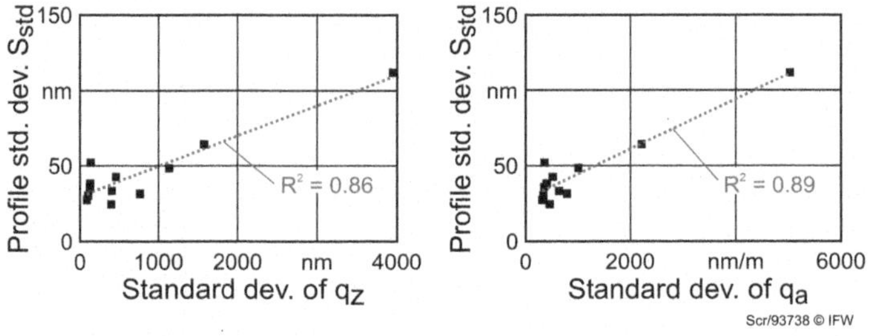

Fig. 20 Comparison of internal signal standard deviation vs profile measurement for q_z (left) and q_a (right)

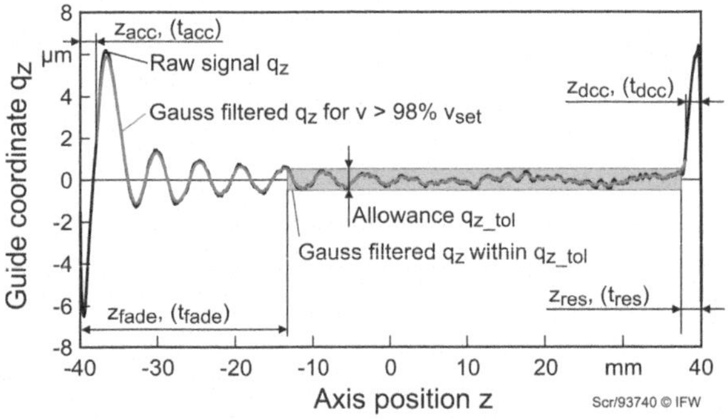

Fig. 21 Definition of the different productivity evaluation times and path lengths

data can be used as a practical tool to predict workpiece form deviations. Thus, the following investigation is based on internal guide coordinate data as they allow for a better sensitivity and more comprehensive parameter combinations. Again, a shaping or line milling process at constant v_c is considered with a jerk limited trapezoidal acceleration profile. Figure 21 shows an exemplary measurement of q_z for a travel range of 80 mm. For further consideration, only the range within which the axis velocity deviates less than 2% from the set-point velocity v_{set} is considered since a constant velocity is assumed to be a process requirement. The path length required to accelerate the slide to 98% v_{set} is referred to as z_{acc} and the corresponding duration as t_{acc}. Analogous, z_{dec} and t_{dec} denote the path length and duration for decelerating the slide from v_{set} to zero. It is assumed that in order to remain below a specified profile deviation, q_z should not exceed an allowance of $\boldsymbol{q_{z\_tol}}$. As the focus is on form deviation, the allowance is applied after low-pass filtering q_z with a linear Gaussian filter at a cut-off wavelength of 2 mm analogously to the profile measurements in the previous section. Based on that, z_{fade} and t_{fade} denote the axis path length and duration required for the dynamic deviations induced by the slide acceleration to decay and to keep within the allowance $\boldsymbol{q_{z\_tol}}$. For deceleration, the residual path length and duration from leaving the allowance $\boldsymbol{q_{z\_tol}}$ to $v = 0$ is denoted with z_{res} and t_{res}.

In order to evaluate the effect of the compensation approaches, the evaluation times and paths z_{fade} and t_{fade} are evaluated depending on different values of $\boldsymbol{q}_{z\_tol}$ for trajectories with different jerk and velocity combinations. The analyzed parameter field includes all combinations of the feed velocities v_{set} of 300, 500, 1000, 2000, 3000, and 5,000 mm min^{-1} and jerk values of 5, 10, 20, and 50 m s^{-3}. An example for how z_{fade} and t_{fade} depend on different values of $\boldsymbol{q}_{z\_tol}$ of up to 2 μm is shown in Fig. 22 for a low velocity of 500 mm min^{-1} and high velocity of 5,000 mm min^{-1}. Due to the high number of parameter combinations, only a selection for reasons of clarity and comprehensibility is shown. The shown characteristics with FF and/or IS as well as without IS and FF are from trajectories with the highest jerk value of 50 m s^{-3}. Additionally, trajectories with a jerk value of 10 m s^{-3} represent the conventional approach of jerk limitation (JL). For both, the figure also shows the values for t_{acc} and z_{acc} as the best possible limit value for each velocity-jerk combination. It can be seen for the lower velocity and high allowances that a high jerk value without any compensations is the best choice of parameters, since higher acceleration time associated with jerk limitation (JL) or the delay from input shaping (IS) are not compensated by reduced fading time. Only below ca. 750 nm allowance, IS gains an advantage as the decay time of the dynamic errors becomes larger than the input shaping delay. For a higher velocity, generally IS is favorable since it effectively reduces the oscillation fading time. Also, it can be seen that FF has higher relative advantage for lower velocities. The reason for this is that FF impacts the slide tilt and displacement mainly during t_{acc}. With t_{acc} becoming shorter in comparison to t_{fade}, the effect of FF also becomes less pronounced.

The chart in Fig. 22 can be used to optimize the process and compensation parameter choice regarding process productivity. However, it also shows that the optimal choice depends largely on the aimed allowances.

In order to discuss the potential to increase productivity by the use of these approaches the solution space for machining an exemplary workpiece is presented. The exemplary workpiece with an extension l_{wp} of 20 mm per line is assumed to be processed in a planing or line milling process. It was shown above that also JL can be beneficial. Thus, all combinations of parameters (jerk, velocity, FF, IS) are included. Further, $\boldsymbol{q}_{z\_tol}$ is set to 1 μm as based on the previous section 1 μm can be assumed to be a reasonable allowance in order to achieve a form deviation of less than 100 nm. Figure 23 shows the time required per line t_{total} and the required axis travel range z_{total}. The time t_{total} is calculated as the sum of t_{fade}, t_{res} and the tool engagement time $t_{\mathrm{cut}} = l_{wp}/v_{set}$. The analog relation applies for z_{total}. The figure depicts resulting values for t_{total} and z_{total} for all feasible parameter combinations. In blue the values for the trajectories with at least one of the presented compensation approaches FF and IS are highlighted. Shown in grey are the resulting values without FF and IS. The most significant improvement in productivity can be seen for higher feed velocities of more than 1,000 mm min^{-1}. This is due to the fact that the tool engagement time for the 20 mm spanning workpiece decreases with increasing feed velocity while the excited vibration amplitude and thus the associated decay time increases. The lowest process time amounts to 0.55 s per line (at $v_c = 5,000$ mm min^{-1}, $j = 10$ m s^{-3}, with IS and FF) with 36.4 mm required axis range. Without IS and FF the lowest process time per

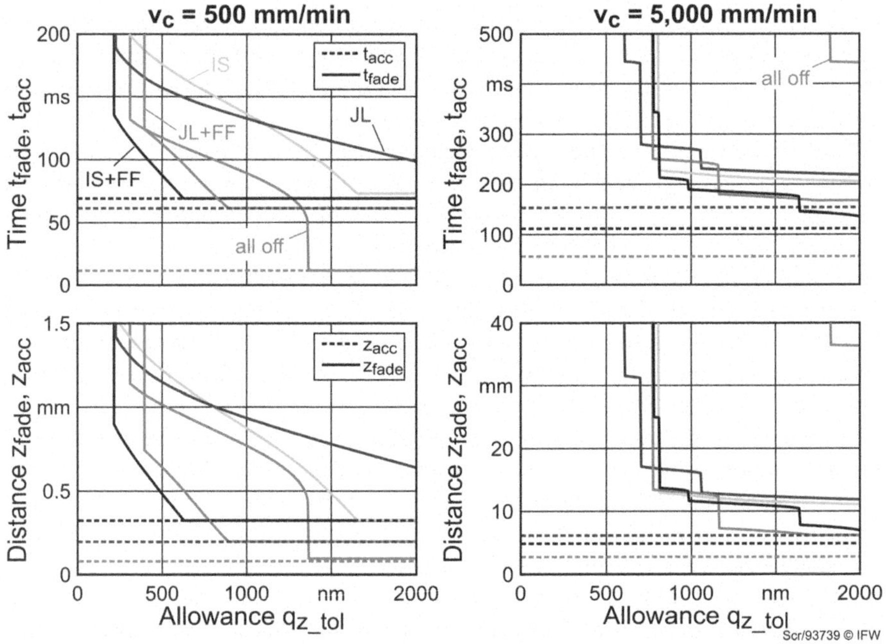

Fig. 22 Times and distances to reach q_{z_tol} for v_c = 500 (left) and 5,000 mm min^{-1} (right). JL = jerk limitation (10 m s^{-3}), IS = input shaping, FF = feed forward

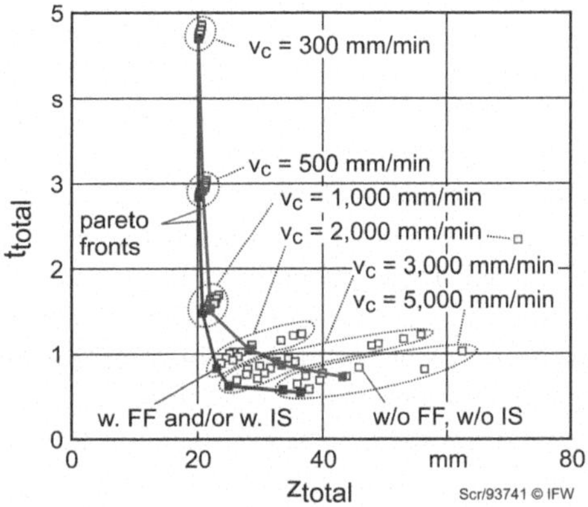

Fig. 23 Solution space for process parameter combinations with and without IS and or FF

line amounts to 0.73 s at a required axis range of 43.2 mm ($v_c = 5,000\,\text{mm}\,\text{min}^{-1}$, $j = 10\,\text{m}\,\text{s}^{-3}$, without IS and FF). This corresponds to a 24.5% lower process time and 15.7% reduction in required axis range. The results show that IS and FF can allow for significantly increased axis feeds in UP-cutting processes and thus in synergy with the other UP-HPC approaches discussed in the previous chapters increase productivity of UP-cutting processes by large extent.

6 Conclusion and Outlook

The increase in productivity with the UP-HPC approach requires the synergistic interaction of the techniques discussed in the individual chapters. In this chapter, approaches were discussed which allow for increased axis feeds while keeping dynamic workpiece deviations within specified allowances. Firstly, an approach for online parameter estimation of axis models was presented. The methods can be an enabler to increase productivity as it can enable the use for more sophisticated control approaches and reduce the effort to identify system parameters manually. To investigate two-axis motion behavior a laser speckle sensor was introduced that provides a high accuracy and flexibility without the need for a containable grid-plate which often prohibits application during cutting in a machine environment.

With increasing feed velocities, also dynamic errors and excitation of vibration are intensified. Thus, it was investigated how acceleration force feed forward and input shaping can reduce these effects and can thus allow for higher feed velocities and productivity. It was shown that for high velocities above 2,000 mm min^{-1} process times can be reduced by around 24% without increasing feed velocity. Taking into account that such high velocities can only be achieved in combinations with the other approaches developed within the UP-HPC research group, the combined gain in productivity is even higher.

References

1. Altintas, Y., Khoshdarregi, M.R.: Contour error control of CNC machine tools with vibration avoidance. CIRP Ann. **61**(1), 335–338 (2012). https://doi.org/10.1016/j.cirp.2012.03.132
2. Bloem, A., Foremny, E., Schenck, C., Kuhfuss, B.: Using speckle patterns in a direct positioning system. In: 4th International Conference on Nanomanufacturing (nanoMan 2014), Bremen, Germany, 8–10 July 2014 (2014)
3. Bloem, A., Schenck, C., Kuhfuss, B.: 2D position sensor based on speckle correlation. In: Annoni, M., Fassi, I., Wiens, G.J., Dimov, S. (eds.) 10th International Conference on Micromanufacturing (4M/ICOMM 2015), Milan, Italy, pp. 541–544 (2015)
4. Bloem, A., Wilhelmi, P., Schenck, C., Kuhfuss, B.: 2D position sensor based on speckle correlation - experimental setup for high-speed measurements and in field tests. In: 11th International Conference on Micro Manufacturing (ICOMM 2016), Paper No. 17, Irvine/CA, USA (2016)
5. Bloem, A., Schenck, C., Kuhfuss, B.: Adaptive state-space model for ultra-precision feed axis. Procedia Technol. **26**, 20–26 (2016). https://doi.org/10.1016/j.protcy.2016.08.004
6. Bloem, A., Schenck, C., Kuhfuss, B.: Dynamic behavior of ultra precision feed axis at increased velocities. In: Wertheim, R., Ihlefeldt, S., Hochmuth, C., Putz, M. (eds.) Procedia CIRP 46:456-459 (2016). https://doi.org/10.1016/j.procir.2016.04.040.
7. Charrett, T.O.H., Waugh, L., Tatam, R.P.: Speckle velocimetry for high accuracy odometry for a Mars exploration rover. Meas. Sci. Technol. **21**(2), 025301 (2009). https://doi.org/10.1088/0957-0233/21/2/025301
8. Denkena, B., Dahlmann, D., Sassi, N.: Analysis of an ultra-precision positioning system and parametrization of its structural model for error compensation. Procedia CIRP **62**, 335–339 (2017). https://doi.org/10.1016/j.procir.2016.06.054

9. Denkena, B., Bergmann, B., Schreiber, P.: Error compensation strategies for productivity improvement in ultra-precision cutting. In: Euspen's 19th International Conference & Exhibition, Bilbao, ES, June 2019, pp. 562-563 (2019)
10. Gill, P.E., Murray, W., Wright, M.H.: The Levenberg-Marquardt method. In: Practical Optimization, chap. 4.7.3, pp. 136–137. Academic Press, London (1981)
11. Ljung, L.: System Identification: Theory for the User, 2nd edn. Prentice Hall, New Jersey (1987)
12. Peters, W.H., Ranson, W.F.: Digital imaging techniques in experimental stress analysis. Opt. Eng. **21**(3) (1982). https://doi.org/10.1117/12.7972925.
13. Schönemann, L., Berger, D., Dörgeloh, T., Riemer, O., Brinksmeier, E., Krüger, R., Schreiber, P., Denkena, B., Hochbein, J., Parsa, N., Schenck, C., Kuhfuss, B.: Synergistic approaches to ultra-precision high performance cutting. CIRP J. Manuf. Sci. Technol. **28**, 38–51 (2020). https://doi.org/10.1016/j.cirpj.2019.12.001
14. Sencer, B., Dumanli, A., Yamada, Y.: Spline interpolation with optimal frequency spectrum for vibration avoidance. CIRP Ann. (2018). https://doi.org/10.1016/j.cirp.2018.03.002
15. Singhose, W.: Command shaping for flexible systems: a review of the first 50 years. Int. J. Precis. Eng. Manuf. **10**(4), 153–168 (2009). https://doi.org/10.1007/s12541-009-0084-2
16. Tobiason, J.D.: Image correlation displacement sensor. U.S. pat. 8605291. Mitutoyo Corporation (2013)

Achievements and Future Perspectives for Ultra-Precision High Performance Cutting

Lars Schönemann

Abstract This chapter summarizes the final results of the research unit that culminated in a common test stand and gives an outlook on possible future developments.

1 Achievements in Ultra-Precision High Performance Cutting

The capability for ultra-precision (UP) machining at a higher performance has been significantly increased within the scope of the German research unit ("Forschungsgruppe") No. 1845 (FOR1845) funded by the German Research Foundation from 2014 to 2020. The term Ultra-Precision High Performance Cutting (UP-HPC) was coined by the research unit. Generally, the feasibility of the individual approaches has been successfully shown up to prototype level, with many results having the potential to be transferred to industrial applications. In order to show the full synergistic potential of all developments of the FOR1845, a common test stand has been set up (Fig. 1).

With respect to the application of multiple cutting edges in diamond milling (see Chap. 2), it has been shown that a defined and localized thermal expansion of the tool holder substrate is possible. For this purpose, a ring light system was designed that allows for the infrared radiation of the applied light emitting diode (LED) to follow the rotation of the tool spindle up to several thousand revolutions per minute. By continuously measuring the roundness of the tool holder at a reference plane during operation, it was verified that the illuminated thermal actuator expands significantly more than its non-illuminated counterpart at 180° spacing. The expansion may reach up to 1 μm and thus allows for compensating typical mechanical alignment errors of the tools. Furthermore, the expansion is controllable using the capacitive measurement of the reference plane in a feedback loop. This has also been verified in cutting experiments, by comparing the thermal expansion of the reference plane with the actually achieved cutting depth of the diamond tools.

On a fundamental machining level (Chap. 3), it has been demonstrated in an extensive experimental analysis, that for metallic materials the application of high cutting speeds leads to a significant reduction of the resulting cutting forces due

L. Schönemann (✉)
Leibniz Institute for Materials Engineering IWT, Bremen, Germany

MAPEX Center for Materials and Processes, University of Bremen, Bremen, Germany
e-mail: schoenemann@iwt.uni-bremen.de

E. Brinksmeier and L. Schönemann (eds.), *Ultra-precision High Performance Cutting*,
Lecture Notes in Production Engineering, https://doi.org/10.1007/978-3-030-83765-5_7

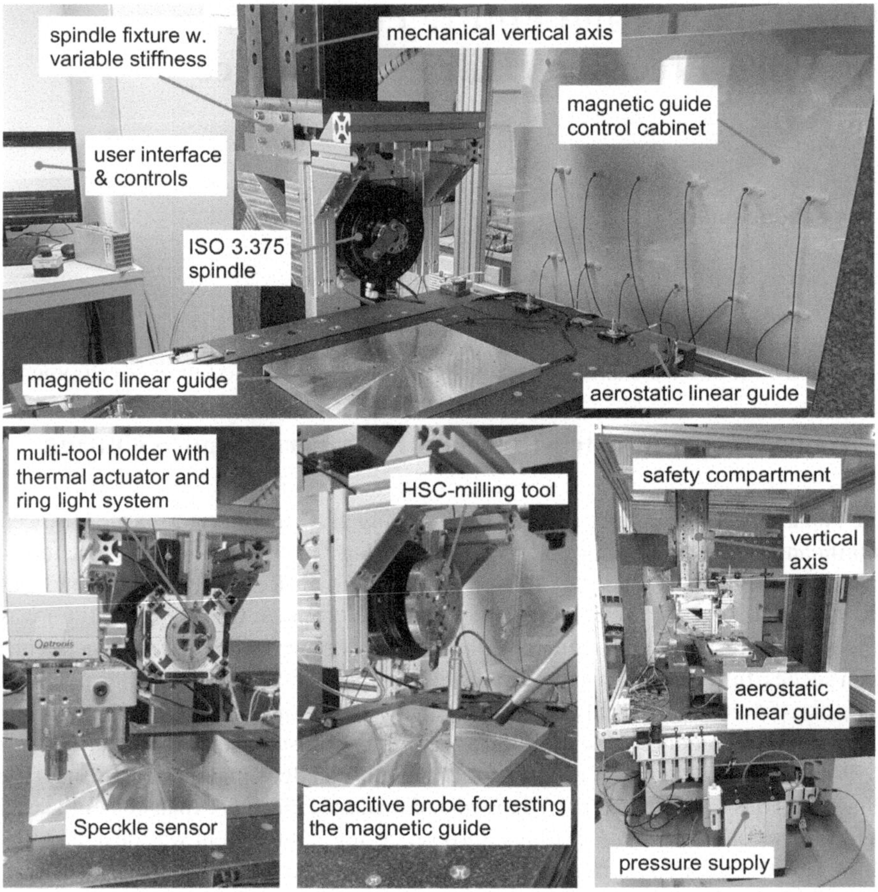

Fig. 1 UP-HPC test stand for evaluating the synergistic performance of all developments

to adiabatic shearing caused in the cutting zone. It is the first time that this effect was demonstrated for ultra-precision machining processes using monocrystalline diamond as a tool material. Along with the reduction of the cutting forces, it was shown that the resulting tool wear is also significantly reduced, extending the tool life in such operations. The short tool-workpiece contact times of UP high speed cutting (HSC) even enable a prolonged machining of steel substrates, although the effect is not as pronounced as e.g. with ultrasonic tool modulation.

For machining brittle materials, a higher critical depth of cut as a result of the increased hydrostatic pressure in the contact zone in HSC could not be generally verified for all materials. Nevertheless, the surface quality after milling was significantly improved for all tested materials when milling at elevated speeds, yielding a reduction of surface roughness up to 91% for selected materials. This may be attributed to an increased ratio of ductile material cutting with this approach, which has been verified offline by an analysis of the subsurface damage as well as during the milling process using acoustic emission (AE) measurements. Overall, UP-HPC has been proven to be beneficial for both metallic and brittle-hard materials.

In order to make full use of the elevated cutting speeds, highly dynamic feed axes are required. For this purpose, an electromagnetic linear guide was designed and built (Chap. 4). This bearing concept not only allows for frictionless movement of the slide at very high accelerations and speeds, but also enables the possibility to compensate movement deviations in six dregrees of freedom (DoF). The realized system offers an acceleration of up to $14\,\mathrm{m\,s^{-2}}$ and a speed of up to $6{,}000\,\mathrm{mm\,min^{-1}}$ with a positioning accuracy of $\leq$300 nm and $<1.9\,\mu\mathrm{rad}$, respectively. By applying a feed-forward control, the impact of dynamic disturbances during acceleration and deceleration of the slide was minimized. Furthermore, the straightness and inclination errors over the complete travel range of 90 mm have been reduced to $<1\,\mu\mathrm{m}$ and $<2\,\mu\mathrm{rad}$, respectively. Moreover, the electromagnetic linear guide exhibits no critical natural frequencies up to 2,300 Hz. Initial tests in a non temperature-controlled environment[1] already showed the capability to machine surfaces with a roughness of less than 40 nm in a planing process using a cutting speed of $6{,}000\,\mathrm{mm\,min^{-1}}$.

Within the FOR1845, significant advances have also been made for the auxiliary processes in diamond machining. It was demonstrated that by using a coupling system with adaptive stiffness, the measurable vibrations of the spindle may be amplified and thereby the sensitivity of unbalance measurements during the setup phase can be improved. In combination with automated balancing systems, a balancing quality grade of *G*0.064 is easily achievable within only a few minutes. For this purpose, two balancing concepts were evaluated for ultra-precision machining applications: a mass-distribution system (spread angle method) based on traveling wave motors and a mass-removing system (fixed position balancing) based on microfluidics. Both systems are capable of reducing the residual unbalance to below the detection threshold of the utilized accelerometers.

On the control side, new approaches for real-time controls with adaptive parameter estimation have been researched. Therefore, the positioning of an exemplary machine axis was modeled and the tracking error between the actual axis movement and the initially identified model parameters was evaluated and compared to a model that could be dynamically parametrized during operation of the axis. It was demonstrated that the latter approach is able to reduce the tracking error from around 10 nm when only using the initial identification to less than 2 nm with the dynamic identification. Furthermore, a speckle-based tracking system was developed that allows for arbitrary machine axes to be tracked in 2D during operation. Moreover, particular attention was given to the control system of the magnetic guide. Here, the influences of dynamic error feed forward (FF) control, jerk limitation (JL) and input shaping (IS) techniques as well as the combination of these approaches were analyzed. It was shown that the settling time of residual vibrations, which are the main source of dynamic errors at high feed velocities, could be successfully reduced by these means. In this way, the

[1] As this project was conducted at the Leibniz-University of Hannover, the magnetic axis could not be set up in the temperature and vibration controlled environment of the Laboratory for Precision Machining in Bremen.

machining time is reduced by approx. 25 % without even needing to increase the feed velocity. As this effect is more pronounced at higher speeds, the combined effect of high feed velocities and reduced settling times has the potential to reduce the overall machining times in UP machining even more.

2 Outlook on Possible Future Developments

Over the past few years, the path to achieving high performance in ultra-precision cutting processes has been opened by various developments. Nevertheless, there is still a lot of room for improvements and further developments.

For milling with multiple tools, only the radial offset of the diamond cutting edges has been considered yet to equally engage all applied tools in the cutting operation. In actual machining operations, however, the lateral shift of the tools is just as important for controlling the surface generation of an optical surface, and it has to be evaluated whether the intended localized thermal expansion of the tool holder can be utilized for corrections in this direction as well. Furthermore, a thermal drift of the systems occurs especially at long processing times, which has to be counteracted by improved insulation of the thermal actuator.

In machining, the potential benefit of HSC cutting has been shown for two important material classes—metals and brittle-hard semiconductors—but there are other interesting materials, like glassy carbon for example, for which this benefit still has to be verified.

While the performance of the electromagnetic guide is already excellent under the given circumstances, its performance can be still improved by applying more precise and more robust sensor systems and also by implementing even more sophisticated control techniques. Also, it has to be taken into account that all results so far have been obtained under uncontrolled environmental conditions (temperature, air pressure, humidity, vibration isolation). Thus, it is expected that in a fully controlled environment the performance of the magnetic guide would increase per se.

The automated balancing procedures are already a huge improvement over the typical manual tool and workpiece setting. However, this only automates one part of the time-consuming setup procedure, while other areas, such as part centering or tool alignment, still remain manual work in many cases. Future work should focus on automating those parts as well.

As for the controls, it has been shown once again that achieving a high speed in the machine axes is only one part of the story and that it is just as important to stabilize a machining axis during its acceleration and deceleration phase as well as to identify and compensate dynamic disturbances during operation. Here, machine learning and the use of artificial intelligence are only starting to be researched for their application in error detection and compensation.

Overall, the road towards true ultra-precision high performance cutting and its industrial application is still long, but we have made significant steps to progress towards this goal.

The manufacturer's authorised representative in the EU is Springer Nature Customer Service Centre GmbH, Europaplatz 3, 69115 Heidelberg, Germany. If you have any concerns regarding our products, please contact ProductSafety@springernature.com

Printed and bound by CPI Group (UK) Ltd, Croydon, CR0 4YY

30/09/2026

02225661-0015